Special Delivery:

The Letters of C.L.R. James to Constance Webb, 1939-1948

Special Delivery:
The Letters of C.L.R. James to Constance Webb, 1939–1948

EDITED AND INTRODUCED
BY ANNA GRIMSHAW

Copyright © Constance Webb Pearlstien 1996. This arrangement and editorial matter
copyright © Anna Grimshaw 1996

First published 1996

Blackwell Publishers Ltd.
108 Cowley Road, Oxford OX4 1JF, UK
Blackwell Publishers Inc.
238 Main Street
Cambridge, Massachusetts 02142, USA

All rights reserved. Except for the quotation of short passages for the
purposes of criticism and review, no part may be reproduced, stored in
a retrieval system, or transmitted, in any form or by any means,
electronic, mechanical, photocopying, recording or otherwise,
without the prior permission of the publisher.

Except in the United States of America, this book is sold subject to the
condition that it shall not, by way of trade or otherwise, be lent,
resold, hired out, or otherwise circulated without the publisher's prior
consent in any form of binding or cover other than that in which it is
published and without a similar condition including this condition
being imposed on the subsequent purchaser.

British Library Cataloging in Publication Data
[A CIP record for this book is available from the British Library.]

Library of Congress Cataloging-in-Publication Data
James, C.L.R. (Cyril Lionel Robert), 1901–89
Special delivery: the letters of C.L.R. James to Constance Webb, 1939–1948 / edited and
introduced by Anna Grimshaw.
p.   cm.
Includes bibliographical references and index.
ISBN 1–55786–627–9 (hbk)
1. James, C.L.R. (Cyril Lionel Robert), 1901–89—Correspondence. 2. Authors,
Trinidadian—20th Century—Correspondence. 3. Revolutionaries—Trinidad—
Correspondence. 4. Historians—Trinidad—Correspondence. 5. Webb,
Constance—Correspondence. I. Webb, Constance. II. Grimshaw, Anna. III. Title.
PR9272.9.J35Z489 1995
818—dc20
[B]   95–37918
                                                                                              CIP

Typeset by Jim Murray of *Cultural Correspondence*, New York
Printed in Great Britain by T. J. Press Limited, Padstow, Cornwall

Contents

Acknowledgments	vii
Editorial Note	ix
Introduction by Anna Grimshaw	1
I. The Beginning of a Journey (1939–40)	37
II. A Symbol of American Civilization (1943–4)	69
III. Uncertainty and Attachment (1945–6)	199
IV. Separation and Limbo (1947–8)	279
Abbreviations	379
Glossary	383
Index of Names	389

Acknowledgments

I very much appreciate the commitment of Simon Prosser and Blackwell in making James's work widely available, including many of his previously unknown writings. My thanks go also to Mike Dibb, Michael Eaton, Grant Farred, Nikos Papastergiadis and Edward Pearlstien for their insights and suggestions. I am especially grateful to Adele Oltman and Candice Clarke for their painstaking editorial work. Jim Murray of the C.L.R. James Institute in New York has, for many years, demonstrated extraordinary dedication to all James matters; and without his support and friendship my work would not have been completed. My close collaboration with Keith Hart has contributed immensely to my understanding of James. I am greatly indebted to him.

Finally, I wish to thank Constance Webb Pearlstien for entrusting such intimate and historically valuable material to me. Her own work in preserving, transcribing and annotating James's letters are the bedrock upon which this publication rests. But it is the generosity of her spirit—her friendship and encouragement, indeed the example of her own life—which animates the book.

Anna Grimshaw
June 1995

Editorial Note

This selection from James's correspondence with Constance Webb represents the vast majority of the letters which he wrote to her, roughly ninety percent, during the period 1939–48. The originals, along with transcripts made by Constance Webb during the 1980s, are held in the Schomburg Center for Research in Black Culture, New York.

The letters presented here have not been edited for publication, hence they contain repetitions, inconsistencies, ellipses and other idiosyncratic features. In certain places in the text, however, editorial interventions have been made in order to assist the reader. These are indicated by the use of square brackets; but I have attempted to keep these to a minimum in order to avoid cluttering the text unnecessarily. James's letters are full of personal names, many of them nicknames or abbreviations. A list of these and the persons to whom they refer is contained in an appendix. An annotated glossary of major characters, providing brief biographical information, is also supplied.

Introduction
Anna Grimshaw

THE LETTERS OF C.L.R. JAMES TO CONSTANCE WEBB, 1939-48

Cyril Lionel Robert James is one of the outstanding figures of the twentieth century. The rich legacy of his published writing reveals the scope and variety of his life's work, spanning as it did four continents and a writing career of more than half a century. In the pages which follow I hope to provide a context for the letters James wrote to a young American woman, Constance Webb, during his first, extended stay in the United States. This remarkable body of writing, hitherto unpublished, is less a record of a relationship, more the spiritual journey of a man unburdening himself to someone he barely knew and yet instinctively trusted. For only one side of the correspondence survives and Constance Webb's presence in it remains something which we, the readers—not unlike James himself—must construct in our imagination. Through his love for a woman, James found a way to articulate much that gave meaning to his own life and work. His letters to Constance Webb, written over half a century ago, stand as a powerful and profoundly unsettling expression of the complex forces which animated his personality. But more than this, the interplay between James's own individuality and the world in which he lived is uniquely revealed by this correspondence. For the political struggles central to the social revolution of the twentieth century, conflicts of race, class and gender, were mirrored by divisions within James himself; and an understanding of the intense personal battles which he fought within himself illuminates, I believe, the tremendous conflicts of our modern age.

Constance Webb, an aspiring actress and model, met James in the spring of 1939. She was part of the audience in a Los Angeles church for his talk, "The Negro Question," which he gave toward the end of a nationwide speaking tour.[1] He was en route to his meeting with Trotsky in Mexico; and the first letters to Webb were sent from the exiled revolutionary's headquarters in Coyoacan. They mark the beginning of the correspondence which James pursued for almost a decade. It consists of over two hundred letters, handwritten, often many pages long, sometimes snatched notes jotted down while travelling or during meetings, at other times extended musings on art, love, literature and politics.

The young woman who prompted such an outpouring from James describes herself in an unpublished memoir as a seventh-generation American of western birth and southern parentage.[2] Her parents were from Atlanta, Georgia; and although they lived for many years in California, they could not, according to Webb, escape their deeply rooted southern heritage. Webb, however, became involved early on in socialist politics, developing a particular interest in the race question. She was eighteen when she met James, who was almost twenty years her senior; but she sparked off something profound in him, and her process of self-discovery became inseparable from his own.

James's letters to Webb chart a journey. The correspondence is anchored in the most intimate and personal concerns of two people; but their exploration of the differences between them, differences of race, gender, age and background, open out to encompass questions at the heart of modern civilization. The fact that these letters were written in the New World is not accidental. Indeed it is impossible to imagine James writing them anywhere else. For he experienced America as a moment of freedom. He was freed, if only temporarily, from the weight and claustrophobia of his colonial and European past; and he felt a tremendous surge in his creative powers.

The Webb correspondence thus documents in a unique way James's experience of America, not least by the sheer volume of letters written between 1939 and 1948. It offers a fascinating insight into the rigors of a revolutionary life, exposing the dynamics of a small political group, its external battles and internal strife; and we are often reminded of the disparity between the size of the group and the scale of its political ambitions (world revolution). But, above all, James's letters to Webb constitute a profound reflection on love and art. Perhaps what strikes the reader most forcibly is the sense that in his correspondence James opened up a free and private space, one in which he could dream, fantasize, admit to needs and desires, explore new dimensions of human experience, discover intimacy, unburden himself, indulge his wit and playfulness—in short do all the things he repressed in his public persona. For James, the revolutionary leader, was never anything but reserved and self-controlled, always a master of himself, the situation and the party line. In contrast, the letters read as a series of dramatic scenarios in which James tries out different roles or voices— sometimes the brave, romantic hero, at others the serious mentor and friend, the indulgent lover, the stern unbending comrade, and even, occasionally, the willing pupil.

It was through his exchanges with Webb that James began to explore, and to seek to integrate, aspects of his personality which were normally suppressed or kept separate—such as art and politics, Hollywood film and the Hegelian dialectic, emotions and ideas. But James's attempt at synthesis, stimulated by the unleashing of an extraordinary passion for Webb, contained in microcosm the much broader and ambitious project he was pursuing to identify America's distinctive contribution to modern civilization. The process of discovery was then for him both personal and political. He recognized that these disparate dimensions of human experience were intertwined as never before in history; and yet they remained separated in modern society and personality, and within the revolutionary movement itself.

We are conscious, almost from the beginning, of the tension between the two parts of James's life in the United States. Hostility and suspicion toward art, culture, civilization and happiness ran deep in the revolutionary Left. No one knew this better than James himself. Moreover, given its place at the center of bourgeois society, the question of human subjectivity or of the uniqueness of the individual personality had long been downplayed by the revolutionary movement in favor of a concern with much bigger, abstract questions. But the denial of individuality which this involved usually resulted in its distorted expression, manifesting itself in the personal rivalry, tensions, divisions and endless segmentation which notoriously plagued such groups. There was often a striking contradiction between the scope of the historical and political analyses attempted by these revolutionaries and the narrow confines of their personal lives.[3]

It was James's experience of living in the New World, specifically of trying to love an American woman, which made him acutely aware of these divisions within his own personality. In the course of the correspondence we become increasingly aware of the discrepancy between what James calls "essence" and "appearance," between his internal state (chaos, the demons) and his external presentation (order, restraint, commitment). The strain of mediating such a sharp contradiction surfaces again and again in his letters. We witness James's endless struggle against illness, the physical incapacity caused by his ulcer and stomach problems; but perhaps more poignant, even than his admission of sexual failure, is our discovery that the strain expresses itself in a shaking hand which, at times, is so acute that it becomes physically difficult for him to write at all.

But James's internal struggle was inseparable from the intense conflicts which he identified as raging at every level of twentieth-century society. It was what he called in his 1950 work, *American Civilization*, "the struggle for happiness," the need to realize the full and free expression of individual personality within new and expanded conceptions of social life. James believed the conflict between individual and society to be most acute in America. For he saw that the highly developed sense of the individual personality and the people's restless energies expended in the search for new forms of collective life were always in conflict with an industrial capitalist system whose mechanized division of labor was inevitably oppressive. "This is the fundamental conflict," James wrote in his 1950 manuscript. "There is on the one hand the need, the desire, created . . . by the whole mighty mechanism of American industry, to work, to learn, to master the machine, to co-operate with others in building glittering miracles. . . . And on the other the endless frustration of being merely a cog in a great machine, a piece of production as is a bolt of steel, a pot of paint or a mule which drags a load of corn. This conflict is staggering in its scope and implications. It goes on all day and every hour of the day."[4]

I came across the Webb letters while working as James's assistant in the final years of his life. When I began to read them for the first time I found myself looking up from the page to glance across my desk at James. It was an instinctive response to discovering something new; and I wanted to look again at the man whose turbulent inner life was now spread before me. Many times I was disappointed. I saw only a tired, withdrawn old man, his frail but once powerful frame hidden beneath his favorite red blanket as he dozed in an armchair. At other times, though, I saw sudden surges of tremendous vitality, indeed passion, filling and animating his whole personality; and for a brief moment he was transformed into the romantic hero of the Webb letters.

Reading the correspondence moved me deeply, provoking intense and contradictory responses. I found the letters compulsive and yet unsettling; and on reaching their dramatic climax in 1948 I felt that I had been drawn into the eye of a storm, that I had witnessed a drama of epic proportions which was almost Shakespearean in its grandeur and its tragedy. The Webb correspondence lays bare both the scope and the limitations of an individual personality. Its tragedy lies in James's final recognition that, although he believes the individual is able to transcend the limitations of society and history, he cannot in fact defeat the demons inside himself. At times James imagined himself striding the stage of world history as universal man; but the heroic bravado is ultimately shattered by the tremendous flaws in his restricted and divided personality.

THE LIFE AND WORK OF C.L.R. JAMES (1901-89)

C.L.R. James spent his final years living in a tiny book-lined room in Brixton, south London. Although he often complained that he had to sleep in the same room as his books, I knew each morning when I picked my way over the scattered volumes of Shakespeare, Thackeray or Arnold Bennett which lay around his bed, that they had been his companions during the long hours of darkness. During the day James liked to read or watch television, sitting in his old fashioned high-backed armchair; but his eye was always half-watching the pencil sketch propped against the desk at which I worked. He was intrigued by what Margaret Glover's portrait revealed about himself. At first he was satisfied to discover that there were no traces in the drawing of his feckless brother, Eric; later he gleaned resemblances to his schoolmaster father, sometimes to the stern, puritanical aunts who had watched over his childhood in Trinidad; but more often he saw his mother, a woman of remarkable elegance, who at the beginning of the century in a tiny outpost of the British Empire had introduced her son to literature: ". . . she was a reader. She read everything that came her way. I can see her now, sitting very straight with the book held high, her pince-nez on her Caucasian nose, reading till long after midnight. If I got up there she was, reading, the book still held high. As she read and put it down I picked it up."[5]

James's early life in the Caribbean was dominated by literature and cricket.[6] As a young boy he watched cricketers from the window of his house, drawn to the individuality of certain players and conscious of how deeply rooted the game had become in the small island society. James, or "Nello" as his mother called him, was a bright, precocious child. He quickly developed a distinctive approach to understanding cricket, immersing himself in its history, assembling a vast collection of books, articles and newspaper clippings, discussing the game with prominent local players; but, above all, he closely observed, and retained in his mind's eye, the different styles of cricket which he saw being played.

In 1910 James won a scholarship to Queen's Royal College (QRC), the island's premier educational establishment. To his delight he discovered that the masters' room contained among its magnificent collection of classical literature the complete works of Thackeray. Unlike the other boys, who returned home for lunch, James ate his sandwiches in the school and steadily worked his way through all the different volumes. From the beginning, however, *Vanity Fair* was the outstanding work. For without fully understanding its significance until much later, James as a boy was instinctively drawn to the passions, conflicts and vivid characters of Thackeray's sharp satirical novel. They left a deep impression on him, influencing his own fiction writing and later becoming the central feature of his mature political vision, as he moved away from any attachment to notions of specialized intellectual or political leadership and increasingly recognized that people themselves were the animating force of modern civilization.

QRC was modeled on an English public school. There was an emphasis on the classics, European history and literature, and sport. In particular, its Oxbridge masters instilled in their pupils the gentlemen's code, an ethos of fair play, of what was considered "cricket." But to the exasperation of his teachers and much to the disappointment of his family, members of the post-emancipation black middle class, James rebelled against the formal discipline of the college. He was conscious of being "a bright boy;" and although eager to absorb everything QRC offered him, he was determined to chart his own course. By the time he left in 1918, James believed himself to be a complete master of himself and of European civilization. But he knew, too, that even as a highly educated black man his opportunities for development were much restricted in the small stratified colonial society of his youth.

During the 1920s James earned his living as a schoolmaster. Indeed for a short time he returned as a teacher to QRC. Among his pupils was Eric Williams, who later became a close friend during James's years in England and America, and who eventually led Trinidad to independence in 1962. But James's creative energies at this time were channeled into his cricket writing and literary activities. Already he had acquired a local reputation as a cricket reporter; but equally he was beginning to be noticed as a promising writer of fiction. One of his first short stories, "La Divina Pastora," (1927) was included in E. J. O'Brien's collection *Best Short Stories* (London, 1928). James subsequently published three other short pieces of fiction in the literary journals, *Trinidad* and *The Beacon*, which he founded in Trinidad with a number of other aspiring writers—most notably Alfred Mendes, Albert Gomes and Ralph de Boissière.[7] James and his literary contemporaries drew much of their creative inspiration from the unexplored, but vibrant life lived by the people in Trinidad's barrackyards. Although conscious of the local disapproval these young writers courted by their orientation towards backstreet life, they were the first to establish it as a rich, native source.

James's own development, initially as a writer of fiction, was intimately connected with his need to transcend the conventional forms of literary expression which he had inherited through his mastery of the formal English tradition. He now sought to incorporate what was distinctive about the Caribbean into his creative writing. James was pushing against the limits of a colonial heritage which increasingly confined him; but he became aware, too, that his own individual experience was part of a more popular movement in the island society itself. For by the late 1920s Trinidad's population was itself beginning to push against the confines of British colonial rule.

In 1932 James sailed for Britain. He carried with him a completed novel, *Minty Alley* (which was published in 1936), and a drafted biography of Trinidad's labor leader, Andre Cipriani whose growing political prominence had caught James's attention.[8] When he arrived James intended to make his way as a writer in London, but his first months living in a small Lancashire cotton town with the cricketer, Learie Constantine, set him on a new course. James discovered revolutionary politics; and the remainder of his life was dedicated to theoretical and practical questions of social transformation. He believed that his relatively late discovery of Marxism, approaching it as he did with an advanced knowledge of European history and civilization, gave him a certain advantage in approaching political problems. It certainly left a distinctive mark on all his work.

In the course of his six-year stay in Britain James emerged as one of the leading members of the Trotskyist movement; he was active in the Independent Labour Party; and he quickly established himself as a powerful spokesman for the cause of colonial emancipation. From the outset, he was much in demand as a public speaker and debater. His appearance and bearing were striking, not least because there were very few black people in Britain at the time, most of them concentrated in London. Indeed, James often recalled later, with wry amusement, how audiences he addressed rarely knew where the West Indies were situated and, believing him to be African, many people commented on his remarkable facility with the English language. But, as he usually responded, it would have been much more remarkable had he not been fluent in the language he had known since birth.

James was an elegant man, more than six feet tall; and he had a reserved, dignified manner. He was always in complete control of himself and his material. At the end of his life he liked to recall his participation in the intense political debates of pre-war Britain, recognizing that his instincts as a young boy to master all aspects of the game of cricket had been an excellent preparation for the rigors of a revolutionary life. Moreover James was confident that his intellectual foundations in the history of European civilization were deep and unshakeable. He had developed an extraordinary memory and an insatiable appetite for reading; and his habit of collecting newspaper clippings and marking up books gave him immediate access to the details of contemporary political battles.

James was well known for his appearance at public meetings. He arrived with his pockets bulging with books and papers; and from these documents he would read carefully selected extracts which exposed the changing positions of his political opponents, most notably the Communist Party. But, above all, what caught the imagination of his audiences was his passion and fluency as an orator; the scope and brilliance of his political analyses; the ease with which he made connections between local political struggles and much broader issues. James had the unusual gift of making his audiences feel part of history. His ability to instil in people an awareness of their participation in the movement and transformation of society was something he retained all his life.

During the 1930s James travelled widely throughout Britain as a political journalist and as cricket reporter for the *Manchester Guardian*. He published extensively in the *New Leader*, the weekly newspaper of the Independent Labour Party, covering issues which ranged from the 1935 miners' strike in South Wales to revolutionary developments in Europe and questions of emancipation from colonialism.[9]

Until 1935, when Mussolini invaded Ethiopia, Africa's only independent country, James's attention was largely focused on the prospect of revolution in Europe. Like many others he believed that the revolution would occur first in Europe, and in its aftermath independence would be granted to the millions of colonial subjects across Asia, Africa and the Caribbean. But the disarray on the Left over Mussolini's imperialist aggression alerted James to the equivocation of European radicals on the question of emancipation; and he was forced, as a black man and colonial subject himself, to re-think a number of important assumptions in revolutionary Marxism. In particular he now acknowledged the importance of building an independent movement of Africans and people of African descent. "Africans must win their own freedom. Nobody will win it for them," James declared in an important article written for the *New Leader* in 1936;[10] and to this end, he joined his old Trinidadian friend, George Padmore, in organizing the International African Service Bureau which quickly became a leading political organization, coordinating anti-colonial agitation worldwide.

James's growing interest in the relationship between nationalist struggles and a broader revolutionary movement was also stimulated by his historical research into the 1791 San Domingo revolution. Breaking out in the most highly prized of France's colonial possessions, it was the only successful slave uprising in history. The blacks moved, in the wake of revolutionary developments in Paris, to demand their freedom and secured it against the combined efforts of the European powers of the day. James's study, *The Black Jacobins*, was published in 1938. Here he exposed the internal dynamics of the slave revolution itself, charting its development against the backdrop of international politics and the changing needs of the colonial economy. Thus within an extraodinarily powerful and compelling historical narrative, James skillfully integrated different levels of analysis, revealing the changing relationships between leaders of the uprising and the people, between the ideas of the French revolution and the actions of the slaves, and between the competing colonial powers (Britain, France and Spain) and the leaders of the slave insurrection.

At the center of *The Black Jacobins* stood the figure of Toussaint L'Ouverture, "one of the most remarkable men of a period rich in remarkable men." James understood that Toussaint, like other outstanding historical personalities, embodied all the conflicting forces of his age. Subsequently in the 1936 play, *Toussaint L'Ouverture*, which James drew from his unfinished book manuscript, he attempted to exploit the dramatic dimensions of this great historical figure, casting Paul Robeson in the title role.[11]

The interpretation which James offered of Toussaint's rise and fall as a revolutionary leader raised central and enduring questions about revolutionary transition; but equally James's understanding of his historical particularity highlighted the new and distinctive features of that age. Toussaint was a symbol of a new world emerging, one in which black people as active political subjects became a powerful force in world history.

James always noted that he wrote *The Black Jacobins* before the Second World War. Furthermore, he was conscious of the links between the book's appearance (and that of his companion study, *The History of Negro Revolt*, 1938) and the publication in Paris around the same time of Aimé Césaire's *Cahier d'un Retour au Pays Natal* (1939) and in America of W.E.B. Du Bois's *Black Reconstruction* (1935). James interpreted this close coincidence of dates as evidence of a new stage in black consciousness, though not even he anticipated the speed with which the old European empires and America's system of segregation would begin to collapse in the face of popular mobilization after the war.

In 1938 James Cannon of the American Socialist Workers' Party (SWP) visited

Britain. He met James and invited him to the United States to address audiences on the European situation as war approached, and to contribute to discussions in the Trotskyist movement on what was then called "the Negro question." Almost immediately upon arriving in America in October 1938 James embarked on an extensive speaking tour. It took him from the East Coast, through the industrial cities of the mid-west, and into California. Toward the end of his tour, James addressed political activists in Los Angeles, California; and Constance Webb was in the audience for his talk, "The Negro Question." Immediately after this first meeting, James began the remarkable correspondence with Webb which is published here.

James's tour ended in Mexico. Here he spent several days in discussion with Leon Trotsky, the exiled Russian revolutionary, in an attempt to formulate a coherent position on the race question. The Trotskyist movement had no clear program or organizing strategy which would link its own revolutionary goals with the political struggles of America's black population; but both men were acutely conscious of the importance of this question to the Marxist movement as a whole. The major issues discussed with Trotsky were set out in a document prepared by James. These included self-determination; the relationship between the black struggle for basic democratic rights and the socialist movement; the organization and recruitment of black members; and the education of existing members about the race question.

James, Trotsky and another comrade, Charles Curtiss, reached a broad consensus on most of the issues they discussed. It was agreed that James would write a regular column in the SWP newspaper, *Socialist Appeal*; and that he would organize a bureau devoted to "Negro affairs."[12] James's work in England during the 1930s had partially prepared him for these tasks. His historical researches had laid important foundations for an understanding of the evolution of the black struggle worldwide; and he had gained valuable organizational experience in George Padmore's International African Service Bureau. But he recognized, too, that the situation in America was new to him in an important way. For James had never encountered racial segregation before. He was acutely aware that his experiences of discrimination as a black man in the Caribbean and later in Britain, were not of the same kind as those which he now faced; and he was apprehensive, being unfamiliar with all the unspoken codes and conventions of a racially divided country.

Before he gained first-hand experience of America's racial laws, making his way back by bus through the southern states to the SWP headquarters in New York, James held further discussions with Trotsky on questions raised by James's book, *World Revolution*, which he had published in Britain in 1937. This time, however, there was sharp disagreement between the two men. Trotsky accused James of "a lack of dialectical approach, Anglo-Saxon empiricism, and formalism which is only the reverse of empiricism."[13] But James believed it was the exiled leader himself who lacked an understanding of the dialectical method. For Trotsky's vigorous repudiation of key parts of his analysis in *World Revolution* did nothing to dispel James's notion that Trotsky failed to grasp the movement of historical events—neither at the time of his great struggle with Stalin, nor since.

The political landscape of Europe had been transformed by the Russian Revolution; but the subsequent development of the workers' state under Stalin was inadequately understood on the revolutionary Left. The importance of *World Revolution* was that it had provided such an interpretation of the critical historical events and the roles played by key personalities. Moreover it articulated a revolutionary position, one which was deeply opposed to the Stalinism of the Soviet Union. In this study of the Communist International, James attempted to examine the process by which Stalin had been able to seize power after Lenin's death and subvert fundamental revolutionary principles. He took Stalin's declaration in 1924 of the doctrine "socialism in one country" as a significant moment. For at a stroke it severed the Soviet Union from the international revolutionary movement; and paved the way for the barbarous suppression of domestic opposition and popular movements abroad.

If James was impressed by the sharp political insights of Trotsky on the race question, he was much less confident of his method and approach to history. James left Mexico with lingering doubts. At the time these unresolved issues did not seem pressing; but they quickly developed into a major political crisis. For, although on his return to New York James planned to give his work on the race question the highest priority, circumstances forced him to respond to the intense debate over the "Russian Question" which was beginning to divide the Trotskyist movement itself.

Until 1939 it was considered unthinkable by those on the revolutionary Left that a political alliance could be forged between Germany and the Soviet Union. But the signing of the Hitler–Stalin Pact urgently posed the problematic nature of the Soviet Union. Was it a workers' state, albeit a degenerated one? Should it, in all circumstances, be defended by the revolutionary Left?

At the SWP Convention in New York held during early April 1940 the status of the Soviet Union was discussed extensively. On the one hand there was the majority faction, supported by Trotsky and led by James Cannon, which argued for the "unconditional defense of the Soviet Union as in no way incompatible with irreconcilable struggle for the overthrow of the Stalin bureaucracy."[14] On the other hand, the minority position articulated by Max Shachtman took an opposing position, refusing to defend the (degenerated) workers' state. James supported the minority. Shortly after their defeat at the Convention, James followed Shachtman and other prominent members, such as Martin Abern, in splitting from the SWP in order to found a new Workers' Party.

For James this was an important moment. The confusion over the status of the Soviet Union sharply exposed fundamental problems which he recognized penetrated to the heart of the revolutionary movement. The situation had been complicated by the fact that what Trotsky symbolized in the struggle against Stalinism was more important for many people, like James, than their commitment to Trotskyism as such. From a contemporary perspective it is often easy to forget that opposition to Stalinism, not least because of its appeal to many European and American intellectuals, was as imperative for James and his political associates as the struggle against bourgeois society.

Just as James had sought in pre-war Britain to articulate through his book, *World Revolution*, a revolutionary Marxist position which was opposed to the Stalinism of the Soviet Union, so too in the United States he began the process of establishing a coherent approach to a number of key questions. He returned to the writings of Hegel, Marx, Engels and Lenin; and over the course of a decade he, with a handful of collaborators, moved steadily away from the basic tenets of Trotskyism. The fruits of their collective work laid the basis for a new revolutionary Marxism. Specifically, they advocated the independent vitality of the black struggle; they argued for a theory of state capitalism as the means of understanding the nature of the Soviet Union; they developed a Marxism applicable to American conditions; and they broke with the notion of the necessity of a revolutionary vanguard party.

Although many of James's energies were absorbed by the demands of such a profound period of study, he remained active in the day-to-day debates and organizational work of the Workers' Party. Much of this focused around the war. For the revolution in Russia, which had followed the collapse of European civilization in 1914, offered an important historical precedent. The declaration of war in 1939 and America's subsequent involvement in it led those in small groups on the revolutionary Left to believe that in this climate they could stoke the fuel of domestic unrest and industrial conflict, and thus open the way for fundamental social change.

James's public profile was much restricted, however, by his illegal presence in the United States. His entry visa, valid for only six months, had been extended once because of the medical treatment necessitated by his stomach ulcer. But James knew that the political circumstances he found in America offered him a unique challenge. He decided to go into what he called "retirement;" and thereafter he was forced to operate underground. Using the pseudonym, J. R. Johnson, he was able to continue to be a prolific writer, contributing to the major two publications of the WP, *Labor Action* and the *New International*. His articles were always distinguished by their passionate language, political precision and extraordinary historical scope. James succeeded not only in educating those inside the movement, weaving together his work on "the Negro question" with central concerns of revolutionary Marxism; but he also played a special role in bringing what had previously been small insular sectarian publications to the wider attention of America's intellectuals.[15]

Although from time to time James's political work carried him outside New York, it was not easy for him to engage in the kind of agitation among industrial workers which many members of the WP carried out during this period. There had been one notable exception, when in 1941 and 1942 James's activist work took him to southeast Missouri. The exact nature of his participation in the sharecroppers' strike for better wages and conditions has never been clear; but it was, as he describes to Webb, a "tremendous experience." Certainly as a black man, moving across the poor agricultural areas of the southern borderlands, it must have been as dangerous as it was illuminating.[16]

By 1943 James emerged as the leader of a small group within the Workers' Party known as the Johnson Forest Tendency. Its name joined James's with that of his chief collaborator, Raya Dunayevskaya (Freddie Forest). Together they had begun a comprehensive study of Marxism, making the question of the Soviet Union an important focus. Dunayevskaya, a Russian emigrant with long experience inside the revolutionary movement, had also developed a position on Stalinist Russia which argued for its interpretation as a form of state capitalism. Later, Grace Lee (Ria Stone), a Chinese-American with a philosophy degree from Bryn Mawr, joined the Johnson Forest Tendency. Pooling their linguistic skills, different backgrounds and training, they quickly emerged as a dominant and formidable force in revolutionary politics. Other prominent members included Freddie and Lyman Paine. Lyman Paine had been a successful architect, a descendant of Tom Paine; and he provided the Tendency, especially James, with much financial support. James often spent weekends and vacations at the Paines' summer house in Northport, Long Island, from where he frequently wrote to Webb.[17]

One of the distinctive features of James's work at this time was his introduction of a developed historical perspective to the American revolutionary Left. He believed it was indispensable to any understanding of the contemporary political crisis which faced the western world; and an important part of his collaborative work involved a close study of the French, American and Russian revolutions. James in particular was able to draw on his extensive knowledge of European civilization, its history, politics, art and culture, tracing its development through the progressive realization of the democratic idea. At the same time, however, he and his collaborators were seeking to move beyond the confines of a European revolutionary tradition and to embrace the unique conditions of the New World. Their work was animated by their unshakeable conviction that the war heralded fundamental social change. Increasingly they argued that the American people would be at the forefront of the struggle to found the new society, not least the millions of black workers at the center of the industrial machine who formed a unique link between American labor and the millions of colonial peoples worldwide.

But the end of the war in 1945 failed to bring the kind of social upheaval, either in Europe or in America, which the Johnson Forest group had anticipated. Nevertheless, James felt he stood on the threshold of an important political breakthrough, as the collective work in which he had been deeply immersed for almost five years approached fruition. Instinctively he knew it would be decisive. For underpinning it was James's study of the Hegelian dialectic, the changing relationship between thought and society, subject and object, which he was confident would provide the philosophical foundations for a new revolutionary position. It was as yet incomplete, but by 1946 James felt that it lay within his grasp.

Moreover, James was at a turning point in his own personal life. For at last Constance Webb was beginning to reciprocate his affections. During the first five years of their relationship James had conducted an extraordinary campaign by letter to win her love. They had met only once after that first occasion in the Los Angeles church; but with Webb's move to New York in the spring of 1945 James was forced to confront the fact that she remained largely indifferent to his advances. Suddenly however, the dialectical law James was seeking to master in his political work came into forceful play. And at the very moment that he resolved to break the attachment we discover the emergence of a new intimacy. By the summer of 1946 James and Webb were living together in New York. They were married at Fort Lee, New Jersey in May 1946.

Between 1947 and 1950 James and his group published a number of important documents. These ranged from an analysis of the growth and fissures of the Trotskyist movement within American society, to questions of socialism, state capitalism and the Soviet Union, the black struggle, history and the dialectic. Most notable of these publications were *The Balance Sheet* (1947); *The Invading Socialist Society* (1947); *The Revolutionary Answer to the Negro Problem in the USA* (1948); *Notes on Dialectics* (1948); and *State Capitalism and World Revolution* (1950).

Taken as a whole, this body of work established an independent revolutionary position, one which enabled James to trace a Marxist lineage directly from the writings of Lenin. For James had come to the conclusion that Trotsky had not just been wrong in his interpretation of history, but that his method for understanding history was fundamentally flawed. Trotsky's thought had never moved dialectically, rather it remained trapped within the old categories of the Russian Revolution. For years the sterile debate between Trotsky and Stalin had clouded these more fundamental questions which were at issue.

But before James made the final break with the movement in which he had worked for nearly twenty years, he and his group first left the Workers Party. A month or so later they applied to rejoin the Socialist Workers Party under the leadership of James Cannon. Although the Johnson Forest group was given considerable autonomy within the SWP, relations were uneasy. Also, the difficulties James and his associates experienced were partly a reflection of the new pressures which increasingly impinged on these small revolutionary groups. The Cold War climate squeezed any kind of radical activity; but equally, it was no longer clear what political role such groups could play in a world transformed by the war. Moreover, James's own position in the United States was no longer secure. The immigration authorities had finally caught up with him, and he had to begin to prepare his case against deportation.

James's situation was further complicated by the fragility of his relationship with Webb. In September 1947, she had left him and returned to California to seek a divorce. Her situation was a difficult one, not least because, as the wife of a revolutionary leader, she found herself plunged into a maelstrom of rivalry and intense factionalism waged among James's political associates; and her anxieties were exacerbated by racial harassment and almost constant FBI surveillance. A temporary reconciliation was achieved between them; and James planned to use his marriage to Webb, an American citizen, as an important part of his case for being allowed to stay. He thought it would make it harder for the government to seek his deportation on technical grounds and force it to reveal the underlying political motives for his exclusion. But James faced a problem. He had acquired a Mexican "mail order" divorce from his first wife, Juanita, a Trinidadian, in order to marry Webb at Fort Lee. The divorce (and hence the marriage) was not, however, recognized as valid; and in 1948 James travelled to Reno, Nevada in order to obtain a second divorce. Webb, now pregnant with their child, remained in New York. They married again in November 1948, and in the following April, their son, Nobbie, was born.

1950 was a watershed year for James. While in Nevada he recognized that he faced the greatest crisis of his life; but he believed he had weathered it, reaching a new level of personal understanding. Furthermore, over the past decade he had established an historical method and laid the philosophical foundations of his future political activity; and he now felt free to explore questions of art, culture and aesthetics. These investigations, however, grew out of the new and original conception of political life which James had developed by the end of his stay in the United States, a conception that had been shaped by the conditions of the New World.

From the moment of his arrival James had been open to the distinctiveness of the United States—its sheer size, its geographical expanse and variation, its revolutionary history and break with Europe, the vitality and independence of its people—and he felt, to his core, the challenge of a new civilization. He was particularly anxious not to repeat the mistake of other European commentators who sought to fit America into "old world" categories, dismissing it as a brash, new society, a cultural and intellectual wasteland deficient in all those features of social life which they identified with civilization.

James thrived in the bustling cosmopolitan world of New York. He moved in literary circles (which included such figures as Richard Wright, Ralph Ellison, St. Claire Drake, James Farrell and Carl Van Vechten); he immersed himself in a study of American history and literature, and he enjoyed the popular arts of the American people. He read detective novels, and comic strips; he listened to radio soap operas; he avidly watched all the latest Hollywood movies, and he followed closely the careers of major film stars like Bette Davis, Rita Hayworth, Lana Turner, Edward G. Robinson and Humphrey Bogart. James became what he called "a neighborhood man," immersing himself into the rhythms of everyday life in order to understand better the expectations and aspirations of American men and women, their social relations, and routines of work and leisure.

This dimension of James's work in America was not indicated in his major publications of the 1940s. It was a personal project, remaining largely hidden from view and revealed only in his private correspondence with Constance Webb. Later, however, James sought to synthesize his ideas, intending to present them in a book, suitable for the general reader, which could be "read on a Sunday or on two evenings." He completed a first draft of his manuscript, *American Civilization*, in 1950.[18]

James's interest in America, like that of his predecessor Alexis De Tocqueville, in the nineteenth century, originally stemmed from political questions posed within the context of Europe. Although separated by more than a hundred years, both writers departed for the New World at a time of ferment in Europe, after the political landscape had been transformed by a major event. In De Tocqueville's case this was the French Revolution; for James it was the Russian Revolution. Each man believed that democracy was the moving force in history, and that a study of America—democracy's most powerful symbol—would cast light on its changing forms.

James, in approaching America as a distinctive civilization, sought to grasp the whole at a particular moment, fusing different strands of history, literature, popular art and the details of everyday life into a work of striking originality. It was his view that the American people were distinctive. Unburdened by the weight of European history, they were highly conscious of themselves as individuals and yet their need for community was equally strong. Their search for new, expanded forms of society able to encompass full, free individuality—the need to achieve complete democracy in all aspects of life—was the most advanced manifestation of what James understood to be the aim of modern people everywhere. This was what he called "the struggle for happiness." He believed that men and women were now the moving force of world civilization, their increasing power and presence the central feature of the contemporary age; and yet, as he recognized, their creative energies had never before been so stifled and fragmented.

James was conscious of the historical moment, writing as the superpowers faced each other across a ruined Europe, threatening repression and destruction on a scale previously unknown in humanity's development. For him, the Cold War rhetoric—freedom versus repression—symbolized the bitter conflict raging within American society. James conceived of his work on America as the first in a series of publications for a general audience which would address the crisis of the contemporary world. His concerns were with no less than the future of humanity itself. The urgency with which he viewed this task undoubtedly intensified his own desire to be allowed to remain in the United States. But his battle to avoid deportation fractured the creative moment. His marriage to Webb foundered; and, as he stood poised to engage with some of the largest and most critical questions facing humanity, he found himself forced back into old forms of political life and association. Although they had once stimulated some of his most original work, they now began to act as a check on his creative energies.

James's ambitious plans for a complex, original work on American civilization were transformed by these circumstances. He was forced to abandon work on his manuscript in order to prepare his legal case; but during 1952, when he was interned on Ellis Island, James took a number of central themes from the 1950 draft and developed them in a critical study of the work of Herman Melville. *Mariners, Renegades and Castaways* (1953) was published as part of James's plea to be allowed to remain in the United States; but he lost his case and was forced to leave America in 1953.

On his return to Britain in 1953, James attempted to extend his enquiries into literature and criticism which he had begun toward the end of his stay in the United States. Before his departure he had delivered an impressive series of lectures at Columbia University in New York, entitled, "The Idea of Personality in Great Literature," in which he examined the work of Aeschylus, Shakespeare, Milton, Rousseau, Melville and Dostoevsky. James hoped to use the ideas he advanced here as an important foundation in a broad project which traced the movement of democracy in world civilization, taking works of the creative imagination as an important source. These aspirations were only partly realized as a body of published work, but his concerns found a new outlet in the independence era of the former colonial territories. For James found that his understanding of Shakespeare, particularly *Hamlet* and King *Lear*, was immensely enriched by the political developments of the postwar world.[19]

During the second half of the 1950s James became an active participant in the debates and political activity which surrounded the foundation of the new African and Caribbean nations. George Padmore had played a key role throughout the war years, coordinating the different independence movements; but his organization had been boosted by the arrival in London of Kwame Nkrumah, a man dedicated to winning freedom for Africa's Gold Coast. James had already met Nkrumah in New York, and he had been impressed by his political determination. He followed closely his subsequent career, a new phase beginning in 1947 when Nkrumah returned home to build a mass movement to challenge colonial power. Within a decade Ghana, under Nkrumah's leadership, had become the first independent African state and James was invited by Nkrumah to Accra for the independence celebrations. Although James remained convinced that the Gold Coast revolution was a powerful symbol of a new stage in the progressive realization of the democratic ideal, he did not shirk from criticizing the later political developments which finally culminated in Nkrumah's overthrow. For, as James recognized in the dedication of his book *Nkrumah and the Ghana Revolution* (1962), "Like Cromwell and Lenin, [Nkrumah] initiated the destruction of a regime in decay—a tremendous achievement; but like them, he failed to create the new society."[20]

In 1958, at the invitation of his old friend, Eric Williams, James returned to Trinidad. He had been away for twenty-six years; but as the Caribbean islands now approached independence, James relished the chance to be part of this unique historical moment. He believed it to be full of creative possibilities, a time of transition when fundamental questions concerning political life were unusually clarified. His highest priority, however, was to engage the Caribbean people fully in the discussions about the form of the new society. As editor of *The Nation* he opened his newspaper columns to debate; he addressed public meetings; and he wrote extensively about the issues he believed to be important, publishing *Modern Politics* in 1960 and *Party Politics in the West Indies* in 1962.[21] But his lengthy appendix to a new edition of *The Black Jacobins* perhaps best illustrates James's thinking at this time. Its title, "From Toussaint L'Ouverture to Fidel Castro," reveals the contours of a Caribbean identity he was seeking to expose.

Although James recognized that questions of nationhood and national identity were central to the historical moment, he insisted on linking them decisively to the modern phase in the evolution of world society. He had no time for the narrow, small-island mentality of the emerging political leadership; and his own political alliance with Eric Williams quickly foundered. James was wholeheartedly committed to the conception of a West Indian Federation, a unified polity consisting of all the islands (British, Dutch, French and Spanish) to be built through popular mobilization. In his view, such a formation would not only stand against the divisive, old-style European nationalisms, but, expressive of the fundamental movement of twentieth-century society, it would anticipate political forms of the future.

James recognized the particular role played by Caribbean novelists, artists and cricketers in laying the foundations for a new Caribbean identity. He believed that the innovative quality of novels written by Wilson Harris or George Lamming, the new styles of cricket played by Garfield Sobers or Frank Worrell, were the cultural counterparts of the popular movement to establish new political forms.

It was in this climate of intense debate that James completed his book *Beyond A Boundary*. But increasingly hounded by Williams and marginalized by the new Caribbean leadership, James left Trinidad on the eve of its independence in 1962. He returned to London, and in the following year his book was published to enthusiastic reviews. Although it is widely regarded as the greatest book ever written on cricket, James announced in its opening pages that it was neither a book on cricket nor an autobiography.

Beyond A Boundary may be considered the only text James was able to complete from the ambitious writing program he had outlined at the end of his stay in the United States. It is inseparable from the project on American culture and society which James had pursued with such imagination and tenacity during the 1940s.[22] Indeed, the letters to Constance Webb and *American Civilization* form the indispensable link between James's early writings and this, his last major publication. For although James returned to London to excavate some of his earliest experiences and explore aspects of his formation, it was with a mature vision. Within this book he finally transcended the divisions of old European bourgeois society: the separation of art and life, culture and politics, intellectuals and people. It had been his experience of living in America which gave him a new integrated perspective on the world, but if he failed to realize it within his own life, *Beyond A Boundary* became its most brilliant literary expression.

In his last three decades James travelled extensively. He continued his engagement with the immense political problems which faced the new independent nations in Africa and the Caribbean, and he was a distinguished participant in radical debates in Europe and the United States. During the 1970s James held teaching posts in a number of American universities, and, with the reprinting of many of his major works, he became widely known to a new generation of young people. In particular he was rediscovered as one of the century's leading revolutionary figures, and he was much celebrated as a black icon. Although he was claimed by different constituencies James always refused to be confined, for his vision was truly universal. In 1981 he finally settled in London, remaining active as a writer and receiving many visitors at his home. James died, after a short illness, on May 31, 1989.

THE STORY OF THE WEBB LETTERS

During the last decade of his life, James attempted to write his autobiography. He sought to make sense of the journey which had begun at the turn of the century in Trinidad, carrying him to Europe, the New World, Africa, back to his native Caribbean and finally to London, where he died. The autobiographical task he confronted required the creation of a narrative which could reflect this movement and reveal the process by which he developed from a novelist and cricket writer to a major theorist and practitioner of revolutionary politics.

James's commitment to this project, however, was never more than half-hearted. He had left it too late, and he no longer had the energy to write something which would be more than just recounting a series of episodes and encounters over nine decades: such a task required a forward momentum which his life now lacked. For James's interest had always been in movement: "Time would pass, old empires would fall and new ones take their place, the relations of countries and the relations of classes had to change, before I discovered that it is not the quality of goods and utility which matter, but movement; not where you are or what you have, but where you have come from, where you are going and the rate at which you are getting there."[23] But at the end of his life he could only recapitulate the past from a static moment in the present. Thus, although he sought to discover the logic of his life's course as a historical narrative, a progressive movement in which previous stages of development were both incorporated and transcended, James's attempts were always thwarted by the recursive movement of the memory itself.

Working for James during the 1980s, I became involved, like others before me, in his attempt to draft an autobiography. It was a frustrating endeavor. I found out that it was almost impossible to get beyond a certain narrative which James had constructed and to which he clung as the single unifying thread of his life. But the movement implied here was illusory, since the narrative was in fact constructed from a series of timeless moments. Instead of exploring the past in order to situate the present and imaginatively create a future, the past had become a timeless place linked to an immovable present; and his mind was able only to shuttle back and forth between fixed points in the past and present. Indeed so powerful was this recursive movement of the memory that James could dictate episodes to me which were identical, almost word for word, to those taken down by the others before me who had compiled notes and chapters towards his autobiography.

The way in which James chose to remember and construct parts of his autobiography was particularly pronounced in the case of his American years. Repeatedly he asserted that his fifteen years in the United States were the most important for his intellectual and political development. He was, of course, referring to his collaboration with members of the Johnson Forest Tendency; and to the important new positions on key political questions which they established collectively. This work laid the foundation for a new conception of revolutionary Marxism. But in drafting this section of his autobiography James enshrined certain key moments, fixing them in his mind as dominant and immovable landmarks in the midst of a complex and contested terrain. His attempt to impose coherence and order was perhaps not surprising, given that in the intense climate of revolutionary politics, one marked by endless sectarian feuds and fissions, participants at any time were always searching for points of stability in an essentially fluid world.

Occasionally, though, something new and unexpected would emerge. Chance remarks and informal conversations during the long hours we spent together began to suggest different interpretations which subverted the sense of James's life as a straightforward linear progression. One question on which he reflected a great deal concerned women. Conscious of his vulnerability and isolation in old age, and aware of his need for domestic companionship with me, James would sometimes talk about his different relationships with women. This was an area where he readily admitted failure. It was nowhere more strikingly revealed than during his American years, where the remarkable success of his intellectual partnership with a number of prominent women was matched only by the scale of his failure to grasp a new conception of human relationships offered to him by the woman he loved. For despite his choice of female collaborators as intimate colleagues in revolutionary politics— indeed he regarded three of them (Dunayevskaya, Lee and Webb) as among his greatest "pupils"—he still acknowledged the depth of his resistance to admitting women into his life on equal terms. At best, James dealt with them as colleagues and collaborators (though he always sought to incorporate them into *his* vision of the world); at worst, he used them as domestic servants.

Once James had withdrawn from any active interest in the autobiographical project, I became free to try and fit together the different pieces of his life in new ways. My sources were what I heard and saw; the published writings; and the notes, jottings, letters and documents which constituted his vast, unexplored personal archive.

From the beginning it seemed to me that the full-length manuscript, *American Civilization*, which had languished unpublished among his papers for more than thirty years, was central to any re-configuration.[24] Certainly my understanding of what James was attempting here was greatly enhanced by the Webb letters; but equally I recognized that the correspondence stood alone as a remarkable document in its own right. It was quite unlike anything else in the James corpus.

Although the correspondence with Webb continued over subsequent decades, indeed until James's death, the later writing was of a different kind. Following the breakup of their marriage in the late 1940s a new sort of relationship had to be established; and the bitterness, dislocation and anger were resolved partly through the shared responsibility for their son, Nobbie. This itself was not easy for either of them, given James's forced departure from the United States in 1953 and the difficulties Webb faced raising a mixed-race child.

Over the years, however, Webb kept most of the letters she received from James. During the 1980s she began to transcribe them with a view to publication. It seems unlikely that at the time of writing James anticipated their eventual publication; but he responded with great enthusiasm to Webb's plans to edit them into a volume. Their publication offers a new perspective not just on James's American years, but on his life as a whole.

There is a dramatic narrative to be found in James's letters to Webb. It unfolds over the course of a decade, reaching a climax in 1948 with James's exile to Reno, Nevada; but the conclusion of the story is to be found later, outside the correspondence itself. The process of identifying the narrative involves a sort of detective work, piecing together a coherent story from a mass of documents, with obvious gaps and omissions. Part of the problem also stems from the fact that, by their nature, letters rarely pursue a single argument. Writers zigzag across topics, returning to some, while leaving others suspended and never fully resolved. Thus James's letters may be conceived as a sort of mosaic, a collage of pieces of different materials from which different stories may be told. The richness of the correspondence lies as much in its elusive, poetic qualities as in the dramatic story it contains. By focusing on the latter, which I believe to be the most compelling narrative to be excavated, I am conscious of sacrificing some of the beauty of the letters, and in arranging different pieces into a coherent linear story, I destroy something of the openness of the text itself. For as we approach the climax we cannot be sure how James will resolve the crisis he faces.

Thus in the account which follows I am not concerned to present an exhaustive analysis of the Webb correspondence. Instead, I attempt to highlight the dramatic narrative and its development, drawing on my imagination and on the work concerning James's American period which I have pursued over a number of years.[25] I trace the story through four parts, each of which has a distinctive character and yet is integrally linked to the overall movement of the whole. At one level this movement appears to be a linear progression, one of increasing integration as past and present are conceived as stages on the path towards a new future. It mirrors the classic revolutionary vision itself. For the near future is conceived of as a moment of breakthrough, or, as James wrote in *Notes on Dialectics*, following Lenin, "LEAP LEAP LEAP"—the movement from quantity to quality. At another level, however, the narrative reflects James's attempt to achieve integration in American society through Constance Webb. In the beginning James imagines that these two historical projects can be assimilated to one another. But—as the correspondence increasingly reveals—they are fundamentally at odds.

This is the crisis that James faced in Nevada. In many ways the climax may be interpreted as containing the whole story of the correspondence itself. The drama of whether James will manage to acquire the divorce from his first wife in Trinidad, find his way through a racial and political minefield, change his personal and political life and complete his work on the dialectic are the elements of his final test. We feel with him that if he is able to weather this crisis the future holds immense possibilities. But as James desperately sought ways of establishing a new future with Webb, he was simultaneously forced back, by the difficulties of his circumstances (not least his gambling), into old patterns of dependency on his comrades. The sheer anguish of James's late writing from Reno reflects the extraordinary struggle he faced, between his group and Webb, between Europe and America, between the revolution and his love for a woman.

The last letters James wrote to Webb in 1948 convey the sense of his being on the verge of a breakthrough. We feel that he is poised to LEAP LEAP LEAP, as he senses a new life lying within his grasp; but at this very moment we become witnesses to James's struggle against the forces of his own personality. The contours of the battle, however, have already been established. In a handwritten inscription to Webb which

James attached to his essay, "Dialectical Materialism and the Fate of Humanity," in October 1947 we discover that he can only imagine his marriage as an American suburban domesticity, a sort of eternity outside of history, at the very moment that he articulates a progressive vision of humanity and the development of world civilization.

The struggle between the old and the new is manifest in the subversion of the narrative's movement itself. Indeed it is suggested from the beginning by a formal symmetry in the correspondence. For the dramatic narrative which sustains the possibility of progress toward integration is framed by two timeless moments of limbo; and these indicate the possibility of the story being subverted by forces not previously acknowledged.

The first letters James wrote while marooned on board ship, traveling from Mexico to New Orleans are mirrored by those he sent in 1948 while seeking a divorce in Reno, Nevada. What they both share is James's separation from the familiar world of his political group, and his firsthand exposure to contemporary life. There was a curious anomaly in James's existence in America, since his normal day-to-day life as J. R. Johnson, surrounded by comrades who catered to his every need, took him away from society, enabling him to elevate an historical vision in which the present is always sacrificed for the future. But outside the cocoon of the Johnson Forest group, James was forced to confront the here and now, the reality of modern society; and on each occasion his imaginative powers as a novelist were stimulated. But the symmetry between the early and late episodes, between the boat to New Orleans and the ranch in Reno, hides a world of difference. For the character we see at the beginning of the story, the great nineteenth-century romantic hero, has become by its end a divided and tormented modernist intellectual.

The early James, confident, powerful, expansive and brimming with creative energy, believed he could integrate the progressive narrative (revolutionary politics) with the here and now (everyday life). It involved the incorporation of Webb into his imaginative vision. As the story of the letters unfolds, though, we are forced to acknowledge that James is not in control of either project in any realistic sense.

Perhaps at the end of his life James, conscious of his impending death, was able to achieve a kind of integration, if not quite the one he sought with Webb in the turbulent America of his most creative years. For in abandoning his autobiographical project, he finally freed himself from the problem of historical narrative.

I. THE BEGINNING OF A JOURNEY (1939-40)

"I made a long trip, 8,000 miles, I think, and saw thousands of people, and millions of things. It was a great experience in every way and you remain my most vivid and intimate personal experience."

—James to Webb, 31 August 1939

The letters of the first period open in April 1939 with James's trip to Mexico; and they close a year and a half later, following the assassination of Leon Trotsky in August 1940. In many important ways these letters indicate the distinctive themes of the correspondence as a whole. They reveal the depth of James's commitment to revolutionary politics as well as his instinctive pushing against the limits of such a life. From the beginning James covered a range of topics, moving easily between the immediate political issues which faced the Trotskyist movement at that time and the personal questions concerning Webb's development as an individual personality, between his commitment to the revolution and his love for Webb. His confident writing style and the fluency with which he achieves such transitions suggests the profound connection in James's own mind between the different dimensions of modern life.

If the early correspondence with Webb establishes the seriousness with which James approached the question of individual self-expression, there is no other body of literature which so starkly exposes James's own personality. The different facets of his character emerge, not just through the content of the letters, but in the various voices which he adopts in his exchanges with Webb. It is the intensity of James's engagement in Webb's struggle for self-expression, however, which is most striking; and from the outset we cannot but feel this to be a battle at the core of James's own life.

These first letters reveal the contours of the political landscape which defined James's work after his arrival in the United States at the end of 1938; and we follow the course of his changing political priorities. But outstanding among the early writing is James's extended account of life on board ship as he travels across the Gulf of Mexico. It is as if, marooned at sea and freed from the pressures and responsibilities of his political life, James is suddenly able to open up his personality. He allows himself to feel, to desire, to dream. Interestingly he did not immediately send the two shipboard letters to Webb; rather he held back, referring to them in later correspondence as "a little book" written specially for her. The book was also, as he confessed, a "love letter."

James creates a short story during his voyage. It is built around sharp observation of certain characters who share the journey with him; and, unusually for James, he too is cast as a distinctive personality within the unfolding narrative. The writing is wonderfully evocative of the sense of limbo which infects everyone, for the ship moves only imperceptibly. Its passengers are trapped, separated from the momentum of their lives and forced to create community with one another. In important ways the experience on board ship returns James to his Caribbean past, specifically to his early aspirations as a novelist. His keen eye and ear for the drama of everyday life are irrepressible; but the account also contains another story, one which he tells through a series of asides to the reader.

Both letters open with a vivid encounter which brings together the major characters around whom James's story is built. There is Tenor (a singer on his way to Rio de Janeiro) and Guitar (an English steward), and the writer himself. But although James humorously describes the life-stories of the crew and his participation in the ship's life as an enthusiastic listener to radio soap operas, we are always conscious of him standing back, a detached observer of the men around him. By contrast, his letters to Webb are a space in which he does not hold back. Rather he imaginatively situates her at his side during the trip, confiding in her many aspects of his personality as if the two of them were engaged in an intimate conversation. In this way, the narrative of James's own personal development unfolds, and we recognize the fundamental shift from a novelist's engagement with social life to a commitment to revolution.

Unlike most of the early letters to Webb, those James writes while on board ship are marked by a striking freedom and expansiveness. These features are enhanced as we return once more to the hurly-burly of James's political life. But already the writing has changed. For although from the beginning James treats Webb as a confidant, signing himself "Nello," the name used by his mother and close friends (but never by his political associates, for whom he was always "Jimmy"), the intimacy of their exchanges deepens significantly during the course of his trip. Of course, the letters written by James while on board ship are an important turning point; but so too is Webb's willingness to share with him her struggle to find a new life, following the breakup of her marriage. This marks the beginning of James's intense engagement in Webb's self-development. Through it he is able to explore his own personal trajectory, illuminating the many facets of his own character within the contours of a revolutionary's life.

Despite the new understanding between them, however, James's return to Trotskyist headquarters inhibited the development of his relationship with Webb. Indeed he is the first to acknowledge that he is unable to write to her as freely as before. For the urgency of the political tasks which now face the movement—the imminence of war in Europe, the need to develop a clear position and strategy on the race question, and the disarray precipitated by Stalin's pact with Nazi Germany—begin to absorb all of James's energies. As his letters reveal, there was a stark contrast between the disorganization within the movement, especially at the level of its leadership, and the scope of the party's ambition. Despite James's frustration with the internal squabbles, he remains convinced that the world stands at a critical juncture and that his tiny party will influence millions of Americans, if not toward the revolution, then at least against their own government.

The letters written during the second half of 1939 offer a unique insight into the pressures of James's life. For someone so careful about his public persona, James is surprisingly candid about the turbulence of his existence.

But the political crisis was not just external. Not only did it go to the core of the revolutionary movement itself, as he makes clear in his comments to Webb on the leadership. It reached the core of James's life as well. His American immigration visa was due to expire, forcing him to go underground in December 1939. James's "retirement" marks the beginning of the end of the first batch of letters, a closure dramatically sealed with the assassination of Trotsky in August 1940.

The early letters of 1939–40 are important in establishing the narrative which unfolds over the course of the next decade. James's first journey through America stands as a metaphor for the voyage of self-discovery that the correspondence itself charts. As readers, we too embark on this journey, conscious now of the key dramatic elements which have been woven into the story at the beginning—James's wooing of Webb, his decision to operate as an underground political activist, his commitment to a revolutionary path. Moreover the different rhythms of his early writing prepare us for the ebb and flow of the story's movement.

II. A SYMBOL OF AMERICAN CIVILIZATION (1943-4)

After a silence of three years, James resumed his correspondence with Webb. The intervening period had been difficult, as James himself had predicted in one of his last letters to Webb in 1940. "It is adversity that tests and makes people. It is easy to sail along when everything is flowing with you. But now we need courage." The changes in James's own character may be discerned in the writing itself. The later letters are distinguished by a new passionate urgency; the writing is intense and yet always controlled; it is focused and expansive. The distinctive formal features mirror the substance of the second phase of correspondence, as James struggles with questions of the individual personality while seeking to grasp the movement of civilization as a whole. These qualities are particularly notable in James's second letter to Webb of September 1943. But it is important for other reasons too.

It is clear that an important shift had taken place in James's orientation. In many ways this shift was symbolized by the letters James wrote as he travelled by boat from Mexico to New Orleans. He was leaving behind the old European style of party politics, represented by Trotsky, and beginning his journey into the New World. The letter of September 1943 shows how James's renewed engagement in Webb's struggle for self-expression was already becoming linked to his own explorations into the nature of modern American society. But if James is confident he can help Webb to find her way, he acknowledges too that there is much that he can learn from her.

It is clear that by this time James had already begun to immerse himself in American popular culture, confessing to Webb his particular fascination with Hollywood films. Originally movies like *Stormy Weather* or *That Uncertain Feeling* offered him a tangible connection with society, breaking the isolation of his private political work; but increasingly he recognized the fundamental connection between his study of the Hegelian dialectic and these forms of contemporary popular culture.

From the letters of 1943 we can begin to piece together the different elements of James's nascent project. His central concern was the relationship between art and society, and he begins by noting, "Like all art, but more than most, the movies are not merely a reflection, but an extension of the actual, but an extension along the lines which people feel are lacking and *possible* in the actual. That my dear, is the complete secret of Hegelian dialectic. The two, the actual and the potential, are always inseparably linked; one is always giving way to the other. At a certain stage a crisis takes place and a complete change is the result." (1 September 1943). James was seeking to illuminate the process by which cultural forms become appropriated and transformed by a mass audience through his discussion of the changing popularity of certain kinds of Hollywood stars; and by contrasting such figures as Charles Boyer and Humphrey Bogart, Greta Garbo and Bette Davis, he is able to suggest important differences between European and American society.

This question of the dramatic personality, how distinctive social features become refracted and expressed through unique individual personalities was of course implicit in James's early fiction. It remained an important feature in his work; but after experiencing American culture, he began to appreciate the potential of the mass art form and the remarkable power and presence of film stars. Among them was Ethel Waters, the black actress who James admired in *Cabin In The Sky*. She became a focus for James as he began to toy with the idea of again using drama to explore the dynamics of society and history through the clash of human personalities. He planned to cast Waters as Harriet Tubman in a play built around the Abolitionist movement of the nineteenth century. James first outlined these plans in 1943; and he expands on the proposed historical drama in the early letters of 1944. Indeed he found a role in the play for Webb herself.

This was not the first time James had attempted to write and produce a historical drama. He was mindful no doubt of the unfavorable critical reviews which his play, *Toussaint L'Ouverture*, had received in 1936. James acknowledges, in his letters to Webb, the difficulties of the playwright's task in achieving the proper balance between character and plot, between human passions and political ideas.[26]

Although the conflict between slaves and slave-owners constitutes the basic narrative structure of the play James planned to write for Waters, it is obvious that his interest lies equally in exploring the internal dynamics of a political movement. Specifically he wished to trace the changing relationship between key characters as the political struggle unfolds, raising questions of leadership and strategy. But importantly, too, James was fascinated by the intersection of the personal and the political; and, in making Tubman his central character, he throws issues of race and gender into sharp relief.

It is hard not to read James's outline of his play as in part a dramatization of his own circumstances. He knew well the powerful emotions simmering in political life: the love, hate, jealousies, rivalries, battles between men and women, battles between blacks and whites within the revolutionary movement itself. And almost from the beginning of his resumed correspondence with Webb, James's writing reveals such tensions.

Despite the deadly implications of the play for James's own life, he humorously develops it as a drama within a drama through an account to Webb of his attempts to approach Ethel Waters. This time he explicitly casts himself as a character in the scenario. James's sense of theater, however, has a greater resonance. For we cannot help but feel that after 1943 James conceived of his courtship of Webb as a powerful piece of drama. He is highly conscious of his stage presence, casting himself and Webb in different roles. At times James also plays the audience. The play is both comic and tragic; art and life have indeed become inseparable in the world of letters.

The letters of 1943 mark the beginning of the second phase of James's relationship with Webb. Although there is a sense of a new beginning, a recognition that each has changed in three years, something remains fundamentally unchanged; and the original spark of attraction between them continues as a powerful and tangible force in the writing itself. The sheer number of letters James wrote to Webb during 1944 is evidence enough, quickly sweeping aside any residual hesitancy in their renewed exchange. There is, however, an important shift in the circumstances of the correspondence. At the end of May 1944, Webb moved from California to New York in order to pursue her career as an actress and model; and in so doing she effectively ended her relationship with the actor, Jack Gilford, who had drawn her into artistic circles closely associated with the Communist Party. For the first time, five years after their initial meeting, James and Webb now lived in close geographical proximity; but despite this, James continued to write frequently—sometimes lines scribbled as he traveled on the subway, at other times extended and exploratory notes by which he sought to articulate the changing historical relationship between art and society.

The focus of the 1944 letters remains the question of the individual personality. But by taking Webb's personal struggle to find the conditions for the full and free expression of her individuality, James is able to address questions that were central to modern civilization itself. These questions, the relationship between the individual and society, between men and women, between the form and content of creative work, between art and life, are of course implicit in James's "politics;" and yet, as he later revealed (in *Beyond A Boundary*), they were accorded no proper place in the political sphere. Writing in one of his later letters of 1944, James notes, "politics, art, life, love in the modern world, all become so closely integrated that to understand one is to understand all." (June 1944).

James's ambitious project concerning the movement of world civilization begins to emerge in the course of the 1944 correspondence. Indeed we recognize that some of the central features are already present in one of the very first letters of that year. Writing to Webb on 5 January, James dissects a recent production of *Othello* which starred Paul Robeson and Uta Hagen. His critical approach here is characteristic, rooted in his early study of the game of cricket. James deals first of all with the details of the production itself, focusing on the interpretation of the Shakespearean rhythms of speech and key dramatic personalities, before considering the broader questions raised by the play. A combination of technique, insight and imagination are the qualities James identifies as necessary to any modern production; and yet in his opinion neither Robeson nor Hagen succeed in elevating the play above the unfolding of the plot itself. James recognizes that a performance of *Othello* in the United States represented a political event. But he is quick to point out that the play does not just pose questions about race in modern society; for Desdemona's defiance of all established social conventions also raises critical issues about gender.

Fundamentally, though, James interprets *Othello* as a play about the relationship between the individual and society. For him, Shakespeare posed the question for the first time in the modern world, writing as he did at the moment in which the old feudal structures gave way to the new bourgeois society. The world of the seventeenth century saw the birth of the individual personality; human beings were now agents in society and history, responsible alone for their beliefs, their decisions, and their actions. According to James, the insights that emerged from Shakespeare's dramatic imagination illuminated the world in which he himself lived, since the America of the 1940s was still, in essence, a bourgeois society; and the problem of the relationship of the individual to it, which the Elizabethan playwright explored five hundred years earlier, was exposed as never before in history.

James's interpretation of Robeson's failure is particularly interesting for the basis of his criticism is Robeson's inability to make the role of Othello his own. By this he means that the modern actor should immerse himself profoundly in the historical drama and yet recreate it for his own time. It is, as James acknowledges later, a Hegelian question—the dialectical relationship of essence and manifestation. Although he does not explicitly refer in his letter of 5 January to his distancing from Robeson, following the latter's close association with the American Communist Party, it is nevertheless possible to read James's criticism as a response to the actor's inability to resist Stalinism. And Robeson's failure to assert his own unique individual personality within the play itself becomes a symbol of the modern intellectuals' failure to respond to the crisis of their time.

This struggle between the individual and society, the means by which the human personality resists the confinement and fragmentation of modern life, becomes the central theme in James's subsequent letters of 1944. He recognizes it to be the animating force of Webb's life. She is a young American woman seeking to find the social expression of her individuality. At first James encourages her to break with her old life in California and to try to make her way independently in New York. Later, Webb's attempts to write poetry and her willingness to share it with James provide a new focus for this question.

James takes Webb's birthday in June 1944 as a symbol of a new beginning. Webb has finally arrived in New York. All the ordinary things to be enjoyed in human friendship now seem possible; and James celebrates with a letter full of poetry. He admits that he is out of practice as a critic; but already, in juxtaposing Webb's work with that of Spender and Shelley, he seeks to understand the distinctive quality of the modern voice. This attempt, pursued in a number of later letters, involves the detailed line by line analysis of the sounds, rhythms and content of Webb's writing and that of her contemporaries, an analysis moreover which is linked to a wide-ranging exploration of the historical roots of twentieth-century poetry.

From the outset James is highly sensitive to the creative process itself. He explains to Webb that the difficult synthesis of imagination and discipline, the instinctive force of creation with the need to find social form, often emerges from intense conflict. But, as James recognizes, there are great difficulties: "The expression of social forces in our time, in art and in life, is a highly contradictory, subtle and complex business. The crudeness and coarseness of the Stalinists here as elsewhere have wrought an incalculable amount of harm." (14 June 1944). What particularly interests James is Webb's instinctive grasp of modern rhythms and language. For the modern poet, expression is always social, but the problem is to create genuine poetic imagery and not rhetoric or argument. And the more James examines the nature of Webb's poetic voice, the more explicit becomes his appreciation of its distinctively twentieth-century American qualities.

In a remarkable letter of July 1944, James attempts to reveal a sequence of formal developments in poetry, from Shakespeare's development of blank verse to Whitman's complete break with the European style. James's understanding of these formal shifts is built upon their relationship to key moments in the history of the democratic ideal. It is a dialectical process in which moments of innovation are succeeded by convention, freedom by conformity, spontaneity by artifice. Thus James contrasts the ordered eighteenth-century verse of Pope with the burst of poetic innovation—associated with Keats, Wordsworth, Shelley and Coleridge—which followed the French Revolution. Likewise he argues that Whitman's free verse has to be understood in the context of America's early democracy before the Civil War and the rise of mass industry.

As James reminds Webb, her task as a modern poet is to find a way of giving expression to the social forces of her age. That task is an immensely difficult one, as his dismissal of "W.H. Auden and that bunch" reveals. But in James's view, the social responsibility cannot be evaded, for the poet's own creativity depends on it. Describing the thrill he experiences listening to a piano concerto of Mozart or Beethoven, James uses the interplay between soloists and orchestra as a metaphor for this relationship between individual and society. The expansion of an individual's creative capacity is, he suggests, part of a dialectical process, and organically tied to changes in society itself.

We sense a growing intellectual excitement in the 1944 letters. It becomes ever more tangible as James acknowledges that questions of art, creativity and individual personality illuminate the philosophical and political problems with which he is grappling inside the Trotskyist movement—the question of the dialectic, the movement of history and the development of society toward complete democracy. At the same time, however, James's different voices or personalities—teacher, critic, supporter, lover, friend—take on sharper and more contrasting tones. Although there are still moments of gentle playfulness in the writing—humorous self-indulgence or whimsical imaginings which subvert the ferocious and rather forbidding political facade—there is now also an urgency, almost an impatience. For we are increasingly aware of the marked inequality in the correspondence, with James's extraordinary outpouring failing to awaken in Webb any significant response of the same order. It is particularly manifest in letters which read as speeches, rather than as parts of conversation or dialogue between two people.

Occasionally though, James is able to achieve transitions between different personalities within a single letter. The ease of this movement, what James calls the transition between "majesty and the sudden simplicity" which are, for him, the mark of the artist (Beethoven or Shakespeare, for example), reveals again his own distinctive skill as a writer. The letter to Webb of 7 July 1944 is a particularly fine example, evoking James, the renowned political orator, who is able to captivate a whole audience as he did in the church in California where he first met Webb in 1939. And yet, despite this quality, the letter also remains a remarkably intimate document.

James begins with a playful response to a model agency photograph of Webb; but quickly he shifts into an introspective mood as he muses upon his own attraction to Webb and everything she symbolizes. The letter becomes a powerful soliloquy, animated by James's awareness of his changing perception of Webb. And in seeking to clarify this, James offers a powerful demonstration of the Hegelian principle of dialectic that he was seeking to grasp in his political work—that subject and object are linked in a moving, historical relationship and that as the subject changes so too does the object. In his final moving paragraph James imagines Webb, the actress, standing on stage in front of an audience. He confesses that "the most secret, the innermost, the unexpected dream come true" would be if she turned first to him, before all others. But, of course, we see that it is James himself who stands on the stage and in turning to Webb he is in fact turning to face himself.

Reading the letters of 1944, it is difficult not to perceive Webb as a sort of mirror in which James contemplates his own reflection. If he saw clearly the obstacles which faced Webb, it was because he confronted them too. For the conflict between freedom and necessity, imagination and discipline, individuality and social form cut to the core of the revolutionary movement itself. Thus, at the most personal level, these questions find focus in James's desire for intimacy and companionship which his political work leaves untouched, while at another level they illuminate much broader historical issues concerning the development of modern civilization. It comes as no surprise then to discover James's self-conscious exploration of his own trajectory in the later correspondence of 1944. He begins to draft sections of his autobiography, starting with the early years in Trinidad, in the form of letters to Webb. This process of self-discovery is motivated by a sense of movement, a future opening out in which the past can be actively woven into the present (and not just recapitulated as at the end of his life).

But at the moment James turns inward to explore the circumstances of his Caribbean childhood, he is also, in other letters, reaching out to grasp some of the biggest questions facing humanity itself. The confidence with which he approaches the latter stems, in part, from his sense that the collective work of the Johnson Forest Tendency is now coming to fruition. In his letters to Webb of 1944, James increasingly indicates the direction in which ideas in the Tendency are developing—specifically on the race question and the nature of the Soviet Union. Moreover, as James makes clear, these questions go to the heart of modern civilization, opening up entirely new perspectives on the development of humanity.

The excitement of these discoveries explodes in a letter which James wrote following his meeting with Richard Wright. Here James celebrates the fact that the novelist, through artistic means, has reached the same conclusion that he himself had drawn from an intensive study of history and politics. And in anticipating the enormous upheaval of black people against American society, James seeks to place their struggle within a broader context. Undaunted by two thousand years of history, he proceeds, in just a handful of pages, to outline the historical progression towards humanity's achievement of complete consciousness, tracing the process by which ideas once considered advanced and the preserve of a few have become the rights and expectations shared by millions of people worldwide. According to James, it was this tremendous movement of civilization which called forth the unprecedented forces of reaction (fascism). The intensity of the conflict is felt at all levels of modern society—in the workplace, in art and literature, in popular culture and, not least, in the intimate relations between men and women.

The letter to Webb about Richard Wright reveals James at his most magisterial, commanding a broad sweep of history and yet remaining firmly anchored in an understanding of the present. This combination of range and depth finds expression in the writing itself. It is controlled and at the same time explosive—the cold intellectual rationalism matched by an extraordinary passion. In many ways this letter stands as a symbol of the early, expansive phase of James's relationship with Webb. As both the content and tone of the correspondence suggests, it was a period in which James was buoyed by a great self-confidence, an inner certainty which stemmed from his profound commitment to a revolutionary life. It gave him the sense, momentarily, of being able to hold together all the contradictory elements of such an existence. Indeed the tension between them must surely have contributed to the wonderful creative energy of the letters, but it was an equilibrium impossible to sustain. For the conflicts are already discernible in the letters of 1944. Not least because in James's imaginary theater, Webb is expected to play the role to which she has been assigned; but those very qualities James finds so compelling in her make it impossible for her to play such a role.

The 1944 correspondence charts James's increasing objectification of Webb as a symbol of modern America. Webb instinctively grasps what James struggles to understand intellectually. This young Californian woman with her beauty, energy, creativity, and desire for an integrated life, comes to embody for James a new stage in modern civilization. It is distinctively American. But equally, as the letters begin

28 *Introduction*

to show, James is faced with a real person, Constance Webb. She has her own will, desire and freedom. His frustration with her is palpable.

James sought to turn Webb into a pupil rather like his others—Eric Williams, Grace Lee, Raya Dunayevskaya, and William Gorman. Her refusal to be moulded in such a way exacerbates the tension between Webb and his closest political associates, which James is forced to recognize. Almost from the beginning it is discernible in the tentativeness or unease in James's writing about his collaborators. Later it becomes more manifest as the collective work of the Johnson Forest Tendency gathers pace.

III. UNCERTAINTY AND ATTACHMENT (1945–6)

James's letters of 1945 contrast sharply with those of the previous year. The enormous optimism driving the early correspondence, the sense of jointly embarking on the same path and riding the tide of history (cosmopolitan black man, young white American woman) begins to dissipate. There are fewer moments of brilliant illumination; and there is neither the same confidence nor control in the writing itself. Indeed, James contemplates breaking off his correspondence with Webb, recognizing that she remains largely untouched by his passionate courtship.

During the spring and summer of 1945 Webb was working as an actress at the Stamford Theater in Connecticut. After seeing her in a performance of Chekhov's *The Sea Gull*, James writes a long letter to her in which he dissects the play, exploring its dramatic structure. But his interpretation, like his earlier response to Paul Robeson in *Othello*, is much more than a critical appraisal of that particular production. It casts light on the forces which animate his own life. For his understanding of the play hinges on what he calls its *revelation*, the moment when Nina recognizes her vocation. "Not fame nor glory; but patience and faith in your work," becomes the phrase which James ponders. He recognizes the difficulties of translation, considering and rejecting "fortitude" or "capacity to endure," instead preferring the simple, though much abused notions of faith or patience. Even in Webb's four lines he insists that her acting should be an embodiment of such a conception.

This letter encapsulates much of the substance of James's exchanges with Webb. His emphasis on the notion of commitment, of a faith or vocation, is at the center of his response to Webb's poetry, to her acting, and to her life in general. Again and again James proclaims his own commitment—as much to Webb as to the world revolution. He contrasts his inner certainty with Webb's hesitancy and equivocation. Moreover he believes that it gives him insight into her life which she cannot possibly have. James takes up this question of faith in other letters too. He gently reminds her that whatever failings she may find in his close political associates, she must acknowledge their profound commitment to a certain way of life. For unlike her, they have decisively turned their backs on what James calls "bourgeois society," resisting its hold in every aspect of their lives, while Webb remains unsure, undecided, tossed hither and thither by her inability to discover fundamental principles by which to live her life. Indeed, for James, Jack Gilford remains the symbol of temptation.

One of the 1945 letters in particular reveals the important shift in James's mood. It is marked by its introspection and hesitancy. Writing after midnight, when the world outside is dark and still, James toys with the idea of whether to respond to Webb's letters. He feels disinclined. To write means to switch on the light and thereby destroy the mystery of the darkness; but that is, in fact, what the letter is about, as James for the first time holds up to the light his own relationship with Webb. Reading his letter seems almost like eavesdropping on an intensely private conversation which James is having with himself. Although on this occasion he stops short of breaking off the relationship, there are other outbursts of irritation, even petulance, which begin to disrupt the progression of the narrative. Indeed, in another letter of October 1945, James confesses that he has destroyed almost all of Webb's letters and photographs.

After almost six years, the disintegration of the relationship seems inevitable. In a letter to Webb of 2 February 1946, James acknowledges that all his efforts to persuade Webb to reject "lights, glitter, self-expression, everything bourgeois" have failed. He now knows that she is unable to commit herself to artistic development in the context of the revolutionary movement. James speaks quite frankly to Webb about what he considers to be her failings; yet the cool, distant and restrained quality of the writing suggests not anger, but resignation. Certainly he never underestimates the scale and intensity of the battle which Webb confronts. It is no less than a social revolution itself.

But it is here that the dialectical law to which James repeatedly returns in his correspondence with Webb becomes manifest. And in the moment that he resolves to break his attachment there emerges evidence of a new intimacy. This dramatic turning point seems to have been stimulated partly by Webb's decision to write a critical essay on the fiction of Richard Wright. It represents a development of her earlier interest in the race question (subject of the 1939–40 letters); and it enables James to take up the familiar position of mentor or teacher—supplying Webb with a reading list and an outline of the method (dialectic) by which she should approach her subject. But it is more than this. James sees it as a possibility for incorporating Webb into his political circle. For the ambivalence of his political collaborators towards Webb is now openly acknowledged; and the brief account James provides of their collective life, admittedly written with some humor, is devastating: "Nettie came specially from Philly [Philadelphia] to see after me. Ike went to Doc B to get Vitamin B and instructions to give me injections every day; Grace and Rae arranged this trip. Then Rae took over getting a new lamp for me. G. arranged for me to see an oculist or something. Both of them went with me on W'y [Wednesday]. Rae stayed behind to pick up the glasses. Grace took me to dinner at her brother's and gave me stationery, etc., she had bought ($12.00) for our work. Nettie helped dispatch me. Rae met me at the train with the glasses—I have them on—and sandwiches. On Monday a.m. both of them meet me—I'll travel through the night—to start immediately on some writing. And that is only half. They keep me going." [1945 Portrait (Partial) of a Man].

James interprets Webb's commitment to a writing project as evidence of her having made a decisive move towards him. He describes it as her coming back, returning as if from a long voyage. April 1946 is a turning point, and a new voice emerges in the letters. There is now a softness and intimacy in the writing, a distinctive sort of tenderness which follows the climax of a great battle. "Was ever such a play written?" James asks in a letter of 27 April. Although he now emanates calmness and control—indeed we sense an inner happiness—we have never been so aware of his powers. He too is conscious of a surge of creative energy, not just in himself but in Webb too. Always watchful, carefully observant of subtle changes in personality, James begins to see the facets of his loved one differently. And yet he still cannot be sure that he has won her.

A series of letters which James wrote while travelling in April 1946 encapsulates this new phase. Here he creates a private space in which he opens up his personality, echoing the moment of freedom he experienced on board ship as he travelled from his meeting with Trotsky in Mexico six years before. Again, from the intimate tone of the letters we feel Webb to be almost at James's side, not just next to him this time, but travelling somewhere with him: it is as though they embarked together on a journey whose destination is unknown. In these letters James begins to admit his desire, his own vulnerability, and his longing for companionship and an intimate life. This is a striking transition. It reveals James as no longer satisfied with trying to incorporate Webb into his world; rather he can now see what intimacy on her terms might offer him. Later he confesses to Webb: "I have been living in a house with one wall closed. Enough of it is cracked for me to see through. And I don't only see what I never saw before but when I look through the other walls, the views that I thought I knew, I realize that I can only see those as they should be seen if all the walls are open. For me this is not only a battle for you. It is a battle for me." (13 April 1946).

Despite their regular meetings, James continued to write to Webb right up to the time that they decided to live together and marry in the summer of 1946. The battle for Webb seems finally to have been won. James's letters brim with joy. There is a tremendous surge of optimism, as he feels the two of them are now embarked on something new, undaunted and fearless of what the future holds. At the same time there is a certain poignancy in the images which James treasures of Webb when apart from her—her different appearances (as wife, lover, friend), the quiet shared moments, instances of everyday companionship and domesticity hitherto denied to them.

IV. SEPARATION AND LIMBO (1947–8)

"What people are in Act IV is always present in Act I, in life as on the stage. You cannot perhaps see it at the time."

—James to Webb, April 1945

The moment of happiness was brief. Barely a year later the letters to Webb chart the beginning of a painful disintegration of their relationship. For the contradictions between the political world which absorbs James and the different kind of life he strives to establish through his love for Webb have never been fully resolved. They quickly surface again as the political pressures on the Johnson Forest Tendency increase during 1947 and 1948.

Writing to Webb from Los Angeles, the buoyancy of James's political mood is tempered by his reflections on the fierce argument which exploded between them before his departure. He is acutely conscious of the distortions such intense work had brought about in his personality, distortions which prevent him being able to respond fully and spontaneously to Webb. James knows that the skills he has for winning people over on questions of politics, his ferocious debating style, his capacity for sustained concentrated work, his rigorous intellect—all these have distorted and restricted his personality. The repression of feeling and emotion runs deep; and the barriers he has constructed between himself and the world seem almost insurmountable. At the moment James feels he is losing her, he begins to realize what it will take to love her. But the battle is now no longer for Webb. It is for James himself.

Perhaps the most intriguing document among James's letters to Webb are the notes he made while seeking a reconciliation with her in September 1947. They are a stream of consciousness—desires, fears, anxieties, pain, frustration, things half-glimpsed and half-understood which reach into his past, into his Puritan upbringing, into the revolutionary life itself. These fragments offer an extraordinary insight into James's inner world.

But there is also a remarkable outburst, scribbled by James on the back of one of his most important political essays, *Dialectical Materialism and the Fate of Humanity*. Here he declares, "This is the man who loves you. I took up dialectic five years ago. I knew a lot of things before and I was able to master it. I know a lot of things about loving you. I am only just beginning to apply them. I can master that with the greatest rapidity—just give me a hand. I feel all sorts of new powers, *freedoms*, etc., surging in me. You released so many of my constrictions.... We will *live*. This is our new world—where there is no distinction between political and personal any more. I would wash the dishes and sweep the floor so as to have you always with me, literally that. 50%. I *want* it that way." (7 October 1947).

James's moment of poetry, reminiscent of the magnificent soliloquy by Mrs. Roach from his Caribbean childhood, which he had described in 1944 in a letter to Webb (What is a poet?) comes from the full realization that the uncertainty, the indecision, the lack of commitment is as much his responsibility as Webb's. Only then could James admit how he has wronged her.

The first letters James writes from Nevada reveal how keenly he feels the separation from Webb. Their battles of the previous year seem to have resolved into a new understanding and intimacy between them. But despite this, James's letters also take us back to the very first ones he wrote to Webb in 1940. For marooned, alone and away from the hothouse of factional politics, which has for so long absorbed his energies, James's writing suddenly becomes freer again, expansive, as he responds to the sights and sounds of everyday life. In short James becomes a novelist once more.

James's letters from the ranch of Harry Drackert may be read as notes towards a novel, or as instalments of one of his favorite soap operas. For there are some wonderful descriptions of particular characters ("Viola is 46, from Ioway [sic], divorced, middle-aged, plump, with a flat voice, and an incurable desire to talk but is so dull that nobody listens") and of the minor crises which regularly enliven day-to-day existence on the ranch—arguments, sackings, various comings and goings. It is no wonder that James understood so clearly life on the *Pequod* as depicted by Melville in *Moby Dick*. This time, however, James does not take up his familiar position as the outsider who observes. He is the central character.

One of the striking features of the early letters from Nevada is James's sensitivity to the racial situation, to the difficulties of negotiating, as a black man, the unspoken conventions of a strange place. This observation may seem odd. But although James refers many times in his previous correspondence with Webb to the race question in the context of the revolutionary movement, it is rarely discussed as a personal experience. The only other occasion we catch a glimpse of what it means to James himself is when he anticipates traveling through the southern United States on his return from Mexico in 1940.

Despite the uncertainties about his situation and the sheer exhaustion of hard, physical work to which James, of all people, was quite unused, the writing for a time conveys a tangible sense of satisfaction. He is freed temporarily from the strains of his everyday life, from being the "leader" responsible for the work of a handful of people and forced to respond to the contingencies of revolutionary politics. James senses that his translation of Daniel Guérin's book about the French Revolution is progressing well; and he is greatly stimulated by the work he is completing on Hegel and the dialectic. Indeed the work on Hegel explodes; it pours out as James works with an intensity he has not experienced for many years.[27]

But slowly James begins to feel the pressures from outside. In September 1948 his job on Drackert's ranch comes to an end; he begins to worry about money; and he allows himself, as a long distance mediator, to be drawn into the scheming and rivalries which beset his organization. He admits, in a letter to Webb on 20 September 1948, that the fine characters of his two leading associates, Dunayevskaya and Lee, have become cramped and distorted through years of intense political struggle against the Stalinists. Moreover, in his absence, Webb too is implicated in these conflicts. The old division between James's loyalty to his political associates and to his wife re-emerges.

The tangled mess of these relations is exposed nowhere more starkly than in the long letter James wrote to Lyman Paine in October 1948, which he copied to Webb. It was prompted by his need to borrow money, something which, until his marriage to Webb, he depended upon the group, especially Paine, to provide. After his marriage, however, he recognized the importance of financial independence if Webb was to feel that their new joint life was free from constant interference and dependence upon his associates. To this end, James took on the task of translating Guérin's manuscript; and he began to plan a writing project which he hoped would raise money to support himself and Webb. In particular he hoped to write a book on American civilization, bringing together for a general audience both his historical understanding and first-hand experience of living in the United States.

But, as his letter to Paine reveals, James's own position was seriously compromised. For while he was in Nevada he began to gamble, playing the slot machines and losing heavily. As he explains, it is the strain and uncertainty of his situation which pushed him into this uncharacteristic behavior; but although James's letter quickly turns into a polemic against the group itself, his writing is marked by restraint and dignity. He recognizes that the tremendous collective work has been achieved at a terrible personal cost. In the midst of the turmoil—of his immigration case, his divorce, the problem of whether the Johnson Forest Tendency should re-join the Socialist Workers' Party—James's letter to Paine is a plea for a new beginning. For the first time he chooses a life with Webb; and acknowledges that his relationship with his group has now to be placed on a different footing.

James's trial in the desert constitutes the climax of the Webb letters.[28] He sees clearly now what a relationship with Webb offers and how he needs to overcome the restrictive divisions which cramp his own personality, the legacy of his Puritan Caribbean upbringing reinforced by his professional specialization as a modern revolutionary. But this new self-awareness does not extend to any recognition of the irreconcilable contradiction which exists between his static conception of married life and the restless movement implied by his political commitment.

The disintegration which followed is as sudden as it is shocking. And James's American period, like the letters, closes with him in limbo once more, marooned in a society of internees on Ellis Island. We must now read afresh his final chapter to *Mariners, Renegades and Castaways*, and recognize that the demons have returned.[29]

NOTES

1 Constance Webb has written a short memoir of this meeting, "C.L.R. James, The Speaker and his Charisma," published in Paul Buhle, ed. *C.L.R. James: His Life and Work*, London: Allison and Busby, 1986.
2 Unpublished autobiography, n.d.(Manuscript courtesy of Constance Webb).
3 As James himself wrote in a letter from Reno, Nevada to Lyman Paine: "There is a terrible discrepancy between the range, the boldness, the philosophical basis, the concreteness of our ideas and the miserable little place that we do hold, both as a group and individually. There is this constant underlying strain, exasperation, impotence and frustration. It is organic." (2nd October 1948).
4 *American Civilization*, p. 167.
5 "Autobiography of a Man by Him," letter from James to Webb 1944.
6 One of the most valuable sources on James's Caribbean formation is his own *Beyond A Boundary*, London: Stanley Paul/Hutchinson, 1963.
7 "Triumph," 1929; "Turner's Prosperity," 1929; and "The Star That Would Not Shine," 1931. "La Divina Pastora" and "Triumph" are reprinted in The *C.L.R. James Reader*, ed. Anna Grimshaw, Oxford, UK and Cambridge, Mass: Blackwell 1992; "Turner's Prosperity" in *Spheres*; and "The Star That Would Not Shine" in *Rendezvous*.
8 Published privately in Nelson as The Life of Captain *Cipriani* (1932). An abridged version, *The Case for West Indian Self Government*, was published by Leonard Woolf as a Day To Day pamphlet in 1933; and it is reprinted in the *Reader*.
9 For a list of these writings, see the bibliography of the *Reader*.
10 "Civilizing the 'Blacks': Why Britain Needs To Retain Her African Possessions," *New Leader* May 1929, 1936.
11 The reviews of Peter Godfrey's production at the Westminster Theatre, London in March 1936 were in fact critical of James's failure to turn history into drama. A reviewer for the *Manchester Guardian* wrote: "It is one of the theatre's paradoxes that within its walls truth tends to become duller than fiction. Mr C.L.R. James justly asserts that his play on Toussaint, performed this afternoon by the Stage Society, is substantially true to history. This faithfulness it must be which has made stirring events seem so static." (March 1936). Another critic for the *Daily Telegraph* commented: ". . . this stage account of the chief liberator of Haiti is written from the heart. But Mr. James

is a journalist (he writes about cricket for a great provincial newspaper) and not a dramatist. He knows his facts, but not how to marshall them for stage effect" (17th March 1936). James revised the play during the 1960s, and re-titled it, *The Black Jacobins*. The full text is reprinted in the *Reader*.

12 Discussions were originally published in the SWP's Internal Bulletin with the identity of the participants disguised through use of pseudonyms. James was J. R. Johnson, Trotsky was Crux, and Curtiss (the Fourth International's representative in Mexico) was Carlos. They were later reprinted in *Rendezvous*. For details of James's writing in *Socialist Appeal*, see bibliography of the *Reader*.

13 The discussion of *World Revolution* by Trotsky and James was also published in SWP Internal Bulletin, and reprinted in *Rendezvous*.

14 *Socialist Appeal*, April 13, 1940.

15 See Paul Buhle's biography of James: *The Artist as Revolutionary*, London: Verso, 1988, p. 82. For a bibliography of these writings, see *Reader*.

16 James was involved in preparing the pamphlet, "Down With Starvation Wages in South-East Missouri" (Local 313 of the Union of Canning, Agricultural Packing and Allied Workers-CIO), St. Louis 1942. It is reprinted in *Future*. For details of unsigned columns in *Labor Action* on the strike, probably written by James, see bibliography of *Reader*.

17 Aside from this small group, other individuals associated with the Johnson Forest Tendency are referred to by James in his correspondence with Webb. They include: William Gorman, Philomena Daddario, Nettie Kravitz, Martin Glaberman, Cecelia Lang, Norman and Selma Weinstein.

18 Published as *American Civilization*, eds. Anna Grimshaw and Keith Hart, Oxford UK and Cambridge, Mass: Blackwell 1993; originally entitled *Notes on American Civilization* (1950).

19 For a discussion of the documents which make up this unfinished project, see Grimshaw "Popular Democracy and The Creative Imagination," and James's "Preface To Criticism," excerpted in the *Reader*.

20 *Nkrumah and The Ghana Revolution*, London: Allison and Busby, 1982.

21 For details of James's other writings, especially his journalism, see bibliography of the *Reader*.

22 See "Popular Democracy and The Creative Imagination," note 19 above.

23 *Beyond A Boundary*, p. 116, London: Stanley Paul/Hutchinson, 1963.

24 *American Civilization*, see note 18 above.

25 Especially in "Popular Art and the Creative Imagination: The Writings of C.L.R. James 1950-1963," London: Third Text no.10, 1990; an expanded and revised version, published New York: C.L.R. James Institute, 1991; *The C.L.R. James Reader* ed. A. Grimshaw, Oxford UK and Cambridge Mass.: Blackwell, 1992; and, with Keith Hart, in "C.L.R. James and The Struggle for Happiness," New York: C.L.R. James Institute, 1991; and the editors' introduction to *American Civilization*.

26 See note 11 above.

27 This work was originally circulated among members of the Johnson Forest Tendency in the form of extended letters. Later a manuscript was published, Notes on Dialectics: Hegel, Marx, *Lenin*, reprinted with a new introduction, London: Allison and Busby, 1980.

28 In explaining his interpretation of the original character, the creative process by which Ahab or Lear emerges in the work of Melville and Shakespeare, James noted: "The great writer . . . conceives a situation in which this character is brought up against things that symbolise the old and the new. The scene is set outside the confines of civilization. What is old is established, it has existed for centuries, it is accepted. But the new will not be denied. It is not fully conscious of itself, but it is certain that it is right. A gigantic conflict is inevitable." (*Mariners, Renegades and Castaways* 1953). James might have been describing here his own situation in Reno, Nevada.

29 James's final chapter "A Natural but Necessary Conclusion" was omitted from the second edition of *Mariners* which was published by members of his political group in 1978. It was only restored to the text in the 1984 edition published in London by Allison and Busby. Wilson Harris offered his own powerful interpretation of James's incarceration in "C.L.R. James as Writer and Literary Critic," a lecture given at the Riverside Studios, London, February 1986.

I.
The Beginning of a Journey (1939–40)

[1939]

My dear Connie,

I am leaving here some material for you. Read carefully the P.C. *[Pittsburgh Courier]* leading article and the column by George Schuyler. That paper has a circulation of many thousands among *petty-bourgeois Negroes*. You can see what the masses must think of their upper layers' [response] to such militancy. Now my idea is that in a discussion one could start with that, point out its correct analysis of the similarity between democracies and dictatorships, but show the utter inadequacy of the solution. Note however that the position of the paper is very far in advance *of everything in America except ourselves*. And the P.C. is the most respected and the second most widely read Negro paper in America. I leave you also a pamphlet on Scottsboro.* It would be well to be able to tell the whole story of Scottsboro, link it to the economic and social situation, then to the policy of the C. P. [Communist Party] (they made a great mess of it) and draw conclusions. *DO NOT, EXCEPT YOU ARE DOING IT FOR SPECIAL REASONS*, ever spend in any talk more than 10 minutes or so on the C. P.

I hope you will do this work and not be put off by inevitable disappointments. The Negroes will like you in time. I am sure of it. Don't ask me why. I *know*. That's all. I am writing in great haste; and regret very much that I could not see you before I left but if you are good, and better, you will drop me a line, Poste Restante, Mexico City. I have told Cornell that I shall write to you and that you can communicate with him about the Negro question. I shall send you the news from M. But, please, let everything I say go no further. Let it be absolutely dead. I shall depend on you, do not let me down. I am very glad to have met you, like you a great deal, and am sorry I did not see more of you.

My regards to your two stalwarts, N and W [Norman and Wallace Henderson],

---

* The notorious 1931 trial in which eight black defendants were sentenced to death for the alleged rape of two white women in Alabama.

and I hope they will cultivate some strong and violent language for all who intrude upon their personal relationship to the rev'y [revolutionary] movement in a personal way. That however is one of the things that must remain between us.

I send you some reviews of B. J. *[The Black Jacobins]* from England. You must tell me what you think, *exactly*, about the book.

Very sincerely,
Nello

PRIVATE & CONFIDENTIAL

Mexico City
Hotel Luxor
92 Revillagigedo Calle

April 15, 1939

My dear Connie,

Well, how are you? Quite well, now, I hope, and full of life and vigor. And, pray, why haven't you written to me? I asked you to in a letter I left for you with Sol's. I said Poste Restante, Mexico City, would do. But such is life! I have a very good friend in England to whom I sent a cable asking for a reply Poste Restante. He, good man has, like you, failed entirely to take any notice of me. I wanted him to send me some money which a friend of mine had sent to him for me. So day after day I went to the P.O., expecting from him the material and from you the psychological hand across the sea. Net result to date. Zero. I hope you are thoroughly penitent.

I am in bed (not permanently) and I have lost my green pen so that writing is very uncomfortable. This pen I use now is, as a rule, only for making notes or correcting proofs.

Mexico is a most fascinating place: charming, pleasant, kindly people, and yet not at all servile. Poor, and dirty, with some tawdry finery but full of life and colour and vitality. I have not seen much, I have been having trouble with my stomach and had a temperature once and had to stay in, but such as I have seen I like. Best of all are frescoes by Diego Rivera in the Government Palaccio (Palace), telling the history of Mexico, and ending with the vision of a socialist Mexico. Karl Marx pointing to it, and everything as a Marxist would like it. Amazing isn't it? And there is also an equestrian statue—a Mexico treasure, fully able to take its place with the ones I told you about. (I still have that postcard for you. I'll send it later.) I have not met Diego. There is a split between him and L. T. [Leon Trotsky]; L. T. is moving out of his house, there have been letters in the press and a general mess. D. R. has left the IV [Fourth International].

About L. T. himself, I shall not say much now. He is certainly a most remarkable personality and it is easy to see a very great orator. Even in ordinary speech he is the orator personified. He agreed almost entirely with my memo on the Negro question. On self-determination, in particular there was no difficulty. If the Negroes want it, then we are in favour, but we do not advocate it. Which, it seemed to me, was always the obvious position. Something was (or maybe still is) wrong somewhere. But I cannot see why there should have been this dispute.

About the Left Opposition and the bureaucracy, we disagree entirely, he North and South, I East and West. I am preparing notes of the discussion and when he has ratified them I shall send you one. But, *strictly between us*, the first day I saw him he said "about 1923, etc., not too much, we must deal with the problems of the future. Give it only an hour or two." Then we discuss it for two hours, and he said "We'll continue another time." At the end of the second discussion, he told me "Write an article and publish it in our press. It is good to bring up these things from time to time." Of course, he still thinks I am hopelessly wrong, but there is a lot more to be said on the subject, my dear Connie, believe me. What bothers me is that I am away from all my books and files (in England) and I don't know when I'll see them. Luckily the question is not urgent. You see it is a speculative question, we have no proof as yet. But one thing I have proof of now very clearly. There are now three positions in the IV International, there is the one I hold which is growing, the old man says that this is "absurd," good. But the editors of the N. I. *[New International]* and the French Quatrienne Internationale most certainly do not hold his position. Of that I have *proof*. This discussion has at any rate cleared that up. I'll send you the papers in time if you want to see them.

I have had meetings here—one on war at the University of Mexico, 110 people. I had to speak in French, which was translated into Spanish. It went off very well and we are to have another on Wednesday. Now I have the pictures of the horsemen, etc., to send, but why no word from you? As soon as I hear from you, I'll send you some things. My regards to Messrs. N and W, and warm greetings for yourself.

N

Vera Cruz

Saturday

Well, my dearest Connie, I arrived here this a.m.; have had a dreadful day but at least all is fixed for my departure tonight. I have 5 minutes and I shall write as much as I can in that time.

Do not worry about whether what you have done is right or not. You will have twinges and spasms of pain and regret but it would be strange if you didn't. What is important is to give your new life a good honest try, as you gave the marriage and see.*

Your life is before you. You can't guess at what it will be. You live and find out. . . .

I am glad you are so enthusiastic and doubly glad that you have decided to let me know how things go. Let me know your failures and disappointments too. But [it] is not easy. . . . No, I have no pamphlets from the SWP [Socialist Workers Party]. *We* also have none. I have written to Max [Shachtman] asking for a Negro column in the S. A. [Socialist Appeal]. No reply up to now. Patience, my dear. They will be jogged into action if not by me then by L. T. He is the keenest of the keen on the N [Negro] question. You will gasp when you read what he says to the party: *(Strictly between us)* It is roughly this: The attitude of the SWP to the N question has been *most* disquieting and unless the Party can find a way to the Negroes, i.e., to the most oppressed, it will degenerate. The Negroes as the *most* oppressed *must* become the very vanguard of the revolution. They will sit up. Many other things too, many many

---

* Webb had ended her marriage to Norman Henderson.

things which illuminate all problems. I shall see you soon, I hope, and shall tell you all about it. You will feel your understand[ing] double and treble and it will be easy to tell it all to you looking at your bright eyes and charming face. By the way, I wrote to Naomi and gave Mrs. G the answer to her message in the letter. She says: When you write... So she takes it for granted that we correspond. I spoke to Lillian Curtiss about you and it gave me great pleasure to see how genuinely well she thought of you.

With love,
N

S. S. Terrible Spanish-Mexican-Indian Name
I'll find it out afterwards

Sunday 3 p.m.

Sunday afternoon, sweetheart, 3 o'clock. The boat is small but riding as in a bath. The sun is as hot as fire, bluish-green, blue and white sky. It has been lovely....

What have you [been] doing on Sunday? You would have been happier here, I hope. It has been a wonderful trip. Two of us alone travelling—the other is a Mexican tenor—a real honest to God tenor—going to fill an engagement in Rio de Janeiro, 30, his first big chance I think, he was enquiring about buying "tails" in New Orleans. He has a splendid voice—sings popular songs—but with a passion worthy of the revolution. He and I sang at one another all during breakfast. I know the lines of many operatic arias, and he sang Mexican songs. I know 11 words of Spanish and he 12 words of English but "love will find out a way" and he and I said it in music.

End of Act I

Act II brings a further surprise. There is a steward here, a little Englishman, who has sailed the seas for twenty years. He too is a musician. He sings Spanish songs and plays them on his guitar. So now he and the tenor and I sang during lunch—and after lunch Mr. Steward brings out his guitar and—Mr. James chiefly audience—the two of them sing and play till 5 to 3. As I write, the steward is trying some of the chords the tenor has taught him, the tenor is looking at a book and all the time singing away, chiefly snatches, and I am scribbling away. We are in the little stateroom, six tables only and if I wore a top-hat and stood up suddenly it would get crushed. Through the door and the port-holes is the sun on the sea, and the ship taking everything in its stride. You know how it is on a ship. You are sick, well, happy, miserable, tired or fit, the ship does not care. It just goes on.

I stopped to find out a train to N.Y. for the tenor. Meanwhile, he sang from Pagliaca and I stopped to sing from Martha. And the steward who was washing dishes came back and is now guitaring away. Meanwhile steward No. 2 is making tea in the little room next door. Am I right in thinking that you would love it here? Or am I just being masculine and egoistic and saying: I would like her to be here and therefore naturally she would like it too. You will have to tell me.

Au Voir for the present. Truth compels me to add that it is getting very hot, and there is no shower, only those terrible English tubs—but still, I think it would be lovely.

Now I am alone here and the guitar is lying on a seat, yellow-faced guitar, brown seat, white table-cloth. You know those pictures by Picasso, though, alas, the pictures are always so much more beautiful than the actual still-life. But it has been lovely ... monotonous but true.

8 p.m.

The ship just keeps going on. Dinner was early, 6; it wasn't so hot after all—I haven't had to change my shirt. And after dinner I sat on the upper deck while the tenor walked up and down, practising his songs very quietly with a little note-book in which he has the words typed. I spend a great deal of my spare hours doing the same—I have now four speeches [I am] working at—one to whites on Negro question, one to Negroes on same, one on war—which may come at any minute—and one specially to Negroes on war. One gets ideas and works them up and jots them down; bit by bit they take shape. It isn't bad fun really....

But I sat on the deck and watched the sun go down—a glorious evening, so still, and nobody about, only a member of the crew now and then, and our tenor strolling up and down.

It went dark and I came in here, intending to make some notes on something; instead here I am.

Monday tomorrow; then Tuesday and Wednesday a.m. New Orleans and once more the world of men again. But these three days, with practically nobody on the ship mean a lot and would have meant so much more if you were here, i.e., if you would like to be here. We are now all four of us listening to Lawrence Tibbett—the guitar player, another steward, tenor and me. L. T. has just sung Largo al Factotum from the Barber of Seville a bravura aria, which half-an-hour ago I was singing to myself on the deck—he sang magnificently—but before and after, i.e., now he is talking a lot of stuff, the silliest patter imaginable. It is an odd combination. For he really sang well. Who cares anyway? Do you? I don't.

I came in here to write lots and lots of things to you. But I have changed my mind. I could say them, but not write them. I wonder if you could imagine what it is like to be on this boat—under these circumstances (there hasn't been a ripple yet); and to sit and dream how lovely it would be if you were here. The stupid chatter on the radio continues.... Not so stupid though.

A man asks a girl to go to his old childhood slum-home and she turns up her nose; he goes in and she meets a little boy who tells her she is not the girl he wants to marry—she is so cruel. He has a cut on his finger. Suddenly he disappears, and her husband comes back. He has seen no little boy but she asks him to show her his finger. There is the same scar. She begs to be allowed to go in, all will be different, etc. Not bad. But it reminds me of something else—a superb story, superbly told by an East Indian girl, wife of an old old friend of mine, a clergyman, also E. Indian in the W. Indies. Here it is.

One bitter night a man was driving a car and missed the road. He went searching and searching and at last saw a light far in. He turned into a drive, with superb gates, and drove in. A liveried footman met him at the door and led himself (and his wife) into the house. They were entertained by an old-fashioned couple and early next morning they left. The last thing the man did was to give the footman a half-crown.

Later they found that a bridge had been broken by the storm and if they had gone on they would have lost their lives.

But next day when they told their friends nobody knew the house. Rather puzzled, they drove out again, found the road, followed it, and finally came to a drive. But the gates though familiar in outline were old and delapidated. They drove up the drive—full of weeds—the place had not been lived in for scores of years. They came to the house at last, broken down ruins—they couldn't possibly have stayed there the night before. It must have been all a dream. They got out and walked up the steps and there—there my dear Connie on the top step was the half-crown he had put in the hand of the footman the night before.

Do you thrill at that sort of thing? I hope so. I do. I know some superb tales of that kind, Gautier, the Frenchman, Poe, and Pushkin, and Ambrose Bierce. They belong to a non-industrial age, and they appeal to that healthy fear of the supernatural and mysterious which even in this age of electric light and no forests just behind our houses, still appeal to many of us. And how beautifully written most of them are! They are a memory of my pre-MARX days.

The funny thing is that this one is supposed to be true—some English paper asked for true mystery stories and this one was sent in and my friend read it there and told it to us one evening just before I left for England in 1932. She is the ablest woman I know and it is a tragedy that she is buried in the W. Indies—clergyman's wife—6 children. But she has a marvellous gift of speech and a great sense of the dramatic. (The tenor has just turned on another tenor from Havana, his "companero" he tells me; the man sings well, this radio fellow and has just sung "Mi amor" with great feeling. Why, oh why, my dearest Connie, aren't you here? There it is again "Mi Amor;" the song is silly, I can feel that, I mean by that cheap, but still for the time it is good to hear.)

I absolutely must stop, or I shall write forever and ever and then my hand will hurt me tomorrow. (The guitar is still on the brown seat.)

I have just looked outside—one star and then a million miles away another, and then two million miles away, a third. But there are dim lights on the deck, and if you were here, we would now clear out of the dining-saloon and go and sit on the deck and we would talk.... Good-night (*No. 1*) and I hope you have had a lovely day, and remembered me at odd moments; and not thought too much of your past troubles. Sweetheart, I must write one more scrap. "Guitar" fumbled at the radio and behold the Seventh Symphony of Beethoven. The slow movement; one of the loveliest of all the works before the last ones. Now the slow movement is over, and they are playing the quick one—the middle part—one day I may listen to it with you.... Once more, good-night.

Darling a tragedy. This pair of Philistines have cut off the symphony. "Guitar" suddenly discovered in a Mexican magazine the fingering of the guitar-accompaniment to a song the tenor knows. So they got very excited and are now hard at it. (Listen and you can hear them.) "Guitar" is a typical cockney, with a little sharp face; how English he looks, but Spanish-America has captured him and he loves these Spanish rhythms and his guitar. So for the last time (I swear) Good N.

Monday

Here we are, sweetheart, 7:45, and I am writing to you already. True devotion, and (for truth must be told) I am 10 minutes too early for breakfast.

I have something to relate. This a.m. I rose at 7 and looked out of the port-hole till 7:20 waiting for the steward. There is no shower and he has to put water into the bath. I got up and went into the bathroom for my own purposes and there was water in the bath, towels, etc. My dear, had you been there you would have been proud of your Nello. I did not hesitate. For about two minutes I pondered. Was this bath mine or not? I weighed up both sides and then decided that I didn't know....

Then I remembered I was a Bolshevik. Would I be deterred and impeded in my progress towards the World Revolution (the radio is playing: I love you truly, old-fashioned and trite but it always brings memories of a rose-garden in Trinidad and the friends of my youth, Cuesa D, playing the piano and Eric Roach the violin). But to return. As I was saying, I came to a decision. And once having decided, nothing stopped me. Without a trace of Menshevism with nothing that might even be construed as Lovestonism (centrism) this hero (darling, it is the *only* word; forgive me if I sound boastful, but I *must* be true to myself), this HERO took the bath. Calmly I poured the water over my shoulders, etc. Did my heart beat at the thought that at any moment I would hear the tenor's voice running up and down the scale outside and calling imprecations on the head of this intruder? Truth to tell sweetheart (I must tell you the truth) it did. But it would have been invisible to the mortal eye. I concluded, not hastily, with dignity, though I did not linger. It would have been foolhardy to do so.

It is now some 20 minutes and I have heard nothing. Audacity has conquered again. The tenor has come in. He smiles, I smile. Either the bath was mine or he is a man of deep deception. Obviously the latter. But will he catch me late at night on the quarter-deck when no one is looking. Oh, no, my dear, 1000 times no; I shall avoid these obscure places and shall arrive safe in N. Orleans to post this letter.

But before we leave the subject, I have to say that I did not show myself inferior. The best observers agree that my demeanor hitherto has showed not the slightest resemblance to that of the traditional countenance usually assumed by stealers of baths. Enough, I must not boast, though it would be lovely if you were here to share my triumph. As it is, the only man I can tell is the tenor, and that would show a lack of proportion.

Afternoon: 2:30

If you were here you would have been out of this. Though I would have been able to tell you after, which I cannot do now. The little Englishman has been telling me tales of his adventures with girls in Vera Cruz, N. Orleans, Jamaica, Rio, etc. Never was an Englishman so transformed. He has the typical Latin's attitude to women; and has accumulated an enormous amount of knowledge. Being a bit of an artist, he of course is happy to hold forth and I have one great virtue my dear: I can listen, for hours and hours. . . . To all sorts of people, especially strangers. And my greatest weakness? Impatience at party meetings and committees. One of my best friends, an experienced Ceylonese, checked me 3 or 4 times at a little meeting we held just before I left—asked questions, wanted to know what X thought or Y—and told me afterwards that it didn't matter what they thought but that I was giving an impression of railroading the meeting and that was bad. He was right; but I find it terribly hard to be patient with party "leaders" who waste a great deal of time displaying "ego" under cover of revolutionary zeal. For long I have made the best resolutions but failed. And yet on the other hand I have sat for hours in America listening to people, all sorts of poor working people, telling me all about themselves. It is indispensable for any understanding of anything. It must go side by side with the books. Well I couldn't help thinking how differently I would have listened to him 6 years ago. He told me many things which interested me as a man. But he told me also some grand tales. Now 6 years ago I was all set for being a novelist.* I had written a novel (it was published. Do you want to read it?) and many short stories. And I would have taken down all these tales—and very very revealing some of them were—and worked them up into a good story. But those days are over. Though I still listen to stories with the same interest. One of them, told with rich and intimate detail, was of his relations with a prostitute in Vera Cruz. She could do what she liked until he came into port, but when he came, nothing doing with any other man. They used to fight, knives, etc. One day he nearly killed her and the next day he told her "You know I am married. If you stay here I am going to kill you one day. So I don't want to see you in this port again. Go to Mexico City." She begged but he said No. And she went. Packed her traps and went and left a letter to tell him she had gone. I could see on his face how miserable he was. It happened only a few weeks ago. Says when the ship comes in now, he doesn't know what to do with himself, thinks of her all the time! It is a funny world. He is a most interesting man—not one atom of class-consciousness but a man of the world, with a spirit of adventure and intelligence above the average. Quite a personality in his way. He is a fine talker and that is one sure sign of a capability to dominate men. He is the kind who would join the revolution, afterwards, and do very well.

Tonight I shall try to meet the Negro cooks for a talk. I had a long talk yesterday with another steward—married to a Mexican woman. Another Englishman. A very serious, capable fellow, told me all about his wages, the ship's profits, wages of women in New Orleans, etc. Does not think of changing society, but instinctively feels that such and such wages are a damned shame—sees through the profiteering, etc.,—this ship flies the Honduras flag to escape taxes. But I'll keep politics out of this letter for the time being. But the little man did say a lot of very interesting things. He explained in great detail the physiology and psychology of the prostitute. I could write a good and startling story especially as I have spent a day in Vera Cruz and have some idea of the locale. But my days for fiction are over. The day? Perfect, a cloudless if somewhat sullen-looking sky, sullen by implication as it were; blazing sunshine, a shimmering sea, and the ship ploughing steadily on. The tenor has disappeared. Perhaps he is having a bath.

The boatswain is the man in charge of the crew, and is a Negro. I was astonished for he has whites under him. The secret? The captain knows the boatswain for years, likes him, and says "As long as you do your work no one will trouble you." But the chief mate is a Norwegian who hates Negroes and if he got the chance he would not only have a white boatswain, but he wouldn't have a Negro on the ship. But the old captain says "No." The illuminating thing is that they all get on very well together. There is never any trouble. They know the captain will stand no nonsense.

Red, the second steward, tells me that he and the captain's steward, a Negro, go out sometimes in N.O. "But when we get into the car," says Red. "I have to go to the front and he has to go to the back." Now Red is a practical man and does not seem to probe too deeply into the why or wherefore of things.

So what annoys him is that "when I go to the back with him to continue our

---

* *Minty Alley*, 1936; see Editor's Introduction, p. 5.

investigation, then the conductor comes after me." Truly, man is an irrational animal.

(The stretches of green island are getting larger and larger. . . .) There are taxis for white and taxis for black, and as few blacks travel by this boat there will be no taxis for them and I shall have to telephone for one. So that is my introduction to the South. People have been warning me and I have said "Oh, I'll manage," perhaps with too much confidence. If I were an American citizen I wouldn't care, but if I get into any trouble with the police bang go my hopes for a further extension of my visa and re-entry after a little trip abroad. Strange, as I near the actual contact, I begin to feel a slight nervousness. I shall get through of course, unless someone goes out of his way to annoy me, but the feeling of uncertainty shows me how terribly the minds and characters of Negroes must be affected, especially those who have no experience or political or historical background to help them, or no consciousness of a way out.

When I see you sometime I shall tell you some things about Negroes, things which I have experienced in my own person, and give you some idea of what goes on in a Negro's mind. (Guitar has been laying the table, singing accompaniments to the radio-tunes. He is a most lively man and he harmonises and displays really unusual musical gifts.)

So now to dinner. And if I do not get a letter from you at N.O. P.O. I shall not forgive you. No, it is no use asking for forgiveness. NO, I said. But as it's you and for a bribe (guess what that will be) I shall magnanimously forgive you. Not guilty but don't do it again. Now, am I not a nice man? I forgive you (with bribe) for a sin you have not committed. Any fool can forgive for an actual transgression, but it takes a man above the average to rise to the heights I have just attained. But, sweetheart, if there isn't a letter I'll swear and it will be lucky that you will not be there to hear what I shall say.

Sweetheart, a funny thing. It is 7 and we have just taken on board the second pilot for the river trip and it seems he brings letters. He brought one for Guitar—from his wife it seems. He was jumping round as usual, but he grinned. Then he fumbled around and at last sat down and read it eagerly; but he looked at me with a knowing grin as if to excuse himself. "I am not one of those soft chaps you know." I was surprised. And the silly goat, ashamed of being happy at receiving a letter from his wife a day before he reaches home, after being away less than a fortnight. You see he has boasted so much about his knowledge of women that he feels he is letting himself down by being so eager to receive a letter from his own wife. He is a happy man, although he does miss his little Vera Cruz prostitute. I shall not forget this little man. There he is again, chattering away to the other steward, but he has his letter in his pocket and sweetheart, I *know* that as soon as he gets away from us, he will pull it out and start reading again.

And now, sweetheart, it is nearly over. We land at 7 tomorrow. We have just had a rollicking 1 radio 'grammes Pepsodent Linoleum something, Walter Raleigh tobacco, and lots more. How I laughed. Such vigour and wit and rollicking humour, and chiefly vigour. You know, England and France, and Germany haven't got it in them. The whole bunch of us sat round and laughed except tenor, who was away, but came late. He couldn't understand the language.

In a few minutes I go in to pack and then look out the port-hole until I drop asleep. I will think of you last before I go to sleep and first thing when I get up in the morning.

It will have taken you a terrible long time to read this letter. Has it surprised you?

It would be very strange if it didn't. But all unknown to yourself you have been my dear companion on this journey. I saw you that afternoon in the church, then that impudent Carlo said at your house "Isn't she lovely?" and I had to rebuke him. You remember? When we came back you were in a red dressing gown and all sleepy and exciting. I was sorry I didn't see you on the last Saturday. I intended to write but very soberly all about politics; and then came your first letter, written very honestly and with a generosity of aspiration and confidence that startled me; then the second—you were so excited about your Sunday trip that you wanted to write and wrote off to me at once. And now I have replied. You see I am a dangerous man to write to. Write him 3 pages and he writes back 23. I have been crazy on this trip I believe, but you are worth being crazy about. It is your fault. You must not write such eager letters and at the same time appear suddenly before lonely men, wearing red dressing gowns and rubbing your eyes like a big baby who needs to be put to bed. It isn't fair, my dearest Connie, if you write such letters then you must wear spectacles, have your hair brushed back and wear plain clothes; or if you must look as you do (Phoebus calls you zoftig—a Jewish word), then you must ask me if I don't just *love* Clark Gable. Not the two together. The result is 23 pages. Till I don't know when; soon I hope. And now good-bye. Is it a hand only you extend to me? No, the initiative is mine, now. So out on to the deck we go and (if I don't write it you will still know, so why shouldn't I) I take you into my arms and kiss you, as we would kiss if we had really spent these days together and it were our last night.

Good night—once more—and yet again, good night.
Sincerely,
N

Suppose I sat and read this over. It might go into the Mississippi in lots of little pieces. Would you have been sorry? But I am not going to re-read it. You opened your heart to me (though a woman always keeps back a little; have you?). I have done the same. You have confidence in me. I have in you also.

S. S. Tegucigalpa (Got it at last)
Night 7:50

I have just listened to a radio-drama. Absolutely priceless, my dear C, absolutely priceless.

Apple Annie was an old hag who had a daughter in a convent in Spain. Annie sold apples but used to write the daughter as a Mrs. Socialite from a swell hotel. Now the daughter is coming and bringing her lover, a Count's son and his father. Annie is in the soup but a tough guy promises to help. He'll set her up as the Socialite for a few weeks. An old stage-trick but it always gives good fun; that's why it lasts.

They have to get a husband and they get one, an old rascal with a gorgeous voice and a choice gift of phrase; but they have to give a reception and the tough guy scours the town to get all the criminals of the town to be Sec'y of the Interior, Attorney General of U.S.A., etc. The rehearsal is rich. But they are all arrested by the police. However the tough guy in chief who can help the police in a case tells the tale to the Mayor and the Governor. They are moved, they come over, there is a small reception, and, wedding bells.

But that was only half the fun. Guitar found it and settled down to listen with me.

(Tenor couldn't understand a word so sat on the deck and admired the seascape.) Now Guitar as would be expected from a man of his temperament enjoyed it from the start (though he knew the story). Twice he told me what was coming and I had to sit on him and tell him not to. But suddenly at a most exciting part, the reception went bad, and we couldn't hear a word. My God, you should have seen Guitar. He raged, jumped up, twisted the knobs, called the radio names, among which son of bitch was the mildest; swore that he knew it would do that. This, the unrehearsed part of the show, pleased me vastly. Luckily, things improved but once more it happened again and once more he got mad.

I haven't enjoyed a radio play as much for a long time. It is years since I heard one. . . .

I am going in early to-night. I'll write you to-morrow, something serious. For the time being, good-night. One kiss only on your forehead. Shut your eyes. Can you feel it? That's all—for the present.

9:50 Here I am again. I have to. For you are concerned. We sat on the deck and sang and played the guitar. Sweetheart, imagine. The moon was up, the sea still and we sat out there singing away and the tenor playing and singing as if on the stage at Rio—those charming rhythmic Mexican songs. I have almost learnt one. It says in parts "Help me to live again," and "Life of my life," i.e., Vida de mi vida. Old stuff, and rather commonplace. But, sweetheart very very moving in these circumstances.

An old man who is a watchman is quite a character here. He has a handsome old face, and he says "good-morning," but he is very old and they say that he is very shaky on his feet for the first hour or so every morning. But he is not musically inclined—not to-night at least. He came and listened for a minute and then shuffled away.

And another big sailor in an armless singlet, the dirtiest I have seen for many years, with all his huge arms out, came and sat on a bale. Then he put his elbows on his knees, propped his head on his hands and beat time with his fist for two or three minutes. Music hath charms.

And you? You were here. Sitting next to me, I had an arm around you, just sitting close, no more. To-morrow is the last day. We begin to go up the river in the afternoon—the wonderful Mississippi. We shall have a last night—they and I and you too, sitting on the deck, watching the lights, and singing, the tenor playing the guitar. Could you be happy that way, just sitting, with an arm around you, and a hand holding yours. I'll never forget this journey. Not only has it been lovely in itself but you have been here with me every hour. You should hear me sing "Vida de mi vida." Good-night, my dearest Connie.

Tuesday 9

A great change in the weather, darling; no rain but the sea no longer ripples, it heaves, very slightly—the ship scarcely feels it—but different it is; and there is no sun. When you look up into the height of the sky there are clouds of blue and white but they look tired and dull as if they have been out too late last night; around the horizon the sky is dull grey, so is the sea, and they merge one into the other so that this a.m. I saw something in the distance, took it for a plane and it turned out to be a ship.

For all the others it means merely a change in the weather. But for me, darling, it means that my holiday is approaching its end—to-morrow I begin to experience in my own person the rural discrimination of the South. I hope to heaven I do not lose my temper. It would be very stupid to do so.

I am sitting on the deck. Guitar has just done a tap-dance and won the applause of Tenor and me. How happy he was to have given us another pleasant shock! He is now polishing the brass of the windows; and hates it. He tells me so but ironically. "How I love this job!" He says "To-day is a field-day." He has the defects of his temperament, a dislike of sustained labour and drudgery. That is the difference between the artist and the artistic temperament. The temperament can feel, but not strongly enough, or somehow else, lacks the capacity to sit and work and work and work. The artist can. Don't believe, my precious, in any short-cuts. It is work that does it. Patient determined sustained labour. "Red," the other steward, complained without bitterness that Guitar does not do his work but stays talking with the passengers all the time. I know the type well. Do you know where? In the revolutionary movement. Quite right, my dear, quite right. Your observation is acute. . . .

Guitar is clever. He suspects that I am writing about him. He sees me writing and writing, he knows I write and he would laugh long at the idea that it is a letter. Men of his type, who have lived so much with prostitutes, lose something. . . .

So he guesses at any rate—and correctly. Worried? Not he. He is happy and to encourage me, he tells me of a woman passenger who wrote a book about a cruise and put him and "all his stuff" into it. No wonder he, tenor, and I get on well together—I understand them both and play a modest third violin—I encourage tenor to sing and encourage Guitar to talk. They compliment me on my knowledge of music, and I am suitably modest. I know more about music than they will know in 50 years and I am merely an amateur (Sol Babitz is a real musician: 100%). But I lie low, sing the songs with them, as if I had spent all my life singing popular songs, and we are very happy. Guitar, however, is a remarkable person, on a small scale, despite his cheap little face. And he is no fool in other ways either. I asked him if he would go to England to fight. He said "Am I a damned fool? My brothers went and what the hell they got? The dole." "Would you fight for America?" I said. "Ah, that's different," said G. "For 15 years they gave me work and food and clothes. I would fight for America." "But," I said, "They didn't *give* you food and clothes. You worked for it. They didn't give it to you because they loved you. They wanted service and you gave it."

He was serving and he stopped. He had never seen it that way before. He considered it for quite a while, then went on with his chatter. But obviously he was a man who could grasp a new idea quickly, think it over and see its force. His job in the revolution would be as an agitator, to go round and sell the idea. He would pick it up quickly and go around among his friends, having drinks and talking by the yard. They would listen, too. But while he could be used, he should *never never* be a member of the party. The revolution will use all sorts, but not in the party. I am quite sure of that.

And so, sweetheart, I shall be up to my neck soon. I shall write to you of course, but not little treatises like this. I want you to do two things for me. One is to send me a picture—a large one, no little snaps. The second is harder. It is to write to me a long letter telling me how you are getting on, what you are doing and *what you are thinking*. I am not prying into your secrets. But I would like to know much more about you. I shall have to decide on my plans soon. I may get a holiday of a month or two; I will come to Los Angeles during that time for one reason only—to spend it near to you. Otherwise I shall stay near to N. York. *You will of course not mention the slightest hint of this to anyone.* Macbeth, whom I met in Mexico City, tells me about his house in the country—there may be others. I don't know. If I were coming I would ask you to make the arrangements for me, I would give the secretary of the organisation my address in a sealed envelope, and I would bring my books and come in like a thief and live like one. Sweetheart, I have been thinking over the Negro question. I have got hold of a book (in ms.) on statistics of the Negro. And I have been reading as best I could on the way. Also I have talked much with L. T., and have been thinking over all that he said. I am now certain that no one in America, none in the party, has ever seen the Negro question for the gigantic thing it is, and will increasingly be. L. T. sees it, I was groping towards it. I begin to see it now, every day more clearly. The American Negroes touch on one side the American proletariat, on whom so much depends in the present period; on the other they and *not* the British or French proletariat, form the link with the African revolution, and they can form a link with the millions of Indians and Negroes and half-castes who form so much of the population of Spanish-America. And not only before but after the revolution. The American Negro will have to do most of the actual contact between Western civilization and the millions of Africans.

Now I shall have to do a few months of intensive study, before we launch the organisation. How long I shall be able to stay here I do not know. I may have to go to Mexico or Haiti for a few months and then seek to come in again. I want the war to find me in America. I shall probably have to go to Africa some time. All these things have to be worked out. I want to be quiet for a few months, perhaps it will be only weeks; and I would like to come your way. May I? *Do not write until you hear from me.* If you are going to work on the Negro question, sweetheart, you are tackling an almost Virgin field, and one that will amply repay any serious work that you do on it. I would like, in fact I terribly want to tell you all about it; but for that I shall have to come to L.A. Voila.

[unsigned]

Poste Restante New Orleans

Friday
Am leaving here Tuesday
morning *or Tuesday evening.*

My dear Connie,

How are you? Well and cheerful, I hope, and busy I expect. I arrived here Wednesday, went to the P.O. Wednesday and Thursday, and not a line from your good self. (The tour is over. Headquarters made a complete mess of everything, and for all they cared, I would have been still in Mexico. You do not build a party that way. I have had to use the deposit money. Will you tell Dr. F [Harry Fishler] for me and give him my thanks. I shall write to him when I get to N. York.

I am not feeling at all well and I am staying here a few days, before I set out for N.Y. It is going to be a difficult journey. But I shall stop in Memphis, and other places and I have already made some good contacts here and gathered some very useful information.

I wrote a long letter to you on board, but I haven't posted it. I must hear from you first. Write to 125 W. 121.

With much love
N

Postmark May 5, 1939
Private & Confidential

Henceforth write always to
116 University Place, N.Y. City.
The letter will be forwarded.

April 24

My dear dear Connie,

Your letter has quite swept me off my feet. I am so glad for you. I know how you feel. The great step forward which you have made and the possibilities it opens for you vibrate in every line of your letter. These are the landmarks and the impulses that count in life. You are giving yourself to your new life wholeheartedly. These are the times when one says in spite of one's-self "God be with you!"

I am sorry for Norman. Perhaps you understand the blow—you can understand it only if you have been yourself desperately in love with someone. To have had you and then to lose you would be a great blow for anyone, but particularly for him, because you were so obviously a stronger personality than he. Of course I knew ten minutes after I had seen you both together; and your restlessness. It is strange how things happen (I shall of course speak very frankly) but three years ago I met precisely such a couple in England, she 26, he 35, she with an unhappy love affair behind her, he, a very fine man exactly as Norman, but ———. I am telling you my secrets, but we fell desperately in love. She was a B-L [British Labourite] too, long before I knew her. She was ready to leave him but he was rich, and I hesitated, having no money. Then when I finally needed, she had changed her mind. He bought a house in the country for her, a new car, a lot of clothes, and was very very patient with her during the time she and I were intimate. After some hesitation we broke finally. She was Dutch, petite, yellow-haired, and very very beautiful. But she took the wrong turning. She had been a revolutionary all her life. He was not. He was a Tolstoyan though sympathetic to the movement. She had left home and worked in the B-L movement for years. The conflict in her was not only between two men, but between the revolution and the easy life. Some time after, I met her and she spoke with cynicism of the revolutionaries in Spain. I was very sorry for her. I miss her dreadfully sometimes, but that is over, I am fairly sure. So you see how it was that I could see immediately how it was with you and though the circumstances were not exactly the same, not nearly the same in fact, I could understand. You are entirely different to her in appearance and style. She was very reserved, externally, and very superior in manner. You are both very different persons really except in one thing, as far as I am concerned, and I suppose you know how selfish men are. While many people exhaust me, especially in my present state of health, I was always glad to see you and talk to you, even if I was tired. And that does not happen often. I know a man in N. York whom I like in the same way—a Negro reporter on the New York *[Post]*. He is very ugly, but whenever I see him, I feel stimulated. Then there is my old pupil, Dr. Eric Williams, whom I taught when he was a boy and whom I have seen grow up and now is D.Ph. Oxford, my devoted admirer and a most brilliant young man. How nice it would be to have you all living near or spending some time together. . . .

You see I tell you all my secrets. So have no fear that I understand, I understand everything completely, so completely that I was very nervous about you, my dear Connie. Just before I left I said to Carlo "Take care of C. You are her friend. She may do something silly." He asked me what he could do. I told him that the least he could do was if you asked him anything to speak the truth as plainly as he saw it. I did not talk to you as I might when in L.A. You were a married woman living with your husband, and you may have noticed that at times I was rather nervous and unsettled. But all is well. Do not speak to Carlo about this, will you? Let it stay right there. Please respect my wishes in this connection.

And now for Das Capital. My dear young woman I have some news for you. One C.L.R. James, reputed Marxist, having thought over his past life, and future prospects, decided that what he needed was a severe and laborious study of — guess! The Bible? Wrong. Ferdinand the Bull? Wrong again. Not Das Kapital? Right. (Loud and prolonged cheering, all rise and sing the International.) I bought the book a few days ago in pesos, and have got down to it. (This is only one volume by the way. There are two more. You made a mistake when you thought you had read them all.) I shall do those three volumes, and nothing will stop me but a revolution. Isn't that odd? What I am after is what you mentioned—a method of thinking, of looking at history. I have it to some degree. But I am not satisfied. And I shall go through page by page, making abstracts, testing paragraphs, making a summary and understanding every line. It is going to be a terrible job. But it will be done. And you? Have you the will and the strength? I am not sure (forgive me if I am rude) but I think so. If I were near to you I would help you. *But you could have attempted nothing better in this stage of your development.* Grapple with it. Let nothing pass that you do not understand. With the very difficult passages write them out in your own words. And if at times you feel despondent, know that C.L.R. J., reputed Marxist, is also hammering it out. *If you master it, you are made for life,* as a revolutionary and as a *person*, always considering it necessary to do practical work. But do not let yourself be pulled away from it. If you wish I shall send you my notes periodically. They may help you, and it will help me to have to send them to you. Bravo! A thousand times, bravo! Six months from now I shall be still at it. I hope you will be there also. Do not be distracted into reading too many books. The party press and, e.g., the Negro Question, and Das Capital. Once you master that book, all the rest will come very very easily.

When the notes of the discussions [with Trotsky] are completed I shall send you a copy with my own comments. Also when copies are made, I shall send you immediately the notes on the Negro question. Keep cuttings, by the way, from the Negro press. You will need them.

Van Loon, Mann and Co. are a horrible mess. But the intellectuals to-day are in this mess chiefly on account of the C. P. The intellectual petty-bourgeois is at the service either of the big bourgeoisie or of the proletariat—the fundamental classes of modern society. With the proletariat strong, powerful, clear in doctrine and powerful in demonstrations, etc., a section of the intellectuals is pulled to it along with the petty bourgeoisie; and the rest run openly to the bourgeoisie (many at any rate) because with the proletariat on the march, there is not much room for wobblers. But with "Marxism" reduced to support of the bourgeoisie by the Stalinists, the ghastly spectacle of Russia, with the bourgeoisie having little resistance, all the babblers trumpet and puff away very happily under the general umbrella of bourgeois society. A powerful party and a militant proletariat would not silence them, but it would get rid of much nonsense, for it would pose the question very sharply: on which side are you. With us or against.

Enough for the time being. You say you are happy. I hope you are. But it is a state that does not last indefinitely. But one can grapple with things, e.g., Marxism, and master them, and that gives a certain firm foundation. But you are very young still and much of life is still before you. I also, by the way, am seeking a divorce. I have not seen my wife for 7 years. She lives in the W. Indies, is a stenographer, and is not interested in the World Revolution. There was some sort of arrangement whereby she was to come to meet me in England, but she saw after a time that I did not really need her and her pride rebelled. . . .

Let me know how you are getting on. Why this destruction of letters when they are written? Scribble away. I was a schoolmaster once, but am no more. You are one of the few persons whom I am interested in instinctively—so scribble away. I shall understand what you call your "scatter-brains," by which I suppose you mean fits of impulsiveness. Corsets are good for the mind as well as for the body. But there are times when one must take them off, don't you think?

With much love,
Nello

About the money, Dr. Fishler is very kind. I cannot say more now except that there is a hell of a mess all round with the money. All my life money has been a nuisance even when I worked for quite a lot. I am now expecting some cables from N. York, Minneapolis, and London, and when I write again, I shall have more to say. But I am well enough, tho (*between us*) I terribly want all this to be over and have a few weeks at least, if not months, to sit quietly, rest and think a bit.

You see. I write always "private and confidential." A long experience has taught me that one's private affairs, even when not very private, had best be kept private. Have you ever noticed how revolutionaries can chatter and gossip?

Washington

Wednesday

My dear Comrade Connie,

Sweetheart, you are perfectly correct when you say that I am very fond of you. But you were very presumptuous. You say that you must be liked "not for an empty pretty face." Whereby you as good as say that I am fond of you for your "empty, pretty face." You do not give me credit for very much discrimination.

You are a splendid person really. It was sweet of you to write me as you did—warning me. It did not make me like you less. You are fighting your battles and with a person of your temperament they will be big battles. More dignity, more restraint. Yes. But they will come more easily *as your character develops*. I could help you if you will let me. You spoke in your letter only of my side. I must not hurt myself, etc. Is that all there is to it? Your turmoil. Is there someone else? You know a woman always keeps back something. (You will hear this from me often.) The affection and regard you express for me are very precious to me. But for the moment leave me out of it. What is happening to you? I want to know. I must wait until I hear from you. Your earlier letters came spontaneously, I felt that I was in intimate contact with you. It meant a lot to me. Now you are withdrawn. Barriers are up. If you can, Connie, break them down. Must barriers always be up between people, even at 3000 miles distance? I waited for a note from you in N. Orleans. I knew that you were upset when nothing came. I travelled very slowly through the South and now I have had my letters forwarded to me here, and I found that at last you had written. Tell me, did you feel that I had been offended and had not written? I would never do that—to casual acquaintances and then only under extreme provocation—certainly never to you. I thought that you had shut yourself in. And I was disappointed. I didn't think you were the kind of person who would do that. I am glad I was right.

In regard to the Negro you make me feel very proud of my judgment (the vanity of men). I knew you would be a great success. But there is nothing as yet. Look at that filthy review of the Bl Ja in the N. I. But I shall do all I can to correct that.

I enclose L. T.'s remarks during our discussions.* They reached me this a.m. *(strictly private. This would ruin me if it got out).*

The complete discussions I shall send to you, *for your eyes alone*. Read them over again. I enclose also my Preliminary Remarks. They will give you the "approach." You cannot as yet form a N'o organisation—*it is not party policy*. But you can form a "group," and (a) discuss (b) undertake united front activities (c) investigate conditions of the N locally. Get the census volume for 1930 dealing with the N. Work out no. of N workers, professional workers, domestic servants, etc., then take the whites, work out the same. Then compare Negro's percentage of the white population with his percentage of jobs. E.G., white population of L.A. 891,736. N, 38,894. N= 1/22. They will be 1/82, e.g., instead of 110 there will be 12, but domestic servants, e.g., instead of say 51,000 will be 220,000 or something like that. Work it all you, you and your group, for L.A. It will form a useful piece of work, and a fine propagandist pamphlet. You can duplicate it or even raise funds to print. This and constant discussion of general principles of Marxism, reading of Negro press, letters to editors (why not one to Pittsburgh Courier) should keep you active with the group until the SWP decides. Write me and let me know. Any problem, however simple, drop me a card, I'll reply at once. Depend on me.

Schuyler is a very clever man, was once for a year a member of the A.W.P. [American Workers' Party] (Burnham's party). He married a white woman who is rich and they have a child who is 7, composes music, plays wonderfully, and I believe has the highest intelligence quote of anyone yet examined. Result? Mr. S sits back and scoffs at everything, is perfectly satisfied with life. But he is in his way militant and I like him for the stand he takes on war. He has no mass following but the petty-bourgeois though some detest him—the earnest ones—at least read him. His articles against the "democratic" war are giving him some political kudos now. Books. The C. P. bookshop has a book by James Allen, a very good book. The N Question in the U.S.A. Aptheker also has one. The Negro in the Civil War. 10 cents. Allen also has one on Reconstruction. It ought to be good, but you cannot recommend it

---

* See Editor's Introduction, p. 8.

except to people who can discount the C. P. tripe about democracy. Begin with these three. Then when I reach N.Y. I shall send you one or two more, and I shall get some pamphlets for you.

The notes on Capital will come as soon as I settle down in N.Y. Want to hear about me now? I landed in N.O. and found the tour all in a mess. (I wrote you that I think.) I was not well so I stayed there a week and made about 25 contacts, and wangled 2 meetings; then I came slowly up through Memphis, Nashville, Knoxville, Bristol, Roanoke, Washington. I made contacts everywhere, had meetings wherever possible. It was all very impromptu—interviewed everybody (without introductions), and came here 6 days ago. We have had about 4 small meetings, groups of people and they have been tremendously successful. I go to Baltimore Sunday for the same. Best of all I have had practical experience of the South. It has been a wonderful experience. I would have written to you from every place and told you all about it if only you had dropped me a line to N.O. But, you silly baby, you thought I was only interested in your "empty pretty face." As a matter of fact, the first thing I noticed about you was not your "empty pretty face" but your very keen pretty face, at the meeting in the church and how excited you were about getting me to answer a question you wanted put. Tell me, by the way, did you write any letters and then destroy them? Now I must close. I am not very well. I am now *thoroughly exhausted*, and am longing for the tour to end. My holiday I may have to put off. There is the convention coming and we shall discuss the N. Question. I shall have to write one or two things immediately. You are in a mess. But imagine me. I have *nothing* to send my contacts. *Nothing at all.* And if I wait on the rest, I'll wait forever. Will you come to the Convention? Or if not, shall I still come to L.A. for my holiday? I shall be studying the N question all the time (Bribe). My dearest Connie, you have very generously thought of me and my welfare. We are a pair. I would do nothing to hurt not myself—but you. Only if you withdraw yourself or suppress things, then you hurt me.

By the way before I close, brace yourself for a shock. Are you ready? Here goes. Day after day on board I wrote you, about the voyage, passengers, stewards, about me, about you, about everything. It is quite a little book. It is also a love-letter, not making protestations of undying affection, or asking you if you loved me, but without doubt it is a love-letter. I still have it. It requires no answer as far as I know, though that of course depends on the reader. It is yours, written for you, written in response to the generous feeling with which you met me in L.A. and wrote at first. Will it lower my position with the party for you to read it? I don't think so. But it is yours, sweetheart, to do as you like with. Tell me to destroy it and I shall. Tell me to send it and I shall. But do not shirk the issue for then I shall be justifiably angry. Often I was tempted to write on my way up here but I hesitated.

If I have caused you any pain, I am sorry. It was to prevent you any additional worry and bother that I did not, dearly as I wanted to.

Yours as ever,
Nello

Be honest and frank with me Connie. That would not hurt me. Dignity and reserve, yes. But do you think that your behavior and letters to me have been undignified? You do yourself (and me) a great injustice.

Do you know I nearly slipped the letter into this fat envelope? It would be making it so easy. If even only to satisfy your curiosity you could read it and at the same time have no responsibility. But I decided, No. I thought that perhaps I was only indulging *myself.* You know the tricks one's desires play on us. I await your ladyship's commands.

Postmark August 31, 1939
Saturday

Well, my precious Connie, you are being addressed from the nation's capital. Yes, I am in Wash'n spending a week-end with the branch. To-night we have a garden-party, friends, sympathisers, etc., to-morrow night Baltimore, Monday night back here, Negro contacts meeting, and then N.Y. Tuesday a.m. I am so-so, working without strain, tho' my hand is very shaky as you see. However, one day before long, as soon as things are settled, I'll go away for a week or so.

"Stalin-Hitler"* has upset all plans and the N'o Dept has suffered somewhat. But my war pamphlet is nearly finished. I had to stop it to do a long article on the pact. It will appear in the S. A. or as a pamphlet. And by the way, young lady, only by the way, what do you mean by this. Quote: If ever you really need me for that work I shall do my utmost to fly to you. Unquote. Do you mean that or is it only a figure of speech?

You are obviously suffering from strain, excessive work, and worry too. And I think that it is the second which is more important. 7:30–5 is too much. And yet I am positive that you could work in my little hen-coop of an office from 10 till 6 and then go to meetings, etc., until 12 and never feel it.

I do not remember who came with Steve Roberts that afternoon. If I had known I would have taken notice. But that afternoon I looked upon them all as a set of confounded intruders interrupting me particularly when I wanted to be left alone to talk to you. When you feel like doing so, tell me some more about him.

Meanwhile, my dear Connie, I am glad that you feel able to be so frank with me, and that you have me so often in your mind. Do you know that there is such warmth and affection in your letters that it is almost as if you were talking to me on the telephone; or if I had received a note and would see you in the evening. You are a wonderful person in that you can give yourself whole-heartedly. It is a rare quality. But it carries certain penalties. Compromises and adjustment become very difficult for such temperaments. The necessity of restraint, of not doing the things one wants to do, of not finding all the happiness one wants to find, the gap between aspiration and realisation, these things tell heavily on an ardent nature such as yours; and at times your spirits must run very low. You think of me because you feel instinctively that I understand. I do, I am that way myself, only much older than you, and now that I am a full-time revolutionary have at least one sphere, and that the chief, where I can concentrate without a backward glance or fear for the future. But you have not found your way yet to anything, have you? (It took me many years.) Your work you love, but it leaves you too tired to read and study and no revolutionary work. There

---

* The Hitler-Stalin pact of 1939. See Editor's Introduction, p. 9.

is a constant disproportion there. It is a part of the pressure which capitalism imposes upon those who want to fight against it. I have been through that and gradually have discarded all my hopes of writing anything else except that which strictly concerns the revolution. And mingled inextricably with this is the personal life. Do not let your previous irresponsibilities worry you. They seem to. Sweetheart, it is a credit to your honesty and sense of personal and social values. But they are trifles really. What matters now is you and your boy-friend. I get the impression that he is a serious person. I hope that he not only loves you but is careful of you. Or is it perhaps that your innermost wishes, thoughts, etc., you conceal, and he does not suspect that you have these fits of unhappiness? You must know or find out exactly.

Perhaps I have written too much. You will decide. Let me know, or not, as you think fit.

And yet I was glad to get your gay reply. My dear, though not as open as before, I am still firmly allied to all sorts of absurdities; but, a very private confession, in the early mornings when I have just got up. And, here, we approach insanity. I am absurd to myself alone or to some imaginary person—the most wonderful jokes (they seem so to me at any rate); or at other times I make speeches. On what? On anything. To the Negroes on Fascism, to a Party Convention calling for a new spirit in the leadership, to workers just before an assault against the capitalist system, on the Nazi-Soviet pact.

Then I sit down and make notes of the things I said and they form the basis of future articles and speeches. Subject, words, etc., come as spontaneously as the absurdities, one excess of animal spirits. It interests me enormously.

I am back in N.Y. after a busy week-end. We have 4 N'o members in W'n now, one ex-Stalinist ex-president of Washington Local Workers Alliance. At Baltimore on Sunday we had a meeting with some 6 or 7 Negroes, militant—responding to our complete line. They will join the party in time. Meanwhile we have to keep contact. We want people—ready to work hard, study, and of a sympathetic temperament. You are worried about not being able to do enough work for yourself. But patience. Read my articles carefully. Put them aside and read them over. Keep cuttings that strike your eye. Buy a journal with one article even if you don't read it at the time. Keep your own files on the Negro question, odd bits from newspapers, etc. I shall send you such things as I come across. Read one Negro paper steadily at least. And little by little, you will get hold of the Negro question. That is what is wrong with so many people. They have no patience. Now it's hard for you at your age and with your temperament. But you are fortunate, for one cannot beg, borrow, steal or learn temperament. But patience can be learnt. So, my precious, for the moment au voir. I'll drop you a line again to-morrow. I am scribbling just as I please, tho' if sometimes I am saying something and then stop suddenly, it is because I am aware that you have first loyalties to someone else. I could write with great freedom from Mexico, without a thought. Now it is somewhat different, hence hesitation, delay, half-expressed thoughts, etc. But sweetheart, don't let the difference worry you. I made a long trip, 8000 miles, I think, and saw thousands of people, and millions of things. It was a great experience in every way and you remain my most vivid and intimate personal experience. Whatever you do, whomever comes first with you, that continues.

As ever,
N

Postmark September 1, 1939
Friday

Dearest Connie,

The war is on, and henceforth everything is subordinate to that. Our party is reacting very badly (Strictly between us). As a matter of fact, it isn't reacting at all. But some effort is being made to pull the centre together. It is no longer a question of Hitler-Stalin and the politically minded. It is a question of mass appeals and mass demonstrations.

The Appeal *[Socialist Appeal]* will be out 3 or 4 times a week. The Negro column will after this issue be a pamphlet on the Negro and War. We shall save the type and print as soon as it has appeared. Everything else is subordinate.

Work for that in your branch and on the Coast. *Whether America goes in or not*, the whole party should mobilise as if for war, carrying the spirit of opposition to the people. We may unloose a tremendous amount of anti-war sentiment and lift our party to the forefront.

About me—I don't know. I am doing as much work as I can on the Appeal. I shall work inside but I may have to come out openly, according as the situation develops. I don't mind going to prison here or in England. But my night-mare is that I will be deported to the W. Indies and be out of everything. If I have to come out and speak I shall probably make a tour—nothing is decided yet—and I may very well end up in Los Angeles. At any rate I shall keep in close touch with you.

I am glad you liked the B. J. though I think you gave it too much praise. Generous as always. It is a good book, however, and needed. It will play its part in the colonial revolution. And the photographs. Yes. But not one, my dear Connie. Two, one grave and one gay. It is not too much is it? I shall expect them. I send the play. It is in a great state of disorder but it can be read. And now, take care of yourself. You should be here, in the centre. There are immense opportunities for work. Men like Lenin and T'y [Trotsky] are sadly, sadly needed. But we shall do all we can. And there is great need of virile active people. I shall write you again during the week-end. Tell me what is happening to the party there and tell me what is happening to yourself.

With much love,
N

Postmark September 4, 1939
Friday

My dearest Connie,

How are you? Well, I hope, I am too. So that is very good. Now, WHAT ABOUT THOSE PICTURES? You must remember that I have actually seen you very little. Shall I write to the photographer? I shall send him a resolution. Whereas . . . My dear, I have read your letters and still have them in my pocket. I am glad that you are busy. I am sorry too that your ex-husband is behaving as he is doing. But these things happen, and too often. I know. But one must not be discouraged by them. As more and more Negroes, not Jews, come into the party, that sort of attitude will be quite a problem. I hope I shall be around for a long time and be able to help in creating an atmosphere where these remnants of bourgeois ideas will not be able to flourish. The single cure is: profound Marxist study and political activity among Negroes.

One has to be on guard. If I were near to you there would be a lot of things I could tell you. Someday, however, some day.

Why haven't I written? Busy? Yes. But not busy in the ordinary sense. Sweetheart, *what* is happening to the Party in L.A.? Here the situation daily becomes more serious. Split on the Russian question and still more serious, a gulf opening wider every day on the question of the regime, Cannon majority against Burnham-Shachtman minority. Against Cannon are Schtm'n, Burnham, Abern, Gould, and practically *all* the leaders of the youth. L. T. intervened on behalf of Cannon. But now it is clear that at least half the N.Y. membership and certainly a majority of the youth are anti-Cannon, despite Trotsky's intervention. I am not going into the rights and wrongs of the case but under such circumstances it is pathetic to see each side laying all the blame on the other. It seems that this quarrel has a long history. But what is obvious is that this time the minority will not give in, will not allow itself to be split, and in all probability has a large majority of the N. York membership and youth behind it. Cannon has made attempt after attempt to isolate one section of it. But Burnham-Scht'm-Abern-Gould-Erber refuse to be split, and the situation is at a deadlock.*

I am a member of the I.E.C. [International Executive Committee] and am waiting to intervene when the question comes, as it must, before the international. But to-date the majority says of the minority "Irresponsible, jittery and unprincipled, subject to social-patriotic pressure." The minority says of the majority "Stalinist, bureaucratic and unable to lead the party." A split on such issues would show the utmost irresponsibility on both sides.

Once documents are presented then I shall be able to write to you more fully. Meanwhile, let me know what is happening over there. I shall keep your confidence as you will keep mine. Did Curtiss move a resolution to investigate once more the nature of the Soviet State, and if so, when? What is the attitude in the Bay on the party regime. The more I hear the more I see that the party, *the rank and file*, must lose the leadership complex, listen to both sides, and *impose* a decision. Here on the organisational question, as it is called, the party must resolutely intervene and assert its authority. It should approach the question from this point of view. If you leaders cannot agree then we shall examine the questions at issue and say "Do this or do that." Later I shall write you again as the situation becomes clearer. Meanwhile, as always,

with much love,
N

Postmark October 18, 1939
Tuesday

Sweetheart, your letter made me feel very guilty. But I shall write you a long letter soon. Meanwhile I hope you got a copy of the internal bulletin I sent you on the Russian question. I sent it at once. To get out the pamphlet was as much trouble as

---

* See Editor's Introduction, p. 9.

writing it. The confounded C. P. changed its line in the middle of things and as we had the type standing from the Appeal, we had to rewrite carefully so as not to make the corrections too expensive. Another grievance against the Stalinists for which they will pay.

Then Saturday night was our party—a success. Good time had by all and about $25.00 profit. And on Sunday came the city-wide meeting on the Russian question in which I presented my report for defeatism—*in the present circumstances*. Max's is not as drastic as mine but we are close and we *routed the majority*. There has been a fine row brewing here and now it has burst out over the Russian question. Then there is a propaganda pamphlet on war I am doing now, it will begin in the Appeal on Saturday or the following number. Every time I want to write there is something pressing. *Between ourselves*, do you know what happened on Sunday at the membership meeting? I was so tired from talking to a hundred people for three minutes each at the party the night before that I was nervous about my speech and for the first time for many years used notes. But I got through very well—in fact after two minutes I found I didn't need the notes. Anyway, the experience was good for me. I realised how difficult it must be for nervous or inexperienced speakers.

You say you miss me, my dear Connie. Not nearly as much as I miss you, not nearly as much. One day we'll meet and we'll talk.

Now for the Civil War and the Negro.

First you must understand the Civil War itself. Beard. History of American Civilization. There are also some points in History of Negro Revolt by C.L.R. James, that British Negro.

About the Negro particularly there isn't so much material. Woodson has a fat volume on the correspondence of Negroes before the Civil War. This should be looked through.

James Allen has a $1.20 book on Democracy and the Civil War published a year or two ago.

Aptheker has a small volume for ten cts. The Negro in the Civil War.

In the quarterly, Science and Society, of some 6 or 9 months ago appeared an article by Gottlieb, The Struggle for the Land in Georgia.

In Woodson's History of the Negro in America there are many chapters on the Negro. There are some chapters too in Eppse. The Negro, too, in American History.

That is all I can think of at the moment. But if you want more you will find some books in the bibliography given at the back of Aptheker's little book.

As you go on, let me know. We had intended to do the same here, had actually begun, but the war threw us off and the comrade put in charge was also seconded for other work.

The pamphlet on the N and war will be out in a few days. The Pioneer Press did some bourgeois advertising, said the pamphlet was out, and has the whole country screaming at us.

Send the photograph—*S* as soon as possible. I would love to see your face once more, even in a graven image. Much, much love, my dearest Connie. I hope you are well and enjoying your holiday.

Before the end of the week I shall write you a real letter.

As ever,
N

Postmark November 3, 1939
By the way, could you send me the address of Macbeth, the Negro lawyer?
Tuesday

My dearest Connie,

And how are you? Your letter sounded sad. I felt guilty, though I don't know that I am *very* guilty. I have been ill—rather seriously ill, though not many people know.

Yesterday, however, I took down a parcel of books I had prepared for you, long long days ago, to write to you and send them. (Look at the poste and see how old it is really. And behold this morning I got your letter. It was good of you to write. It was my turn this time. You will have got a great and, I hope, pleasant surprise by now. The S. A. will have an article every issue. I know the paper looked "white." But it wouldn't any longer. *Every issue.* Until I drop. The N. I. will have a Negro no. in November. A pamphlet on war and the Negro soon; simple, straight-forward. I shall write it myself. And a Negro Bulletin for inside as well as outside the party. Little by little we shall build it up. It is hard work. But the hardest part is over. Do not expect too much. Be patient. We'll win in the end. A tremendous victory. We shall lay a foundation—a few Negroes here, a few there—many of them reading our paper, etc. Then, as the party gets really strong, a mass party and carries out some mass activity—scores will come tumbling in. I hope the article in every issue will make your work easier and make you happy.

Why are you sad, sweetheart? Aren't you happily in love anymore? I used to think of you as very happy, very lively, bright and gay as only a woman in love can be. I was a *little*, just a *little*, bit jealous, but glad for your sake. I have your letter, I wrote to you in the Gulf of Mexico still. It is, I am sure, in parts a silly letter. But I do not mind writing a silly letter (in parts) to you. But I hesitated to send it. I thought not of you, but of "*him.*" You couldn't show it to him, and why should I encourage you to keep a secret. So there the document is, a thesis undelivered. And God, how happily I wrote it. Three or four days, the Gulf of Mexico like a pond, moonlight at nights and Nello sitting scribbling away and wishing to Heaven that you were there.

Now about me. After Convention I was in bed for 8 days, going to see the doctor every day. Then I went to Newhaven on holiday. I had a good time but cut it short and came back to N.Y. to start organizing the Negro Dept. I am up about 18 hours a day, and flourish on it. Office all day and meetings at night. But I feel very well and not at all tired. The ulcer I ignore, and it is as quiet as a lamb. Every other week-end I plan to go away for a visit to a branch; last week Newhaven, week after Washington. Why *do* you live so far away? My stay in the country is still uncertain. I may have to go away for awhile and then come back again. But as long as they do not trouble me I shall not trouble them.* That is fair, I think. I cannot speak outside private discussions. Otherwise, I would soon be on tour again. That is easy enough and necessary. And I would spend 6 short weeks in California. I wouldn't spend a day less. But at present it seems so far away. Yet I have some plans and as long as the immigration authorities are not unduly inquisitive, I shall find my way to California

---

* James refers to the United States immigration authorities.

one day. Two persons I have to see—one is Antoinette Konokov of Boston, she is 70, a veteran of 2nd, 3rd, and 4th Internationals. A most delightful person and a great revolutionary. She liked me a great deal. I sent her my Bl Ja, and she wrote a letter to me about it which made me quite pleased to read. She is one person, and the other is——. Can you guess? You see this is the end of the page, and therefore I can drag it out. Yourself of course. But it is easier to go to Boston than to California. Though how that is to be managed I don't know, yet managed it must be.

And aren't you coming to the Fair? You know one day the Negro Department is going to be very big and very powerful and I shall send for you to work. Will you come? We will pay $15.00 a week. They always pay the girls very badly but not in my office! You would love it though. Especially now when everything is beginning. You know to see it grow. Like a baby. And grow it will. My dearest Connie, you should be here! In the first fortnight we didn't have an office. Now we have got a little cupboard (I couldn't lie down in it). But it is *our* office. Alternately two girls type on afternoons and Birchman, an Indianapolis comrade, is here too for the time being. But I can't talk to them as I write to you ever. Then there are meetings at night. We have to rush for dinner or sometimes we have an hour and find a quaint restaurant. Morrow and I found a Spanish one the other day and sit and talk for a bit. And then back to work again. And if you have a good room, and *one* real friend, then it's the happiest life. But those aren't so easy to get.

Now I shall write to you often. But you must let me know how you are getting on—not superficially, really. I am your *friend*, you know, and there is little I would not do for you. Have no doubt about that. I shall drop you a line in a day or two again. You have written one or two things in your letter that moved me very much. And whether your love affair is going well or not I would come to you if I could. But meanwhile I'll write to you.

With much love,
N

Wednesday

Just going to dispatch your letter. Down to office at 10 to 9. But Stanley, Managing Editor of the S. A. beat me by 10 minutes. When I am dictator, my dear Connie, 10 o'clock will be the deadline for these dear Bolsheviks. I was trained in the bourgeois world, and the haphazard methods of some of these gentlemen amaze me. That is not the way to run a *headquarters*. But Abern and Stanley are first-rate office-men. An office must be run properly. Till later. The Marx I shall write to you about soon. Now I shall drop you notes at odd times, send you papers, etc.—if I can freely. I don't like to feel barriers in between.

N

A disappointment. The editorial staff of the S. A. had *three* articles from me, three. Yet they left out the one in the second issue. So that no article appears. One needs patience, my dear Connie. I am so disgusted.

Monday

Dear Connie,

Just a hasty line. I expect that I shall hear from you soon, but am not going to wait for replies. Tho' I want to get a letter from you, bright and full of courage.

62   The Beginning of a Journey (1939–40)

Saturday I saw Article No. 2 in the press. And I'll eat the editors alive if we miss another one. I am doing my best but they are hard to write. They are primarily for the party, but still I must bear in mind the Negro readers. And it is always difficult to do two things at once. Later I shall write comments on things of the day. That will be easy.

Myself, I go on, very busy, but sometimes, like yesterday, wishing to go to the country for a few hours, or to the pictures with a friend—someone with whom I felt at home. Then I quite shamelessly think of you.

I read a play yesterday—a revolutionary play by a young Negro from Chicago—produced by the W.P.A. [Workers' Party of America]. The boy does not spell correctly. But he is a natural born dramatist. I shall send it for you. Just let me know. It dramatises the situation of the Negroes and the solution. The last scene is tragedy of a high order, the death of one idea but the birth of another. It will do you good to read it. It did me.

I send you some absurdities.* Do you love absurdities? I do. Well, sweetheart, I laughed till my tummy hurt me. And I am positive you would have laughed too.

An apology. I have not been able to touch Karl Marx yet. But I shall, before long. Never fear. Meanwhile you carry on.

So take care of yourself. I'll drop you a line or many lines as the spirit moves me.

With much love
N

Postmark December 12, 1939

Darling,

Quite a crisis, not political but personal. I have had to leave the office and go into "retirement." But I shall carry on from there, and hope for the best. Write to me, will you? Write to Bill Petersen. 116. Enclose the letter in an envelope marked Goldberg. *It will come to me.* Write to me as Bill.

Meanwhile, just say nothing to *anybody* (Now, mind you!) I'll write to you about the Workers' State and everything in good time. But—absolute silence.

Much love,
as ever,
[no signature]

And where are my photograph*S*, please? Perhaps you don't think I want to see them really. If you knew how glad I would be to have them you would rush out and take 3 and send them at once. Write soon.

Drop me a line c/o Dwight MacD 117 E. 10. Put the letter in an envelope inside marked Nello.

April 4, 1940

My dear Constance,

Writing in bed; *on the very last day* of work in S.F. I fell ill; and have had a difficult time since. I was ill on the train, ill in Chicago, and now, am in bed here; no

---

* newspaper cartoons.

Convention for me, no discussion at caucus, nothing. I have now to rest and recover. It will take me some time I am afraid. What I shall do and where I shall go are uncertain as yet. For the time being I try to be as still as possible. That is why I did not write before and cannot write much now.

Remember me to all the friends, L; B; J; M; A; everybody not forgetting Ed's family and Sol Babitz's sister. Shirley I gather is here; I shall see her if I can but I doubt it. Everybody shouts at me "Go to bed and stay there." Tell Edward I shall begin soon on Roland.

And for yourself,
As ever,
N

Will you ask Jordan to write to me. I have nothing to say.

c/o Dr. Eric Williams
Howard University
Washington, D.C.
My dear Constance,

How are you? Well I hope, and Brother Edward? Full of vigour and doing good work for the party and making lots of money at the studio? Yes? Good.

I am spending a few weeks in Washington, trying to gather some strength. I wrote to you some weeks ago and hope you got the letter. I am due to leave for L.A. at the end of May; for some months at least I hope to be on the coast. I had a private letter from a candid friend in N.Y. about what has been going on during the past few weeks in the W. P. [Workers' Party]. I was immensely pleased to learn that despite a few set-backs we have done splendidly. I took good care to write to a rank and filer who I know is critical. So you can pass the word along.

Of myself personally there is no news. I am reading some books and following the war news in the press. The British Empire is in the most critical spot it has ever been in. If Adolf makes one more successful raid, e.g., Holland, then the political current will swing so strongly against Great Britain that anything could happen in Europe—and something will happen in America. It seems clear that neither Republicans nor Democrats will take responsibility for war before an election; but the preparation of the people in the press is terrible. Every day at least two, sometimes three articles, columnists, etc., are making *the idea of entry* as something inevitable, familiar to the public mind. It is some of the most brazen propaganda I've seen for a long time: brazen, because the sentiment of the American people is over 90% against. What is the press doing in your part of the world? If you are not too busy, read it for 10 days and then write a short article 500 words for Labour Action.

Remember me to all the friends; drop me a line and let me know how things are going. A letter would be very welcome to yours as ever

N

Postmark January 4, 1940

Well, my dear Constance, here we are. I am late but forgive me. We had a fierce battle (on a small scale) to get the N. I. out for Max's meeting to-night. The result is, it's out with a nice crop of typographical errors. I did not make them. I should have insisted on reading the last proof. But———. I shall post you a copy airmail. That is what I have to say about the war. I hope you will feel some sort of understanding greater than before and to understand is to be more confident. At least so I have found. When you read it think that I was telling you all about it. If you were here, I certainly would. So much for bourgeois society. About ourselves, the revolutionary movement and the workers, I shall write later. But, my dear Constance, the same power which enabled the Marxists to see the future so clearly 20 years ago, is the same which gives us confidence for the revolution. It *must take place*. Win? I can't say. We can work. But capitalist society is going from barbarism to barbarism. We must fight it. But you fight it best (and you can be happiest) when you have turned your back on bourgeois society *completely* and identified yourself with the movement, going up with it or down with it. Between the two one suffers terribly. Especially in crises like this. Is that your position? I think so. In fact, I am pretty sure of it. You see, I have been in the same position myself. Let me know.

About M'sieu Burnham. My dear, nothing to be disturbed about. Nothing. Did you know that his passing never stirred the movement more than a ripple? For a man of such great ability and one who had played so outstanding a role in the party and during the faction-fight his defection should have caused a storm. *Cannon & Co. were counting on that*. Those idiots didn't understand what was happening under their noses. The party was seeking a way out. Burnham and *Max were being borne by a current*. They were not leading a split. They were pushed into a position by the development of events. I have traced it in "The Roots of the Party Crisis." But all movements need leaders. Max responded splendidly. When the thing had started, Burnham *drew back*. He shrank from the responsibility of leading the split, because though he had managed to dodge responsibility before, the new party would need him. He now had to face the question—are you coming in full-time or not? He could dodge it no longer. And we could see him bend and finally break under it. Nothing became him less than the manner of his going. He stayed away for weeks immediately after the split—just didn't even come around or phone. Then he turned up with the most god-awful document you ever saw. He didn't believe in Marxian economics, he didn't believe in the Marxist theory of history, he didn't believe in the party, he didn't believe in Socialism, he disavowed everything he had preached for five years: Reasons? None. None at all. Theories he had taught for five years he dismissed in three lines. Now, my precious, I know Mr. James B. very well. He is an intellectual of intellectuals—professor of logic and philosophy, advocate of scientific method, a man of reason to the point of arrogance. Very good. But now at a moment of crisis in a movement of the highest intellectual traditions, Burnham comes to the conclusion that he must leave. That is his privilege. But to write the rubbish that he did. Thereby he proves that *he did not leave on intellectual grounds at all*. Had he genuinely developed differences with us he, being who he is, would have set them down as clearly as any man I know, except L. T. That he didn't, that he wrote so badly is proof that it was a miserable rationalisation of his wish to get out. He was tied strongly to bourgeois society—wife, children, job, *social life*, easy living. Marxism never completely enveloped him. He wouldn't let it. Hence the pitiable figure he presents to-day. A man of remarkable intellect and great strength of character—has crawled out of the revolutionary movement by the back door; to-day stands nowhere; to-morrow will have to stand with the bourgeoisie, for our society offers you no third choice in this crisis. Either for Wall Street's war or—Fifth Columnist. Now Burnham in his middle thirties, in his prime, has to begin all over again, to swallow all he said and thought for nearly ten years. To-day he has no opinions. To give the bourgeoisie the benefit of his talents, to make a way for himself—not in any vulgar personal sense—but as a man of his talents and sensitivity would need to do, to live at all, would be terribly difficult for him now. He is a remarkable example of what happens to a gifted intellectual in our difficult generation. He almost made his way into the movement and *just failed*. Strangely enough, I have come to one conclusion about Burnham's career. One thing could have saved him. If he had fallen head over heels in love with a woman in the movement, whom he would have followed around, who would have made him enter into the spirit of party life, who would have given him some emotional, personal interest in the movement, apart from his intellectual convictions. But, poor man, he loved his wife, I think, and therefore always remained a stranger to the party—never had any emotional pull to help him take the final plunge. Some of what I say may sound as heresy. Only to fools. The way to the heart of the rev'y movement is sometimes straight and sometimes tortuous. I am sorry Burnham didn't make it. Sorry for two reasons chiefly. One is that we needed him. He was far and away the ablest man I have met in the labour movement—with native ability, education, character all combined. Secondly, it is a tragedy—for Burnham never knew what I learnt—that all his doubts, hesitations, etc., could have been solved only one way—by plunging boldly in instead of forever standing on the brink. For once you break with bourgeois society, put it and all its works behind your back, life changes completely. You become part of something, and it is the greatest thing in the world. You lose that terrible sense of being divided, of dissatisfaction, of guilt, of never knowing what to do, of being internally torn by the two forces of society striving within us.

Now here I have written so much about Burnham. I didn't intend to. But there it is.

Confidential: Write me, my dear Constance . It was quite a gap not hearing from you for so long. Max is back. He tells me that I am wanted for a tour—semi-incognito, including L.A. If I do come, I'll make a long stay. Maybe then you'd take me for that drive we were to take, before I went to Mexico. You remember? It was many and many a year ago in a country by the sea. That a maiden there lived whom you may know by the name of . . . etc., etc.

As ever,
Nello

I have a lot of jokes to tell you about myself. I have an apartment. I am stocking it myself—I buy icebox, Babbitts, dust-pan, soap, toilet-paper, eggs, sheets, old chairs. I wash up the plates and wash down the frigidaire. I defrosted it yesterday. Hell of a mess. I clean forgot that ice becomes water which must be disposed of. And Christ, I nearly forgot. I'll tell you if I haven't before. One of my secret desires has long been to *own* (no socialism business, *private property*), to own Beethoven's last quartets, 5 of them; to own *all*. They are without a shadow of doubt, the greatest music ever written. I would love to play them for you over and over again until you began to see inside of them. They are not easy but patience and perseverance do wonders. Well, a man I was talking to the other day, a party member, asked me if I liked them. I told him what I thought of them. He said "I have all five. I'll lend them to you for as long as you like." He has done so. And now I have them. I hadn't thought

that possible until Socialism. I have, my dear, acquired enormous confidence in the future. What I want I'll get. God is with me and history.
R. J.
520 W 150
N.Y., N.Y.

Postmark July 18, 1940

J.R.J. c/o Lyman Paine, 136 W. 65 St., New York

Tuesday

My poor, dear darling,

You have been having it hard. It is too bad you are so far away. I could have made it very easy for you. Strange, the political situation has got past the defences of many who are stronger and more experienced than yourself. For myself (no boasting, sweetheart) I feel ten times the man I was. I understand things so much better and I am working for the party better than ever before. Some weeks ago we had a party meeting. Many were in the dumps. They asked me to speak on the political situation and then ask for donations. I spoke just what was in my mind, and the result was $1,000. I have just written an article which takes up a whole number of the N. I.

But, my dear Constance, this noble Bolshevik whom a million Nazis could not demoralise (that's the way I feel at any rate) is quite often very sick and tired at all the difficulties the revolution places in the way of one's private life. Sometimes I feel like a motherless child a long way from home. Seeking sympathy? No. I merely tell you this so that you will know I understand exactly how demoralised one can feel, and the temptation to run away from it all. But I don't let it overwhelm me, and you must not let the hostile current sweep you away. If I were near to you, I would not let it happen. I could prevent it, I am positive. Well we must do what we can even though all these miles are between us. . . .

This is not a letter. It is just a note to let you know how glad I am to hear from you and to know that you went to a meeting. I shall write on Thursday, a long letter. But you shouldn't have waited so long. All you needed to do was to send me one line, one word even, e.g., Miserable. Constance I would have written you a cheerful letter at once. Now tell me, what about that picture you promised me? And those that appeared in the N.Y. magazines. Which? Send me one or two or all? Or the dates? You are not treating me fairly, Constance. I register a protest. I see you have changed your name. What is it? Conspiracy? Holy wedlock? Or what? I would like to know. So, till Thursday or rather Friday for you.

As much love as always,
N

Postmark August 21, 1940

Washington

Wednesday

Sweetheart, you have heard the terrible news.* I came here on business and after

---

* The assassination of Leon Trotsky in Mexico on August 21, 1940.

a meeting last night, and a long talk with the friends, went to bed happy. Now this morning this awful news. It is the greatest blow we have ever received. One by one they have struck down all our best people and now the old man himself. The news is bad but if he regains consciousness at all and can fight he will fight for his life. He has always fought for what he thought worth fighting for.

I owe you a letter. But we have been so pressed—that's why I had to come here—that I didn't have time to write it properly. But don't let this get you down. I know how you have been feeling. But it is adversity that tests and makes people. It is easy to sail along when everything is flowing with you. But now we need courage.

As ever,
N

October 1, 1940

My dearest Constance,

You have not written. But I forgive you.

I am going to hospital on Thursday. I shall probably be operated upon in a week's time. I must get rid of my ulcer or it will get rid of me. I shall have a nurse in the sanatorium after I am cut and it wouldn't be you. Sad. Take care of yourself physically, emotionally, and politically. The world we live in holds tremendous changes in the near future. Don't be taken by surprise.

As much love as ever.
X N

II.
A Symbol of American Civilization (1943–4)

Postmark August 26, 1943

My dearest Constance,

At last I am able to write to you. You got my night-letter I hope. I left N.Y. the next day and am now out of town, living alone by the sea, absolutely alone. There are people around and some of them I know, but for the most part I sit here and read a little and just keep still. I have not written because I could not write—just that literally. It is a long story. I'll tell it to you.

Two years ago, three in fact, April '40, I left L.A. I'll forget neither one of the dances we had at the party, when you spoke to me, not in words but in actions which I well understood; I did not reply. And next morning when you came to see me off with Eddie, I remember too how you looked. But that can wait. There was a letter or two and then—blank. I noticed that in the last letter or so you were using a married name. I had written to you about Burnham you remember, you had written about music; then I wrote saying that all sorts of dangerous times were ahead. That was my last letter. You did not reply. You will I hope tell me why. At any rate I was on the verge of my first serious illness. For the last half of 1940 I was in a bad way—I went to hospital for an operation—two days before there was a division of opinion among the doctors and I finally decided not to. An operation might or might not cure the ulcer and the risk was too great. I came out in December very much shaken. I started writing and going round again and had a bad year working but ill half the time, though keeping it to myself. I sent a message to you by Jack Widdick. No reply. Did you get it? In addition to the stomach trouble I had nervousness of the fingers—writing with great difficulty. It was very trying because I have never had so much to say as during the last few years. However, I made good use of the illness. I made a thorough study of *Capital*—at last, and thought of you much during it. Do you remember? There are about a dozen people now who are at work on Volume I and by December after a steady year they will have finished it. However: late in 1941 I left N.Y. and went into the wilderness for 10 months. *After I hear from you* I'll tell you about it—a tremendous experience involving thousands upon thousands of workers, black and white, and much travelling over hundreds of square miles. The whole thing passed off splendidly but when I came back I was seriously ill—that was August 1942. I was in bed and out until December 1942 when I fell ill in the street, was lifted home and operated upon that very night. My ulcer had perforated. The operation was completely successful. I made a marvellous recovery. And after a few weeks of recuperation I started working again. But I dictate most of my work now. Writing is sometimes very difficult. These few days were pretty bad. But I am better now than I have been for years.

Now the foregoing might make you think that the last three years have been very miserable for me. Far from it. I am very strong really, but have taken advantage of it and now I am having trouble to readjust myself. It is clear that I need someone to take care of me but I am very individualistic in my habits and personal outlook and unless I feel that I can share my life completely with someone, am unable to contemplate even the idea of a temporary association. I will marry a wife, neither a nurse nor a cook.

But while this illness and the unsatisfactory circumstances of my personal life have worn me down somewhat, on the other hand these last three years have been very wonderful for me. I have at last got hold of Marxism, economic (Capital) and philosophical (Hegelian dialectic). I don't know all I want to know but I have covered the ground, and not only in theory but as a result of it, in my daily work, really can see that I am in command of things. These last three years have been the most exciting intellectually of my life and if I could have studied only because I was ill so much I don't regret it. I welcome it. Many and many a time I have thought of you in connection with it. I know that I could teach you a lot of things. Further, I am not alone. I have a few close collaborators. They are doing magnificent work. They are young and full of enthusiasm, in no hurry to show off themselves. At the same time, bourgeois society goes so rapidly to pieces in Europe and Asia that we feel we are on the verge of great events. I feel my enforced isolation and semi-retirement. But that I cannot overcome. So I submit philosophically. There have been great battles and some of it has been wearing but that is politics. I do my share from outside, and on the whole am satisfied with the past and very confident of the future. That's all there is to me. Later I shall give you more detail and send you some of the things.

But, my dear Constance, I have missed you. You were my first friend, you know, in a personal way, that I made in the long trip around the U.S.A. I have rarely looked forward to anything as I looked forward to seeing you on my second trip to California. And yet, as far as our friendship was concerned, my visit was a failure—a dismal failure. When I see you again I shall certainly tell you why—the truth, the whole truth and nothing but the truth. I may write it. That depends on you. But I can assure you that it was very difficult not to talk to you. Maybe I was wrong. One day you sat with your legs over the edge of the chair eating raw carrots and cottage cheese for lunch. I never concentrated so hard on politics as I did that day. And do you remember when I offered to read some Shakespeare for you? Did I look an awful fool? I know I felt like one. What you thought or what you think I don't know. Perhaps when you write to me, you will let me know. If not at once in time.

I have read your letter often. I am glad to know that you have been thinking about me. As I told you in my wire I have never ceased to think of you. I have my own instinctive judgments of people and I liked you from the first moment I saw you in my meeting on the Negro question in the church. Now I shall expect to hear from you soon. It is a different Constance. That I know. I can tell from your letter. You must write to me freely, this time. At times I may dictate parts of my letters to you. You will understand why. One more word. Are you still as beautiful as ever? Tell me honestly. I'll take your word. You know your single weakness—the possibility of weight. It doesn't matter very much as long as the step is vigorous and the carriage is good. And both of these you have. Tell me all about yourself—without shame for you have nothing to be ashamed about. I want to know and whom can I hear from better than from yourself? Tell me all about yourself. And me? I am much the same. I have aged a little—grayer in the temples, a little thinner, not much, a little more serious, a few lines in my face, but since I have come here they have almost disappeared; my hands are more nervous than before, but I am much the same, quieter externally, more explosive inside; and very very sure of what I am doing politically—of myself as a person, doubtful and more than a little worried as to my future. You see. There it is. Autobiographical sketch but for Constance and Constance *alone*.

I send you my love, unchanged after three years of silence. Write to me at once. My regards to Eddy, fortunate enough to be near to you all the time.
    As ever,
    Nello

I am hoping for much from your letter. My regular address is
R. James
520 W 150
New York, New York
But write to me:
R. James, General Delivery, Northport, Long Island, N.Y.

Send it Air-mail. I would like to hear from you here. For if you write me a real letter—I know you will—I would like to answer it from here.

Once again, much love and know that your letter with its promise of renewal of our friendship made me very happy.

P.S. If, however, you are in any doubt about time then write to the N.Y. address. That is safer.
520 West 150
N.Y. New York

        Sep 1st 1943
My dearest Constance,
Your letter was a whirlwind, a complete body-blow. As I read it, in the street, I wanted to stop and tell everybody. For I believed in you, Constance, I knew you were altogether an exceptional person. But the will to decide, to take action, to force your way through, that my precious, is something that is rare and so valuable. Sweetheart you must forgive me. That you would vegetate. No. I didn't think that. You obviously had the spark of dissatisfaction which moves people. But what exactly you would do, I didn't know. But now. Wonderful. Absolutely wonderful. I am what you know. Never more so than now. But believe me when I say that if you were my wife, daughter, or sister, I would say the same "Go your own way. Find yourself." You are finding yourself, my dearest Constance, in fact

you have gone a long way. There are dangers on the road, as there are on every road (Here I came to a full stop.)

I got your letter at 12. I came home and started to write. Then I decided to stop and swim. The house is on the water when the tide is in. I got into trunks and sat for an hour dangling my feet in the water—thinking, thinking of the European revolution, of the Negro question, and of one Constance, actress. I was looking at my feet in the water and then out across the sound and my thoughts just went their own way. I have just dipped and am back again.

So, my precious Constance, doubly precious now, I'll tell you what I think. You ask for my reaction. Here it is. I am thrilled beyond belief and proud as if I have done something. You write "I read every book I could find on acting" and again "I was a monomaniac about acting." Sister, that is life and living and finding yourself. Stick to it and squeeze it dry. The feelings that surge and must be expressed are the pulsations of a life within you more powerful than in the average person. All people have it. Capitalism stifles it. But with some it is so powerful that it breaks through. You achieve or you don't achieve. But the thing that matters is to live your life, to express yourself as long as it is not ignoble or mean or actuated by cheap motives such as getting a lot of money. You seem uncertain about my understanding what you are doing and why. Some pseudo-Marxist has been getting at you, telling you that what you should do is to join a party and work in a factory? Just tell them to go to hell, that's all. I worked at literature for years and made my own way to where I am. I made my own way. Not a soul contacted me. Nobody taught me. And, thank Heaven, I find that I am still making my own way while so many others are floundering around, repeating.

Now you are a creative person and express yourself to society in a certain way. Sweetheart, no revolutionary of any sanity or experience would dream of your doing anything else—*as long as you did something about it*, which you are doing. The wishy-washy who sit around and *talk*, they are detestable. You are serious about it. To be serious about an art is a contribution to society. You are young. Very young. In two or three years you will know more clearly what you are doing and what you are expressing and what are your prospects. Perhaps longer. Meanwhile, sweetheart, your chief backer, supporter, press agent, inspiration, and rooter is just me. And particularly with those who say that you should join a party, pass them over to me. I'll destroy them or give you the weapons to blow them to bits. That is, if you need them.

And that being so I can tell you more plainly than most could what the dangers and difficulties are. I'll speak in your own terms.

During the last two years, illness and other difficulties have caused me to spend a certain amount of time at the pictures. I rather despised them—Hollywood I mean. I don't any more. The rubbish I look at would astonish you. I can sit through almost anything. When it is very bad I see why it is bad. I have, on the other hand, seen Now Voyager 6 times and will see it if necessary 6 times more. The reason? I work at home. At times I *must* stop. The only thing that keeps me quiet is the movies. So at all hours of the day or night I go where there is a picture, often the nearest. That is why I see some over and over again. And I am learning plenty, I can assure you. If you were near I'd talk to you about it, day after day and being a woman and quick you'd teach me much that I am missing. But meanwhile here goes.

The movies, even the most absurd Hollywood movies are an expression of life, and being made for people who pay their money, they express what the people *need*—that is what the people miss in their own lives. That explains a great deal I think. Why the popularity of the Western? Because young people who sit cramped in buses and tied to assembly lines terribly wish they could be elsewhere; if even, not consciously, yet when they see it they respond. That is the fundamental principle. Like all art, but more than most, the movies are not merely a reflection, but an extension of the actual, but an extension along the lines which people feel are lacking and *possible* in the actual. That my dear, is the complete secret of Hegelian dialectic. The two, the actual and the potential, are always inseparably linked; one is always giving way to the other. At a certain stage a crisis takes place and a complete change is the result. We can take that up another time. Now as I watch the movies and the stars and see who is popular and who not, certain things begin to emerge. *The* great stars are all *characteristic* people, selected by the masses who pay their dimes, because they represent something that the people want. Charles Boyer and his predecessor Rudolf Valentino. American women in particular are fascinated by Boyer, a typical representative of the Latin-Gallic civilisation. He is not merely a great lover. The people do not express themselves clearly. He is a Latin gentleman, smooth, cultured, suave, with an air about him that is the result of a thousand years of European civilization. I would love to watch him with you in the same picture three or four times and work it out thoroughly. Jean Gabin in French pictures is a finer actor than Boyer. He is a failure here, I think. For one reason he is a tough guy. And when Americans want a tough guy, they have their own Clark G and Humphrey B. That is their own, the real *American* type, as different from Boyer as men could be. This type also the American people want and they get it. At least when they see it they sieze it. Note Ronald Coleman, before Boyer. He is *English*—not as finished as Boyer but reserved, no fanny-slapping, "hello baby," type; slightly insipid if you ask me, but full of appeal to people who would love sometimes to be treated with courtesy and restraint and a certain grace.

The women are equally characteristic. The exotic charmer—they rush to Greta Garbo and Marlene Dietrich. Of the three women who to-day are really at the head of their profession—Bette Davis, Ingrid Bergman, and Greer Garson—they are a wonderful study in types. Ingrid B is a Scandinavian, a typical representative of one of the very finest examples of European bourgeois civilization. The Scandinavian countries and Denmark acting as food producers or agents for the great imperialist powers had all the advantages and none of the responsibilities (great armies, navies, colonial oppression, excessive political corruption, etc.) of imperialism. Hence they produced some of the finest people in bankrupt Europe. Note how closely Greer Garson approximates to Ronald Coleman, though she is in my opinion a better craftsman than he. But Bette surpasses them both in my opinion. This *American* woman has something that neither of these representatives of the older civilisations have—a tremendous vitality. She is not so fine a person as I. B. is—you can feel it; and GG achieves some extraordinary effects with the greatest economy of means—but B. D. is simply terrific at her best. She sweeps on like a battleship.

Lana Turner is no fool but she is the eternal bed-companion. There is always one on the screen. Men want such. But Ginger Rogers is more interesting. She has a wonderful figure, but I have noticed how lousy she looks in evening dress. Style she has none, but she is plain, honest-to-goodness, American lower middle-class, one of the people, and the American people love her for it and I don't mind the silly pictures she plays in, but I see what she represents. Jean Arthur is another, a highly skillful young woman who aims at portraying a social type—I think more consciously than do most of the others.

Now, my dear Constance, I may seem to have wandered far from you. I don't think so and I am sure you don't. That is one reason why your letter thrilled me so much. You seemed to have been travelling along the same road I had been travelling. You inside, I outside, a fellow-traveller so to speak. It seems to me that success depends on two things, (1) what you have in you (2) what the public wants. Of course there are a thousand things in between. The road up anywhere is strewn with wrecks, of people and of ideals, but these are the things which matter (1) what you have and (2) what the public wants. Now the second seems beyond your control. It isn't. The more powerfully you develop yourself, the more you strive to bring out all that is in you, the more genuinely yourself you are, for being yourself in any art, is a hell of a job (I know that my dear C, I have seen and felt the process at work), to repeat, the more genuinely yourself you are, the more you express your own genuine personality, the easier it is for people to recognise that you express something which is inside of them. Often they don't know it. The artist, writer, actor, painter expresses something by strenuous effort. And people say "Yes, that's wonderful." They mean "I have felt that all along."

Now you are you. Go your own road. I mean something to you. Good. Something in you feels the need of contact with me at three years and three thousand miles distance. That is you. You were busy at one time and thought of me but didn't write. I understand it all, my dear Constance. I have been through it myself. (At present by the way, I am deep in, guess what, the films and sociological analyses of Beethoven. My discoveries there would astonish you.) To return. Your life, your interests, your sense of social crisis, your political consciousness, all these, sweetheart, are *you*. Live them through. As long as you have one dominating interest to which, drudgery and all, you subordinate your life, as long as you *transmute all your ideas and longings into hard work at your art*, you will in time express something—you. For the rest, no one can control that. It is idle to worry over it. But you are young. I would love to see your work, not only once but over a period. But go your way. You are young as I was saying, socially conscious, with a better background than most, for any knowledge of the movement, my dear, is a wonderful background. All those turgid feelings that are stirring in you, tell them to me. I can feel through the lines what intellectual and creative passions are moving through you. Tell me all about them. I'll write to you often. It will at least help you to find yourself, the you that matters so terribly to you and *maybe*, may matter to a lot of other people too. This is enough for to-day. To-morrow, maybe, I'll go on. About something else. But I thought it best to let you know at once and at some length how close I am to you in what you are doing, how thoroughly I can enter into it, both for your sake and for the sake of the thing itself.

But now, dear lady, one more point. You say that you will send me some *pictures*. Now, Constance, I have a standing grievance against you. You never sent those you promised. I am waiting anxiously for these. You are, my dear, a very beautiful person. I can point out, I daresay, faults here or there. But the ensemble is lovely, very striking, very human, very vital, with emotional depth, and, I always thought, intellectual power above the average. Maybe I'll tell you more another time. People didn't seem to think so. They used to say "What can J see in her? She only has a pretty face." Dopes. If even you hadn't embarked on a career for yourself there is plenty in you which these superficial idiots cannot see. But what they can see, I can see too. And with your kind permission, I shall await the *pictures* immediately.

Many, many more things to be said. I'll take up something else to-morrow. But—*ATTENTION* "It is hard for you to write" you say. "It will be better after one or two more from you. I am still as fond of you as always." Then you continue. Please, sister, on this point, I am determined not to fence any more. It has gone on too long. Whatever you write, dearest Constance, I'll reply to you accordingly. But, as you must see, the initiative is yours here. If you take time, I will understand. In one respect, I have an almost infinite understanding of not everything that you do, but why you do things. It is simply because I am anxious to find out what you are thinking and why. It is, now I think of it, precisely the same feeling I have for the working-class movement. The workers do this, they fail to do that. I am disappointed but not mad. I say, why? Maybe it was because—. I may say: Don't do that again. See what happened. I may even say: If you do that, there will be a mess and as far as I can stop you I shall. But, permanently, what you do and why concern me and always have. And why, Christ only knows. So that imagine when I see that you have the will to decide and to do, be the sphere large or small, I am as pleased as Father Xmas. But, my dear, dear Constance, take your courage in both hands and write. If, sweetheart, you wish not to, then tell me so. Know, darling, that in any case I am your good friend. Do you know? What would astonish the vulgar and the barbarians and what would be hard for many to believe? I have never tried to kiss you. Think back and see. Never. And would I like to? What do you think? Why have I never? That's a long story. That, in fact, is *the* story. *When I see you next, I'll tell you, first thing*. I don't care if you have 20 husbands. That much is settled in my mind.

But maybe I can understand you better if you wrote to me in a way that makes it possible for me to write back to you. I have the utmost confidence in you. Have you in me? You ought to by now. If, my dearest Constance, I didn't think of you, always of you, I would long ago have made such violent love to you that one of two things would have happened—you would have capitulated entirely to me, or you would have asked me please never to write to you or speak to you again; not necessarily in anger, but merely because it would be better so. My life is all of a piece. In politics as elsewhere, I look and weigh and hesitate, looking for some line, some clear path. As soon as I see it, I go my way. Immediately after my illness I was strongly urged to come to L.A. All arrangements were made. I *nearly* came. If I didn't finally you had as much to do with it as anybody else. And yet under other circumstances I would go to my friends, and tell them quite plainly "See here. I want to see a friend. If it's the same to you I propose to go to L.A." I wouldn't hesitate. As I look back at life, I see it as woven threads of development, one thread is the gradual shedding of fear. By degrees, I am now (almost) but not quite, afraid of nothing, except this miserable ulcer of mine. And even that I can sometimes snap my fingers at and tell it do its worst. So, precious, it's up to you.

And by the way, give me more details of your work; always give me *details*. How long is the sketch? What part do you play? What part would you *like* to play? What actress do you like? You once told me "Wuthering Heights, the film, is mushy."

Constance, you great big baby, if you only know what a terrible give-away that was. Why? Because it was a great love story. All the world loved it, intellectuals (who are very finicky) and common people. And the moment anyone said "Mushy," the inevitable question is "Why?" Who is she not to be stirred and moved by a great love story? There is something wrong, *not* in the story but in the *person*. What? Who can tell? Sometimes people think they are perfectly happy and then to a sharp eye there is an indication that the perfection is not so perfect. A husband or a lover who is really interested in his wife or his mistress, who does not take her for granted, notes these things, wonders why and if he looks can generally see. But I must stop. Your letter has made me so happy I scribble on and on. Good-bye. Close your eyes. Tilt your chin. There. On your little rosebud of a mouth. A chaste salute. The tide is all in a dither outside and it is all very wonderful except that you are not here.

As ever,
N

By the way, it seems then I may ultimately write my Madame Roland for you? How strange!

This house, the platform, wind, air, sun and the sea, and the sound in front and to right and left. My table is filled with a mass of papers and cuttings about the war (I'll write you a *whole* letter about that. I have had a great triumph.). The surroundings are commonplace—not even a radio or a phonograph and yet I sit here and you are 3000 miles away and it is a wonderful day. You know, periodically, I stop and think. How wonderful life can be! Not could be, in the future. But now. (By the way. Last night I was reading Romeo and Juliet. Balcony scene.

Nightly she sings on
yon pomegranate tree.

Did you do Shakespeare? How wonderful life can be, even in the midst of a crashing civilization. And I *know* that to sit here and read Shakespeare with you would be an intense experience in my life, read it, not as that day in L.A., as a defence, but this time as an expression. I am sitting and watching the water and feel a strange inability to say what I want to say. Let me try again. I am political. I live at present in daily expectation of the beginning of an upheaval in Europe, marking the beginning of the socialist revolution. I think of that many hours every day. It keeps me alive. It governs my every activity. I feel life is worth living on account of that. I want to give every drop I have in me to help the cause on. And yet, if someone were to say wish 2 wishes, I would say (1) the socialist revolution and (2) to sit on the platform with Constance and watch the evening sun go down. The connection may seem to some monstrous. It isn't. Somehow the intensity of a personal experience, even at this distance, the sense of beauty and companionship, which are so very rare, such things even when exercised only in imagination and over a continent's distance, seem to give a personal meaning and significance to the great struggles opening up in Europe. If you don't understand me, I'll try again another time. I don't often try to express myself this way. I am, as all the world knows, very reserved. Maybe that is why you mean so much to me. People are always seeking self-expression and where they can find it they stay. It is hard to find. I love you very much. Good-bye, this time. But *definitely*.

Now. P I C T U R E S P L E A S E

Also lady, I am not possessive, but very demanding. Face, and all of you; from head to shoes. See, I like how you look. And I want to see as much as possible *so be generous.*

                                    Monday [October 1943]
My dearest Constance,
    Truth above all things. (That is to say as far as possible.) I was bothered at not hearing from you—wondered what had happened. I thought of writing again; then hesitated. I should have. But it takes time. And, as you say, we are getting acquainted again.
    By now you will have received the news, i.e., you will have seen the film. I have no fear for you at all. Your camera man is a man of insight and good taste. When he says that you don't need good luck, he means that you have the capacity and the determination. He must have seen scores and scores of people come and go. These pictures may be not what you expect, though personally, after reading your last two letters carefully, I am pretty sure they will be O.K. I know you and I can see how you have been working during the past year. And when I think of the multitude of inane young women whom I see on the screen, who presumably have passed their screen test, I know what your camera man meant. As soon as you get the news, drop me a line.
    Last night I went to the movies. Saw Stormy Weather (3rd time) and That Uncertain Feeling (Lubitsch, Melvyn Douglas and Merle Oberon). I was with two friends who had not seen Stormy W. and I wouldn't spoil their fun. These days I never never object to looking at a picture over again and even again. Well The Uncertain Feeling I found dull. But there was Mr. Sig R [Sigmund Rohmburg], your recent partner. He was there only for a few minutes, but he gave me quite a thrill, for two reasons 1) I like him very much 2) you must have got to know him very well. Tell me about him some time. He was in a picture To be or not to be, as a German officer who used to say "They call me Concentration Camp Earhardt!" He really is a very comic man. And in another picture, with Errol Flynn, where some airmen, stranded in Europe, escape and get home, he played the part of a German sargeant. He was most diverting. The Stormy Weather is a very interesting picture. Bill Robinson's villainous countenance is a sight to see especially as a romantic lead! But Lena Horne is a problem. She is a beautiful creature and of course strange. But she singeth not neither can she act. In fact her strictly dramatic personality is thin almost to the nonexisting point. Yet she gets across. And I have been wondering why. As far as I can make out people like her because she is a nice, simple person trying very hard to please. Ethel Waters, however, singing and acting in Cabin in the Sky, gave one of the most satisfying performances I have ever seen in my life. The musical comedy business is, as far as I can see, very difficult. She triumphed. Tell me what you think of her. In the last bars of the lyric Cabin in the Sky, there was some virtuoso singing that you hear only on the concert stage in lieder by Brahms and Hugo Wolf. If you haven't heard it, please do. You know she was a terrific success in Mamba's Daughters*—straight drama. I may meet her sometime. If she comes back to N.Y.

---

* *Mamba's Daughters*, 1939.

I'll make it my business to do so. The good lady should play Medea in Euripedes or Lady Macbeth. You know I love the tragic drama. I am just waiting to see Paxinou in For Whom the Bell Tolls. Have you seen her? You say you tend to underplay. I would like to see you and watch you do the same thing two or three times over again. Then I'd know quite a few things about you. I am so glad that you are acting. All children and young people whom I know I encourage first and foremost to do as they please. But my secret passion is music—piano playing. I would love my daughter to be a fine player—as far as I am concerned. But next to that I would love her to act. (Did you ever know that, by the way?) I would have been glad to put acting first. But then I would be a liar, and lies must be kept within bounds.

And *the* acting which I think is the hallmark is the classic drama. When you say you repeat Hamlet to yourself I wonder at many things. I am always doing it. Hamlet, passages from Othello, Midsummer, Lear, The Merchant, Romeo and J, Macbeth; and singing snatches from Beethoven. Sometime I'll tell you the passages in Shakespeare that I am always reading and repeating. I am going to read the plays you say you have done. But meanwhile Shakespeare will be borne in mind. I have known two great actresses—Sybil Thorndike and Flora Robson. I saw F. R. periodically in London. I even gave her a copy of my novel—we lived quite near and she knew some people I knew very well; also when Paul Robeson was rehearsing for my play she came once or twice and talked. She is a very gifted woman but unhappy when I knew her. The other, Dame Sybil, is a terrific personality. She liked me very much and told me about acting and how she worked. She wanted me to come to see her but I wouldn't go. Her son was an officer in the Navy. She was a fanatically pro-English (in a nationalistic, chauvinistic sense) and I was afraid that if I went there the conversation might develop into directions where I would either have to say something very unpleasant, or pretend that I was different from what I was. So I never went—to my regret. She was a fascinating woman of a tempestuous temperament (she used to throw bottles, etc., when she was angry) but disciplined by work like a Prime Minister. She said that she read and worked at Robert Browning every day of her life—he was so hard to interpret. Anyone more different from Flora R, it would be difficult to imagine. Poor Flora, as far as we could tell, was terribly frustrated. But Dame Sybil was happily married, after 25 years of marriage was crazy, like a schoolgirl, about her husband and children. I saw her once as Volumnia in Coriolanus. She just took the centre of the stage and you saw nobody else while she was there. She didn't hog the show. Simply that was she and you had to take it or leave it. I took it.

So there we are.

I have been gossiping. I have other things to write to you about—particularly the comrades whom you know. They have been very unfair to you but I think you have been unfair to them too. One must live, and let live. But the more truly and intensely and comprehensively one really lives, the more one lets others live. If anyone wants to be a travelling salesman, or a girl wants to be a mother and bring up children as much as I want to master Marxism, then who am I to say No—or to criticise? In a day or two I'll tell you what I think about that. Meanwhile you have, I hope, sent the pictures along, and will also send me the news of the test as soon as possible. Meanwhile I think of you and as I sense your eagerness I live again the days of my youth and excitement and discovery of myself. Then will come, inevitably, another stage, when you discover the world around you, its infinite diversity and "accidentalness" and yet, miraculously, the fundamental logic of society, the "necessity" of its development. As Hegel says: All chance is the expression of necessity. And all necessity expresses itself by chance.

All my love.
N

By the way, young lady, you say some curious things. Your wishes I respect. But what do you mean when you say "We have a kinship which goes far beyond a physical relationship." Suppose a man were to say "I have a hunger which goes far beyond a beefsteak." It would be poetic, but not true. Follow me. One of the fundamentals of logic is that if A = B, and B = C, then A = C. From there wonderful things have been done. But do you know what is its basis? A dog looks at a figure in the distance and he says that man wears a red coat. My master wears a red coat. Therefore that man is my master. He is in reality working according to logical principles. The logic, which is the proud creation of human brains, in reality is only the reflection and transmutation of the ordinary every day processes of life. However high we soar we are rooted. And the connections, though mysterious and sometimes insoluble, are nevertheless firm and very strong. Physical relationships are of many kinds. So are mental and emotional affinities. Sometimes they are split. Most people have to split them. Capitalist society is the most vicious of all societies in that respect. (If you have ever seen a picture called Dreaming Lips, with Elizabeth Bergner and Raymond Massey, let me know. I'll write to you about that some day. It is very important and if I don't soon, remind me.) But to return. The split is a matter of regret, it is often the cause of tragedy, it is, today, a social question, where the social necessity expresses itself in all sorts of individual accidents, chances, and forced accomodations. One may accept them. Or refuse to. Some people say and I don't know if it is true, that the conflict is the source of the personal drive of many a powerful personality. I can't say Yes or No. But this I know. An affinity which is beyond a physical relationship is not stronger but weaker than an affinity which is rooted in it. I am speaking here without prejudice, but merely expressing what I have seen in life and in books, and experienced in my own life. But one can say more in ten minutes than one can write in ten hours. Voila.

I'll write you too about my work in time. Plenty of time. My wretched hands shake, but I am sitting on top of the world really. I am like you. I can only do my best. The rest lies with the people. But ready I am now. And I'll explain it all to you before long.

"Nightly / she sings // on
yon / pomegranate tree."

Write it for me as you say it. I want to know.

By the way, do you know that Charles Laughton, that loud, vulgar, over playing filmstar played a Macbeth in London underplaying in the modern way so that he created a sensation; and that he once played Molière at the Comédie Française and won golden opinions, so well did he combine the French classical tradition with his own individuality. What has caused the deterioration? Till later now. I'll write to you about the comrades.

W'y, [November 11, 1943]

My precious Constance,

Darling, you have me worried. "A Terrific strain on the heart and muscles." What does that mean? Was it only while your were down with it, or is that sort of strain going to be recurrent? Please let me know in detail. Take care of yourself, *precious*. You are very precious to me, you know. How precious I'll tell you the first time I see you, and will write it at the lightest provocation. I have been in bed more or less since Othello. I am badly shaken in health, sweetheart, badly shaken. But I got your letter today and am writing you at once. If my handwriting wobbles, it is because I haven't written a line for over two weeks. But I must write. I am sorry you have been suffering pain, darling. I hope it's gone for good. Tell me all about it, do. When I lie in bed or crawl around I look at your tennis racket picture and think of you, beautiful and radiant and happy. So you mustn't be ill for your sake and for mine.

No. I didn't curse you. I have never done so and never shall. Your place with me is safe, you know. I may get angry and close up for awhile, but think ill or ungenerously of you? No. Knowing you and feeling your interest in me is something I have always kept apart. And when I heard from you again and you said that you had remembered me always, then that sealed it. You know it's a rare thing to be able to feel about someone, "There I am, safe. Whatever I do, whatever lapses I am guilty of, I know that there I can turn." So it is with me for you, and do not ever doubt it.

About the play. I am glad you did yourself well. That is what matters to you now. It closed down—worse luck. But you opened up. That's it isn't it? And the reviewers? Why no clippings sent to Miss? W H Y? That people approached you is no surprise to one envious citizen thousands of miles away. If I were near, I would approach you too Constance, blond or brunette You remember Juliet apostrophised by Romeo, Every cat and dog and every fly can see her but I have to do without her. How true it is. *Worn out your theories.* I know this blank feeling when you have discovered something only to find it was discovered long ago. Marx and Engels were always doing that to me. But to discover it yourself is a vastly different thing from reading it. You develop you own analytical and creative powers. You strengthen your gift and in time you tackle the problems of your own age, which are never the same. Go ahead, darling. Let me know some of them sometimes. I have the *Encyclopedia Britannica* near my bed and often I read Stanislavsky's essay on acting—a masterpiece; I know it is—he is a Hegelian, a master of dialectic. I saw it once and followed his argument beautifully. Next to it is an essay by Max Rheinhardt, passionate and turgid, but lacking the mastery of structure, the relations of the essential to its manifestation which Stanislavsky shows. I'll explain it to you some day. It is a theory of knowledge not needed by the artist but indispensable for the theoretical writer.

About the telegram, dear heart, it said what I thought. The mistake was not Freudian or whatever it was. You see, my sweet Constance, Freud's theory is a theory of the *sub*-conscious. I don't know what is happening in my subconscious but Freud believes that is 2/3 or 7/8 or something like that of the mind. All I know is that if it is even one-half of my conscious, then my subconscious is in a very bad way. Poor fellow. He had better remain sub. For if he were to emerge, then things would Happen.

Names for the cartoons. I agree with you. I love the argument one best. But the one where the skier performs the miracle I have seen before. It is, I think, a masterpiece of the ridiculous. You know, it grows on you. There is something of genius in the impudence of the artist.

Take care of yourself, darling. *Please.* You may come in March? I wouldn't tell you what I think of that. Let it wait. This much you should know. I have been ill, sweetheart, very ill, and am once more shaky. After the last operation, some of my friends wanted me to go to California, L.A. I nearly came, but though I love California, I would have been coming to see you. I thought over things and then decided: No. Now I am working hard until January. (I lie in bed and dictate.) Then I shall have to make a serious effort to regain my health. I shall come to California and stay for a long time. If you are coming to N.Y. I shall stay here. You must let me know in good time. As ever, all my love.

N

About the blonde change! I'll have to see. Luckily I knew you brunette and the meaning of that word luckily, I'll explain one day, I hope. You meanwhile try to work it out.

Did you get a letter from me about our friends in San Pedro, etc.?

December 15, 1943

My precious Constance,

Thanks for review of Othello. No. I hadn't seen it. But it is a good review, that reviewer knows what he is about. I regret to say that most of the others wrote bilge. So you also go in for close personal observation of yourself. I do it all the time. It is the only way to understand *other people.* If you have a good grip on yourself then you "get across" the full power of all that you have in you. I was reading Stanislavsky in the Ency Brit. [Encyclopedia Britannica] and he says a lot of things about physical and nervous control that apply equally to the public speaker as well as to the actor. If Carradine is lousy then he is no good for you.

I have already sent you a sweater. Quite an adventure for me. Of course I chose it. Whom would I ask except yourself? I worked on this principle. The first thing you put down is what you have subconsciously in mind. If someone said to me "Wish a wish" automatically I would say "I want to see Constance" or something connected with you.

Then I go to Bonwit Teller's. That means it will be good. I can't choose things for their value so I have to be sure that it's O.K.

So in I go and I say "sweater please." Size? says she (middle aged but neat and trim). I say 14 and was sorely tempted to add—hips only 12. But I suppress it. However, one day, one day, I'll buy something for you which will enable me to describe you in detail, with the utmost propriety.

So next, for colour. White I say; but then I say "Pink and coral." White is virginal. And I regret to say, "virginal" bores me or at least does not interest me. It suits adolescents or old men searching for their youth. Then I remember a coral sweater you used to wear. So I say "she probably has that colour." So I point out to the saleswoman "What about that one over there?" So she brings it over and I say "This is it," and I hope it is.

Can I afford it? My dear, dear Constance. You are very good to ask. Can I afford a plane-trip to L.A.? Of course I *can't* in the abstract. But if you wired me "Come as soon as you can. I want to see you!" Then sure as day I can afford it, immediately.

And who will not act that way for you is not worthy of you. So anything I send you please know that I have immense pleasure and satisfaction in doing so. I please *myself.* Enormously. I have written a long letter to you about what a woman can mean to a man, how contradictory any deep emotion really is. I wrote it for Thanksgiving, but at the last moment didn't send it. Why? Because you *might* misunderstand it. Sometime I'll send you some gloves, and then again, a scarf. Lovely things for me to send. Because I wish I could be a scarf which you wrap around your neck and gloves which hold your hands for hours at a time and (with apologies to the Hay's Office) I would very much love to be your sweater. Do you remember

    heaven is
where Juliet lives; and every cat,
and dog,
And little mouse, every unworthy thing,
Live here in heaven, and may look on her;
But Romeo may not.—More validity,
More honourable state, more
courtship lives
In carrion flies than Romeo:
they may seize
on the white wonder of
dear Juliet's hand,
And steal immortal
blessing from her lips;
. . . .
But Romeo may not; he is banished, —

Do you understand now? I have been reading Shakespeare often. The N. Yorker reviewer completely misunderstands Desdemona. My dear Constance, if I spent a week reading that play *hard*, I would write an analysis of the *play in general* first and the relation of Desdemona to it. It could be a "revelation." One day I'll meet you and we'll talk about it a long time, and I'll tell you what I think. It is one part I want to see you in. There is more significance to Othello and to Shylock *to-day* than to many of the other plays of Shakespeare, except perhaps Julius Caesar. I saw to-day the Nonesuch Shakespeare, 7 vols. $145.00. Beautiful as a dream. It is not often I wish I had money. But like this afternoon I did. I would have bought 2 sets, one for you and one for me. Then read it and refer only to pages when I write. But, my precious, I have given you already the moon, the sun, and all the planets. If I cannot give you a beautiful Shakespeare, then you must be patient a while.

My enforced vacation approaches. I shall have to employ my time somehow. I could spend long hours talking to you or, rather, listening to you. I so much want to hear all that you have to say—to *know* you. But while I struggle to get my health back I'll have to employ myself somehow. I am toying with the idea of writing a play (*Mum's the word*) for Ethel Waters, that superb natural and mature actress.

It will be a historical play—Civil War. The central character will be Harriet Tubman. I have a short biography of her which I shall send to you if you wish to read it. I shall bring in all the conflicts of the time, but all represented by characters. There is to be a girl in it—a Southerner, who will make a rapid transformation from southern prejudice to an extreme revolutionary position. I have seen this transformation quite a few times in real life. She is very brilliant, well-educated, and of passionate temperament (I do *not* mean sex). I should say rather intense. She falls madly in love with an escaped slave. The Abolitionists of those days had very friendly relations with escaped slaves who became great agitators, writers, etc. On the edge of the abolitionist movement but very much in love with her is our aristocratic wealthy liberal—who is dilettante, in sympathy with the movement, gives money, but maintains a semi-cynical attitude. (He is based on a character in the history of the time.) She takes up women's rights, temperance reform, etc., all the revolutionary ideas of the time. He is in love with her as I say and as with so many weak men, she is all he needs to make him join the movement. (You know the type I daresay. I am drawing heavily on my experiences in the movement.) She, however, loves the slave. And our aristocratic character hates him. He tries to be above race prejudice. He thinks he is. But this is a weak spot, a weak spot with many men where women are concerned. Now the ex-slave is *not* an intellectual. He is handsome, a magnificent physical specimen, a man of action, a fighter with Harriet Tubman in the Underground Railroad. He is in love with the girl too, but for the time being he only pays her attentions as a dumb man does. He gives her flowers, does everything he thinks will please her, but he says nothing altho' she tries to make him speak. The general environment is awkward for them. In their circle the atmosphere is political—Garrison, Wendell Phillips, Frederick Douglass, John Brown, all come into the play which is a *political* play. But the *political* ideas must be expressed through *living people with all their passions, loves, hates, jealousies, etc.* I have one scene sketched. Here it is, very roughly.

Winthrop, the fellow-traveller, visits the girl, and the Negro boy is working in an office in the house. He meets Winthrop when the latter comes in. W is polite and well-bred. The Negro boy is quiet. But the antagonism is clear. The girl comes in and the N leaves. She smiles at him and clearly indicates her preference. She detests W for his ill-concealed feeling of superiority to the man she loves; and she expresses it by "attacking" him for his dilettantism. He is irritated. She refers pointedly to the dangerous work the Negro boy does. W loses his temper slightly and makes a sarcastic remark about N. She flares up at him. He capitulates, and tells her he loves her, it would be different if she . . . etc. She is softened a bit but says No. She can't. Is there someone else? "Yes" she says boldly and they look at each other and they know what is unspoken. Our aristocrat then makes a really nasty crack about her preferring that Othello (or some such remark) to him! "You love *him*!" Then she gets really mad. W gets cool but is raging.

[Line drawn through next two lines, below]

"You will have to kiss him you know, not merely admire his heroics, and bear more. Yes, bear his children, little mulatto children."

[narrative continues]

He says

"Presumably Othello's repetition of his wonderful adventures in the South have quite fascinated Desdemona. But life is not all politics and heroics. You will have to live with him."

"Yes," she replies "and kiss him and bear his children, little mulatto children."

He breaks down again; says he was rude, but "You couldn't mean it." She says

84 *Symbol of American Civilization (1943–4)*

"I'll show you." She asks N to come in. He comes in. Then she speaks

"I want Mr. W to know that we are in love with each other. He doubts if such a thing is possible. I thought he should be the first to know."

She goes over to him and kisses him, makes him kiss her by holding him close. Then, her arm in his, turns to W and tells him that under the circumstances it is usual for gentlemen to leave. W leaves.

The Negro, slow-speaking and a bit confused, looks at her for an explanation. She leads him to a sofa.

"Do you love me?" she asks. He tells her how much and soothes her doubting pride. (This is 1860 you remember.) But he is ex-slave, doubtful. She is a woman, confident, rich and accustomed to having her own way. She is a bit mad with his hesitancy.

Are you afraid? or words to that effect, she asks him.

He laughs. He is not afraid of anything. But——.

Then she speaks, curses all the prejudice. She'll break it down. She will live her own life with the man she wants, etc., etc.

They kiss passionately. She says she'd love to kiss him at the main corner in Charleston, Carolina, for everyone to see. He replies that it would be the last kiss they'd ever have, but that if that was the only way he could kiss her again he would be ready.

Then he asks her. Was W rude to her? For if he was, he would break every bone in his body. She turns on him again. He must not do anything of the kind. Remember. Keep his hands off W. That is exactly what W would expect, brute force. Fiercely she insists that this he must not do.

You see, of course, how sensitive she is on this point and why.

He agrees. "Whatever you say, honey. But," he adds, "You can argue and talk. But I have been a slave and I know these people. They'll come round in time. But I'll have to take that Winthrop by the scruff of his neck and shake the life out of him, he and all his kind. That is the only way I'll ever feel myself his equal and that is the only way he'll ever respect me."

After a pause she says "I think you are right. But, please—shake anybody whom you like but not Winthrop. I shall deal with him."

I should have mentioned before that the great political conflict of the time, among the Abolitionists, the basis of the play, is whether abolition can be won by peaceful means or revolution. Harriet Tubman and John Brown said "It will be war." But Garrison and others, including our heroine, thought otherwise, though very bold and resolute in their agitation, etc. You see the political implications for those days and for now. Now tell me if you like it, tell me *plainly*, as I shall tell you what I think of your verse when you send it. I shall have to see E. Waters and ask her first if she'll do it. The second character will be this girl. And every *personal scene*, love, hate, jealousy, generosity, will illustrate some *political aspect*. If it is taken, do you know who would play the part of the girl? You must keep these notes around somewhere. I have no others. I am busy with politics but the ideas come and as I cannot tell them to you—sweaters, scarves, gloves, and every cat and dog and fly on Doheny Drive are more fortunate than I—I scribble them to you instead.

As ever, all my love,
Nello

Thank Eddy for his kind regards. I hope he is well and I know he is happy.
I send this one ordinary mail. No haste about it.
R. J.
520 W. 150
N.Y. N.Y.

[December 1943 or
January 1944]

Dearest Constance,

Thank you for them. They are quite lovely, some of them very beautiful. I'll tell you which one I like most when I know. I see that I was wrong about "rosebud." The pointing finger gracefully informed me. The little one was ravishing—terrific. If you "camera" like that your fan-mail would be mountainous. The sun-suit with glasses is exciting and the hair-do, back-ground, etc., make a fine picture. The Trocadero one is not as "glamorous" as the others. Pardon the word. Yet somehow I saw you there behind the pose—a little pale as you can be at times. You, you know, behind the pictures. Was the Bonwit Teller one a great success? *I* loved it. In so many of my ways and thoughts I am incurably bourgeois. It was dainty and demure, but demure serious not demure mincing. I didn't know you had it in you. So I can't decide. If I were compelled to make a choice I would choose—I just don't know. It was sweet of you to send them. You say you will send others—please do. They bring fresh to me you as I remember you, in so many different attitudes. Also much more. I'll tell you when I see you.

This has been a dreadfully hard day. Politics. You know most of it, I *hate*. It is the most degrading profession that I know. Without qualification. There is now a serious fight going on in one organisation I know; so to-day some half-a-dozen people sit down to think out how best to circumvent the other side. Six solid hours of talking, scheming, planning, fighting as if you were matched against your bitterest enemies and not comrades. It goes on and on and never stops. Some get innured to it. I never have and never will. But it has to be done and it is not a thing that one can play with. Do it or get out. It is not necessary to go under however. Souvarine, one of L. T.'s enemies, once wrote of him that there was nothing "mesquin" about him—nothing of the rascal. At 60 you could still say the same of him. He remained untouched inside. One of the very finest men I ever knew was a Belgian, Le Soil, veteran of World War I, Bolshevik, Trotskyite, shot by the Germans last year. Hard as steel, honest as the day, gentle and very kind. But they are rare. So many become after the years toughened (not tough), cynical, and unscrupulous as any capitalist. And yet they all are closer to a true revolutionary than anyone outside. I'll tell you why. You see they are a people apart. Somehow, for all sorts of reasons, some of them very remote, they have seen into the inside of society, beyond the surface and have had the impulse to do something about it. They give their lives to it. And anything that anyone gives his life to is worthy of respect. When it is a question of resistance to the tyrannies, injustices, and crimes of capitalist society to-day, with the enormous power wielded by modern rulers, then, whatever their personal deficiencies, all these people belong to the salt of the earth. If some of them, particularly the young ones and the rather inexperienced, show intolerance, it is a by-product of their fundamental certainty that what they are doing is not only important but the most important thing that anyone can do. The sacrifices, the devotion, the readiness to do *anything*, these my dearest Constance, are a perpetual source of wonder to me. Most of them are the most astonishing young people. How irritating, how profoundly ignorant some of them can be, I know. I lived in the bourgeois world, many phases of it, before I got to know these people. I can therefore compare. I know them in Britain, in Paris, from Germany, Holland, Belgium and various other places. They are the same—the very salt of the earth. So though they irritate you, look a little beyond, think a bit and you will see. They are as passionately devoted to their business as you are to yours. Normally I stand no nonsense from people who criticise my friends. But with you that's O.K. I tell you what I think and what I think you ought to know. If you were near to me I'd make you understand—just make you. I hope I shall have some success at this distance—3000 miles but not so far now that I have your pictures. (Any that you have, send. I cannot have enough.) Furthermore, the type is a type you should study and try to understand—for your own sake. It is since 1917, a very characteristic type of our modern civilization. It will increasingly be so for quite a few years. Study it, watch it, learn from it. One day you may be able to do it justice in your own way, help others to understand it, and if you are a great and mature artist, you will help it to understand itself. As far as is possible, never let anything fundamental irritate you.

Yes, I remember P. A. very well, certainly a charming person, of more than usual distinction. The day after I saw her that August I fell ill and never got out again until December for three days—and then operation. You must explain to her for me. I liked her very much but, truth to tell, when you were around, I had eyes for no one else. And though I have philandered, I might do so in New York or Kansas or Chicago, but not in L.A., nor even in Frisco. I would think it a sort of sacrilege, and infidelity. You know what I mean? And unfair to the girl too. Because I wouldn't be giving her even that minimum of attention, real attention I mean, which a woman must have in any sort of relationship, however temporary. So, *between us*, although I saw Miss P, I kept away and maybe she thought I didn't like her. But I did. I hope she succeeds with her painting. She has a fine personal quality and if she has technique enough to transfer it to canvas, then she'll do well. And so, my precious, I must leave you.

You say you are in a new show. *What* show, young lady, *what* part? You say please to spoil you a little. Sweetheart, what I would like to do is to spoil you a lot. Now it is up to you. Frequently I am reading and I say Voila. Here is something Constance should see. All sorts of things. Jokes, funny pictures, and sometimes striking pieces of information or just beautiful writing. I could send them to you. But if you are going to be spoilt you must be spoilt systematically. Just how often would you care to hear from me? State your terms, precisely, and without timidity. They will be obeyed as far as lies in the power of your devoted admirer.

N

The other day I saw a column dealing with Eleanor Roosevelt who it seemed wore a grass-skirt when visiting some natives in some island. I laughed loud and long, and thought of you. Want to see it? Send me a warm and tender greeting, and I'll pay up on the nail.

January 4, 1944

My dearest Constance,

To-day is my birthday. I am 43; much older than I should be in some respects, but thank heaven, full of life in others, in the ones that matter to me most. One of them is loving you. Do you know? You make me love you more every day; your last letter did.

Sweetheart, I am glad that the sweater came first on your list. To be first with you, at least in one sphere, on one occasion, at one time. That is a precious victory. Over whom? Over fate that conspires in so many ways to keep me away from you. But let me tell you. I regret nothing. I am glad that you have lived and developed the way you have. I respect you more.

Now for the why and wherefore of this. Xmas eve I saw Carlo. I questioned him about you. He has insight into character you know, rather diseased and distorted, but very often penetrating. He described your life to me. He told me how really beautiful you were, and Carlo is an artist with an artist's eye (he is very gifted you know and can make a good bourgeois living any time. But he tells the bourgeoisie to go to hell, which is one reason why I respect him fundamentally).

Well he described you in great detail and your life and your prospects and your friends. Carlo is no fool and he knows that whenever I see him I want to know all about you. He knows why and I do not in the least pretend that I am disinterested or merely enquiring in a "friendly" way. Now I don't believe in the "starvation" theory of art, least of all for a young and beautiful woman for whom her appearance counts so much. But as you know, I watch the films and I look at the stars and particularly I look at the starlets and see you as one. What Carlo told me didn't seem quite right for you—for the stage. It would have done for you as preparation for a part with Robert Young but not for Paul Lukas, for a society screen drama but not for St. Joan. Now get me right. I merely listened to Carlo and questioned him. Naturally this was at second-hand. I understand you—not perfectly. God forbid. I am not so young as to think I understand any woman perfectly. Secondly, whatever you understand perfectly is, for you, dead. It cannot possibly stimulate you. But I understand you, the you that matters infinitely more than Carlo does or ever could. For that matter, as far as that is possible for me now I would wager that I understand you as well as anybody and probably more than most.

Anyway, I was doubtful. I didn't say anything to Carlo, I couldn't write to you. You would have got mad in all probability and said "You listen to gossip about me and come to conclusions about my life and prospects as an artist. You are unfair."

So I am worried. Then I got your letter and I know that I am right, on both points. Carlo sees only the surface and even below, but not too far.

When you write that you will save some money and come to N.Y. and make the rounds and try to get small stage parts or stock or something, my heart gave a great leap. Human nature is very treacherous. It is possible that deep down I am being merely selfish and thinking of myself and your being here. But I don't think so. For if I had never set eyes on you and your case had somehow been brought to my notice I would have said exactly that.

1) Get some *money*, for sister, without money, in New York, then God help you. You will have a rough and tough time. And perhaps suffer some hurt, deep inside . . . who despises money is a big fool that's all.

2) But having got some money, then tie it round your waist as a life-saver and jump into the deep, open sea.

Every day I see it. Most of the people *who matter* have been in and fought their way through. Let me give you an example. I have in mind a politician, a gifted man, in his way, devoted, experienced. But he joined the CP early, a big party, with funds from Moscow, the prestige of Russia, etc. To this day he has that mentality, of looking at things from above. As the crisis sharpens it handicaps him at every turn. Perhaps you understand. If you don't let me know. I'll explain more. But you usually do, without my explaining too much, like my friend Bill Williams.

So, precious, make it. Come. Save the money and come. I wish you were near to me. I would tell you something and then kiss you and you wouldn't resist. It is just this. Thirteen years ago, 1930, I was 29, married and in the W. Indies. I had been practising writing. And I said "Enough of this. I shall save 200. I shall go to London, and take my chance, come what may. I'll make it." I didn't do exactly what I intended to do. But I found my way to myself, and my place in the world. I am still finding it, and parts of me, my inner self, you are helping me to find.

So when you say you are going to do what you say you will do, do you understand why I love you so much more, why I say I understand you. It is just me, all over again. And I was so certain that Carlo was wrong.

And now, my precious stop disparaging yourself to me. None of your letters is silly. None. Do you know you write wonderfully well—exactly that—wonderfully well, with a directness and simplicity that only a professional writer and particularly a journalist can appreciate. The dress I would love to see you in. It is not trivia. It matters to you and to me also. Do you wish to know one of my secrets? I would love to spend a day, a whole day with you buying a dress, and shoes and stockings and everything to match. You write what you want to write. That's *you*. And that's what matters for me.

Now to some business.

1) Politics. I have for some weeks now, had put aside, three articles which deal with the war. I shall send them to you now. I shall send them ordinary mail. No hurry. Read them at your leisure. Read them carefully. Keep them. Then I shall send you regularly cuttings from the press, with short notes. All your problems I shall take up.

2) I wrote to you on Thanksgiving Day. I have decided not to send the letter. I wrote on December 15th that I send you in another envelope. In it I make reference to a play.

3) Some weeks ago I wrote to you about a holiday I am compelled to take. I want to come to California. My plans are these. I have to get away from politics for 3-6 months. I have to see after myself. During that time I propose to write a play—for Ethel Waters. But I shall only write it if she wants it. She, like all Negro actors and actresses terribly want plays. She lives in L.A., I hear. I propose to come, speak to her about it, show her reviews and pictures of Paul R playing in Toussaint L'Ouverture, and come to terms with her. If she accepts, I shall do it. If she does not, then I won't. If she accepts, I shall make one condition. There is a part in it which I have you in mind for. I shall tell her so and she will have to agree. Otherwise, nothing doing. The play is very clearly worked out in my mind, characters and all. If you are interested, let me know, soon. Also find out her address for me. I shall send her photostatic copies of the photographs and reviews as a preliminary to finding out if

she is interested. I shall send them to you also. If nothing comes of it, then nothing comes. But I don't mind your knowing what I am doing, with all its chances of success and failure.

If it is all worked out then I shall leave here early in Feb'y or thereabouts. That puts everything in order, I think. I love you.

Yours as ever
Nello

The picture I shall send. I want it to be a good one. If you like it half as much as I like yours (with the finger pointing*) then I'd be satisfied.

*Are you slightly sadistic? You could have devised no more exquisite torture than precisely that pose? Was it done before or after? And your eyes in that picture, Miss Flirt? I would accuse you of the most malicious coquettishness, except that I have seen them like that once before—that night I passed in from Pasadena—red dressing gown and Constance all sleepy. I remember it as yesterday. You know with your husband and the other man who lived with you, and some idiot who was with me; and you among them. It was like Cleopatra in a suburban drawing-room. I looked at them and then at you, or rather at you and then at them. It was *horrible*. That is the only word. I felt like lifting you up and saying "What are you doing here? Come away from these people. They mean nothing to you. Come with me." It is one of the most powerful impressions I have ever had. And like all things that have ever mattered in my life it came in a flash. I saw it to the end. How far you have reached now, I don't know exactly. I can guess, but I'll know when I see you. Some of my friends are giving me a "secret" party to-night. They think it's secret. But I know all about it. Anyway I'll keep up the pretence. They'll make it very pleasant for me and I love them very much. But to-night I'll have my own party—Constance in red, sleepy and therefore giving herself away, all instinct and feeling and unawakened passion and power—and me, an intellectual to my finger-tips, but arriving through observation and study at what you know instinctively. It would be a wonderful party—a voyage of discovery and understanding, constantly to discover and to understand, the eternal instinct of life with the understanding of civilization. You see why I love you?

January 5, 1944

Enclosed I send you the programs of Othello. I am thrilled at the idea of your doing Shakespeare with Carradine. Fight for it, Constance. Fight hard to make it. It is presumptuous for me to give you advice but I think I understand something about Sh. I want you to know what I think.

The other day I saw an interview with Carradine in the press. He said that he and the late John Barrymore used to read Sh. He read too "colloquially" in J. B.'s opinion. In his, J. B. read too lyrically. Both were *wrong*. Pardon me the dogmatism. I have felt Sh in my bones too long and am studying him once more. I have also seen some superb Shakespearean actors and I have some opinion.

The English tradition is the best. It aims at preserving the Shakespearean rhythms, the finest in the world, and *at the same time* making them natural. In other words, you have to do both what Carradine and J. B. were doing. It is hard, hard as the devil, but it can be done. I heard J. B. do a speech from Hamlet and another from Richard III on discs. He was theatrical. The best I know is Forbes Robertson on some old

90 Symbol of American Civilization (1943–4)

Columbia records. Get them if you can. He is old, but rhythm and expression are perfectly matched. To do this is a triumph. It is worth doing. Shakespeare in drama and Beethoven sonatas in music are the supreme test. Few succeed. If you would care for me to listen to some discs and send them to you let me know.

You see, I saw the Othello. It has created a tremendous stir here. In my opinion it, particularly Paul R, was lousy. Not one of them, except at odd moments, had the Shakespearean rhythm—not one. I was shocked because Margaret Webster and Uta Hagen were both trained in England. To hear John Gielgud or Edith Evans is to hear a miracle of rhythmic beauty *and* naturalness. Without the first, there is no Shakespeare.

Robeson was rotten. He is a magnificent figure, a superb voice, and as usual with him, at moments he is overwhelming. But in between his lack of training, his lack of imagination, were awful. For long periods he stood in one spot and *said* the lines, just said them. Dynamic development of the part, there was none except the crudest. And Shakespeare is dangerous for the amateur. Without strong feeling you slip immediately into melodrama. A great actor gives a grand sweeping performance in effect, but every line means something. Every phrase can stand by itself. It is built up into a whole. For long periods Robeson lacked grip. I knew he was just going on, to shout at the climax. I wish I could see it with you two or three times. How I would love to. Then I'd tell you what I think and you'd help put me right.

What made R's failure so noticeable was a magnificent performance by Jose Ferrer. Never once was he just swimming along with the stream. I never saw him working hard or sweating. He had an all-over mastery. But he had both the imagination and the discipline to make every line tell. I have never seen anything better. E X C E P T. The rhythm of Sh was entirely absent. You know in one scene after Iago has planted the poison in O's heart, Sh makes him soliloquize: Not poppy, nor mandragora, nor all the drowsy syrups of the world, shall ever medicine thee to that sweet sleep which thou wldst yesterday.

Now lines like these are a test. Sh did not write that music for fun. The music emphasises the dramatic climax. It must ring. You must hear it. Where on the film an orchestra emphasises the dramatic values, Shakespeare orchestrates himself. Ferrer didn't have it. Just as in a film if the music came suddenly it would be an obtrusion, but instead it is there subdued, to come to a climax at the correct moment and then die away again, so it must be in Shakespeare. I have heard Gielgud do Hamlet lines: Angels and ministers of Grace, defend us. Dramatic passion and lyric beauty were fused. You could not separate them.

One thing the play has done however. It shows that Othello was a black man—who felt his colour and his age were a handicap to him. The mess that colour can cause in a happy married life was particularly clear and the whole American Negro question was highlighted by the play. *Politically* it is a great event. It was also very interesting. I could see it often again. It was a distinguished performance, and Robeson's remarkable gifts and personality were very much worth watching. But the play on the whole fell short. A word on Desdemona. She frail and young and sweet, then when righteous indignation forces her to stand up to him, there is a terrific clash. You should tremble for her. Even at times her fire and innocence should enrage and yet over-awe Othello, only for his rage to mount higher. What should break her is her inability to convince him she has not been unfaithful. You should get a glimpse of this spirit in her defiance of her father and it should come out in the quarrels between them. That would give the last acts a grim power. But Uta H simply bungled it up properly, or rather Margaret Webster did, for the responsibility is hers. Desdemona is a "revolutionary." She crossed the colour line. She spurned the rich and curled darlings of Venice. She married a middle-aged man. She ran away to do so. She is a modest maiden but she has a fiery spirit. When Othello turns on her, she should, after a time, *fight back*. That spirit must appear again. She loves him but she must resent his accusations. Now if the Moor as he usually is, is a big man, a soldier, a terrible-looking African (in his rages) and she is as Uta Hagen was, bowed down before O. She was merely pathetic. Someone had poisoned Othello against her. That was all. It all depended upon the plot, upon the trick that Iago played. That wasn't good enough. . . .

Successful as the play is it could [have] lifted off the roof if a Desdemona with technique and insight and imagination had been able to rise to the necessary heights. I repeat. It was not merely the trick, the plot. You should have been able to see her very personality making Othello mad.

You see, my dear Constance, Sh like Beethoven is a man who has not yet been fully grasped by bourgeois society.

The world made a great stride forward in the 17th century. Bourgeois society began. Religion was the dominant mode of feudal society. Luther (although he didn't know what he was doing) removed religion from heaven to earth, from the priests and the Church to the heart of the individual man. The first great bourgeois writer was Shakespeare and coming when he did, he posed for the first time the relation of the individual to society. Hamlet remains for ever the prototype of what we know today as the petty-bourgeois liberal or radical. In politics for instance he is for the revolution, he sees it intellectually, but he cannot bring himself to take part in such violence. He ruins himself and all around him. The Jewish problem—it is perfectly posed in the Merchant of V. The race question, and with it the marriage of a middle-aged man to a young girl. The demagogue and the masses—Julius Caesar. To-day society is profoundly different from Sh's day. But it is bourgeois society. And whereas in feudal days the Church decided what was right and what wrong, with bourgeois society the individual has to decide. To-day more and more great classes make the decisions but the conflicts are sharper than ever, in fact they are at breaking-point. Now S was a dramatist, no sociologist, so he individualised them. Every man looking on them to-day can see them not only in individual but in social terms. Yet whatever society is each man must make his individual choice. So to-day we see these plays and in them is mirrored the life of society. The artist therefore can play them and the managers stage them with a penetration and breadth that comes from 300 years of social experience. As Hegel says somewhere, an old man repeats the same prayers that he did as a boy but now they are pregnant with the experience of a lifetime. So to-day we look at Shakespeare but we have not solved the problems he posed and we can see them as he never could. And in this period of world-shaking crises they are all around us, insisting on solution as never before.

Finally, the more I think of Sh and Beethoven the more I see that the rhythms and the tonal qualities (of B) are organic to their work. They felt the tragic quality of society, Shakespeare after the Reformation and B after the French Revolution. The rhythms are a response, deep and tragic, to the tragic quality of life in all periods of great social ferment. There is a well-known piano piece by Beethoven that children play Fur Elise. Listen to it. You hear something never heard in music before or since; same with Sh. You see now why I think you should as an artist move heaven and earth to work at these plays. Whoever after years of work grasps them, penetrates into them, and recreates them for this age, will be doing the work of a giant. I know that you have it in you. I read your letters and I see that. You see Carradine and make him take you, just make him. Then you'll come to N.Y. and we'll read the plays and you'll do parts for me to see and you'll be graceful and lovely and full of power and I'll be terribly happy; and if I can tell you a few things which will help you to see deeper into them, I am sure that when I see you there are many many things I'll understand about Sh for the first time.

Take care of yourself, mind you.

January 25, [1944]

Sweetheart,

Your long-awaited letter arrived most opportunely. I was in the midst of a violent political struggle—in many respects crucial. The letter came to me—I had to send for it—ten minutes before a debate began. I needed nothing better. I cannot explain but you will be glad to know that against enormous odds, I and a few faithful supporters won a tremendous victory—we succeeded in our aims beyond our most extravagant hopes. We worked hard—very hard, but more important, we had *faith*. Someday I'll explain that to you. *Faith*, so misused by Christianity that the idea, which has in my opinion, strictly materialistic roots, is lost in the modern world.

Anyway——. About yourself, darling. Where exactly do you stand re Arsenic and Old Lace? Did you go on tour? I read your letters very carefully. But I am confused. You said you would come in seven months. Now you may come in May. Possibly you don't know exactly yourself. But I am making some plans, as I have explained carefully. I want to make them in relation to your probable movements. Sometime in February I wish to leave here. I wish to come to L.A. But how long I'll stay depends upon you. Do give me some more precise idea, as far as you can.

I am glad you like the idea of the play. I shall send you in greater and greater detail the structure, the essential conflict, the manifestations of these, how they express themselves in people, real human, wonderful, miserable, noble and vicious human beings. I am depending on you. Of course I want you to find E. W.'s address for me? Are my letters too badly written? About Carlo, I thought I had made it clear. He gave me the impression that you were "settled" living very "comfortably," and I was worried about it. Because your letters showed an essentially different person, the Constance whom I knew. (By the way I haven't the slightest objection to people who live comfortably. Socialism hopes everyone will.) But I couldn't quite see Cleopatra continuing to live a suburban existence. There was a clash. So when your letter came saying "I am going to plunge into the deep and take my chance" I said "Wonderful. That is exactly what I hoped and expected you would do." You see, Carlo was not so dumb. He is as you describe him, but he has penetration. He is no fool. He saw a conflict between your life and your aspirations but, as so often, he misunderstood not the conflict, but you. That is why I described how I was exactly in your situation and then broke out of it. Read my letter again. It will be easier to follow now. Perhaps it will help you to understand me better, perhaps help you to understand yourself better. I was very glad I spoke to Carlo. Work it out and see. Then write me about it.

Now about my love for you. Darling that is my problem at present, not yours. You have mighty problems of your own. I can guess at them. There are many aspects of life that are to me very mysterious. One of them is the electric spark, something in the blood, that flares when two people meet. It did for me with you. As far as I know, it did for you with me also. Perhaps I am here entirely wrong. But I don't think so. I have never asked you. I shall when I am ready. I have carefully refrained from doing so.

Now sometimes this happens to people and the person who stirs it is for one reason or another "impossible"; sometimes the person is a phoney and then the original spark dies or is almost extinguished. But, my dear Constance, it is one of the most powerful things in the world. I have known people happily married with children who have cherished for years mere memory of a short acquaintance with someone whom they knew in their most secret life, was the person who instinctively mattered most to them.

A woman usually knows herself at about 30. The latest generation matures earlier, perhaps about 27. For myself, I got to *know* myself in 1936. The last few years have taught me much. The last few months of correspondence with you have completed my education. How can I begin to explain all this to you by correspondence? If you think carefully over all this, however, you will understand although if I judge you correctly it will be as much by instinct as by reason. No harm in that.

Now here is a problem for you. All my friends for years now have been worried about me. They want to see me married or at least settled. They know that this will be the salvation for me. It isn't that I am sex-starved. God forbid. They know that I am not. They are quite right however in thinking that that is what I need—to settle down. I know it. But I can't. I cannot settle down with anyone who is not everything to me. I can't do it. It is no good for me. Briefly the person must be able to make me think more of her than of myself. Then I would make her part of my own life and to help her in hers would be a way of life *for me*. I don't want anyone who would just be nice to me and love me. I *need* someone in whom I would be so interested that doing everything I could for her would be a need of my own life and my nature. It has taken me many years to find this out and to understand myself. You have helped me to understand it so you might as well know.

Now there are two women I have never met personally. One is about 32—Italian, tall, very beautiful, black hair, bourgeois, European cultivated. She plays the harpsichord and the lute—Corelli, Lully & C. She dresses beautifully, is very wealthy, has a beautiful apartment—is in love or fancies herself in love with a two by four milk and water idiot. She is a type I know and very much appreciate, the type you come home to. She knows a friend of mine and the friend described her to me and I suppose if I pressed the point I could meet her. We would have a lot in common. I know that. I have met people like her before in Europe. If I settled down to cultivating her acquaintance, we might become very good friends. I could appreciate her and she could me.

The other is totally different. She is an American—about 33. She is a widow—the widow of the brother of a good and close political friend of mine. She is tall and graceful—but her father is a judge—old American family, typical Anglo-Saxon type—good firm character, no graces to speak of. She doesn't know what to do with herself now. She has been watching us talk and is drawn to our political ideas and action. She has learnt a lot lately and is likely to plunge head over heels toward *us*. I like her. She needs to go to a hairdresser and get a good hair-do to begin with. She is snobbish too, but she is a solid person—and could be very attractive. She is by the way as scared as hell of me. I talked to her the other day for two or three hours, then asked her to go out with me. She thought it over and then in the cool direct way I admire her type for—she said "No. You are slick and insidious. You put across your ideas and I find myself agreeing without knowing. I am going to keep away from you." Too bad for her to say that. Altho women are so clever that she may well have said it purposely. I don't know and I don't care. But she wouldn't want to be someone to come home to. She would want to do all that I am doing—to live. So there we are. That is the truth. The first, as I say, I have never met but she was described so carefully to me by the friend who had met her that I divined what the description meant.

So here I am, and there they are. I am *not* asking you what to do. I am not asking your advice. I am talking with you. I talk to nobody, absolutely nobody, about my private affairs. But you are different. I'd tell you anything, young as you are and little as we have spoken really. Now tell me what you think. And tell me very frankly.

About the politics, all in good time. When you have read those let me know. I'll write to you about them. But only when you have studied them and let me know your impressions fully.

Meanwhile, with great restraint, I'll continue to tell you how much I love you. So don't worry about my loving you. The time to begin is when I ask you to love me and to come away with me. And if and when I do that, sweetheart, it will be very very different from all you have known of me in the past. So meanwhile write to me and let us get to know one another, more and more. Write to me a real long letter that takes up some of the things I have said. Meanwhile I send you one kiss—3000 miles away—I can make it a dozen at this distance. As usual,

      All my love,
      N

I wrote this yesterday. I read it over a few minutes ago. How inadequate it is. The things it says are true. The things it does not say are so important that the whole letter is one-sided, so one-sided as almost to be false. You will have to fill in the rest. How false it is your intuition must work out. Sufficient to say that there is scarcely an hour that you are not in my thoughts. I am slowly from your letters, which are very revealing, building up what you are, how you are developing. Carlo's conversations helped. It seems now that I have two major interests in life, one socialism, as expressed for the moment in the party which, from my position, I analyse and watch over in all its relations from morning until night. And 2, myself as a person which is expressed, very partially at present, in you. And the party at times makes me mad and tires me out, and periodically lifts me up very high and whatever it does, that's O.K. with me, though when it does what I think is wrong I do not hesitate nor do I mince words in saying what I think. And with you, sweetheart, it would be wonderful if it were the same. I do not idealise you. Far from it. If I were near to you for any extended period there would be some wonderful, some magnificent quarrels, with Constance talking 90% and Nello 2%. The other 8% would wander around until you would take it and in the end finish up with 99%. If I am not very much mistaken, most of the men and people in your life have spoilt you? Am I correct? And in all probability have been scared of you, worried about you, afraid lest the power of temperament (it is now expressing itself in your work) should run away if not actually, then that intangible way in which people living together, kissing, sleeping, are slipping away from each other. For my part, sister, if things were fixed as I wanted them, nothing would give me greater pleasure in life than to see you going ahead full steam, working at your career, absorbing the admiration which I know you love, being your own constant, inconstant, deadly serious, scatterbrained self. So, my constant nymph, I watch you, and without in any degree losing my head over you (I carefully have refrained from doing so) I know that you are the most wonderful phenomenon that has ever come into my life. If I had you to be kissed often, to listen to you instead of talking to you (do you know what that means? Think it over. People are always asking me questions. They are always listening to me. Then I listen to them, for what they have to say. But except for one or two kids I know and perhaps one or two persons, how many people in my life have I listened to because not what they said mattered but because they mattered. There I think is the whole question, especially if you understand me, how preoccupied, self-centered, self-contained, devoted to my own pursuits, as I am.) As I was saying, you would be kissed, listened to (not necessarily because of your wisdom, though you instinctively say many important things, but as far as I am concerned because you said them), watched over as a father watches over his child, or better still as a bird watches a fledgling trying its wings in flights which become bolder and bolder; and my precious Constance, whenever necessary, spanking you hard. As far as I can see, you would need it not often, but periodically, and it should be a good one. (One is fast becoming due by the way. In about 2 weeks I shall know.) So, dear lady, if you read this long letter carefully in its two parts, you will understand things a little better. The first part I could write only because of the second part. The second part is what Hegel calls essence. The first part is what he calls appearance. Both are true. But the truth of appearance can only be understood in the light of the truth of essence.

I am always adding bits to my letters. I saw *The Cherry Orchard*. Eva le G. [Eva Le Gallienne] and Joseph Schildkraut. I also saw Helen H. [Hayes] in Harriet. The first was wonderful—a wonderful show. If only you had been there with me. Always it is like that. If only Constance was here with me. I have the programs. I'll send them to you in time and all that I saw and thought since. I shall write you quite an essay on *The Cherry Orchard*. I hope you have seen the play or know it.

[February 4, 1944]

Well, my wonderful, I played a little trick on you. I wrote this on the same day that I wrote the other letter. But I posted it different mail. I didn't want a whole wash of mail arriving at the same time, for many reasons. This letter will contain notes about the play.

Let us start from the beginning.

The play will represent a conflict between slaves and slave-owners, an exemplification of the age-old conflict between the oppressed and oppressors. It will, therefore, be of exceptional interest in the world of to-day and particularly of to-morrow. It will be a historical play, dealing with forces everybody knows about roughly, slaves, plantocracy, Northern politicians, abolitionists, fugitive and slave laws, race-prejudice, Abraham Lincoln, emancipation, etc.

Now the trouble with all such plays written by both amateurs (99%) and talented play-wrights (1%) is that (1) either they know the history and the politics, etc., and write a political tract or (2) they write something full of stage-craft, but with no understanding of history and of *politics*. Politics is a profession. Only people who know about politics can write about it. Politics is made by people, people who live for politics, but who hate, love, are ambitious, mean, noble, jealous, kind, cruel. And all these human passions affect their politics. They take one position to-day and change it to-morrow because they are anxious to win a post or fear to lose a job or wish to be revenged on somebody. That is true but that is the appearance. But the essence of the thing is different. Political and social forces change the circumstances in which people live. Thus at a certain time when slave-owners are powerful, ambitious politicians seeking jobs naturally support slave-owners. When the slave-owners by economic and social forces are losing power, *equally ambitious* politicians, *still seeking jobs* attack slave-owners.

This is to put it very crudely. Then there are idealists who go their way, irrespective of material gain, but are subject to vanity, prejudice, etc. And the rank and file, simple, honest people, following one leader, now another, etc., etc.

Now the job is to translate the economic and political forces into living, human beings, so that one gets interested in them for what they are *as people*. If that is not done, then you will have written perhaps a good history, good politics, but a bad *play*. Now I propose to write a good *play*. Ordinarily a play of this kind has no chance of popular success. But in the political atmosphere of to-day this kind of play has a wonderful chance. The proof is Paul R in Othello. The "Negro Question" was at the back of the interest in Othello; that and Paul's reputation. With an actress of the stamp of Miss E. W., all that is needed is her approval and interest. She can make it. In my opinion she has here a duty to perform, not only to herself as an actress, but to the stage and the American people. She is a magnificent actress and can here create a tradition.

Now the basic conflict is between slaves and slave-owners.

Harriet Tubman will represent the slaves. In the play she is about 45, unable to read or write, thinking only of the slaves and freedom; so bold, so courageous that she is famous even before the Civil War, earning her living by washing and yet a guest at the homes of Massachusetts aristocrats for days at a time because she is the link between them and the slaves. I send you a small biography of her. You will see how dramatic her life is.

Opposed to her is a *slave-owner*, a fictional character. He is not a devil. He is *not* a bad man. He is an intelligent, sober, highly political person. He merely says "There are 3 million slaves. They are the basis of the economic life of America. I have 300. They are my property, sanctified by law. Abolition means economic ruin. I do not propose to be ruined. I do not propose that the country will be ruined. I shall fight." The basic clash is between himself and Harriet. Harriet by the underground railroad steals his slaves and he representing the slave-owning class is driven to find solution in Civil War.

Then come three famous names, William Lloyd Garrison, Wendell Phillips, and Frederick Douglass.

They are agitators and revolutionaries. Garrison and Phillips are the pure pacifists. They believe in moral suasion, agitation, education, they will convert people by words. Garrison is the leader, a fanatic if ever there was one. He is for the abolition of slavery, of drink, of cigar-smoking. But he hates politicians, he hates violence. Wendell Phillips is more reasonable. Harriet follows their leadership, but at the beginning of the play, Frederick Douglass splits with them. They were preaching: No politics, no violence, abolition of the union. F. D. says "No. Henceforward I am for political action. I am for the maintenance of the union. I shall start my own paper."

Garrison becomes bitter against Douglass. You know how the splits take place and how fierce those who are working in the same cause can be against each other.

Harriet is sympathetic with Douglass but follows Garrison and Phillips. So workers follow leaders of the moment. Now come some subordinate characters, subordinate politically but *dramatically very important*.

There is a white girl from the South, idealist, who joins the abolition movement and works with Garrison. There is an escaped slave, a young man, serious, taciturn, a man of action, devoted to the cause, who works with the movement but follows Harriet, who helped him to freedom. These two are in love with each other. Then there is a young politician, fictional (on the whole), who is sympathetic to the movement, but whose main aim is political ambition. He too is in love with the girl from the South. He and the ex-slave hate each other because of rivalry over the girl and the racial question is clearly posed *inside the movement itself* centering round the girl.

But this politician represents something very important. He is a follower of Seward, the Secretary of State in Lincoln's administration and Governor of New York. Seward hates slavery, he is for abolition. *He brought up in his house as his own daughter, Harriet's adopted child.* He knew Harriet well, gave her money to buy a house and protected her.*

But he was a man with political ambitions or, if you prefer, he did what he thought was best for his country. Anyway, Seward's political life is there for all to read. He was always saying the most drastic things against slavery but always climbed down when the Southerners threatened Civil War. In other words he was a characteristic *liberal*; all through the play he vacillates. But he comes only into one scene. The vacillations of Seward are represented *by this young lawyer*, and the conflict is expressed dramatically between the rivalry over the girl, the ex-slave, and himself. The girl is a follower of Garrison, remember, and is always denouncing *politicians* and this young lawyer is a politician.

Harriet's daughter (she is a historical character by the way) is in love with the ex-slave too. She is a typical bourgeois Negro, well-educated, hating slavery, but following Seward in all his vacillations. She is always suggesting to the ex-slave to break with Garrison and the other fanatics and follow Seward's more "realistic" politics. Thus she will get him away from the influence of the white girl and win him politically to liberalism. Harriet is a great believer in Seward who has helped her so much and who has brought up her adopted daughter as his own child—a very important thing in race-prejudiced America. The climax comes with the John Brown raid. America is thrown into an uproar. The South threatens secession. Seward as

---

* [Note by C.L.R. J.] All this is historically true.

usual says "Retreat. Cease provocation. Slavery is evil but we cannot have civil war." Everybody is taking sides. And dramatically the thing is expressed by the arrest of the ex-slave under the anti-Fugitive Slave Law. What to do? His owner is the slave-owner from whom Harriet had rescued him. Seward says that they must buy him back and the boy must go to Canada. They *must* have peace. *His adopted daughter says the same thing.* The boy himself says No. He will stay and fight the case. He is not going to Canada. Harriet says they will fight the case and if they lose she will rescue him by direct mass action.

The white girl now moves away from Garrison and pacifism and she is for direct action too. Wendell Phillips opens up a merciless political attack on Seward. The young lawyer takes Seward's position. Lines are clear. For everybody knows that this means Civil War. (You will be surprised to know that a case of this kind actually took place, and that Harriet actually carried out a most daring rescue of the arrested ex-slave leading the people and taking him away from the police and the soldiers.) See Biography p. 29 on. The upshot is a successful rescue. Harriet breaks politically with Seward her benefactor and sees that her daughter's chances of happiness are ruined. But she lets nothing stand in her way. Wendell Phillips persuades Garrison to adopt the new position, political action and civil war. And the play moves to a triumphant conclusion, in which the young ex-slave, however, is killed at the front.

All the political ideas I know are as sound as if from a political thesis. But as best as I can, they are expressed in people. Harriet the leading character undergoes a slow evolution from hatred of slavery, the beginnings of direct action (underground railroad), follows the pacifists, looks to Seward her true *personal* friend who made her ex-slave daughter a lady, then realises that the moment for action has come, breaks with Seward, and joins Wendell Phillips who overcomes the more fanatical and impractical aspects of Garrison.* In the conflict between her personal affiliations and her political duty she does not hesitate. That is her personal tragedy. But for a long time she hates the white girl, not because she is white but because she knows this girl stands in her daughter's way.

Then there are all the subordinate conflicts, between the white girl, revolutionary and Seward's adopted daughter, Negro bourgeois; conflict in Seward himself, how far are his vacillations due to ambition, or to a sincere love of peace. He does not know, he is a sensitive man and it tortures him; conflict between Seward, the practical man, and Wendell Phillips the idealist, but *in revolutionary times*, it is idealism which becomes the most practical thing; conflict between the brilliant, witty, clever, dandified young lawyer and the uneducated but quiet, strong-charactered ex-slave; conflict between the sincere, brave, and idealistic white girl and her determination to win Peter, the ex-slave and the prejudice among the abolitionists themselves—they say "Yes, all men are equal but——"; and Harriet's hostility to her is hardest of all. But she fights and actually wins though the war defeats her. Then I hope to bring in a real vicious Southerner, head overseer to the slave-owner and a Negro abolitionist, a detestable character who tries to make love to every white woman he meets; these and many other subordinate conflicts but all of them somehow are swept forward in

---

* [Note by C.L.R. J.] This is the "moral," the way political events force people to revolution.

the great historical movement towards the Civil War and emancipation—unknown to them historical forces are shaping their political lives and their personal preoccupations. It is an enormous job of course, but I see it as clearly as I saw The Black Jacobins and once I see it I know that I can do it. By the way, near the end, there is a scene during the Civil War itself when Harriet and the ex-slave had a raiding party against the slave-owner and all the slaves on the plantation pour into the hall of the great house and he and Harriet and Peter meet face to face at last; with the roles reversed. Voila. I feel to-night that I could go on forever.

You are very near to me. Sitting while I tell you about it instead of writing. If you were here I would act it all out for you and you would be very excited, wouldn't you. Of course, you would. That's one reason why I love you. And to-morrow you would say "But, Nello, you know I think that it would be fine to introduce here such and such an idea." Now, my precious Constance, just see why I am so confident that if E. W. will agree, there is a real play hidden there. On another occasion I shall give it to you act by act, scene by scene. Naturally one changes these things as one actually gets to work. But the basic ideas are there. The play if written will be written around Ethel W. I admire her beyond idolatry. But once her part is fixed, then the other part will be written for you. Then, later, I'll write a play for you, for you as the centre—Madame Roland. That is a long time off, however. Dreams perhaps. I don't care. The point is that I am ready to go through with this one—to come to L.A., to see E. W. and to place the whole business before her. As things are, I can write it only if she will do it, after I have talked it over with her. Otherwise my work in life is political. However, if you were near me and wanted it done, I'd do it, to please you, as long as you helped. Then it would be one long pleasure to work it out day by day with you and then merely publish it. In years to come it will be played. But for the time being the thing is to aim at getting it done now. I'll write to her and then I am quite ready to come. Please do not, by the way, discuss it with anyone. There are very good reasons for that, very good reasons I assure you. By the way, just one word to get things right. I intend to write a magnificent part for Wendell Phillips, a splendid, brilliant and very neglected American. As usual, all my love. Can't you imagine how much I miss you, when I read and work out these points by myself and know how much more it would be if you were near to me. Imagine working out a scene together, one of your own, how you would want it one way and I would want it another and how I would stand up for my way—on principle of course—the *highest* principle and how you would have to persuade me—I would be willing to be persuaded. In fact I would sit back and say "Persuade me, sister." And I would stand an awful lot of persuasion. But when it came to how it should be acted then you would be boss. "This way," you would say, from principles higher even than mine. And then it would be my turn to persuade. My dear Constance, when I turn my mind to it there never was such a persuader as me. Could you stand a deal of persuasion? I think you could. You would be very disappointing if you couldn't. Dreams, but life, real life consists of struggling to make dreams into reality. According to how I hear from you I shall be ready to leave here in a few weeks—three or four—tho' I don't know how easy it is to get a seat on the crowded train. Bessie G is going home in May and she told me that as soon as she gets home I shall stay with them—if I stay so long.

One last word. You know Judy—Bessie's little daughter, my good friend, a most dazzling child. I have loved her from the first day I saw her—she was about 8 weeks or something. I am going to write a story for her—a serial, a most WONDERFUL serial. Whenever she writes to me she gets an installment. And she is to have the privilege of telling me where the next chapter will be laid and what the old characters must do and what the new characters must be. This is the toughest assignment I have ever undertaken, but God willing, I hope to keep the little treasure happy and interested. If I am in difficulties I'll call upon you for an episode and some pictures. I have an idea that you could do very well with pen and ink sketches. Enough for one day—Good-night.

[unsigned]

520 W. 150th
N.Y. N.Y.

[March or April 1944]
Monday

My dearest Constance,

1. You are taking the plunge. Loud and prolonged cheering. If you stop and listen you can hear the echoes of it across the continent. I rejoice for you. Your teeth are shivering? Bite them hard. You come along. You have your aim. Fight for it and never never settle for less. The schedule of the up-state people looks fine. That is what I have always read and heard actors say. Stock is the best school. Night after night, part after part. When I hear you say the same I somehow feel that it is O.K.

If it doesn't materialize, your summer parts, then you try to do what you can do elsewhere. Let me encourage you.

IT IS A TOUGH ASSIGNMENT

As tough as could be. There is only one more tough, and that is to make your way as a painter. But who cares? If things look really gloomy at any time, come to rest your weary head on my shoulder. I have nothing except me. But I'll stand by you. There is Constance who wants to make her way in the world and there's me who will stand by her. That is No. 1.

No. 2. I shall see you. I shall hear you speak. You know, that is to me like a new milestone in my life. Middle of May or end of May, and then once more after 4 years, we shall breathe the same air. I want to see you badly, and hear all about you. You have been and still remain for me, even at this distance of time, the woman who most fills a huge gap in my life. Therefore to see you is an event. I remember you in a 100 different ways, dear and distinct, in a thousand different remarks, gestures, episodes. I'll explain some of them to you one day, when you are ready to hear them.

No. 3. and this, my dear Constance is very important. Precisely because you instinctively mean so much to me, I am really mad at you. Good and mad. I send you a draft of my play. Not a word from you. Ethel Waters has been at the Zanzibar, months ago. You write that "immediately after" my request you found out; and never told me.

I have been in contact with her secretary. I have a lot of news. The synopsis of the play has been drafted and it is now being typed. As soon as it is finished I am to see someone from the Theatre Guild to discuss it.

I am now on a vacation in order to try to get my health back. I may have to extend it for another three months. During that time I propose to write the play if I get the slightest hope of its being played sometime. There is a part in it I have written specially for you.

I would have liked to send you the various drafts and ideas I have had. Not only because I love you and your presence and the idea of being in communication with you stimulate me enormously, but because the stage is your business and you have some grasp of politics, I would have loved to have you in on this with me.

And instead I get hastily scribbled notes from you, and the task one began and not finished. Now tell me, my pet, what is it that you are so busy doing that you cannot write to *me*? Tell me, please. I would like to know. Especially about things which you ought to be and I feel, are really interested in.

I have been reading historical plays, analysing them, reading history, dramatising it, looking at innumerable pictures, trying to see how best the job could be done. And you, of all people, whose help I would cherish more than anyone else's, you ignore my draft and write me half-a-letter.

Now my precious senorita, you know what I think about you. You know what I have always thought about you. There are things between us that have never been spoken. I know them. I have heard about you too. Everyone who knows us knows that what happens to you matters to me, to put it mildly. But for that very reason, for all these reasons, and many more, I could not possibly indulge you in this way. I love to write to you. Try and grasp this. I am an extremely busy, self-centered person, but somehow I look upon you as half-a-woman, in fact in many respects for me, *the* woman; but also in some respects as half-a-child. In our friendship I am the responsible one. I have never been able to feel any other way towards you. Perhaps you understand me, perhaps you don't, but I think you do. And much as I would like to write to you and tell you everything and work out things with you—you have proof enough of that by now, I should think—I shall not do it as long as you will not spend at least an hour or so every week and write me a genuine letter. That is why I haven't written. If we were lovers, every day of my life that I was away from you, you would hear from me—every single day.

My letters to you, dearest Constance, are part of me. They are not anything like the letters that I could write to you to-morrow, or under other circumstances. But such as they are, they are as much, in fact, far more of me than I give to any other person. Voila. I have said enough. I love you. I wish I had a lot of money to buy you a diamond bracelet, just to see you preen and prance around in it, you vain, lovely creature.

Yours as ever,
Nello

Bessie has been here and left this morning for L.A. with the children. Judy and I had a wonderful time. She is a marvellous kid. I wish you would see them before you leave. Bessie tells me a lot of things about you—among others that you are wonderful with kids. Let me boast a little. So am I. It only makes me love you more and feel you warmer than ever in my heart.

April 8, 1944

And so, my wide-eyed baby—here we are.

My hands shook awfully last night and are shaking to-day again. I have just had a tooth out. Also, at the mature age of 43, I now must wear glasses to read. I shall have them on Saturday. I am fed-up. I have had 3 examinations during the last weeks. Despite shaking fingers all agree that my basic neurological reactions are still sound.

I am much amused. For without their tests I know that. How do I know? I know. And I know what is wrong with me, too. I shall cure it all in time, I hope. Now as to your melancholy. I had fits, badly, for years. I don't get them as I used to. I know when I stopped, and I know why. I'll tell you sometime. It may help you. I shall tell you the results too—most astonishing results. Now I have no fits of melancholy at all but only an underlying nervous tension through lack of any intimate companionship—there are a few pretty girls around and a number of attractive ones. I am not unattractive to them. I am a rather unusual combination, I am 40 odd and have obviously travelled and seen the world and read a great deal—and at the same time in my attitude to life and my outlook I am quite young, do not live in the past at all and haven't the faintest trace of complaint against the world though I know it for what it is.

Furthermore, I am known as the most fanatical of Marxists, but never make a fuss about it except where it is necessary to do so. Women seem to like the combination of maturity and a buoyant temperament, of devotion to my own business and yet not going around expecting everybody to do as I do. But, my dearest, I can go only so far with them. I am painfully honest in my sexual relations with women. A girl fought me for two years because I would not even in the most intimate moment tell her that I loved her. I wouldn't. In fact I couldn't. And when after 2 years I told her, under repeated badgering, it was a hopeless failure. I couldn't even for the moment pretend. I am in my own way as fanatical about it as I am about socialism. Moral reasons? Absolutely none. It is simply that somehow I feel that I can only give myself body and soul completely to some woman with whom I shall have no reservations. So I live in my outward life, which is dominated by a single purpose. I could not pretend about it. And so, unfortunately I think, I have to live in my personal life dominated by the single relationship. And women are very clever. They sense it—sooner or later. Then they try to break my reserve. I just can't do it. That's all. So that, though many of my male friends hate me and envy me because I get on so easily with women who show their preference for me distinctly as opposed to some of the others—it is quite a joke in our circle—I am in reality a very lonely, very solitary being in that respect. I expect you are the first person I have ever told. I was very much in love with a girl in 1936—Dutch, a ravishing blonde, small but carrying herself like a queen. She was married. We were friendly for a year or so. After our first day together I told her to tell her husband. He wouldn't give her up. He was very rich. He bought her a heap of clothes, built a house for her in the country, gave her a new car; but his winning card was that if she left him he was finished. So Candida finally went back to him. My dear, no one who has not lived a full life can appreciate what is in books. Curiously enough, though I loved to go to bed with her, that was something which mattered less with her as far as I was concerned than with others whom I knew before or have known since. But we had wonderful times—finding out good and cheap restaurants, talking, going to book-shops and fiddling around with books—she was fluent in English, French, Dutch and German—she had a wonderful eye for people and when she said she didn't like a person, I learnt to be very careful of him. Well, it ended. I was sick for a year at losing her but then I came to America. Since then I have thought over it a lot, and have learnt much. And now I know that why I lost her was deep-seated and decisive. Beautiful as she was she felt instinctively that physically my need for her was not overpowering. In that respect she wanted me more than I wanted her. And as she was not a half-way person she hesitated and finally said no, we had better part. And now, the more I study things the more I see that reason, analysis, etc., go a long way but ultimately you reach a stage where something fundamental in everything defies analysis. There is something that Hegel, most profound of bourgeois philosophers, calls "impulse." He nearly drove himself crazy trying to rationalise it. When you have examined a political situation to the last degree there still remains an intangible where one man will say "Let us retreat" and another will say "Let us go forward." True, at a really critical stage you will find a greater number saying "advance" than you will find saying "retreat" But why of 100 men, those 70 will say "on" and that 30 will say "back" is ultimately indefinable. And so a man standing on a platform speaking in 1939 looked at a girl in a red coat who stood up to ask a question and looked at her again and has never forgotten her since, has kissed other girls and thought of her while doing so, and knows that if the most wonderful women of all the ages were lined up before him to choose, he would go along the line looking for her. When he found her the competition would end at once and if he didn't find her the fair damsels would scratch his eyes out for he wouldn't be too much interested. So there is this letter which began with the intention of describing the interview has wandered on. Forgive me, darling. I'll write that story to-morrow.

But your fits of melancholy disturbed me and I know you are the type [who] would feel it with an almost physical pain. When you come I'll tell you what exactly was wrong with me, and how I got over it. The political movement and the consciousness that I had found a home at last saved me. That is why I am so anxious for you—I know you are coming to seek your place in life. But the other you will find in a man's arms. Until you find both, you will find life hard. Be honest with me and I'll help you all I can. I have a son you know. He is 30 years old. I watch over him like a trainer and a prizefighter. Of course, he is not my son really. He is a young West Indian, a scholar of repute who wrote a superb thesis at Oxford for his doctorate—The Economic Basis of the Slave-Trade and Slavery. For nearly 12 years now, I have watched him come along. He sometimes is very thoughtless and selfish. But I don't mind. Seeing him develop pleases *me*. So, you witch, seeing you come along and fight your own way pleases me. But you will never be happy with those sensitive, quivering nerves of yours—all artists have them—until you find somewhere you can without reservations of any kind, say "Darling, kiss me. I love you." I know what I am talking about, sweet. I know. From what I have seen and from what I know, you have been nervous and uncertain of yourself as a woman. Have you got over it? It isn't worth a moment's thought. Those men who have had the inestimable privilege of being your lover and couldn't hold you, should be put up in a line and shot. To put it briefly. A man should know that you were a precious flower whom it is his business to tend But he must not hang his happiness on you. His happiness must consist in making you happy. It is so in love. Women of experience have told me that they grow tired of a man who is so *obviously* having a wonderful time when he is with them. You will know what I mean. She wants to abandon herself completely and can only do so—perhaps it is biological, perhaps socially conditioned, I don't know—and can only do so when she is conscious that she is being watched over all the time.

Now this letter must stop. My tooth has not ached—not a bit. So, my wonderful Constance, if you are not sleepy, read my letter again and then go to bed, rather, to sleep. Believe me, sweet, if you try to stifle your excitement and your work in the day-time by study and reading, you only stimulate yourself more. Read over my old letters, read other love letters that you have—calm yourself deliberately and gather your nervous strength and energy for the great invasion. People will want to see you or want you to come to see them. Cut the list to the bone and if necessary cut the bone as well. Go to sleep. Turn off the light, hold up your face to be kissed; so; once more; and then off you go.

As ever, darling, all my love.
N

Remember? In bed. Ready to sleep. Do these letters, help you to sleep? I hope they do. If they do, I love you. If they don't, I love you still. I gave you a list to choose from. Or do you want to choose new subjects? Or do you leave them to me? Or shall I write you one love letter, just *one*? You know the prospect of seeing you does things to me. Do you mind?

Postmark April 20, 1944

Well, Sister-who-is-soon-to-be-seen,

I was thinking of my last letter to you and it worried me a bit.

You are coming to N.Y.—on the big adventure. December 20, you are relieved of one man who was your husband. That is always a strain and a break, a wound, sometimes realised, sometimes not, but the wound to the emotional sensibilities is always there. It affects the future life. Now you are all ready to come for the big step and my letter might have given you the impression that here at this end was a hungry monster all ready to start bothering you about one thing. Now, precious, I won't. There is a job to be done. You are to get going. That's what you want. And that's what I want for you too. It will be one of the great moments of my life when I see you take a call, go in, and the audience insist on your coming back. That is success—though the part may be small. But nevertheless I love you. And, that you know and that's that.

1) You *sleep*. Sleep *plenty*. On sleep I am one of the most learned men living, in fact a recognised authority, having had to do without it so much. So, my precious, sleep. Work as hard as like, but sleep. And when you don't sleep, I'll see, and I can assure you that I shall tell you without mercy exactly how awful you look.

And now for some N E W S. Carl Van Vechten—I shall take you to see him and his photographs one day—told me to take the synopsis of the script to Miss something Marshall of the Theatre Guild. It's a long synopsis—60 pages. It isn't as I would like it yet, but the play, as a play, is there for anyone to see. I shall not send it to you. You take it easy. When you come here I shall give it to you or better still, read it for you, and act some of the parts, you my audience of one = 1000. So on Monday, I go down to the Guild in 52nd St. I am to see her 2:30–5:30. Now I have been singularly fortunate. I have never had to do any hanging around in Editors' ante-chambers. I reached England in 1932, I was working for the Manchester Guardian in 1933 and my books were all taken almost at once. In fact but for politics I would have been a writer now, pretty well established. My publisher's wife, a wonderful woman, whom I would have been glad for you to meet, begged me almost with tears to settle down and write. I said NO, and look at what is brewing in the world to-day, a fine sight I would have been with two or three books or a play or two to my credit and hanging around the political world, as all these other writers do, treating as amateurs, what is the most serious business in the world to-day. *Politics isn't always that way.* From 1871–1905 politics was *not* the major concern of men. But to-day, any man who can and has the instinct and doesn't, well, he is in my view, a pretty poor creature.

Anyway—a long digression. But I am just talking, indulging the old ego, you know. You are sitting at the dressing-table and I am brushing your hair. Do you know? Men have some curious ideas. To me *one*, only *one* but an important part of connubial bliss is to brush my wife's hair every night. 100 strokes, every night; and it will shine like stars. Anyway—can you keep up, or are you sleepy? Once more; I am sitting in the Theatre Guild outer room. So a girl comes out and says Miss M is not there and she doesn't know when she will be. She wears red, has her hair in some sort of snood, glasses, medium height, plumpish—ve—r—r—y nice but definitely not attractive. Will I wait? Yes, I will.

Now, this, my precious, is important for me—and for you, too. Emotionally, I mean. This office is The Casting Office. There it is, in print. And I who carry you about in my thoughts all the time, find myself sitting in the ante-room of a casting-office, immediately become very much aware of my surroundings and you. (Ah, you miserable creature, you are not sleepy any more.) So there we sit, you and I. A woman comes in, 35, well-preserved, net stockings, well-dressed, handsome, she smiles at me. Actress? I don't know. Miss M not there? She goes. But she takes a little peep at me just before she takes the lift. I peep back. Half-an-hour. Then a man. Actor all over, small. Handsome; good sports clothes, about 50. He says nothing but sits waiting. He is as serious as hell. No job for some time I guess. Then comes Miss M's secretary, tall, glasses, commonplace, but capable-looking, a bit of a spread around the hips and a professional smile. Miss M has come. The man goes in.

Then comes the catch of the day. 5 ft, a beautiful blonde complexion, and *genuine* blonde hair to the shoulders, not bad-looking, but fresh and eager. Her neck is too short and she'll be awfully fat in a few years I think, but she has youth now. She speaks first. "I have been waiting two hours." Now this is very friendly, for I am a Negro, and again, never even smiled at her.

I asked her if she acted. No, she sang. She sat waiting, all keen and tense. I looked at her. And then I almost fell for her. She started singing to herself, snatches of some song. You could see that she *loved* to sing. She wanted a job but she wanted above all to sing. Then the actor came out and she went in and I wished her luck (to myself).

Then came a young man, actor type too. 5 [ft.] 9 or so; olive brown complexion, dressed in brown, long curling lashes like a girl's, a delicate oval face, very very handsome and though somewhat "girlish" with a tremendous breadth of shoulder which made you see that he was really quite a man. He looked at me and wanted to talk, I could see. But I looked at him, and didn't bother. So he got out a play by Ben Hecht and started to read. Then the secretary came and asked me would I come in? Now what happened? Come to this theatre next week and see the next episode in this thrilling serial.

Now I am going to find out if you have really been listening to my gossip or only pretending. If you want to hear what happened, you drop me a card—saying *Please*, tell me. Naturally if I were on the spot I could be bribed. And, my dear Constance, I try in my external life to be honest but if you know how corrupt I am in private, how easily bribed, it is terrible. My immortal soul has long lost all hope of regeneration. So, bribe me, at a distance, with an immediate card saying Please, tell me. Well, I mustn't talk to you of love so I won't. All I say is I love you. Good-bye.

As ever,
N

God have mercy! Some 15 pages! I intended to write 2. God above is my witness. I intended to write 2. Forgive me! And believe me, sweet, I have some writing to do all morning; and I look at it and do something else, and say how I shall begin in half-an-hour. It is your picture that does it, sitting before me, with the tennis-racket, your forefinger pointing to your lips. Now *definitely*. Good-bye. No, not a word, not one single word. I am A D A M A N T. Good—*Bye*.

[April 24, 1944]

Constance darling,

Here are two clippings. The one deals with a play in which you will be interested. If you have no time to read it now, slip it in your bag. We'll go to see it sometime, I hope, though I warn you in advance, except on *very special occasions*, I am a standing room man more often than not. When you come round to it you will see that in lines which I have underlined, the critic is deeply struck with the idea that the audience wanted more politics. These dopes understand little except the technicalities of their own jobs. The other clipping shows that the political cleavage which is showing itself in every department of human life is now raging in Hollywood, your own native bailiwick. More and more it will condition life. I have seen this thing in other countries and it is on its way here.

A N D N O W, sweets, a request. You say you are going to surprise me. Darling, don't. Don't. Tell me when you leave, and the train you take, so I'll follow you on your journey all across the continent. When you reach [New York] you let me know. Perhaps you have friends here whom you want to meet you or whom it is important that they come to meet you. If that is so, good (tho' I really mean bad). If not, let me meet you. At any rate I'll know that you are in. Then you send to tell me when we shall meet or arrange for me to call you. So that I'll be ready for you.

Do not forget, dear sister. To see you, in New York, after all these years, and all that has passed between us, is a great event in my life. I wonder if you know that, or how far, if you do, you can appreciate it.

Will you do it for me? I am rather staid and reserved as you know. That's why I love *you* for one reason. But this time? No. Let me know. Life, you know, dearest, is for me a wonderful spectacle. Every succeeding year I see how powerful are the compelling *laws* which dominate human existence and human personality. I am watching some of these laws at work now in my own personal life and the lives of others. And funny thing, it is when you see the laws and recognise that you are subject to them, it is only then that you have real power to mould your own destiny. As Engels says "Freedom is the recognition of necessity." One necessity it is important to recognise is the necessity of your own nature. I have recognised mine. I think you are on the way to recognising yours. You are swimming out into the sea. You know that famous sentence in the Bible "men who go down to the sea in ships and do their business in great waters." To appreciate it, one must think of the miserable open boats of those thousands of years ago, the uncharted seas, the mystery and adventure of every voyage. The sailors took their lives in their hands on every great voyage.

Little people trembled and stayed at home. Others, however, went down to the sea. You are coming down to the sea. A cargo, tiny, unknown, whose disappearance would hardly leave a ripple on the surface of the great ocean. And yet to yourself, the most important boat among all the innumerable boats on this sea, and, to me, an infinitely precious ship and cargo. The journey you are attempting is for you and for me and I don't know who else but people to whom you really matter, as important as the journey that Columbus began across the Atlantic, those hundreds of years ago. Poor Christopher won immortal fame, but died a beggar, with nothing but the memory of bitterness and personal frustration to darken his declining years. Now our boat, yours and mine, is to get safely to port sometime, artistic aspirations, and personal development fought for and conquered. We seem to have wandered far from my asking you not to make our first meeting a surprise for me. I am living every moment of it with you. Let me. My way. When are you reading this letter? Late at night or when?

All my love, darling, as always,
N

April 28, 1944

Too much love is not good. So to business.

We ended where the folding doors are thrown open. There is one biggish room with desks in different corners. In one corner is my little blonde singer and I believe, and sincerely hope, a contract was being signed. Then you will see this room in time I am sure—to the right, a very small room, 10 ft by 6, a desk and one or two pictures, and at the desk Miss Marshall.

Now Miss M is a tall woman, with a hat. You see she is not purely a business woman. The hat shows that she is actress, society woman, what you will. But the face is interesting, long, firm chin, goodlooking, about 50, lined but not unpleasantly. She is a native American—if I can use that misleading phrase. But it is important. She wears a suit, gray. She sits back and looks at me, smiling but businesslike. There is a chair on which I should sit. I don't. I never sit unless I am asked to.

So I stand 6 ft 2; and it's a bit awkward for her, so low down. Particularly because I am very grave in manner. I am giving away nothing. For this is not art. This is business. I learnt that years and years ago. It is a thing to remember.

Who had arranged the interview? (The radio is playing the last movement of the Mendelssohn Violin Concerto, one of the most wonderful passages in all violin music. Horn taking a countermelody against the violin. Terrific. We'll listen some day.) I say Carl Van Vechten arranged it. Oh yes! Would I sit down? She says this a little guiltily. Thank you. I sit. Have I only an outline? Then comes something typically American, and most *unEuropean*.

She says. If it is an outline we cannot do much with it. Often people bring us a good idea, but when it is worked out it isn't suitable.

A European would take it more from the point of view of art. What is the play about? etc. Have I written others? The European would be just as much business-woman, mind you. But the cultural *tradition* permeates still. I tell her I have an outline. It is 66 pages. The play is there, roughly and crudely but it is there.

She says: Well we shall read it. But we buy only a finished play. (I hadn't come there to sell anything. I was after Ethel Waters.) I tell her what the play is about and

I say I want E. W. Had I seen her? No, Carl Van V had told me to get an opinion from some reliable theatre people and with that I could interest E. W. C Van V thinks E. W. the greatest of living actresses. I don't go so far but I think that given a great part she would swamp all her most famous rivals, some of whom I have seen. She has had 25 years of hard work at every kind of vaudeville, musical comedy, nightclub, and has had to fight her way. She is now in her prime, aching to act, but she has no plays to suit her.

I don't explain all this but I give a little outline. Miss Marshall who is very quick catches on quickly.

She says: Well, we shall read it here and tell you if we want it. She will give it to their reader. She rises to get him. I see now that she is slim, figure still trim, tummy a bit protuberant (after all she is in the late forties) but vigorous and assured. So far so good. Then enters with Miss M, Mr. Grasser, I think the name is.

Sweetheart, at sight of him the whole complex society in which we live, comes rushing into the room.

Mr. Grasser is a Jew, a fat, obsequious Jew, about 40, or less or more. He shakes my hand obsequiously but does not look at me.

At once I understand everything. Grasser is without personality and without charm. He probably works 18 hours a day. He has probably read all plays in four or at least 3 languages. He has probably seen everything worth seeing during the last 15 or 20 years. He reads all the notices. But he has in addition a specially Jewish characteristic. He is not an American, any more than I am an Englishman. But he has (like me) been educated in the American culture and is in it, though not of it. He sees it with detachment. This and the extraordinary *commercial* instinct (note I say commercial, i.e., trade) gives him an almost infallible instinct for what the public wants. In journalism, criticism, publicity, films—the Jews do wonderfully. In the film business they come to the front and handle things themselves. In the theatre also they do. But I have seen it repeatedly this combination of "native" American or Englishman or dominant race and behind him a very specially gifted member of the oppressed, most often the Jewish race. Orson Welles showed it in Citizen Kane where the tycoon had as his man of business Bernstein a Jew. One of Roosevelt's most trusted personal advisers is a Jew named Rosenman—same type as Grasser. I knew Grasser would read my synopsis and that his opinion would carry.

So we three talked. I said that I had some experience in dialogue—the first play with Paul [Robeson] had been directed as much by me, amateur as I am, as by Peter Godfrey, and during rehearsals we had changed things about and I had learnt a lot in the only place where you can learn certain things—on the stage itself. I told them too that I had corresponded with the critics of the Times and the Observer, the two best known in London, and they had given me some hints and were very pleased with the play.

Grasser knew them at once Charles Morgan and Ivor Brown. It is the sort of thing he would know. So finally addresses are given, etc. We say goodbye all round in very friendly fashion and I bow myself out. That is Monday before last. Monday coming will be 2 weeks. I haven't heard anything.

Some of my friends are in a feverish state of excitement. I am not. I have had 6 years of this business in England and I have learnt to take it easy. C Van V says if they don't like it there are some other people to try. Meanwhile I have clarified the play and structure and characters are becoming more and more clear. If they wish to talk business, I am ready. If not, I shall improve the synopsis and send it out again. There is as I told you a fine fat part written with you in mind. But one has to learn to take things without too much excitement and worry. I can't do it with everything, but, important as this is for me, I am quite philosophical about it. I have wrestled with the thing and drawn on my ten years experience of the political movement—ten intensive years, and I know what I am writing about. There are all sorts of problems connected with it. Isn't it a miracle of miracles that the stage turns out to be your business, that you have a living vital interest, a modern practical experience as a player, and that you are—you. Whom else could I have "chosen" more suitable. There are all sorts of psychological problems in the development of character too which I shall have to work out in detail, and on which I want your opinion. So, sister, au revoir. I wish I were with you the other morning sitting in the sun. It is one of the great things of life. Do you know this, sitting or lying with someone and *not talking*, just knowing the person is there.

And lastly, sweet, I am so glad that my letter the second one, came quickly, and that your head is once more high on your shoulders. That's where I want it to be, always. And far from my doing anything which will cause it to wilt a little, I want you to be so sure of yourself with me that when the world or others press on you, you say to yourself, or rather feel: O.K., my friends, but Nello is with me and him I know you can't touch. So now, nothing in your sweet head but to work and sleep and be all ready for the great push. Strange how much I know about you in some ways, and how little in others. Your 3 brothers. Who and what are they? Isn't life funny. Here now I have an intense interest in 3 men whom I have never heard of until this morning when your letter came. You will tell me all about them. And your mother? By the way, you tell me that you don't think of yourself as Cleopatra. I never said you did. Which is something else.

> Fie, wrangling queen!
> Whom everything becomes,—to
> chide, to laugh,
> To weep; whose every passion
> fully strives
> To make itself in thee fair
> and admired!
> No messenger; but thine, and
> all alone,
> Tonight we'll wander
> through the streets and
> note
> The qualities of people.

So Antony speaks to Cleopatra. But he lost himself and everything he stood for in her. And so they ruined themselves. Life is more than that. But without that there is no life. Or worse still life becomes work and a feverish succession of attractive women (or men) who attract until their newness wears off. No, my precious, you are Cleo—though much more than Cleo. All that is bursting in you to come out I know and have always known. And I would be the Goddamndest and most selfish fool that ever was to try to grab onto you and mould you to *my* purposes. That is what men under 35 do. No, sweets, I want you to be Cleo, you have it in you, but Cleo for me. I love you.

Go to sleep. Sleep is important for everybody but for you, Constance Webb, at this time, for what you have behind you, and for what is before you, go to sleep. I know you. Go to sleep.

Love,
Nello

R. J.
520 W 150
N.Y. N.Y.

[April 1944]

Do you know, Constance Webb, you are the most amazing creature I have ever met in my life, not the strongest in character, that I don't know, nor the most profound, nor the most brilliant, nor the most beautiful, but simply the most amazing. And you don't know it. Of that I am positive.

I showed your picture—fingers to lips—to a girl the other day. She said, "Oh, Hollywood!" I said "Yes. how did you know?" She said, "Oh, it's obvious." And we left it at that. Now Rae, my good friend, Bessie's sister, doesn't know you. She has seen the pictures in my room. The other day she was criticizing some pictures, discerning character, etc. I said, "What about this one? You would say 'no character', I suppose?" She said, "Exactly," but then she added, "Bessie says, however, that when she makes up her mind to do something, she can do it." Said I to myself, "One up for Bessie." Now I read one or two of your letters, especially this last one. Where have been hiding your poetic gift? You suddenly hurl them, these poems, at me, and I am literally flabbergasted. I have told you before that you write very well, when you write. Extreme simplicity and directness. So that what you have to say carries no excess baggage. It is a rare virtue in writing. The rest depends on the development of your personality, your contacts with life, your gift for hard work and concentration—at writing. I observe it with the feeling that I have for you, but I observe it with a critical eye too, as writing is my business.

Now you show me what is much rarer, the same simplicity and directness in creating the visual images that are the basis of poetry, coupled with an extreme boldness in the attempt to make sounds visible, all very clear, very simple, and yet very penetrating.

And you say casually you have been writing for two years.

Now, my doubly and trebly precious Constance, I have read little modern verse—T. S. Eliot, D. H. Lawrence, fairly closely. Eliot is a traditionalist for all his modernism. I do not know whom you have been reading, in what school you have been brought up; I would like to know. But your *literary gift is unquestioned*. How much? How deep? I would have to see a lot of our work to know. Furthermore, that depends on how much you *want* to write. But if it should so happen that you terribly want to write, then the drudgery that accompanies or rather precedes mastery, comes naturally to you. But write you can. The rest is out of our hands, out of yours, too, for the intellectual *passion* out of which good work is born, as far as I have seen, comes by nature. You write with an instinctive sureness that betokens the natural craftsman, and with you it is obviously the expression of strong feelings. Send me some more.

And your analysis of Candida. Sweetheart, I have read that play off and on for twenty years. I have seen it twice. I read it a fortnight ago—twice—thinking of you, and of me too. Do you know that I never got the last *two* words. All day long I thought about it. Then I came home and looked them up. Your are perfectly correct. The words are, "Ah, James!" The Ah tells it, particularly because Marchbanks has refused to kiss her. And of course, it was always clear that when she told Marchbanks to say, "When I am 30, she will be 45," she meant that the age disparity was for her decisive. You know Shaw cheated in that play. He made the artist nineteen. He gave her two children, and a helpless husband. Your divination is splendid. This subject I have spent some time on during the last year, particularly in connection with another play—Dreaming Lips—an old film with Bergner. You see the theme recurs in art and in life. Day after day I see it around me. It has profoundly affected my own life. Your are in it too. Do you know it forms a part of all women, *all?* It is your life too? Candida was not giving up *all* her life. The instinct for both types of life is strong in most women. She gave up, however, what, *were she in difference circumstances*, she would most certainly have chosen.

We'll talk about it one day, the social roots of this particular problem, and its solution ultimately. Meanwhile, we all fight it out. You say it is perhaps the self-destructive impulse that hangs you on to the neck of some man, and at the same time another part of you drives you on to some fulfillment.

I do not believe in the self-destructive impulse. I believe that man and woman are shaped by society and that woman has the task of bearing children, of finding the security and the steadiness and peaceful companionship which goes with it. All society and nature drive her in that direction. But at the same time life calls to her, and to some vital creative women it calls strongly, and to all it calls to make life an adventure, not dull routine, but the development and creation of the self, physical adventures, intellectual adventures, sometimes the tremendously satisfying adventure of being part of a man's life, when that man is doing something that is not merely earning a living, Marchbanks, the poet, or the violinist in Dreaming Lips. And often she is caught between the two. I have repeatedly seen *in life* the woman snatch for a moment at the life of the artist or companionship with one, and then be pulled back. She is afraid, or too old, or something. Both in Dreaming Lips and Candida, and in one episode in my own life—one man says to the woman, "If you leave me I am finished." And last week a girl told me that this is the hold her husband had on her.

You have fought your way out. But you may be caught again. The solution, of course, is to find both the man who gives security (I am not speaking merely of money, though that counts). I am speaking of an emotional security, which feels that here, with him, I am safe with all the love and protection and confidence that a woman needs, and at the same time, *in the same person* find that creative drive, that consciousness of living for something out of one's self, which all human beings need so strongly they cannot do without it.

In a socialist society, a man will not be a drudge, scared of losing his job, suppressed and crushed from birth. He will be stable, because society will be stable, and yet he will be able to develop the creative capacity that exists in every human being to some degree or other. Then a woman, with the privileges she will also have, will not be continually torn between two men as she so often is today, or worse still, be continually dissatisfied until some of her desires die, starved.

There are so many, many things, darling; so many, many things. I read about them in books and plays. I see them happening every day of my life—*every day*. I know three couples now, if not four, where this conflict is raging. In others I can see it suppressed. I can only observe it, speak very rarely about it, never fully and completely. How can I? You see when I say I love you, what I mean? For art is not a reflection of life. That is a half-truth. Art is a part of life. There never was life without art of some sort. To understand art, one must live. And there are some people for whom the division is not distinct—one fuses into the other. The great revolutionaries, L. T., e.g., made no distinction between his life and the great science and art of politics to which he gave himself. So with the truly great writers, actors, composers, and all the sincere ones, though some of them play only humble parts. Sometimes the price one pays is heavy. Whenever Lenin heard Beethoven's sonatas tears would come to his eyes, and he refused to listen to them. He had no kids, and wherever he saw kids he went and played with them, throwing them up and catching them and laughing all over his face. Now with all sorts of barriers between us, I see in you every day, such immense possibilities of completion in my own life, that, but for the fact that your own happiness and development are more precious to me than my own—for I have found my road—I would long before this have parked myself on your doorstep and refused to move until you opened your door and let me in. You remember what Viola threatened to do to Olivia, in Twelfth Night.

> Make me a willow cabin at your gate,
> And call upon my soul within the house;
> Write loyal cantons of contemned love,
> and sing them loud even in the dead of night,
> Holla your name to the reverberate hills,
> and make the babbling gossip of the air
> Cry out Olivia! O, you should not rest
> Between the elements of air and earth,
> But you should pity me.   (Act 1 Scene V)

I heard Edith Evans do them once. How lovely they were! So, sweet, good-night. Tomorrow I shall write to you the conclusion of Act 1 Scene 1, where the hero (me) faces the dragon (Regina Marshall). The audience, for me, the most important audience in the world, is interested? What more can a playwright want?

One last word, darling. This is a difficult time for you. I know it. I live my life and yours, alas hitherto, only in the spirit. New York will be very exciting and strange. You know, I have been through this. So go to sleep. If I were near you, I'd *make* you go to sleep. To study and to read? Totally unnecessary—if you can manage it. Go to sleep. I know you, my infant.

Here I make you an offer. Accept it in the spirit in which it is made. Until you leave, I'll write you a long letter every day, I'll cut out comics, press notices, scraps of politics, all sorts of things. When you have the evening free, you come home, go to bed, read them. Amuse yourself, then go to sleep. Take it easy. What do I ask in return?

That you love me. When? At your own pleasure. At present you have the great excitement and the road to find. So while you must know that I love you, let it stay there for awhile. Is it a bargain? "If I don't read or study at night, I am miserable and can't do the day-time business." Now, Constance, that wouldn't do. Read, yes, study, a little. But your letters breathe the excitement that you are in. That is life, but sleep and take it easy. Can I help you? Will you try?

Read them at night, when your are in bed, all curled up. They can be on anything you please. You want to know about my first reactions to New York, to London, to Paris, when I was a little boy, how I set out for the big city, what I think of Russia, how much I love you, you choose. But calm yourself. I'll even send you bits from Capital or Hegel's Logic and explain them and apply them to personal lives. But meet me half-way darling, for your own sake, and being for your sake, for mine also.

Loving you more than ever,
N

Postmark May 25, 1944

Well, my rhapsody in blue, I want to tell you a story. It is one of the great stories of the world—certainly one of the 10 best that I know. It is from the Bible—the story of Naaman the leper (NAAMAN). Your generation does not know the Bible. So much the worse for you. Naaman was commander-in-chief of the King of Syria, and he suffered from leprosy—the white kind. They were a fine pair of rulers in the days when individual leadership counted so much and they were loved by their people. Among the servants was a slave girl who had been captured from the Israelites. She, like all the others, was much concerned about Naaman's disease, and one day she went to Naaman and told him that in Israel there was a great prophet, Elijah, who could cure Naaman if anybody could. When the King of Syria heard this, he was glad to see one more chance and he wrote off to Israel, telling the King that he was sending Naaman to be cured.

The King of Israel was terribly scared. He called the Council together and he said "How can I cure this man of leprosy. The King of Syria is picking a quarrel with me." Obviously he feared that this was only an excuse for a little imperialism. But as usual he had to accept and he put the matter in the hands of Elijah.

So one day Naaman arrives with a great retinue and they lead him to Elijah. But the old prophet had only this to say "Wash in Jordan seven times."

Now Jordan was and still is a notoriously dirty river and the idea that the commander-in-chief of Syria should wash in Jordan seemed a dirty joke about a serious question. Naaman grew angry and uttered some very famous words. "Are not Abanah and Pharpar, rivers of Damascus, greater than all the waters of Israel?" He asked if he could not have washed there and be clean instead of coming to the filthy river of Jordan.

Watch those words, precious. Repeatedly they pop in the mind, in all great historical and personal crises. They are one great artistic expression of a situation constantly recurring. Are all my tremendous efforts, my studies, my sacrifices, my desperate seeking of a way out, day after day, are all these to be brushed aside for some simple commonplace solution? Naaman was mad. But he was, like a great leader, on good terms with all his staff. One of the older ones said to him "Master. If the prophet had told you to do some great thing you would have done it. He says to wash in Jordan. Why not try it?" So Naaman agreed. He washed seven times in Jordan and when he came out his flesh was like that of a little child.

You can imagine! Here, to the minds of those days, was not only a cure, but proof that the God of Israel was the true God and the God of Syria a false God.

Now Naaman was a man of high integrity and he faced a terrible dilemma. What to do? Perhaps his own words, as far as I can remember them, will best explain his crisis and his solution.

He told Elijah "I can see that your God is the true God, and that our God, Rimmon (RIMMON) is false. But I am not only Commander-in-Chief of Syria, I am a personal friend of the King. When he goes to the temple of Rimmon I am at his right hand and he leans on me. When he bows down I bow down with him. *I cannot destroy that faith.* All I can tell you, Elijah, is that I recognise the God of Israel to be the true God. And when I bow down in the temple of Rimmon, know that in my heart I bow down to the God of Israel."

In those days, religion and statesmanship were one. To have raised the question of substituting Israel's God for Rimmon was to threaten the very foundations of the state, to break up what was clearly a good and capable government. *Naaman couldn't do it.* But he did his best.

Sweetheart, every day a man bows down in the House of Rimmon. Every day. In that superb tale the conflict is pitched on a very high plane. Naaman was not seeking any personal end. He was not defending his personal status or possessions. The whole story shows that he was above that—at least as far as he knew. In all its simplicity and the apparently childish mentality of those primitive peoples, a fundamental social and therefore personal problem was posed and, as far as was socially possible, in those days, resolved. There are many such tales in the Bible, profound beyond 9/10 of the popular stuff to-day, but so disarmingly simple that their significance and the artistic power escape you. Shaw uses one in Candida. You remember Morell is almost maddened when Marchbanks reminds him how David's wife saw him singing and dancing before the people and *despised him in her heart.* Many a man's wife sees him making politics, writing, organising and being famous and fine before the public. But she who lives with him, knows him, can see through him for the faker that he is, how much he is living on past reputation, how little he means what he says, how opportunist he is, how the idealism with which he began has been transformed into concealed but shameless self-seeking. I gained an insight into the superficial character of a well-known political leader by a joke his wife made at him in my presence five years ago. Last year, under the pressure of the crisis, the veneer cracked and what he really stood for became clear to all who wanted to see.

Am I preaching at you? God forbid. Every day of my life I bow down in the House of Rimmon. But I know that I have to. I look and see how much I can bow down without losing myself altogether. At a certain stage I say "No, I shall bow down no further." I see other men bowing down. I read how other men bowed down, I see the consequences, I read how they recognised their necessity and faced it, what they gained and what they lost, the strengthening of experience, the deepening of character—the perpetual battle with life as it is and not as we would like it to be. You know the first movement of the Eroica well? The next time you happen to hear it listen carefully to the fierce outbursts of baffled rage at contradictions which

Beethoven could not resolve. In the midst of the smooth almost caressing melody, Beethoven suddenly lets out with some fierce chords—the whole orchestra, bang, bang, bang, bang. And does it once more. But he battled with it, organised it, and then lo and behold, in the Fifth, he made that his main idea and mastered it completely, and having exhausted that, went on still further to the Ninth and then took personal refuge in the last quartets.

Au 'voir. You were lovely yesterday and sweet; did me more good than all the vitamins and doctors. The argument about the T's [Trotskyists] and the S's [Stalinists] is not so important. It is beginning at the wrong end. One day soon I shall write some notes for you about the things that really matter, the basis of our society, the relationship between life and the practice of art in our time. The true significance of our age is that all aspects of life are so closely tied together.

I'll call you over the week-end about next week. I have seen both Turtle* and Othello. And the enclosed implies that all seats for Turtle are gone. I saw it standing. Meanwhile I'll make enquiries. By the way, two things. The end of the Naaman story is most amusing and instructive. I'll tell you sometime. And secondly: The play I am doing: at every turn I face the problem. Shall I bow down? Shall I bow down? And I wrestle with it. How much can I dare to put? And believe me, I am having a good time. Harriet [Tubman] believes in God. Good. She shall talk about God. She shall talk simply about God. But when she is done, God will appear so much like the force of historical development that even He would not recognise himself. A religious man and an historical materialist would both be able to listen to her and draw whatever each wants from it. Quite a job but difficulties are made to be conquered. In other words I am trying to bow down and hold my back straight at the same time.

History is a stream with the broken vertebrae of those who tried to do that. But who cares? I like your phrase that you wouldn't settle for less. I wouldn't. The play *will* be popular and it *will* say what I want to say. Or there will be no play. I started with other intentions, but I am too old to change and I don't want to change. The weather outside is gloomy. But for me the sun—the sun of California—shines high and bright in a blue sky. Salud!

[unsigned]

R. J.
520 W. 150
N.Y.

[June 1944]

My dear niece,

It is all the paper I have on me, sweet. I am in the train, subway. I have a letter for you at home, nearly finished, I was going to post it to-night, but it is all about politics and society. I'll send it another time. I have been fooling around for a day and a half. Tuesday night I didn't sleep at all. It happens sometimes. So I got up about 7, very tired and went to town to see some friends—Freddie and Lyman Paine.

They are without doubt the most wonderful couple I know or have ever known.

---

* *Voice of the Turtle*, three act comedy of 1943, John van Druten.

He is working in a plant somewhere—10 hours a day. He started two years ago, and now he is about 42. His hands show the result but otherwise he is doing well. He thinks as I do, and is devoted completely. An astonishing person really. One of his ancestors signed the Declaration of Independence, his father is a clergyman, a theoretical and mild socialist, and the son is what he is. He is a Harvard man, and the family is a New England family, American to the bone. He studied architecture and did some brilliant work. Then he gave it up and now works among the workers. He remains a New England Yankee with a good hard head, shrewd and penetrating, educated both in a bourgeois and socialist manner, very tolerant and understanding. I expect he is my best friend altho' [about] my really private life I say nothing. He is a native son, and as such not only my friend but very interesting to me.

His wife is a different type—one of the most wonderful persons in the world. She is a Jewish-Romanian, came here as a child. She worked at jobs—factory, etc., until she came to New York. She is dynamic as a plane with six engines, of remarkable independence and strength of character, and does not mince her words. She understands people in a way of her own and is very attractive. She is without formal education but curiously enough has had a few very brilliant New York intellectuals trailing after her. She is somewhat uncertain of herself in intellectual matters, but only a real intellectual can appreciate how sound are her instincts and her judgment—and particularly her sense of values.

Well, two years ago she fell seriously ill, and now is only half her former self. The wonderful life they lived is deranged. Her business is to keep quiet and she can't. Her husband is sick with anxiety about her, but says nothing. Only his manner to her has changed. He is even rough with her sometimes and I know it is because he is so worried about her. I'll tell you more about them one day. They are the friends of mine I particularly want you to meet sometime—people you meet once in a generation.

And now, my precious, instead of 8 every day, take only four. The N.Y. heat is like nothing on earth. It kills you. Furthermore the noises and excitement and speed of the city wear you out. And worst of all, you are unconsciously making an adjustment to the new life, strange people, new impressions, new surroundings, new ideas, new hopes, new fears. It takes a heavy toll of energy and is a drain on the nerves from the mere fact that it is all new. Great cities have a personality of their own. And I know what London and Paris did to me. New York I took easily, very easily, and as far as possible I suggest that you do the same. It is hard to do that, at your age, but it is just as well. Do I sound like uncle. O.K. I am uncle too. But that is why I was begging you to sleep before you came. Sleep, sleep, sleep. Because I know what the impact of a great city is—especially on a person like yourself.

So some producers wouldn't even see you. So much the worse for them. The chief thing is to keep steadily going, not only in actuality, I know you will do that, but *in the mind*; a certain steadiness, a mental confidence that takes all setbacks in its stride. I know I was pretty near forty before I acquired it. It is *not* poker-face. Because many a poker-face is boiling inside. It is with many people a natural or semi-natural thing. But it can be partially acquired. Life becomes very much easier then. Sister Paula seems in a rare mess. It is a pity a nice girl like that cannot find some man on whom she can lean, emotionally, and at the same time who wouldn't try to boss her or create storms about revolvers, shooting, and what not.

About your writing late at night, Christ only knows what to say about that. If you must, you must. That is all. If it is inside then it is better out of you. It is no use talking about that and saying "ought" or "ought not." When I see more of your work I'll tell you what I think. But I want to see more, very much.

Forgive me if I sound too much like uncle. I have been through it you know and what with (a) modelling and (b) producers and (c) our friends who want you to bow down and (d) the urge to write, then I feel worried about you.

By the way, let me tell you something and I wouldn't flatter you—not one little bit. There are many handsome women, at least quite a few; there are a few beautiful women and, very rarely, there are really lovely women. D. H. Lawrence once wrote about this and altho' he did not use the same classification that I do, he understood the business. He said that Mrs. Langtry, Lily Langtry, the actress and mistress of Edward VII of England, was exceeded in good looks by a thousand women. Yet she had the extraordinary quality of loveliness that made men and women follow her when she appeared in public. It is a bloom, a vitality, something that not only pleases the eye but warms the heart. Now you have it, far more to-day than in 1940. Tina who knows the human face I expect from her work, was very near to it when she said that she thought not sculpture but colour suited you best for portraiture. Of course she missed it really—it is not colour although colour is the first thing that meets the eye. Many people have good colour. I do not wish to exaggerate but the word is radiance and yet at the same time, at your best, it is combined with a simplicity, directness and abstract quality for which the only word is child-like. You know it will take me some time to get to know you as I should. But two things matter to you. Again Tina, as a professional, hit the nail squarely when she said so much apparent beauty had no foundation, and she implied that your foundation was health. So it is. But it is not the health of a doctor's examination. It is vitality and in your case that is a combination of physical health and exuberance that combine to make you vital and radiant.

B U T—you must take care of yourself. You must not have those circles under your eyes. Sure you will get rid of them. But they should not be there at all because once they come they come back too easily. And taking care of yourself for you, is not so much not working hard but holding yourself well in hand. Am I right? The second thing is character or as people like to call it in America, personality. That, my dear, you will have to work out. But people can read it in the face as the years go by, what you really are. I look at people quite a lot—men and women. I know few really lovely women and handsome men. The Arabs have a saying that a woman is sometimes beautiful when you look at her. But a really beautiful woman when you look at her she is more beautiful and still more beautiful and still more beautiful always. I knew one such—curiously enough she was a member of the English Trotskyites. Her name was Lee Bradley. She had wonderful bone structure, a marvellous head, the same bloom that you have and when I knew her, in her thirties, a superb dignity. Have you ever seen pictures of Joe Louis's wife—Marva. I have seen her snapped by newspaper men under the worse conditions—her facial structure is so good that it is impossible for her ever to come out badly.

But there is nothing else to the face. It is empty. So take care of yourself, my sweet. Take it easy, *inside*. And outside it will shine in your face. I shall send you some flowers for your room—to make you feel good. I take no denial. When you leave there, leave them, give them to the elevator man, or to the telephone girl. During the week I shall send you a poem I have read. It is a little terrifying but it bears on this subject and you will appreciate it. The political letter can wait. Now, no cramps, please, not one little one. I can take care of myself. You are something very precious in my life. New York is a different place now that you are here. I am conscious of you every minute of the day. Every time you score a point I throw my cap up and shout Hooray. I'll call you often to hear how you are doing. Dinner will be wonderful. I know a small pleasant place near to you. Just tell me when. I am doing fine—troubles up to my eyes but I take them one by one and have learnt actually to enjoy difficulties.

Only take it easy—inside. A great city is a terrific impact—hammering at you in all sorts of ways you are unconscious of—the people are different—and at the beginning especially it is as well deliberately to give the personality some time.

Yours, this time,
Uncle

Oh, good news. I have seen a beautiful apartment. Far away but quiet. I hope I get it.

June 10, 1944

Wishing you, my precious, many happy returns of the day.

No one who wishes you this will wish it more sincerely and more profoundly than I do.

We shall celebrate I hope on Wednesday. Please oblige me by just letting me go my own wilful way. Think of how long it has been and how little I have been able to meet you in the ordinary associations of a simple human relationship. I am loving it, hugely. So let me be.

I send you some verse as the beginning of the celebration. The first poem is in somewhat traditional form but fine nevertheless. The writer is not afraid or ashamed. The other verses should interest you also (I hope). They interested me.

I Think Continually of those who were Truly Great (Stephen Spender)

I think continually of
those who were truly
great.
Who, from the womb,
remembered the soul's
history
Through corridors of
light where the hours
are suns
Endless and singing. Whose
lovely ambition
Was that their lips,
still touched with
fire,

Should tell of the spirit
clothed from head to
foot in song.
And who hoarded from
the Spring branches
The desires falling
across their bodies
 like blossoms.
What is precious is never
 to forget
The essential delight of
the blood drawn from
ageless springs
Breaking through rocks
in worlds before our
earth.
Never to deny its
pleasure in the morning
simple light
Nor its grave evening
demand for love.
Never to allow gradually
the traffic to smother
With noise and fog the
flowering of the spirit.
Near the snow, near
the sun, in the
highest fields
See how these names
are feted by the
waving grass
And by the streamers
of white cloud
And whispers of wind
in the listening
sky.
The names of those
who in their lives
fought for life
Who wore at their hearts
the fire's centre.
Born of the sun
they travelled a short
while towards the
sun,
And left the vivid
air signed with

their honour.

The others follow. Read them carefully.

Life as a chase*
One maddening surge
Ebbing and flowing
Fighting and
losing
Continually growing.
Rootless being of no
past,
Clinging sadly to a
life
without race memory.
Asking, attacking,
claiming birth.
Inside my bed swift
water wings beat upward,
I giant-like emerge,
but even as the
face
strides up and confidence
lays bare my cheek,
I, inner core, stand
back and mock
impotent me.
You, the God who
constant economies name as ruler;
Women building your
empire place doll-
like exteriors
over resoluteness so
your manness will
be served.
Heartbreak is seeing
a sunset and only
knowing it is
beautiful.
... the light
that holds
  A gleam sprayed
unknowingly

---

* Poem by Constance Webb.

And my grave will
be
strewn vertebrae
   Shiny bones each a
little skull
   but on each glinting
still my truth.
My love, how to you
can I bow
What false words
shall I say
And turn my truth
   shined face
   for your kiss.
What enemy to myself
lives within.
Why truth, why
   integrity, why inner
   ache.

Well, my mistress and my pupil, there I have copied out for you some verse. It is *genuine*. And genuine authentic poetic writing is rare. There is also genuine sentiment and in one or two, perhaps more, real passion. I am reading them slowly and I have to do other reading too, because I am much out of practice. I shall also, in good time, and with your kind permission, talk to a friend or two about them. For the moment, however, and on this your birthday, read the following lines.

He has outsoared the shadow of our night; Envy and calumny and
   hate and pain,
And that unrest which
   men miscall delight,
Can touch him not
   and torture not again;
From the contagion of the world's slow
   stain
He is secure and now
   can never mourn
A heart grown cold, a
   head grown gray in
   vain;
Nor, when the spirit's
   self has ceased to
   burn,
With sparkless ashes
   load an unlamented
   urn.
and, only two lines this time,

Stay yet awhile! speak
  to me once again;
Kiss me, so long but as
  a kiss may live;

They are from Adonais, Shelley's lament on the death of Keats.

Intensely personal; the greatest of all lyric poets in my own opinion, a man for whom abstractions were more real than "reality." Yet his wife wrote of him the following: "To defecate life of its misery and its evil was the ruling passion of his soul; he dedicated to it every power of his mind, every pulsation of his heart. He looked on political freedom as the direct agent to effect the happiness of mankind..."

The bourgeois writers misrepresent Shelley. I know that it was from the power of his *social* passion that sprang the power of his intensely *personal* lyrics. He understood art too well to try to express himself directly in all his work. But I am convinced that no purely personal passion could have resulted in such perfect lyrics. By the nineteenth century that was already impossible. Not a line of social implication need appear in the verse. But to-day more than ever the strength of any individual is his social strength. Your own conflict is as old as society, only nowadays it isn't disguised. It is open. *In addition*, you carry the burden of an oppressed sex as I carry the burden of an oppressed race. You write best when you feel the conflict most keenly—some of the latest ones, scribbled on Chief paper, have real fire. *But* (one of my big buts) only when to express yourself in this way becomes an irresistible and consuming passion, dominating all else, will you acquire the mastery and sweep which will enable you to handle the detail with the firmness and precision needed to express the complete idea. Have you got it in you? No one can know that. I believe that the only proof of the power is the unwavering determination to persist. It may be in acting. *But a flame burns in you—that is without question.* Those who love you for yourself and not for themselves can help you. But in the same way as the flame came from God knows where, so the power to develop it can only be your own and in the last analysis depends upon you. Never settle for less and you will have no regrets. I feel somehow you won't.

You have a short nose. It amuses me very much. I make constant jokes at it.

Love,
Nello

June 14, 1944

Well, precious, how are you? Lovely, I know. Well, I hope. You seemed very well, yesterday. I am up to my eyes in work. Here is a letter I wrote to you since last Sunday. By accident it deals with what we were talking about yesterday—one aspect of it. And curiously enough the ideas of society which I had written to you about, and which I have been working on for two years, suddenly demand expression in reply to Laski.* Life is moving very fast these days. You scarcely think of something before

---

* C.L.R. James, "Laski, St. Paul and Stalin," *New International,* June 1944; a review of Laski's *Faith,*

there it is. The inter-relation of everything is a fundamental characteristic of our society. Every day I see it more and more. How closely related are the life I live, the things I think, and you—will sometime or other become suddenly clear to you. I haven't the slightest doubt that your ideas of acting, *if valid* (I don't know) are very closely related to modern society and to one of its expressions, modern poetry. Laski does not understand *anything, in general* for he understands nothing in particular. If I understand you at all, and it is difficult to be sure you understand, your theory that you as an actress get hold of the *essence* of a play or a part, and depend upon your grasp of that for its *manifestation* in concrete action or movement. Is it so? I hope it is for if it is I understand it. I have been trying to explain. It is my fundamental idea which I have grasped from Hegel and Marx. If a man loves a woman and seeks to do this and that to please her or to show his love and do what he ought to do, it *may* go well. But if to love her and show and do everything is a necessity of his own nature—then his love for her is a *manifestation* of the *essence* which is in him. A worker defends democracy not because he ought to but because it is a compelling necessity of his life to do so. Make what you can of this. But once you know something well, very well, then a general principle is easier to get hold of. And politics, art, life, love, in the modern world, all become so closely integrated that to understand one is to understand all. But that is very hard.

That Elizabethan stage-conventions were most favourable to poetic drama is indisputable. Patent make-believe leaves us freer than scenery to receive impressions through ear and mind, and its effect upon actors is even more important. Unsupported by plausible surrounds they are forced to draw upon themselves to create the illusion of reality. Thus they not only tend to act more from within, but they are able to modulate with less embarrassment from realistic dialogue into those passages and speeches which can only be given their full emotional splendour and significance by *unnatural* delivery. The crucial test of an actor or actress in any great Shakespearean part is not only the degree to which he or she succeeds in making a vivid consistent character out of it, but whether he or she shows a true instinct for those moments when psychological interest should yield to poetic interpretation. The extent to which the play as a whole rivets our attention depends upon interpretation of character—which shows how vital that is; but its power to exalt us, upon the imaginative rendering of its poetry.*

Desmond McCarthy on a recent performance of Hamlet. It is a problem. He is correct—to a point. Shakespeare is the greatest of bourgeois writers. Individualism is therefore carried to its highest point with him. Undoubtedly, Shakespeare felt as D. M. writes. But what to do with Sh *to-day*?
When I ask that question I do not mean that we sit down and work out the answer in the head. No. Some modern person, really modern, with ideas and values which are part of his time, and with the knowledge of his time, reads Shakespeare and draws out what is implicit and important *for us*. That is one thing which the Robeson Othello partially did, and which could only have been done in America. It showed the race

---

* Reason and Civilization, 1944.
A newspaper clipping which was glued to the first page of the letter.

question. Similarly a modern performance of the Merchant of V should show the Jewish question. It is not at all accidental that your Mr. Carradine did what he did with his Shylock. He was making one modern response—and a very genuine one too. I don't know who can do the other. That is where the Margaret Webster Othello failed worse than I think—it failed to show what we, as modern people, could see in Desdemona's character. She was breaking social prejudices on the race question. She was breaking them on the position of woman. She demanded the right to go with her husband to the wars. That the Elizabethans could not have seen the full implications of her character is their business. We are not Elizabethans and it is no use pretending that we are or trying to think as they did. Thus with the proper insight, due to the age we live in and a sense of its values, the ones that matter; with knowledge, to prevent crude anachronisms and vulgar "modernizations," and with artistic restraint, a good modern actress and a good producer would recreate a Desdemona that would mean something. And the final test? If Shakespeare came back, after he had walked around a bit and seen things, he would be fascinated by it, especially when he saw the young people all eagerly discussing the thing from their point of view. But to all this our Shakespearean company was as blind as a bat. But it will come one day. They at least have done their part in one sphere. For that they deserve much credit. The rest will follow. It always does. It always does. It always does.

Why am I so sure? It would take a lifetime to explain that. But in 1935 in Paris, the Popular Front and the Fascists fought nightly over a performance of Coriolanus, until the government stopped the performance. Yet a year or two later I saw Sybil Thorndike as Volumnia in the same play. She was wonderful. Took the centre of the stage and played everybody off—and not grabbing, but simply because she was what she was. Yet she was personally a "progressive" woman, despised race prejudice—she liked me a great deal and did her best to be friends but I wouldn't, much as I liked her. She also voted for the Labour Party. Yet no one would have fought over the Coriolanus she played in. So that Carradine, a reactionary, but with a powerful social passion, makes his Shakespeare more alive and more modern. You see what I am driving at? The expression of the social forces in our time, in art and in life, is a highly contradictory, subtle and complex business. The crudeness and coarseness of the Stalinists here as elsewhere have wrought an incalculable amount of harm. They ruin everything they touch, and even where they do some good work they use the prestige and influence to do more mischief than ever. But thank Heaven, their reign is beginning to crumble. The intellectual reaction against them, from the left, is well on its way. Small, a little nervous, especially among those who do not see historically but feel as artists, such as our friend [Richard] Wright. But it is on its way—in Political Economy, in History, in analyses of the arts, everywhere. I hope in the course of the next two years to deal two substantial blows myself and to assist in the production of two more. My truth, Miss poet, will not be confined to my vertebrae. Not on your life. By the late fall, my friend Bill Williams's book will be out*—I have read the page proofs—a masterpiece. And I am sure Wright's book will hit some powerful blows. By 1945 a book of mine should be well under way. And it is not at

---

* Eric Williams, *Capitalism and Slavery*, 1944.

all accidental that the three of us are Negroes. But that is another and a longer story. Good-bye. I love you most terrible and awful much. And I sat down to read a bunch of English papers to write an article and saw this passage by McCarthy and thought of you at once and have neglected my work most shamefully for the last hour. But I am now feeling fine and shall proceed to write my article and it will be I am quite sure better than it would have been for the thought of you is very warm inside of me. Which to the vulgar must be a very shocking thing, but to me is the most natural thing in the world and very good for the article in which the glow which pervades me at the thought of you will I hope be translated into the most vicious blows against the enemies of our peace.

[Postmark June (30?) 1944]

Well, my little bundle of surprises, how are you? Well, I hope. Your friend, Murray, is a very genial host. He was very kind and polite, not in a superficial but in a very genuine manner. He is a bit of an Englishman.

When will I ever be able to talk to you enough? (This is a thing to say!) But I went to the museum on Wednesday for the pictures are back. They had taken them away for the war. I had a wonderful time. For the time being I am most interested in this one. One day we must go there or if you go take a look at it carefully for me. There are innumerable things to talk about. But for the moment let us stick to poetry. Some of the things you wrote at L.I. [Long Island] were good, very good in fact. I am looking at it quite objectively. *But one day you will want to express something very badly. It will be a big idea, about 100 or 200 lines perhaps.* Then you will have to get down to the *structure as a whole*. It will possess you. You will have logical sequences for which you will have to find poetic expression. You will search for them. You will read up your previous work and transfer old ideas to new uses. You will battle and grapple and sweat. And behold, it will be a fine poem. *Of that I have no doubt.* For you have all the hallmarks—except the dominating passion and excitement to do just that. Let it wait. So meanwhile we can think of a few things.

Here is a list of what distinguishes "modern" poetry—"imagery patterned increasingly on everyday speech, absence of inversions, stilted apostrophes, conventional end-rhymes, 'poetic' language generally, except where used deliberately for incantatory effect," "freedom from the ordinary logic of sequence, jumping from one image to the next *by association* rather than by the usual cause-effect method, emphasis on the ordinary, in reaction against the traditional poetic emphasis on the cosmic," "concern with naked consciousness and the newly identified 'unconscious' as against 'the soul'," "concern with the common man, almost to the exclusion of the 'hero' or extraordinary man," "concern with the social order as against 'heaven' and 'nature.'" Note that you do all of them to the manner born. You just think that way naturally. Now what interests me is where you got it from. For two reasons. First because it's you. I want to know where you read and what you read that gave your mind that particular impetus. Secondly you do it so naturally that I am wondering if it is not the natural language of your generation by now—of those with a poetic gift I mean.

You feel at home with Muriel Rukeyser. Good. I know some of her poems. They are very fine. B U T. Listen.

In the square a crowd listens, carrying banners. Overhead, boring through the speaker's voice, a plane circles with a snoring of motors revolving in the sky,
   drowning the single voice. It does not touch
   the crowd's silence. It circles. The name stands:
   Scottsboro

Now, sweetheart, she is a fine writer. She has a discipline, a mastery of her technique, and a concentration which you have not got, though some of your love poems have unity. Yet those lines, if you had shown them to me *would never have made me feel as I do about your possibilities*. You *understand that? Never.* Take again that poem of Spender's.

I think continually of those who were truly great.

Read it again. I sent it to you. The method, the vision is commonplace. Take this by S. V. Benet on the Dictator:

We thought we were done with these things but we were wrong.
We thought, because we had power, we had wisdom.
We thought the long train would run to the end of Time.
We thought the light would increase.
Now the long train stands derailed and the bandits loot it.
Now the boar and the asp have power in our time. . . .

It is in an anthology. But it is not really good. It is rhetoric. It is a speech. Now what your verses show is something else, the capacity to create images, which images when disciplined by structure (and the structure, the *genuine* structure, can come only from passion and dominating purpose) these images themselves create the impact *emotionally* of a powerful logical argument. You say that in acting you master the inner action, the essence, and then the manifestation, the outward movement shows itself. Poetry is, in effect, the reverse, at least the best lyric poetry. The genuine lyricist does not argue or declaim. Somehow his mind is such that he produces backwards, the images, the ideas, all combine to give the total effect. Of course he may begin with a general idea. That is his business. But as he works it out the result is not argument but a series of wonderful vignettes of music, pictures, and what not.

   Above the cold
      Cordilleras hung
   The winged eagle and
      the Moon:
   The gold, snow-throated
      orchid sprung
   From gloom where peers
      the dark baboon

That is a rather obvious but very lovely example. Sometimes it is in the sheer magic of simple words. The Lady of the Lake begins like this

The stag at eve had
  drunk his fill
Where danced the moon
  on Mona's rill

(Now note)

And deep his mid-night
lair had made
In lone Glenartney's
  hazel shade.

Compare that with the beginning of another of Scott's poems,

The Minstrel

The way was long, the
  wind was cold
The minstrel was
  infirm and old

Sheer doggerel. Now you do the real thing and surprisingly often, in the modern manner. I read again

Rootless being of no
past,
Clinging sadly to a
life
without race memory.
Asking, attacking,
claiming birth.

Do you know what I think of that? I think it magnificent. I don't care to what it applies. But the images are vivid and unmistakeable; and the last line, *asking, attacking, claiming* have real power. But it is only a fragment. There are many such. I copied out some for you on your birthday. So there we are. What will you do with it? You will do what you have to do that's all. So meanwhile I'll scribble to you notes and you will scribble down your impressions as you feel. In the poems you scribbled at L.I. are some lovely lines.

Here I stopped for a day. By degrees I see certain things more clearly. One of them is as follows.

Last night I read your poems through again. I have been behaving very stupidly, hesitating, weighing, recognising your poetic gift but anxious lest my judgment be affected by my love for you. But to hell with it. I think three or four of them are completely beautiful as they stand. That is my considered judgment. And giving evidence of a quality that is rare—judging by the poems I have been reading in anthologies—"Best Modern Verse," etc. So. I have got it off my manly chest. Phew! Strange. If it had been someone else I would have read and after a time come to some decision easily—if I had read at all. But I had to be quite sure. I tested them out in all ways I could. I read other modern verse, I read Shelley, to check up, and now I am quite sure, quite quite sure. I shall write to you some things you ought to know—and remember. Then one day we shall sit and I'll talk to you about them. You are a very rare, very precious creature, and you will have a hard fight to find yourself completely. When I think of some of the things you have put up with, I cannot understand it at all. You submitted obviously from some inner need of your own nature. The need perhaps for sacrifice to a cause. I don't know you well enough to be sure. But this I know. With a tempestuous temperament you have a rare talent—at least one, and some of your actor friends say you have another. And on the one hand, you wish to be admired and loved by everybody and "be something." And on the other there is an equally powerful devotional strain. Yes, devotional. To sacrifice yourself to something or someone, to be ascetic, yes, Miss, to be ascetic, if I am wrong tell me, losing yourself in something far from the flesh-pots of the world. It isn't new, my dearest Constance. Many of the greatest saints—I am using words which are open to grave misunderstanding but I trust you—many of the greatest saints began by wild outbursts of joyous riotous living, and then suddenly were "converted." Then there are the others. I have seen them in the revolutionary movement. They joined early, denied themselves, and after years, went back to bourgeois society, eager for what they had missed. The two trends are in every human being. Lenin, one of the "saints" could never listen to Beethoven. He would weep. It upset him, opened up sides of his nature which he needed to suppress. Each of us in his own sphere fights the same battle, some on a very very small scale, of course, some on a larger, until some equilibrium is established. Am I correct? Do I read you aright? Is it in any way news to you? Do you know it all already? And if so, what. *If it is so*, then you will live and *the world outside* as much as your own development will shape you to some climax, whereupon a new phase will begin. One day I shall show you some letters from a friend of mine—he writes to me out of his daily needs. But it is a very powerful drama that is being fought out in and around him. You described my letters once as "spontaneous" and "generous." Perhaps they are. But my dear Miss Head-Over-Heels-in-Love, they are much more than that. I am in love with you because you are lovely and sweet? That attracted me. It could never hold me. There are all sorts of depths and facets to your many-sided personality which concentrate for me in one single person an enormous number of aspects of the world. To suppress any one of them would be a crime—like cutting off one of your arms, only much worse because the amputation would not be visible and the damage it would do would be terrible. "Spontaneous" and "generous" indeed! You are something I have been looking for all my life. You must not underestimate my love for you. For the time being, it is content to show itself only when I write to you. It is wider and deeper than anything you know or have ever dreamt of. Of that I am quite sure. As your sense of values matures and strengthens you will see that. As you know me better you will see how much you as a person mean to me who looks at the world in the way that I do, why it is that to see you developing in all ways means so much to me. Friends innumerable have told me "Why don't you get married? Why don't you get someone to take care of you?" The reason is simple. Despite all appearances

I don't want someone to take care of me. I want someone to take care of. I need something inside—not outside. And as so many people cannot understand how the Nello that they see can be at the same time a fanatical and unreasonable to the extreme adherent of Bolshevism—and how fanatical only a few people know, altho' some have guessed and a few men I have worked with in action know and would give their lives for me. In the same way I love you as passionately as any man ever loved any woman. I wonder if you know that. I doubt it. Meanwhile I must see to it that along with the politics—real politics—we work out something about the poetry.

By the way. I know something now. *The* picture of you that really matters is the one where you stand in the field in the long dress. One has to learn and learn slowly. That is the person you want to be, isn't it? That is the final person who is inside of you somewhere, asking, attacking, claiming birth. You can be that person, but it is going to be hard. All I know is that now I'll give all the pictures I have for that one.

        N

Thursday. 14th and 8th
6 o'clock. And no cramps. As
if you didn't know, you
enchanting faker.

R. J
520 W. 150
N.Y. N.Y.

July 4, 1944

Darling, I left you and had ravioli and meat-balls in order to catch Cover-Girl at 6:15. I wanted to sit quietly. I wanted to see it. I thought it would give me side-lights on the Cover-Girl I know. It did. To some a silly sentimental typical "Hollywood." Not to me. I watched it with profound interest. Then I came up town—and had dinner—at the Spanish restaurant where we had moule. Then I bought some envelopes, came into a Riker's and here I sit. I shall go home to sleep when I have finished this.

Dearest heart, this afternoon I have never seen anyone so lovely. Some shyness, yes shyness, at first, then your radiance blooming and tenderness. Then we spoke. Do you know? Your face and your eyes gleamed as you said that your decision was taken; and you agreed that the life that was strong and invincible came from the inner confidence. There are a few moments in one's life that stand out. This is and always will be one for me. What a week-end it has been! July 4, 1944. Independence Day for you, sweetheart, independence day for you.

I read your poems again and again. For me they are a recurrent miracle. Excessive praise? Because I love you? Want to flatter you? Listen:

Teach me, only teach, love
As I ought
I will speak thy speech,
love
Think thy thought
Meet if thou require it

> Both demands
> Laying flesh and spirit
> In thy hands
> That shall be to-morrow
> Not to-night
> I must bury sorrow
> Out of sight
> Must a little weep, love,
> Foolish me.
> And so fall asleep, love,
> Loved by thee.

That was Browning. Some 60 years ago. A woman dedicated herself then to a man. Now read again (a similar sentiment in a line from your poem)

> My life is no longer
> Mine . . .

A woman gives herself to a cause. The free verse, the modern attitude, the social consciousness characteristic of our age and needed by our age. But the poetic spirit is the same, transferred to a higher stage of development. I had quoted the Browning to you on Sunday. Now I see it reproduced, by a woman, in the world of 1944, the terrible world of 1944. The images too are as good as Browning's in that poem. Dells of refrigerated coolness. The door unhinged and swung back. But the same feminine final response. Where he says

> Must a little weep, love
> foolish me

You say

> But sometimes I'll weep
> And wish it mine.

Now do you see how sure I am and why. Over and over again I see the genuine poetic and literary instinct, and in a field which I understand.

> My hands touch no
> Braille

has beautiful lines. The first 6 lines are perfect. The single words, lines 2, 3, 5,

> if my life is no longer . . .,

are indications of an instinct for using the modern medium which amazes me in one so uninstructed. But what you write is as nothing compared to the spirit that I saw in you as we talked for a few minutes. You say I understand you. It is because I watch you and watch over you so carefully. I shall make mistakes with you. When I do, be lenient with them. For such as I am I am wholly yours. Be strong and fight for your own road. You see it. Follow it. All that I can do to give you insight I shall. What you mean to me, perhaps you will be seeing more clearly now. It will be difficult, I know. But when in doubt, lean on me and have confidence in me. For your happiness, your complete realisation of yourself mean everything to me. Whatever happens.

No dust can fill
No bitterness distill

I shall work on my article again to-morrow. I shall strive to get it as clear as possible. This one is for you. I thought of you every second that I wrote. I am hoping you will like it, that it will give you courage and inspiration. Then in a day or two I shall write to you a letter which will be my response to the great step you have taken. I love you and know now that I have never loved anyone else but you, because I have never known anyone like you, and know that I never will again.

I shall be sitting waiting for you to-day and every day as long as I can get away.

Love,
Nello

Postmark July 7, 1944

Well, St. Monica. Why St. M? I don't know at all. Only I have your picture up in front of me—the new one. Alas, such is man. I do not look at the others at all now. The best view I have hitherto liked of your face is full. But this profile fascinates me, not only internally—this picture signifies much—but externally as well. And it brings St. Monica to mind. Who was St. M? Wouldn't you like to know? And wouldn't I like to know too? As far as I remember she is in a famous Virgin of the Rocks by Leonardo, a magnificent painting in the National Gallery in London. Or she is the unwilling heroine of some scandalous episode related by Anatole France. His method was to rake up all the scandal he could about the saints and discuss them with a straight face thus discrediting Catholicism. But, whichever she was, I don't care. I have christened the picture St. Monica and Monica it will be. After all it's *my* picture. And do you know her second name—her surname? It is Conover.* Monica Connover. And Monica battles with Connover who wants her to be Chu-Chu Connover, or Wendie Connover, or Angel Bangs Connover; but Monica gave Connover a most angelic bang on the nose last week—and I believe that Connover is restored to his proper place. But he is clever is Connover. He appears in the most unexpected and seductive disguises. But Monica, dear, dear Monica, she stands before me, lean and trained and ready, alert but confident, smiling even, hands clasped but not too tightly. Connovers! beware. You see, sweetheart, I am a poet too. Style? Modern. Very very modern, treating of only contemporary phenomena, e.g., photographer's models. Verse? Free, very free. Never was verse so free as mine. Ah,

---

* Webb was working for Harry Conover's model agency.

darling. If only you could see and feel how much I love you, the verse you would write would shake to pieces all who read it. Do you remember Ferdinand's speech to Miranda?

For several virtues have I loved several women, but she, his Miranda, was compounded of the best of each previous woman. Why should it happen to me? I don't know. But it has. Look at it. My life is political, a very special branch. You are political through and through in the best sense of that word. As you see, poetry is for me a very living, a very vital part of my life. You write poetry. I cannot and never could. But through you I write it. I love the stage, have hankered after it for years. You belong there. All the creative instincts I have had to suppress or ignore are alive in me again in you. I love, or rather admire lovely women, who have an instinct and an interest in clothes and style. My friends know it and laugh at me. You and your particular style I have admired from the very first moment I saw you. You are young and gay and American, without the English or continental desire to "waltz," but ready to "cut a rug" instead. I love it. Nowhere in the whole wide world could anything like you appear but in America of the post-war, and I am pretty certain that you are a special product of the West. Observe the points I have made. See if they are not all literally and soberly true—for me. Think then what it would mean to me to hold you in my arms and love you. Ferdinand being what he was saw in Miranda what she didn't know was there. I say that these things and others too exist in you—for me. Others could love you. But how could they know you—all that comprise you. They can't. You must know that, Constance. You must. And me? I am as confident as I am of anything, as confident as any man can be of anything that in a personal way my whole life has been a preparation for you. Poetic? Yes, but not less true but more true on account of that, just as Ferdinand's extravagant words come true in me for you. Daniel Webster made a famous reply to Hayne in Congress a century ago, a reply made on the spur of the moment, which laid the foundations of American nationalism. When asked how he was able to do it without preparation he replied that his whole life had been a preparation for it. Politics? Ten years of it and, thank heaven, I came to it with knowledge and understanding of bourgeois society. I have, particularly during the last four years, made a complete examination of the whole theory, helped by some splendid people. And from the theory has come insight into the movement in economic, in philosophical, and in *human* terms. I couldn't see you four years ago as I see you now, far less appreciate and enter into your political life, and help you in the special way you need. Same with the arts. It is only two years ago, as a result of illness, that I began to go regularly to the pictures and began to see them and reflect on the relation of the arts to life in a society so "collectivized" as ours. Even the theory of your acting is the embodiment of a profound philosophical principle which I have only mastered a year or [so] ago—the difference between essence and manifestation and the relation between them. It is during the past four years that I have learnt to know what it is to need, and now to love a woman, for her own sake, because nothing else I know can ever satisfy me. I belong to the twentieth century. I have a comprehensive view of life. I become more and more interested in all aspects of life, as in our modern society all aspects of life become more closely inter-related. I can only completely love someone on whom and with whom I can exercise all my powers, and that means someone who is such that she continuously stimulates me by her own manifold gifts and responses to life. There is not an ounce of spontaniety, generosity or romantic passion in all this—or rather what is spontaniety, generosity and romantic exaggeration is in this case sober truth. That is the miracle of it. How it has happened I know. It is only on the surface an accident. I have recognised it for what it is. It is for you to do so. Always, this is the third time, when I see you some man is around. If when I came the first time no man was around, we would have understood one another better. But what has been has been. And what will be will be. I wasn't ready for you then. Some sure instinct kept me away. But nothing will keep me away. I shall go only when you tell me to go.

And now about your work. (Do you remember how four years ago I planned that we should study *Capital* together? Always I have seen us working together.) But now, thank Heaven, we do it from your own angle. I look at you again and see you standing on a stage, speaking to thousands of people, just as you stand here before me now, telling them what? That is exactly what you are deciding now, these wonderful days, when the whole world is racked with pain, of death, and I am sure, of birth too; when at the same time I am being recreated anew, wonderful days when a man who has looked at the world for many years and seen many women and felt that perhaps he chased a dream, sees it suddenly sitting opposite to him and smiling. I hope they are wonderful for you too. And when you stand facing the people what will you say? That depends upon the people as much as it depends on you, far more on them. But that does not prevent the responsibility for yourself being yours. Poetry, acting, whatever it is, Monica has to say something.

Now first you were born and grew up after the Russian Revolution. Do you know what that means? The mental world in which you grew up *as a child* was the widest and freest the world has ever known. The greatest group of men the bourgeois world has ever know were Ricardo, Goethe, Shelley, Beethoven, Hegel and that group. They lived in a world which had been illuminated by the French Revolution. Think of all the things you have studied and read and talked about from early, what you were doing, at 15 for instance. But, unlike the Europeans, you did it without fear, without perpetual anxiety, even without hunger, i.e., without these being a major and permanent part of the society around you. This makes some people dilettante, they are mentally stimulated by the great release of ideas but somehow do not feel them deeply inside. Your own beautiful nature, your early life, all that go to make you what you are, have saved you from that. You are a serious person. But you have more than that. You have gifts—one of them is a talent for writing verse—a very rare, very precious, gift. It is at the same time a gift for an art *which is one of the most difficult in the world.*

Why am I so sure you have it? I explained a little last night in the poem about giving yourself and Browning's poem. Here are some further observations. You know Shakespeare was the greatest of all poets. He was a great dramatist, he was a great master of human character, etc., etc., but he had this gift to begin with, of vivid imagery. I shall underline them. Look at each one.

To be or not to be—

(a very powerful simplification)

whether tis nobler in the mind to suffer

> *The slings and arrows of outrageous* fortune
> Or *to take arms* and—

see the boldness with which he says to take arms against *a sea* of troubles. Then two lines later

> and *by a sleep* to say we end
> *the heart-ache*

Now come two

> and *the thousand natural shocks*
> that *flesh* is *heir to*

Now I am skipping

> When we have *shuffled off* this *mortal coil*
> *the whips and scorns of time*

A little lower down

> conscience doth make cowards of us all
> *the native hue of resolution*
> is *sicklied o'er* with the
> *pale cast of thought*
> and *enterprises of great pith and moment*
> with this regard, their
> *currents turn awry*
> and *lose the name of action.*

It is terrific, isn't it? Stroke after stroke. Sometimes two in a line. There is nothing in the world like it anywhere else. *It doesn't matter what he is talking about.* It is not "dramatic" in the ordinary sense. There is knowledge of life but the way he sees it, the images in which he expresses it, that is what matters.

Now you see things *that way*. The horses stamping ecstacy, the doors that you open (July 3), the path wide that narrows, the amoeba and the pivot, the dells of refrigerated coolness (a superb image for a night-club), waggon-ringed, the horns of the car-noises, fringed unicorns. They are numerous all through. Some of them are very beautiful. All are fresh and spontaneous. How much is there of it in you? I don't know. You don't know either. But you write three or four poems at a time when you are moved. Every poem has some. But it's no use arguing about that.

Point 2. Immediately after Shakespeare ends the passage I quoted he makes Hamlet say (Listen carefully)

> Soft, the fair Ophelia,
> Nymph, in thy orisons be
> all my sins remembered.

It is a famous phrase. But its beauty is not only individual. It is dramatic, a contrast in mood and therefore in manner with the preceding. Nobody could do this as well as Shakespeare. Over and over and over again he feels that the moment has come for a change. Here is one of the best I know.

> The cloud-capped towers,
> the gorgeous palaces
> The solemn temples, the great
> globe itself
> Yea all which it inherit
> shall dissolve
> And like this insubstantial
> pageant faded
> Leave not a wreck
> behind
>   (Now)
> We are such stuff as
>   dreams are made on
> And our little life is
>   rounded with a sleep.

The majesty and the sudden simplicity. Sometimes it is vice-versa. All sorts of changes. (Beethoven does it in superb style.) Actors too. Orators too. But it is the mark of a writer. The feeling that the moment has come to change. I know this well for I practise it—I shall show you many places in the Black Jacobins. Often the change is harsh but turns out natural as often a laugh is from someone in tears.

Now, dearest, I who have spent many many years feeling these things—15 to 33—and never lost the habit of feeling them as I read, regularly am delighted when I see them in your work. The change to: No dust must fill, No bitterness distill—to the rhyme, the almost perfect interweaving of three strands in the one about the voice over the ridge falling on the bleeding heart, and best of all (I am quoting from memory)

> Lovely lyric of unreal
>   perception
> Sung by poets through aeons of fervored love.

And then a really dramatic and yet brilliantly ironical transition to a modern woman's protest, in modern verse, emphasising the contrast with the two lines above which are in the best 19th century tradition. That whole poem and many others have an instinctive sense of form. And that is a terribly difficult thing to have in so treacherous a medium as modern verse.

These things then you have, the eye for the image, the instinct for the moment, the sense of structure. You have plenty of them too, and what is most wonderful, you have them without instruction of any kind, without organised study. Some faults I see. But any fool can make errors. I don't tell you about them, first because I am never sure and will only do so when you are yourself in doubt. I exercise this restraint not because I am tender with you, or wish to "encourage" you. God forbid. The way to "encourage" anyone is to take their work seriously, if even to attack it for 20 pages. For no one attacks something for 20 pages unless it is important. Which is why people who say, i.e., Trotskyism is a small, insignificant, sect and then organise international campaigns against it make me laugh. No I don't mention them because it is *your mind* that is finding itself and *your mind* that must be developed. If even I were perfectly sure of certain mistakes it would be a great criminal error for me *now* to intervene and impose my mature and integrated personality and ideas on yours. Over and over again an artist, especially in so subtle a thing as poetry, makes certain mistakes repeatedly and out of it at last gets the new idea that is seeking expression. To cut it off is perhaps to stifle something. If Delmore Schwartz or W. H. Auden showed me a poem I would without hesitation, after studying it, say what I thought freely. My job now is something else. It is to try to create the arena in which your own poetic personality will take strong roots and grow. That I shall tackle next time. When I say that my whole life seems to have been a preparation for you I speak the sober truth. I was going to buy the anthology and read it with you. On reflection I said No. But you, in relation to society, for you are a manifestation as I am, as all of us are, that I know about and will tell you. That is true for all of us. Then you read and follow your own tasks and will talk about them and exchange ideas. All I can do is to save you a lot of time and fumbling and make the general road clear for you. You follow it in your own individual way. And so, selfish me, you will continually charm, delight, and startle me. Next time we shall take up the question: How "deep" is the gift you have, how far can you go, what can you do, always remembering that you have another profession.

(To be continued)

I think I should let you know how wonderful, how exciting all this is for me. Ten years ago something came into my life and altered its whole course. Everything previous seemed only preparation. Now someone has come into it—actually here, I can speak to her and watch her face, and gift of all gifts, she is an embodiment of my interests and pursuits from 15–33 and also of the things which during the last ten years have dominated me. Just as I make the connection between them, and see them fused, you appear; Constance was my embodiment No. 2. Then Constance changed to Embodiment of No. 1. Even then I loved her. Now Monica is 1 and 2 combined. If I see you stand on the stage one day speaking in your own particular voice to many thousands, I shall be happy and proud. But if when you finished you turned to me before all others, then that would be the most secret, the innermost, the unexpected dream come true.

[unsigned]

[1944]

I agree. Her [Muriel Rukeyser] weakness you analyse perfectly. What she and her type represent, that too you see. Modern man runs away from the deeper emotions. Society and science are so developed that he can no longer hide from himself what is and what ought to be. So his art becomes increasingly more abstract and his emotions undergo a similar transformation. All this is very sound but needs history, a knowledge of literature and of philosophy to develop as it should be developed. But even with all this, no one is any real good without creative insight. (That is a bad phrase for insight is a creative act.) That you have. The world is simply waiting for work of that kind.

But there is something more important for you. *Why does M. R. write that way?* She learnt from the creators of modern verse. But she is "proletarian," she is at least "progressive." She wants to be read by thousands, and hundreds of thousands. Yet she writes as she does. Simplifying her images wouldn't do it. If the images were "right" they wouldn't have to be simplified. Every poet, or most, until they are mature, has to work like hell to perfect his style. But that effort for perfection is needed even with straightforward verse as Housman. No, the images, the form, the finished work (it must be finished in more senses than one) are the final expression of the mind. The mind is sensitive and strong. It absorbs a certain type of impression and rejects others. These are transmuted into a complete personality. Soon the personality begins to select images and impressions. That is it begins to impose its own stamp on what it meets. The outside world still shapes the personality however—until growth stops. But the process is a dual one. Now who is Rukeyser? What were her original gifts. What life does she live? Who are her friends? What are her aims in life? What dominates her?

I don't know. But I can sum it up—my guess—in a phrase. She is probably *for* the working-class but not *of* it. There are two people who are very important in this connection. Engels was a Manchester business man. He dressed well, was at home in any drawing-room, *rode to hounds* (he said he was preparing for the revolution—the cavalry) and led a bourgeois life. But that was on the surface only. Every thought, every line he wrote was permeated with the spirit of the working-class. *His mind lived in that world.* He was a great scholar. He made no concessions to the uneducated in his serious work. But somehow in the most abstruse of his reasonings you are conscious of the fact that the role of his class dominates him. Now I suggest M. R. does not think that way. W. H. Auden and that bunch. They, none of them, think that way. So they can simplify their images as much as they please—they cannot get very far towards being popular in the best sense of that word. Another is Gorky. He was a man of letters, revolutionary, but living the life of a man of letters. But he came from the people and remained one of them. In his case all his early life, the formative years, had been spent with them. In Engels's case you have a mind that in its youth grasped intellectually the importance of the workers so powerfully, and spent so much of his life developing the ideas, that his bourgeois life never touched him.

To be "popular," to do what you want your poetry to do, you cannot "simplify," and if organically you do not think in terms of the people, then your popularisation will become either sentimentality or blood and thunder shrieking of the r-r-r-revolution. This is not "prophecy." It is a logical argument. Now in your work *since you came*, there is little of this in it before, shows that you have a powerful impulse in the right direction—not right, because I think that is right, but because if the poetic or "personality" impulse is not that way—then the work will be infallibly like M. R. or that type. No. The poet to-day who will be popular must have the highest standards, must *not* write down, must work out his images and ideas and stick by them, however strange and new they are. But if he is organically of the people, then the work will be popular in the best sense and if not read immediately in thousands must ultimately get the ear of the people. Poetry for the workingman. Yes! But the poet must be so much a part of his time, and that to-day means particularly in the U.S.A., the hopes, ideas, aspirations, weaknesses of the great democracy, the great mass, that altho' he write of love's young dream or dialectical materialism, the mass of the people will in time feel it to be their own. That is why I have tried to tell you over and over again. You are very gifted. This letter shows me that again. You have all the signs, all, of the truly creative personality, you are in the best environment of the age, that orientation to the working class, not as something to save you, but as something you feel part of (without that we have the T. S. Eliots, then the Audens—*who have done their work*). All that you have. *But*, the individual to-day is so subject to the life of society that your problem is the development of yourself. You write a sentence that makes me feel to squeeze you: "Ordinary man must feel the impact with no effort on his part and be stirred into the realization that he is MAN (with capitals because of the greatness)." That is the whole secret of present society. It took me years to learn. The productive capacity is solved. The problem is not a higher standard of living or no unemployment. The problem, and dear lady, this will rejoice your heart, the strictly scientific, *economic* problem, the solution of the capitalist crisis, lies in precisely the recognition of man as MAN. That is Marxism, that is Marx's philosophic theory, that is his economic theory, that is his political theory. The act out of the revolution makes him man. That is the central theme of the book Grace [Lee] is to write. In these days when your mind is opening you will have to feed it, and strengthen it and exercise it continuously in that direction. If you build your mind and your character and absorb this in every pore, given your already fine endowment and orientation, your writing future is golden. The difficulties in your way I have told you about. You will have to fight it out. I'll help. But the fight is yours.

What great excitement writing and thinking is! Yes I know. I live by it. It is a sign of your vocation, the sign, Miss Monica. You jump along miles at a time. You are to me profoundly interesting. I doubt if anyone finds anyone else as interesting as I find you. You say reading poetry, etc., is almost a sexual act. You discover great truths by instinct. They are. They are like the act of excretion and the sexual act a form of release, of accumulated life. One absorbs, transmutes, releases, and then carries on the process again. So that the highest (pardon the word), the most profound expression of the sexual act and the relationship of which it is the final consummation consists precisely in the combination of all human functions, the most primitive, elementary instincts and animal intimacies combined with the fusion of the highest most elevated reaches of consciousness. Only then is the relationship complete. But in bourgeois society people do their best with scraps. Your letter was very interesting for many reasons. It is the first letter you have ever written to me. Shocked? But it is. Think a bit, Miss Poet. Sure it is the first. I hope, in fact I am confident, there will be others. One must have patience. And it illustrates something which is the structure of all my thinking and outlook on life. You wrote it because you wanted to—for your own sake. Then one day you will say "But I very much want to see Nello. I must. He lives 2 hours away at the top of a hill that one has to walk up. And I am sleepy and tired and have no time. But I really have to see him to talk about something." Then you will. Or you won't. That's all. That is not all there is to things. But that is the essence of them. And of writing poetry too. You see what a philosopher I am. I repeat. I am a philosopher. Now Frosty doesn't know that. Neither does Constance. But Monica should. So Monica should not take too much trouble to emphasize pupil and friend, etc. You mean well. But it is not necessary. Take it in your stride. And that you should think it necessary to do that—please don't. You are madama, to me a phenomenon, a little miracle, a perpetual real life motion picture, a human and social drama, with the end unknown, but the problem posed. And no audience was ever more filled than myself to-day to appreciate this example of the comedie humaine. Better still. I can from my seat in the front row, even take part in the play—warn you who the villain is and when he is coming, shout at danger, cheer your successes, weep at failures, when the curtain goes down speculate on the next act. Sure I would like to be the hero. I have been looking for just such a play and just such a heroine all my life. That I have found it is one great victory. For the time being, the play must go on. In fact for always, the play must go on. In fact

The play's the thing
Wherein I'll catch the
conscience of the King.

Which, my wonderful, is very profound. I am pleased with it.
[unsigned]

[1944]

The truth is far more powerful than these half and half fakers can work out.

I (forgive the ego) fought battles with intellectuals on Song to Remember. I had one standard—great art had been brought to the proletariat. I judge *every* picture, for pictures are for the people, by that first. Most pictures are vulgar. This one, even if vulgar (and there is a case for this one) was vulgar + Chopin. Imagine people sneering at the Iturbi vulgarisations—as if that mattered, and note the cheap, weak defence.

Iturbi will have a place in the history of culture. He went to Hollywood. The others didn't.

The picture exceeded in results my greatest hopes. Not only in Hollywood but everywhere the masses loved it. I'll talk to you about the picture itself one day. But the social facts are: the great music companies sold so much that they are ready to subsidise pictures around the great composers. On the way are Beethoven, Rachmanninoff, Rimsky-Korsakov. Music, great music, will become a possession of the people. *It is revolutionary.* Why? Because the more the technical discoveries of capitalism bring culture to the masses, the more they resent the degradation and humiliation of their role in *production*—the grinding slavery of the machine.

Again. Today an intelligent worker sees the same films, reads the same bestsellers, hears the same radio speeches, same newspapers, etc., as the bourgeoisie. An intelligent working class girl can dress and look like anybody else, more or less. The gap between the classes is becoming increasingly narrow. If even the great millions are down below, the fact that the more favored representatives of their class can reach out to these things, makes the desire for them not utopian but something that can be got by 30% increase in wages. Thus the musical "renaissance" is part of the development of the proletariat.

Finally the logical method is important. Note how it happened. A Hollywood director notes the great success of the Tch'y Concerto in B Minor in The Great Lie.

He, *to make money*, works on a new kind of musical. (I'll tell you about him later.) He produces this film. Why? *Because the masses are craving for something new.*

Now if the masses didn't like it, the idea would have died. *They gobbled it up.* This proved that among all the novelties being presented to them *they wanted this.* Result, they get more and more. In two years they will know about *music.* Lenin would have loved this. He said once "We must get millions of reproductions of the great pictures and distribute them so that the proletariat will get culture—know what the bourgeoisie knows." Thus we see a great dialectical law—the capitalist seeking profit or Marlene Dietrich seeking publicity with pants, opens up an avenue through which the masses recognise something and at once appropriate it—with all sorts of distortions but yet a step forward. Thus the chance, the appearance, the accident is the capitalist seeking profit. The social necessity, the social movement is the mass grabbing at culture as today it grabs at everything it can.

So history moves. Where class relations are where they are today, things of accidental importance can have great repercussions. It looks like chance but it is social necessity, and every great necessity expresses itself by chance. We'll see this law often—it is a great discovery of Hegel and the lifeblood of Marxism.

O.K., prize pupil, you'll learn and learn and then one day you'll know more about it than I do. That will be a great victory for you and for me.

Love,
Nello

July 6, 1944

Well, my roaming pigeon, have you fluttered back home by now? Was the gay world bright? Were you moved to verse? Or did verse move to you? In other words, did you inspire verse? It need not have been written. It need not have been even spoken. It can be looked. To paraphrase favorite lines from Keats

Heard verses are sweet
But those unheard are
sweeter
Were you conscious as you came home, that you were making
the journey homeward to
habitual self

Keats again. A line which can be held up as a perfect example of what poetry is.

Did you? And did you? And once again, did you? Did all which you did amount to a good time? Did you get my messages? I sent them by mental wireless, one every five minutes and I only was that restrained because of war-time regulations. You *must* have got them, because they were carefully marked: Return if not delivered. If they are lying around unopened, they will be a terrific shock for who receives them. They may be blinded and deafened.

By the way, do you know—but of course you don't. So why should I ask? I have just had dinner and am back home sitting in my chair, leaning back and scribbling. It is 8:30. Very quiet. The radio murmers. I am just scribbling; facing me is Monica, my friend Monica; do you know her? I have been writing a poem for her. It is in the shape of an article. I made up my mind to celebrate Monica's coming of age—July 4—by doing the best I could, the very best, with an article I am writing. I have written and rewritten and shaped and reshaped. It is a dedication. You remember Anatole France's famous story Le Jongleur de Notre Dame. He was a contortionist, and he had been made to see the significance of the Virgin Mary for mankind. So they found him doing his tricks before her statue, alone in the cathedral. It was all he had to offer, he said. So I shall just slave myself to death over this article. It wouldn't even be addressed to you. But you will know when you read it. I wish you could see Monica as I see her. You can't. Nobody can. She is simply devastating. You know the truth of the object is in the eye of the beholder. It is a famous Hegelian paradox that when the see-er changes, the object also changes. "But in the alteration of the knowledge, the object also, in point of fact, is altered; for the knowledge which existed was essentially a knowledge of the object; with change in the knowledge, the object also becomes different, since it belonged essentially to this knowledge." (The Phenomenology of Mind, P. 142.) A tough passage, but true. So to see Monica demands knowledge. Lack of knowledge cannot see Monica. You see what Monica does to me? She stands opposite to me and makes me look up—Hegel. Vastly comic but true. She does other things to me too. A most wonderful creature, Monica. And, dear Constance, no jealousy of Monica. If I love her more than I do you, you introduced me. You know my weaknesses. I love you too. *Of course I do*. But I shall always think of you as having introduced me to Monica. About the knowledge and the object. When you (knowledge) change, the object (me) is also seen differently. Ah, you didn't think of that did you? Lady, beware of me with Hegel in my left hand and Marx in the other. I am dangerous. I carry out great encircling movements which in true Hegelian fashion transform themselves from subjective (the mind) into objective (the body). First encircle the lady's mind, then the lady's body. Pardon me, madame, this is philosophy. To believe the subjective alone is the philosophy of Berkeley, pure idealism, and according to Lenin, reactionary. And pure materialism, Hume, is also reactionary. But from the ideal as an indispensable concomitant of the whole, to the material, whence to the ideal on a higher plane, whence once more to the material on a higher plane, etc. That is the true dialectic. Marx adapted it to his purposes and I to mine. Look! Monica is smiling all over with approval. (That girl has sense.)

Well this can't go on forever though I wish it could. One day I am going to write you a letter—or rather to Monica. I shall order a quire of paper or a ream. I don't know which but the larger one. I shall also order meals for a month or two. There shall be relays of post-men at this end and at yours. And after a period of training I shall begin to write. God! how I shall write. What will it be all about? I shall illustrate. A famous Eastern monarch said he wanted to know the history of men. So he appointed a monastery of learned men to study and write. After 20 years they brought the results, numerous volumes on the backs of numerous camels. The king was busy and looked on this mass of material with distaste. Go and shorten it he said. Twenty years later an old abbot came again, with one volume on one camel. But the king was dying. Alas! he said. I cannot read it. I shall die without knowing the history of men. Sire, said the priest, I can tell it to you in one sentence. They were born, they suffered, and died.

So what will my long letter be about? Shall we save the quires or the reams of paper, the post-men, the writing and the reading? Yes. It will all say: I love you.

There as a true artist I should have stopped. But, alas, a man in love cannot be a perfect artist. His art suffers from a certain excess—an incapacity to tear himself away from communion—in ink and on paper, my God!—with the beloved. But Monica, who is my friend and counsellor frowns and signals: You should have stopped at the last page, and then smiling again, says. Stop at this one. I argue: P. 13. Bad luck. She is adamant. So I leave you.

Love,
Nello

[1944]

Glory be! Where did you spend Sunday! I discovered by my well-organised system that you were out of town. So was I. I spent it at Long Island. You remember the house on the L.I. sound from which I wrote you my first letter last August. I was on vacation there. Well! I came out this weekend, exhausted from an article I had written during the last few days. I got the book on Wednesday, read it W'y afternoon in about 2 hours (it is short), *wrote* 4000 words, then rewrote them, every one, and gave it in on Saturday. It dealt with material I have never written down before except to you, and to mobilise it in a complicated argument was not easy, particularly because I hadn't the faintest idea I would be called upon to use the material so soon. The trouble was that my hands are bad, and I had to write very slowly, like a kid of 6.

So Saturday night I arrive here and Freddie and Lyman [Paine] and a friend are here already and we have a good time. I am horribly tired and sleepy but feeling good—I love water, sea, river or lake and the company is very good. Three people come in, a worker who has done some studies in playwriting and his wife, a German refugee and a friend. The friend is a refugee too, lived and worked in Germany, Switzerland and France. He is an engineer but he studied at Geneva under Werner Sombart who wrote a famous History of Capitalism, before 1914, practically accepted Marxism and was a figure in his day, until he capitulated and joined the Nazis! Our friend did his doctor's theses on—guess. "The business side of the theatre in Germany." He did it as a relief from engineering! We talked of Europe and he speaks excellent French as he ought to, having studied at a French University.

The house is on the water and I lay in bed looking at the stars and listening to the water. It was wonderful. I remembered the weeks I spent here, when I first remade communication with you. It was quite an anniversary. Everything so still—a relief after the weeks of abusing Laski.

Next day, today, some English people turn up. They are living here. I spent a lot of time with them last summer. The wife knows Laski very well and we abused him heartily. We talked about England and the old Europe that is gone.

I know Normandy well enough. I spent a holiday there in the fall of '38. A country hotel—I was translating Souvarine.* I knew a girl in Rouen who came over every morning at 9, helped me in the translation. We had lunch and dinner and walked in the woods. I took her to the bus at 9, and went back and read Maupassant until I fell

---

* B. Souvarine, *Stalin*, trans. C.L.R. James (1939).

asleep. We would talk to odd people—but walked or sat around chiefly. Now that countryside is being torn to pieces. The trees will never grow again, not for decades. And the girl—I don't know if she is alive. I have her picture—I'll show it to you. She was half-Norwegian, half-French. I think she went to Norway. If she did then she has, I am almost certain, been killed in the underground movement. I know the type—very quiet, with a slow smile, but as determined as hell. She wouldn't give way to Nazis. I remember it all well because that very October I sailed for New York.

Later tonight I was talking with Lyman who has travelled all over Western Europe. I told him of how I loved Paris—of having dinner with a friend in a restaurant on the leftbank, from which we could see Notre Dame—the wonderful food, the quiet—the overshadowing cathedral. I asked him if I was mistaken, but I had an impression that nowhere did I ever feel the same atmosphere in America. He is American through and through, but he said no—it didn't exist here, and he told me of Florence, where Clarke's men will soon be. What will happen to Europe I don't know. I know what I hope, but *that* Europe is gone. Even if capitalism should last for some time, it can never be the same again. There are things I regret, things I would have loved to show you one day. I hope to God they do not destroy Paris—Bastille Square, the Tuileries, the Louvre, the Luxembourg, Champs Elysees, the Arc de Triomphe, Montmartre, Place Blanche, Place de l'Opera. The sense of history in every inch, the wonderful food, the social grace of the French people, their pride in their famous capital, bookshops (they say more in Paris than in the whole of England), the open-book shops on the Seine—a great capital throbbing above and when you look over the bridges on the Seine down below white sand and people—fishing! To say nothing of Versailles which is the most wonderful place in the whole world I think.

At 8 o'clock I went down into the little town and called you—it would have been nice to speak to you from here. But you were away so we talked again of the old world that is passing and I was impelled before going to bed to drop you a line from here.

But though old France is going, the France that meant so much to European civilization will not perish. It is being reborn in the spirit of the great masses of the French people. They resisted and they led the peasants and the middle classes. The other day a member of the Underground said at the Assembly in Algiers that France had never had a free uncensored press until the underground press. That sentence will live in history—it lights up the whole fraud of class relations. Today the French masses are not dominated by the French bourgeoisie—and they reject the Germans. Thus, with their minds clear and able to think their own thoughts, they have recreated the nation underground so to speak. The press is brilliantly written—I have read much of it—such wit, such style, such fire, and the merciless satire of the French. No advertisements, no libel action, no big overhead, anybody who has a typewriter and is prepared to risk his neck can write and publish, and everybody reads. There are literary journals, journals on the arts, poetry, music, political differentiation, all sincere, powerful, vivid, and free as never before, despite the soldiers of Hitler and the police of Laval. How Roosevelt hates them! He is terribly afraid of the people who are maintaining the best traditions of the nation, but in a revolutionary manner, potentially dangerous to all.

Voila. Enough. The night is mysterious, as it always is, though in town we lose the sense of it. You must come out here some time. They will be glad to have you I know. To sit on the little portico and look out across the water, mixing hosannas to

Nature divine with anathemas to the mosquitoes. There are not too many though, and we'll make still another contact with another aspect of life. Those in favour say Aye. Nello (loudly and firmly) Aye. And you?
N

Lyman left early this morning and Freddie and I are still here. It is raining—such a rain as you never *see* in town. It beat down upon the water and churned it up and wind and rain roared together at the little house and the big dark clouds closed over as if to say: Go ahead. Beat them up. Blot them out. I'll prevent anybody from seeing. For the few minutes I had a very strong sense of what primitive man must have felt in the face of Nature. For we can never recapture that sense of being entirely at the mercy of natural forces. For a moment we can get a flashback. That's all. But the mechanized world is too much with us. Now it's all over, for a time at any rate, and I can see at the other end of the sound the *aeroplane* hangar of the Vanderbilts. I shall go into the village and use the *telephone*, I'll take the *train* in; and *bus or subway* home, where I'll turn on the *electric light* and the radio. Nature in its original form cannot dominate man, but what W. B. Yeats calls "mechanized nature," i.e., capital, the means of production, that dominates man entirely now and he will conquer it as he conquered primitive Nature or this far more dangerous enemy will destroy him. Now somehow or other the poet must feel this menace and translate it into terms which his fellow creatures in this age will understand. People are waiting eagerly for a voice or voices. By poetry I mean nothing too narrow. It was said Rachel, the great French actress, that when she sang the Marseillaise you could see the gaunt, hungry, marching masses of Paris and Marseilles. Somehow we have to get into our bones today some feel, some sense of the great forces at work in modern society and then express them through our personality such as it is. This modern world; our world. As for a moment I caught a glimpse into the thought processes of primitive man, and even the Greeks, it made me see only the more clearly what our world is *not*. For Heaven's sake, do not misunderstand me. Shelley, the passionate idealist and lover of political liberty, wrote

> I am the daughter of
> earth and water
> and the nursling of the
> sky
> I pass through the pores
> of the ocean and
> shores
> I change but I
> cannot die

He was a master of Greek, Latin, German, French, Spanish and Italian. He hesitated whether to become a poet or a metaphysician. So that out of his intense awareness of his own time and his technical mastery and knowledge of his art came the power of his work, and its strangeness. I wrote for Heaven's sake, do not. . . . Sorry. It was rude. But, you know, one lives in a world of controversy, of statement and counterstatement and, alas, deliberate misstatement. So unless one is very careful or if one is in the least tired, the routine of the particular mind asserts itself and Juliet or Cleopatra becomes the recipient not of emotional responses and spontaneous communications of mind to mind and heart to heart but of arguments. "For Heaven's sake do not misunderstand me!" Too bad. But so we are, what with the world we live in and the things and persons it makes of us. Now, you, fair lady, by some trick of fate, humanise this intellectual barbarian that is me, not with the restraint and reserve that I formally exercise towards people in general, but for other reasons, quite, quite, other, other reasons.

Now I am going to do my work. Stern and unbending I shall leave dalliance aside, dalliance being you. Have you ever been called dalliance before? You told me you wanted me to write about politics. And I said yes, but. In reality I always write about politics, or nearly always. The ordinary arguments about this and that group are so sterile! Neither side understands what [the other] is talking about. A political attitude today is a philosophy of life. Little by little, and then with sudden flashes of insight that complete in a minute the work of a year one masters the fundamental movements of our age, sees it in relation to past and future and becomes intellectually and emotionally a part of it. So that when a man comes along and talks about a progressive capitalism, or another babbles about a new faith, or still a third talks about suppression of rights as if it were something you could turn on or turn off at will, then the reaction should be deep, immediate and not only social but personal. Otherwise all the goodwill and energy in the world means only mischief and corruption. Hence Laski talks the utmost nonsense about T. S. Eliot and James Joyce. So, however far I may seem to leave politics, I am really on that subject, i.e., an understanding of society. Once and for all, good—bye.

[June or early July 1944]

Darling,

Here is the stuff. *I want you to tell me very exactly what you think of it.* I have just got home—after calling you yesterday. Tired isn't the word. I was very sorry to think of you sitting tired after a day's work. I know it very well. You know I was tired too, but all I needed was a bath, whereupon I park myself somewhere and am full of jokes—really good ones, made up on the spur of the moment. Or early in the morning after I have had breakfast in bed—but then I saw you, sitting alone and tired. Anyway I came home—to a meeting in 30 minutes. I was tired. But as soon as I came in I heard a concerto—Bach, piano and orchestra. Now I'll tell you a secret. (I am full of bribes and secrets and mysteries, but only in a small circle.)

The secret is this. When the *first* movement of a concerto begins (piano concerto, Mozart or Beethoven), I sit impatiently waiting until the orchestral introduction comes to an end; then there is a pause and there follows the piano. The end of the orchestra, *the pause,* and the entry of the piano form for me a combination from which I receive a thrill beyond description. Why? God only knows. To further mystify the question, I then wait for the end of the last movement—usually a quick one. There is a cadenza, then a long trill, as part of the cadenza, and then, under the trill, the orchestra comes creeping back. Such is my life. Why? I don't know. But that is only half the story. This is the other half. I know in my bones that this "method" was worked out over the years until the composers and players arrived at this final stage. It signifies something. In concertos the soloist is "a leader," the orchestra "followers." There is some organic social "relation"—not a fact but a "relation" which is expressed there. What it is I don't know. But I know that I will know sometime. Forgive me for chattering so much about myself. I am tired that's all. And I am being very tired that's all, with you. My friends are here now. I shall not be tired. I shall be very energetic and decisive. Then when they are gone I'll be worse. Poor miserable me! But I shall go to bed, and read Shelley and read some of your poems. You know Shelley is at the opposite pole to modern verse, but yet is an almost perfect poet. I read him and get behind the lines—seeking *him*. And I read you for the same purpose. I am finding out a lot of things. And about your not being able to talk to me, Miss Redeemed. Let it slide. You will in time, if what is inside feels that it must come out. The number of things I have to tell you. Millions. They will last forever for new ones are always turning up. Good-bye. Final. You see my strong irresistible will.

Good—bye. Good—bye. Good—bye. Yours *firmly*.

N

[1944]

Well, Miss Firm, your letter made me feel very good, and very sorry for you. But more good than sorry. You would have had to face the conflict and the pain sooner or later. Either this or the gradual awakening to the fact that you were once more stifling yourself and that part of you which mattered most. It hurts. I know. I wish I could console you. You asked me to write. I feel the request like an arrow. I didn't because I decided not to. I thought I would wait a bit. But sure I shall write, and keep on writing. About the poetry let it wait. Once you are mistress of yourself and some inner composure restored, you will write terrifically. Nothing will stop you writing. You are a born writer. I told you so last year after your first letter. Remember? But the test of a vocation is the ability to submit to the drudgery it involves. The more you write and see your capabilities the more you will feel the necessity of getting more and more down to it. And remember this, please. Nothing I say to you about yourself, about anything that you do, is either untrue or complimentary. Some people use such extravagant expressions in every day life that one gets skeptical. And when a man is in love—then everything he writes must be sifted. But you will in time learn to trust my opinions about you, I hope; by which I mean not accept them but always take them at face value. I study politics and I study you. About the job, persevere. That's all. Never let anything pull you down or shift you. My experience—almost as many years as you have lived—is as follows. Life goes up and down—sometimes a long way up and a long way down. Always it changes. It changes because it is its nature to do so. Constant change. Now when it is going down the thing is to be conscious of the fact that it will go up, to lose as little nervous strength as possible and to be patient. Then one is ready to take advantage of the inevitable up-turn. That is what happens to the weak. They get demoralized and give up. Over and over again their chance was waiting round the corner. What I am mad at is that just now when everything should have been held in check so as to be sure you had all your strength for your work, you should have been thrown into this. That is, in my opinion, unpardonable. The translations of L [Lenin] are usually accurate. No one would dare, or has dared to alter what is already so widely published. But nothing in any library can alter certain facts.

L stated that the present period beginning 1914 is the period of imperialist wars and proletarian revolutions. This period we live in. He said that the decline of the system would continue into barbarism unless the proletariat overthrew it. This was the economic analysis of *Imperialism*. The political conclusions he drew in *State and Revolution*.

Now since 1917 we have had nothing else but continuous revolution, counter-revolution, economic crisis, and decay reaching now to barbarism.

1918 German Revolution
1918–1920 Continuous revolt all over Europe
1923 Ruhr crisis and revolutionary crisis in Germany
1926 British general strike
1927 Revolt in Austria
1925–1927 A tremendous revolution in China
1933 Fascism in Germany

The rest you remember more easily as you were grown up. In 1929 there was an economic crisis such as the world has never seen before. In 1939 came [World] War II which has almost destroyed Europe. Now who can look at this dreadful record of waste, blood, destruction, the barbarism and brutality and not see that the decline of the society has reached stages undreamed of fifty years ago. And what do our so-called Marxists* tell us. This is the time to re-build capitalism. This is the time to support the "progressive" capitalists. It is a shame for people to say such things in the name of Marx and Lenin. Here for thirty years, since 1914, we have had the system tearing itself to pieces. It never recovered from the crisis. Six years after, it "solves" the crisis by the war. The proletariat pays, in labor and in blood. The French bourgeoisie disgraces itself before the whole world. It abandons even the national defence. The workers take it up and write imperishable pages. To-day de Gaulle, nephew of Petain, ex-monarchist, a military maniac, is at his wits' end to check the appeal for drastic changes in French society. France is bankrupt. Isn't this the time to declare to the masses: Socialism. But our friends find all sorts of excuses. Nobody says to attack for the seizure of power to-morrow. But to stand in the way, to preach the regeneration of capitalism, that is a crime for which the proponents should pay to the utmost. Europe is crying for socialism. The old order is disgraced, bankrupt, ruined. The European peoples are ready for a change. Churchill and Roosevelt are the enemies of this change. And their ally is Stalin and all the Communist Parties. Who can argue against this?

It is a fundamental principle of Marxism that the workers must have their own party—their own Labor Party. It is the first stage to differentiation from the bourgeoisie. You have the Republican and the Democratic Party. We have a Labor Party. Perhaps the leaders are reactionary but the workers to know this must have their own party. That would be a tremendous step. It raises politics to the height of the conception of class. Are our Marxists for this. No, as every reactionary for 100 years, they are busy tieing [sic] the workers to Roosevelt. In 1940 when Russia and Hitler were allied, Browder said that the U.S. was the country above all suited for a quick transition to socialism. That is in one sense true—the productive system is magnificent. But this "quick transition" will not be accomplished except by workers.

---

* the Communist Party led by Earl Browder.

No one can make them act. Historical events do that. Maybe another big depression. But at any rate Marxists preach unceasingly the necessity for class consciousness, for independent labor action and organisation. The Marxist prepares the workers subjectively for what history prepares them objectively. But our "Marxists," what do they do? Prepare for cooperation with Morgan and other capitalists. That is to snap the rope for the workers' necks. All this was true for Browder as soon as Hitler joined Stalin. Then in June '41 it is not true because Hitler attacks Stalin. Now Stalin and Roosevelt are collaborating it isn't true. But if there were a split to-morrow between these two, then at once things would change. Isn't this degrading? Is there any reason to it except a complete subservience to the Kremlin and a refusal to study and to think seriously? Except for a brief interlude during the Hitler-Stalin pact this thing has been going on since 1935. It is now nearly 10 years. And the voice of socialism, the proletarian education for Leninism, that these people have betrayed, dragged in the mud, heaped with lies, and have been the bitter enemy and murderers when possible of those who advocated them. In 1905 and before and here and there afterwards, Lenin, writing about Russia used to say that a bourgeois-democratic revolution was on the order of the day. He was *wrong*. These old documents are now fished out and these statements used to prove that the thing for to-day is a bourgeois revolution. Those who preach this are rogues. Those who believe it are fools—honest, sincere, self-sacrificing—I don't care. I have sympathy for a worker who labors all day in a factory; or for an intellectual who has a merely sympathetic interest or "wishes to do something." But for anyone who takes politics seriously and professes to guide his or her life by it—No. Be serious about politics or leave it alone.

Anything you are in difficulties with, send to me. Just say, such and such a book, such and such a page. I'll find it and by phone or letter I'll help you out and you'll be able to riddle your opponent with bullets. Don't put up with this shameful nonsense for one minute. Stamp upon it, break it into bits, don't tie the bones in stacks in the sun; let them bleach out in the rain. To compromise or pamper or be tender to this is to encourage misery, deception, organised crime, to help to lead thousands upon thousands of fine people into ultimate disillusionment. Do you know the hundreds of thousands of people who joined these folks and left bitter, cynical, disillusioned? Look at what they have done to R. W.?* No, my precious, you were 1000 times right. The thing now is to take the offensive every time. You are not on trial. You haven't betrayed anybody. You are not spreading lies and nonsense. Once you decided to speak, speak out. Keep me in touch and together we'll strike a blow for liberty and honesty and intelligence and truth. They matter. That is why Marxism is so splendid and why young people and young writers need it to help them grow.

Courage, precious. I could hear from your voice last night you are doing fine. It hurts but anything else would hurt more. This will hurt. It cannot harm you. Whatever you wish, command me.

Yours always,
N

---

* Richard Wright suspected that his publisher's decision to drop the final section of *Black Boy*, which dealt with his Communist experiences, was due to its unwillingness to offend the Communist Party.

R. A.
Apt 2A
405 E. 55

[July 1944]

Let us make this abstract.* I prefer it that way. Further. Once the underlying principles are grasped, the individual application is always easy, given the necessary will.

A modern woman, a woman born after the Russian Revolution and World War I, a woman born in America, is a certain type of person. Her relationship with a man, even in her own mind, is something different from that of a person who grew up in a different age. The generation before her had to fight the theoretical battle for sex equality. This generation hasn't got to fight that battle, the theoretical one. *It grew up with it in its bones.* And if, and when, through personal weakness or difficult circumstances, it capitulated, *it was conscious of defeat.* A woman of 1924 who submitted to the dictation of another will, however much disguised, however sincerely (and I very very rarely accuse anyone whom I do not know, and few whom I do, of insincerity), when she submitted it was to a large degree a battle in the head; she had grown up fighting if she was a progressive woman at all in revolt. The Suffragettes fought a revolutionary struggle (and I am sure had a fine time). This generation is different. It has grown up looking upon this freedom as normal, as accepted. I have seen submission, after keeping itself quiet for a dozen years, break out in the most furious revolt. I know two women now, two sisters, in the thirties who tell me "that they don't want to be bothered with any husband." A man, yes. A man they must have. They will not stand any nonsense from any man. The men they meet are "normal" men—who want a wife and kids. What these girls are saying in reality is that they want a husband who does not relegate them to a secondary position where they have to submit their will to his. One has been married twice. The other once. They are not intellectuals. They have merely arrived at a certain maturity and unbeknown to themselves, are expressing the changed position of woman in the modern age. That is the ordinary, regular, normal, type of woman. Some of them make the best of it as wife *"because of the children."* Over and over again I see this and hear it. And I regret to say that many men I have seen want kids as the surest way to keep the wife quiet. Very very often, however, the woman loves the man. Her deepest instincts are aroused by him. And life in capitalist society being what it is, she suppresses something that is smaller for what is to her larger. Fifty years ago Shaw saw that very clearly in Candida. Fifty years ago! In backward England. And Candida was still a wife. Marchbanks wanted to worship her. She was to share the dramatic, high-lighted, ups and downs of the life of an artist, an adventure. That is still, very often, the conflict to-day.

But with the increasing opportunities that modern production (and the development of the ideas based upon it) gives to women, a new type of woman arises. She is called a career woman. The name is stupid but nevertheless very revealing. A man

---

* Webb's relationship with the actor Jack Gilford had broken down.

is never a career man. That is his right and privilege. He can have his career and the finest fruit of his successful career is wife and children. But the woman is called career woman because her "career" in modern society demands that she be placed in a subordinate position or even renounce the normal life. The social dice are loaded against her. And the plain fact of the matter is that the social dice are loaded, not only in the economic opportunities, *but in the minds of men*. The man cannot take it. I know my own sex reasonably well. And with the best will in the world a man, a good man, unconsciously demands that a woman submit to him. It is what he wants that matters in the end, not what she wants. Some men are crudely egoistic. Others are not. They believe in equality. But the practice of society dominates them. It must as long as they do not consciously oppose it, consciously and intelligently and always on the alert. Nevertheless the "career woman" can fight and given real ability, and luck, can *sometimes* win through.

But if a woman is an artist, then in the early days in particular, God help her! Virginia Woolf, no mean artist in her own way, and a woman who had every advantage, social and financial, has summed it up in the very title of her book on this subject. It is called A Room of One's Own. That is what a woman wants, who is an artist: a room of her own. It is the devil's own job to get it. A surprisingly large number of women who are physically and emotionally normal just go their way and take love as male artists do—a strictly subordinate affair, sweeping them out of themselves for a time, but pushing it into its place as soon as it interferes with them. But they are not satisfied with that, as a rule. But society being what it is, and men being what they are, they make their own adjustment. They do not think in social terms. They are not socialists. They are not acting for or on behalf of society at all. They are acting for themselves. They are seeking to live their own personal lives. But their personal lives are what they are because of social changes and social movements. Those who do it instinctively, who in all ways battle for their own way, are expressing a social movement which is highly progressive. Those who do it, conscious of what it means to society, and of what they represent, are very much stronger (the individual life becomes part of a collective movement). When they see it they express themselves more clearly to themselves and to others. They become in their own way, and in their own sphere fighters for a new society. It isn't that one does this or that "for socialism." No. One does this or that because in society as it is to-day, a substantial number of people are created who to express themselves and live the life that is in them, refuse to be bound by the old traditions and ideas. The very fact that these people appear in increasing numbers is a sign of the break-up of the old society and the emergence of the new, both of which always take place at the same time, and are one movement. It is not "I would do this—for you, but I have to do this for socialism." It is "I must do this, for myself, and not to do it is treason to myself, and to the others who are all fighting with me in this sphere, and to all the millions who in their various ways, are fighting their battles, which together constitute the struggle for the new society."

So it is for the "career woman." So much the more for an artist, a woman conscious of gifts. Socialistic or not, she must fight for the development of herself. It is a duty she owes to the fact that she has gifts. But, and this is your case, if the woman is completely conscious of the social movements, identifies herself with one part of it, and finds that she has a talent which can help, then that is argument enough. Nothing must stand in the way. Nothing at all. There are two reasons, both intimately connected. First one has a duty, the highest and most difficult type of duty, the self-imposed, which springs from no external compulsion. It comes from "inside." But this powerful impulse from "inside" is merely the response of a resonant, sensitive personality to what is taking place outside. That is the essence of the personal question. As a result of this, however, an individual becomes more powerfully individualistic than ever. The stronger the collective force which the individual is expressing, the more powerfully individualistic the individual becomes in that he or she cannot suppress that individuality for another individual. One may try to, may succumb to temptation, to strong personal feeling, one may even for a time feel reconciled, one may even gradually become reconciled, and be even "happy." But if the original impulse is strong and organic to the personality—then a hell of a mess is the result. There is always the gnawing consciousness of a wasted life, frustration, sometimes a resentment that lies dormant and grows with the years. Candida can give up and live. But if Candida were herself an artist and a creative person, then utterly apart from the sense of duty (which is particularly strong in an artist in 1944, with a social bent), apart from that, I say, purely from a personal point of view, there is danger. To put it crudely, the very attempt to secure a "happy," "personal" life may be the road to life-long personal unhappiness. It all depends upon the personality.

But the personal life remains. It will not be suppressed. If suppressed it wears the artist down. Of that there is no question at all. Some compromise is necessary. It is always so in life. The point is: which matters most to the individual person. Now before I go on with this, I should say that the ultimate decision as to whether a particular choice was successful or not does *not* rest with the person. If society moves forward, the collective movement is fighting, great decisions being taken, great sacrifices borne, the person who has "retired" is miserable. If, however, the social hopes are set back, no progress is being made, then "retirement" is more acceptable.

That being understood the personal question can be looked at separately.

You love a man, but you have your own life to live, you in particular have a special life to live. You want both. That depends on you—on what you really want. But in the society in which we live it depends far more on him. What does he want of you? And by him I mean your man in general as well as in particular. I don't know. You will have to find out. And it may or may not be easy. Forget for a moment what you want. What does he want of you, this man of yours, be his name Jack, Willie, Nikolai, or Jean. He loves you. Which you? 99 men out of 100 would be satisfied with you as you are. You are young, vital, terribly attractive, a perpetual delight to have around, to make love to, to take out, to have a kid or two or three, to be constant companion; to be "progressive," to develop mentally up to a certain point, to be "progressive" to share your husband's "progressive" activities; to be his second half. You can even, within limits, have a career (although as far as I can see the average "career woman" has the career pretty well based *before* she commits herself). Now if that is what your man wants—and it is quite legitimate and normal—then except you are very very lucky, you are in a bad spot. You may overcome it—chiefly by having an exceptionally brilliant *material* career, that shines so brightly that you become the dominant partner.

Does a man want anything else? Some men do. Not many, but some. Very often, or quite often, a man of not great ability himself, is dazzled by his wife. He is anxious to see her become "something." "Something" is one thing to one man, and one thing to another. Here I can, I hope without prejudice, interject a personal note. For me, especially after the last few months you have been here, you as wife and mother, and general better half, attractive as the prospect would be, would be a terrible let-down. I trust to your good judgment and understanding to follow me when I say that even if such an opportunity was offered to a man who has lived in rooms or an apartment alone for 12 years, I would unhesitatingly reject it. I see my intimate personal friends and associates, I am older and more experienced than they. They look to me for intellectual leadership. But all of them are personalities in their own right. I love them for themselves but each one is himself or herself because he or she pursues some goal, with me but independent of me; every year there is a tremendous growth, things done, things learnt, the natural gifts constantly expanding. I have watched one now for 10 years, the other two for three or so. Their growth and development have been terrific. They are my friends, I respect them enormously. (Both are *very very* fortunate. They have *no* financial troubles. But they would overcome even those.) When we meet and talk there is no condescension neither open or implied. Do you think I could stand that my wife, a woman with gifts precious not only to herself but to what I believe in, should be wife and mother and "very intelligent—she understands all her husband's work." For me *No*.

But I am an extremist. A political extremist—not in this case. It is because *that is what I want*. If I thought it "right," but didn't feel the personal need for it, I would not, could not stand up for it. I explained this to you a long time ago. I want a woman who is a personality in her own right—the more powerful the better, the more removed from my own field the better. I can stand up to her. I am not afraid. Now all men are not as extreme as I am. (I know one or two gifted women. Unfortunately I don't like to look at them just for the pleasure. In these matters I trust my instinct.) If they are not as extreme as I am, yet men are on one side or the other. I know men who think more or less as I do. I know three or four *in my own circle*. Rae's [Raya Dunayevskaya] husband is one. He is no Marxist. Given this, sometimes it's hard for him; at times he feels the strain, terribly. But so far, he is for her, stands by, helps her, would love to have kids, etc. But he sees Rae's ability and fine character. He loves her. He loves her for her sake. The struggle never stops. (He, by the way, is a man of *exceptional* ability.) But he wants to see Rae be what she can be. As I say, I know others. But they are few. Now you have to find out, and decide. I don't mean to-day, to-morrow or next week. But find out if your man, whoever he is, wants, above all, you as he knows you (and that is enough for most men) or you as you want to be. If he loves you for your sake, not what he *says*, but what he really needs for his own sake—then despite all difficulties you can make it. If not————. Another way to put it. Does he need Constance or Monica? (It is very very difficult to see Monica and to know her value.)

Now a last point—philosophical, but for that reason, more profound than the rest. To-day our world—for the conscious ones—is becoming more and more fluid on the surface and more serious below. Take as an example verse. Where before the rigid forms disciplined the poet externally, to-day the free verse gives an enormous range, allows far greater power, but is a trap for those who have not got a powerful, internal discipline. In reality it is much, much harder to write superb verse in the modern style than in the old style. "Society" gives more privileges even to the writer but demands greater responsibilities. Same in social life. Formal manners are much looser. The result is that real social distinction depends far more on character and natural consideration and tact than when everyone was a little Emily Post.

Marriage is the same. The old relationship was simple. The woman was to be faithful. The man was not to neglect her. They compromised, etc. But the lines were broadly established. To-day, *among people who can afford it*, that is going. Both he and she have a greater freedom. She has a career (sometimes). She goes around with other men if she wants to, up to a point. They often live separate lives. But this freedom only means that the mutual bond below is infinitely more powerful than anything the old relationship could show. From the very beginning it is firmer. Many girls I know have taken life as it comes until they meet someone and said "Here is what I have been looking for. Here I stay." *Everywhere in modern life it is the same.* And that is what must be understood, Miss 24 years-of-age American, with advanced ideas and a certain talent.

Now there are one or two purely personal things. To live this type of life takes some money. It can be done, without much. But as a rule it needs money. It calls for much self-denial. Some can't take it. In the end they seek another partner if the other is too far away, or too distracted. But altho' this is a problem, it is not the main problem. A man is always ready to say "My work demands that I go to Europe for a year." Behind that is the idea that he is *supporting* the family. But if his wife says "My work demands that I leave you for 6 months" then he as a rule can't see it. He can see it if his wife is a gifted person, *who is making a success that other people can see*. Or if he genuinely thinks she has possibilities of being such a success. But otherwise he says "Why bother?" Only what he actually says is "Darling, I can't bear you to go. Think how I will miss you." All I can say is that *the* test is whether man or woman wants the best of the other to such a degree that they bear being apart for the sake of the times when they are together. And life isn't terribly cruel. There always come good breaks, when people have long times. No. It is like the professional revolutionary. Life is hard, full of denial, but any other life lacks so much that you cannot dream of it.

Lastly you and me. I do the best I can. I hope this is of value to you. I believe in people understanding things fully. I think that with this you can make the case that you have to make. I have an idea from the extracts you read to me that you are not putting your side well. There is only one reason for that. You are not *seeing* it clearly enough but only *feeling* it. From your verse I can see how strongly you feel. Artists are above all people of feeling. (And revolutionaries too, that I am learning every day.) But you should now be able to express yourself as an individual, for we are all individuals, but in a more objective manner. Also you should be able to meet arguments more firmly, clear away the fog which personal passion can always place over a discussion of this type. Do you see it more clearly now? If you don't, tell me and I'll try again. The chief thing is to understand yourself. Once you do and can express yourself clearly then you should do everything possible to go back there [to Hollywood] by the means you mentioned, Harry C's trip. Don't go in a confused state of mind. Go because you want to. But go also because you have to settle these things—for your own peace of mind. I hate to have to tell you that. But if you meant nothing to me I would tell you the same. If I had any claim on you, then we both would go. But I haven't. So I try my best to be as objective as possible. If I don't succeed completely it is because I am leaning over backwards to see your case as objectively as you deserve. You see I want Monica, not Constance, though Constance is wonderful enough, enough to tempt any man.

Keep your head high, cornstalk fashion. Do not settle for less. However much the pain and the frustration, they are but phases of life and can be borne and overcome, and not too much harm done. But your own inner self that is just blooming, that you can harm. Don't. You can harm it in two ways. By capitulation. I don't for one moment suspect you of that. But you can do it too by a compromise which will gradually close in on you. Your road is hard enough, to be Frosty, Constance, and Monica. Curiously enough I love all three; I loved Constance because among other reasons, she had a touch of Frosty, and a lot of Monica. She should never lose all three. But Monica must discipline the other two. Monica is very precious, one in a million. And the only way for Monica to win is by trusting her instincts, *but* at the same time explaining herself to herself very clearly. Then she acquires confidence and can meet all demands, can even compromise (for we all have to), but only up to the point where the compromise is not dangerous. All I can say is: I love you. But not to bother you or bring pressure to bear on you, don't take it that way, but to help you. Father-complex I suppose. We all have obscure needs. Have you ever looked for yours?

[1944]

What is a poet? I'll explain. When I lived in the W. Indies I lodged once with a woman, a Mrs. Roach. She was not educated. She spoke English with the French patois accent of the peasant people. She was a gentlewoman, but language was not her strong point. She had a brother, a drinking, shuffling, guitar-playing idler, Francis. Francis would not work and what was worse got himself one day into trouble with the police for keeping a brothel or helping to keep one. Mr. Roach was the City Cashier, and this would have meant a terrific scandal. And Mrs. R, a woman with a high sense of social propriety and a very moral woman in addition, was outraged. Passing through the yard I heard and saw her talking to Francis.

She had a shawl around her shoulders and she stood straight like a tragic actress. She said "Our parents brought us up together Francis, spent time and money on us. But from youth you went your gambling, guitar-playing way. Wine and women, that has been your life. You have disgraced yourself and disgraced us enough; and now you may have to go to jail for keeping a brothel. Look at the white hairs on your head, Francis? Are you never going to change? Thank God, our dear parents don't live to see you as you are," etc., etc.

She had never spoken like that before. I never heard her speak that way again. But for the moment she had uninterrupted fluency, a wonderful rhythm, dramatic pauses, etc. I, a very literary person in those days, listened amazed. What caused it? Intense emotion, it was bursting in her, a subject she knew well, had long meditated upon. At various times she had said this and thought that about Francis; other people had discussed it with her. Then under a powerful stimulus, this last disgrace, she became for the moment a poet. She was on a very high level of emotion and to batter Francis into some sort of discipline she needed a very high level of expression. She found it.

Perhaps for once in her life—perhaps two or three times. Then she slipped back to her old level.

The poet, my dear, is so constructed that this height which ordinary people reach only on rare occasions, is the general level of his or her consciousness. That is the quality of the personality. Mrs. Roach *had* to speak to Francis. If she didn't she would burst. You know the expression. Same with the poet. He has to speak. But inasmuch as we are social creatures his need of expression takes certain forms which others have used—thus he or she writes verse, free or rhymed, wants it published in a magazine or journal of poetry—all the things which poets do. But all that is merely form. Two thousand years ago he would have played a harp and sung songs. The thing that matters is the urgent need to express the personality. There is nothing wrong, in the slightest, with that. You are a piece of earth, matter, with a highly charged consciousness. By means of such, when the consciousness is of a superb character, e.g., Marx, Hegel, Shakespeare, Tolstoy, Michaelangelo, society as a whole is moved forward. Science, art, literature, philosophy these are part of the means of production. Yes, exactly that. People see their world and understand it and themselves better and humanity moves forward. But the personality has greater or lesser gifts—nerves, will, desires, strong heart, etc. But the society around shapes the person. A great poet in the 18th century can do no better than Pope. The age is the "Age of Reason." Shakespeare would have been a Pope. We express ourselves best when we express some powerful social current. One day I'll tell you how closely Shakespeare was related to his time, to the rising bourgeoisie, how much his work owes to it. He lived among them—he merely expressed the tumultuous thoughts they were thinking. He was superbly gifted. But his age was bursting with new ideas, new desires, new sensations. It educated him in general. But he educated it in particular. By merely living among his people he learnt what they had to say. His high tension, his need for expressing it, dramatised it so that they could see and hear and feel. From highest to lowest that is the relationship between the artist and his age. But of recent years, this relationship has become clarified to an unusual degree.

People all belong somewhere. If an artist expresses the people around him, then he expresses the violence, the class-consciousness, the political clash, the soul-shaking problems of the day. For good or ill that is the age we live in. The artist may express it, in fact, will express it how he likes. But if he is to be fertilised by the life around him, then this is what he will express. Arthur Koestler, Malraux, Richard Wright, the Lewis-Auden school, even that dancer Pearl Primus, their work is directly social and political. I cannot conceive of any other work to-day.

Now, sister, that sets you an awful problem, and that is worrying you and will continue to worry you. And as I learn more about you I am more convinced than ever that deep down there is a terrible conflict raging inside of you. Pop (Mrs. Olive's husband, you remember?) listened to your poetry and told me the same; he said that whatever happened to you, this conflict would continue to tear you to bits. Why do I write so freely? Because you are you. I have confidence in you. Whatever you do I am standing by. I not only love you for me, but now you are something valuable, precious, *whom our side needs*. I didn't know that until I saw your poetry. Finally, I have been through it myself. And I wish I had known.

Now as I have said I believe you are finely gifted—you are a natural for poetry; gift for phrasing, quick emotional response (that's your stomach trouble), and power.

That is wonderful. But, miracles pile up, you are irresistibly drawn to "the people." The future is theirs. Nobody, or very few, have expressed the tumultuous ideas, sensations, etc., which are about to burst out from them. Poets haven't bothered with them in the past. Now if I were a poet I would go down on my knees and praise God that he (bless His kind heart) had given me these two precious gifts. But in addition you have, I think, a fine critical sense—for the best criticism is a form of creation. Your weakness is a lack of formal education in poetry. That, however, is the simplest weakness to correct. And your critical sense will help you here. With will and effort you can learn. Now this as I say is a conscious age. The things to be learnt are no longer theoretical. All the great social and political truths are being lived and experienced. To-day for example the criticism of literature demands an understanding of society. You being what you are can learn rapidly and your social ideas and poetry can be fused so that your whole expression of yourself can, in time, acquire enormous power. I for one will stake my critical judgment of society, of art, and of personality on you.

Furthermore, and this is so important for you and your difficulties, all this is stirring inside of you. You may not be totally aware of it. But if it is to come out it is inside—and as I read your first verse I know what must be going on inside of you. You need to express it and the world, the big world, Warsaw, China, French babies, the American workmen you pass in the streets, all are hammering at you, telling you they want you to say something for them, they want you to sit and study so as to be able to say it well, they want you to read some books—they haven't time, knowledge, nor the gifts—and tell them what is in them and what these books mean. They are telling you to come and live near to them, be with them so that they can teach you and you teach them. They tell you—I was only a medium—come and live, free, independent with all its responsibilities—the new life we all want to live. That helped you to break with Jack, to refuse to satisfy his needs at the cost of so much. This world is calling to you.

But you are caught in another. The particular profession you have chosen—acting—is tied up with that world. You could perhaps compromise with the Stalinists and make the best of both. But alas! the very honesty and simplicity which is one secret of your poetry—*particularly for this age* prevents you from making that compromise. You cannot have it both ways. A poet may be a very dishonest person—but he cannot be dishonest about the sources from which his poetic inspiration springs. That is death. So you are torn, and the fight goes on inside of you. Further, you are young and lovely and the bourgeois world is ready to do a lot for you. I do not mean merely dells of refrigerated coolness. No. But a civilized existence, pleasant surroundings, interesting people (not middle-aged millionaires), but people who have done things, seen things, who do them still, travel, opportunities to learn—and charming intelligent attractive people, a happy home and children. Only a fool who didn't know the world and some people who have looked at these things from the outside and whose envy has turned to hate, only such people would underestimate these things. The only people who can push them aside, cheerfully and easily, are people who are dominated by an idea and a need for expressing it that is far more powerful than even the opportunities which bourgeois society offers to ability or gifts that it can use.

So in the heart of my dearest, very much loved Constance, the precious Monica has taken a seat and refuses to be driven away. She has won one great victory, a victory that set all the bells ringing and the great outside world cheering. It was our victory. They don't all know about it yet. But they will soon. It leaves you shaken. But it should. It isn't *a personal* conflict. No, no, no my darling. It is a social conflict that is expressing itself in you with great intensity, precisely because you are what you are. *Noblesse oblige.* The greater the gifts, the greater the responsibilities.

What is to be done? First of all to see it, recognise it, analyse it, so that it doesn't wear you out inside. There are shades and angles I don't know. But by and large I think that is it. Secondly, get physically settled. I am so glad you have moved. You want to be somewhere away from what is past, knowing that you are going to be there some time, and thus giving your particular temperament a stable base. Then go steadily away at your modelling and acting. I repeat. Go steadily away at it. Nobody can take away from you the power to write. *If you get settled*, then you can read and write as you have been doing—that body of work, all things considered, is an amazing achievement, and I choose my words. The conflict will continue of course, but if you face it, frankly, calmly, and openly, and just let things work themselves out, you will be doing the best thing possible under the circumstances. You need to be settled so that in your spare time you do another burst of poetry—it will be deeper, wider and more splendid this time I am sure. Then you will see your way consciously and make decisions as the conflict presents itself. Now here, now there, now in this form, now in that. *The thing is to know.* And count on me. At present what I want for you is to see you get a part on Broadway. Once you get it, you wouldn't have so fierce a conflict any more. Sounds funny. But it is true. Proof? I wanted to write books. But as soon as I had written one or two, I was "happy." I said "Now I can do as I please. I wanted to write. I can if I want to. But now, after two years of conflict, I know what I want to do."

And sweetheart, if I had wanted to go on writing, nothing, at least nobody, could have persuaded me otherwise. You have your own life to live. Live it your own way. But try to see it all round and give the best that is in you a chance. That's all. You are everything to me Monica, Constance, and even that gay baby-doll Frosty. There isn't a man living who doesn't appreciate even Frosty too. You are all three. No accident in the vulgar sense has sent you my way and sent me yours. You and your career mean a lot to me. Near to me or far, I need you for myself and my own development. So take it easy. Face the problems as they come. And I shall always look at them from your point of view. And I do it because that is what I want.

All my love,
Nello

July 10, 1944

Part II (Continuation)
You and I, and all of us are manifestations of our age. The sensitive, active ones are acute manifestations. The C.I.O. is a manifestation and the New Deal and Wendell Wilkie, that Republican with a "New Deal" program. They all express the basic problem of our times. What is to be the future of society? When Henry Wallace says that the coming century is to be the Century of the Common Man, he expresses it. Wallace, Vice-President, would not dare to say that without the permission of the

President you may be sure. You and I know what the real solution is. The common man must continue to complete democracy. I and some others have taken an uncompromising stand. By economic analysis we maintain that it is impossible to have an advanced *economy* with a totalitarian *state*. The abolition of private property does not make an economy progressive. Workers' democracy or economic crisis and reaction.

This desperate conflict is not in books. It is in life and everywhere it expresses itself. As I say in Fascism, in the New Deal, in the thousands who join the Stalinist party, and in you and in the heart and life of every single person. None of us escapes it.

Now you, young, idealistic, serious, American, with certain poetic gifts (to confine ourselves to that) begin at 15 and react to society in a certain way. At 20 you feel a pull in another direction. The reasons do not matter now. You are pulled away and you do the things you did. You say you felt like a traitor. Good for you. But your personal life is tangled up in it. Meanwhile you have been writing verse, from some inward need. What need? You write chiefly love poems, that show talent, a capacity for writing. But the conflict now shows itself in another place. You want your independence as a woman. You know I presume that that in its way is a struggle for the new society, small, isolated, insignificant but it is just such, multiplied by millions, that make a social movement.

You decide to come away. It will help your profession. It will help your struggle for independence. But now on the train or immediately after, you write two poems—which show a tremendous advance and show real power. Language, images, sense of structure, dramatic contrast are stimulated by the conflict. You in your own individual life feel the pressure of the forces and in your contradictory position become a manifestation of them.

However some people react powerfully to one side and are stimulated by that. Some react to another side. You show every sign that your powers are stimulated by one force—the revolution.

During the last few weeks my dear Constance you have written more valuable stuff *as poetry* than all the rest. In every sense the range of your impulse and its form of expression are deeper and wider than before. You are deeply, deeply aware of the change.

> But I am not returning
> I shall grow
> You saw lace edge and
> too late feel *relentless*
> blue
> I cannot be silent
> I am not afraid
> and out of me shall
> return
> A *new* life
> I defend you because
> You are *my life*

I perhaps *gave you
up* to-day....
But I gave you up
I see the path...
and see it is mine
the path I *must* follow
my feet follow
Their pointing....
My life is no longer
Mine
I gave it....
Though my love
Asks not
My returning
I cannot go....
I must not return....
I must remain alone.

The other three poems are completely *objective* descriptions *of other people's behavior or states of mind*. You do not come into them at all. The best of them is a perfect fusion, perfect as far as the fusion goes of yourself as poet and the workers' struggle. That poem can be printed in any modern anthology. Of that I am quite sure. Do you now see yourself as a medium of expression of contending forces? The forces appear sometimes in the shape of people with definite aims and desires. But they are the expression of forces nevertheless.

And do you note that *for you*, the definitive victory of one particular force in you, suddenly released capacity in you, strengthened your talent, drew you out of yourself and projected your ideas and desire for *self-expression* on the expression of objective things? It does *not* matter that the description of objective things came first. You were following a certain line of development. Even on such short evidence, and of course your whole past, it is clear where your artistic path lies. You will, I am sure, write love lyrics again. Mayakovsky, the Soviet poet (have you read him?) wrote some amazing ones. But your poetic impulse and stimulus even for writing lyrics will come from your inner sense of harmony with something. Read again that list of quotations I made. Any *stranger* of critical insight after seeing the repeated insistence on—I cannot be silent—I am not afraid—I shall not return, etc., would know at once that not only an emotional but an intellectual crisis had been reached and passed.

Now if you want to do justice to yourself you have got to stay where your heart tells you. All poets do not need that type of stimulus. Keats did not. But Shelley would have died rather than give up the hopes and interests and passions that made his life. Byron the same. Both died in exile in bitter conflict with their own people. You may write good verse, even poetry, about other things and about a different life. You can be a fine actress and a poet as well. That is not at all impossible. If poetry is in you to the exclusion of everything else then it will mould you to its will. The extent of your talent I do not know. Nobody can know that, though for my part, to-day, without seeing another line, *if you decided to make writing your main, your only purpose in life*, I personally would stake my reputation on your ultimate success. But whatever the degree of your talent, it is my confirmed opinion that for it to develop you need a mind completely free to follow what it is so obvious is your direction. Easily done? My dear, dear Constance, life is not so simple. Contending forces are not so easily overcome. In fact the opposite forces are of enormous power, particularly if you are in the professional position you are in.

Who are the people you will meet? What are the books you will read? Who are the intimate personal friends with whom you will discuss life and art and society? The people whose lives will influence you and whose lives you will influence, books, music, pictures, love, passion, friends, vacations, parties, social analysis of one's self and one's friends, long intimate conversations, the significance of which sometimes come back only long long after. These for you, as a writer are the formative years. Cut me out of the picture please. Cut Jack out. Your problem still remains. You agree? I think you do. The main reason of course is our friends. The circle which "the left" creates for itself at any critical time like this has been corrupted and poisoned by them. They are deliberately destroying the conception of workers' democracy. I shall always remember Richard Wright telling me how isolated he felt. But he was lucky enough (and strong enough, for I hear now that he fought them all the time) to go his own way and reach maturity before the blow fell on him. You will have it hard. *You can count on me.* But to give your mind a chance to grow and develop is not going to be easy for you.

That a man says that he is completely amenable to your following your own path means little. Just you think for a moment and see if that settles your problem for the next few crucial years as far as your education, in the widest sense of the development of your personality, is concerned. A talent needs room and warmth to grow. I repeat. The extent of your talent only time and work can tell. I repeat again. If you came to me and showed me this work and I didn't know you from Adam I would say. Writing is your career. Roll up your sleeves and get down to it.

But there is more to your particular case, I being what I am. You remember my telling you in Part I that you are an American who had grown up after the October Revolution and in the intellectual atmosphere created by that tremendous event the world over. That always interested me in you. I told you that, I think, before I knew you even wrote. (You will find that the things I say I mean.) Now after many years I have started reading poetry again. I tried to explain to you a certain sequence the other day, Kant to Hegel and then Feuerbach and Marx using their technique. I see it in Eliot to W. J. Turner and Dorothy Wellesley and then I see the school of Cecil Day Lewis, Auden, Spender, MacNeice, Madge using the technique discovered by these writers and most of them, embracing communism and writing from that point of view. This is a profound movement in history and art. The writers who reject society make great discoveries in *method*, which their followers in time, who accept a social regime or part of it, apply in *content*. Now, as I see it, the Auden, MacNeice bunch are all about 40 years [behind] or so. They are English gentlemen, Oxford, Cambridge, classical culture, great learning, etc. That generation was never a part of the working class. They accepted communism as a social philosophy. They would I am sure have fought on the barricades. But they remained intellectuals who had come to an idea. It was not their fault. They wrote finely. They expressed their generation. To-day, disillusioned with Stalinism they are or seem intellectually dead. They are not identified as L. T. was with the fate of the class.

I feel all over and my recent studies point in this direction, that the generation which grew up in childhood after 1917 is different. Poetry has another stage to move and they will make it, for there are always poets. This generation of poets, if rebels, will be completely a part of the workers. They will not be sincere intellectuals who will come to the movement. They will identify themselves as individuals with it. Your poem about you being their voice is a beautiful confirmation of this idea which I had before. But fine as that is, the process must I think go further. I believe that just as Marx, the fastidious, learned, highly cultivated, intellectual did the profoundest abstract thinking but always as a member of the mass movement, so I think the new poets to amount to anything, will be cultivated, study their art, but see themselves always as *a part of the movement* which Auden, etc., never were. This does not mean joining a party. You know my views on that. But it means a *complete permeation of the mind with the philosophy of the movement*, a sense of oneness with it as it rises and falls, *familiarity with its problems*, knowledge of and feeling for the strength and weaknesses of workers in general and individual workers. It means in other words a declaration of war against bourgeois ideology in one's own mind. Now here you become very very precious to me. If anyone had told me about you and you had no teeth, weighed 180 lbs and were 5 ft short, I would have come to see you. For I think your whole bent is towards just such a development. I believe that (let me put it carefully) a type of talent such as yours, with the social orientation in you that shows itself so strongly, is just the type which will do the best kind of poetic work in the coming period. Furthermore I believe that such work, if finely done, would prove itself a powerful *concrete help to the cause*. What the extent of the talent is no one can say. But it is of a type and you are the sort of person, who with the necessary *opportunities and devotion* have the best possibility of clearing out a new path and giving your undoubted talent the best room to develop. Am I clear? I shall return to this in the third and last letter. Now as to your being an actress, that would not by itself prevent you writing fine verse or even fine poetry. Not at all. It is possible that the emotional creative power may be expended in histrionic creation. That is possible. Many poets and great poets, for years did other things and other jobs. But they were not draining their emotional power by an art so exhausting as acting. But there is another side to this question, a social side. The modern specialisation is a sign of social degeneration. Engels points out that in all great critical periods of history, the "pure" writer had no place. In all the great stirring periods, the writers were all doers too. Shakespeare was worse than an actor. He was an actor manager! Walter Raleigh, Essex, Thomas More, Erasmus, Luther, Donne, Milton, were men of affairs and of literature. So was Lassalle, Goethe and a dozen others. These were men of enormous power of course. The point that Engels makes and he is perfectly correct is that the *social forces* in turmoil manifested themselves even in gifted individuals in various ways. There is no earthly reason why you shouldn't act and write, though undoubtedly the best thing, *in all probability*, is complete devotion to so exacting an art as poetry. That, however, time and your own development will decide.

No, your problem is the problem of finding and keeping the personal and social milieu which will enable your particular gifts and your very special and very very precious orientation to develop. I know and knew some of these younger writers. Not one of them has the "feeling" for the workers that you have. I read their work, have been reading it in recent weeks (I owe that to you, as I owe so much to you). Gifts they have and fine qualities some. But somehow your temperament, your early experiences, your life from 15 to 20, have given you an impetus in a certain direction which I believe gives you a special opportunity to develop yourself and to make a real and very rare contribution. The trouble is as I have said, to be able to develop it, and that has nothing to do with acting.

Finally, darling, one more literary point, you have another field which is almost untouched and where I think your talent would find a wonderful opportunity to make the best of itself. That is the Negro question. The writings of white people on this are an obscene joke. This is not surprising because nearly all the Negro writers are almost as bad. They are bourgeois, and black or white, their writing is cursed by the bourgeois mentality. Wright got away from it and his work is a testimony. Now *L. T. understood it to its bones*, through his great knowledge of history, of social manifestations and his intuition. Long ago I spotted you and used to tell you that you could do great work here. I see hints of it in your few lines on it. It is an almost virgin field, of enormous importance, and you have an emotional insight, which, with *study and experience* could give your talent a great opportunity. You have to open your mind, to give your imagination room and scope. But that again is not easy for you.

So then there is the question as I have thought it out, as objectively as I can. Naturally, in so uncertain a question as art where the subconscious plays so large a part, *the most closely reasoned arguments can go very far astray*. But I think I know you a little and I think I know something about the relation of the artist to society, particularly in this *highly conscious age*. I think I know something too about the artistic needs of the age in which we live. Your gifts are yours. All I am trying to do is to indicate an arena, a field of endeavour, a *method* of progress, by which you being what you are and the world being what it is, you can best develop the talent that you undoubtedly have.

As I say, it will be hard. Anyway you take it, you will have great struggles. But all students and my own lifelong experiences too, personal and otherwise, have taught me that only through struggle is strength attained. The chief thing now is for you to get a good acting job? Meanwhile take my word for it, you have made such rapid strides in a few weeks along with all your other problems that I am amazed and delighted beyond all expectation. You seem suddenly to have opened a closed window that opens up extraordinary and unsuspected vistas. I was your friend for your own sweet sake. But now I have a duty to do all in my power that will make available what you have to contribute. Small or large, it is genuine and therefore precious. And this responsibility I feel here neither to you nor to me, but for its social value in a striving world. Next time I shall take up the final question of the *general* direction in which you should read or at least investigate possibilities. It involves again first your being an American. Very very important this here, and secondly how best to *strengthen without narrowing* your particular orientation. Finally there is the connection indicated between the closely related art of writing verse and speaking verse—*which is the actor's business*. For some years now I have had ideas on this question based on social analysis and reflection on the literature of past times. I'll tell them to you and they may start you thinking—you are more than anyone else ready for them.

You know I have three special "pupils." There is Bill Williams. He is a Ph.D of

Oxford. He has already written and published some brilliant work and this fall will appear a *superb* book on Capitalism and Slavery. Grace Lee is another. She is also a Ph.D Columbia in Philosophy. She is Chinese and I hope within a few months that she will have ready a book on Dialectical Materialism. That question we are going to settle once and for all. The third is Rae [Raya Dunayevskaya]. Her special field is Political Economy. As soon as time permits she is going to settle down to a definitive work on the American economy. When you see Bill's book you will understand the quality of the work that is being done. If you have time I can show you essays by all of them. First class work and they are all just beginning. Now I am as confident about you as I was about them and when I began with them, with every one, *they had no real idea of their own talents*. Now in their particular fields they are all smarter than I am and teach me things I could never have had time to learn by myself. Once you can manage those difficulties that I have indicated—and I can assure you, darling, they are very *real*, I can promise you that in a year or two you will not know yourself. But you will have to fight. Are you a little depressed at the difficulties? Monica will conquer them. Meanwhile here is something, from Shelley, to cheer you.

Good-Night

I
Good-Night? Ah! no; the hour
  is ill
Which severs those it
should unite;
Let us remain together still,
Then it will be *good* night

II
How can I call the lone night
good,
Though thy sweet wishes
wing its flight?
Be it not said, thought,
understood —
Then it will be—*good*
night.

III
To hearts which near each
other move
From evening close to
morning light,
The night is good; because,
my love,
They never *say* good-night.

Then he wrote it over in Italian. Just a little bagatelle, but very graceful and tender, don't you think? As I write to you, late sometimes, your presence is very real. Almost I say. Don't let us say good-night, *yet*. Ponder over that and perhaps you will write a poem about it which I can read instead of Shelley's. It is now 20 to 3. I am going out for a walk, down to the river where we sat that first Sunday. It has been a favorite haunt of mine.

As I count up and number the pages I am astounded. 49. But the subject is important. I'll finish next time.

Love,
Nello

[July 1944]

Part III
We now approach the question of what you should specifically study and how. It isn't easy because strictly speaking you can really study only what appeals to you, either in the sense that it is immediately attractive, or altho' it is drudgery, you feel deep down inside that there is something here which you must study. That is and remains true. At the same time, however, you are as we have agreed, 1) American, 2) You are not an academician as Shelley, T. S. Eliot, or Auden, 3) You have instinctively a certain orientation towards the workers at a time when they are filling the social and political stage and affecting every kind of art or thought. This dictates a certain trend in reading and study, i.e., in thinking. Fortunately the Whitman essay said half of what I had to say. You should read it repeatedly.

The sonnets, rhymed verse, concentration on the beloved as inspiration, etc., mark a poetic expression of a certain stage in human society. It is connected with forms of language, with a continuing literary tradition, etc. But the dividing lines are clear. The 16th century in Britain saw the maturing of the magnificent blank verse form—the Shakespearean. I believe that this form so sharply opposed to the stanzas of Chaucer marked the greater freedom of expression which was required by a new and more expanded society. Shakespeare and the Elizabethans needed a new verse form to express a new world. After that outburst, verse slowly swung *back* to the artificial couplets of Pope. Listen

> Know well thyself, presume
> not God to scan
> The proper study of
> mankind is man

and again

> Some men to business, some to
> pleasure take
> But every woman is at heart
> a rake

The verse is the verse of an ordered society. They have left behind them the Shakespearean blank verse line. But immediately after the French Revolution, Keats,

Shelley, Wordsworth and Coleridge broke away from the type of verse Pope and the XVIIIth century specialised in—the change had been coming a long time—and once more English verse became a medium of great freedom.

I am sticking here to England, and I am stating *briefly* general ideas which would have to be formulated with many qualifications in a formal thesis. *But of their general validity I have no doubt at all*. Now the importance of Whitman is this. He consciously saw that the society of America, *without the European roots*, and more democratic in its social life than any European society needed a new verse form. *He was a great student of the European tradition*. Don't forget that please, miss. He knew he couldn't start afresh. *He knew and said that without them he could not have written as he did*. He was neither ignoramus nor dilettante. But he broke clean away and every year sees his work growing in importance. He is the greatest literary force in America because he broke so consciously. *At the end of his career*, the Symbolist movement in France started the revolt against the traditional bourgeois verse from which has come Yeats, Eliot and the whole modern school. Note something specifically American. Whitman broke away *in confidence*. The Europeans broke away in disgust. Why did Whitman not have a greater influence? This is a historical question. In the nineteenth century there was real popular govt in the U.S.A. The big bourgeoisie did not dominate as yet. It really seemed as if democracy could function.

Unfortunately the Civil War victory let in big industry. And the popular masses were slowly disciplined by big capital. Thus the social system became more and more like the European.

After the war America made one notable contribution—the fiction of Hemingway. He broke the literary convention and brought the speech of "the people" not only into dialogue but in his very narration.

Now to-day it seems to me that the studious American poet, with the power and devotion can take verse a long long way. The American democratic tradition, the life of the country to-day, the power of the workers, the approach of a new social order based on the working-class demand new rhythms, new forms. But you can't sit and make those up. Whitman knew European verse, he knew America, he *participated in its struggles*, he knew American democracy both in theory and practice, and soaking himself in these he caught something of the spirit of the country and this gave him his style.

Now you have to do the same. The traditional verse you must read and study. The democracy of to-day is workers' democracy. The America of to-day is the most wonderful country in the world, its problems, the problems of the people, must be your problems, the philosophy of the working-class movement you must understand, and as you live these things, deeply and sincerely, they will express themselves in your writing—even in love lyrics. This does not mean joining anything. But it does mean that your thoughts, your ideas, your hopes, must move in a certain direction. *Get that right*, strengthen your mind, develop it, exercise it, in that way, and according to your talent, it will express itself in the verse. Is that clear? Now to be more precise. Do I say Read this or Read that or Read the other? No. But I say, e.g., See what you can get out of Whitman, read books about him, if you find him interesting, try to place him in American history. Follow him as far as your mind leads you.

Then take Whittier. He is another unacademic American. He wrote as a valiant fighter in the cause of abolition. For thirty years he placed his poetic gift at the service of the movement. Read him. His Songs of Labor are, in my opinion, quite commonplace. Why? His Songs of Freedom I have not read. What was his concept of freedom? His verse is in parts commonplace and naive. Yet he has 1 columns in the Encyclopedia Britannica. Why? Then there is Herman Melville. An American if there was one. Try to find out why his Moby Dick is what it is.

In European literature there is one man worth your while. He is Burns. *He is your type*. No classical education, a ploughman, but a magnificent poet, *a poet of the people*.

Then there is Shelley, master of languages, a European university-trained type, the opposite of Whitman, of Whittier, and of Dreiser, but a man in whom the spirit of liberty and revolution burnt strongly. You should read him carefully. Try to study him. I wouldn't mention any more now. But those are your ancestors, the people whose special tradition you are to continue and develop as far as in you lies. And, of course, you continue to read modern verse, anybody you feel interested in, any school you feel attracted to. Then there is literary criticism. You will find people whose criticism stimulates you. I recommend only one—a book I have never read. It is Essays on American Literature by D. H. Lawrence. I know that Lawrence well enough and I am sure with a lot of nonsense, he will say some extraordinary things, which will stimulate thought and expand the mind.

Then there is philosophy. To-day you will find it a necessity. Whitman was a *Hegelian, by the way*. The philosophy of the day is dialectical materialism. What you need is some grasp of it as it applies to social evolution—man, nature, and society; is there a movement in history? If so what, whence, whither, how, to what end? If you don't get that then you will begin to read Isaiah, St. Paul, and Christ knows what. Some of my ideas on that subject you have read. I am working on that steadily. You will read some more in time. I have other articles written. Others are being prepared. These permeate the mind, give it direction, exercise it and strengthen it, give you a base, give your outlook some structure, and then the poetic images, the dramatic contrasts, etc., not only begin to get a deeper, consistent pattern, but they become more significant, more vivid, more all-embracing in their scope. You reach out at bigger things *structurally*, and the poetic talent rises to meet the demands which the expanded personality is making. What makes me so hopeful for you is to see how after a few weeks here, everything has jumped.

To sum up. You have to read such books and investigate such problems as will give your mind the background, breadth, and impetus necessary to attempt to do for America to-day what Whitman did in 1860. *He was very conscious*. You have to be far more conscious than he. The age demands it. But the age also provides the material and the social premises. The various points for elaboration are innumerable. To take one. Whitman emphasized that he wrote as an individual. That is not accidental. Bourgeois society is essentially the production of individuals. To-day the individual can be individual only so far as he is a member of a collective unit. The individuality of to-day is a higher individuality but it rests on a very conscious collectivity. Everywhere you see it. A worker in 1860 had as his highest aim to become his own boss. That was the American dream. To-day he may say that in words (though he rarely does) but his aim is through his union to gain collective benefits. No one can sit down and write verse expressing that. But to see it and feel it, and understand it makes a poet write in a different way. And so on, and in various multiple ways. If I am not mistaken your acting method is the same. It is all a reflection of the age.

How will you do all this? What about the techniques of verse? Take all that very easy for the time being I would say. Read and write as best you can until you are settled in a job. But I can only end by saying that the energy, the strength and the determination to master the technique can come only from your own internal needs and their imperative desire for expression. Sometime we will talk about these things. But this I think concludes what I can contribute at present.

Love,
Nello

NB also *Method*. The "truth" of something is its opposite, e.g., the "truth" of capitalism with its socialised production, freedom of assembly, right of free press, etc., is socialism. (This is the dialectical terminology.)

July 28, 1944

Well, my native song-bird, I must write to you. I don't wish to write, physically. My hand does not feel like it. But I am full of a lot of things, chiefly disappointment at not being with you for four or five long hours on Friday. It is a miserable business. I get these horrible spells—since my operation in December I have had two. I must stay in—lie in bed for a few days—it passes. But during that time if I am in an apartment then I am in a gorgeous mess. I can't get myself anything to eat. When I do, it is anything I can get and I eat it in my room. I read voraciously then—newspapers a lot. They accumulate. I am really very dependent then. Nobody came on Wednesday—I seemed to be slipping back into primeval or at least colonial frontier days, particularly because my things are still scattered over the apartment. It will take me a long time to fix them. Then to-day three people came—Gloria and Lois, two girls, two sisters, old old friends of mine. And then Rae came in the afternoon; and the four of us had quite a time. Then Rae alone remained. Then she left. One book-case is up now with the books. I am horribly *weak*. I think of you. That is me.

But I have been doing other things. I read Moby Dick on Wednesday. It was an experience. There are many pages, many, in that book which are among the most amazing I have ever read. They kept me and have kept me in a state of almost continuous excitement. Have you read the book? If not, put it on your list soon. You can have my copy if you wish and can stand my markings. I saw it in an old furniture store and bought it for 25 cents. I am convinced now that as the history of America must be studied around the Civil War—leading up to it and from it, so American literature revolves around Melville and Whitman.

So to-day when Rae left I couldn't take it any more and went to the library a few blocks away and got 6 books, 4 on American literature, to read about Melville. It is nearly 12 and I finished the chapters on him half an hour ago. I wouldn't tell you what the books were, for it's no use only telling you about books. But if you think you will be, or are interested in Melville, then sometime or other we'll go into him. I have to study him. The book I shall write will be American History and the Negro and I shall fit the Negro into the framework of the history. American economic and historical development I have the outlines of. I shall have to study the literature and then when I have it all clear I shall write the *political* study. For politics embraces all forms of the life of the community and a serious political study is nonsensical without a grasp of the *whole* life of the country. But as I say, it has been an experience. Some few things, however, are important for you at once. He was typical of the finest American writers—he was without formal education, and he wrote of the people, in this book. He had a colossal *power*, but he lacked the discipline of study. You remember that poem we talked about on Monday—I was feeling pretty feeble on Monday, so I may have been a little distant, subdued—the one beginning

Though my love
Asks not

Look at it again. It is a lovely and quite *formal* lyric. The verses are (1) Lines 1–4 (2) Lines 5–10 (3) Lines 11–13. The interior form despite the "freedom" of the verse. That is what matters. But what was most comic was when I showed it to you, you said "Is that bad?" You enchanting ignoramus. That is what is good. That is what is so very very good. But—in this highly conscious age, you will in time have to learn to recognise them yourself—dactylic meters, hexameters, pentameters, alexandrines, the Shakespearean iambic, internal rhymes, assonances, subtle alliteration, various types of stress, and unstressed lines; and from these a sense of the structure of the smaller forms and then of the larger.

This is why your inspiration, the breadth of your mind, your culture, using the word in the broad and not the narrow sense, your struggles with life, all these give you an impulse to write in a certain way at a certain time. Now, instinctively, this will dictate a certain *type* of form, as all unknowing, you slipped into the "formal" lyric in that little poem. But you should be able to recognise it yourself and work it out. Sometimes the whole impulse is clear from start to finish. But sometimes it isn't. Whether it is clear or not, it is your unconscious artistic instinct which will create and ultimately decide. But by and large it is well that you know always what you are about. That will come in time. One picks it up easily enough. But I *think* that you shouldn't worry about that now. Just keep on writing. I notice that you have dropped one or two things you used to do before, e.g., an *excessive* use of "seeing sounds," etc., a deliberate rejection of the normal human responses—it is fine when well done. Some of yours were artificial. I was glad to see them disappear naturally. Meanwhile you just go on as you are. I want to see you settled, with a good job. Then to embark on some studies. No hurry, as far as I can see. Nothing good was ever done in a hurry. Quickly yes. In a hurry, no. When that time comes, I shall place some more ideas before you.

Meanwhile as soon as you are able, send me as many of the poems as you can, typed. I want *all*.

Meanwhile, my precious, I believe in you more than ever. You have a long long way to go. But you have all the signs, general and particular. There is first of all your general orientation. We have talked of that. That is the road for anyone who will do good work to-day. Not because you have it you will be good. That is the Stalinist third period insanity. The point is that, without it, no one to-day can be really good. Certainly not for long. A talent is a talent. But it must have room. There is no room anywhere but in that direction. Secondly, you have it *beginning in 1944*. The next few years will make you, as they will shape all young people. See to it that you follow your instincts and find the atmosphere in which your natural tendencies will flourish and mature. Periodically in small things and large you will have to decide: Shall I or shall I not? Wherever possible follow your own star. It's yours. And that way lies growth and power. For writing poetry at any rate. I shall say this often. The world presses hard upon you, in a 1000 unseen, subtle, enveloping ways. I hope I have not disguised the fact that the odds are *against* you. Terribly against. But we fight, don't we? So much in general. I believe in you. But also I see other things which I find tremendously exciting.

1) You are interested in love, sensuously, and sensually too. (I knew that the moment I saw you—actually the first moment. It was one of the first things that struck me.) Now few people are though they can be taught. More women are than men. But very few modern people are. They are interested in a man or in a woman, and in the expression of their own desires. D. H. Lawrence worked hard to correct this, but he was a Protestant Englishman and he screamed until sex-life became a new religion. The French are interested in love too but there is an atmosphere of "gallantry" with an undercurrent of "vice" which is repulsive. Americans and modern Americans have a more healthy attitude than most. But the old pagan sensuality, what Christianity destroyed (you know Swinburne's lines. Thou has conquered, O pale Galilean. The world has grown grey at thy breath) as I say, that old pagan sensuality, will come back to the world again. It is *not* licentiousness. Highly individualised modern people are as a rule licentious because they can do no better. But the sheer delight in the body and love-making for its own sake—you are fortunate in your temperament and in your age, you can in time write here with depth and penetration and help to open up a great field of human life. (I could teach you a lot of things here, but no, you go rushing off and don't give a fellow half a chance.)

2) You have a strong sense of affinity with people in general. As you walk along you feel communication with them. No one can learn this. But as you learn more about yourself—a long job, sister—and more about people, the communication you will express will be more intimate and more powerful. *All of us to-day have so much in common.* We live the same sort of life. We are a "collective" community. We are moulded by the machine age—California, New Orleans, Chicago, New York, London, Warsaw, Czechoslovakia, Hungary, are all very different, but yet are, in 1944 "One World." The poet is an individualist, but since the days of the Hebrew prophets and the Greek epic poets I don't think there was ever a time when one man was so much every man. You can in time do wonderful work here. Shelley loved humanity but was so far from so many. Whoever walks along the street and feels warm spontaneous kinship with the other millions hurrying along and can dig it out and make it concrete and vivid that person can awaken a response in many many hearts which feel these same sentiments but is only vaguely aware of them in this mechanical age. I have just stopped to read over

I love your hoot
The air shafts

and half way through, another one, the passage beginning

As I pass and
You stop your work . . .

Do you know something? I feel that the one beginning I love your hoot, is actually closer to the workers than many of those which take the more direct political line.

Get me? Of course you do. I feel that in time as you really grasp deep down the social affinity, your identification with the people will be far more profound and will express itself with infinitely more power than at present. It will be as spontaneous, as poetic as the "hoot" poem, and yet coming from deep down inside the poems will have a political depth which will express itself in the images, the ideas, the whole structure.

You see why I believe in you. These are grooves along which your personality runs. There are others. Another time for those. But these two are good—very very good to go along with. I am quite sure of them, first because I know you and saw them in you before you wrote a line, and secondly because I know how they fit into our time. I am horribly tired. Isn't it disgusting? I loved your dress on Monday. Is it the same powder-blue? I don't think so. It fitted very "slick" or is the word sleek? The powder-blue had "decorations" in front which this one hadn't. Tell me all the doctor says. I hope those caps don't show. I am so tired I can barely finish. But the worst is over. I'll be out in a day or two. Meanwhile I'll wait for another day when I'll see you for 4 hours—not one.

N

I forgot to tell you something. See that German situation? For over 18 months I and a few others fought a tearing-down fight that the centre of things in Europe was Germany—*though there were no signs*. We were abused, hounded down. We would not budge. Now we are all on tenter-hooks waiting. I must explain it all to you when I see you. This is in pencil (couldn't find the pen last night) but it is very very important. Long ago I sent you the two articles and Eddie took them. I think it would have been good for you to have gone through that experience with us. but you can live it retrospectively perhaps. I'll tell you.

[July 1944]

Autobiography of a ManbyHim
Price: Priceless
First Edition. All sold out.
Publisher's Blurp
The publishers have pleasure in presenting the first installment of this auto*by*. Our readers say that in these troublesome times it provides a necessary escapism. It far exceeds in interest our recent best-seller and

PTO [please turn over]

American classic: From Log-Cabin to Home Relief. The author wishes his identity to be kept secret. He therefore regrets that everybody knows who he is.

All [the word ladies is scratched out] women who wish further details must send stamped and addressed envelopes and photograph. Birth certificate is not necessary but the photograph must be dated. The author will *not* give any press interviews. But he will speak on the radio anytime he is asked and will answer all questions.

All rights are reserved, i.e., the readers can do what they like with the book as long as they do not bother the author.

Chapter I.

I was born on Jan. 4, 1901. My mother says that I was a very lively child, moving about continuously in the womb. I am very proud of that, though my pride has no scientific basis. My first memory is at the age of about 4. My mother brought myself and my sister, two years younger, in a cab to North Trace. The train brought us to

Princess Town and then a cab carried us the 6 miles to North Trace. My father had gone there to be a village school-master. I sat in the cab looking out. Then I remember in the first days going to the wooden latrine. It was new, built of pine-wood which smelt very strongly as pine does. I remember too that one day my brother and I were allowed by my mother to run out into the street and bathe naked in the rain. I remember too that a teacher at the school boarded with us. I do not remember him at all except that one day a girl, a young woman, came by a cab and my mother hid her in his room. Then he came home from school and she led him smiling mysteriously into the room. I followed. When they saw each other they embraced. I had never seen people kiss for so long a time. I stood amazed. It meant nothing to me, except that they kissed so long.

One night my aunt, my uncle's wife, came to stay with us. She was a beautiful woman—not handsome but beautiful. She and my father went for a walk. I heard him call from the street "We are on the hook," meaning that her arm was hooked in his. I was vaguely aware that my mother did not like it. Those are my first memories—of that house. We left there when I was about 6.

Then we moved to another house, nearer the school. It was a small house, shaped like this. [Drawing inserted]

It was about 25 feet square. Room 1 was not ours. It was a store-room for cocoa, after it had been shelled. Room 6 was (I think) connected with 1. Room 2 was the drawing room. But a paper blind made a little room of 4 for me and my sister. I slept in one bed, she in another. Room 5 was my mother's bed-room. My chief memory is of my mother sitting reading and I lying on the floor near her reading until it was time for me to go to bed—9 o'clock. She was a very tall woman, my colour, with a superb carriage and so handsome that everybody always asked who she was. She dressed in the latest fashion   she had a passion for dress and was herself a finished seamstress. But she was a reader. She read everything that came her way. I can see her now, sitting very straight with the book held high, her pince-nez on her Caucasian nose, reading till long after midnight. If I got up there she was, reading, the book still held high. As she read a book and put it down I picked it up. My father read nothing—a book a year perhaps. My life there until I was 9 centered around books and games. When I was about 7 I sat up late one night and wrote a poem. About 8 verses of four lines each in imitation of a poem in my reading-book. Why I felt to write I do not know. No one wrote that I know. No one had ever said that people wrote. Another day my mother put down the Last of the Mohicans. I picked it up and read it. I read as she did—straight through except I saw a chance of playing cricket or shooting with an air-gun. When I finished the Last of the M I got a copy-book and began to write a story of my own. But after two chapters my mother read it and said it was exactly like the L of the M and I stopped. I know now that this was the worst thing she could have done. She should have told me to go on and I would have written it to the end I think. But I don't know.

Books, books, books. There was a rainy season and a dry season and in the rainy season we got fever. So we were sent to Tunapuna to my grandmother's, every rainy season, for some months. There I used to climb to the top of the wardrobe by way of the window-sill and take down the books. I remember "The Throne of the House of David." I read it to pieces. And I remember too an extraordinary book—a prize novel, for a prize offered by, I think, the Herald of New York. It was a green book, a modern novel, and it had style. I didn't know what style was. But it is one of my most powerful memories—the strange effect this calm, detached writing had on me. I must have been about 7. Long before that I had appropriated my mother's Shakespeare. I couldn't read it all. But there was a picture at the head of each play with two lines or so describing the picture, giving the act and scene. I looked up each one, over and over again and read the whole scene. The one I remember, the only one, is the quarrel between Brutus and Cassius. My father bought me the Pickwick Papers and I read that too when I was about 7. When I didn't read I played cricket or ran races or went shooting birds with my air-gun, or shot at a tin-cup or a bottle. I was a dead shot at about 7 and for long after—with my air-gun and after a time I didn't use to aim but shot from the stomach. I wasn't aware of my physical surroundings. They didn't change sufficiently—the wet season wasn't very different from the dry. I wasn't aware of social distinctions. We were all Negroes. The house in Tunapuna had two rooms, one divided by a paper blind. My two aunts and my grandmother lived there. They were very poor. The house was about 12 feet by 18 feet. There were holes in the floor, the house was so old. It had a thatched roof, and the rain came in. My aunts were in their early twenties. My grandmother was about 65. They washed clothes for a living and my aunts also were seamstresses. Very good seamstresses they were. But they had a very hard time. I remember chiefly the fleas at nights. Never seemed to sleep when I was there. But my father sent money and we were well fed.

I shall try to keep my impressions in harmony with my age. I lived in North Trace and in the wet season I went to Tunapuna. I went to school and read and played and read. I don't know that I thought of anything else until April 26th 1909 when I was eight—a great day in my life.

But until then there were some personal developments. I thought my parents knew everything and were always right. I still remember that one day—I was walking across the drawing-room in North Trace—it broke in upon me that I had a judgment of my own opposed to theirs. I was about 7.

Then came the Sunday cricket. Some Chinese people lived near to us and there were boys, Kelvin, Buller, George, and Aldrick. We played every day and Saturday. But they had a grocery store and were busy selling on Saturday. On Sunday afternoons there was a big game in the grass patch behind the house and all around came to see. My mother who was a Puritan said I was not to play on Sundays. So on Sundays I sat in the drawing-room and listened to the game. God. How my heart used to hurt me. Every Sunday. Then to make matters worse my father would go and play. My mother said he could do as he pleased—he was a man. I was to stay in. I felt bitterly the injustice of it.

Bitter too were my experiences with my brother. He was the last and about five when I was eight. He was a sickly boy and lazy and not too much inclined to play. When I had no books to read, for I read them without stopping until I was finished, I would beg him to play with me. Sometimes he came. Now at cricket one bowls the ball and the other bats. Then when the batsman is out the other takes his place. My brother would never play unless I allowed him to bat first. If he got out at once he would say he wasn't playing any more. I used to cry bitter tears (I remember them now). It wasn't fair. He had cheated me, and the idea revolted me. I complained to my mother. She sometimes compelled him to play—a stupid thing. He would play for a while. I batting away. Then he would stop before getting me out and once more the bitterness began. I gave him two innings to my one. No use. He always cheated me. He cheated naturally and I was naturally honest and fair-minded. I believe those days left an indelible mark on me. I went about a lot. Wherever he went, to play cricket himself, to see friends, to see games, my father took me. Everybody said I was a handsome bright boy, but I merely remember that. It had no effect on me. I was happy I think but for the sense of injustice I have described. I didn't love my parents. I loved nobody. I didn't hate them. I had no grievances. I just didn't feel to them as I was supposed to. Once when my mother was near death I cried because everyone was crying and I thought I ought to cry. But I knew I was faking. They were very kind to me. Simply I was like that. I had sex experiences but I do not feel to go into those as an honest statement demands some intimacy. I think so, at least. I believed in God and went to Church regularly. But it was routine. I was very well trained. My mother saw to that—respect for elders, good manners at table, modesty and self-respect. My father made about forty or fifty dollars a month and was always desperately in debt. But he always dressed my mother well and we never needed anything. My mother kept us scrupulously clean and kept the house the same as did my aunts. I was somehow aware that we were not common people or laborers. We kept a servant, a girl sometimes, sometimes a woman. White people meant little to me. The clergyman in North Trace was white—a Mr. Reeves, an Englishman, and he drank I remember. His wife was stylish and like most of the white women wore a veil. The colored people I knew didn't wear veils. Only white people wore them. But my mother wore one. And I used to hear my parents talking about the way in which her clothes compared with Mrs. Reeves's at church. My father played the harmonium at church and took the choir-practice and he and Reeves ran the church. One day the Reeveses invited my mother to lunch. It was an occasion. The white parson had invited her to lunch. There was great preparation and for days afterwards it was discussed. But I had no strong feelings on the subject. They were white and somehow special, but my father was the schoolmaster and I was his son and everybody made much of me. There were some white planters in the district, a few, who used to speak in a friendly way to my father. There was a German named Conrad. I don't remember him but I remember his wife—a tall, slim, elegant, handsome woman. I heard my father say once that she called herself Mrs. Conrad but he didn't think they were married. One day, my mother was very ill and she came to see us. I remember how well she carried herself and the dress going up to her ears with whale-bones in the neck. She was a mysterious woman. I don't think she kept company with the few whites in the district but I am not sure.

There was also a girl once—a girl about 11—brown-skinned, very handsome. I remember her to this day and if I were an artist I could draw her picture easily. One day all of us were playing police and thief— your cops and robbers. We ran into the forest; found ourselves alone and stood looking at each other—just looking for two or three minutes. She and I understood what we were thinking. Then the others came and the moment passed.

There was another curious episode. I got hold of an English history book by a man called Ransome. It was dry fact but I read it from cover to cover over and over again. But the English always won all the battles. I resented it fiercely. I used to read and re-read the few battles they had lost. I conceived a fanatical admiration for Napoleon.

A friend of my father's had a picture of Napoleon pasted on his wall. It was always a great day when my father took me there specially to see it. I used to stand and watch it—enthralled. Why I do not know. Nobody ever discussed history or literature or writing with me. But I read that history and hated the British for always winning and loved Napoleon. So I lived my life till I was eight years old and four months. I was a happy boy I think, active and very intelligent. My parents worked hard on me when I was ill as I was not infrequently. I had no love for anyone. I went to school, did my work, read all books and played. On April 20th my father began to teach me for a scholarship. Next time I'll tell you about my father and what he was and how he taught me. I hope you find this interesting. The life of the people, the physical landscape, the ideas, meant nothing to me. Later they came home to me. In time I shall describe them, but only when I became aware of them. If I may, I say that in a different environment I would have been a different child. I learnt everything. But there wasn't too much for me to learn except in books.

[unsigned]

August 8, 1944

Dear Monica, solitary saint on my calendar, there 365 days in the year, your three fat envelopes were very nice to see, to feel, to open, and to read. Old ones and new ones. Some of the new ones are slight. One or two very good and, personally, I find some very *very* interesting. Do you know what I have discovered? You need confidence. And you'll get it in time. To tackle your subjects, all aspects of your thoughts, boldly. It is almost a physical sensation, sometimes, the bound the mind gives. Suddenly after groping, a light and a new path is opened, or the narrow path that seemed to be going nowhere opens broad.

I am scribbling in the subway, work overwhelms. Things are happening so fast—Europe, Germany, Philadelphia, Reconversion—and all sorts of internal problems. You say you shudder to think what your life would be without my friendship. They are very generous words. But your friendship, even that alone, has meant much more to me than I even thought it would, and I expected a lot. In all this tension and activity you are something I can turn to and immediately lose myself and, strangely enough, very strange but true, the knowledge of Monica, striving valiantly against "the world, the flesh, and the devil" gives me a wonderful courage. I have plenty in certain spheres. I am not affected seriously by even great defeats. I need and receive "inspiration" from nobody. Usually it is in reading and getting insight into problems of historical development that I get a great life; also from spontaneous mass movements, or by work in which the writer or artist does not consciously know what he is doing but, guided by imagination, portrays great social truths. I get a wonderful kick from those. But even meeting the Old Man [Leon Trotsky] didn't "inspire" me in the usual sense. But by some trick of fate and psychological complication you do. I see you battling along and I feel quite a glow. And if you stumbled badly or fell by the wayside I'd feel it very much. I would feel not only a personal but a social blow. What would it matter on a world scale? One girl more or less gone over to the enemy?

No. I don't think so at all. I believe you have plenty to contribute. But you have become for me a symbol. Does this add to your burdens? Take it in your stride.

By the way, you have made two conquests. And, sister, *I* can appreciate them. Rae says that you are even better looking than your pictures. But—and this is more than the first. She says frankly that she had had the impression that you were dumb, and that you are nothing of the kind and are not only intelligent but have considerable poise. Now I assure you Sister Rae is very critical about women and their intelligence. She is not snobbish. She is just critical and particularly with women, being herself the most independent woman I know. But as for Brother Bernardo. That is the most merciless critic that there is (only to Rae and close friends. He is a very polite man). He and I discuss Greer Garson's profiles and he does not find women good-looking easily. It is a standing joke. But Rae told me with great glee that he approved of your appearance. She and I were both astonished.

Now don't get me wrong. Don't let me give you a false impression of my friends. They do not set themselves up in judgment. But both are very intelligent, have seen a lot of the world and keep their standards high. Bernardo has nothing to do with Rae's writings. He does not accept her principles. But when he does read something he looks at every comma and scrutinises every blot. If they had been merely polite about you, well so much the worse for them. I have my own judgment in these matters. But that they not only like you but admire you, that is wonderful! Sure see as much of them as you can. The two of them and Lyman and Freddie are people whom it is a pleasure to know and gives you pride in the human family. Without any strain they live naturally and easily by principle.

I have now drunk a strawberry malted and an orange soda. I am in a cigar store. I shall now go home and read some of your poems before I go to bed.

I was glad to see you on Saturday. You looked very well and very sweet. But I noticed signs of strain upon your face. Take it easy. You are doing fine. Knowing the circumstances, your conflicts, difficulties, etc., or at least having a general idea of them, I think you are doing fine. You have come a long way. Sure you have plenty of hills to climb, plenty, but so far you have nothing to complain about, on balance, and much to be modestly proud of. So take it calmly, ready for a few *hard blows* and ready too to jump like a tiger, fit and strong, at any chance you get.

Some day this week you shall get what I am sending you for your birthday. Mind you make it a success.

I am, dearest Monica,

Always yours,
N

[1944]

Roosevelt, Wallace, Wilkie, Dewey are only manifestations. The action, voice, gesture, that you make at a particular moment is a manifestation. It represents the essence, your general conception of what you are doing. To judge it by itself, would be an error.

Same with Roosevelt. He is to be judged by what he represents. The essence of society so far is the division into classes. Society is a natural organism, a very high stage, but a part of nature nevertheless. The class division is the division between matter and consciousness, physical labor and intellectual labor. The work of Roosevelt is governed by what he represents. More than that. *It shapes his character.* The moment one begins to speculate as to whether he is a good man or not one is lost, not only politically, but psychologically as well.

Class struggle as the essence of society is a very profound *philosophical* conception. The survival of the fittest, the Darwinian conception for nature is reproduced on a higher plane in society as the struggle of different *groups*, and these groups are distinguished by their role in production, proletariat, petty-bourgeoisie, bourgeoisie. Today the chief, the imperative necessity is to help the proletariat arrive at consciousness of its maturity. Hence any agitation or propaganda or writing, verse or prose, which leads it to think of leadership as residing elsewhere than in its own bosom, as coming from anywhere except out of its own depths, is a blow against it. It cannot continue Democrats today, Republicans tomorrow, Democrats day after, Republicans after that, etc., ad infinitum. That is why we call today for a Labor Party—a political party based on the unions. All the progressive petty-bourgeois intellectuals and artists; farmers; Negroes; the discarded old folks; all need *to follow* this party. The task of the intellectuals in particular is to break down all the intellectual ties with bourgeois society and clear the minds of the great masses of the people. The chief thing is to reject Roosevelt and Co. *in toto* and *a priori*. Class is decisive. One day I'll tell you how after the French Revolution, the revolt against Hume, led through Kant, Fichte, Schilling, Hegel and Feuerbach to Marx, step by step with an inevitable logic culminating in the doctrine of the class struggle. It is a fierce doctrine, harsh and unforgiving, chiefly, however, because the ruling class make it so.

What is most exciting is that that sequence from Hume to Marx which I have been studying for the last three years and which has had an effect on my thinking and on my personal life beyond all explanation, this I find repeated with an almost photographic exactitude in modern poetry. Yes, modern poetry! The sequence from T. S. Eliot to Auden, Spender and Cecil Day Lewis is a repetition of the sequence from Hume to Marx. It is and must be so, for the human mind having said A, must say B. I would never have looked at it all, not unless I was ill, but for you. And the sequence I would never have discovered but for W. B. Yeats. Some years ago he wrote an essay which I read lately and have been reading steadily since. *He knows poetry.* That was his job. He analysed it with the eye of a master. And as he traced stage by stage the development there before me was the classic philosophical sequence. Hegel had traced it in ancient philosophy, had himself been the completion of the greatest example of it, and now here it is again. The book that my friend is preparing will trace this in philosophy and history. For years people have argued about dialectic. They don't know what it is. This book will challenge them all. But the perfect exemplification which Yeats gives in his analysis was a great thrill for me. In fact it is so far the best exemplification. And there in the very heart of it, tangled up inextricably with it is yourself, living, warm and lovely. Do you see why I call you my little miracle? One day we'll have a jam session—you and me. It will begin with philosophy—the method of thought, i.e., logic, the inevitable development of ideas, and we'll reach poetry by that road. Then we'll see as clear as day what the concept class means and what the absence of it has meant to poetry. Always remembering however that the poet reacts to life *emotionally*—and without that, though he were the wisest man in the world, he could not write a line of verse. But the more humanity develops the more the emotional response depends upon a conception of the world which does not so much guide the poetry, but releases and expands the personality, integrates it, opens horizons, and thus gives the emotional responses a range and depth and power impossible otherwise. This, sweetheart, is to live. When the disciples asked Christ about the world to come and the places they were to get in it, he told them "The Kingdom of Heaven is within you." They could not understand. They just *couldn't*. The glory of life in our age is that this intense, individual, personal life can, in fact, must be lived, in harmony with the great social forces that are now striving to carry humanity over the last barrier. When I say I love you it comes from very, very far.

If you read the Guernica thing carefully, you will see that Clark* understands but, chained by the Stalinist doctrine, is in the same position as Picasso is as a painter. *He cannot draw the argument to a conclusion.* He cannot grasp why Picasso is so confused. In fact Picasso sees far more clearly than he the futility of the nonclass opposition to Franco.

All my love, darling. You see it is not a phrase "all my love." It just is that—if you understand me.

[unsigned]

September 8, 1944

Well, Monica, 100% Monica, there is one citizen whom you have made to rejoice greatly—and that is me. Do you know that this morning you sounded like a different person from the girl I have known these five years. Some uncertainty and (I can't find a word) had left your voice and it was calm, assured, genial, and lovely to listen to. (You *ought* to act very well. Your emotional responses are translated almost automatically and very intimately into your physical expressions. It is a good base.) Confidence and command of yourself and you will do many wonderful and useful things. What were you feeling so deeply happy about this morning? I have often wondered about your acting. Now at least I know one part of it. But I have never heard it before and we have talked many hours on the 'phone. If you can command it always, then you have one very beautiful weapon with which to conquer. I tell you when I heard something like it once before—the very first day I called you. But there was a hint of artificiality—and after a minute or so it dropped away. At odd times I would catch a hint of it—but very briefly. However it was there all Sunday morning, and I could feel that it came from deep inside somewhere. I have spoken for many many years and I know that only rarely do I get the best out of myself, but with me it is usually ill-health. But with you I think you will need a deep inward assurance to get the best out of yourself. The night of the broadcast the voice was clear and natural, but it lacked the arresting resonance and complete fusion of all tones which I heard on Sunday, i.e., this morning. Now I know and Stanislavsky writes in the Britannica in his masterly essay how difficult it is to have that complete physical control that enables the actor to use his voice, and make his movements as he ought to. He thinks, and I agree, that most of them are far below standard. Robeson has a magnificent natural organ—I rehearsed him for a few weeks and the voice is a miracle—but he lacks real sophistication in its use. He has nothing like the diction and feeling for words that Bette Davis for example has; and the beautiful style and real distinction

---

* Kenneth Clark, influential British art critic and historian.

that Mary Astor can show when she has a part that suits her. But there is a lovely voice-quality that is inside of you somewhere; only you have to cut away everything that impedes it until it is part of your natural, i.e., developed self. Naturally it means hard work but unless I misjudge my Monica, it means too a hard struggle for an inward grip which allows the whole personality to express itself and not only a part, or worse still, parts fighting each other. What a long story about a few words heard on the 'phone! But the voice of everyone matters—an actress's voice matters more than most, and the sudden unexpected beauty and all its possibilities for you startled me, and made me think a lot of things.

The train is near N.Y. I have been lifting logs all afternoon and I am most gloriously tired. But also I feel very very happy and "uplifted" and you have made me so. You know all the odds were against you. I don't think 9 out of 10 would have counted on you. It was what in our jargon we call a "tough assignment." I saw all the difficulties clearly—only too clearly, but I have and always have had an invincible confidence in you that you will come out right. (How far that confidence extends I'll tell you some time.) But yet it was an awful, in fact a terrible strain. And I felt, I confess it freely, very very tired when you left and I knew for certain that your very precious self was safe and you were in command. You have great gifts. No one, absolutely no one is fit to guide and direct them but yourself. Furthermore at the present time, you being what you are, they are a responsibility.

One more word. As you think over things it may seem to you that certain developments were accidental, that things did not work out as you wanted them to—exactly, that even you do not or did not command your destiny but circumstances, some[thing] fortuitous shaped them. These often cause an honest and sensitive person much genuine concern and self-searching. They are not as important as they seem really. Wherever there is internal conflict these things *always* happen and tend to obscure the fundamental issue. As one looks back after a time, one is able to see that the series of "accidents," even some unlooked for and unwelcome at the time, formed in reality a certain logical pattern which moved in a particular direction towards a climax. The thing to do as soon as possible is to strip away the unessentials from the concrete fact itself, and then with this as the centre, other things will find their proper perspective and natural level. I hope this will help you. It is my own experience and may help you to clarify your own. Meanwhile all my best wishes for you. You are very lovely, very sweet, and a very fine person whom it is a great pleasure and education to know. No letter will be opened more eagerly in the whole wide world than the one containing your six poems. I expect a big jump and it is so wonderful to know that I shall not be disappointed.

As ever,
N

I am sending this to V.A. [Vanderbilt Avenue] as it is late and may miss the first post down your way.

Special Delivery

September 13, 1944

Darling Monica,

Your letter was fine. One day I'll show it to you. Very simple, very clear, very confident. Now I am just going to continue my autobiography. Off to the West Indies

1908 (you'll get another letter to-morrow). You remember North Trace—the little village, and the schoolhouse and my parents and me, and my brother and sister. The schoolhouse was about eighty feet by forty, with a few maps on the wall and benches. Everything was very primitive. There were about 120 children, boys and girls, most of them bare-footed for they were very poor, Negroes and mulattoes chiefly. Few white children came to such schools and when they did not for long. There were some Indians and a few Chinese, for the island has a very cosmopolitan population. My father was the Head Master and there was a Head Mistress. She was always in charge of the infants. Then there were about half-a-dozen other teachers of varying degrees of ignorance. The school was divided into standards, Standard I, II, II, etc., up to Standard VII. We were taught Reading, Writing, Arithmetic, Geography, Singing, and Drill, a form of physical culture. The chief thing about the school was the yearly examination and to this day that examination and everything connected with it stands out in my memory.

First of all the pay of the head teacher depended upon it. He was a government teacher, but his pay was divided into three parts. About thirty dollars a month was the regular pay. Then every three months he received a capitation grant—so much per head for those who attended. This might bring in about thirty odd dollars a quarter. Then the examination was marked very good, good, or fair, as the case might be. Very good meant so much per pupil, good meant less, and so on. This could come to a tidy sum—about 100 dollars, known as "the bonus." And a series of good capitations and a good "bonus" meant not only money, but promotion to bigger schools in the towns. Furthermore the bonus was a lump sum—you could do things with it. All life was governed by these financial circumstances.

The examination lasted one day. They were carried on by an Inspector of Schools and his assistant, a woman, who examined the infants. They, in 1909, were always white. For months we prepared and then on the day they came. The examiners took a kind of tour. North Trace to-day, Prince's Town the next day and to place after place day after day. The chief part of the examination was the written part; all the standards had for example Arithmetic Cards with sums on them. Now my father was an able, conscientious teacher. But the teachers took no risks with their bonus. The cards were imported by the examiner from England. Groups of teachers got together and imported cards from every maker of cards in England. They all had all possible cards. When the tour began, the first teacher passed the word along that this year, Mr. Robinson was using Craul's cards or Johnson's as the case might be. At once the teachers all along that route had their pupils furiously working out those cards over and over again so that when the day came and they were handed out each pupil knew his sums already. If the cards were of a kind which had different sums for each pupil, then we were so arranged that we got the cards we had prepared for. If we didn't get them, we changed them, with the help of the teacher. No arrangement or rearrangement of the boys and girls could stop this. Same with the geography and the grammar. Thus there was this cheating going on in every school, scores of them, for miles and miles all over the different circuits. The curious thing is that no one considered it immoral. I never did until I was about 20. I never thought of it. Teachers and pupils all cooperated to pass the examination and do well. My father was not lazy. He taught hard and well, but he was not going to take the chance of getting a good instead of a very good. So it was everywhere.

On the great day the Inspector and his assistant came. They were usually very incompetent. They never discovered that they were being cheated. They all had weaknesses. One loved singing. My father therefore always had some fine songs for him. Another one fancied himself as a military man. My father gave him a long and special drill. You could be sure that he would give a V.G. [Very Good] Then a clever teacher would give them lunch—a wonderful lunch with champagne. One of them always got tipsy. He would be sure to give a V.G. and so on and so on.

I remember only one of the examiners—a Miss Doyle. She was, guess what, you will never guess, a beautiful woman. This sounds trivial. I assure you it was not. She was small, dark-brown hair, slender, elegant, quick in her movements. (It is thirty-five years ago now and I saw her once.) But everybody in the teaching business on that circuit spoke of her. When she came in there was a murmur of admiration. The women teachers raved over her. When the examination was discussed, her beauty was always mentioned, as a constituent part. There was no lasciviousness about it, no envy. The teachers were servile to the inspector because he was authority. They loved her because she was lovely and gracious. It was a glimpse of something "artistic" in a dull, drab world. Part of the charm was her speech, nothing very wonderful perhaps in itself but standing out against the dull heavy rustic accents. My father was not servile—he had a formidable dignity against all white people. But he was a careful, shrewd man. On examination day some or most teachers wore their best clothes. He did not. He wore a plain white tunic. Let the inspector be dazzling and the best-dressed man in the show. I remember his deportment during the exam, as we called it—a mixture of dignity and deference. He always got V.G.

All the bonus and all the capitation came to him. But he gave substantial sums to the staff. They knew that he would and worked hard. Some head teachers were mean and kept it all for themselves. He never did and if he had wanted to, my mother would have raised cain. Later, many years later, this business of capitation, etc., was stopped. The authorities condemned it and paid a man his full salary every month. Everyone agreed that it improved matters all round. But the thing I have described went on for many many years all over the island.

Of the teachers I remember little. There was a man called Leben—a black fellow who always wore tight shoes. Often they were so tight he had to cut a hole at the side. Why he wore them so tight God only knows. Perhaps the local cobbler just couldn't get them right. I know I often suffered martyrdom from badly made shoes. The other teacher I remember was a Miss Todd. She also was an experience. She was not handsome, but she was brown, and very very stylish. She had a face like Miriam Hopkins, with a broad mouth; and she had a mole. She was my father's head mistress for years and there was an affair between them. I only worked it out years after. But altho' my mother knew she could only hint to my father that she did. I was always vaguely aware that something was going on but what it was I didn't know.

So for a year or two I read books and played games and went to church and was one of the 100 odd children who came from miles around to the school. I was the schoolmaster's son and therefore had status. I was bright as a new shilling and everybody said I would be sure to be something one day. It didn't matter to me. I just lived along. Then on April 26th 1909 my father called me and said he was going to teach me specially for a scholarship. I said Yes. I didn't know. I didn't care. But things happened. I'll describe them next time.

Now I hope you'll go straight off to sleep with your mind drained of your troubles for the time being. See me one Monday morning I think it was, all clean and scrubbed, over thirty years ago, at 8 o'clock, with my father beginning special training of me. An hour before school 8–9 and an hour after 3–4. You were not born then, darling. New York, California, Los Angeles, Hollywood were not in existence. If they were, I wouldn't have known. A little island 50 miles long by 30 broad, a little remote village, a little school, and in it, a little boy looking at his father and waiting to be taught. The years would pass and I would get to know a lot of things, and meet a lot of people, but chiefly I would get to know Marxism and meet you. It began on April 21, 1909. Whenever you feel for some distraction let me know. I'll tell you about it as Scheherazade told the tales of the Arabian nights.

                         All my love,
                         [unsigned]

R. J.
Apt. 2A
405 E. 55

[1944]

Well, my darling, how are you? To-day, Sunday, has been a most curious day. It is lovely, very bright warm, temperate. The weather has been so vile lately that this surprise packet was welcomed by everybody.

Being out late last night I sleep till 12. Then begins a very curious day. I lie in bed and day-dream until 3. What do I dream about? You guess. Right. You have guessed correct the first time. So that goes on until 3. Now curiously enough, I am not talking to-day. I just lie and dream. Sometimes I carry on conversations with you—the most BEE-YU-TI-FULL conversations. I ask the questions and then I say the answers for you. You can imagine how satisfactory they are to me. Do you always agree with me? No, madame, no. But then I have to persuade you to see my point of view. There, my dear, you score heavily. For being a reasonable woman you appreciate highly the dialectic I bring to bear; being a nice woman you welcome all the effort I make to ensure that the process of convincing is pleasant. And would you believe it, Constance, strange as it may sound, it always works out right in the end.

But is that all? No, No, No. Sometimes you tell me things. I listen. I am not sure. You envelope me with arguments (and arms). Sometimes I am stubborn, but, and this is hard to believe, I am convinced. But that is *not* all, no, fair lady. Sometimes we quarrel. Yes, you say. I say No. You say: Yes. I say No. That is final. IM—POS-SIBLE. Good. We part politely but coldly. All day, however, I am not so good. So by the afternoon I go out and call you; not there. But when I come back I get a message from you. Urgent. So I call you back. Conversation goes slow at first, but then I say: About this morning—. You say, Oh, I was about to mention it. I say: You know I was thinking it over. You say: I, too, and I thought there was something in what you said. I say: Wonderful. Darling, as long as you think I am right, I can say that there will be no disagreement. We decide to go and eat somewhere early and all during dinner I make so much love to you, only by looking of course, that you blush pinker than the roses I have brought you. So—to return. That was a digression.

So having digressed we begin exactly where we left off. I take it easy. I have a horribly dull breakfast. Then I go and sit on the bench. The other day I wrote to you about lying down in the sun and not talking—well, this is *exactly* how it was to-day. I could have come home and written you a long letter. I had plenty to say. But I didn't. I just wanted to sit around. So I sat around. Then I had dinner; went to the show, came out half-way and here I am—9 o'clock deciding that I must write to you. Is it a very dull account? It was a dull day. And yet I wasn't bored, not at all. If I had been in the least bored I would have come home and worked. But I wasn't. Nor did I think of you actively. I had no conversation with you. Nor did I think of all the things I know about you and add them together so as to understand you as thoroughly as one human being can another. In some vague but very sure way I was aware of you near to me, sitting or rather being near and just watching the hours and the people go by. You speak in one of your letters of the physical ache you feel sometimes and then you act or write. But the ache I have and it is not *almost* physical, but sometimes the heart hurts actually, if not for your physical presence but for the knowledge that you love me. You know it used to be said. The man's desire is for the woman. The woman's desire is for the desire of the man. I believe that that is true no longer. Women ask for more these days. They desire the man too, as well as his desire for them. But the man cannot help being influenced by the increasing range and confidence of woman's independence. And he too needs the woman and the desire of the woman. Needs the second because a woman to-day is more, far more of a personality, has so much more to her than a woman of 50 years ago. Do you know that you are in your way quite a phenomenon to me. You are an American woman. To you that is nothing. Sweets you are a member of the most independent, most confident, most demanding type of woman in the world. This country has never had feudal or Catholic traditions. Secondly, the enormous economic opportunities offered to women in the U.S.A. (far far from "equality" with men) but still, enormous as compared with even advanced countries like Britain and France or Germany. An American woman is far more of a complete human being than most Europeans, though in their very narrowness some Europeans achieve astonishing grace and charm. Then the American woman in the home and out of it has such advantages in the technical organisation of society. Constant hot water, shower, beauty-parlors at every corner. My dear the *average* European woman does not have these things; the average middle-class Englishwoman does not. All these mean so much more to the personality of the individual who uses them, unthinkingly. I can see the effect of them in general and on you in particular. In Britain under similar circumstances you would be a different person. (One day I'll tell you some of the advantages of the more traditional and technically backward civilizations of Europe.) Then you are neither Jewish, Mexican, Italian, Pole or Negro.

Have you ever stopped to think what that means? America is the most fanatically race-conscious country in the world, and it affects the personality of all—particularly the Jews, the Negroes, the ones most obviously discriminated against. They are conscious of difference and if they have grown up in an atmosphere where this difference is oppressive, or live in it, then they are twisted some way unless they wrestle with it and acquire a philosophic attitude—which is not easy. You are entirely free from the one danger—being Irish and other things. The opposite affection, arrogance or patronage (sometimes very subtle), you have cast aside through your own warm heart and your experience in the movement. It needs more than that but you can begin where so many others never arrive. Again I believe from reasons of climate and origin, the people of California are freer and less governed by tradition than in most parts of the U.S.A. You are "pure" California aren't you?

Then you are young—nearly 20 years younger than I am—you are the pure post-war (1914–1918) generation. And I am always watching generations. The present 15 year olds are terrific—one I know discusses with me homosexuality, hetero-sexuality, etc., in a most scientific manner. I listen, show no surprise, and she likes me immensely. You know I live and let live. You are closer to me but still I am much in advance of you—20 years is a long time and the way you, with your background, upbringing, etc., react to things is fascinating to me, even if I didn't love you.

But—sweets, privileges bring responsibilities. And as you reach out for life and full freedom, you acquire the complexes and difficulties of freedom in a capitalist society. Your mother—I speak hypothetically and historically—would have been satisfied to do her best with her man. Even Candida was wavering in 1895. And when, as in your case, you have an immense vitality and certainly creative talent of some kind, then you are in for a fight. By the way, something I forgot. The "rawness" which is part of the American rapid growth and vitality, you have little of—reading and your friends—I don't know them yet—have helped you. So altogether, you have a little outline of how I see you—not only your face, your lips, your figure, your walk, the things that make my heart beat at the thought of you—after 4 years during which I know you have improved in all ways—but also everything you represent. I'll tell you *a secret*. Previously I always admired most women from the Continent—they were always full of charm, they had a certain style and those who grew up in post-war Europe were very free too, as a result of the 1918 revolutions. I also admired greatly the films of Rene Clair—all grace, French wit, tenderness and sentiment combined with insight into human nature. But I have now lived here 5 years and little by little I have learnt to understand more and more of this huge country of yours. To-day I admire a film like the Glass Key more than I do Rene Clair's. We'll talk about that. And I begin to realise too that the American woman, though she lacks so much of what her European sister has, is broadly speaking, a more compelling and a more charming, yes, charming, personality than her European sister. The causes of these things go deep. But one learns about society in a woman's face as well as in economic documents. To know you and to love you and most priceless of all for you to love me would not only be a personal treasure to me but is also an education. You are to me an ambassador of American civilization—and you don't know it. So much the better. Its size, its immense and wonderful panorama, the powerful proletariat, the Negro people, all these have held me fascinated but I remained obstinately British in my personal standards, ideas and tastes. I still am and in many things will always be I expect. But during the last year I have read American history as hard as I could—I have been ill so much—and then your letters began to come, not very long, not *too* frequent, but simple and direct. I pieced them together and you become at one and the same time a perpetually fascinating woman and a symbol. But, such is human nature, the pupil (me) terribly wants to kiss the teacher (you). I can assure you, dear lady, that after 12 years of teaching and study of the highest and most learned authorities, that both teacher and pupil progress best when the warmest personal relations are established. Am I trying to deceive you? I am. Without shame. But the fact remains that that is what the great pedagogues of education say. Now I am going to bed. This letter has become unconscionably long. But remember. It is for you to read in bed and then go to sleep. Remember. Get into the habit of sleep and stick to it. Particularly now. I love you and think of you always.

N

P.S. I had a look at the digression. Isn't it terrible? And have you copies to send of the national magazine and the color page. I would prefer them to a Rembrandt.

Postmark October 16, 1944

How are you, my precious flower? That cold, is it going away! I suppose you know that you should stay in as much as you can. Particularly at nights. You will have to put off those jitter-bugging parties for a while. And the new place? Fixed O.K. I hope. Two weeks is quite a time. One can settle down for two weeks. And do and grow a lot in 2 weeks. If you can get that apt. for the next few months that would be lovely—you would get a chance to get settled without having to look for furniture—now.

Guess where I am—in the subway—going to meet R. W., his friend R [Ralph Ellison], and two others.* I am hoping for the best—something solid should come of this ultimately. I'll keep you in touch. Just note. The N.A.A.C.P. has million members; the Negro Digest sells 90,000 copies monthly; a class started at the Schomburg Library (135th St.) has over 250 enrolled. The Negro people are once more taking the lead in political action. It is against that background that you must see our meeting to-night. All of us are fully capable of helping to guide this movement towards the social problems of America as a whole but it can do so only on its own basis. The political clarification depends upon me. . . . Well we'll see.

And now for a nice week for you. Settled as far as possible and, my miracle, doing one thing at a time. Like Jack, I have needs you know. One of them is to see you settled and on your way. I have a suggestion. In the next month or so, what about 2 days instead of one for producers? Very systematically. If, however, you don't manage a job after a good steady effort, then the hell with it that's all. Another time the luck will turn. And you have plenty to do meanwhile. Just take everything in order and calmly. For the time being don't worry about money. Just go steadily on looking for the jobs. And as for your capacity to do things—your fear that perhaps you have no "ability" really. Forget it. You have plenty—enough for two. But apart from that, ability is not to be considered in the abstract. The field to which you are impelled is so vast, so untilled, begging for people to come and gather what is there, that people without a tithe of your imagination and creative energy could do distinguished work far less you. Soon I hope to give you a practical demonstration of what has been done in that field, in a quiet unpretentious but very effective manner. No. It isn't your ability you have to worry about. If I have ever met anyone who has it, it is you; and ability of a rare kind; no. Lie in bed at nights peaceably as far as that is concerned.

---

* James, Richard Wright, Ralph Ellison, Horace Cayton and St. Clair Drake were working together to prepare a book proposal about the race question in the U.S.

The thing is to be able to harmonise the divergencies of your personality and be able to concentrate your powers. And that means work and patience. The goal is important. But when we live happily enjoying the *road to the goal* that is a great victory.

Do you know you are sometimes quite a Madonna? Very quiet, head to one side, all you need is to have your hair parted in the centre, and pressed down flat. Then you look very domestic, full of no ability at all except to do what you are doing at the time—Saturday it was arranging poems—and altogether so sweet that it almost hurts looking at you. When you feel well, do come again. If I were a poet I'd write what it means to me to have you with me for a few hours. It'll take me a long time to know you—but the journey is full of delights, surprises, and all sorts of fascinating facets and features. It makes me quite excited even when I am alone. It is a chase—you grow and I follow and as I am catching up, you slip away again. What I am waiting for now is *after you are settled and have come to terms with yourself on the recent past*—an outburst of poetic energy where you will surpass the June and July poems as much as these surpassed the L.A. ones. You will.

All my love,
N

R. A.
Apt 2A
405 E. 55th
N.Y.C.

October 28, 1944

Look at what I saw in the paper to-day. Very interesting, isn't it? Look at the forms he uses. And it is interesting to note who he is and that he had an audience which listened for an hour and fifteen minutes. Already the great debate is beginning. From now on, as never before in history, people will ask "Why? Where are we going? Why do we live with such high ideals and low practice?" And we shall take part in it. We have something to say. And we shall take care to say it in a way that gives it the best chance. [Russell] Davenport has a fine face. But he is a muddled bourgeois. He says "Why didn't we act?" We have to say why it was impossible for us to act. And *you* have to find words that make people feel in their bones how wrong it all is. Some time or other you may spend half an hour over Mr. Davenport.

Tired? Almost automatically I was going to write, darling. Just because I feel that way. I wonder if I know that fatigue. I think I do. It is nervous strain and worry. I used to have it terribly for years (*Now be calm*). And one thing it did was to intensify my ulcers. What happens is that internal conflict (which goes on and on even when we are not conscious of it) exhausts energy and nerves. You have had a period of great strain; acting lessons; fighting with Eddie; meeting Jack, fighting to get away to N.Y., clarifying your view about Jack, all the excitement and struggle over jobs, prospects, the coming back of Jack and the break; the moving, and now thinking it over, the anxiety over the future—the plain material anxiety first—one has to live—and a girl, in your situation in particular—and then the anxiety over the whole new life; and poetry bubbling and bursting to come out. I live these through with you every hour. I am not surprised that you are tired. That is why I shall do everything that I can to relieve you of some of the strain. If you meet me half-way you will always have some money as long as I have some. And by meeting me half-way I mean not making it difficult for me. I know how hard it is to do that. But please know that when you are in a mess like that, it takes the hell out of *me*. I want nothing from you that you do not passionately want to give. I am not waiting around to reap a reward some day. Above all I must not add to your responsibilities. Do you see how hard that would be for me in particular; for me because I understand your troubles in general far more than you do yourself. I cannot *feel* them as much. That would be stupid for me to think. But I know the depths of what you are going through and I want to help you and I want you to let me help you. I may be wrong but I am pretty certain that the fatigue is tension. I think so though it is very very difficult for one human being to penetrate into the depths of experience of another. And therefore the thing is to relieve tension as much as possible. One way is to feel sure that you will not be broke. We'll do all that we can about that. Another way is to clarify your mind about Jack—boldly and with energy—even writing it down. Point 1. Point 2. Point 3. In this way you do not give way to it, but you use your strength to overcome it and put it where it belongs. And finally you must learn to find some rest—relaxation. Quite often I wish I were not in love with you but the idea soon passes—for if I were not I wouldn't feel your life so closely. But it might ease things for you—I want you to come up here more often and to go walking with me—or go somewhere and walk with somebody—in the country—become physically tired in the cold air and drop into a bath and go to bed. In the old days, I listened to music with a friend, went to see my friend Bill Williams and his wife. It acted as a kind of poultice. I think that when you came up here that Saturday afternoon it did you a world of good. You come and let me fuss around you, talk about what you like or don't talk. If I am tired I'll tell you so—for, dear lady, I am sometimes very very tired. You can even work on the poems with me. But that will only help you if your mind is at ease with me. I must tell you quite frankly that if you are secretly on the defensive it wouldn't be so good. But that in all sincerity is what I think. Tired, tired, tired. And you have no physical ills. We must break up that somehow. Of course a job will help. But we must be on the alert so that if a job does *not* come we don't think the world is coming to an end. And this fatigue does not build up reserves of strength. It is in these moments, repeated too often, that one slips into folly. And all things considered, my precious Monica, I don't think—anyway let that pass.

And now about you and me. Let me tell you a few things. I am here illegally—though I have registered as an alien and signed up for the war. When the war is over I don't know where I shall be. I may have to go away—they may ask me to leave—compel me to. To stay here *may* mean the kind of semi-underground life I live—cut off from the platform and free activity.

The last five years have told heavily upon my physical and nervous strength. I have used them well, I think. I have mastered Marxism to its roots. I know where I am with it, economics and philosophy. I have also mastered the elements of political organization. I have learnt also what it is to love a woman. I have learnt that through study, experience, and a lot of time to think. You also taught me that, particularly during the last year. I have been lucky in my friends, but particularly in you whom I consider the most wonderful woman I have met in all my life—most lovely, most gifted, most full of possibilities. You are a rare person, very rare, but you have had bad luck so far. You have weaknesses. If you had had better luck with your men you would have been able to overcome them by now. But I with my knowledge of the uncertain life before me and all my handicaps would be the last person to harm you, to encourage you to do anything which would add another to your bitter experiences. Do I want you? More than anything else on earth. But only if you say "I have seen the world now and I know that I can never be happy unless I am with you." Whatever you wish from me to help you along you can have freely—only be honest with me—as honest as you can—for honesty is a struggle, a constant struggle. My personal feeling is that you demand so much of life and love that you will not find it easily. But that you will have to find out for yourself—who else can find it out for you?

I tell you all this—and I shall tell you other things too as the necessity arises—to see if I can reassure you—get rid of any sense of "responsibility" to me. For the idea that I add to your troubles—particularly now—is intolerable to me. I want you to lean heavily on me, come boldly to me, and have no sense of embarassment, in fact to glory in the fact that I love you so much. It is your right, your privilege. It will be some small return for all you have meant to me, the things I hope to see you do, and, for me the two things are inseparable, the person I hope you will be. Let's see if we can work it out that way—that you do to you what you do to me—relieve tension, feel that you are not ever alone, see the world as a bigger, better place, have confidence in oneself and the future.

Just some news. Rae went to get some copies of the magazine, the American Economic Review. They had only one. They had *doubled their order*—but altho' they came in on Wednesday night by Thursday a.m. all had gone. They have sent for more. But they don't know if they'll get them. They have never sold so many copies before, all because of some Russian articles in it. Three years hard work, in the dark so to speak, going only by faith and a belief in truth, fought for against many odds and now, a contribution and recognition. Courage, my miracle. You cannot fail.

Love,
Nello

[Undated, 1944]

The Dialectic of Nature, Engels, International Publishers
Part 2. The Renaissance and Reformation.

It was the greatest progressive revolution that mankind has so far experienced, a time which called for giants and produced giants—giants in power of thought, passion, and character, in universality and learning. The men who founded the modern rule of the bourgeoisie had everything but bourgeois limitations. On the contrary, the adventurous character of the time inspired them to a greater or lesser degree. There was hardly any man of importance then living who had not travelled extensively, who did not command four or five languages, who did not shine in a number of fields. Leonardo da V. was not only a great painter but also a great mathematician, mechanician, and engineer, to whom the most diverse branches of physics are indebted for important discoveries. Albrecht Durer was painter, engraver, sculptor, and architect, and in addition invented a system of fortification embodying many of the ideas that much later were again taken up by Montalembert and the modern German science of fortification. Machiavelli was statesman, historian, poet, and at the same time the first notable military author of modern times.

Luther not only cleaned out the Augean stable of the Church but also that of the German language; he created modern German prose and composed the text and melody of that triumphal hymn which became the Marseillaise of the sixteenth century. The heroes of that time had not yet come under the servitude of the division of labor, the restricting effects of which with its production of onesidedness, we so often notice in their successors. But what is especially characteristic of them is that they almost all pursue their lives and activities in the midst of the contemporary movements, in the practical struggle; they take sides and join in the fight, one by speaking and writing, another with the sword, many with both. Hence the fullness and force of character that makes them complete men. Men of the study are the exception—either persons of second or third rank or cautious philistines who do not want to burn their fingers.

Voila. I wrote to 52 Van—but I called there and they said you hadn't been there for the day. Here is what I promised you a long time ago.

5 o'clock. We are at Rae's. G., R, I and another friend. We have just worked out the basis of a defence of Germany—pointing out its great contributions to civilization in the past and the necessity of its incorporation into the Europe of to-day—a serious contribution—the only contribution I fear that will be made to any serious understanding of the problem of Germany.* It is going to be fine. As we talked I felt very very pleased. One person writes but in the world in which we live all serious contributions have to be collective; the unification of all phases of life make it impossible for the single mind to grasp it in all its aspects. Although one mind may unify, the contributory material and ideas must come from all sources and types of mind, approach special information and personality. The best mind is the one so basically sound in analytical approach and capacity to absorb, imagination to fuse that he makes a totality of all these diverse streams. That is what I am anxious that you get in good time, by making the effort that will be needed and at the same time, not wasting time on inconsequential and merely "interesting" stuff. Look forward to it. It will be fine and very satisfying to all those who really feel the necessity of "One World."

So now you are well installed I hope. For your sake and for my own. I live through whatever confusion you are in and therefore genuinely and sincerely rejoice when some stage of stability is reached. For that reason, to help *me*, please organise your self, clothes and shoes, etc., for the winter. For if you get ill, then both of us are ill. Fanciful? No sister, the truth of imagination and emotion, which, for those who feel it, is more powerful for joy or for sorrow than many material experiences.

I have just spoken to RW. He wants to see me about many things. I *think* I have won him over to doing what I wanted him to do. He says his mind is open now and he will do what the group says. O.K. I have now to persuade the group. He asked about you. He said he had read the poems and wanted to speak more about them. But he thought they were "fine." That was his exact word. We will send him some more and then one night have a grand talk, all of us, about it. We must send some copies for his wife specially to read. She was very cordial. And I hear that [St. Clair] Drake has been won over.

---

* J. R. Johnson, "Germany and European Civilization," *New International*, November 1944.

The letter rambles. What was I referring to in the puzzle? Not little Julie. No. I thought about that, sure, and I spoke to her on the 'phone. She is well and says she remembers me. Which I hope is true. But my strongest personal response to the whole evening was when you sat on my left on the sofa, and read the paper, while Dick and I talked. You weren't listening, weren't paying any attention to us at all. But for that very reason you seemed very much at home. And by the curious contradiction between appearance and essence, which is a fundamental of thought, I was more aware of you then than at any other time. You were just there. And by being so much at home, I think this is it, there was the illusion that you were there to stay, you were going to be there for a long time. Same but not so intense when we were going home. I was tired, said so, and kept quiet. No need to talk, to make conversation, just sit and feel that you were near. The future? To the devil with the future. Live the present fully and intensely and know what you want. The future shapes itself.

Your friend is nice. I mean exactly nice. She is terribly in love and proud of her husband. That is always very nice to see. But I make bold to wonder. How old is she? He is 21 and must be very young. He looks so. In five years time I wonder what she will think. A kid or two will help them. I know nothing, of course, about them. But simple as she seems, a woman, an intelligent woman, after five years or so begins to realise herself. It takes a man or men to make her do so. This husband at 21 business is not so good very often. Anyway, I wish them luck.

I am glad that you feel O.K. inside—that as you say in your letter, you have got rid of any basic depression. I can see that in your face—the difference between last night and that other evening that we dined in the same place was enormous. There is a word for it—but it seems that your metabolism reacts very immediately to stimuli—the effect on you of things and events is very immediate. Sometime or other I'll tell you why I think so in more detail and discuss your past.

This letter must now come to an end. Work. G., R, and I have just dined at a Spanish Restaurant. I have been writing it at intervals all afternoon. I hope you are having a fine time with your a.m. coffee. Will call you later if only to know that you are safely installed.

As ever,
N

My hand is v. shaky to-day. I am still tired.

[Undated, 1944]

Sweetheart,

I hope you are well settled and not too much worried by the moving. Usually I hate it but I would really love to help you.

News. Wonderful News. I went to R. W.'s house as soon as I spoke to you. I was "cautious" because he was just outside the booth. We talked for 1 hours. First, he has broken with our friends—told me with emphasis that he has no political affiliations whatever. But I am not rejoicing in the ordinary political manner. I wouldn't do that in a letter to you, darling.

It is from what he told me. For years I have wanted to talk to him more than to anyone else in America (political and literary) because from his books I felt that he understood the Negro question. I was equally confident that no one else whom I knew did, except a few people whom I had preached to for years. I knew I was right because a) the Old Man had always said that he had never *studied* the question but from all he had read and heard it seemed to him that the intellectuals and the Marxists in America were all *wrong* on this question. Secondly, I knew Amy Garvey, the wife of Marcus, and she knew the whole thing inside out, with her political limitations of course; thirdly I had done close study of the San Domingo Revolution, and had learnt the essence of the question there. Now R. W., with an artistic sincerity for which I could have kissed him has worked his way to a real grasp, and is now engaged in correcting the proofs of a book* for which the whole intellectual public is going to abuse him fiercely. He tells me that he is almost completely isolated and I think he sees quite clearly the chances that his great reputation will suffer a serious set-back. But he is confident of his truth and he is giving all he has. It was a wonderful meeting.

I knew about him—tho' I didn't know how far he had gone. But he didn't know that I held the same views—all he had read was the Souvarine. Briefly, the idea is this, that the Negro is "nationalist" to the heart and is perfectly right to be so. His racism, his nationalism, are a necessary means of giving him strength, self-respect and organisation *in order to fight for integration into American society*. It is a perfect example of dialectical contradiction.

Secondly, however, the Negroes represent a force in the future development of American society out of all proportion to their numbers. The repression has created such a frustration that this when socially motivated will become one of the most powerful social forces in the country.

Finally neither white America *nor black America* has faced the Negro question for the deep fundamental thing that it is in the life of *the nation as a whole*.

He has worked to it artistically, I through history. But our conclusions are identical. We shall meet again. Four years ago . . . but I will tell you this. Anyway, it has been a wonderful evening. If you have read Native Son and remember Bigger Thomas, compare him to the Peter I outlined to you, frustrated, fierce, unreasonable, overstepping the bounds. We'll talk about it. I have been wavering about writing a book. But now I shall hesitate no longer. By the time they have recovered from his autobiographical novel I shall hit them across the eyes with a historical study. You should have seen him grinning all over as I told him what I thought of his work and how long I had wanted to tell him but had avoided him. This is just an hors d'oeuvre. The real letter follows.

By the way, RW was rather despondent. But he is wrong. The tide is turning. His own work is evidence. So is mine. So is the book of Gunnar Myrdal.** But what pleased me with him is that altho' he sees it as an individual artist, he drew the full and complete conclusion and went at it with the throttle open. You know history does move. The thing is to see it.

All my love for you.
N

---

* Richard Wright, *Black Boy*, 1945.
** Gunnar Myrdal, *An American Dilemma*, 1944.

Let us try and see if we can get the fundamental question, the essential question right. It isn't easy. But until that is right nothing is stable and one fumbles along.

What are the standards, ideas, values, by which we live, and by we, I mean society as a whole, which, however, expresses them through the individual personality, the individual personality conflicts and problems of every living soul, writer, actress, revolutionary, worker, waitress, to the extent that he or she is conscious. Unfortunately for some, we live in a conscious age, not only an age of revolutionary upheavals where every "accepted" idea is in question, all accepted ideas are in question whenever the social conflicts reach the period of explosion. The distinctive feature of our age is that mankind as a whole is on the way to becoming fully conscious of himself. All the great revolutionary periods, the Renaissance, the Reformation, the French Revolution, all meant some further progress towards more complete consciousness. We are now on the eve, historically speaking, of a complete realisation of the purpose, meaning, and potentialities of human existence.

Your business in life is to find yourself. Whoever suggests to you or hints that you "ought" to have remained in or should join a serious political organisation is an idiot. A man or woman should do that for one reason, and one reason only, because that is the way he or she *must* live. People who do not feel that compulsion have no right whatever even to think of it. The average number at most of those who feel that way in bourgeois society was in France, in 1937, 300,000 out of 40,000,000. In Germany, 1932, 400,000 out of 60 million; in Russia *October 1917*, 200,000 out of 170 million. It will never be proportionately more, never. It usually is much less. *But* every educated person, every serious artist, every young person to-day has to come to some conclusion about the world. It *ends* with conflicts about Stalinism and Trotskyism. It does not begin there. So, darling (you know these words slip in naturally. It is an effort to repress them. Why should I?). So, darling, see if you can get what I am driving at. It will help you, I am sure, in everything, problems large and small.

We are the fruit of 2000 years—not to go back further. The classical world was very different from ours. The large mass of men were slaves. They were not considered as human. To-day every person is theoretically a human being, with human rights. They are often deprived of these rights. But at least, theoretically, they are ours. It took the ruin of the Graeco-Roman civilization to establish that. Christianity was a revolutionary movement which said that every man and woman (for there were terrific fights before women too were included) (the cult of the Virgin Mary is no accident), all men were equal in the sight of God, all were his children, and would be again. We may not all be Christians but theoretically to-day every man has the possibility to be as good as any other man.

After the establishment of that principle we had centuries of semi-slavery and serfdom, and the growth of a new civilization of the Middle Ages. Its greatest exponent was St. Thomas Aquinas. Life was very poverty-stricken in those days. Nature dominated man. He could not master it, so he lived in expectation of the future life where the theoretical equality and happiness would be made real. One thing, however, St. Thomas expressed—the *unity* of civilization under one God, and his representative the Catholic Church. Europe has never lost that concept. But it was only ideal. To-day, however, for Europe and the world, it has become a compelling necessity. Civilization will be unified or it will perish from imperialist wars. The ideal has become real. Then came the humanists of the Renaissance,

Erasmus, Petrarch, Sir Thomas More, and others. (Sir Thomas, a very holy man, said "that a wife should be good *and beautiful*, so that she should give delight to her husband." I have always agreed with the gentleman.) They established that the good life should not only be celestial but human—here on earth—hence *humanists*. This was a tremendous advance, due of course to the developing process of production.

The next great stage is the Reformation. The movement that began with Luther established man's right to decide his own course to heaven and, as far as possible, on earth, and established *individual responsibility*. For St. Thomas, humanism and individual responsibility were not only impossible but heresy. He could not have understood those things at all.

Let us go a little more quickly. The American Revolution (Declaration of Independence) and the French Revolution went further. They proclaimed liberty—the *political* rights of man.

By the middle of the nineteenth century we have something new—the rights not of man in general but of *labor*—the working man. Marx led this current of thought.

To-day, in advanced countries, labor of right demands universal *higher* education, safety from unemployment, state medical attention—you know them all. Now look at that worker whom you see in the subway, the bus, or moving properties in the theatre. An ordinary person, full of prejudices, not knowing very much, etc., etc. Viewed historically, however, he is an extraordinary person. He believes:

1. That he is as good as any other man. He is a worker because he has no money, etc. But if he could, or anybody else could, the road to anything is open to him. It is the driving force of *Christianity* when it was a revolutionary force.

2. He thinks that somehow or other, and this is true above all in Europe, that the civilisation of our day must somehow become unified. Two World Wars and one great Depression have taught him that. St. Thomas's great theoretical principle is now a matter of life and death with the average worker in the street.

3. He may call himself a Catholic, but he is a confirmed *humanist*. He believes that the good life is here, on earth.

4. He lives and works side by side with Catholics, Methodists, Episcopalians, etc., and would not dream of persecuting his fellow-worker for his religion. He may, for political reasons, use religion or be stimulated to use religion as a weapon. But he never thinks of religious persecution purely for the sake of religious persecution. It took Europe almost a century of blood and destruction to learn that. St. Thomas, fine intellect and splendid vision that he had, could not have understood this at all.

5. The worker believe in the Rights of Man. Before the end of the 18th century the finest minds of civilization did not believe that. Millions of workers are far more advanced here than, e.g., Spinoza.

6. The idea that all men had a right to the best possible education, that unemployment, and medical attention, etc., were the concern of the State, all these things would have seemed like madness to Kant and Hegel. They could not have understood it.

Thus to-day the average advanced worker accepts as legitimate certain human and social values which make him as a human being infinitely superior to men of past ages, infinitely his superior in intellect, learning, and nobility of character. His values instinctively, and weakly as he holds some of them, are the only values that count to-day. I repeat. There are no other values of any significance whatever. The slow accumulation century by century of the thoughts of the great philosophers, which they could only hold often as ideals, are now the common property *as a matter of every-day life* of millions upon millions of ordinary people. And the tremendous ferment in India and China and Africa show that owing to the progress of technique, the steamship, the plane, and the radio, poverty-stricken, starving backward millions of Oriental peasants are now demanding these things for themselves. People call this a materialistic civilization. So it is. But its true significance is that things which hitherto a few idealists and sometimes certain classes preached in distorted form, are to-day the desires of the masses everywhere. *"Idealism" is being forced into material form in the lives of the people.* There never was a more highly civilized age than ours—never were the basic ideals of a good full life so desperately desired by so many people.

Now, by a dialectical law which one day or rather many days, we shall, I hope talk about, this unprecedented movement towards a more profound civilization finds itself in terrible conflict with the existing social order. It always has been so. Fascism is nothing more than the attempt to suppress it. People say this, but do not appreciate its full significance. The German Fascists struck at every principle I have outlined. Men were *not* theoretically equal. The good life was not for man but for the state, etc., etc. But, in the crisis, certain startling truths emerged. What people thought was the heritage of *all* civilisation was defended only by the working-class. (They defended it badly but they did their best.) Not only the capitalists but the middle-classes to a large degree showed that in the crisis, desperate for a way out, they were willing to abandon everything. The teachers, the journalists, the actors, the clerks, the whole bunch or large numbers followed the Fascists. *The workers did not.* They were taken by surprise in Germany. But in Spain for instance they fought magnificently. *They alone were uncompromising defenders of the great heritage.* I am not idealising them. They defended it because it was their daily lives they were defending. For you and me, as a class grouping, democracy in its fullest sense, was or seemed to be, an ideal. The European middle-classes were prepared to let it go because they were suffering so much. The workers, *precisely because they were suffering*, could not let it go. All theories must be proved by practice. Mussolini and Hitler had all the power they needed. Look at what they have done to Italy and Germany. To make it personal. You are interested in artistic expression. But the Fascists in crushing democracy ruined the artistic life of the nation. There is no art to-day without freedom. And without the freedom of the workers *there is no freedom for anybody.* That we all must hold fast to.

Let me explain it as concretely as I can using the great experiences of the last dozen years.

In America we have about 13 million organized workers. With all their faults they are the most fanatical defenders of freedom of speech, freedom of organization, the Rights of Man, etc. They must be. Now they know nothing of Martha Graham, of Eugene O'Neill, of Hemingway, of Ernst and Dali, of the men who are sincerely striving in philosophy, in political economy, etc. But if the workers should be defeated and lose their privileges, then so cohesive is the structure of modern society that everything else goes. No work in any of the arts or sciences (this has been proved) can be done in a totalitarian state; once the workers' power is gone, a blight descends *and must descend.* The men who have to keep the workers quiet in a modern society must control film, radio and press. And he must see that they serve the ends of keeping the workers quiet.

So that Martha Graham and O'Neill and the rest who perhaps do not think of workers at all can think at all and work and develop solely because the workers' organizations exist. The peculiar thing is neither group worries over much about the other (except for a few here and there). But the intellectual consciousness of society rests with the great mass, that and the great heritage of Western civilization.

Now anyone who thinks at all must know this and never forget it. More than that, his duty is wherever possible to try to make the workers conscious of it. The more conscious they become, the safer the great values of civilization are. That is why when people talk as some people we know do they are committing crimes of the most abominable kind. Some may do it professionally, some in philosophy, others in art, sometimes the connection may be remote, but always, always, always, the task is to develop the consciousness, the independence, the sense of destiny, the sense of responsibility, among the masses of the people. Anything else serves the forces of reaction which aim at the destruction of this enormous power which faces them. The relation I have outlined here is broad and rough. In reality it is very intimate, affecting personal lives, sex relations of the most intimate kind, the development of personality; as Wright and I talked to-night (I am finishing the letter) point after point came rushing out, about Negroes chiefly, but I see them every day, in the simplest things, in the *voices* of people, the songs they sing, the clothes they wear, and the terrible struggle for self-expression, self-realisation. Most folks give up. One reason is because they do not comprehend historical necessity. As Engels says, Freedom is the recognition of necessity. The necessity within which a modern life can be truly and fully lived is the recognition of what the working-class means in a modern society, to be able to trace this relation in all its ramifications (they are innumerable) and to live up to them bravely, courageously, and with the inner confidence which it brings. Compromises one has to make, but with a clear understanding one knows pretty soon how far one can go. In all forms of art to-day, *all*, this consciousness guides the really significant people, the people who ten years from to-day will amount to something. Details of this I'll talk to you about in time, when we can. It isn't easy to grasp. It took me years and years. But I have it now and I don't care two damns of the opposition. I am sure "inside." If for you to be sure "inside" takes you away from me, then, sister, go in peace. I want you very badly, as badly as I have wanted anything, but you have to live your own life which will bring you nearer or further away. Your "revelations" to me yesterday were no surprise. I knew. But I am glad you said it, tho' it makes no difference to me at all, fundamentally. I love you more than ever. One day you will understand. Thanks for the picture. It is lovely—closer to you than anything I have yet seen, but not quite you. Not one of them is you. I doubt if a set picture can ever get it. It will have to be a snap. But this is near enough. It looks sophisticated and aloof but somewhere in it is some of your child-like simplicity. You know there are two kinds of simplicity—the simple direct one you have sometimes, and the same simplicity which is the result of much experience and strenuous living. All artists have the first. No one can be an artist without it. All great artists arrive at the second. That is their maturity. So Marx and Lenin by tremendous studies and experience arrived at profundities which expressed the thoughts and aspirations of the simplest workers. So, as I believe I have written to you, Hegel says that an old man repeats the prayers he repeated in childhood, but now with the experience of a life-time.

Ten years ago I talked about the workers. To-day I say the same. But God! What a difference. Same with a woman, love, happiness. I am going to bed now, 3 o'clock. Take care of yourself. Remember that whatever happens to you happens to me.

Love,
Nello

Postmark November 27, 1944

Well, precious, your letter has caused me a vast amount of interest, speculation, and amusement. For example. You say as cool as punch "Since my independence . . ." Now that is wonderful. And you say it in the most naive, matter-of-fact fashion. Like the United States, you have a day when you began. You seem to calculate events from that day also. Wonderful! Please get the date right and let me know. We'll make it a personal July 4. Celebrated every year.

Now listen. You used to wear your hair this way in front. It was "pretty." You looked like many other girls who had their hair "nicely" done. Then one day you go somewhere, "accidentally" they suggest or you suggest a change. And now. You look a very different person. You look like someone who has had a July 4, the you that functions "behind a mask" is a little, in fact, plenty more obvious. You look more of an intellectual, using the words in the best sense of the term. Now, do you think that was "accidental?" I don't. The occasion may have seemed a chance. But the choice of that particular shape, the recognition that it suited you, the decision to continue with it, all these are the result of subtle but definite changes of personality. Perhaps I am wrong. But, in general, that is the way movement in every sphere expresses itself. Necessity always expresses itself by chance. And chances added together comprise the expression of necessity. So stage by stage I read your letters and watch you, listen to the things you do and say, and watch you on your road. There are vast areas I know nothing of. But the grasp and understanding of a personality is a huge job. I have a lot of fun doing it. And I repeat. Your letter intrigued me enormously. When I say you are doing fine I judge by lots of things but none is so significant as the chance phrase "since my independence." Now, don't get scared of me. Please. Don't get the consciousness that I am a kind of psychological gestapo watching your every move. No. It is all in love and affection—two very different things—and the fact that for good or ill, you perpetually interest me.

I send you two clippings. One of them, my precious, precious Constance, shows how far you have come, the jaws from which you have escaped. Look at that attack on the German people. Look particularly at the way in which the Nazi women are identified with "the nation." Nowhere is the propaganda against the German nation so vicious, so unprincipled as among these people. A friend of mine has written an article about it. I shall send it to you. This attempt to destroy, to degrade, to smirch in the eyes of the civilized world, a whole nation, is, in my knowledge, unprecedented in European history. And as for being a part of socialism!

Furthermore the mass murder of German men for the second time in a generation makes the position of the German woman one of the great social problems of the coming period. In England for some reason, apart from the war, at least between 1932 and 1938, there was a larger number of women than of men, particularly women about the age of 30; who would have associated with the men of 40, but who had been killed during the first war. The results were terrible. These women were driven to accept the crudest advances—men were fresh in a most offensive manner. I remember a Frenchwoman writing about it in the British press. The disproportion affected the manners and the emotional development of a whole generation. If even some sections of the German women have formed such a league, it is decidedly *not* prostitution, and in any case it is a matter of social analysis, like the way the American kids give themselves to any soldier—grasping at the fundamental experiences of life which they fear will evade them. But this gloating by the Stalinists—as a preparation and cover for economic dismemberment and political domination. And all this mess is rooted in the economy of the U.S.S.R. and the contradictions and corruption which flow from it. Not the least of that corruption is the political miseducation of those unfortunate American youth who follow them.

The other clipping is about C. Lee.* There are two currents in society now. One is towards integration of Negroes—an inevitable accompaniment of economic development which places a common stamp upon all workers, compels them to recognise that they are all wage-slaves. But *simultaneously* it drives reactionary elements together. Always this dual movement in everything, society, personal life, art, until one of the two trends wins a victory, and then the new movement begins on a new basis. One day we'll go into it.

My hand is better but I have to ration it. One thing more. You seemed disturbed about the profundity and range of Gide's knowledge. You wonder how with so much life to be lived one can know so much about books. There is no need to. Gide is an example, and in my opinion, the last great example of a type—the man of letters. Not only writing, but literature was his business. To read and analyse books—that was his life. But as I told you to-day, he lived—very intensely and over a wide range of experiences. But books were his business—as it was never the business of Tolstoy, Dostoievsky, Tchekhov, Mark Twain, Hemingway, or for that matter, Shakespeare. I believe that you will in time be able to do your full share of interpretation of books, ancient and modern, on the basis of historical materialism and personal insight. That is a part of your own education and the education of your generation and of the workers too. That is a strictly creative job. But encyclopedic knowledge—No. You just read what interests you, study what intrigues you. I send you books and articles—will send you more. Most of the new ones I will not read first. You form your own opinions and tell me. The one way-dialogue in which A is always telling B is a trap both for A and for B. Guard against being dominated by anybody. I am on guard but you be on guard also. The general analysis of life and society, the method, the range of social thought and its relation to personality, that is a scientific matter. All that I know I'll tell you. And that you can and should learn as much as you can from me. I'll save you as much as I can for too often people waste a lot of time, reading a lot of useless nonsense. By careful reading and reflection you can educate yourself and train your mind without being any kind of encyclopedia. But your personal reactions to poetry, etc., hands off by everybody. You read, you ask, you listen and don't listen, you think over, you accept, you reject. What you will do no one knows, not even you.

---

* Canada Lee played Bigger Thomas in the 1941 stage version of Richard Wright's *Native Son*.

Do you know that Stravinsky's early music was in the style of Tchaikovsky and Chopin? I could multiply that example by dozens. Just be sure that it is in you and that if you work it will come out—of that I am supremely confident. One good habit by the way is to have your own books, write notes all over them, keep your own clippings, etc. Sometimes an idea comes which needs rapid research and revision into one's own past reading. *Don't lend them out. Don't.* They are your work, for other people they are play.

I must stop now. Why do people love you? Try to answer that question yourself? And you are always surprised! I must work that one out. But, dear sister, there are some people who wouldn't love you, who will hate you. You will have to conquer them. Life is an adventure. And if one learns the rules, then it becomes a great and wonderful adventure.

As ever,
N

Connie, about letters. I feel as if I haven't seen you for a long time, a long long time, and at last we are back where we were. Just being able to sit and write to you a long letter, as a few weeks ago. Do you remember those I used to write to you in the summer? When you ran up and down to Brooklyn—to Brooklyn! and I used to get bunches of poems. And all the confusion. I hadn't seen you for 4 years. And what a confusion it was. And I used to sit and write—just write and write and write. I am laughing now, rather grimly, as I think of it. You know, at my age, a serious man, shaken up and torn from my inner tranquility by a slip of a girl; and Jack, who with all his virtues, was what I knew he was; and when I saw the verse and recognised its potentialities—and felt in my bones that you could be lost—that was a mess. At the same time, dear sister, I was in the midst of a desperate political crisis, which had lasted 18 months without ceasing—that is another story, I *think* it is settling itself now though I am not out of danger. I am tired in my bones. But not worried, not in the least worried. Just tired. And worry is much worse than fatigue. It has been a great relief and very pleasant to write to you this letter. My hand will be in a mess to-morrow (it is now 4 o'clock) but I don't care. It is my hand and I do as I like with it.

R. A.
11A
405 E. 55

III.

Uncertainty and Attachment (1945–6)

[January 1945]

Well, sweets, how is the cold. You are watching it, I hope. I cannot help wondering why you get them. Some people are susceptible to colds. If you are, then that's that. You will need a lot of love to keep you warm, that's all. But sometimes it's malnutrition; you know, not lack of food but careless eating; sometimes it is lack of resistance due to absence of sufficient rest and sleep; sometimes it is the same thing due to nervous strain, internal conflict or what not. How is that thing you are taking to prevent you eating too much. Now comes a very profound question. Have you been to the doctor? And the answer I suppose is No! I think you should. Just tell him your case history. What you are doing and what you are not doing; also there is, I think, an anti-cold vaccine. Don't let this go on until spring if you can help it. Do you take vitamin pills? As for me, this noble citizen, my tummy hurts me, I am fighting a cold and am on the verge of victory, tho' the situation is still uncertain. But I am cheerful enough. I am well behind hand with my work and see no means of catching up under two or three weeks. But God above us, I do not care too much. As was said at a great historical moment "I have other fish to fry," said fish being you.

So far we stand thus. I am in love with you; you either screaming in anticipated pain whenever the subject is broached (known in military circles as the offensive defensive) or telling me that you don't want me to be hurt, either now or at some future time. As if I am some new born babe wandering around, reaching for the moon, and getting ready to be hurt because alas!, the moon is so far away. That, we agreed, is squashed. No more of this "You will be hurt" business. Take it to its logical conclusion. Constance (solemnly) "Nello, you will be hurt." Nello: "What! Hurt *badly*!!" Constance: "Very very badly." Nello: "My God, if that is so, if I am going to be *really* hurt, then I had better retreat and save my precious hide." Constance: "You are very wise, my dear *dear* Nello. I feel *so* relieved." Shall I go on? I could write pages and pages of it, with asides like O'Neill's play. No more "You will be hurt." Kids are hurt; grownups are hurt, too, but when obligations, spoken or tacit, are not kept to. Neither of us fits into either category. We are not kids, there are no obligations. I am free to fall in love tomorrow and say "Constance, you are divine, but I love Priscilla now."

There remains then only your being hurt if I raise the subject. And why? Why should you be hurt? A nice situation. I must not hurt myself and I must not hurt you. A big T A B U. Let's go behind it and see what is there. I am in love with you, not abstractly, not aesthetically, not soulfully, but plain, honest in love with you, want to get up in the morning and see you sleeping next to me; or go about my business during the day and feel you always inside of me. There has been for years a great big empty hole inside of me and no one has ever fitted into it; you do. And every mortal thing I can do to win you, I shall. You don't want to hurt me. Good. I'll tell you how not to. Don't force me to carry this wound, unexpressed. Does it hurt you to hear it? (this is becoming pathological, almost psychiatric). If it does, tell me why.

I have told you how much I love you, and why. I'll tell you again and again and again. In fact I would love nothing better than to spend the rest of my life telling you. But look at it from the other side? Why should you love me? Why should you be my girlfriend? You don't love me "that way." Good, for the time being I accept—for the sake of argument. But you have loved other people "that way" didn't you? You surely did or thought you did. You genuinely and sincerely loved Jack. You loved Eddy too. You told me as much. *But you outgrew them.* Hitherto, however, if I am not wrong, you have always been the woman chosen. You never chose. *It looked as if you chose.* But in reality you were chosen. And you then proceeded to try to give everything you had, only to find out that there wasn't there what you wanted. It is, my dear Frosty, a familiar process unworthy of Monica. That, by the way, is a smug sentence. But language often does not express the idea. Because we speak in moral terms and metaphors "unworthy," when what we should say is that such actions do not help Monica. They happen, I know. We are all poor weak creatures. But that doesn't make our actions necessarily wise.

Now I say that I was made for you. Maybe you wouldn't see that. That would be too bad, for you and for me. I tell you something which I have noticed. From the time I first met you to this day, there is scarcely a person who has seen us together (whom I know at any rate) who has not somehow expressed the idea: a wonderful pair. Doubtless some bourgeois would say "Monstrous." And the louder and more emphatic their "monstrous," the deeper my inward satisfaction would be. The bourgeois instinct is very sure. It is as follows: "That vital attractive woman. If she goes with that man, she is lost." They are quite right. They feel that you will be lost to them. While our friends feel "If she goes with Jimmy she is won for us. And J, who goes around by himself all the time, or philandering, and has obviously never met anyone to hold him, here is someone at last who will stabilise him."

But you say: "No. I don't love him. So what can I do."

You don't love me? But sweets, forget me for a moment. What about you? What do you want? I'll tell you some of what you want. You want lights and gayety and admiration and care—freedom and no bother about money and fame and a thousand other things. But you want something else too. You want to sacrifice yourself, to be conscious that you are living a life that matters, that will win the approval of serious people, something about which you will have no regrets, which will open out always wider perspectives, something you could cheerfully die for, something that you feel is as good as anything else that anybody is doing. It is a sense of a historic drama and you want your place in it. You also want to charm and fascinate, but you want also to understand deeply and exercise your intellect, to know that you have reached and are penetrating into the very depths of life, as far as the best of your contemporaries. I may be wrong. But I think if Eddy had had some serious ambition of his own, if for instance he was an absolutely devoted party man, living for it, sacrificing for it, studying and writing for it, and intent on it, he could have held you. (Thank heaven he didn't. You would not have had a chance to develop, unless he had developed you.)

Such is your inner life as I see it. And with a person so impetuous, so eager as yourself, who wants so much, I believe your love life to be the same or even more so. You want to give yourself completely, to express yourself as violently and without reservation as you want to live. (Leave me out of all this for the time being. For you will love someone on account of *you*—not on account of him.) All these violent contradictions in your personality can be organised in life, this one suppressed, held in check, forever, for the time being, compromises made, etc. (For years I have left books, poetry, music, painting, the drama aside. They are a part of me. Kids too. I have let them slide. I had to.) One makes these compromises but in so instinctive a person as yourself, you will constantly be hoping and, unless you are very lucky, always making love with half of yourself. Most women compromise. I have seen them do it. Do the best they can. Weigh and consider and let X/4 go for the sake of 3X/4, most often let 3X/4 go for the sake of X/4. I have a case in mind now—I know many. I doubt if you will. Your reactions after you met Jack on his return represent a blank realisation, which, all the circumstances considered, will always remain, with your sudden outburst of verse last summer, a wonderful illumination for me. I said to myself "This girl is immature and does not recognise her own capacities in clear terms. But she is after something—snatching here and there, hoping, ready to burn herself out if she finds it and recognises that she has found it and that something is me."

If you were to make love to me, is there anything in you that would be unrecognised? Answer, please. Or wouldn't things be discovered? If I had tried to make love to you that Saturday afternoon in 1939, when you didn't come and went home to Fresno instead, what would you have said? Answer please. Is it because you don't want to think about these things that you set up such a barrage whenever I just bring up the question? Why, after two years, did you write to me to share your great discovery of yourself? When you said that for two years every day you thought of me, wondered how I was, if I were well, doesn't that mean, at the very least, that I am a part of you, fixed, whose presence is not even necessary to be remembered every day? You remember those two weeks, the second time I spent in L.A.? Do you, sister, Am I just a conceited male or was there electricity in the air? I know I felt I was on the verge of a precipice. And if I had stayed at the sculptor's house instead of at yours I would probably have fallen over alone, or with you! That Saturday you began your break with N [Norman Henderson] as I heard. There was a crisis with Eddy—of some sort when I was there—he at any rate gave every sign of it; then the crisis with Jack—if I am not a part of your life, then who is, I would like to know.

But you don't love me. Now you are growing up. Have you ever sat down and thought out what it is you want and where you are likely to find it. It may be very

near. And oh, the difficulties in the way. I am 44! Terrible. An old man. Oh you enormous infant, in fact you embryo. You should see my wonderful grey beard. One day I'll let it flourish specially for you so that you could see it and run away at sight. (But nothing in you would be unrecognised, silly. That matters much. More than my declining doddering years. Can't you grow up faster and see that?) If you [. . .]
[missing page]
[. . .] I accept society, only to be able, I hope, to crack it wide open.

Worst of all I have red principles, a small persecuted body, not only hated by all but for that reason torn by factions, a daily grind that wears you out and makes you sometimes unfit for human society. An awful prospect. I am no catch. Too many disadvantages. But that, dear Monica, is precisely why I just will not take no for an answer. You are now set on your road. You are working hard, satisfying one part of your nature. But the other—and I think in fact I am sure it is the stronger part—and the real you, the something which drives you on, that satisfaction which you crave, which you have been running around looking for, and which you want served nicely on a platter—everything fixed as you like it? You are looking everywhere. It is here waiting for you. It is up to you, not to me. Precisely all the difficulties and the bother are what you need to be in contact with, something that with all its faults and disadvantages, matters. In fact, unless I judge you wrongly you will find yourself at home at last because of the difficulties. For all I have to say for myself is that I matter. I am something because I represent what is infinitely greater than anything else. It makes life tough externally. Inwardly it makes me as strong as 20 men. You need it badly. You can find it with me. I have helped you to see many things. But this may be the most difficult. However, battling with you is far more to me than the most marvellous reception from other people. I love you. One day I'll tell you all the things you have taught me, about myself and about you and about life in general. But that must wait. I love you very much. Why don't you love me very much?
[unsigned]
P.S. Now if you tell me any stuff about my being "hurt" I'll really be mad this time.

[February 1945]

Well, sister, can't get you anyhow on the dial; so have been reduced to leaving my name—a phoney name—Jimmy—because as you once said: I am no Jimmy. Correct. But it will serve.

How are you? I presume that your being not at home so often means that you are better. It means too I fear that you are gallivanting around—the word in my dic means: going out when you should be lying at home, contemplating. Let me know how you are soon.

And a nice acting job? Any news? But the chief thing is that you keep well and cheerful.

I have a long letter to write to you, but you must be well and I less busy.

Sister, we are sizzling around here, sizzling. I'll tell you on the phone and when you have some time you will be able to get the stuff. All I can say is that every conceivable problem is thrown open now—the social crisis is expressing itself as a political crisis, and my friends and I are challenging the false, the reactionary conceptions of our opponents. Strangely enough it can be stated in very simple, human terms. 1) The Negro struggle has a validity, a strength, a democratic, a "socialistic" value in itself. 2) Socialism is inevitable (when we cannot say) but there is no possibility of further suppressing the development of the individual human being. The economic analysis finally resolves itself into your conception of what man is, where he has come from, where he is going and why. 3) Russia is capitalistic, because the social relations between man and man have the same repressive results on human personality as fascism.

We feel that all along the line inhuman conceptions dominate our people, due to a false conception of philosophy, economics and history, *which expresses itself in their concepts of people and political organisation*. Naturally the whole thing is very complicated. Marx had a *scientific theory*, but it expressed and depended upon such a conception of the development of man as you never saw, and now the whole thing is wide open and I am engaged in making the first statement that has been made among us and all near to us for over 20 years. It is a hell of a job but I am confident for I see no one else to do it, and my friends are priceless, good brains and strong hearts. So we are at it, all of us and in a month or so the work of a few years will receive its first comprehensive expression. Bill was up for the weekend. Already he has a superb piece of work done. All we need now is revision. It is about the idea of a university for the W. Indian people.* And when I tell you that story and you see the work, you will be thrrrilled. And not only the work but the strategy—superb I think and a great victory is at the end waiting for us. I don't see how we can fail. And you plenty of time. "No poetry since Jack." But who had the poetry you or Jack. No, no, no. It will find its way. Remember. You develop slowly. That is the type you are. Patience. When things have settled down a little I'll write you the letter. It is very clear in my head. And when I see you I have lots of news.

N

[April 1945]

My dear Constance,

I have tried to get you but failed I am sorry. I continue to be up to my eyes.

I came to the play [The Sea Gull] on Wednesday. I brought no one, as the friend I was coming with missed me at the rendezvous. Thus I have only my own impressions, unchecked by anyone else's. Furthermore, Chekhov has always seemed to me the most difficult author in the world to stage. But I read the play two or three times and that I understand thoroughly from a literary point of view.

First of all after Act I I had a wonderful time. And if I can make it again I will. I liked being there. I believe in what I hope will be a not too distant future people, relieved of distressing daily cares, will be acting all over the place, groups of friends for their friends, all very small and very intimate. . . .

Let me give a general impression. Act II I found dull. The actress's son I didn't like. Not at any time. He seemed to be acting too hard. It was a difficult part for a

---

* Eric Williams delivered "The Idea of a British West Indian University" in Atlanta in April 1946. He argued for the development of a popular educational policy in the Caribbean tied to the extension of democracy.

young American to play. I have seen people getting into trouble with Marchbanks in Candida for the same reason.

But in addition in Act I I seemed to see the particular difficulties which beset all Chekhov. I felt over and over again that there were points in the dialogue which were being missed by the audience. There seemed a faint joke; or sharpness which had been somehow blunted. This is not the first time I have noticed it. I think first that he is very difficult to translate. I am told that even Gogol's The Inspector is a riot line after line *in Russian*. And Chekhov is so quiet that the flavor is unseizable in any other language. Secondly I don't think the players were good enough to overcome that difficulty. As soon as action got under weigh they showed themselves very capable. But time and again I found that here, here, there, here, something was meant which wasn't coming over. It wasn't a question of laughs at witty dialogue. But sombre though an opening act might be there is always a sense of intellectual and emotional excitement and anticipation which I missed. I have never seen the Moscow Art Players but I believe that it is right here that they would excel. This of course would be to see them in Russian; altho' I don't know a word I'd learn off the play and would know. I have noticed the same lack by the way in a performance I once saw of Uncle Vanya; and I gather that there is a danger of producers, in the attempt to correct this, pushing the players over into burlesque.

From Act II I was very happy until the very end. I am an amateur of course but I loved the sets; and I would like to know more of the person who did them. Nina was most exciting to watch. Until the last act, the very last part, I was impressed. However, towards the end of Act II, I began to feel that there wasn't sufficient variety of mood in the portrayal. You know. It is a law. What people are in Act IV is always present in Act I, in life as on the stage. You cannot perhaps see it at the time. But it is there and the pitch of eager, hero worshipping youth was not sufficiently lowered at times or heightened at others not in relation to others, as when she was frightened by her first love, but in relation to herself. There should have been hints which those who know the play would have seen, and those who didn't would have remembered. What is her personality by the way? Is she by natural temperament the same type as the early Nina. Was she a "natural" for the part?

Tregorin is most certainly a portrait of Chekhov himself—as author at any rate. He did a fine job not brilliant but sound and very sincere. I don't think he *quite* got the double movement the superficial lightness but the deadly seriousness which was below; the posing before the girl but the recognition by a very intelligent man of what he really was. But as I say I have seen it only once. I would sure like to see him again.

I liked personally the wife of the noisy steward. A charming woman, a charming actress. Her daughter was in a difficult spot in Act I. That original difficulty was very evident in her case but as the play went on she became more convincing and by the end I believed in her.

Now for the "fat part" the distinguished actress. She was wonderfully cast and did everything particularly in her big scene where she wins over Tregorin. But somehow I got an impression of routine. You know she was a great or at least a fine actress. Her charm was all charm. I think there is more to it than that. This is a very profound play. Chekhov is describing a type he knew well in fact he is analysing the artistic temperament *in all its manifestations* in all. Now the thing about these women is that superficial, selfish, and often ridiculous as they are, and Chekhov spared nobody, not even himself they have an irresistible power. At moments even their enemies, and very serious people who see through them feel it. I have seen a woman, socialite, sleeping with every man she fancied, selfish, deceiving her husband in a very cheap way, meet a man who was a puritan, a distinguished surgeon, and who knew all about her and disliked her. Yet for one evening under the nose of his wife he was swept away by her transparent flattery and her genuine charm. She was not ridiculous in any sense. You notice the same listening to a real demagogue. When you read his speeches he is a complete fool. See him in action and he is no such thing. I think the actress read the character too lightly there was more to that woman than she gave her.

Up to Act IV I was very happy and Nina in the last act held my attention all through. But when I came out I felt that she had missed driving home *the* great lesson of the play. Here I think the producer is to blame and altho' all I have written so far is what I *feel*, here I am speaking of what I *know*. Listen, young lady, because this concerns you. There are all sorts of artists in this play mature ones, young ones, the boy who will kill himself, the girl who will fight her way through. Some of them are unpleasant people; the two successful ones, one is ridiculous and even mean. Tregorin is selfish and fine writer as he is, lacks all genuine feeling. That is why he is not as good as Tolstoy or Turgenev. He was not cruel to Nina he just was incapable of recognising what was in her. What he saw he liked.

But these two successful ones and Nina who is going to be successful have one thing that matters the capacity to endure. They love fame and glory and are eaten up with vanity and selfishness, but whatever their personal and social weaknesses, they have this inward strength, this passion which makes them the artists that they are. I have known many artists of a certain type, revolutionaries. They are artists in their own way. And despite all the ambition, the rivalry, the meanness, the human weaknesses, the ones who matter are the ones who have the "capacity to endure" who cannot be deflected. That is what Chekhov is saying. That is what the play means. That is what makes them something. Otherwise, these are a very sorry lot of people and the woman whom I like, and the unloved Masha and her faithful husband and the philandering doctor and even the steward with *his* passion for his horses, all these are superior social beings to these artists. That had to come over. It didn't. Note how carefully Chekhov sets the stage for it. Nina has had and lost her child. She has had a terrible time. She still loves the unlovable Tregorin, loves a man who is no good and hurt her personally, hurt her in her love for her art. She knows how that boy loves her and she feels it is something valuable, precious to her. She knows that her love will make him. Chekhov knows the greatest temptation is a happy comfortable life. Nina quotes Turgenev warm, comfortable, in your own home, while the storms of life rage outside. She did that splendidly in her own style. So far she was fine and the rapid changes of mood, the conflict, old memories, regrets, new possibilities, she was not only good but inspired by which I mean she felt it deeply.

But it is there in that room that her own vocation comes home to her. Not fame nor glory but patience; and faith in your work. With all due respect to producers and all the rest, that is a revelation, not merely a climax but a climax *in opposition, in contrast* to all the rest. She played it as the highest wave of a rising tide. It was that but it was plenty more than that. It was as all climaxes should be, the end of one thing but the beginning of something new. *How* it should have been done, I don't know that is not my business. But it was not done.

I tell you why I think it was not done. It is a terribly hard thing to know. It is only within the last two years that I have been able to grasp fully what that signifies. Hegel says somewhere that an old man and a boy repeat the same prayers but the old man with the experience of a lifetime. Someday you will I hope know what those words mean.

Even the translator it seems to me broke down here; the translation I have says, not *fame* nor *glory* but *patience*. One must have *faith*.... Young translates "capacity to endure." I doubt if Chekhov would have written that there. Note the words fame, glory, faith; in between "capacity to endure" seems horrible to me. You need a simple word like the rest; patience seems commonplace. But it is better than "capacity to endure," which I think destroys the feeling. We are dealing with simple fundamental things. (If you can get someone to look up the Russian, please do so.) I think I know what Young wants to do the word is fortitude but that isn't good enough. I think patience with all its weaknesses is the word. The actress would have to do the rest. Nina did her best but the success of that play for her and for all the others would depend on this, that all who saw it would go home saying "not fame nor glory but patience. One must have faith." The whole play seen in retrospect must revolve around that. I doubt if many would do that. Unfortunately, however, when you read the play this must hold you tight, live with you, penetrate into your subconscious and shape everything. I would love to dissect this play those characters and work it out but I have other things to do. And in any case to work it out is one thing but I am neither producer nor actor; and the strictly dramatic effects would elude me and if even they didn't I wouldn't know how to express them but what Chekhov means that I know. And producers and players must know that too or they miss. Yet don't misunderstand me. Nina is a gifted person a true player, and she did wonders with what must be one of the most difficult roles for a young actress in the whole of the repertory.

And you and your four lines, or was it three? I tell you what my impressions were, difficult as it is with so little. Appearance [Act] I was most impressive not to the audience in general but to me who was watching you. Concentration in particular good. Appearance [Act] II the byplay with mirror and the ruble quite good too, but I felt there might have been some rustic admiration before this dazzling woman. Perhaps it would have been out of place and it is very hard to do anything under those circumstances. Appearance [Act] III where you all were waiting anxiously for the Doctor to return you were one of them and *not* a peasant girl. Your reaction was more or less theirs. *What* you should have done I don't know sister. That is not my business. I am neither producer nor actor. I am that lordly person the audience. All of you exist to please *me* and to convince *me*. I have the impression that you didn't take the part too seriously. Did you? Only four lines? But four lines are four more than zero. Not fame nor glory but patience and faith even in four lines.

So there. I am very busy and I would have preferred to see the play again before I wrote. This was particularly necessary because playing is your *business* and you have been on the inside of this one from the start. All of you know more about this play than I shall know if I read it 100 times. But I liked it immensely and tho' I felt *the* point of the play was missed yet who cares? I have enjoyed myself and learnt plenty.

Now remains something much more important. When it is all over you tell me what you think.

> Your expectant pupil
> Love
> Nello

I have some things for you. When we meet I'll give them to you the Sonata, Opus 111 and some papers.

Now I have torn the sheets badly. Sorry. Please fix them.

> [Summer 1945]
> Sat'y, no Fri'y.

Here is a lovely mess. I am sitting in the front room, and looking thru' the panes of glass. I can see house-tops, lights and a dark gray-blue sky. In one corner is a moon. Perfect—every inch of it. It is 1:15. Quiet. I have been sick the last few days—but I have a respite from pain, these last two hours. All is still. But to write to you, I have to turn on the light. That ruins everything. To write or not to write. I had better write. So out goes my peaceful landscape.

I had better write I suppose. But first—Northport is out—nowhere to go. I have a better idea. Why not come here? Two or three days or a week—you wish to talk. So do I. What could be simpler? I'll scour the town and get a radiogram. Records. And food. You'll have a room for yourself, and every night you can put two book-cases, the oak-table, and the trunk across the door. That will surely allow you to sleep in peace as I shall most certainly be doing.

Decide: Yes or No, before you go on reading. Have you ever been candid? Yes. *Not true*. But one can within limits. I shall be.

I have had all your letters and read them. I have not replied. Why? Vacillation, fed-up generally—yes, you included; engrossed in my own affairs which are in a very critical stage, *very, very* critical; ill; but the last is the least. I can always overcome that when other things are O.K. Let me trace a sequence. Why do I do it? Why shouldn't I? Letter No. 1 says things are fine. You have a job, etc. I am rooting for you. *Always*. Nothing can alter that. *Nothing*. I call you but there is some confusion. You are not there—back-stage or on stage or something. I call again—you and Stu are on stage. O.K.

But I notice a strange disinclination to write. Why? Every man is his own best subject for psychoanalysis. I ask myself: Why? I get immersed in a terrific political crisis. I am not using words lightly. The long antagonism has perhaps reached a show-down. I think of it day and night. I work out plans. I discuss....

Comes a second letter. Why don't I write? You miss me. "Write me a letter." Write you a letter.

I say: I'll be damned. She misses me! I must write her a letter. Not a note. But a letter. I know what she means. A letter. Does she think I just sit down and write off letters. I write letters because I want to—not because people ask for them. I wrote letters to my wife, before I married her—three years. Every Friday. That is 20 years ago. I started again two years ago—then I stopped. My hand, dear Madame, is pretty bad. And if I don't feel like writing I just can't (not always but quite often). So I just don't write. I am busy. The political crisis continues. Then I have personal troubles, then financial troubles. I am having it tough. But I don't mind. I can manage my affairs. I'll come through.

But I say a few things to myself. I could I suppose strain a point and write Constance. She is ill and perhaps lonely. I am sorry for her. But sometime or other I have to take hold of myself—for myself. She does not love me (Do you wince? Why should you?) O.K. If I never loved you at all I would still be interested in you. But here I am at my age (44 and flourishing) in a line with a West Point Cadet and brother Stu. West Pointer I don't know. Stu is a nice young man. But that suits them. It doesn't suit me. I have been thinking this a long time but now I take it out and face it. I say to myself: J, this does not suit you. Norman Henderson, youthful indiscretion. Eddie, Christ knows why. But still—. Jack—you know what I think. But now, *NO*. It is wrong—for me. For you. Christ, No. For the rest. Good for them. Let them line up. For me. *NO*. That is it. It is symbolised but only symbolised in the letter I should write or don't write. I have one or two friends. They would not think the same of me if they knew everything.

Then comes letter No. 3. You have seen something about yourself which I knew you would see. You want me to write to you. But I don't. It would be unfair to me. You wouldn't be unfair to me. I would be unfair to myself.

For four years I have carried the image of this woman deep inside of me. It is time I tore it out. Hostility? Bitterness? Not as far as I know. I have not the slightest trace of it. Only it's time I stopped philandering around and dreaming dreams of you and seriously begin to think of someone else. But responding to you, not in words, but emotionally, every step you take, that I must not do any longer. I must get out of the habit. And, perhaps, I don't know, you should get out of the habit too. There are things you should understand. I am a very lonely, very self-centered man. The problems I have to solve dominate me. I am 100% political. But I happen also, unlike Dick Wright for instance, to be intensely interested in the world around me, all aspects. I am like you—greedy. Unfortunately, I felt that I could give you a wonderful time and myself one at the same time. There are reaches and depths of relationship which I have experienced in scraps, here and there, this girl, sexual compatibility; another one, listening to her talk about pictures, music, and her art; another one, hearing her talk about people; another political sympathy; sometimes a combination; another one, I liked to look at, and so on. You, my cantankerous Constance, combine them all; developing, growing, and you can say what you like, I know you liked me once. Terribly in love with me? I am not so conceited. But you liked me enough. (NO. NO. NOT TRUE.) O.K. You think what you think and I think what I think. I was certain that I could make you happy—not despite but because of all the mountains of difficulties. But you insist: No. Good. Possibly after wandering around for another year or two you may think differently. (Constance. Violently. NO. NO.) Sister, you are an infant, emotionally *un*developed, but growing up all the time. That is to your credit. How and whom you will continue to develop is another story. You are a bit scared already. One day at Dick's he said of Farrell that he had been married twice and if the second was a failure then something was wrong with him. I saw you wince. Also you told me as much the last time you talked to me—you talked very very well. It was a pleasure to listen to you. You were very honest. You looked very sweet. You smiled once or twice—a dimpled smile—not the one for photographers— but a very modest, self-conscious one when you are pleased and reassured about something you felt a little doubtful of. You are scared. Don't be scared. Dick is wrong in that generalisation. But at the same time you should watch your step. You are going to find it difficult to find someone to whom you can give your innermost self unreservedly—you want youth and gaiety—you have had so little—and physical exuberance ("whip-like." You teenager. But you want somewhere to express all the tempestuous intellectual aspirations that burn inside of you, and you want to feel that you are learning something and at the same time teaching—that is only a part. You want them all and when you don't get them you are disappointed and recognise "unrecognising arms." It isn't your fault. Only you have to know yourself and recognise what matters most to you. If you are not careful and discriminating, then you may lose confidence. You have been an unlucky girl. Because confidence once gained is not often lost. This is a long parenthesis but it contains multum in parvo, which you may look up in the dictionary.)

To return to *me*. I called you. Your voice was wonderful—like that day at Northport, a Sunday—but I suspect you were just a little on guard so to speak. I wanted to arrange with you to meet.

Then I got very ill—tummy—and I lay in bed and thought all the things I am writing—to be correct this is a small summary.

To put it in a nutshell. If I start to write to you, I have to think. What shall I say? What shall I not say? Every now and then, in fact quite often, I wish to say I love you, to tell you what I think of you, what you mean to me; that you were in love with Jack somehow didn't bother me *very* much. It didn't check me, dry me up, set up conflicts. As a matter of fact, those letters were only half of me. I was somehow untroubled and confident that in time an intimacy would grow—and I would be able to write to you, without any reservations at all—whether you were 2 yards away or 2000 miles. I read only last week a superb letter by D. H. Lawrence—utterly magnificent so easily misunderstood but so true. Now that I look back I see that I have never even talked very much to you about me—a form of selfishness. But I took great delight in you.

So, sister, that is it. Why this candour? My way is to keep my mouth shut and go my way. I offer all I have, or as much as I am allowed to show. Why should I bother you? But to-day things happened. My house was in a mess. I got someone to come and clean it. It looks lovely to me.

Bill came from Washington to see me. We talked. He progresses mightily. What a good pupil to have! And how I wanted you to be my star pupil! But Bill came and I am very pleased with him.

I had lost my passport—a hell of a mess. I found it.

My financial troubles are solved.

My personal troubles are now under control

Politically the crisis is being tackled with energy and with boldness. Chances are good. We may lose but I don't think so, and in any case we'll fight as our great ancestors would have fought. We are all *confident*. . . .

My tummy has stopped hurting for a bit. I said: After all, why should I equivocate with Constance—with Monica. Must people go through the world never saying what they think. I have told her so much more than I have told anyone I may as well tell her this.

Oh I forgot. In the clean-up I was arranging your pictures and the one I love after the Monica [is the] one standing in the park with the bag at your feet—turned up. I looked at it and felt very friendly.

So I sat looking at the moon—I had fixed, within limits, everything. Three strenuous weeks. But there was one thing remaining. To write or not to write. So I have written. Strange business! I know now I was right in writing. I am very exhilarated. It is clear this business has been brewing in me a long time. That is what the years bring. Patience.

By the way, your birthday. I hadn't forgotten it. I have for you the Myrdal volumes.* But, let me confess, I said "Hell, why should I jump to it? They'll keep." Now that is bad. I said to myself. "You, you are behaving in a mean manner and to whom—the one person you shouldn't do it to." It made me think plenty.

Also Lyman has *three* books by Clive Bell, including the famous one on Art. But, *between us*, gifted, sensitive, and full of knowledge as these critics are, they lack the social basis and their talents run to waste. You have never been to a gallery with me. You have never been anywhere with me. You are scared aren't you? I hope you didn't think I was so dumb as not to know—you big infant. But you would get out of it in time as you get out of most things. So write to me a long letter, or write to me a short one, or come and stay with me two days or two weeks (the *food* will be good and not fattening) or two hours. Up to you. I have been through three trying weeks, and you were the most trying of all. But this noble citizen, i.e., me, is now feeling not so bad. I have turned off the light and the moon is gone—let it go. And so, my miracle, for you still remain to me, a miracle, for above all the others, a perfectly gorgeous creature and Monica, as well, I wish you good-night.

N

P.S. I wanted to come to see you act. I terribly *wanted* to come. But illness dogged me. However, I know *now*, that something else was bothering me. Send me a wire please—home, 4F, telling me if you are in this week and I'll come. I want to see you act—I want to know if you are actor or writer fundamentally. So send me the wire please. My warm regards to Stu—and if you misunderstand anything I say in this letter about him I shall be very disappointed. But you never disappoint me for long.

P.P.S. I was numbering the pages and I started to laugh. Why? She said imperiously "Write me a letter." Well, here is a letter. Which reminded me of something else. A famous Shakespearian critic once divided Sh's career into various periods, comic, tragic, disillusioned, etc. Another critic sneered. Said he. Imagine someone going to S and asking him for a comedy or a love-story and S saying "Sorry. I am in my tragic period." Whereupon the critic made the devastating reply: "No? But when they asked him for a love-story in his tragic period they got one—only it was Romeo and Juliet." Terrific I think. And somehow I think it applies. Somehow I think it applies. My tummy continues to pester me. I need to lie in bed and be fed at regular hours. I am down at Lyman's to-day—Sunday. I wrote this letter Friday. Any more news?

NO.

NOW....

---

* See p. 190.

[July 1945]

Say, sister, what kind of a letter and post-card do you write to me?

1) About you and me. As usual, conventional expressions, conventional sentiments, dashed off at great speed. You have written to me directly three letters in your life—perhaps four. The word correspondence you know = co (together) respondeo (answer). See? Answer, *together*. You have many things to talk to me about. You "hope" to spend a few days. And what am I to do? "Hope" you come. Sorry. I am engaged the weekend of August 2nd (or thereabouts) from Thursday to the following Thursday. I have not had my vacation. I'll fix it to suit you if you come. That's OK with me. But either you are coming or not coming *and fix a time*.

2) Your card about the acting is *awful*. Luckily I know you—knew you most during those wonderful days last summer when you wrote that verse day after day and I was wondering how long it would go on.

Look here, sister. I get a message saying: don't come on Monday. I don't come on Monday. I can't. I can't come on Tuesday. Ill. I crawl out on Wednesday. I stay a whole day thinking about your work. I brush aside all superficialities and try to penetrate to essentials. Much against my better judgment I write to you. I thought it would be better to wait. Saturday I come back again and watch you again. And what do I get on Monday—a card, with "not an excuse but an explanation." Scribbled in great haste, as usual. Now I was going to write to you again about the performance. I shall do no such thing until I receive an *answer* to my letter. If you are too busy, O.K. Let it wait. I don't think you even read my letter properly. You certainly did not understand it or you wouldn't have written that card. Listen, sister, listen. Sit still and pay attention to what I am saying. I am referring to a concentration that is in your "subconscious," a concentration that you show repeatedly when you write verse, when in some of the poems, good or bad, there is nothing fundamental between you and what you want to communicate. This was *absent* on the stage. It is a serious charge to make. I can probe it with you. But *with you*. Not by myself. You must meet me half-way. I know all about the multitudinous correspondence you have always carried on. Cut out half of it and really *c*orrespond with me. None of them could possibly write to you about your work as I would. But no scribbles and superficial excuses and remarks. Write that way when I tell you that I am now free of your spell. I don't appreciate it but if that's the way you feel, OK with me. But about your work. If I am to take it seriously with you, you must take it seriously with me. I have been reading and re-reading Stanislavsky in the Ency Brit [Encyclopedia Britannica]. One of the greatest essays I have ever read.

I understand him. I understand him I am sure better than most professional actors would. Both because his method is profoundly, dazzlingly philosophical, both in a social and logical sense—apart from Hegel and Marx—it is the most brilliant piece of pure dialectic I have ever seen; and secondly because having spent so many years in all kinds of speaking and listening to people speak, I can feel inside most of the things he is talking about. I can help you to understand yourself and to concentrate and to work and *to learn to bring it all out*. And in doing so, I learn a great deal that is of interest and importance to me. *But* I shall not do it unless you cooperate. That is not correct. It would be more true to say that I cannot do it unless you cooperate. How can I? As a matter of fact if I write you four pages you should write back eight.

Or is it, where I am concerned, even in regard to your acting, you take me for granted so much that you don't even bother.

N. E. NEW ERA. A new era has begun.

3) Here, dear sister, dear dear, sister, I have to restrain myself. You see all those dears. They are a euphemism for what I really want to call you, which is a frivolous, stupid, thoughtless, irresponsible, young fool. You have never heard me curse, have you? You don't know that I can, do you? Sister, *dear, dear, dear,* sister. If I ever did you would cry. And I am very near to it. This is why. I see in your letter the following sentence.

"I am not too well either this week—a nervous stomach and pains like mad. I have a great sympathy for your stomach now."

Keep your sympathy for your own stomach. You will need it. Months and months ago I warned you. I told you in as plain words as I could. Do not fool around with that. For Jesus Christ's sake do not do it. Let me tell you what you are on the road to.

1) It will, in time, unless checked, make you self-conscious about every meal you eat. This means that in the most natural and necessary of all functions you will be unnatural and continuously exercising conscious judgment. *It will affect in time your whole outlook upon life.* You will be as sensitive as a thermometer to anything which affects your personality and will develop abnormal egotism.

2) It will drain your strength away, little by little. Particularly in acting (as S-ky points out) by absorbing your physical energy it will cut off from the psychic processes. You will be most of the time below par and have to strain.

3) It will alter your appearance—particularly under your eyes and skin-texture. Your hands will shake.

4) It will periodically set up toxins in your blood and give you halitosis. Fine lover you'll be.

5) It may affect your whole nervous system and by giving you periodical insomnia get you into all sorts of bad habits—drugs, dissipation, and at periods either throwing yourself into the arms of any man available or excessive masturbation. I have studied this business. I have had this trouble since I was about 7. It may be that the symptoms are the result of early childhood difficulties. I don't know. But we know for certain now that its seat is in "the head" and not in "the body."

What is the best way of impressing you sister? On my knees with flowers, or by slapping you about the face? Or alternate doses? For I want to impress you now. You have to do three things.

1) You have to get not "my" doctor—but the best stomach specialist you can put your hands on—and find out—peptic ulcer, duodenal ulcer, mere spasms or what. Get X-rays. *Find out what it is.* Think over *all your symptoms* and tell the doctor. Particularly the X-ray so that if there is a duodenal ulcer (Mussolini, Leon Trotsky, Antony Eden, and many others, too numerous to mention) if there is one, you know.

2) Doctor or no doctor. At the first sign of "pains like mad," *cut out everything except what you have to do.* Take short walks or rides and go to bed. If you have a dear friend who is soothing or someone who is pleasant, ask the person to come and stay with you and talk to you.

Diet. Not unpleasant messes. But plain, good and simple food—eaten with rigid regularity. Eden didn't, couldn't take part in the *election* campaign. James Roosevelt is a walking skeleton and every few months has to leave the army and go to hospital. Harry Hopkins has a permanent room in the Mayo clinic. "Pains like mad" indeed! You ought *now* to act, and then go home and lie in bed or sit in a big chair—for that stomach in your head.

3) *This is the hardest of all.* Learn to control yourself. It can be done. When you get excited, and the blood is racing and your stomach muscles twitching, fight it down. Give yourself the job of calming them down. Just restore them to normal. *It can be done.* Fight for self-mastery. Calm yourself. This is a long and difficult business. But it will help you in everything you undertake, in art, in life, in love, and wherever else is important. But for the time being in your stomach.

Now my conscience is clear. I cannot do any more for you. If you don't listen to me, you will go to hell without a shadow of a doubt. The thing is to be fought and conquered *early*—by physical discipline—technique and mental control. Master it *now*. You have had illnesses—all of them signs of nervous strain. Even sinus, some people think, is a sign of a neurosis. Though I have no fatalistic early childhood determinism about neuroses. Even your acting as I saw it shows a lack of coordination of your ability. Yet you have grand concentration—when you decided to make it as a model; when you wrote verse last summer; when you talked to me the other night—when you wrote me a letter about Muriel Rukeyser—but you have to learn to concentrate yourself—and first of all to master that fluttering stomach of yours.

So will you, dear, dear, *dear* little woman (substitute the correct words, my *precious*—my infinitely precious) you know what I really want to call you—will you read this letter carefully point by point, and do what I tell you?

You can-

a) Come or don't come *but decide; don't scribble inanities*

b) Write or don't write about your performance but *decide; don't scribble inanities*

c) Never, never, never think of your stomach troubles as "pains like mad." I shall not refer to this subject again unless you raise it. It is too serious. And I am sure, my dear Miss Selfish and ill-mannered, that you are glad to hear that though still weak I am much better. *Thank* you. Don't apologise.

Love,
Nello

I almost forgot. So you expected a letter! So you thought I was dishonest—only a "form of dishonesty." Ho! ho! Was I? I don't care a damn. Look who is talking! You *try* to be honest. *Untrue.* Absolutely untrue. Now *I try*—or I tried—will you? Proof? *I spent time on it.* I tried to find out. I waited. *I analysed.* I tried to express myself. I tried to make sure what I felt. I hesitated. I *wrote. I tore up.* I let it ride. If I was dishonest, I was honestly so. I took pains about it. But you? You were neither honest nor dishonest. Just indifferent. You offered neither love nor even friendship. You needed a shoulder. You can still have it but you must come part of the way. It isn't or it won't be there *whenever you feel you want it.* Your conception was not even bourgeois. It was feudal—lady-love and knight-errant. Degrading to both of us. Certainly to me, at my age and with my responsibilities. But I am not ashamed. I was so lonely and had so much locked away inside of me for so many years. And you had so much that I needed so badly. I am positive you don't know what I am talking about though in ten years you will. But it was wonderful while it lasted. And chiefly last summer. Envelope after envelope. True you didn't write direct letters but you did better. I was in communication with you. Jack! You were kissing him but to hell with Jack, I thought. I refused to let that citizen intervene between you and me. You were writing him letters saying I love you but you were writing poems to me or to be more precise, for me. You don't know that? Whom were you writing them for—I would like to know?

Democracy—Richard Wright—independence—women's rights—walking along the road and feeling in tune with workers—pulling yourself out of that Stalinist influence which would have corrupted and corroded you. Those long conversations on the telephone. Up to the day when you came to Northport and we sat in the station talking. How I loved you. You were at your best then, Jack or no Jack. It was a wonderful correspondence then because natural. You were not indifferent. You wrote for me—you wanted to hear what I thought—you wrote again and sent it off—you fought a great battle—and won a great victory. As I write about it, I am thrilled again. It was a marvellous episode. I hope you remember those months as I do. They were terrific. When you went away with Jack. Almost for the first time I was aware of him as a serious rival. Hell, I said. That man is going to take her away. But really I didn't believe it. And sure as day came a poem—"unrecognizing arms." I said, that Jack is a dead goose. He has failed her. Whom was that poem written to? Not for Jack. Nor for the public. No, you *had* to express yourself and you wrote it and sent it to me. I repeat. Those were wonderful, wonderful days. I don't think you appreciated them. You were giving, giving, giving in one way, all you had. And if you had had the least little bit more of courage and not so much overburdened by worldly considerations and childish notions we would have soared even higher. You said you would come and spend a week-end without a chaperon. You did. Yes, you did. YOU DID. I can see you sitting on the divan—you had touched up your hair and wore it high—and a reflective look in your eye as you considered it. And then you said to yourself "Why shouldn't I?"

YOU DID, and you said "I'll come."

YOU DID and as long as you continue to deny it, I know that you are not trying to be honest. Just another of your multitudinous fears.

So, sweets, a-dee-oo for the present. As I said, I came again on Saturday to see you perform. (About that not a line until I hear from you *properly*.) But with your hair up, at times you looked very forlorn and youthful and protectable—brave and trying hard but in a world that was pressing hard upon you and in which you needed help. It was a sudden but very powerful impression, more personal than anything else. These last pages I am smoking and looking out of my window periodically. Tranquil as a lake. I had been so worried. I look at your Monica picture and Monica isn't worried—eager yes, but confident. *Superb*. Victor Serge once wrote that walking along in Russia you periodically saw a man or woman, middle-aged, calm, with a dignity and courage that would have walked up to a cannon's mouth—they were the old revolutionaries, dedicated to a life of struggle against Tsarism. A whole generation of magnificent people—you look like one of them in that picture—a young one, but one of them. Saturday night somewhere in Act III it was or II I think (they skipped a scene) I suddenly got that impression of you I mentioned. No[t] Monica but Constance, fighting hard but uncertain. Somehow or other you will have to resolve that contradiction. If you can capture the inner confidence and power of that picture and the calm self-control—for it is you, it came from you; and harness it to the fire and energy and singlemindedness you showed when you poured out all that writing last summer—good good stuff, crude though it was—then you will be terrific and surpass your expectations on the stage—with hard work of course. Was it because you were fighting for something that mattered? Something beyond yourself, something that called for sacrifice, for giving up the tangible for the intangible? that made you feel life was a great battle and you were on the right side? And now? What are you fighting for? Are you satisfied with your aims? Do they dominate you? Those week-ends you spent quietly in Brooklyn—just getting yourself together, thinking, reading, mobilising yourself? Wasn't there something which gave all your life meaning and purpose and cohesion? Not Jack. No. The struggle with *Jack and all he represented*. The letter you typed and read and re-read. What a little crusader it was! And you sat quietly at the week-end and gathered yourself together. And when the time came, well fortified, you routed the enemy. Why were the arms unrecognising? Because you demanded so much more recognition than six months before. Of course. Now you have to pull yourself together again, get courage and, more important, conviction, aim at something that will stiffen your back and raise your head, as high and proud as in the picture; and find strength to discipline that stomach and everything else.

39 pages. I am thinking that this letter will be a surprise to you. I was reading Heine the other day. You can say with him.

> Thy letter, sent to reprove me,
> Inflicts no sense of wrong;
> No longer wilt
> thou love me, –
> Thy letter, though,
> is long
> Twelve sides, to tell
> thy views all!
> A manuscript in fact!
> In giving a refusal
> For otherwise we act.

Isn't it lovely? But it's *merely* lovely. I sat and wrote and as the ideas came I wrote them down. Everything I say I mean and why shouldn't I tell you what I think. I say all that I think and am not bothered about it. Ignore it if you will—I wouldn't mind. It may help you. But about the future and the work—I can help you if you help me. And I must say. Thanks for the memory. You will never know what it meant to me day after day to get those poems—I have never even tried to tell you. It has been one of my greatest personal experiences in fact, apart from complete emotional and physical union, undoubtedly the greatest personal experience I have ever had. I only wish you could have felt the same about the whole business. So as I sat writing and it all came back to me—the same summer days I expect, in spite of myself I wrote. No. That's not true. Anyway it doesn't matter. Here it [is] as I wrote it. Lots of success and strength.

Yrs, N

Postmark July 24, 1945

You still have two weeks there. They are very precious. Don't throw them away. They will be valuable for experience. So work hard but don't attempt to become a Sarah Bernhardt in a week. *Don't fret*. Calm yourself and look at everything you can. It will all come back later. Master the inner excitement. Master it. *If it is too much for you then tell somebody pour it all out. But don't let it eat you up inside.* Somebody is slandering Stanislavsky. In his Britannica article, Volume 22, P. 37 he says

"The same growth of consciousness and fineness of internal feelings must be worked out by the actor in relation to his vocal equipment. Ordinary speech . . . is prosaic and monotonous."

Then he shows what the genuine artistic speech can be. He knows that it is *internal* in its origin. But he concludes

"The perfecting, therefore, of the phonetics of speech cannot be limited to mechanical exercise of the vocal equipment but must also be directed in such a way that the actor learns to feel each separate sound in a word as an instrument of artistic expression. *But in regard to the musical tone of the voice, freedom, elasticity, rhythm of movement and generally all external technique of dramatic art, to say nothing of internal technique, the present day actor is still on a low rung of the ladder of artistic culture, still far behind in this respect, from many causes, the masters of music, poetry and painting, with an almost infinite road of development to travel.*["]

Now this is clear enough. Voice, movement, gesture. This has to be learnt. Are you going to travel that road or do you want the road of Lauren Bacall? Earlier he says . . . in an artistic condition, full freedom of body plays a principle role; i.e., freedom from that muscular strain which, without our knowing it, fetters us not only on the stage but in ordinary life, hindering us from being obedient conductors of our psychic action. This muscular strain, reaching its maximum at those times when the actor is called upon to perform something especially difficult in his theatrical work, swallows up the bulk of this external energy, diverting him from activity of the higher centres.

Now this freedom is learnt. It is to be worked at. *You are stiff.* But whether ballet is the thing for you I don't know. Dancing it must be. Perhaps expressive dancing. But dancing and voice. Those are imperative.

And when I say dancing and voice I mean dancing and voice—not playing with them. Or in some City class. I mean tutors—good masters. It means sacrifice of money and of time. You have to learn "to scorn delights and live laborious days." This will help to loosen you up and give you a chance to express yourself. But all this is external technique. What you need most is what Stanislavsky talks most about *internal* technique the training of the intellect *and of the emotions*.

Another day we'll talk about that. But look on page 1 of this letter. And in the quotation see his phrase "the fineness" of internal feelings. He says again *his individual emotional experience*, by its limits, actually leads to the restriction of the sphere of his creative genius.

It is the life you live especially when young its intensity and the breadth and grandeur of your experiences. But a girl in a tea shop can have tremendous experiences. Beethoven and Mozart *deeply felt and understood* are emotional and intellectual experiences. *Serious* trouble is too. And he says again of the actor . . . he must judiciously develop his imagination, harnessing it again and again to new propositions.

Now how much of all this have you done? As I watched you I could see how amateurish you were, and, what is the same thing, in acting, how stiff, how inhibited, how much you needed to *unloose yourself*. Now I know you, your energy, your ability, your observation, your insight, your imagination. (I know your weaknesses too. Your sense of values, in human personality, is often very very weak. Norman Henderson, Eddie, you *married* them you know. That was terrible. That you didn't make it with either is not worth two minutes thought. That you were so indiscriminating as to *try* that is not to your credit.)

But you have as you say a wealth of creative talent. I know it from your writing and from knowing you. This last letter I wrote to you this morning about the poetry in the summer of 1945 (I hadn't the slightest idea that you were despondent) should show you that this is what I really think. I have said it and I will say it again: Of all the people I know and work with, the young people Bill, Rae, Grace, Willie (who is so *brilliant* at times that I smile even to look at him) you have the greatest natural ability, the greatest creative power, the most genuine imaginative vision. Now are you satisfied? Remember the inscription in Bill's book I sent you. You think that is just talk? But *you are the least selfless*. Every one of them, every one, cares not one damn thing for the bourgeoisie and all it can offer not a tinker's dam. Bill is bourgeois but he thinks of his books and his ideas and principles *first*. Grace is consumingly ambitious but only in our circle. She wants nothing outside. Now *you* are torn. *What do you want?* You can be a gifted and accomplished writer, doing tremendously important work in 5 years. You can be a fine actress in 5 years. I know that. As soon as I saw you I knew exactly what was wrong with you; and you have expressed it yourself in this last note it is there, untapped and your lack of technical training inhibits you externally; and your emotional and intellectual lack of development I called you emotionally undeveloped and I mean every syllable of it your innumerable fears, fears for your future, fears the years will pass you by, financial fears, fears of public opinion, e.g., of being seen with me in public, fears for your moral reputation (you tell me how you went to Stamford first and you and Stu got *two* rooms a long rigamarole story, as if I cared; fears lest you are not honest fears lest you have not got the capacity to make a success of marriage, fear that prevented you coming to spend that weekend which you promised you *did* promise; take it back if you like, but promise you did; all these fears limit you; on the stage, the real power of your personality limited and chained. You are not growing. I told you I could help you. I know I can. Naturally with writing you are less inhibited. You are more naturally writer than actress. But even with the stage I could teach you *how* to work. But I shall not for one moment do more than my share. I stand by what I wrote yesterday. You and your dear "friendship!" Absolute baloney. You have built up a fine mechanism between yourself and me. I know it. I have proof. I am your standby, your "father complex," that is me; but meanwhile you waste yourself and run your emotions ragged and cheapen them and stultify them with Norman Henderson, Eddie, Jack (who with all his qualities turns out in the end to be afraid of you) and now, or tomorrow, God knows what riffraff. And what is so Goddamned annoying is that I have known and know charming and intelligent women who, as between any of your swains and me, not only would not hesitate, but would be indignant yes, my dear

Constance, would be indignant, at the suggestion that they could for instance have chosen Eddie instead of me. (Now, you see, I can tell you things I wouldn't have told you before.) You *wasted*, threw away, three years with him. Do you know that? And everybody, *everybody* wondered why. And a great deal of all the restraint and inhibition and cramping and doubts and lack of emotional growth and lack of freedom which I saw on the stage comes from just there those years thrown away; in one fundamental respect, Jack added his precious quota. Which of them helped you? NONE. And you are a very feminine person, dependent upon a man and will be until you gain confidence in yourself by loving freely and being loved, not hiding and suppressing and being afraid that he will find you out or being afraid that you will find him out. Well you have to clarify and organise yourself is it a talent you want to express or is it fame and your picture in the papers? The two are not the same. That conflict is deep inside of you. And if you are going to *act*, then you are going to have to loosen up yourself, move your limbs and your shoulders as if they had no bones, and develop your intellect and emotions so as to be able to give them full play and transmit them. I don't know what the public saw but I saw all through you and around you after 15 minutes never saw you so clearly, *you*, what you really are, what you can be, the stupid blunders you have made in the past, I saw everything. At any rate you learn. It is to your credit that you recognise that you are in a mess. How deep a mess I shall explain to you with great precision, for that is the only way you will be able to come out of it. Only, I warn you once more, dear sister. You must make up your mind to break the habit patterns you have formed in regard to me. I have written this letter because of your talent after the work you did last summer and the way you did it I respect you. Personally I prefer that you write because you have, after long and hard work, so much to contribute directly to our side of the barricade. But you prefer the other road. I don't know if you are right. But you have too much ability not to make a success of that too. So for old acquaintance sake and because as I say of what you are, I'll help you if you wish it. But no "indifference," no troubles and difficulties for me and good times and merriment with other folks, no "problems" for me, and celebrations with others; above all no scraps of letters and long screeds to people who are not worth two damns to you, because if they were they would have helped you somehow, directly or indirectly. And none of them, not one, has been any blasted good to you. You stood on the stage amid the other performers, forlorn, lonely and miserable. I am on the whole a poor psychologist but you, you are my washpot, to use a phrase of [Arnold] Bennett. I see through you, not everything, but plenty. I saw you last Wednesday afternoon and knew. Now you have to get out of all that and the first thing, or at least one thing, is to get out of your attitude to me for your own sake. If you cannot do that, for your own benefit, then we will soon be episodes in each other's past.

Now let me hear from you. It will do you good. Find time. Do not scribble. Where do you think *I* get time to write to you? Have you ever stopped to think of the work I have to do? Have you ever stopped to think of that? Well, I have to. Henceforth it is not what you are that matters with me but what you do.

As I am about to put this letter in the envelope, it struck me that it was quite like old times. But it isn't. Times change. In fact it's very different from old times. You have made a change too. Your letter, which provoked this one, shows that you have reached a turning point too in your road. Be sure that you examine it well, to find out where you have come from and where you are going. And please tell me why was I *not* to come on Monday?

[unsigned]

[1945 Stamford]

Dear Sister,

1) The election. It is tremendous. The labor leaders are scared "pissless" to quote Freddie's altogether priceless expression. But the rejection of Churchill and all his works just in the moment of his greatest triumph! They have, the British people, laid the responsibility for the war at the feet of the Tories and have shown that for them the wartime "unity" was only for the war, that they hated them all the time. It is a trumpet call to all European labor and U.S.A. labor too. . . . There are so many things to say.

2) I stood at 7th Ave at 7:45 and a girl came up to me—familiar but I couldn't immediately place her. Paula Aragon. I had to send you a wire and to meet someone at 8. I asked her to come with me into Western U. I wrote the telegram. The man came up and read it out LOUD she asked me to remember [her] to you. Of all curious coincidences! She, at that time, and under those circumstances. She came in two or three days ago. She *will* paint she says. She has already a small apt, bathtub in kitchen, heating by a stove but paint she will. She says she will write to you.

Thank you for your letter. I shall wait for the rest. You will have to make a great effort really to meet me halfway. As these last few days have shown, I am very sensitive to you, more sensitive to you than I have been to any other human being. Read my letters and then think of you, parts and everything. I saw you sideface the night of Sylvia's concert and I saw signs of dissipation. Yes dissipation. I wrote to you about it and then tore up the letter. I suppose you are over that now. I think you are. That sensitivity is a very precious thing. But you can destroy it if you do not want it. After all it's yours.

N

By the way I owe you very *very* much. It is as well, it is in fact, necessary that you know that. You should know that and I don't mean in words but inside of you be conscious of it and know to what extent you contribute though so far very carelessly. For instance I have been a dilettante but alert observer of actors for some years I have concentrated more on speakers. But watching you on the stage has been of immense interest to me. I have been running through practically every play, every actor who made an impression on me from 1921 arranging my ideas in order comparing, sifting, and as always, analysing, probing. I have worked out everything, all leading up to you and around you. I hope it will be as exciting to you as it has been to me. You did practically everything *wrong* this is presumptuous of me but I feel so certain of it. And I am equally confident that with hard work and righting yourself *inside*, you can turn all the power that now tears you apart into creation and knock that Stamford audience absolutely silly. You had, in my view, the second best part you *were apart from the bunch*. It was intensely dramatic even melodramatic. Listen to the big boaster which is *me*. *If* you had had a year's steady training and I yes, ignorant, untaught me, could have spent a weekend with you with that part, you would have been dizzy at the effect you would have made. True or False? When I see you I'll talk to you for an hour and you'll see. Get the script, by the way, if you can *both plays*. Try hard to get them. Enough. . . . I wouldn't say that to or of anyone else in such a business. But I understand you (in certain respects at least) and see what you are doing too clearly not to feel confident enough to tell you. You will decide whether I am correct or not.

P.S. I was very sorry to hear your bad news. But sit quietly, my dear Constance, and master everything, being sure always that you are going to work it out. One must grow up sometime. And you have immense power. If you don't discipline it, it will destroy you, or ruin you for anything that matters. But handle it, learn to handle it, and you will not only go places but go good places.

[1945]

Well, my little songbird, I await your woodnotes. I hope I get them before I see you. I hope I see you this afternoon.

Do you know what the time is? 6 o'clock. I have worked continuously from 3 o'clock this afternoon with two intervals for meals. Unfortunately, I have an appointment at 10, here though. Then I have another at 1:30, and I must have lunch in between. I hope I shall catch a snooze before I see you. This article has been very lovely to write. Meanwhile I am thinking of you. Do you know what exactly. The strangest melange. The last time I met you in the street—my first glimpse of you, in high heeled shoes and that black skirt, making you look all tall and willowy and your face very gay and looking very pleased to see me. You know we walked away from Bill and Georgie. And I had intended to walk with Georgie and let you walk with Bill. For a moment I forgot them, my guests. And secondly, your decision not to go back now. It is very hard to disentangle one's own subjective desires from an objective situation. All I can say is that you seem to be growing and expanding like a young tree, shooting up and spreading branches. I am even a little scared at it. For your acting comes first and the chief thing is for you to be settled. But when you say you will stay I am glad for myself but glad too for myself in another way the indescribable and far from merely personal pleasure at seeing you finding yourself and realising the immense possibilities within you. Sometime I shall explain this to you in detail. I cannot bear to think of you being cramped or checked in any way. Every step you make I mentally throw up my cap. I am terribly eager to see the poems. I wonder what they say about life, what they say about you. And I think about you in a black skirt and high heeled shoes and wonder if I shall see you this afternoon; and if you will wear the black skirt and how you are working out your personal problems. And I say "If you are sleeping well, it's O.K. But if you are not, then that's bad." I have suddenly got very tired. Who cares? I think I was tired when I began this letter. Is it an absurd letter. I think it is. I don't care. Do you? I love you very much. I am sorry. A moment of weakness. But is it? I don't know. Perhaps it is a moment of strength.

I intended an ode
But it turned out a
sonnet
I intended an ode
But Rose crossed the road
In her latest new bonnet
I intended an ode

But it turned out a
sonnet.

I didn't write it. Austin Dobson did—an English poet laureate. Ode, bonnet, sonnet. Skirt, bonnet, sonnet. No good. I am terribly sleepy. I must stop.

[unsigned]

[October 1945]

Well, precious, here are some ideas on things—chiefly books. You have to read Wordsworth's Preface to Lyrical Ballads—not long, a few pages, but get it into your head and the best way is to have it. Also Dryden's Essay of Dramatic Poesy. Then Shelley's essay on poetry. Francis Thompson's Essay on Shelley. Not one of them too long. Later you will pick up some Greek drama—and then read Aristotle on Tragedy and Poetry. The chief thing is to get the dialectic development. T. S. Eliot has an empirical conception of it. You have to get it in its outlines clear. Don't worry yourself about gobbling them all up. But gradually have them around. The chief thing is to get them cheap. One day we'll run in at a place I know and see what we can pick up. But know the names. Then stop at bookshops or piles of books outside and see what you can pick up. You will in a few months have the whole conception, concrete and clear in *its development*. Then you will be able to see all around Dick; and when you read Parrington and these other moderns on U.S. literature, etc., you will be able to learn from them and see through them too.

The thing is to grasp the method so that these learned men (and they are learned) when they read you, will say what they said when they read Bill "I would never have believed it."

Now one thing I am always repeating. Take these in your stride. For example, in Proust there is one section I want you to read for me—it is his analysis of the mind of A France. In Joyce's Ulysses there is another section—or rather 3 or 4 sections which I would like you to read for me, and we'll discuss them. That is all for the time being in those long books. If you want to read them O.K. But it is these sections that are vital for your work and the building up of your general conception and the culture, that vast culture which Hegel says the poet needs more than any other artist.

Then along with that steady accumulation you read all the poetry you want to, how and when, Aeschylus, Patchen, Ella Wheeler Wilcox, *follow your own bent*, develop your own ideas. Be as willful and capricious as you please, that's *yours*. Trust to your studies of serious things to shape your natural instincts. For *work*, stick to Dick. The time is ripe. Between him and me and your own dear self we can strike a great blow for freedom, and make ourselves supremely happy.

Some time I'll tell you about yesterday. Incidents, *perhaps* slight to you, were for me of great significance. I was sulky—with cause. But I shouldn't be sulky. But then that is not certain. Some people think one should be if one wants to. Perhaps the best thing is to have so strong a universal that one does not need to be *too* sulky. I looked at you after dinner—and you know what I thought? What kind of men have you known who had you and let you get away? It fills my mind these last few hours. You are, I repeat, a miracle, by nature. But when you want to, you can use this and be wonderful so that you envelope your companion with an overwhelming impression of beauty, intelligence, honesty, grace and winsomeness. You live on different levels of personality, of an extraordinary range. They need a governing unity—you have discovered it.

As I watched you yesterday I saw them all following one another in great rapidity. I thought for a while after dinner that you deliberately set out to be as "nice" as possible to me. Before very long, however, whatever its origin, your presentation of yourself had reached the climax I have described on the previous page. I wish I could have a film of you during the fifteen minutes before we rose from the table. Words and gestures and smile (a new one) and a glow, everything you were, or much of it fused. To be able to wake those moods in you, all of them and others I do not know, to be able by one's own native and developed personality to make them spring to life in you, not consciously, but as a natural response, that would be—something. And there are only glimpses of you, you are not yet organized. Only now you are beginning. But the possibilities are dazzling and immense. Organized in regard to society, organized in regard to your part in it, and organized emotionally, and all the facets or phases of your personality having free play as free verse has free play, free but not loose, because of the deep organic logic that governs the apparently spontaneous manifestation, a logical anarchy. When the circumstances are favorable I speak like that—without preparation and I speak best then. So, miss, do you see? Write me back and tell me that you see. You make me want to write fiction again, to capture you and pin you down on paper and tell the world—look.

Dance every day if you can. Keep on with that. Never stop. You need it. More than you know now. Go ahead, my sweet, and be more wonderful every day. It takes a whole day to catch a good glimpse of you—a day and other people, lots of people too, Dick and Ellen, and the Negro artist and Freddie and me—and all this you need to make you aware of yourself. There are ten million things I want to talk to you about, ten million places to go with you, ten million people to see with you. There seems to be an infinity of relations and a few hours in a few years that will never, never encompass 1/10,000 of a unit of them. You never talk much or write to me of love. Shy? I am too. You are afraid? I'll meet you half-way. Politics, society, art, but boy meets girl. Those millions of pictures and novels—what a craving they try to satisfy. Love as our parents knew it, as King David knew it, as modern people know it. Perhaps there will have to be too many reservations. Freddie is closest to me. She talks of you—she says definitively that you are now deadly serious about what you want to do. But I'll never be able to talk to her until I talk to you. It is an adventure, isn't it? And to think that you might have gone away. But you couldn't. I know that.

I was sulky. But you played the gramophone spitefully loud. Did you or did you not? Or at least didn't turn it down? Frederick the Great (and he was great) to spite Voltaire, his guest, wouldn't let him have early morning chocolate and V retaliated by stealing wax-candles from the palace-hall for his room. O.K. I withheld the chocolate. Did you steal the candles?

I called you—you were not in. Madeline says—later. I have worked continuously since I left you. I am now dog-tired. I shouldn't be. But so it is. I am better tho'.

When shall I see you? And the picture? Soon, please. I want to put it up near my bed—strong and vital. If you have a lot of old pictures send me some—please or bring them. I destroyed the old ones—everything or *nearly* everything. But Monica and the little "essay" on Rukeyser, defied me. I couldn't do it. I couldn't send them back. And how glad I am.

Grace is staying here. (I am saying good-bye and dragging it out.) Nowadays I do not go to the pictures at all. Every spare hour I spend with you, and cannot afford to enjoy myself elsewhere. But Grace says she wants to see Love Letters. Ho! Ho! Ho! She says she wants to. So—I sacrifice myself. I shall go and have a good time. But I'll miss you.

Love, Nello

[1945]

Portrait (Partial) of a Man
7 p.m. Wondered about you—cough gone? Good day?
Tired, my dearest Constance. Tired so I can not even go to bed. Wandered about, called you a few times.
I had something on my mind. It expressed itself as a problem I have to solve. What exactly was the relation of Kant and his synthetic logic (I'll explain one day) to his age. For days it is on my mind and I cannot forget it. *It is the last link in a chain.* I'll get it, but its *tough*. I have an analysis of the Critique of Pure Reason in my pocket. I read it in bits. But I just can't make it. Why is it important? We have solved the main problem of historical materialism. Rae and I have mastered the basis of the economic theory. She is eating it up. But for some 70 years dialectic has remained a closed book. Everybody—even L.D.,* paid lip-service. (L.D. understood, but never wrote.) Grace is a graduate (has a doctorate) in philosophy. And we are on the verge of solution. This alone holds it up. There is a curve from early Greeks to Aristotle; a curve from Descartes to Kant; then another from Kant to Hegel. By and large we have all, but the key is Kant. Look at these dates
1776 Smith, Wealth of Nations
1776 Declaration of Independence
1789 French Revolution
1780 Critique of Pure Reason
1784 "Beginning" of Industrial Revolution
Dialectic is on its way. The social crisis means all problems will be posed in the most profound terms. In Russia thousands of copies of Hegel's logic are sold every year. If I get this then the road is open.
So I am tired. At 9:30 I go to the Roxy. Hazel Scott made a grand appearance—last time she was lousy. There was a good comedian. And then Gene Tierney in Laura. Very good murder film; also one good character study. Her face reminds me of you, but she is getting fat since the baby, tho' I notice they have trimmed her thick ankles. Some superb acting (dramatic style) by a maid. How good so many of these middle-aged women are!
Songs in the show keep running thru' my head "I walk alone . . ." Silly words, trite melody, but somehow I know why people listen to them. They sure can mean something at times. Then another one—so mediocre I have forgotten it by now. But it hit me like a Shakespearian sonnet. Then I come for the train and I am writing in

---

* Leon Trotsky's original name was Lev Davidovich Bronstein.

it. I hope to God that Kant thing doesn't bother me to-night. I am so tired I can hardly hold up. I am very sorry but I am too tired to resist telling you that I love you very much. You know it already so it doesn't do any harm. You remember?

> But if the while I
> think on thee,
> dear friend.
> All losses are restored
> and sorrows end.

You know I heard this afternoon that my mother died and was buried a few days ago. I pushed it away. I was too tired already when I heard. I was all taut and busy and I knew I could put it away for some time. But now I feel miserable about it. I am not overwhelmed with grief. I have been away from home and lived alone too long. But I had always looked forward to going back and seeing her once more. I was her eldest son, wayward, but people always talked about me to her and she loved me very much. I have not cried and I shall go about my business as usual—but something in me has gone. A hope I cherished and a little, a tiny flame. I would have liked to see her. Conceited as it may sound I know she would have been happy. She had had a stroke for years and wanted to see me before she died. The others were near her. In these few hours I have discovered something. Life is so *hard*. It batters you into shape, toughens you. When your mother dies it's bad for you. Another tie to the simple ordinary things of life goes. Take care of yourself and you write your mother often. I don't feel too bad really.

[1945]

[Beginning of letter is missing.]
Another point: Try to see the author's attitude and sympathy even in the books where he is not writing in the first person (UTC and NS). [*Uncle Tom's Children, Native Son*]

Now the logic is a line consisting of opposed contradictions which develop. But—and this is the point—the logical development, or arrest of development, or distorted development, for *life* gives all—these must be sought in the material itself, e.g., the growth of the Negroes as a nationality in the U.S. It begins in 1863. It does not begin in 1776.

After the abolition of slavery the Negroes form the Republican, i.e., the revolutionary party. They seek complete citizenship. After Reconstruction they recognise that there is no hope there.

Then note. They explode in the Populist movement. They organise themselves, one million strong in the Southern Tenant Farmers' Alliance. They come out as a "nationalistic" unit. But when the big nation-wide Populist movement begins they join it. You get Revolutionary Populist Movement + Negro Movement. The Negroes are more ready for drastic change than any other section of the Populist movement. They see more clearly the need for a change.

Populism is defeated. The Negroes sink into despair. The war brings them North to serve capitalism.

But as soon as they come North and are free of the Southern tyranny they take another step forward to "nationalistic" consciousness—the Garvey movement. Republican Party—Populism—Garvey.

Now the Garvey movement became as absurd as it did because the American proletariat was not ready to offer revolutionary leadership. If the American proletariat had said: We hate this society as much as you. Join us in action, the back to Africa would have faded away.

Last stage: Finding a certain freedom in the North and being compelled to live segregated lives, they build a separate life. The Negro communities spread from a few thousand to hundreds of thousands in the big towns—have Negro press, Negro churches, big NAACP units, tremendous growth of Negro consciousness and out of this comes the Negro "regional" literary movement. Then in 1932 the Negroes, en masse, join the New Deal. They move as a unit, being so well organised among themselves. To-day they are very conscious of themselves and are, as Negroes, profoundly dissatisfied with the Republican and the Democratic Party. They are nationalistic as never before but their nationalism is aimed at breaking into American society. When a mass Labor Party is formed, they will join—they are ready for revolution whenever the proletariat is ready. But it is as if they were an oppressed *nation*. Now watch it

Immaturity — Join Republican Party
Disappointment— "You are not a part of the nation."
First self-conscious organisation
   Southern Tenant Farmers—
   Join Populism
   Failure
Second self-conscious organisation
   Garvey—Join? Nothing.
   Dissipates in Nonsense
Third self-conscious organisation
   Not spectacular. But the whole Negro community is organized and
   conscious of itself as Negroes
Negro Community —New Deal. Tomorrow?

They have grown up. They will continue to be more and more nationalistic *until* they break into full participation into American life after the revolution when the nationalistic instincts will begin to take the opposite trend.

Now where is the *contradiction*?

Here.

The historical contradiction of capitalism is the contradiction between the development of the productive forces (labor and capital and chiefly the spread of machinery) on the one hand and social relations, i.e., the relations between people. Thus the more capitalism develops the sharper grows the antagonism between the classes. But the Negro's relation to whites is part of the social relations—and the more capitalism develops and drags the Negroes into it the sharper becomes the contradiction between the development of the productive forces and the social relation between white and Negro. Thus after slavery he joins the Republicans—as an exploited tenant-farmer he joins the Populists. As a raw laborer fresh from the South he joins Garvey; on the basis of the positions gained in industry he builds up the Negro community. And when capitalism gives them jobs in 1941–1944 they take an offensive (in Harlem and Detroit). So the complete logical presentation is: contradiction between the development of the productive forces and the social situation of Negroes—not whether they get more or less privileges but their sense of resentment and readiness to resent it. This contradiction is the logical movement and its growth to maturity is the increase of the contradiction. But as it is easy to see, the increase of the contradiction is due to the Negro's getting into industry, trade unions, etc., and gaining so much confidence that he organizes to fight for his own rights. Thus he is being prepared to solve the contradiction by his increased power to take part in social revolution. That is an example of the dialectical logic applied to history.

Now you can trace it in a fictional study. The point is to find the basic oppositions in a book or a series and trace them. You read and will work it out. All this will come in for your study.

Now I have been thinking. You looked brighter to-day but Saturday you looked forlorn and lonely—just as you did that day on the stage in Stamford. I know why. You must come more definitely and powerfully towards us. You must come and we'll work it out and go and see people—people like us, Dick and James Farrell and another boy I know, Bernie Wolfe, and even the rude Dwight [MacDonald]—we'll go and beard him and make him talk—and other people. You asked me about politics, the other day. Good. Let us meet some people. Freddy and Lyman. At first you will be only my friend—but have confidence in yourself—Freddie liked you. The others did too. But they cooled off—they felt you didn't really belong and they felt that you might be hurting me. That's a long story which I will tell you soon—and get it out of the way. It's something you should know—it will teach you a lot. Then you should come and go with us to party meetings—big ones where there are a lot of people. Let the friends feel that you really are coming—people always give so much when they feel that there is response. Our people are generous, but jealous and suspicious—as they have every right to be. I have ten years experience in this field and having been like you once I think I understand your problems. Friendship is only words if we do not talk. These last eighteen months have been months of violent struggle and achievement for you—your conquest of yourself as a woman (Jack), your conquest of a place as a model; the proof that you have a gift of rare value; and now a choice, a decision between the bourgeoisie and the proletariat. You are going on and on. You still have some difficult rivers to cross. But you need some solid ground now. You need some sense of stability and you need recognition and achievement. That is one reason why I am glad you decided to do the R. W. thing. Don't mind if at first most of the ideas are mine. In my first book every idea worth anything came from L. T.. I didn't mind. I now have my own. Bill, Rae and the others started as you are starting. You have a rarer gift than any of them—creative imagination and logic (how many people you think would have grasped so easily the difficult and complicated ideas that I told you this afternoon. How many?) You have the energy, the temperament, the driving power, and the ambition. But the conflict is greater in you precisely because of that. That is why you must come, firmly and decisively. Some of your difficulties are due to me—I am sorry about it. I have plans for you—to go to Philadelphia and speak to some people—to go to Buffalo and speak to Tim and his friends—they are all our people—so much to give us—if we only find out for ourselves. They will be difficult at first—get through to them as so many of us have got through and then our lives' pattern is set. So will you come? I don't like to see you as you were on Saturday. You need to concentrate yourself and get all the power that is in you functioning in one direction. The process is largely subconscious and step by step you have been following it through. Now you have reached far enough—only a little effort is needed. I want to emphasize this. Because of your ability I have no doubt whatever—I repeat—last summer was the most amazing intellectual discovery of my life. But the split in your personality—that is your weakness. About the modeling—as long as you take it in your stride it is as good a way of making a living as any—better than most for you have time to work.

That is enough, for the time being. I have a story to tell you—a horrible story with a moral. But to write it would give it too much weight. One more thing. Strictly between us. You need what Virginia Woolf calls a room of your own. Get it. If it is only one room. If you are in need of money, a lump sum, I can get it for you any time you want it—$100. My own. I'll tell you where I got it. I am not being altruistic. You belong to us. And to see you well set and on your way means very much to me. I am a very self-contained person; in addition compelled to maintain a watchful reserve with everyone—however friendly I may appear to be.

Friday a.m.

One day I'll give you a little—a little idea of what goes on, and the way I live and the part you played in it. Yeah! *You.* My fault entirely, well not quite entirely. But I should have warned you. Yet I was diffident and nervous as—as whom—as you. It is a wonderful day—ill on the ground, gloomy sky, but still and sure of itself. It says "So I am. Be damned to you."

I am curiously uncertain. This letter is long enough. I have a lot of things in my head. But why embark on a long journey on paper. Nettie, by the way, is very taken with you and she is *very* acute. She made some observations about you, some of which are embodied here. So long, see you later—to be precise, Monday a.m. by phone. In an hour or two I'll be at it incessantly until I leave Sunday.

By the way. I forgot a most important thing. I want to borrow the typewriter for awhile. We need a heavy one for some documents—many copies, etc. But you must have one of course. We'll talk about it on Monday. Meanwhile, however, I suggest that you call Grace HA 9/9806 and talk to her about it. Tell her what I told you.

THE END
FINIS

Fooling around—loath to stop; yet hand not good; ought to stop; long pauses after every few words; ideas sprouting—how I got here, e.g., Nettie came specially from Philly to see after me. Ike—you remember—who pushed you around that night we were at your place—went to Doc B to get Vitamin B and instructions to give me injections every day; Grace and Rae arranged this trip. Then Rae took over getting a new lamp for me. G. arranged for me to see an oculist or something. Both of them went with me on W'y. Rae stayed behind to pick up the glasses. Grace took me to dinner at her brother's and gave me stationery, etc., she had bought ($12.00) for our work. Nettie helped to dispatch me. Rae met me at the train with the glasses—I have them on—and sandwiches. On Monday a.m. both of them meet me—I'll travel thru' the night—to start immediately on some writing. And that is only half. They keep me going. A great battle is on. We are doing fine—in fact wonderful. The last few months have been dramatic and exciting to a degree. And they have performed mightily on all fronts while they nursed me back to health and now keep me going. NB: remember to ask me about those two girls, who they are, what they are, etc. Exceptional ability, strength of character, and devotion. Then there is Freddie. What a story! A sterling character if ever there was one. And all of us with the petty-bourgeois streaks in us, all of us, for we have to fight daily, the heritage and the influence of the capitalist environment. But we fight it collectively. On the whole, they are of singular purity of character. It is a world you should know about—curiously small in some ways and yet capable of hitting blows that are felt in far-away places; with some of the most strenuous thinking and writing that are going on anywhere in the world—in at least four fields of worldwide importance we have made outstanding contributions and bigger ones are on the way. Dick and JTF [James T. Farrell] are very close and we must make JTF closer. Already we have influenced them and we have a quantity of material they need. All the threads are in my hands. I forgot the historian (you know) and the musical analyst. You realise my responsibilities? They, the responsibilities, don't worry me. It is my health (and my bad habits) that wear me down sometimes. I don't tell them, my friends. How can I? When I say that I need you, you understand? For over and above all—literature remains my first and perhaps best-understood interest. Maybe this is what I have been fiddling around with since last night. When I see you lonely and uncertain (Nettie swears you are), I see where you belong—what you are searching for. Fill in the gaps. And don't hesitate any more. Don't think of it as giving. Think of it as finding—plunge. Detroit is here. Salud!

N

P.S. What a letter! But the thing I am moving to is this. One goes by stages, fighting blindly, but going the right way. Then comes a time—dialectically, i.e., logically—when one should gather up all forces and strike hard. I believe you have reached it. A clearing up in thought and action, when a sufficient momentum has been reached to take all obstacles or at least root out the old, even tho' it bleeds. In politics as in life these moments arrive. Do you feel it now? Did you? We'll discuss it. For one thing do you think of your break with acting as "a failure"? It is the reverse. It is a victory—a very great victory. You'll look back and see what a blessing it is you weren't caught there by an early success. I remember with Jack—there were complications that made you feel you were the result of circumstances. You were not. It would appear to be. But an internal necessity drives you, the result of external circumstances. The proletariat, for example. It has not allowed you to settle down. It fills the papers and the radio—insists that you pay attention, pulls you back to it. . . .

[1945]

Well, my pearl of great price, how are you? I hope you are well, and not tired. I tell you what I would like to do now in fact what I am doing set you on my knee, you being as you were Saturday evening, red pants and that beautiful blouse, and make a lot of love to you until you were quite relaxed. Why? Cause I would like to. And also, because I want to talk to you. To talk is to write. Anything serious with me is writing. If I were married to you I would still write you letters serious ones and when I was very gay—gay ones. Wouldn't it be wonderful? To sit opposite to you at breakfast and see you open a letter I had written and posted. I would be quite embarrassed. This is going to be a long letter. It will last a few days, I think.

Immediately you say "Ah! Stan." Sweets, you know how I think. Stan, Willie, Jack, Ivan it's all the same to me. I shall make a few remarks about Stan who is only an *expression* of something. I am concerned with you. I am sorry you wrote about Stan as you did. It was not permanent, etc. You are in control of the situation, etc. My belief is that the situation is well in control of you; not Stan but the situation. In any case if you are seriously in love with someone at any time, I am interested. But otherwise I am not. In fact I very much do not want to hear about it. I'll meet anyone you want me to meet or talk to anyone. But adventures or explorations of yours in that department, no thank you. I am in love with you, you know.

No, this is something else. I have been thinking of it for some time, in fact from the very beginning. And Saturday night climaxed it. Saturday night was not a success. In fact, it was a distinct failure. And small things, accidents, acquire significance in the light of big ones. The play has made a move a subdued but highly significant climax. As audience and participator I want to clarify it. Act I is over. Act II is beginning. I love you because you are adorable, but I love you too because you are serious. I can talk to you, sister Monica, because you are really very profound and can see the individual and the particular in the general.

There are, as all the superficial idiots repeat without understanding it, two classes in society, the bourgeoisie and the proletariat. Most people unconsciously belong to one side or the other. The petty-bourgeois wander around in between but until the proletariat moves and moves violently, the petty-bourgeois usually incline to the bourgeoisie. The conflict, however, goes on without ceasing. In the heart of every single man, revolutionary or not, that conflict exists and is fought out every day, every hour. When one becomes conscious of it, and is a serious, conscientious person, then there is hell to pay.

You began by aligning yourself on one side. You wanted, you still want to express yourself. You have great gifts you don't know the half of them. But you have them, and they stir you; also one of your gifts is a great need for emotional expression. The origin of all this is unnecessary to go into now. So it is.

You align yourself and almost at once you marry. You are set, politically and emotionally, on the proletarian side. But soon you realise that you have made a mistake. You break and you marry again—Bessie told me that you were all upset, eager and even distracted until you had married again—some fear drove you. The man you married did not help you. He neither established you on one side of the barricade nor on the other. You just floated along until you decided to do something yourself. You did it—you broke away, studied, got a perspective, and followed it. Splendid.

19 out of 20 would have been unable to make it. But you mature slowly. Meanwhile you take up with Jack. You are in love, at last. You are sure. That battle with Jack was tremendous. I should have told you at the time what was happening.

Eddy was the petty-bourgeois complete, Hamlet, sick in body and sick in mind. Jack was an actor and a 1944 Stalinist. Nothing could have been more dangerous for you. He offered you a compromise—it looked wonderful. You would be an actress—in the same field with him. You would have the same friends, the same interests, the same pleasant life—work and effort to achieve amidst stimulating surroundings. At the same time you would be political and revolutionary—in contact with "the movement" actually participating. But there wasn't much risk. You were not *opposing* bourgeois society. The Stalinists of 1944 were bourgeois to the bone. Life was and is wonderful for them. They have the psychological satisfaction of working for the cause and at the same time of accomodating themselves to bourgeois society. You loved Jack, the way his hair grew, or the sound of his voice, or the soundness of his character—or all three or what not. *But all this was taking place in a certain social and political milieu which intensified it and made it look so lovely that frankly when I think of how you fought it and got out of it I cannot admire you and love you enough.* You saw Jack. I saw bourgeois society, disguised as Stalinism, pulling at you, with the tremendous power of attraction it exercises, especially when disguised as Stalinism. The two of them do that to the workers, offering them allies, "progressive forces," pacts to preserve peace, etc., all in the name of Marx and Engels, and the socialist society in the far distance. The same thing was being offered to you. The workers accept and when they reject, as they reject a National Service Act, do so because of their harsh experiences with the class-struggle. Your battle was fought on another plane. You had only your integrity, your consciousness of what was right, this consciousness, however, being the result of early political training. If I helped you, I did so not only because I loved you and want to see you go the right way. I knew that I represented something which was entirely opposed, the mortal enemy of what was pulling at you. The independence also was part of the same struggle. It was part of my creed. You won—and after reading ". . . no bitterness distill" and some of that verse, I was certain you would win. Henceforth (for me) you are comrade. As I read your verse I could see that your struggle with Jack was mixed up with personalities, but in essence it was a political struggle—bourgeois and proletariat. For me also it was your whole future as a political writer at stake. When you came through you did two things—you organised and won yourself and you won me. For good and all. You could fight and win, a hard battle with all the odds against you.

What did you face now? The acting career, the fight to establish yourself—and at the same time the desire, the need to retain your base—the proletarian (Trotskyite if you will) base which was the background of your struggle with Jack. You want both. You feel the need of both. But your career drags you in one direction; your environment, your friends, the people you meet, the completely bourgeois base of the sphere in which you move—not only base but superstructure. I have told you before. It is not unpleasant. It is seductive. In Europe it has collapsed. But in the U.S.A. it still functions. You want it or it draws you. It is the career which is your magnet. But bourgeois society is all-embracing, bold, brutal and yet subtle and insinuating. It says "You can have your career, but at a price. I don't give anything unless I am sure that I get something in return. Some few manage it, but very few." So while you go one way, you are friendly with me and with R, and with L, and F, and with G. You are not too sure of what they think about you but you know that here is something which matters to you. Your instinct or your reason is quite sound. Without us you would in time be lost. The difficulty is that as you will have guessed or worked out, we all are deadly serious people, cut whole, headed in one direction, and judging everything by that, in the last analysis. Saturday night you wanted, if I am not wrong, to be one with us, to feel that you were with your people—you wanted to talk about things, for us to talk about them with you. It just couldn't get going. G. has a habit of directing conversations in a channel where people not close to us feel outside. She does it particularly where women are concerned. But I can usually handle all such situations. But on Saturday I was not myself. I was preoccupied with me and with you and just couldn't settle down and make it right for you, as I have done repeatedly on far more difficult occasions. I have noticed it before. You raise questions of strikes, political activity and problems, etc., but somehow, with the others, it doesn't come off. I know what I know. But they don't. And that is why, and with all my personal entanglement with it, I let you down on Saturday. L and F were perfectly aware of it. It may seem a small thing. It is not. It is an indication of your whole problem—and your problem is mine. There is no question at all that [with] great will and effort and some luck [you] can make it. James Farrell is an artist but with an unshakeable political base, which is in fact, his life. Richard Wright is even more so. And there are others. Most of them are Stalinists but the two I mention are not. J. F. is defiantly not so. You have me—but you also have yourself to deal with. And as all social forces express themselves in people, your problem is personal in a peculiar way. It is in this connection that Stan concerns me. Otherwise for me. No.

I noticed in your Xmas note to me that you talked about being glad to meet these young people whom you meet and finding out that they were not anti-Negro, not anti-Semitic, not hostile to wives working, etc., and you could have screamed with joy. I didn't say anything. It was a natural reaction. Then came your realisation of the fact that they were your own age, you had a good time, you were relieved of the pressure of being on the side of persecuted Jewish people or people with Jewish persecution complexes, etc.

All that I understood, and know how you felt, and was glad for your experience. It was fascinating to listen to you and see you growing up and watch you having a good time with them and yet analysing them critically, and with a good basis. (Those times I look at you and think of the past and love you to fill the whole world.) But it is time to see those things in a certain perspective. The liberal ideas of the young bourgeois and petty-bourgeois are liberal ideas and no more. Even L sometimes is apt to wander off in psychological probings. It is unfortunate that Stan is mixed up in this, but Stan or no Stan, the truth is that the proletarian line, the thing we stand for is stern, hard, and in some respects, quite merciless even to us who seek always to guide ourselves by it. *The anti-Negro pressure, the anti-Jew pressure, the anti-working class pressure one never escapes from.* Never. At every turn bourgeois society imposes it upon you, insists that you declare where you stand. All of us have to make compromises—I, as a Negro, constantly make them on the Negro question above all others, but they can only be made because of a firm settled determination and consciousness that an active struggle is being carried on against the whole business. You think perhaps that some of your friends are not anti-Negro because they go out with Negroes or invite them to parties. Others can think so. You must not. I remember the old man is reported to have said once "The Negroes in the South will one day revolt and half of the party, instead of jumping in to help them will hesitate." Someone who saw him said that he said it with deliberate emphasis. And that is among trained, devoted people. The bourgeois pressure penetrates everywhere. You have to fight it daily, hourly. The only way in fact that one can really become anti is to become pro something else, not avoiding but going out to meet the enemy, challenging him, seeking his attacks, digging at him when he is not attacking. Otherwise so all-embracing is the pressure that not to attack is capitulation and slow infiltration.

Frightened? It is frightening. But the thing is to know, to see to the roots. It breaks weak people. It strengthens strong ones. They have constantly to be strengthened to strengthen themselves. With clear vision, insight, and understanding you can walk in the camp of the enemy and (perhaps) escape disaster. But it is false to think it easier than it is, you get swallowed up and lost. Your problem is *not* whether you can act and write. That, difficult as it is, is a minor problem. It is whether you can live in bourgeois society and make your career there and keep alive the flame that is in you, and deepen and broaden the instincts and the actual knowledge which you have, and which are infinitely the most precious part of you. They are the more precious part of you for me, they are for society in general and, unless I am very much mistaken, they are the most precious part of you for yourself and your own happiness too. Perhaps I am wrong, in this last part but I doubt it. You married and you married again and you very nearly married again, all in rapid succession. In fact you were as good as married. But you gave yourself to unrecognizing arms even the third time. I believe that at the back of all this is the conflict which reached its climax in your battle over Jack. If I weren't in love with you I would have told you this long ago. But I am so much older than you. I like to see you finding your own way and fledging your wings. My background is British, not American, which means that my temperament is enclosed in a traditional reserve. Also you were supposed to be getting over Jack. Now, however, you are on the warpath again, "looking for a fella." Your preliminary skirmishes, I repeat, I don't want to know about. But you, the fundamental you that I know and care about, that I must let you see as I see it. It is time. (Tomorrow I shall continue. It will be more personal—in fact highly personal.) Funny; my hand has been bad—very bad. But I decide to write to you and it becomes good. That's why I call you my miracle, red pants. If there are things that are not too clear, or gaps, we'll clear them up in talking. I am up to my eyes in work, and cannot reread or revise as perhaps I should. But you have always understood me in the past and I think you will now.

        Love,
        Nello

Return address Farrell, 340 East 58th Street, New York City

                Postmark February 2, 1946

My dear Constance,

I am very very sorry you are ill and I am glad you are better.

First thing is your poetry. I have made a close study of it, poem by poem, line by line. I have examined it historically, what it represents in social development. I have read it to a few people—chosen. I have compared it to the work that is pouring in on me from all sides—the most recent a Marxist study of the evolution of jazz, written by a man with whom I shared a flat in London for three years—a brilliant masterly book, better than Bill's. I know now that you belong to us, in that field—poetry and literature. You will have to work like hell, but you belong to the proletariat. You have something that it needs, that all of us need—something new, and very precious. I can help you—if you are serious. I'll talk about it with you any time you wish. This is unreserved, no strings attached. I'd do the same for anyone who turned up with half of what you have.

But apart from that, my friend of many years, we haven't much in common any more. We may have again but not today. Your last letter from California told me what I knew. You say that you are leading a selfish existence and when the revolution comes you'll join up. It wouldn't do. It proves the superficial—and I use a moderate word—attitude which you have both to the revolution and to your work. A genuine creative impulse in any field is accepted by all of us as something to be respected. If the person has great gifts the attitude is that he or she should be helped to develop them—we recognise that our road is not for everybody. But when you say, and more when I see you, seeking your own road, selfishly, then that is very bad. What are you seeking? I'll tell you. Lights, glitter, self-expression, everything bourgeois. Everything you have to give you give to them. All that bourgeois society demands of you for your success you are prepared to pay. To the proletarian movement you give nothing. To salve your feeling of guilt you read and talk to a few people and say, to me of all persons. When the time is near I'll come. It is terrible—false to us and false to yourself if you wanted merely to fulfill your impelling urge. But I don't think the urge is artistic—I think it is an urge to success. You are of course entitled to do what you like with your life. But I have the same privilege. Thinking as I do, there is nothing more between us.

When I called you it was to let you know that if you talked to Freddie she could arrange an introduction to Bill Fitelsen for you. He is well placed on Broadway and is openly one of us. That was all. But you talked and I replied and it may have seemed to you that I had changed my mind. I haven't.

Will you find your way out of this? I think you will—you always have so far, but it isn't something you can play with much longer and I shall not help you to play with it. My advice to you, and this is not personal, but political: Give up all that you are doing—get a job and write. The atmosphere in which you live is corrupting you. I worked for years as a press correspondent—I see no difference in that and what you have been doing. Both of us served the bourgeoisie—and I have never taken a snooty attitude to modelling. But you cannot stand it. I could. I ignored all the people and all the invitations and all the sincere offers—and as soon as I finished my work ran to my own people. There are people among us now who do just that—but they carry on their profession, stage work too, and then dash back to us. They belong. You don't. I say, turn your back on them. Get a job. For that matter I could help you get one. And settle down to work at what you have to give us. The proletariat needs what you have. Are you going to work for it only when it can give you rewards? Everything that you have that distinguishes you, apart from your natural gifts, you have learnt from us, from your proletarian, Marxist background. It can make you into something that matters. The proletariat, particularly the American proletariat, is going places— it is the greatest social force that history has ever known, and on its shoulders rests the destiny of this whole vast country and the overwhelming influence it exercises in the world. You know that, you feel that, but you will not tie your destiny with it. You want it to offer you something. No, sister. You must offer it all you have. The Kingdom of Heaven is within *you*. He that shall save his life must lose it. Lose yours. The proletariat is going places. Come and go with it. As it is, if you grasp hold of it you can do splendid work and as it rises it will lift you with it. But if you don't, then you may become a successful actress—like X or Y or Z. That you may become, but I doubt it, because you are torn and cursed by wavering. All artistic processes are for the most part subconscious. Your powerful desires and energies, your sensitiveness, the mark of the poet, precisely those things make you such a battleground where the bourgeoisie and the proletariat struggle for mastery. You are choosing little by little and you are choosing *wrong*. You are choosing wrong because you have to make excuses to yourself and to me to stifle the gnawing pain that you are choosing wrong. Great actresses are not made that way—not in 1946.

About you and me, forget it. The meanness and cruelty with which you behaved to me and which made me realise that our friendship was over, I am now convinced sprang from what I have been writing here. I have offended, embarrassed you? OK. I wouldn't do so any more. That is why I can now say to you what I would say to anyone in your position. Of all the gifted young people I know you are the most preciously gifted. But to use this come to us. Otherwise I simply haven't any time to spare and besides will not encourage you or anyone else in playing with revolutionary ideas. I don't play with them and I shall not encourage you whose road I can see so clearly.

So there. Do you want to talk it over? I am willing—not only willing but anxious. You at least know what we will talk about, so that there will be no false pretences on either side. You can come and stay over if you want to—but we shall talk business. If you are uncertain and want to hear about the poetry and all that I think I'll gladly spend one, two, sessions with you explaining what your possibilities are. But I shall not chatter with you about acting any more or your modelling prospects.

It is a big problem, a great decision I am putting before you. One thing I must explain; tho' I think I can trust you to understand, I cannot risk it. There is a certain arrogance in this letter. I am laying down an ultimatum so to speak in which the reward, to a vulgar person, can appear to be, my friendship. I would be very sad if you made that mistake. I am writing here as someone who is, as you know, always on the lookout for what will help what I believe in. For me it is the biggest thing that there is—including everything; and I rejoice when this magnificent book on music appears—because it is *ours*. It is a blow against them. It belongs to the world the workers are building directly or indirectly. I feel responsibility and I have helped many to find themselves. I look upon you as one such. I in the name of something am speaking to you in the name of something. That explains my attitude. If it were anything personal it would be intolerable. I wouldn't speak to a child in that way—least of all to you. I am hoping, sincerely hoping, that you will turn towards us. It will be a fight and some bitter pills to swallow. But seek for the best in you and you will find it.

       Yrs
       N

I had almost forgotten. I read your poems to 2 girls—graduates, very intelligent, just out of college, members of the W. P. and cultivated in many fields. They were thrilled—and spontaneously asked me to tell you please to go on, that they understood and admired your work and that they would be advocates to spread it wherever it appeared.
R. J.
Apt 4F
1306 Chisholm
Bronx

Postmark February 3, 1946

Your letter encourages me to be frank with you. You must continue to express yourself. Don't keep it locked up inside of you. Write and write again. You will master it and it will become a part of you but a part conquered, and absorbed.

There is a dialectical law here. Everything is in a state of contradiction, opposition. Within an individual as in society, the classes struggle. When you fought with Jack for your independence *the classes* struggled—the bourgeois role of woman—going round with Jack while he performed or the proletarian, socialistic role, i.e., freedom and equality. Two different social conceptions met. There was only the possibility of a struggle because of the existence of the modern socialist consciousness.

Now a contradiction has to be resolved; the Hegelian word is sublated—remember it. It means that when A and B struggle A is above, B below. B gradually grows until B overcomes A. But the result is not B + A but something new, C, in which *A is incorporated*, i.e., Capital and Labor. Capital is above, dominant. Labor is subordinate. Labor grows as cpl grows until labor in a struggle becomes dominant. But the result is that cpl, the mass of machines, etc., is incorporated into a new social order subordinated to its former slave, strengthening it.

Now when you won with Jack, the ideas that you had of devoting yourself to a man and finding a fulfillment were not destroyed, abolished. They were incorporated in a new Constance, but subordinated to your socialistic conception of what a woman should be.

You had bourgeois ideas of self-expression. You fought—you have won. But you haven't lost the need. Only it is incorporated into a new person—subordinated to something else growing in you, the something that fought Jack, and is making you change. But it is a hard struggle. The social transformation is a revolution—it shapes society. In an individual it is the same. And when big battles are fought and great victories won, it must hurt—parts of you are being torn out, some cut away, and what is good being forced while cut and bleeding into new positions. You settle down in time, an infinitely stronger person. But now you are convalescent. I feel very deeply for you. I wish I could help you to ease it a little. It will go *and come back again*. But it will be conquered.

And I shall continue to be frank. To-day all my plans, etc., are flowing the correct way. Politically all the breaks we could hope for have come. That is a story in itself. Personally my affairs have taken a turn for the better—my friends are all busy seeing after me. They get money, they want me to have a typist, a maid for some hours—I can only watch them and marvel. Lastly, you, my most precious pupil, and from whom in one way I expect the most, more than from Bill, have come back. But I am tired—in a way that I don't like. I don't tell the others. I work and God! how the work has grown. But I feel a fatigue deep down that worries me. My hands are very bad, and the sight and consciousness of them has begun to affect me. I am getting ready to do everything—take injections, get a good lamp, see after my eyes again, try to organise my house. They are even getting a radio-gram for me. They spoil me really. I'll try to pick myself up again, feel good inside. But this last year has been bad. Politically, analytically, etc., it has been tremendous. But I—well I have told you. I suppose the mere fact that I have to tell someone is a sign that I am weaker.

Your work and your new orientation should give you more time. Come and talk to me whenever you can. I'll tell you everything I know about your work and place all my ideas at your disposal. I have many, collected and worked out over the years. On literature, in relation to society; and examples of how to work out the logical ideas I described early—to work them out requires as you can guess great sensitiveness, subtlety, and both imagination and discipline—otherwise they become caricatures. I know that you can handle them in time. So come often. It is a pleasure for me to talk to you and it stimulates me in a way that relieves me of the constant pressure I feel. Don't mention this to anyone. Don't read into it more than there is. But when you write that you nearly came back on Saturday night it suddenly struck me how glad I would have been to have you back and to talk without the idea that you had to leave—to have no sense of time. So let it go at that. You will understand. So, my dear friend, let us do what we can to restore losses and end sorrows.

Yours,
N

One must do what is right I said to myself. If it were anybody else you would go out of your way to nurse this fine talent and help it to find itself. That is your *duty*. Do it. I finally compromised. I said. If she is serious she'll find it out and write. Then I'll speak the truth as I see it. And the rest is up to her. Well, here we are and first your letter and then the knowledge that you are back again, and on a plane so much higher than before, makes me feel very close to you and very happy that I have made this experience with you and have so many exciting ones ahead.

P.P.S About Dick Wright. It's a deal. It will take three months at most. You know, I am selfish. I am looking forward to seeing another burst of activity as 1944 summer. And if this occasions it I'll have a swell show watching it.

R. J.
4H
1306 Chisholm
Bronx
Zone 59

[February 1946]

The development takes place with an inexorable logic. As soon as I left you yesterday I caught something about writers on the cover of the New Masses.* Here it is.

These people are mobilising for another assault. They have come to a dead end—through their crude, rough, disloyal handling of literature and Marxism. But now that the postwar crisis is on they are clearing their decks. Much that they say is true. But they do not understand the problem in its depths. You have come just in time (if you hadn't come I would have felt defeated as I had not been for a long time, as far back as I remember in fact; for tho' we gain slowly, once we (our group) [do gain we] never lose). As I say you have come just in time. Everywhere on every field, the mobilisation is taking place.

---

* A political journal with literary pretensions associated with the Communist Party.

One thing, however, you can learn, again from these folks' experiences. Until you work out your own talent and develop your own powers, don't let the party line worry you very much. You have to keep political company in the company of people who are socially and politically minded, but your profession comes first. And your profession means your craft on the one hand, and on the other, the study of society, of which a political party is only one manifestation. That is what these swine did—prostituted literature to politics. It is a testimony to Dick's high talents and strength of will that he fought them and broke with them. Of course you will be in it, you will read and you will know—but your special assignment is to find yourself. The verse is your own business. I can help a little, perhaps a lot, but the social study—as I tried to explain to you, Proust, Eliot, Joyce—and you will have to read them—were marvellously equipped. Delmore Schwarz on T. S. Eliot shows why and how. But *that* equipment is no good today for the young writer. He needs an ordered instead of a disordered internationalism—must have a sense of the social integration of all things, see society as we see it, and as you show how you can, with work, see it. Then you will meet a child crying over a flower and write a modern poem; or do a critical essay that illuminates; or observations about life. If not, you are like Mauldin, instinctive but lacking depth. The Stalinists only appear to be changing. In reality *they cannot change.* They said: We will use art as a weapon in the social struggle. Now they say: We must *not* use art as a weapon. They cannot say. Let us study, let us build such a body of thought and ideas, such bold imaginative conceptions of democracy, such realistic analyses of society today that our artists will find even in the desert of bourgeois society a milieu where their personal individual talents can grow and flourish. The whole necessity to defend Russia poisons them at the root. This generation, your generation, must start again unpoisoned. Dick is so wonderful. He fought them and beat them and cleared a way— to be revolutionary and anti-Stalinist. Others have taken courage, chiefly Negroes. But Jas Farrell fights a gallant fight and is making headway. Rae gave them two resounding whacks in political economy and slowly we get evidence that the blows have gone home. The field is open. I am glad to get you. Patience, thoroughness and soon both friends and enemies will know that a new soldier has entered the lists. As we talk, I'll explain to you what is happening. I am glad that you are keeping up your dancing.

[unsigned]

[February 1946]

This is letter No. 2.

Christ have mercy, where were you on Sat'y night. Tonight. In fact an hour ago. We saw L [Love] Letters. My second time. It was an experience. I missed you. I wanted you during and I want you now. Listen. I am a fan of J [Jennifer] Jones. She has a marvellous face, and a great talent. Her face is all bone-structure, curves and planes, Negroid and Mongolian; wide eyes, a good strong nose, wide mouth and a lovely curved cheekbone. She has the goods. Now the film is typical, good bits, cheap sentiment, etc. But this time I was struck by what J. J. was doing with her lines. They were commonplace. But in emotional scenes by sheer acting, emotional power but restraint, she gave them a genuine poetic quality. Over and over again it happened. Then it struck me. *This is our modern poetry.* Remember T. S. Eliot and his poetry coming back to ordinary speech. Now Dryden did it—and Wordsworth, whom *we must read*, did it—and stated the case in the Preface to Lyrical Ballads. Now we have come to a new age. The symbolists and the free versifiers have prepared the ground. We have said this before. But there before us, before me, the thing was being done. Naturally, everything contributed. But I grew terribly excited because I know that what by voice, intonation, inflexion, gesture, etc., she was doing, you are doing by plain pure writing. Yours is a thousand times harder. But it is the same thing. She is your age, older probably, but your generation. She is bourgeois and as far as I know hasn't an idea in her head. What she is doing will vanish. But the particular quality I find in your poetic work I found distinctly in her treatment of the trite lines she had to say.

That's why I so wanted you to be there. We must see the thing together and I hope you will see what I mean. *I missed it completely the first time.* But it was as clear as day to me this time. But I wouldn't write that to anyone. I talked about it to Grace but I doubt, in fact I am sure, she couldn't have got what I was driving at.

We do not speak here [of] Shakespeare. But we feel that way and we have to use the prosaic sharp disjointed urban speech of our time and make people feel as Sh wrote. Wordsworth did it in his day. Now, more deeply all into it. J was using the actress's arts. But *chiefly* rhythm and inflection. Now I am seeing every day that rhythm is an expression of the human "soul," which is of course social. But the great rhythms of history—the Greek hexameter, the Elizabethan blank verse, the heroic couplet, all are social. But as Hegel shows, the modern ones are connected with social development and therefore connected with each other in a process of development. I shall trace them with you, I have it *I think*, and then you will just eat it up. Sufficient for the time being to say that the rhythm is the rhythm inherent in a particular language, i.e., in a particular culture, which is constantly being distilled from the particular stage of "normal" speech at the time. Thus when we read Wordsworth, and the poems that matter are not many and simple, we shall see a rhythm that is related to Pope behind him and Tennyson after him. It is, I feel, English, and the gradual discovery by a nation of its most intimate language—a growing to maturity. That is why in Eliot there are all these poets, these quotations. He feels the need but lacking a positive *universal*, his very rhythms are chaotically and crudely introduced. His universal is not merely not positive, it is negative, destructive, not *creative*, lacking perspective. Now I think that your rhythms today can express, not negatively, but positively and coherently all the previous ones fused. The basic structure will be simple speech, the poetic quality Jennifer was getting across. But I have noticed in many places a return to rhyme and rhythms of previous times. Stravinsky does the same in his concerto (written in the style of Bach here, Mozart there, Rachmaninov there). Joyce does it but they all do it critically, evocatively expressing nostalgia. But today the people's speech, the basic common language, distilled into poetic rhythm (and of course imagery) becomes the basic structure while all sorts of echoes of the previous rhythms and the things they represented can become not only echoes but positive expressions of the aspirations towards the freedoms, powers, sentiments, etc., of previous generations enjoyed by only a few. All that of course is beyond Sister Jennifer. She is no poet. But that in expressing in her own way a strongly felt artistic emotion she should so strongly remind me of the things you are doing was a revelation that makes me feel only too clearly that you are expressing something that belongs to this generation, that is deep down in it.

The logical working out of it hits me with great force because I was working on the incomparable Hegel and applying his ideas to English poetry. I am a bit scared that when you listen you will not hear (and see) what I heard. But we must try. Remember the last pages of Dick's Bl By *[Black Boy]*. It is the same sort of thing. Now previously (I think this sums it up) they got to that only exceptionally, only in very high and special moments. Now that is our regular, only it is much closer to the ordinary. But we reintroduce our modern distillation of their old ones. Naturally this can give you no qualities you did not have. But it can release them, widen your range, and strengthen your confidence in seeking to make what you are trying to make. I haven't explained it too well. But I wish (1) that I had talked with you about Hegel and ancient and modern verse; (2) that we had already read the Dryden and the Preface by W [Wordsworth]; (3) that you had heard JJ; (4) that all the books were here and you were here. A lot of ground would have been covered. This is now a horrible mess. I shall not sleep. But I shall read about Senator Claghorn. Do you know him? Life has a priceless article on him. Why weren't you around? I hope you enjoyed yourself whatever you were doing—for if you didn't then I would feel horribly cheated. When will we have some real *time* together? But remember, we must see LL *and together*. If you have seen it already so much the better. Then you can listen undisturbed. I would like to get that script.

Goodnight.

See the miracle. You, summer 1944. Me. Grace. "Jimmy likes Hegel. He is always reading about poetry for that Constance. Here is a book. I'll get it for him." I read—revelations. I am all sensitised. I hear JJ. I recognise something. Miracles all. Chance. But governed by necessity, the necessity that drives all of us to seek something. Madeline seeks it in her personal life only and settles for less I regret to say. But we seek because we have to. And though you are necessity you are a miracle nevertheless. I think I'll sleep by the way. I feel less excited. I have it. But here is for the Senator nevertheless.

[unsigned]

[March 1946]

Tell me, sometime, sweetheart, I want to know. You are worried about something fundamental? No, that is not it. You have a feeling of insecurity? I am not speaking of the horrible chatter of the pseudo psychoanalysts. They go around, insecurity, neurotic, inferiority complex. I mean something else. I have mentioned it twice before—the day at Stamford, the first day you came back. (There is another mood, by the way, that I see quite often; no, not so often—eyes blazing and your head up when I sometimes open out some perspective of something. I mention this because it is part of the other.) It is a curiously forlorn look like a baby wondering what next. I have seen it only twice Stamford when you were in a great dilemma about acting and this last time. I mention it because once before when you were ill I noticed the same baby-like dependence. I said "Go to bed" and you said "Yes" as if you wanted someone to tell you what to do. It was at Madeline's (how is she, by the way?) I noticed the same today to a much lesser degree.

Now there is insecurity and insecurity. I remember once for a long time I was insecure about money—always wondering if I would not be stranded, etc. That fear is gone. Confidence in myself, sureness of my ultimate aim, a circle of friends who I know value me, these killed it. But I had it badly for years and years and years. There is another kind. A deeper kind that strives for certainty.

Oh what a dusty answer gets the soul—when hot for certainty in this our life

That's what some think. But it is the battle for certainty that produces some of the greatest philosophical works. I told you yesterday.

But there is even another kind. The uncertainty I felt in politics, how things would go. Now I am absolutely calm and confident—I don't care what happens. I don't know about you, my dearest Constance. You are ordinarily strong, powerful, sure of yourself—able to hold your own easily. Some of the girls hated you—they accused you of being pretty but dumb. Yes—pretty but dumb. For the life of me I cannot understand the blindness of some people. But they accused you also of ogling men—dying to be admired. They took particular care that I should hear this—this by the way not among recent acquaintances of ours but people who knew you years ago. They wanted to save me from you (Funny, isn't it?). I just stared at them or told them mentally to go to hell. I have never for one moment since I knew you ever taken you for anything else except a superior person—though what you really are I didn't know until later and I know now that I shall never completely know—that you will go on unfolding. It is a wonderful prospect. I'll tell you about it another time—lots of other times.

To return. You have a need for approval and admiration. As long as it does not dominate you—make you do what is wrong when you know it is wrong—that is nothing terrible—the need. It stimulates splendid work and heroic action very often.

But I wonder if there isn't something else? I was reading your poems last night—some of them standing up so strongly.

No love can fill

No bitterness distill

A *powerful* piece of work, strong and beautiful. But do you sometimes wish to be a kitten tied with a bow? You remember the spires and the childside of your nature? Somewhere deep down are you afraid and wish to be protected? You have told me about your childhood and what you missed. There is nothing "wrong" or "weak" in it. If it is so, whatever it is, it helps you to be the person that you are—and I above all who can't say that I know you, but certainly know more about you than I know or ever have known of any human being, I don't want to change an inch of you. You will develop, yes. And change. Yes. As society and your own internal qualities change you. That is part of the excitement that is you. But this aspect of you that I mention puzzles me. It does not worry me. Not at all. I have the most perfect confidence in you. I have learnt it. But it sends a sword through me whenever I see it or hear it—not only a sword tho'—a tremendous tenderness for you. And I wonder. What is it? Are you lonely? Some people tell me that I am—a separate person. But I am not scared at all. At least if I still am, I don't know it and have got a rock for myself—my views and actions. I know now that I was always lonely, I know that with you I can never be lonely as before—I am not only in love with you (let it pass, it can do no harm), I admire and respect you—not only your character and your many-sided personality, but, being the intellectual that I am, your intellectual power. Immature as you are theoretically, I recognise your superb gifts. But as I get closer to you I recognise that the "impossible" idealism which makes a revolutionary refuse to accept the world, kept me lonely and unwilling to give myself except in bits to any woman because I felt the individual somehow always inferior. With my intimate friends, gifted and vastly superior in many things as some of them have been to me, I ran the show. But you, strange as it may seem to you, I meet on the level and not a little astonished at the things you say and do. You haven't the faintest conception of what you will do once you are settled. I know. And that plus all sorts of other things make me know what I was missing before. I think it is this—that in strictly intellectual matters, and there is where I live, I was always aware that I could do what the others were doing—if I devoted myself to it. You understand I am sure. Actually I couldn't. But it was not beyond me. But what you do I couldn't do if I tried a hundred years.

A long digression. But not really. Do you feel very lonely? Is it that you wonder if you will ever do anything? If that is it, put it aside—you will. Only you can prevent that. Or maybe it is some fear implanted by an insecure childhood? Or perhaps—I don't know. Perhaps you will get rid of it with some achievement. As far as money is concerned, ignore that for the time being. Never worry about your rent for a moment. But that will only lessen something that is deeper. You will know. Perhaps you know it. Whatever it is, my precious, and it may be many things, it is nothing to be frightened about. I'll write about it tomorrow. You will do things and gain confidence and be mistress of your own self. Nothing else matters.

I hope your hand is not painful and that you rest easily. These are Nettie's notes for you. Others will come.

This letter is only partial. It is inadequate. I would like to write for you such letters as were never written before. To sit down and write to you, as I cannot even write for the proletariat but as I will write for them one day when they are ready. They will unloose power from me, the power I feel surging in me. I know it is there but only their actions can bring it out. I know I will. And I know too that I can't until they do. Same with you. Same with you. Curious the affinity I find myself always making now with you and the proletariat. I can explain it if I worked at it. And I know that somewhere there is a logical connection, that if I write to you, I will in time write better for the proletariat. And if the proletariat does act and a voice is needed to give its actions their fullest implications, I not only know that I will do it, but that then I'll write to you as never before. No one will ever write as I shall write then. No one. The revolution is a release of power—and release for me too, in every direction. You see what you mean to me? I could not write this to anyone before. I didn't know it. And even if I did I couldn't write it. Tho' perhaps the knowledge and the person go together. Poor Shelley. I understand his frustrated spirit.

       Love,
       Nello

           Postmark March 28, 1946

How are you? No pain I hope—no worry. To-morrow will be a bright day. I shall see you. And I hope, on Saturday—afternoon and evening? But whenever you can.

It is 11:35. I am dead tired, worn-out. Work, work, work. To-night I went to see Bill and Margie, two ordinary rank and file workers. They talked to me for 2 hours. They said everything (but everything) that is in the American Resolution—in their own way, from their own experience, that is in the American Resolution. I sat fascinated. For they and others like them sit still and do not talk. They listen to the others. It is all above them—they feel bewildered and scared—but what they and other workers think, that they know. These two listened to me one day and then came straight to me afterwards. Now other people told me "I have been around for eight months and I have never heard what I expected 'til now." I'll explain it to you one day—its great significance—for me and for you. You should know Margie—a wonderful person. Oklahoman, blonde, tall, not well-educated, but experienced, very intelligent, and in her instincts and actions revolutionary to the last drop. She wants to leave the place where she is working but before she leaves "she has to make it a fit place for those who follow her to work."

I am in the train—no paper. I just posted you a book. Read in particular Preface to Lyrical Ballads by Wordsworth and then Tintern Abbey. When I'll post this I do not know. I had such a letter to write to you—about the poetry of Shelley and the love poetry in particular with a note on Keats. But it is near 1, I am still 20 minutes from home and I am ready to fall asleep here. I am OK but I haven't been sleeping. I go to bed at 2—fall asleep at 3:30 and am up about 9. For days and days I haven't had enough sleep. Pressure on all sides. But I lie down to rest sometimes for half an hour or unable to sleep and I think of you—just say "OK: Now, Constance." You never fail. Quite often it consists of thinking through some problems connected with you. But it is an oasis in a desert. You will get the book in the morning, I shall call you, and then I shall send you a wire which you will have got by now. Shelley will wait till to-morrow night or sometime. But I'll see you. You will be lovely and sweet and knowing that there is a bond between us will make me very happy and proud of myself. I feel myself bubbling over but I am too tired. However, one thought. Get close as close as you can to the workers. There is all the power in the world there. To-night I felt it again. Bill and Margie. I want you to feel as close to them as I did. Perhaps you will be closer—are already. But more of that later. I am now staggering to bed. I hope I shall dream of you. But I have done so only once in a year. I wonder why.

Home at last. I tried to get you this afternoon but you had left. Your landlady answered—dripping with good-will. I trembled for you.

I hope you had (why now) a good time at Sylvia's concert, which means that she sang well.

I want to register this letter to you. So must finish it at once. I propose, precious, that you take a holiday this week. I wouldn't argue with you. You know by now what I think. Only this a.m. I got your letter which said how happy you were and how you loved the place; then too, your cold is getting better you say. Which means you must get rid of it completely, taking advantage of the enforced rest. You will judge how far you can afford to take off time from your modelling. But as far as expenses for a week are concerned, I would say take it—you need it. Think of it, a whole week not to be bothered—to finish up that cold and sort yourself out internally. If it will help you to decide, know that if you do, you take one worry off the mind of one bothered citizen.

All my love,
N

Your letter I shall answer soon. Thank you for laboring to write it. I spoke stupidly about it on the phone. I had just got it out of the letterbox on my way to call you. I reacted traditionally. Dear me! But if you feel the content that way I am satisfied. Now I think of it, I think that way myself. I'll explain it in detail. But in essence it is this. L & T [Lenin and Trotsky] had only the Russian prol't, small, surrounded, backward. It achieved miracles but create the new. It would not. But this prol't is the greatest the world has known, the greatest social force history has known with such a wealth of creative power bursting in it, that if we tune ourselves to it, if we prepare ourselves, if we resolutely and continuously clear our minds and eyes of the never-resting film of bourgeois prejudice, then when the time comes and these people act—as they are acting already—we shall be lifted high. We could write as our ancestors could not—for we shall see it in the concrete . . .

I'll have a talk with you about how you are going to keep that place going. $15.00 a week is not too much considering everything. You have to manage until the summer; then through the summer until your work begins again. You should aim at a real good summer, working at writing, living happily and comfortably, developing your powers. When I see you on Sat'y we'll talk about it. Meanwhile————.

N

R. J.
4F
1306 Chisholm
Bronx

[March 1946]

Look, my precious, for everybody's sake, take care of yourself. This is not an ordinary admonition. It is something special from me to you. People use words that express their feelings for the moment and are sometimes extravagant. I have tried to avoid that with you. But I spent yesterday with you, just another of these wonderful days, not only wonderful in themselves but full of all sorts of promise. I do not know of anyone, have never met any young woman, am not interested in meeting any young woman, altogether so lovely, so precious, so wonderful as yourself. I don't think you are perfect—far from it. But all sorts of social and historical conditions have combined to produce just you. Your future depends upon many things which none of us control. But as far as you are concerned personally, you have never failed to rise to it. I am building up a great confidence in you. Unlike so many many people, you constantly show new and unexpected sides to your character, your talents, your personality—and all with not only depth but opening up wide vistas and perspectives. I am not afraid of making you conceited and have exaggerated opinions and expectations of yourself. I am learning to trust you absolutely, your judgment and your instinct. Conceit lies not in what one thinks of one's self. It lies in going about the world expecting everybody else to think the same. No, You are 1 in ten million. *But,* but, but, but, but—you must get rid of such a thing as illhealth nibbling at you. I don't like it. You must look as you did that day you came with Paula's sister—in the silk suit—radiant. She said what a commotion you created in the surrounding population. You created one in me. And another night—after coming from Sylvia with Bill and Georgie—you on one subway, I on another—you in a black skirt and white blouse—tall and a little tired but fit and keen, as if trained, very much like in the picture. Nothing forlorn as that day on the stage at Stamford and the first day you came back. I had finished (Turn over) the letter when I came back to this page and started to finish it. However you look it is the same to me. (I'll tell you some other time your characteristic attitudes.) But how you look matters to me because it is often an indication of how you feel—and also of how other people see you. On the whole you were best that day—when I first met you at 14th and 8th and Bill and G. were behind us. I want you to look that way again, fit and gaunt and ready to discipline material. Also that night where we sat on the floor and you looked at me and said Hello! And I just had nothing to say. You remember? I do—often.

The other sheet is somewhere. It is 9 p.m. I am "resting." Lying down. I have to so much—I write slowly. I can't see after the house and when I lost the money I had to get rid of the maid.* I am pretty helpless. So I am bothered about you. You must not go this way. You have been ill too often. You look strong and healthy but you catch things. And you hate to tell me about the stomach. Don't. Tell me. You must talk to someone and it should be me I understand. Get rid of it. You have many things to do. And one of them is to get rid of worry. I can't help thinking of that day when we walked down the step and the street and your feet were heavy. Your eyes yesterday. They weren't good. Enough. I wouldn't harp on the subject. But please, my precious, precious Constance, when I say precious, and miracle, I mean them, and that implies for you a certain responsibility. I want to see you handle a big piece of work, with mastery and power as an artist shapes clay. I want to see you shape your ideas into a bold structure, handling all the details with strength and sureness and a formidable discipline and patience. So that ordinary people will feel the impact and good critics will say "Boy, here is a force." So you will? Write and say that you will.

By the way, you must criticize the resolution freely, say what you think. I leave it entirely to your own good judgment and regard for me to know how to speak your mind. Particularly the little doubts you may have. Tell me. There may be something there. If you are wrong, you will learn. But express yourself. Now I must stop. I am altogether, not overwhelmed, but "permeated" with you. Every time I see you, talk to you, observe you, I feel my internal recognition of you as a superior person grow. You must understand what it means for me. For perhaps the first time, not perhaps, I am taken out of myself, not by things, but by a person. I am as sensitive as they make them, but here again I am not scared or apprehensive of your critical judgment. I am not defensive against it. About me, personally, I mean. I need you not to live at your expense. I am beginning to think that a lot of my hesitation with you in the past was due to a lot of things but one of them, just this feeling that you would only be a contributor to me. Perhaps it was only a cover for fear. One never knows. But I rejoice in the revelation of the strength of your intellect, your insight and reserves of character. With you I am beginning to find myself. Something I could not do alone. I use you not as a prop or for defence against reality but to break down barriers and get rid of defences. I don't know what I will find but I am not afraid. Sometimes I wondered if my personality, so mobilised in a particular way for a particular purpose I wonder if it would not suffer if I tampered with it. But I recognise that to be defeatist. Why should anyone be afraid of knowledge? Why should anyone be afraid of life? If

---

* [Note by C.L.R. J.] Not because I was broke. But because she might have taken it.

you read the resolution, you will see that I seek to formulate politically a comprehensive approach to life, of the vast stirrings and seeking for full personality which in the U.S. above all characterises the people. *We are today a stage higher than in 1917.* K. M. [Karl Marx] has said that you can judge a civilization by the posture of women[;] you can judge an individual by what he needs from women. I read it three years ago. I have never forgotten it. In reverse I saw Madeline's case [in] that astonishing far-reaching remark of hers. I have to learn, for the world outside reflects itself in me only so far as I can embrace it. I hope that sometime I shall get some of our girls to write with sensitiveness and yet with political sharpness about women. You will, I know, poetically and socially, perhaps in time politically too. I mean well, I know. But that is only the framework. . . . As in everything in my life the personal is always a reflection of the social. You are a peculiar combination of personal individuality and social manifestation. I cannot help marvelling at what I call the miracle, and the wide horizons knowing you daily opens up before me. The wonder is that I know as time goes on you will grow and expand, a constant source of new wonder. All that has happened. I wouldn't change a thing. So it was. Well, this is the result. Who am I to think that it could have been arranged differently. A warmth and glow suffuse me when I think of you and all the exciting things I know are going to happen, all opening outward.

N

Why have I never told you? My time in the U.S. is very uncertain. Nobody knows when "they" will say: "You. Get out. We don't want you here anymore." It has hung over me for years and now that the war is over, nobody knows what and when they will do. I never could bring myself to tell you. I have done or tried to do all that I legally can. But there isn't much. The only thing to do is to go on. I have made up my mind and politically I have mastered it. I go right on as if it were all settled. But it keeps me in a state of personal uncertainty that I think somehow, somewhere, eats into me. But of late I say, "To hell with it. I do what I can." But I want to tell you everything I can, to learn from you all that I can, to get as close to you, to know you as much as I can so that whatever happens, I take you with me and leave with you as much of me as I can. I am not too much worried about it anymore. Little by little, no, by great jumps, I'll tell you everything.

I'll call you in the a.m., but that will be before you get this. All my love for you, my own, special, miracle, all mine for the time being, until the world begins to know about you. I am anticipating, *how* I am anticipating, your analysis of Dick and then when he reads it seeing him look at you with a new respect and recognition that here is something he missed. I am nursing it. Then we'll go off and gloat, somewhere by ourselves. Ho! ho! ho! Then after, when you speak, he will listen respectfully. Ho! ho! ho!

Postmark April 1, 1946

Well, my pearl of great price. The truth is always *concrete*. You never know what a word or phrase really means until life fills it for you. Do you know I have repeated the phrase pl of gt price, a thousand or a hundred times and never thought of what it meant. Now I know what the poet meant—what did he mean? Simply what he said. A pearl—a precious jewel, rare and beautiful, of great price—people would pay enormous sums for it. That's it. That's you. You had a bit of a cold by the way, Miss Beautiful. When we were coming home I noticed. We shall have to chase that intruder down to his lair and root him out. He has other places to inhabit and not your lovely self.

Look. Yesterday I watched your face and silhouette from all angles. You looked, my p. of gt. p. *wonderful. Almost,* though not quite your own self. And a wonderful smile that glows from inside and looks—I can't describe it. I saw it for the first time when we had dinner at the Oviedo that day we spent with Dick and Ellen [Wright]. I have never seen it before. Saturday I saw it often. Yesterday it came and went.

After the meeting. It is morning. 8:30. I had a good sleep. I hope you did. I am in no hurry to tell you about these last few days. My values change. I look at myself and I think the opposite of what I thought. You know my great discovery? Guess. I love you? NO, elementary. I AM A COLOSSAL IDIOT. See, I said to myself. You, C.L.R., continually wonder how Norman and Edward and Jack let her go. Good. But you, C.L.R., you *nearly did the same thing*!!

I am absolutely amazed. Now suppose you had! Do you know? A lot of things I would never have known. Never. I know that. At least. I see no prospect of it. For one thing I would never have known—*you*. Henceforth no more superior criticism of Norman, E. and J. No, sister, that's over. I tremble to think that historically I might have been linked with them as one to whom you came and was found wanting. Ho! Ho! C.L.R. is now a wise man.

Fly around little birdie, but no getting away. It will be far easier to find you wherever you are than to replace one third of you. Now I have work to do. Good-bye.

By the way. Tickets for Wednesday. *You* must see it. Please. If one ticket is very expensive, get it. If not, get two. But always be prepared that at the last minute I cannot come. Also the Antigone. This may be pleasure but it is duty too. I'll call you. But Thursday—Monday—holiday for you. *We must make it something.*

It's a raw day. Take care of yourself.

> Thus in a season of calm weather
> Though inland far we be
> Our souls have sight of that
>   immortal sea
>   which brought us hither
> Can see the children sport
>   upon the shore
> And hear the mighty waters
>   rolling evermore

I don't know if I have the metre right. But you remember the passage. Now look at what happened.

I was very much moved by the passage and drew it to your attention. I knew it and loved it at 17. It is in the old tradition of English prose. It is very wonderful to me—to you too, but it strikes many chords in my mind. Now you liked it. But you were struck by something else. In the primal sympathy which having been must ever be. You responded to other parts of the poem.

Every great poem, especially of a great poet, has elements of the past and elements of the future. You caught hold of the ones that signified the future. I love it all. But the older rhythms mean more to me, with so much more of classical English literature in my head.

I noticed the same once when we were listening with a friend to Chopin. I liked the singing melodies of a Ballade, he the quicker, more modern passages. I tried to find out why and made it. That is why I am so careful in listening to what you have to say. It is worthwhile for its own sake—always. But I am a different generation, with a much longer background of knowledge in my head. (In much I expect it will be the same.) Catholic in my tastes, and always eager to see the response of someone like you, and particularly you. So that now I am well set and have no fear any more, of subconsciously even, unduly influencing you in literature. Most times your responses though fundamentally the same as mine have a different emphasis, a different perspective. And it is most exciting, most stimulating. You keep leading ahead, Miss 1946, and I watch the direction and analyse why. Isn't that fun?

I tried to get you this p.m. and again to-night but I failed. Was sorry to miss conversation with you even for a day. I hope we can meet on Wednesday evening. In any case, Thursday or Friday—we'll see each other as much as possible? You are responsible you know. Saturday and Sunday were two wonderful days, full of all sorts of beginnings, confirmation of anticipations and immense avenues opened up. I thought that talking to you on Saturday night was a new experience for me, entirely new. Isn't it odd? At 46, or rather 45, I have *one*, just one conversation to look back to in which I felt I was really communicating not all of myself but as much of myself as was available—no part of me consciously or unconsciously held firmly in reserve—this is mine, private, and I shall certainly not let you see it. There was none of that. As we talk more I shall tell you a number of things which should be interesting to you for my sake and your own, and for your reading and writing. And Sunday! *Absolutely different*. I was the same personality. Was I? You seemed an entirely different person, taking to it as a duck takes to water. Good. This is now Tuesday a.m. Spent the night at Freddie's. This is a terrible letter. I wrote most of it at a meeting. Freddie says "C has a lot of poise, but in reality is uncertain." She is far behind. It is going to be a long hard fight, but Saturday night going home in the taxi I knew that the problem was well in hand. You reminded me in profile of the picture at home—in the field. But there was a stage further. There you were looking up, in general, you were aiming at something. Now you sat still listening, sure, confident with the job not in the distance, but in front of you. I have seen so often athletes just before their turn comes sitting in dressing-rooms waiting. You were just like that. Mr. Insecurity? He is a dead goose. But he doesn't know it yet. And—me too. Alas, me too! My doubts about myself that I have conquered or at least restrained with so much effort. They are a dead goose already too. I know since you know when. Difference between us is that I have mastered a few things and *once I see it*, I am confident I'll get there in time. One more conquest lies before you and then the world is yours.

Money worries you? OK. For the time being you must build up a little account. Ho! Ho! To solve the problems of the individual soul, build up a little account. But—did not the great Stan IS Lavsky say "start off on the material and build up." Proved. And I say too. The artist need *not* be like Tregorin—not in the 20th century in the U.S. when he need not be an individual but a representative of the proletariat.

Bill and Margie—wonderful wonderful people. We have so much to teach them but oh! Sister, if you know how much they have to teach us—if only we have the patience and the ears to listen. But to do that you need a good universal.

Thank you for being very sweet to me? When? After I left you in the subway Sunday night. And by the way, never a backward thought, never an uneasy self-questioning. This spring and summer and fall are yours. You are the Queen of the May. Want to buy some lovely and not too cheap something. No conscience probings. Buy it. "I oughtn't to, etc., etc." You are young only once.

When have you been free and easy and happy and thoughtless as youth ought to be? Sure of the world around you, of your home and parents and friends? As a kid, no. With Norman and Eddie? No. With Jack? No. Stalinism gnawed at your conscience. My dearest, dearest Constance. Now is your chance. Remember. It is *not* in your bank-account, nor anywhere else. It is in *you*.

So let it go. I am standing by in case you stumble. People learn to swim by swimming. Let's see what you can do with yourself between now and October. See what you can build up inside by then. Now you can build for yourself a house in which to live, a house you never had before. You want to help me? Do that. You will, I know you will. I sit here and am singing inside.

R. J. 4F
1306 Chisholm
Bronx

Postmark April 5, 1946

I have half-an-hour in the train to Pen. It shakes. So does my hand. But you must get this tonight.

I say you are, or rather I know no one like you. I say: let them look all over the world. I stand pat. You wonder; maybe I exaggerate. Let's see.

Look at our world, sweetheart. See it as Dorothy Thompson* and so many others see it. It is barbarism. Not only bombs and famine but impotence in the mind. They are caught in a narrowing circle. They cannot think. They are driven in on themselves, corrupting their minds by the limitations of their thoughts. I once wrote of Winston C [Churchill] as having as fine a *natural* endowment as L. T. But this bourgeois limited by bourgeois ideas and the bourgeois decay has made no single contribution to modern ideas and if it were not for the war would have died a failure. L. T., I said, joined something which had room.

Now I know England and the U.S. Tell me where any of their *young* people for the last 12 years have done anything—tell me. Dick. Nobody else. Absolutely nobody. Talents, gifts, of course they have. I know that. But the bankruptcy is complete.

Then some splendid ones move over to the Stalinists. And tell me, my miracle, whom or what have they produced in the last dozen years. Browder? Foster? Bob Minor? Paul Robeson?** Any history? Any volume of criticism? Any poetry to speak

---

* American journalist and columnist.
** Prominent figures associated with the Communist Party.

of? Any political analysis that enlightens anybody? Sweetheart, *they kill everything they touch*. There is nothing growing in that soil. It cannot produce. If it does sprout they kill it—they do not, they cannot nourish. I have watched this for 12 years. I saw Auden, Spender, MacNeice and the rest perish. Didn't you?

Now I look at you. What do I see? I see you through spectacles which have watched pupils and young talents for nearly 30 years. I knew that yours, the untrained, is the finest I have seen. But I have seen Bill and Gorman. I have their work. I saw it grow. I know that it is an individual talent which has grown out of a certain attitude to life and society. But you, with talent greater than theirs have a terrific *background*. Your years with us are the driving force of your life. You have fought off Stalinism, a dangerous attachment, bourgeois flesh-pots, the inheritance of your personal difficulties in early life, step by step I have seen you, by instinct almost, fighting them and defeating them. You are an *honest* person; with superb drive and energy. In addition, a by no means negligible thing, and I haven't to prove this, you are an extremely attractive woman.

Now I ask you. Tell me where at 25, where could I hope to find another like you? As an individual, as a person, I would be the God-damnedest fool on earth to say: Maybe there is someone else. In China? Maybe. Let the Chinese look for them. But this is not only personal. It is a social judgment. Read over my past letters, especially since you came to N.Y., and a little before. Where will you end? That depends upon the American workers. If as you can, you fight your way to them completely—put your talents where they can affect you, then your future is safe, and if they go places you will go. But I my precious, love you because you are all this—I see it. Let the riff-raff question my judgment. But you have no fear.

           Love,
           Nello

R. J.
4F
1306 Chisholm
Bronx

        Special Delivery
           Postmark April 6, 1946

I have no paper but scraps. I am now on the train. I gave your letter to a man (porter) to post. I hope he did. I'll continue here.

You see what I think of you and why. Talk to me about it again and again. Now to me and you. First me. Look at me.

I am 45.

I am not a healthy person.

My hands shake.

My beard is terribly gray. I can very often look my age.

I don't know when I will be yanked up from here and told to get out with no possibility of ever coming back again.

I am a Negro, which means that an association with me will be tough for anyone.

My life with women in the past has not been good for me. I am just beginning to learn.

That is me. Not all of me, the best of me you know. I'll come to that later. But that list is a formidable one, and there is no need to exaggerate them for someone with your outlook and possibilities. Furthermore talking and writing are one thing. An intimate life is another. The two are connected. To-day I believe that they are closer than I thought—formerly I was merely in love with you—now you are a well of inspiration and an embodiment of some of my deepest ideas and longings.

But I can see it as someone in your place could see me. Good. The conclusion I draw *to-day* is this. If in a year's time you should say "I have seen someone. I am in love," the *only* thing for me to say is "I have had every opportunity to win you, to make you feel that your life will only be complete with me—that you will never find recognising arms but mine. Yet I didn't make it. The differences, the obstacles were too much. You have fought and overcome many barriers. But this is your intimate personal life. You have decided. So be it."

Before yesterday, I felt that *for some good reason of your own*, you were never giving me half-a-chance. I have some little idea now of what they were.

But the idea that if you relaxed with me, if I held you close and kissed you, you thereby were committed and soon (Good God! perhaps in an hour), I would be pressing you to go to bed with me, asking you to come and live with me; that next time this would go on, that our friendship would be dominated by my constant desire to express my male need for you—that I hope is, if not dead, in you, is dying and the debris will soon be cleared away. What, my precious, could I ever have to *reproach* you with. You are unjust. For the last two years, have I lost anything? Have you taken and not given? You think if it were to end to-morrow, I would regret anything? As usual you underestimate yourself. You underestimate what you mean to me, actually and symbolically. Can two people live their own lives and have so much respect for each other, given so much, have so much respect for the *developing* personality as not to wish to limit, to constrict, to hamper, to bind the other? If you are going to come as I want you to come it will be because you feel that in my arms you are most yourself (and that means plenty) and that it is so much to you that the price must be paid—other things will have to go. I believe that your personality is such that you will search far before you will find anyone with whom you could so completely express yourself as with me. Reich I am sure has given you some idea of what is contained in the simple word orgasm. I know (only negatively, alas!) that he is right. I have lived dissatisfied for 25 years. I have chosen. I have decided. But I could not find it in me anywhere to reproach *you* if you decide not to choose me. I am not trading with you my interest and attention and friendship in return for your surrender, and then if you don't, to feel that I have not got my share, I have been cheated. If you think that you are harming yourself. I know it. I have done it in the past. Perhaps I had cause. I don't know now. But you have no cause to feel or to think so with me. I am 45. It has its disadvantages. But it has its advantages too.

This is one.

Listen. If you made love to me, gave me all you could, and then left me I wouldn't, I wouldn't reproach you. Isn't that what I marvel at in the others? They had their chance and lost—the fools. If you gave me only a part of yourself, then it is my business to make you come further. I can't see it any other way. This is a matter not of our future—it is a matter of *now*. That is and must be the correct relationship between us. Dig into yourself and see what barriers and constrictions are created, how wrong it is, for you to carry in your mind, to have carried, the conception that you had to be on guard lest you deceive me. Sure I know you had cause. I know you were fighting instincts and doubts and fears—Oh! yes, fears too. (Don't you think I have them too?) But at any rate those must go. You do as you damn well please. But *that counts both ways*. One last word for my train is arriving. I accept responsibility in this. I am not Sir Galahad. But I am accustomed to accepting it. And far more important. I am a "settled" person. I know what I want. I have an axis and a profession and a course. You haven't settled yourself yet. Here in particular you don't know, you haven't any clear ideas of your future. You haven't even cleared up the past as yet, have you? That is the difference and that dictates my role. It is the same that I see in regard to your work. And confidence in you? That terrific childlike boldness which I see in your literary work explodes every now and then in your personal statements as when you said, in passing "I know I can get on without you, now." It is magnificent. The chief thing is to sweep away the rubbish that clutters up. But a great part of that rubbish was contained in your defensive attitude. That is on the way out? Good. (I'll continue this as soon as I can.) Meanwhile I hope we'll meet Saturday afternoon. I'll call you in the a.m. I have all Sunday free for you and am engaged Saturday evening for some time. The choice is *yours yours yours*. I know what I want and where it is to be found. You don't. Find out.

            Love,
            Nello

R. J.
4F
1306 Chisholm
Bronx

[April 1946]

 Still on train. Breakfast. A lovely day outside. God! How I would love to see your lovely face opposite to mine this morning and the miles flying—going somewhere. What a companion you would be; not only for that journey but for always.

 My dear, sweet, good, lovely, wonderful miracle, miraculous too even in your weaknesses. Darling, you must come out of it or let me come in—that shell of yours. The wounds need air. How bold you were. I said "Writing it must be" and a special delivery—"Writing it shall be." Decision. You are offered the job in Berkeley Square. "No," you say. You go out with the agent. Job, he says. "No," you say. Firm in your heart I am sure. Of that I have not the tiniest doubt. Will you do the analysis of Dick? O.K. you say, I am scared but I will, and you tackle it as bold as ever. You cross the line. You come back with us. You know where you belong. Sweetheart, why go it alone? You are hurting yourself far more than anything I can do to hurt you. These are grand and exciting days for you and for me—great decisions made, risks gallantly taken, steps affecting our whole lives. You are living now, more than you ever did before, strengthening your character, deepening your responses to life, knowing what so many others have gone through and will go through, storing up experience which you will translate for others. And yet you hesitate, you lay down injunctions about affection, when your whole nature is crying for it—at a little, a very little of it, what you had hidden from me so long, from *me*, came out. You hid it from *me*. If anyone had some claim to know, it was I wasn't it? Whom could you tell who would understand? Nobody. About the acting and your hopes and the changeover to writing. About Dick and his work? About the revolutionary life and the old life. Even about a simple thing like finances. Man or woman, is there anyone to whom you could come and open your heart to? Is there anyone who needs your happiness, your relaxation, your confidence, as much as I do, needs it for himself. Don't you think of me sometimes? Do you think of what I want, of what I need? I have some relaxation the few hours a week I spend with you. At no other time. But when you cry, and come to me and are gay, and then go back home to cry again, what do you think happens or will happen to me? There is not a part of your present life—the things that matter and the past that remains with which I am not connected. Is it for that reason that you fight me so hard, put up barriers, lay down ultimatums, and then go home and be miserable? I do not say that you are miserable because you put up barriers against me. I say that you are miserable because the natural flow and outlet for you in these seething, draining days is me—in my arms, talking to me, giving yourself a chance. There are all sorts of things we have to talk about, clear up the past (you and I are interested in emotions as personal and as emotions) get to know each other, hopes, dreams, aspirations, problems, fears, build something, double the happiness and halve the pain. And if in a day or in a year, it leads to something, or doesn't, or half-way, or wherever it does lead, what are you afraid of? Afraid of life? With the whole stage set for a depth of communication, a community of interests, a real expansion of life, living as how many people could live, how many, you build up barriers to safeguard yourself. You are wrong, wrong, wrong, wrong, wrong.

You spent a week-end with me once. On the Saturday evening at about 7 we were on the divan or is it a bed? I held your hand. You knew I was going to talk to you. You appeared resigned, bored, willing to go through with it. I was never farther away from you than at that moment. It may have been genuine with you. It is a technique with some women. The way out of it is simplicity itself. All you have to do is to say "The hell with it. If that is the way you feel, you can go to hell your own way and I'll go mine." They usually come out of it. But I left you alone. I said what I had to say. You tell me now that all that time you were lonely, doubtful, suffering, fighting, with bitter memories and doubts for the future. Maybe you used to go home and cry. I don't know. Maybe you talked to someone. I don't know. But now it is different. I am closer to you than I have ever been to anyone in my life—without any reservation I make that statement. And I try to think of your relationship with Jack—how far apart you two really were for all your closeness. What did he know of you? He called you a liar. Think of that. He accused you of preparing to marry him but at the same time carrying on an affair with me. Imagine that. He didn't know how sensitive you were. He either didn't know of your years with Eddie (and if he didn't it is his fault) or if he did he was utterly oblivious of it. While you stayed at his house he kept you in the same, a worse nervous tension day after day. Tell me, sister, how close could you ever have been to a man who understood you so little and to whom you gave so much. A man tires of a woman or falls in love with another woman and then treats the first one badly—not always but often enough. Jack didn't tire of you. He just wasn't a man big enough to satisfy all your needs.

Have you ever been closer in your life to anyone than you are to me? "You may see someone." Who? Someone whom you will go to bed with, carefully shutting away the life that matters. You read Reich and learn 0. Where is this man? One who will understand your political views not only on the surface but deep down, understand the kind of life you want to live. Where is the woman friend to whom you can speak? Madeline? She drains you dry. Every time you speak of her for any time at all I see that. Maybe you have friends I don't know about, friends who understand you. I doubt it. And yet there it is, instead of coming to me you stay at home and cry.

I am not asking you to marry me, darling. I am not asking you to promise me anything. I am not asking you to commit yourself. I am not even asking you to go to bed with me. I am asking you something else—I am asking you to come and be natural with me, be intimate with me, and to hang the consequences. If you could get rid of that fear of consequences we could go places—all sorts of wonderful places where only two, and two perfectly matched can go. Will the situation be any better in 6 months? It wouldn't. How could it be! When I think of how nearly, after all these years, I lost you for good, I shiver. Your letter tells me how you sat in the night-club, admiration, attention, an adoring escort, drinks, dancing—and how you wanted to get home. I should hope you did. You remember dells of refrigerated coolness. That does not suit you anymore. Not you, Constance, not you. But then you come home to your room and the lights on the river. No, sweetheart. Not that either. *You*, to come home to an empty room, to be alone. You need someone. I know. You need love and affection, a constant sense of nearness, someone to draw strength from. I am sometimes distracted with loneliness. I go to the pictures—3 times a week. (I don't any more.) The children used to come. I asked them to stay. I have lived that way for years, with interludes of love-making, some of them quite passionate. But do you think that if the opportunity had come of meeting someone like you I would have missed it? I would have gone where it led.

(Before I forget. What did you have for lunch yesterday, and to day?)

You cry alone, you scan the horizon, you sit in a nightclub, wishing to get away from the admiration of women and the attentions of an adoring escort. You endure all these things and more, you suffer, but one thing you insist on that you and I keep away from each other. Now let me tell you something, Miss. I am in love with you. I have been in love with you for 8 years. I nearly settled down with a girl some years ago, and just couldn't, because tho' you were married and I wasn't hearing from you, I was loyal to what was only a memory and a vision and preferred to live as usual rather than settle for less. I want you, you understand. I don't look at another woman these days. Maybe to-morrow I will. I don't know. But to-day it is only you. I tell you what I want. I want to spend hours and hours, whole days in bed with you, talking to you as people can talk only when they have made love to each other, or know that they can when they want to. Once every week at least I need that from you, and will face the world after with complete calm and confidence. Everything is fused in you for me, your lips, your lovely body, your smiles, your sweetness, your brilliant mind, your revolutionary temper, your integrity, I don't know where one begins and another ends. Don't you think, do you think ever of me? Or have you got accustomed to my patient waiting? I am patient, I can wait, I can lose and continue to love you and admire you, and help you where I know I can help you, but this crisis has been a long time coming, it is here, and I shall not stand aside and see you unhappy, tears, boring yourself with excitement, and then running away from excitement, aching to lay your head somewhere and feel around you arms that recognise you, and yet so determined that come what may it must not be me that you declare: I don't even want affection from you. Is everything between us so much in itself and so little in comparison with what you have got from other men you say you slept with? What is it that makes you so determined to keep me at a distance, when you need someone so badly particularly now, and I am near, who knows and understands and went through everything with you. I can, I have to stand aside and accept your wishes. But I want to know. I want you to ask yourself and then tell me: Why do you prefer to keep your real conflicts inside corroding you, and seek distraction in alien places, rather than come to me and say "I am in a mess. I am winning my victory. I know I am winning but it is costing me much. I am not in love with you. I don't promise to be in love with you. But the love and kindness you have for me I need it now. Also I know how much you need me, how much whatever I have to give you will mean to me. Here I am. Be gentle with me, be kind to me. Don't rush me into anything. But I'll meet you half-way and if I feel like it all the way. If it does not succeed then you and I after all these years have too much in common to be bitter. At least we will have done all we could to help each other. And if it does come to it that we have to part, at least we weren't afraid and didn't torture each other and ourselves."

You will see me on Tuesday. I'll call you in the day. Those violets are on my conscience. I wanted you to have them while I was away. Courage, baby. Courage. Look. You'll write wonderful poems or a book about it someday. I am your opponent, your antagonist, and yet I am in your camp too. Remember I was in your camp conspiring (in ideas) against Jack's wish to enslave you. And all the time I loved you so much. But you were so much in love and yet you were fighting with such spirit. I tell you what to do.

WONDERFUL IDEA. You come into my camp and help me to plan strategy against you. Isn't that brilliant? We, you and I, would be IRRRRR-e ZIS-TIBLE against you. And your punishment—my peace terms, my reparation. For the first year the conquered power shall come and be in the arms of the conqueror and talk or not talk until she goes to sleep. The conqueror lays no other conditions, restrictions, enquiries, promises, demands, or other upon the conquered except to be honest and straightforward and confident in the good-will of the conqueror. Try it for once, sweet enemy!

[unsigned]

P.S. I laugh at myself. Hear me talking boldly—the conquering hero! I am racked with pain—nerves tense and exhausted with a great program before me. But I shall win my battle here. And if even you affect me I am a stronger man because of you. I love you, darling. I wish you would try—just try to be natural with me, the warm human being that you are. Exclude others from that—not me.

[Undated, 1946]

My lovely darling,

Little pieces of paper with black marks upon them come to me enclosed in another piece of paper with pictured stamps. I open and read, in fact before I read, the knowledge that it is on the way, the messenger saying "Special delivery" your bold writing—all this sets off currents in me that are not only wonderful in themselves, but astonishing to contemplate. I think of previous trips when there was nothing. And now, everything, everything, is altered. I do my work here as well as ever in fact

Uncertainty and Attachment (1945–6) 255

infinitely better. My friends and enemies both feel a certain *weight*. It is a concentration of the impact. I am so sure. And I do it all from an inside fortress. In there I am impregnable. I love you without reservations. I feel myself one of the most fortunate of men. I feel that I am the man for you. I am proud of myself for it, have that personal confidence which my political confidence needed, feel that no aspect of life is now shut away from me, am confident that you will recognise what all this means for me and for you. I was here last August, same place, same circumstance. You spent the preceding days with me. You remember? They meant much for me. But this time? Darling, a world has intervened. It is as if my previous life was some sort of preparation, a long immaturity. Yesterday I was talking to someone whom I want to persuade to a point of view. I was as fluent as resourceful as ever. But there was something else. I watched her as a person, was not so nervous, sized up her reactions, tried to fathom what she really was like, what she was thinking. Of course I always did that before—but with a sense of strain. Now it was easy. We talked for two hours. She left and promised to come back. I was physically tired, psychologically as fresh as ever, in fact stimulated. I thought of you every interval of you as there with me. I am conscious of you inside of me all the time. There was an emptiness before and I literally ate myself to pieces. But now that it is filled I am learning to be calm, not for people to see, but for myself. And thank goodness I know that it will never, never be empty again.

You write of a certain type of relationship which you have always thought of as ideal. You write of it as something you have always wanted. Darling, please just cast aside the cobwebs of the past and it is here for you to take. I shall have and you shall have many adjustments to make. But what you want, what you have hoped for is what I want and what I have hoped for, nothing less, dreamt of it while you ran about, a straight-legged little kid in California suns and laid the foundation of the marvelous specimen you are today. (Do you know, of course you know, you have beautiful straight legs, larger than is fashionable, but perfectly proportioned?) I want the independence too, feeling that you have a life of your own, the constant spectacle and wonder of a personality always developing, seeing life through my own eyes and through yours. But at the same time, there is no independence with dependence. Nettie's quotation from Hegel is profound truth, in logic and in life. You realise that too, it is clear. Nothing else really matters. Nothing else. When you ask yourself: Why all these years has Nello meant so much to me? Why did I not break with him when Jack was pressing for it? To ask the question darling, is to answer it. That is the way with all fundamental problems. And that is the final answer to your doubts and hurt as to why Jack "rejected" you. Don't you see what I told you? You rejected him. Not in any superficial sense either. I didn't know the details, but I had watched you during the previous months and I knew.

You were writing poetry that summer, a burst of creativeness going on side by side with your finding your independence. But while your physical passion was for him, these which mattered most to you, were for me. I told you so once. He was out of that. In those spheres, not only I came first. There was no one else but me. And looking back now I see that this and this only could have been the source of a curious fatalism that governed my relationship with you at the time. You say that in writing to me about us you are working at Dick. You are right. You are doing some of the most important work of your life in clarifying all this. This is the impact of life upon you—politics, art, and the life of the heart are all indissolubly intertwined. You are the instrument on which society plays. Your writing is your organised response. How can your responses be strong, comprehensive, embracing, unless you have organised and clarified your deepest personal experiences. See the effect it is having on me—and this is just the beginning. In your letters already I see the effect on you.

The dialectic is here functioning in all its superb clarity. At one and the same time, you are getting rid of the old hang-overs, you are ready to ask Jack for your letters and examine that past; *and* you are beginning to ask yourself the fundamental questions about me. All affirmation is negation. All negation is affirmation. To see your past as it was is to begin to see me as I am for you. And dearest heart, as I see your thoughts unfolding, your rejections and acceptances, not by any logical *system*, but empirically on the basis of your feelings and experiences, and at the same time when I see how strictly logical the process is (for there is no logic so logical as the logic of empiricism) I realise the deep honesty and sincerity of your character. If, in the past, I have had doubts, but impatience, yes, impatience, at what seemed to be your incapacity to see certain things, your determination not to ask yourself certain questions, it is because I didn't know how rare, how sensitive, and how passionate is your desire for truth and integrity, how bitter the pain when you felt you had tried and failed. You say you never felt protection such as I give to you. That I accept whole-heartedly. For me to see you as you are, and not to surround you with all that I can give of what you need would be to degrade myself in my own eyes, to know that I was a third-rater, and in a very important sense, so much the less a socialist. I shall work out these and many other things with you. I see myself in time developing a depth of comprehension and a human sympathy which will expand my own work, which will be indefinable perhaps but will enable it to reach people it didn't reach before, and in places that were formerly shut off. You will do the same. I, the old I, far less the new one can do that for you, if you come to me.

I love you and I want you? How else could it be? All sorts of men want you. You have so much delight and pleasure to give to any man. But you in whom so much of my life and ideas is concentrated, do you see how desperate it is to feel that you, as a woman, are separate from me. If you were dry and wizened and dull-eyed, I would love you. But you are not. You are a vital, passionate, lovely, dazzling woman. If you are that to so many men, think of what this must mean to me, who see all the things I see in you, embodied in your superb physical self, not physical self, but the loveliness and the bloom and the dazzling quality that makes men look at you. When I think of some air force officer kissing you it seems to me a sacrilege and a waste. It has taken me years of hard work and life and experience in many countries and in a great intellectual and social tradition to appreciate you and to love you as you should be loved, to love you as you need to be loved, as you must be loved if you are to be what you have in you to be. You are now on the threshold of your fullest development. Your previous life has been a preparation. You have experiences behind you of life, of art, of politics, of men, of joy and sorrow. You need completion. I am not, I don't think I am jealous of men in your life, glimpses and indications that I have had. I look at one or two I have seen and I feel pretty sick. I say: They could find other girls who suit them. This is Norman all over again. And I used to say: Constance, my precious, wonderful Constance, surely you must see them as I see them. But now that I know you so much better I understand it, but at the same time want you so much more to help you put an end to it for my sake because I love you, and for your own because it isn't worthy of you, darling, not to-day when you know what you want, and when it is so near to you.

There is such a life waiting, just round the corner, a human life. Come and let us see. I want to revel and delight in your loveliness, of mind and body, but I want your love and your passion. Your trust and your confidence. I want you but I don't want to grab on to you and thrust you under the sheets. But I want you in my arms, talking to me, giving me a chance and giving yourself a chance to break down the inhibitions so that then you can act freely. I trust you—to recognise what you want. But we are so close and still so far apart, a distance which only you can cross and which I want you to cross with decision and boldness and the gallantry you have shown on so many occasions.

I hope Tuesday was a success and I am sorry you have family troubles. You must tell me more about them when I come. I want to know. I think perpetually of the hours in which your lips will seek mine as passionately as mine seek yours, of hours of calm, all passion spent, now perhaps of hours in which lying in my arms, all the painful past is washed away and a new Constance, more miraculous than ever finally emerges. In other words, I think of you, body and mind and character always interfused, at your loveliest and best; but never absent from my most enchanting pictures of you is: what did she have for lunch and is she getting rid of that sniffle? One day, the days, the days ahead, I'll tell you why among other reasons I am deeply certain that I love you—discuss it with you in all its implications. You are the only woman, the only one, whose sniffle does not detract one iota in my thoughts of you. Huysmans, the French novelist, and D. H. Lawrence, and I think Anatole France have written along these lines. Constance my dazzling goddess, with the sniffle. I am just aching to put my arm around you and hold some kleenex to your nose and say "Blow. Blow hard. Harder. Good."

To His Coy Mistress

Had we but world enough, and time,
This coyness, lady, were no crime.
We would sit down and think which way
To walk, and pass our long love's day.
There by the Indian Ganges' side
Shouldst rubies find: I by the tide
of Humber would complain. I would
Love you ten years before the flood,
And you should, if you please, refuse
Till the conversation of the Jews;
My vegetable love should grow
Vaster than empires and more slow;
An hundred years should go to praise
Thine eyes, and on thy forehead gaze;
Two hundred to adore each breast
about thirty thousand to the rest;
An age at least to every part,

And the last age should show your heart.
For lady, you deserve this state,
Nor would I love at lower rate.

But at my back I always hear
Time's winged chariot hurrying near,
And yonder all before us lie
Deserts of vast eternity.
Thy beauty shall no more be found,
Nor, in thy marble vault, shall try
That long-preserved virginity,
And your quaint honour turn to dust
And into ashes all my lust:
The grave's a fine and private place,
But none I think, do there embrace.

Now, therefore, while the youthful hue
Sits on thy skin like morning dew
And while thy willing soul transpires
At every pore with instant fires,
Now let us sport us while we may,
And now, like amorous birds of prey,
Rather at once our time devour,
Than languish in his slow-chapt power,
Let us roll all our strength and all
Our sweetness up into one ball,
And tear our pleasures with rough strife
Through the iron gates of life;
Thus though we cannot make our sun
Stand still, yet we will make him run.
             [unsigned]

[February/March 1946]

Alone with you at last. Train back to home. You and I travelling somewhere. I have been writing you this letter for days. But I had to write the other two—my orderly mind had to clear away the debris. But that is one—gone. As I think of you now at this moment a glow fills me. I go warm all over, as if a lamp were lit inside of me; and the warmth expanded me.

I am in love with you and am very lonesome for you. Constance winces a little. Now.

I am in love with you and am very lonesome for you.
Constance winces a little less.
I am in love with you and am very lonesome for you.
Constance winces slightly.
I am in love with you and am very lonesome for you.
Constance does not wince.
Instead takes a friendly offensive. Well, so you are.

Good! And I am going to talk to you about it.

And you are going to talk to me too. No more closed off places. No more apologies, explanations, excuses. No more. I'll be rational and you will be.

I stop and look out of the window—flat plain, snaky river, and some houses on a street. But I do not see them. I see you—always Cleopatra in a red dressing gown in a suburban drawingroom. How incongruous you looked—half-sleepy and a dissatisfied twist to your mouth. It was the second impression that I had of you—the first—in a *red* coat—at the meeting. I got the first full impact of your temperament and your loveliness as a woman. Two women have spoken to me of you as I like. Bessie and Mrs. Olene of Northport. They said "She is a lovely creature." That is it. A lovely creature. You are other things but that too. Look at the sequence. 1. Your eagerness at the meeting. I responded to it. 2. Your interest in me as a person—the others wanted to know about what *I knew*. You saw *me*. It was after a long hard tour. Politicos had pushed me around—meaning well of course, but mentally. 3. You came out that night. I looked at the two men, your two men. I remember saying something like this. "What the *hell* is happening here. Look at this girl and look at them." Near the house, if I am not mistaken, was a bridge over a river. I crossed it lost in thought, but I remember the conjunction. I have carried that image ever since. Wordsworth, in the din of cities and in lonely rooms, was always remembering nature; and when in vacant and in pensive mood. For 7 years I have remembered you that way. Wished that I could have chased all of them out of the house, just told them to go, get out, and pulled you down on the rug, held you close and talked to you. I know you now better and I know that I was right then. If I had been able to make you sit quiet, once they were gone, and talked to you, got through your defenses, you would have talked to me in return. For what you are now was in you then. I wasn't good enough—didn't know enough, was too selfish, but who knows? You could have drawn out of me the things that were there, waiting.

You slept on Thursday. You jumped once or twice. I put my hand in yours. You clutched it tight and held on to it and slept. Harry went away. I didn't lust after you. I wanted to lie down, put my arm under you, and let you sleep on my shoulder, sleep until dark. Reich is wrong when he condemns outright the male instinct to pierce and thrust hard at a woman. People play all sorts of games with each other and we all carry heritages of previous ages and manners, particularly in the dark jungle that sex is. But his analysis of what that signifies is so correct that I wonder at his penetration. I want to talk to you for hours, to hold you in my arm, to quiet your nervous twitches, to make all those little fluttering nerves in your stomach keep still, to see your face without lipstick and your hair dishevelled, all the strain that life stamps upon a sensitive person gone, to have periods of silence and say and hear you say inconsequential things, and somewhere in the midst of all this and as a part of it make love to you, with no reservations, no fears, no worries about the future. Time past is time present and time future. All that we have been through would combine to make that present what it would be and if we had got rid of barriers, and it takes time, even in love-making one has to learn, then every present would contain the future. All terrible hampering doubts about the future are but expressions of inadequacies, lacks, fears of the present, the result of unresolved conflicts of the past.

Tell me, does all this mean anything to you? Not what it tells of me only, but does it stir you, make you look into your own self. For you can only receive what is in you, either there already, or existing in elements which can be combined into an entity by the stimulated imagination.

Sir Thomas More the strict, moral, old precursor of socialism, said that in his Utopia a man's wife should be beautiful so that he could have delight in her. I stop again. The words I want to write you know (a notice by the track. Guess the ad. Just guess. Bloomer Girl! Exactly. How inapprow-pree-8! Now a play called Girls without Bloomers. See this evasion of an issue. How I grabbed at it; and could have used my literary facility to do all sorts of things. I wouldn't. You would be for me a dream of delight. I have made love to you a thousand times. Once only in a dream. And then it was this way. I just said. Enough of this nonsense and held you and kissed you and you capitulated. See that word. All the history of society and women's place in it is there. And in reality she does not capitulate. That is a pretence—the fictitious place she held in social practice contrary to reality. But that is how I thought about it. And it was terrible. But no more of that. And you see to it that the capitulation idea is out and keeps out.

Your voluptuous self would be an endless source of delight to me. You know you are a wonderfully endowed individual. All you need is an internal security to coordinate yourself. What you would be in bed I don't know. But I tell you what I would do. I would marry you first in a country where there was no divorce and find out about you afterwards, about you and me. It would be a hell of a long chance to take but I would take it cheerfully. I have never been jealous of you—never. Only I have looked and wondered, never at any of your men but at you. What could Constance find to please her in those men? What could they bring out of her? After real love-making, for an orgasm as Reich so well knows is the climax and center of a far-reaching relationship, after real love-making every tension, every mental tangle, all difficulties should be gone—life begins completely again. Two pages ago I reached N.Y. I have to go. The 1 from Philly simply flew. So, sweetheart, take it easy, by quick leaps you will get control of yourself fully. Learn to deal with one man and you will be on the way to easy handling of all. I am on my way. Last night I was absolutely untwisted inside, took it easy, was not fatigued after but was powerful without straining myself at all. I propose to clear away all my jungles. My hands may shake but I am not going to shake inside not with anybody and least of all with you. And if you whimper I'll write: I love you and I am lonesome for you fifty times and tell you until you get accustomed. It isn't you. It is a hangover, planted there by society and some third-rate men. For that you need the knife. Once that is away we'll look each other in the eye you and me and not only see each other but see ourselves. Afraid? I am not. I am burning up. Lose friendship? You silly person. The other way is the way to lose it. Don't you see? I love you and send you a thousand kisses from the very tip of your head to your pink toe-nails.

[unsigned]

[April 1946]

I could not get the violets to you—I wanted very much to. But I have been held back by a series of meetings, one after the other (everything going nicely) and my stomach tearing away at me. You saw I couldn't eat yesterday; it continued all to-day—savage pain, bitter taste in mouth, and a nervous tension. Something to carry around I can tell you. But I am accustomed to it, accepted it—until recently. I am now mad at it—one thing, however, I never never lose my temper on account of it, though I sometimes curl up in bed and am very quiet. But I *always* reply when spoken to. A model patient. But a patient nevertheless. Some friends of mine are discussing something. I am supposed to be listening. I am, but I am so tired and have such a bout of work waiting for me when I get home, that I have to write to you now. By this means I catch the mail and, I hope, present myself for breakfast.

(Mr. Speaker drones along. Awful; simply awful; it is very painful to listen to. One has to have faith to think charitably of some of these gentlemen.) Let me shut him out by thinking of your face as I saw it yesterday—watched it for hours after dinner—in repose, in animation and with the wonderful smile, the new one, new for me, I have never seen it before. It is something to carry in your mind as a man carries around a photo in his wallet—he knows that it is there and can take it out whenever he wishes. (Mr. Speaker goes on. I cannot tell you what he is saying. But imagine—by damn, I shall not even ask you to imagine what he is doing. Why should this barbarian intrude into a communication between you and me. "You" he says "confuse two things. . . .")

So back to you. I have so many things to tell you—I don't know where to begin. Here is one.

I am thinking of going away with you. Every spare minute. I think of it as a week spent in the country somewhere, just at this time. I ask only one thing of the great gods—that I am well, not feeling as I do now. If that is OK I look forward to a wonderful week. Doing what? First from my point of view, exclusively. Being near to you, for hours and hours every day (not *too* near) but being able to see you whenever I wanted. On an evening when we say good-night, I know I will see you in the morning. Isn't that wonderful?

No. 2. I see you in the morning, then at lunch, lazy in the afternoon perhaps, radiant at dinner, quiet and contemplative as the evening goes on, talking quietly, animatedly about politics, writing, people, then you and me, a constant kaleidoscope, always your lovely face, with its successions of smiles, your exciting figure moving actively around—or stretched out luxuriously somewhere—but you, always you. How I'll get to know you—what memories I'll take away. For oft when on my couch I lie . . . in the din of cities (and meetings such as this) in lonely rooms . . . I shall have another gallery of pictures of you to flash upon my inward eye.

Does this seem extravagant to you? I mean every syllable of it—every single syllable. It seems to me so true, so literally true, that I cannot believe that you don't see it as I do. I stop and look up at the ceiling—nobody knows why. I can see you in ten ways in less than as many seconds or even less than that. The more I see of you the more I see what a treasure of possibilities of beauty and grace, charm and vivacity, intimacy and insight which you hold for me. You agree don't you?

I have confidence in myself to this extent—that I feel myself able not only to respond to but to stimulate not only the present facets of your personality but to develop them, constantly to make you extend yourself further, probing and leaping forward, feeling your powers, intellectually yes, but not only intellectually, as a person; that is the thing I do to you. You are a flower that blooms best in the sun. I am your sun because I take such perpetual delight in seeing you expand and develop.

I don't do it to please you. I do it to please myself. It pleases you of course and I am happy at that. Can I give you that feeling of constant development and enjoyment of all your ideas and all your senses? That depends on so many things. And that is the sphere where I have the advantage over you. What do I want from you that you cannot give me? As far as I can see, you are able to give them all to me.

There are difficulties and even dangers—I know that well enough. But given an even chance I think those difficulties can be overcome. What are they? I'll tell you soon. But as I say, you to-day, now, give me the promise of everything I have ever dreamed of. Everything.

I know I cannot do that for you. All I can hope for is that I can offer you so much of what you feel you need that my deficiencies will seem to you worth bearing with. And yet that is not all. I feel that although one adds and subtracts and weighs, yet there is in a mature person, an instinctive recognition that his or her fate is entangled here. It is based on experience, experience of past relations, of needs which were stimulated and not satisfied, of personality fighting for a medium in which to express itself—and if this is felt strongly enough then advantages and deficiencies seem not worthwhile weighed in the balance—in fact deficiencies then sometimes become a stimulus for greater feeling, greater desire to help overcome—developing and unleashing great wells of love and tenderness and a desire to help. Thus if the fundamental impulse is strong enough the very fact that so much is missing in one person can give the other a greater consciousness of strength, of power to achieve, of real expansion of personality and participation in living. You get it I am sure. It is true of me in relation to you also. The weaknesses you may develop (and I say may, because fundamentally I am convinced of your strength) I am all mobilised to help you overcome them and feel fit and ready for a battle I can win. If only I could feel that you see me as I see you, what a life it would be.

The discussion is now over. I am in the subway. Quite a change. All the time I was writing I was following the talk. Pretty poor stuff but the best we have. Something has just struck me. In my life and the life of such as me we have advantages, the *chance* for the finest, keenest thinking in the world; but we have to put up with much that is third-rate, shoddy, much that is cheap and grimy. And you? You will irradiate it with sunshine. I stop. Why do I say such things? I simply cannot help it. I should moderate it—should not be so extravagant. But I just can't see immoderation or extravagance here. It is the simple plain truth.

See it as I see it. My apartment is not wonderful (it can be fixed and I'll fix it). But at best it will be a place that the $50.00 a week clerk will despise. I go to see Lassiter and the kids. Our people in comparison with what they have to do are few and pitifully inadequate. Poverty and frustration can bring out ugly streaks. Except for those who really glory and revel in ideas, the life can be hard. And then I see you—as last night or reading to me. Not in silk or satin, perhaps a red dressing gown that cost $25.00. But just you. And I say you irradiate the whole gloom that may be there. Is it extravagant? Tell me.

And remember: hamburger or lamb-chop for lunch.

All my love, and I wish you knew how much that is,

N

Postmark April 7, 1946

How to do it? I don't know. I just have to trust my instinct, that's all, I'll be as honest as I can, and truthful as I can. I'll make blunders. You will be kind. I shall also make some wonderful discoveries. People may have discovered them before. I will discover them for us—and they will be wonderful.

This p.m. you were just at your very best—the woman I want. A little greyness under the eyes—I want it away but I don't mind it too much. But otherwise superb, and very calm, talking easily about difficult things, and able to watch me at awkward moments—and all the time so lovely and sometimes so sweet, that the moment itself was a treasure. I ask myself: Why can't that be enough? Isn't it splendid enough? There is music, there is art, there is nature, and here is a wonderful person, in a specially warm, intimate understanding related with you. Why press for more?

Because I must. You went and after you left I went upstairs and fell asleep. Everytime you leave me I feel that you are going into an alien world trying to take you away or keep you. Sometimes more strongly than other times, sometimes very little. It is stupid, irrational and I trust you absolutely. But I too have hangovers. However the Logic was with you. Guardian and representative of the new society and of me.

I held you as you left and you fought instinctively. You felt I wanted to kiss you perhaps passionately. I know now. I am not disturbed or repulsed by it. I understand. But all the more reason to talk about it. Think not of you but of me. Unless you had indicated some feeling for me, had come close to me, for me to try to force kisses of any passion upon you then in the passage would have been—the only word I can think of is disloyal besides being insensitive. Your recognition of my intentions towards you will cure you of these reflexes. Another time we'll talk about men and American men in particular and their relationship to girls. But you must have absolute confidence in me that I will do the right thing, that under certain circumstances if there were too few beds and you had to choose one you'd come unhesitatingly into mine to sleep.

You remember when you were leaving last Thursday. We had kissed earlier. I held you for a moment as I put your coat on. (When you come and when you leave and to be close to you, for you to be on the crook of my arm, may mean little to you. It is a world to me.) I kissed your cheek. You turned your face towards me and I kissed you. Otherwise I wouldn't have. Why? Because I know your dread of committing yourself. And if you spent an afternoon necking with me, next time I don't presume to start again where we left off. I have always felt that way with you and now that I know your story and see how it is with you, I feel it more than ever. It is not a concession I make to you. It is how I want it to be. I hold you to no promises, anticipations, implied agreements, and the whole cursed legacy of bourgeois sex relations. I hold you close for a moment, just to feel you near to me. If I were in love with Freddie, I would do it to her, tho' she is L's wife. And whatever her response there would be no misinterpretation on either side. We have to learn to be at ease with each other. We have gone a long way. It can be achieved.

You will be aware of what I want. It will embarass you? I doubt it. It could no more spoil our friendship then my wanting you. But it will help you or rather help me if you remember this. What I want from you can not be stolen, or given and taken back, or misunderstood, or mistaken. I know enough of you to know that where your personality can find its fullest, most complete expression in passion, then I wouldn't have to be looking for it with a candle. You have never expressed it yet. How could you? Where? With whom? I know that if you did with me you would know yourself for the first time, as you are discovering yourself day by day. You think I would mistake a kiss after a pleasant evening for that? Tell me. Write and tell me that you understand now. Other men may kiss you, a lovely creature, intelligent, vivacious, etc. You respond to one degree or another. I do not kiss the same woman. For me you are the most enchanting creature I have ever known, who has stirred me as not five other women put together have done; who has made me admire her and her sex for her courage and tenacity, who dazzles me constantly with the insights and the sparkle of her intelligence, who is altogether gifted with special gifts that our cause as a whole needs badly to-day, and in whom I see such a concentration of gifts, qualities, partly social, partly personal, as to make me glad to have known her, shiver at the thought that I nearly drove her away through selfishness and blindness, and enjoy every moment with her or thinking of her, whatever it may cost.

That is what I hold and place my face next to, what I want to feel lying quietly near to me, talking. I couldn't grab on to you and kiss you and kiss you and *suspect* that you would think you were being imposed upon or that I was rubbing my hands saying "Ah that means if we go on like this soon we'll be in bed."

You give me plenty now. Whatever you give to me I shall be grateful for. Little to you, it opens perspectives, ideas, memories in me, I being what I am. But you mean too much to me for me ever to mistake any affection or momentary embrace or gesture for you, or for a promise of you. You couldn't promise yourself to me for some future time.

So far. By degrees. We'll work out something. And if even from deep incompatibility our friendship does crash, these things must be taken philosophically. I for one will never have any regrets. That is why in that respect I have no fears tho' I have others.

I have to see you more often. I want to see you. There are things too you will see. I shall express myself many times in traditional phrases and shall express traditional attitudes sometimes. But I shall get to it in time, unadorned. I have got to things in the past. I love you.

[unsigned]

R. J.
4F
1306 Chisholm
Bronx

Postmark April 13, 1946

But like a bird (a large one I admit—let's say I am a Viking bird) who hops at the treed circle far from your hand, who pecks at twigs and grass keeping one eye always upon you even when catching an ant, sees the grain, the yellow in your palm, but stays far away, soon comes on hopping forward and back, steps seeming to retreat more than advance, head still watching, faintly turned to one side as if to catch your movement before it has left your mind and so fly away to defeat you. Coming closer, shy, frightened, darts up fast to take one grain and rushes not back a foot but across the entire circle back to the edge once again to eat and watch. Better than the ants, again the approach and the eating—But a breath, a tremor on your part and the bird goes—to the circle, no—to the air because it knew all the time that man was going to pounce. Knew all the time he was a lover of birds' tongues minced. So, the man holding the grain, wanting only its trust, wanting just to see it close must resist the impulse to smooth out a feather, must subdue the curiosity about whether birds like to be scratched or patted like dogs, must just be there with the grain many months to combat the bird fears, the jungle, the other birds, the bird friends who lie with ants eating out eyes with feathers clumped in stiff mounds.

Sweetheart, this is it. Read it critically. The sure firm grasp, the clean unburdened writing, the imaginative power, for you never saw all of this anywhere, and something that you do superbly and is the mark of the poet—the image complete in itself, concrete, and yet in every line expressing the emotion. The integral humor "birds' tongues minced" and then the conclusion that embraces the whole—friends with *ants* eating out eyes and dead—not dead but with the feathers stiff.

This thrills me and clears up a great problem as everything truly beautiful does. As we work this out we are not leaving the writing to settle the personal to go back to the writing. No. In settling this, in probing it, in working it out, you are clearing up the obstacles in the way of the writing. Poetry is emotion recollected in tranquility. What deeper emotions have you ever had than these? What more serious problem have you ever grappled with? I have but one road to your heart—that road by which you will find your deepest and truest self, the self you have to find to express. Otherwise I am nothing—for you. And you, being you, to find yourself means to get rid of everything which stands in the way of your finding everything in you which reflects and corresponds to the socialist way of life and shedding or keeping in control everything that pertains to bourgeois ideas. Your personal struggle, your social struggle is for you the realisation of yourself, in organising your weapons to take your place in the ranks.

Try it this way. Your youth, your beauty, your desire for a happy home life and children, security for them, seeing them grow, all that instinctive life and normal society would give you as of right, that you could get so easily, the relations with your brother, your mother everything, they stand in jeopardy. One step towards me, just as an experiment and maybe it will be irrevocable. Isn't that it? For life with me will be a battle. I know all my disadvantages, social and personal. Social and personal combined, they frighten even me. But they are or will be as nothing if you find in me with all my weaknesses the personification of what you have been seeking and will seek all your life. You are afraid of the mere idea of an association with me. I tell you that I love you and it hits you like a blow. Why? That is the question. Why? Because it touches your rawest tenderest spot. Uncover it, look at it, see what you see there. Even your new-found freedom, before you have enjoyed it, you may lose that too. Darling, I have had 15 years of freedom, in fact 25 and it isn't worth a damn. For that kind of freedom means absence of responsibility. And that is no way to live. It isn't. I know. You dry up inside. Better to try and fail and hope for better luck next time than be that way free. You didn't have to fight your way *to* the others. You had to fight your way from them. This is different. Your deepest feelings are involved because there is nothing that isn't involved. You are sensitive and discriminating and

I love you for it. But, after all, unless something very vital was at stake, involving not only your past with men, but your *whole* past, the idea of "smooching" with me would not be so terrible, so important an event for you. On V.J. Day we were all in the street, L, F, you and I, and we were about to hold hands. You shivered and only felt you could make it when you held on to Lyman with the other hand. I felt not the slightest anger with you—only worry and love for you that you should be so deeply sensitive—wanted to help you. And afterwards we stood on the little platform above the staircase and I held you by the shoulders and you were calm and thoughtful and sweet. It was a very sharp contrast. I wondered why and knew the wounds inside—for a person with your principles. Now you are looking at them. Look fearlessly. I am not afraid of what you may find. I trust you. Let us see if what I think is there is there. Remember too what I told you about Jack long ago. Things work by contraries, especially fundamental things. It seemed at the time that Jack rejected you. I knew that you were rejecting Jack. His cruelty, his refusal to protect you, were his retreat, his armor, his defense against you, his refusal to accept you as you were. And all the mistakes you made, the hesitations, the incapacity to express yourself, all were nothing compared to your fundamental stubbornness, your refusal to capitulate to him. This is more serious than your affair with Jack—infinitely more so. And the same contradictory process is at work. As for me I have doubts and difficulties, too about you. You don't suspect that do you? But I have them. They are as great as yours, except that I have twenty years of half-a-life behind me and I know. I am not merely in love with a splendid woman. That is of great importance in any man's life. It is that I have been living in a house with one wall closed. Enough of it is cracked for me to see through. And I don't only see what I never saw before but when I look through the other walls, the views that I thought I knew I realise that I can only see those as they should be seen if all the walls are open. For me this is not only a battle for you. It is a battle for me. The dangers for me, my dearest Constance, are as great as the dangers for you, equally as great. I'll tell you. That's one thing in loving you. I have no fear of telling you everything. That is one priceless gift you have given me. And I think that your real battle in regard to me is a battle for yourself. It may seem to revolve around: how miserable it is that I have slept with others and cannot sleep with him. There are aspects to that too. A girl I knew who had never met a Negro before and was attracted to me at sight, for some days afterwards sat with me in the dark and begged me to be patient with her, as she had to get accustomed to me. But for you all these are in my view only manifestations of something far more serious, something that has reached the most secret places of your consciousness. Darling, darling, these last few days I am loving you so much that————.

I can't even write it, I can't say it. It tires me, the constant glow and warmth inside of me. I can't express it any way that I know. I hope I am strong enough to handle it, make it serve me. I can't explain now but I will later as feeling clarifies into ideas. How can I do anything else but love you for what you have done to me. There are a million things. Never, never in my life have I taken care of myself. And now I want to, bitterly regret never having done so, wonder if it is too late, but feel that with your love, not with your help, I could. Perhaps it is an illusion. Perhaps. Perhaps I am too far gone with selfish, self-centered living. But I am willing to begin again, and like a baby, learn from the beginning—so many many things. But I regret nothing. For the things that I have are the things you need if only you could see it. And if I have them, even the absences and gaps which you will fill, they are because I have been what I have been.

[unsigned]

R. J.
4F
1306 Chisholm
Bronx

Sunday April 21 [1946]

To the loveliest girl in the World
No Stamp. No address needed. . . .

Darling, I am longing to see you, altho' I know I shall do so in three hours and a half at most. It is now 2. I shall write for a little less than an hour, then fly to eat, dress, shave, meet you, spend two hours and then———.

Sweetheart I am fine. I have pains, but I am fine. A tremendous and I mean tremendous calm has settled over me. I am carrying on an internal reorganisation, something automatic. I'll cure these pains in time. For the rest I only know what has begun to happen to me. It will take its course. Meanwhile I think only of you.

I say that perhaps I interpret you in the light of my ideas, my longings. I do that. But I interpret something, someone, who fills and develops those ideas in a manner that leaves me quite stunned for long moments.

See. Thursday afternoon you were Constance Webb, 18 years old, shy, entertaining her *first* boy-friend. Constance the writer, Constance with an understanding far beyond 18, but still the ingenue, with a touch of Frosty too. You weren't playing a part. You were shy. Though you had jumped a year ahead of our conversation on the 'phone. As soon as I left, however, you wrote me that wonderfully intimate letter of your dreams.

Next afternoon I meet another person. You welcome me, with a little effort as *the* boy-friend. Constance, 18, is dead or left behind, outgrown. You don't only accept me yourself, you as naturally and easily as if we had been going together for 2 years, let everyone see. There is not the slightest trace of constraint. But you are not proprietary. I see you helping Gene, being nice to Conrad (and observing him closely), filled with responsibility—a valuable guest. Later you become a propagandist, following the discussion closely, your instincts as right as rain and your illustration of the engine clarifying the position. You are a real fanatic, ready to defend the position and push it against its enemies to the last drop. Your criticism of Freddie is motivated by the same desire that nothing should stand in the way of the cause. I feel how much you are one of us. You belong. Particularly our enemies would know that.

Going home I see another aspect of you. With eagerness and great confidence you analyse swiftly and precisely and with sureness in selection of the detail Freddie's responses to you and you to her—the dangers involved for me, and for you as part of me—what you will have to do. Sweetheart, I look at you and wonder. Where the others labor around the point discussing and analysing and tossing it back and forward, there the speed of your reactions and a certain cold-bloodedness in the decision, shows that with all her experience of people, and her real intuition, Freddie has no chance with you. You will be in complete control of the situation and she will recognise it.

Saturday morning you come up bright and early. Punctual too. There is a situation, small but not negligible, with Grace. We whisper and I see you as feminine as the feminine, confident as hell over manifestations. This, you say, means this, and that means that. You handle the breakfast situation, competent, deft, and at ease. You are a housewife. Capable and piquant, because our little public does not associate you with any such thing. And lovely, even in slacks, you don't look like a housewife. Friday night and Saturday morning so far you are Constance Webb, married. The ingenue has never existed.

Then I come upstairs to the roof. Darling, darling, do you know what? You reek of sexual abandon and voluptuousness. Has the cricket become an elephant? But you do, darling, or rather you did. And no Frosty Webb or young bride either. But a woman, a mature woman in her prime, knowing what love is and what it means to her, the world excluded, the incipient Cleopatra of the red dressing gown eight years ago now full grown. The impact was terrific. It wasn't love, I am wrong. It wasn't passion. I am speaking of the effect. It certainly was not passion. It was just sex as Clark Gable is masculine and Marlene Dietrich is "woman" so you were. Do you blush? Why? I don't mean that you were lying there full of desire? Far be it from me to presume, dear Madam. . . . No, that's not it at all. You were just the embodiment of something, that's all. You just were. I could not love thee, sex, so much, loved I not so much more. Imagine how I register one after another of these pictures.

We come down to eat. *Sweetheart, you change completely.* You are now Portia, an adoring wife, silent for the most part, listening, looking at me, letting me deal with the others, watching them for us both, watching my miserable attempts to eat. I didn't know you were suffering inside, sweet, otherwise I would have broken it up. The others were a little embarassed by our intimacy, you were statuesque.

Then the last few minutes before you left. You sat on the bed, near to me, thinking. Then I realise, saw once again, what an extraordinary individual you are. You said nothing special, but I got a long and continuous impression—it remains—of deep power, purity of spirit, in Sophocles old phrase, seeing life steadily and seeing it whole, an illimitable confidence, not personal and yet personalised in you, as if nothing could ever shake you from that calm, not so much determination, not at all resignation. But of the twentieth century, 1946. I think of the anti-Tsarist Bolsheviks and of a statue by Rodin. When I see it I shall show you. It had something of the old Greek statues too, but it was 20th century, it was feminine in its recognition of injustice but not the faintest trace of bitterness. I don't do it justice. But it will come to you again and I shall see it. It was no passing mood. It was you, Monica, but a long, long stage beyond. I don't know that mood yet.

This is between Thursday and Saturday; and all the time I see you loving me with a talent for the expression of love, admiration, affection, and confidence which by itself would distinguish a woman.

So, darling, there it is. For the time being it is mine and mine alone. I am grateful for it and I treasure it. In time it will belong to others—this personality of yours transformed into literature. Two things you need now.

1) Hamburger for lunch
2) Rest and quiet.

Both are to keep that wonderful mechanism in perfect order. My love you have, always, and have had from the first moment I saw you though it has grown as I know you better. How much it has grown between Thursday and to-day! Sleep well.
[unsigned]

April 24 [1946]

Dearest Heart; It is long long after midnight. As usual when I am in bed all day sleep is difficult. I have read a little. I think of you and I feel like writing to you. On what. I don't know. But to think of you is to unloose my most secret, my most spontaneous, my most generously flowing thoughts. Let it be that way. What am I thinking? First how perfectly lovely you were to-day. Perfectly is the word. Clothes do make a difference. I still love best my tousle-haired Constance, but to-day your dress and the whole ensemble, including your hair style, your energy, or rather your vigor and grace———me (——— means no word. I could say overwhelmed. It would be wrong. No word to express *exactly*. Let it go.) I saw what a lovely, sophisticated, beautiful woman you are. The dress was wonderful. The length in particular seemed to give your legs just the right curve, and you yourself—with that lovely hair-do, simple but shapely, struck the right, the perfect note. There was not the faintest trace of self-consciousness about you. The others were aware of your physical splendor—Grace in particular. No one could deny it; no one could miss that you were beautifully dressed, with taste and care; yet, and this pleased me so much, no one could hint the word—bourgeois. Your profession has given you a great training. Yet you retain a natural simplicity. I shall not forget you as you were today for a long time. Frosty Webb!—my precious, a thousand Frosty Webbs and a 1000 dollars could not make you what you looked to-day if there was not all the character and intelligence of Constance behind it.

When they left I held you in my arms and you kissed me—a long long long way from yesterday. But to-day you had moved forward again—two dimensions—I saw and felt that I held the woman two years of N York had made you, for to carry your clothes that way is a little triumph; and in your kisses I felt the new Constance, our Constance, the old jungle almost cleared away, and your true, honest, passionate self, with your usual directness and vigor, striding towards self-realisation. In 24 hours you bestride 24 months. My lovely darling, *who*, who, could kiss you as I can, or with whom could you exchange the kisses that we exchange? Who as he holds you can feel for you what I feel; to-day you were a new person—I couldn't see you walk around on Sunday and I was too busy with another aspect of your personality and our love to see what I saw to-day. And conscious as I was of all the other yous, I kissed you as no one else could, felt you, in my arms and in my heart and for the moment possessed you completely. Yes, possessed you, felt all you were, and met gladly how far you had reached and felt that you had reached so far to me and because of me, and if even you were being freed of the old and as I hope, are henceforth free of it not only for me but for always, yet your progress so far has been mine. I held and felt against my heart with her lips on mine someone who belonged to me and me only.

Now I am tired. I must go to bed, or rather, try to sleep. Tired. That is my weakness. *Inside* I am tired no longer. That has miraculously disappeared. Gone for good. That dragon you killed. But physically I am not so strong as I should be. The years of illness, and of frustration have left me shaken. I have learnt—the things I have learnt you know. I have learnt to love you, to recognise you, to take care of you. But I have paid. I looked at your superb physical vigor and style to-day, and wished that there too I could match you. But you fall asleep so easily in my arms, the love with which you are enveloping me already is so tender and so warm, that here too I know that you are the one woman in the world for me. I love you, darling. And I would love you as much if you were only half of what you are. I hope you have had a fine day, that the sinus is not troubling you and that you look as lovely as you did to-day.

I want you to buy me that robe we talked about, and I want you to buy some things for your trip next week with the balance, things to bring with you, buy for yourself. I mean anything you want. But, please, darling, show me what these special things are when you come. It would give me great pleasure to know what you chose. But to-day I forgot to ask you, how things were with you, if you had all you needed. People were around all the time and I hadn't the chance. If you are the least little bit not absolutely OK, then forget the trinkets and be sure to have a large hamburger for lunch. And the eggs! Anyway, take care of yourself.

[unsigned]

[May or June 1946]

Dearest,

The love and confidence and power of your letter overwhelms me. What, sweetheart, did you think my answer could be. Come. Come to-night. Pack up and leave that place. The difficulties are enormous. But we'll fix those up en route. That such a person as you should feel towards me as you do makes me see my personal past in a light different to how I have seen it in the past and tells me that my future is safe. People are here, I only scribble this in intervals. But my life is in your hands, yours in mine and both of us together with our people against *them*. *They* are all I am scared of, not their hate, their disdain, their persecution, but the legal power they have over me and may exercise over you. But we'll match our arts and our love against them and wait for our day.

All, all my love,
N

[1946]

Dearest, how did the battle go to-day? The never-ending constant struggle against the enemy, which hits straight blows but also never ceases to infiltrate. I'll be calling you in two hours or so. Meanwhile here is confidence and solidarity even if you sustain a minor defeat, for all defeats now can only be minor.

Let me tell you, for you deserve to know. I have never, never, felt better in my life on a platform than last night. Physically I was below par, much below, but my control over myself and therefore over the audience was never quite so good. I didn't let them have all of it. Only as I went on I discovered how much of my old form (in Britain) I had rediscovered; how much I have learnt during the past years here; and how coordinated I am inside—nothing fundamental worrying me, neither political nor personal. It has been working in me for the past few weeks. I was fully aware of it only last night. Later I shall begin to organise my writing to suit. That will perhaps be harder. But it will be done. I used to tell you how I was certain that I was on the eve of vast discoveries about myself. Here they are, the first, and they are big enough. L. T. was always reading Freud. It is a pity we do not know what his ideas were. I suppose he dared not write them down. I can to you. There is one thing now I have to be ready for—not so much be ready for as to work up to it. To be well-integrated into an organisation, resting upon and interlaced with the proletariat. Then when it moves and shakes the world, if I have kept close to it we'll do something. We shall write, and we shall speak and perform miracles of organisation. Man is a complex animal, but above all social.

Darling, you have not only done these things to me, you have taught me so much, the actual experience with you. It has within a few short days immensely widened and enriched my knowledge of myself, of women, of American society, of relations between men and women, yesterday, to-day and tomorrow. And at the centre of it all is your splendid self.

There is such an integration as amazes me. I see you dressing—from the tub to the last dab of lipstick. It is enough to go on with. If you were completely dumb, if you were only a week-end episode, it would be lovely and wonderful, something memorable, never to be forgotten. And in addition to all this—you.

I looked at you yesterday—it is always so interesting to look at you. I noted your concentrated attention—theatre or whatever the cause or origin, it is an extraordinary faculty. I noticed it even when others were speaking. You sit still, practically not a muscle moving. I saw a hint of it that day when you came from the roof and had lunch and watched me. When you are disturbed inside the strain must be terrific. But when you are OK inside then your grasp of what is taking place must be equally strong. The difference between you and certain people I know, is in that respect, enormous.

And, after, your concentration of attention on me (without being impolite to others) was not only personally delightful but as I cannot help doing with you, a phenomenon to observe. You must tell me all about it darling. I want to know. How and when you developed these characteristics, became aware of them; do you know other people who behave in the same way. I don't. From start to finish yesterday you displayed a *formidable* poise and ease, in fact that of a person many years older than yourself and yet obviously and without strain devoted to me. It was quite a performance—something to see.

About you and me, just we two, I cannot write now and may not be able to for a long time, for some time at any rate. I am thinking of us, thinking of you in your new role as my wife, with all that this implies. The results are already apparent in me—the first fruits of them that slept as the Scriptures say. But I know already that starting handicapped as we did inside a week we are infinitely beyond where I expected we would be—and before long shall reach places where it would ordinarily take months and perhaps years to reach. My nervousness about myself and you is almost entirely gone. Somehow everything, everything, works out. The very inadequacy of your previous experience makes insignificant the difficulties I anticipated with you. Your intimate life really begins with me. I am sorry for the pain and brutalisation you have suffered in the past, but it makes all your realisation of yourself associated with me. No man will complain of that and not me, least of all with you. I must go now. I have a horrible week. As you saw, stealing a week was welcomed by everyone who merely put off everything until next week, i.e., this week. But I'll deal with them—kindly but firmly. I am looking forward to calling you in an hour and seeing you (to-day) when you get this. All my love.

To be truthful I am tired and, what did you have for lunch yesterday and what will you have to-day?

P.S. Went to bed—and got up to call you and some others. But I was so awfully tired that Ceil said "No, I had better stay in bed and she would call anyone I wanted to." I thought it over and then decided that it would be a mistake to force the point, both with you and with her. I have work to do by 6:15 and then have a long meeting (journey down and back).

Let me reassure you, darling. If I could get a period of real quiet with you, I'll be able to make it. But at 10 this morning M [Martin Glaberman] was here pretending that he had mistaken the day and the stream began. I took it peaceably before. Now I am not so much resenting it as actively organising mentally against it.

I wanted to find out exactly how things had gone to-day—whom you saw, etc—and how you felt. But it will wait until to-morrow. Love to you, my sweet.

[1946]

What is in your letter, darling? I don't know but I am hoping. . . . I am in your room—ours. Bill is here—next door. It is about 11 or 10 or something. I have been sleeping but thinking of you all the time for I barely dozed off.

First about a letter to you. See here darling (I am seeing you all day as you welcomed me on Saturday evening—gorgeous, magnificent, in that white dress, something to dazzle any man. That is how I am remembering you these last days). But as I was saying, I haven't written you *a letter*. I can't. It is going to be a long time, weeks and weeks before I can. I know something now which I haven't known since 1943 when I began to write to you. Those letters were written by someone else, the man I was—letters pent up in me for God knows how many years, not the facts, but the feeling—aroused and stimulated by a succession of women. I saw you and recognised you, but hesitated at first, made a gesture, made many but only let myself go when you wrote in 1943. Darling, please, stop to think a bit. Where did that superhuman energy come from? I look back and wonder, as I think of the never-ending stream and never, never, never once did I ever have to push myself to write. In fact all the time I was restraining myself. And now, with you in my arms, the goal of over twenty years achieved, over 20 darling, in fact more, for I have needed and wanted you since I was fifteen, dreamt of you, created you as I lived and understood more (all this you will know in time). But now that you are mine, a new period has begun for me. It came over me as soon as I recognised weeks ago that you loved me. The tension of years, of years and years, subsided suddenly. It has left me a wreck. Yes, a wreck, like a man just operated upon for a deadly tumour or something. He knows it is gone, he is happy, confident for the future, knowing that "the thing" is gone, that now he will live. But just now and for quite awhile he is an invalid, convalescent, and cannot even do the things he could do before he was operated upon. That is me. You see, darling, not only you were wounded and suppressed. You went through and are now finding yourself. Think of me as going through the same, in my own way. I knew it and expected it and told you often that I was prepared for strange developments—in me as well as in you. The proletariat prepares itself for mastery by struggle, sacrifice, defeats, partial victories, but by violent convulsions that shake it to its depths. With writers and artists it is the same. And with people who really live it is the same. We are in it. We have exceptional gifts, particularly of temperament, you and I. We affect the life around us, have an impact upon it. But it shakes us too.

So darling remember how I love you, how I admire you, and how my arms are always waiting for you. I read your letter to the publisher. It was not a good letter to a publisher but it was a wonderful letter to me. But you must do more than you are doing—for your own sake you must do it. You have not lost your soul sufficiently to save it. You still hesitate a bit. You have done splendidly—miraculously, but I mention it only as a fact, not as a reproach. Although your kindness and growing affection to me equal your love, you have not even yet caught on to the fact that loving you is a tremendous experience for me, new, and has shaken me in a way that makes me need your insight and penetration and enveloping affection and sympathy as much as you need mine. And if your work tears you to bits while you should be grappling with the new experience, imagine what mine is doing to me.

Do you know for the last four weeks or so I have written practically nothing—not only not to you, not to anybody or for anything. And at this time! Just think. I am physically incapable of it. I have had to rest and be quiet for a day, fall asleep for an hour, before I could do as much as this. So, darling, you understand? You will I am sure. And I must tell you too a horrible suspicion I had. Did you *really* have that paying job to-day or did you only say so because you wanted not to have me be bothered about you? I said—I said a lot of things to myself. Perhaps the best thing is to tell you all about it when I see you. And you were going to the Waldorf—with how much money?

Is this a gloomy letter? Not for me. I am happy to write it—to the most wonderful girl in the world—that I know already, I need no proof. I trust you absolutely and think only of how fortunate I am to share everything with you. I hope you went or will send flowers or a telegram or something to your friends if you think the occasion needs it. And I hope you had a good time, darling.

I am giving this to Bill to post. I just lie in bed, worn out, but knowing that my disease is behind me and that health, i.e., full life is ahead. Also somehow, some way, next week, I have to get away for a few days—three or four even. I'll be back on Thursday a.m. I'll call you as soon as I come. I think that we can dispense with my coming with L and F, don't you? Bill will be here this week-end. But I have to see you as soon as possible. Just to see you. You will not fill up all the week-end will you?

All my love,
[unsigned]

[late 1946 or early 1947]

Just a line. No. Any number of lines I choose.

How are you? Not as anybody else asks. But as I ask and you must answer. Well, happier? A stage beyond yesterday? Another dragon being carted out, slain? I want to tell you. I have come to a conclusion (tentative) about you. I think you need love more than any human being I have ever met. I watch your face even. It is sometimes pale and lacking, at moments, I think, when you feel quite alone, even tho' I may be near. Then I speak to you, you get reassured, and in a moment you are lovely beyond dreams. The writing too, the more assured you feel of being loved, the more powerfully you write, the more subtle the more unexpected your flights of imagination and probes of insight. You, yourself, need an enclosure. Nothing to worry about. Why and how we are what we are is not too important so long as we understand ourselves.

It was a lovely day yesterday—as lovely a day as I remember. We can have so many many more. Ours to have as we wish. The greatest, the truest, the most necessary pleasures and satisfactions of life need no elaborate paraphernalia, just two human beings, themselves, not a stitch of civilization on them, but the whole accumulation of civilized knowledge and sensitivity and response inside of them. Such is our life, darling, that is what the preparatory years have done for us—not for A or B or Y or Z, but for us, for you and me. Look at yesterday—just our personal lives. Poetry, music, literature in general, politics, and society, the forever stretching green fields of love in mutual exploration and discovery, these were in the background, but we could spend hours just discovering ourselves, you and me. I knew this, and the reality slight as it is surpasses dreams, as it always does with anything that matters. Naturally I am glad that you are beautiful—you were chosen for that among other reasons—but it wouldn't matter too too much if you weren't. When the spirit in you shines out in your eyes and face, and in time, in the pressure of your arms and your body against mine, I experience and shall continue to feel what no money can buy nor power win. The perspective is infinite. The gates of hell, darling, will not prevail. They cannot prevail against us two, for neither of us will ever be alone henceforth. That power I feel all over me already. I want to be quite quite sure that you feel it too. Never, never alone anymore. Isn't it the answer?

[unsigned]

[1946]

My lovely darling,

Philly bound—on train. I am writing you as before, but a world lies between the last trip and this one, between that letter and this.

Sweetheart, I love you. Last night I did not love you less because of our troubles. I loved you more. I see how sensitive you are, and I draw the conclusion that I must take greater care of you than ever. I see you with tears coming into your eyes when you obviously did not want to cry—and I know how deeply moved and upset you must be. It is obvious that it will be a long time before the old wounds heal and you get rid of the pain you have accumulated. I am not irritated or resigned to it. You are my personal proletariat, so splendid, so wonderful, of such importance to my whole scheme of things that any signal or sign of distress only mobilises me more to love you and work at it with you.

But some of what is troubling you is a heritage of your past. You do not know what a woman, and a woman such as you, can mean to a man. That no one has taught you, or rather shown you. So you disparage yourself. They grabbed on to you and poked at you. They enjoyed your society. They wanted to marry you. You know in words how much you mean to me. You know it intellectually. But you ask—do I want what you have to give? It means that you think of me as merely someone who wants much more of you than the others did. But still a type of wanter. I want your intellectual qualities and your development. I want those. They were not interested and so far I am vastly superior, but (it seems to me that all this is what you think) I still remain someone apart, a man, who weighs his own life-interests against what a woman has to offer. You on the other hand feel that you are on the road to giving yourself so completely that you dread the terrible risk involved—I couldn't possibly be to him what he can so easily be to me. And your whole past and the fears for the future, fears for a repetition on a higher scale tear you to bits, in addition to all the new sensations and the difficulties.

Now understand this much, young lady. You are in so many respects a human being so infinitely superior to me, that I am waiting for the time when you take me over to teach me. Love and affection—not kisses and sleeping—but the daily hourly interchange, the kindnesses, the thoughtfulness, the generosity, the watchful care, the concern, the instinctive loyalty, the readiness to sacrifice not only life and comfort, but one's own idiosyncracies and prejudices and ingrained habits, the overwhelming and enveloping devotion and passion—sweetheart, I am a hack, a practitioner compared to you. I know my past and the influences that have moulded me. I know the drain my illnesses and preoccupations have made on me. I have much to contribute to our relationship. No one has so much to contribute to you. But as between you and me, love, affection, tenderness, warmth, understanding, protection, you are the one not me. You have them; like some deep, inexhaustible spring that is only now bubbling and heaving preparatory to pouring out in an irresistible flood. You are going to be the senior partner. Your youth, your emotional vitality, your poetic imagination and insight, I am the one who should be nervous when I see them and what they will be as soon as you find yourself. You are one of the most dynamic, comprehensive personalities I have ever got near to, and your life is all of a piece, literary, political, emotional, all the power is fused, you turn it on here, all of it, then there, all of it, always your whole self mobilised, and what a self! The moment you said that you loved me and began to write, I realised from your letters that you will have to teach me how to love, how to be generous, draw out my capacity, so starved and limited for continuous affection and tenderness, develop me, as a human being. You haven't got to learn that. It is in you. I know the difference—how clearly it appears in our recent letters is very obvious to me. I am worthy all things considered. But just as the young poet is superior to the wisest critic, so in our personal relationship you are superior to me.

This is the truth. You don't know the things that are in you. I do. I am waiting for you to realise them. A whole new world awaits us, but you are the leader. Luckily I know it, glory in it, am waiting for you to assume your rightful place and responsibility. And you must assume it. For that is your field—the field you above all must explore in order to develop your personality and your special powers to the utmost. Once again I give you the idea. You will work it out, darling, in your ideas and you and I in life. Perhaps when you grasp it it will help you to overcome the shrinking your past has imposed upon you. That is what I think of you. That is what I am waiting for. You will begin to see it soon, and as you realise how much not only in quantity but in quality you mean to me, you will gain in confidence and power. You see your present doubts and difficulties as weakness. For me they are merely the preliminary pangs to the birth of your strength. The real one who will have to learn is me. I send you all my love. I am unlessoned, unschooled, unpractised. I am the Portia. When you understand this it will be a great day for you and for me.

[unsigned]

[July 1946]

Here we are. I have just heard from you. I shall get down something of what I think, tho' writing is still foreign to me. I labor and labor to write—physically labor tho' it is mental too.

I just wander around missing you. I have discovered why I went to the movies so often the last two or three years. Somewhere, somehow I found in them some substitute for you. I would like to see what goes on in a man's mind, really. Being what I am I made use of my visits. I analysed the movies to the last degree possible without actual study. I have worked out reams of theories and ideas. I have learnt vastly about the U.S. and the rest of the world. But the moment you "came along" I didn't want to go again. The moment you leave I am wandering towards them again. But now instead of analysing them I look at myself. What am I seeing here? Not Ann Sheridan. I wouldn't go down to the third floor to see that sister—she is by the way lop-sided, and she is an insensitive somewhat coarse-minded woman. Between a picture in which she appeared and one in which Walter Houston appeared I would choose Walter every time. But there I was on Saturday and again on Sunday.

But, thank Heaven, I miss you but I am not unhappy—not at all. I am not miserable—in fact I am faintly happy. I know I have something, something that matters, that I haven't to take care of lest I lose it, something that is to say that is in me growing without my control. It isn't primarily to kiss you or to make love to you or to talk about books and life. It is just hearing you grumble about the picture, and your violent reaction to the Stalinists, and your wonderful desire to finish the article in Time. At odd moments I have had such relations with people, glimpses of it. Once I told a girl "X, for heaven's sake, don't *bother* me; let me read." She stood amazed. She said "Well, well. I never thought you could say that to anyone. It was so intimate and friendly." She felt that for a moment I was at home with her. She was as acute as they make them and as much of me as she could see she understood. I never let anybody in. I didn't wish to be bothered. Now you are in, and it is the funniest thing. It is concerned with your looking like a kid, your dirndl, low-heeled shoes and no stockings are a part of it and aforesaid grumbling, etc. Strange. You know what I think? Your red slacks are not so homely as the dirndl. They have a "glamorous" appearance. *Rolling* them up at the bottom does not fool me one bit. And shorts mean legs—long legs and shapely that I watch—subconsciously most of the time I am sure. Also that you made the dirndl. God! What sort of early domestic memories of a small West Indian island with its primitive ideas are sleeping in me and that you bring out—if I were a novelist I would pursue this to the end. But you have found it not because you the domestic are it but because you were exactly something else. Because you were that something else and I felt it safe to have you around, you are finding me and I am finding myself. I love you very much darling—very much. And I know something. I am not going to worry about us any more. I just have to love you, that's all and do all I can to make you happy. The rest will come, what and how I don't know. We'll just see, that's all. I am glad you are not going back for awhile to slave for the capitalist system. We'll work out something, but you will stay at home as long as you like. I thought so but I left it to you. I am eager to see you back, sweets, just to have you around. Well not that only but to have you around. I like it.

N

IV.
Separation and Limbo (1947–8)

Airmail Special Delivery
April 16, 1947
[from Detroit, Michigan]
Please hand over to G.

I did not speak to M and J [Marty and Jessie Glaberman] on Sat'y evening. It was too late. Sunday I began at about 2. They listened, then said point-blank "No."
1) We had possibilities of gaining in the W. P.
2) What *new* thing had occurred to justify this new step?
3) It would affect unity.

Johnny Z came in his usual nervous but steady, intelligent self. He said "no" too. We had dinner and they left. After dinner I talked to Jessie for 3 hours. In the end she began to see the points and said I had "a good case." JZ and M returned at about 11 and we settled down again till about 2. By the end I had I think convinced them. I showed above all that we had a splendid case to make. J did not say anything. But M and J showed that they had no more arguments against.

To-day, Monday, Dave, a sympathiser of the J'ites and a member came. Also one of our own people. It lasted from 1 till 5, when we went to the faction meeting 5:30–7:30. Kurt and Rachel Simon, M, and we took Dave with us. I told them of the provocations, the political reason for them, and our decision to wage an all-out struggle.* J did not come, neither did Morgan. But I am to see J to-morrow. Dave was pleased with us, he gave us 2 bucks. We now have a very close friend.

Then upstairs to a Branch Meeting. Ben H had called me up and asked me to speak on unity and I thought it better to go. Full House. I spoke for about 50 minutes, using our resolutions.

Then the riot began. They wanted to know. Was unity off?** The SWP was cold?

---

* [Note by C.L.R. J.] Unity on the American Question and that quote on Cannon—bureaucracy in building the Bolshevik Party.
** See Editor's Introduction, p. 32.

Whom did I think responsible? Cannon's propositions for no discussion. Did I agree? They were a bunch of lawyers. You have to take my word and Marty's. They were exasperated to the last degree—I was "evasive" and "demogogic." Sample.

Do you think our conduct justifies the SWP in feeling that unity must be reconsidered?

Answer: I believe unity is assured. Max said "Don't get panicky. The SWP may or may not be angry at our circular. I don't know. I can tell you, however, who was angry. I was," etc., etc. I gave them an awful run-around—expanded myself on the "theory" of blocs; told them with quote how gladly I would vote to condemn bu'c coll'm [bureaucratic collectivism], retrogression, etc.

They were in one respect like lunatics. On the question of the regime in the SWP I, they said, took it lightly. I asked them what did they propose? Zero. Then they wanted to know if I was in favor of Cannon's proposals for the Congress outlined in his circular. Then they argued bitterly about what was in the circular. A copy was brought and after they read them aloud they found *they* had little to oppose. I asked them if that was what they called taking the organisational question seriously.

The last question: Did I propose to split or did I propose to continue the policy—they were disturbed. And they undoubtedly were.

My reply:

When the WP Plenum decided to accept me, R went to see JPC to tell him that if it was a maneuver we would not collaborate. That is still our position. (Murmurs of relief)

But

(Consternation)

The attitude of the WP PC [Political Committee] to us is such that we have had to tell them that we shall not continue to make protestations of loyalty, etc., or discuss what steps we should take to end an "intolerable" situation (consternation and confusion). That we are discussing and we shall let you know (reassurance but vague doubts).

Ben Hall came and said "I don't understand it." I said "It is very clear" and left him.

They are now in a blue funk. They fear to be rejected by the SWP and to lose us. Marty was very satisfied and so was I because the consideration they show him was absent. They showed their claws and he had to admit it. I was very rude to them also—said I would form a bloc of myself alone with anybody, to denounce and drive out of the movement retrogressionism, bu'c coll'm, etc. They sat and took it. On the way home Wilson said: "Now off the record, I want to tell you Jimmy. Don't do anything wrong, which in the long run you may regret." He was friendly. The others didn't know what they wanted to be.

Marty on the way home has agreed to support the line. I see JZ to-morrow. The faction will subscribe more than $25.00. I shall know to-morrow.

I hope J says O.K. But even if he doesn't D[etroi]t is safe. For wh[ich] Allah be praised. (I have read a scandalous letter by Murray. I shall deal with him in person.) This letter is a warning to us.

Sat'y Evening

Darling,

I read my Philosophy and Phil's* moving dedication. It isn't true, of course, but I appreciated the superficially personal but in reality deep concern for the pro't which prompted him to write it. The book is splendid—and is the best introduction to Hegel and dialectical thought which I know. Now isn't that lucky for you?

I was tired but read, had a lovely dinner, read Life and now am writing.

Sweetheart, I love you more than ever in the old days. I am beginning to understand you and beginning to understand myself. I do not regret one single second of my marriage—not one. You irritate me often and I am now working out which is you and which my peculiar self. Usually it is me. You are lovely and full of love and loyalty and a desire to help. And you have all the ability I thought you had. I look back and add and subtract and see clearly that I am responsible for much. I shall do all I can to make you happier and happier.

I shall not be able to write at too much length. I have to do that document on tour. It has to be *something* and that and close contact and reports with my people, will keep my shaky hand busy. But you are always in my thoughts and you are a part of me as never before. I want you to feel very free to do as you please when I am away. Of course you have your freedom. But to go off to M's and stay for a few days or to go to the R's for a week-end or so. I'd be glad to know that when you finished your outline you went. Or Emma's. I'd be happy to know you were moving around and not stuck at home.

I hope this time to make a model tour, and not arrive back home tired. By taking it easy and exercising strict control over myself, I think I can make it. I'll keep you posted.

Episode. Sister Stewardess, plump and friendly. Sees my books and my preoccupation with them. She came for a talk—told me about herself—Shelley, Keats, Van Gogh, etc. It was easy to talk to her. I was a little shaky in the last 20 minutes but finished strongly.

The trip so far has been wonderful. I have had astonishing success so far, both in the arguments and the finances. I can foresee nothing but success but I keep my fingers crossed.

And now, darling, I have to ask your forgiveness and you must believe me. Tonight is Monday night. This letter I started on Saturday night in the plane. I intended to finish it and send it immediately on landing. Sunday I was at it for 10 hours continuously; to-day without a break from midday to now, midnight. I am writing now so that Martin may post at 5. I ask myself: Why didn't I find a moment to finish the letter and send it? Why do I ask that question? Because I think you are asking it. (I tried to phone last night and again to-night, but failed to get thru'.) Last time I was here I would have made the letter for sure. Such is man? *No.* For to my wide eyed interest I have been thinking of you every single second of the day. It is most peculiar. I thought at first it was guilt, or worry about the letter. But no. It is just you. I see

---

* Phil Romano collaborated with Grace Lee to produce *The American Worker*, a first hand account of life in an automobile plant. It was published by the Johnson Forest Tendency in 1947.

you two ways—in the black dress as you were just as I left you—nothing about the dress. Just how you looked—misty-eyed I thought. And then you up in the morning in Harry's old dressing gown and going to the bathroom—just as you get up. Isn't it funny? All day long I have them both in my head—these pictures of you. Otherwise I have not remembered you at all—I haven't talked to you, I have not thought of your outline*—I always look upon that as giving no trouble—I have worried a little if you were too mad at not hearing from me immediately, I have thought of the spring for the bed and how we must have it soon, I have thought a lot of how valuable for you will be the Introduction to Hegel's History of Philosophy. I have wondered whether to include my reports in your letters or send them directly to G. or R. Nothing very long about anything. I haven't even wondered what you were doing. Only like two pictures put up in the back of my mind—you in the black suit and getting up in the morning and stamping off. Not a second has it been absent. Make what you can of that. Not a second. No. I sometimes get caught up in argument and nothing else matters, but I know that it is there and when I return I know that they have been there—they never moved. That's all, nothing more, nothing less. It has never happened to me before. I haven't another line to say. I love you that's all. And never, never again shall I not talk. Put that out of your mind, precious. That's over. I may be silent or preoccupied. But keep myself to myself? Never. And do you know something else? I have never, not once, talked to you or about you in the old way in the street or by myself. It is completely gone. What a relief. The lacerations I was committing on myself. All my love darling, I shall write again to-morrow. So, precious, take care of yourself—please. Have a good time. Don't worry about anything. I like to think of you as happy.
[unsigned]
R. J.
Apt 7. 158 Orchard St.
New York, N.Y.

Postmark April 16, 1947

On board—to Chicago

Well, sugar-pie, we are about to leave. Two hours to Chicago. (Stewardess said 1 hours; man next to me looked up and said No: 2 hours.) I don't care. So long as I can write to you and you don't ever feel that I am too far. I asked Rae and G. to give you the news. I cannot write everything over and over again—my hand will not allow it, and I write once fully. The stewardess, one (there are 2) has just told me that my pen may leak when I get up in the air, so I may have to use a pencil. I'll be real mad. I love my pen. I lost it last night and found it to-day. I am looking for a present for you. I ain't got one yet. April 18 I get to Frisco at 7:44. Start again for L.A. at 9 and will be thru' by 12. About your mother, I don't know what to do. I wouldn't like to miss the chance if it should arise naturally. You can talk on 'phone if you wish—pardon, that is impossible. Wire, if you wish.

---

* Webb was preparing an outline for an essay on Richard Wright's fiction.

There is a baby in front of me. Either it is suffering from acute something or it doesn't like flying. It yelled like hell till the plane started whoozing. Now it's stopped.

I love you. I fear I shall be sick. I get sickish after 3 hours or so. And to-day of all days I had lousy food. Had dinner with Murray. He had frozen chicken, peas, carrots, etc., all cooked, etc. And his baked potatoes were like the Russian masses in Petrograd 1917. They had a hard core at the centre—Bolshevik. So I expect the worst. To hell with it. Nothing may happen. L.A. to-morrow noon. This is my 3rd. Wonderful, how I was glad to come back in '40. And how I used to dream of coming out to see you. It is the most romantic spot in the world for me. (I am an ass. I just pushed down my chair and don't want it down yet but—Whoop! I dipped; but don't be sorry for me. I am smoking so I ain't dying—yet) a man helped me put it down. So I wrote for 2 minutes, looking silly and feeling so. But now I have straightened it. You should see the people travelling, nearly *all* business men and petty bourgeois, sailors and soldiers, wives and babies—I have not seen one millionaire nor screen-star. Just had a [drawing of a wavy line]. But I am flourishing. I shall recommend [another wavy line] for air-sickness, chicken hash and uncooked baked potato—what a joker I am.

Ho! I was laughing at you. I make rapid jokes and sometimes you can't follow or try to lamely and I said one day "Darling, I am too quick for you." And you said "Yes" resignedly. Cheer up dull student. And how about that outline? Don't show it to anyone before I see it & tell you about it. Phil's book is wonderful—and you will read it. And he will too.

I shall write Bill soon. I know why I said that. I am expecting some money from him.

Well, honey-bunch, I love you very much. I am now so far from flinching that I have been racking my brains if Willie will have the sense to send your letters on to L.A. or make me wait for them. He and his lovey-duck Phil [Filomena Daddario]. How glad we shall all be to see each other. And I shall value William's views on many things, in fact, on everything.

I am beginning to feel tired. I had an awful night (my friend has begun to solve cross-word problem). And a discussion this p.m. at wh[ich] I learnt something but not much. Murray, as you will hear, has proved recalcitrant. O.K. with me. We'll try and try again. But if he continues to tail after the W. P. he will suffer that's all.

So, sweets, I am so in love with you, so quietly, so contentedly you never saw. So kisses and hopes for letters from you soon. I hope *everything* is O.K. darling. Chicago soon.

N

L. Paine
629 Hudson
N.Y. N.Y.

On board L.A. Plane just about to leave. *2 p.m. W'y*

Postmark obliterated, 1947

Hullo, my precious, this has been a wonderful day—light, bright and yet cool—a beautiful breeze. Bessie & L just left me at the airport. (For you alone) G. told me that they both were very unhappy the past 3 days. This thing in my neck might have been a malignant growth, and my time would have been short. But examination showed that it was something on top of something else—this one being a tumor on the salivary glands. It ought to be taken out, says G., within a few weeks. 4 or 5 days in hospital and then a few days quiet. I am glad you told me—very glad. You take care of me and you must take care of yourself too. Now I shall post this at Frisco so that it gets there quick.

There has taken place here during the last few days, an astonishing political demonstration wh[ich] deserves the close attention of the c'ds [comrades].

1. The two minority members, BG and EW [Everett Washburn], on whom the burden fell carried out a job of organization, political strategy and tactics that for energy and adaptability could not have been bettered. It began when they insisted that I change the schedule and begin with the debate on Russia on Sat night. After that, to practically the whole branch, we had Sunday: The Fundamental Basis of the M'y [Minority] Position, Mon The Negro Question, T [Trotskyist] Unity.

Four days on such subjects gave me unequalled opportunity to test out ideas. The Majority was routed and by Tuesday had politically and morally disintegrated. They had one cry "anti-Cannonism." We have won over

1) Bart Abbott longshoreman, a stalwart of the [San] Pedro branch
2) Helen A, proletarian type, his wife

We have bound to the movement with a new understanding and perspective Washburn, M.Manon, E W's wife, a petty-bourgeois intellectual of great potentialities who at last "understands what it is all about" and showed that by her stream of unceasing questions, all pointing to the correct problems.

We have drawn closer to us a Mexican worker, Mannie, a genuine proletarian, hanging on to the party but sick to death of its ways. Two young students, very active members, have been intrigued by the ideas, followed closely and are now wavering. Another longshoreman says he likes our positions and will study them. Two ex-SWP'ers who attended all gave us money, asked our advice as to what to do and have offered us a meeting of sympathisers, Negroes and SWP'ers in Minneapolis—either me or anyone I recommend. They have some and want all our material.

There are the diehards in the branch and some ex-SWP'ers, democratic fanatics and one or two waverers. *If it were possible to have here for a few weeks a very developed c'de we could have a solid basis in this branch.* The importance of that is this. The branch is feeble beyond belief, and right here the SWP has its second largest concentration, about 75 or 100, in the country. *The official Minority in L.A. can be ours if we act with boldness and care.* The present branch gabble about anti-Cannonism but have no basis for really helping to build a fruitful unity and a genuine democratically functioning branch with the SWP here. They will be just swamped.

All we need is someone able to carry on where we have left off. Our 2 c'des here are too modest. B has learnt to make extremely effective organisational interventions exposing majority maneuvers. She did it at each meeting. E speaks like a genuine *American* Bolshevik—no theoretical frills but simply and straight to the point. But they need help, for themselves and for the contacts....

The usual Collier's, Posts, Life, etc., should be sent to [San] Pedro regularly. Yet we must not badger them. Now you have it. *Please* do an exemplary job.

Bart's address is Helen's. Manon's is Manon Washburn, 918 W 75, L.A. 44 Ca

We are safely in, darling. I'll wire you and post this. *I love you.*

[unsigned]

L. Paine
629 Hudson
N.Y. N.Y.

Postmark April 19, 1947
Sat'y 5:30 p.m.

Sweetheart, I only now have time and truth to tell, energy to write what I wanted to since night before last. I am all bandaged or taped rather but have had not an inch of pain. I cooked fish for lunch to the admiration of the surrounding population, and I shall prepare eggplant (it is in the stove now) for dinner. Judie is looking on.
JUDIE IS VERY SWEET
She read this and made a blushing gesture. Thursday night while writing I was thinking of you. I remembered with remarkable vividness how that night of the great quarrel how uncontrollably you cried. And after a time I said: She likes an audience— she knows Grace will hear and she cries loud and talks loud. I didn't think that only. But I thought that too. Then I went inside and you followed. I remembered how you fought—insisted that I listen and speak to you; I knew at the time that I was not responding—wooden and obstinate and stubborn. But I knew too that my saying you wanted an audience was spiteful and mean. Then you sat on my knee and were very tired and wanted so much or rather needed so much for me to take you close and love you. I remained distant and made only a few gestures. But you won a great victory—I talked; and when I talked a whole new world began. Never never again.

The whole thing lives at the back of my mind for days. Then suddenly as I was writing it came to me and I saw how I should have acted, even then. Why? Am I old? I face it squarely. I have had no practice in meeting people on that level. I have done things for people, spent and spend long hours doing things for them but the spontaneous human response, giving myself, at least as I should have met you that night, I am no good at it. I have to learn. It isn't an easy job. I note on the way round how powerfully I give myself to my audience in speech. Day after day, morning, noon & night, without an effort unless I am very tired I speak. Friends & enemies alike feel the impact. I wonder if that capacity developed over so many years does not dry up a man. I am not doing one thing except examine the matter as scientifically as I can. Then there is the fact that I do feel it—I felt it as strongly as anyone could—nearly two weeks after. Over and over again I feel an emotion for you, to say I love you, or you look wonderful, or that was profound, or clever—I feel it. I don't say it. Then I say I should. Then I say a young man would or a man different from me would. I end by shutting my mouth and going on with my business. That's me.

Living here is wonderful. The lovely house. It suits *me*. The air and light and bungalow-style houses of L.A.; the connection with you—I would love to live here—to spend 3 years—3 months. It would be the making of me and of us. I must hope, we must hope and manuever.

I hear you are in with Rae. Wonderful! I only hope Grace does not feel rejected But it cannot be helped. Love to Rae and John and everything for you. I love you.
N
L. Paine
629 Hudson [N.Y. N.Y.]

Separation and Limbo (1947–8)

Postmark April 16, 1947

Hullo, sweets. I learned from Willie that your letters were on the way to me. I am all anxious to see them; and if they are not fat, there will be one fed-up citizen.

Bessie, house & kids are wonderful. I am very happy here & Gogol is his quiet, kindly self.

I am just doing this in preparation of a letter I shall write later. I am in G's office. He is going to cut out my nuisance, he & Bessie. As soon as I leave here I want to post. Then when I get home I can write.

OK? OK?

G & B say that there will not be much to it. And guess whom I saw & who is coming to-night to hear me on the R. Q. [Russian Question] Fishler. Gogol's office is in the same building. F is "in bad shape personally," I hear.

So I love you. That's the news.

N

I had written & enclosed in envelope. But now THE OPERATION is over. I am all taped up and am a sight. The intruder was "friable," some insignificant scraps of stuff. Then, when I return, Nesson. Bessie sends her love. And who else? *ME.*

N

L. Paine
629 Hudson St.
N.Y. N.Y.

Postmark April 21, 1947
Tues, 1 a.m.

Hullo sugar-pie. I am in Cleveland, in a hotel with bath. I regret to say I left razor, tooth-brush & paste in Detroit. I am mad. 4 bucks at least; and my presents lost. But I shall get them later.

Why am I writing you now. I have a stiff day to-morrow. Discussion 11–4. Dinner 5–7 (same) meeting 7:30 till God knows when. In other words continuous talking; and not talking, i.e., restraint, wh[ich] is very hard when I am listening to nonsense or extravagance. I find Murray here terribly disoriented. It will be a major effort to pull him back. He has all sorts of illusions about winning people in the W. P.; and by the way from what he says, he got them from the arguments that Grace & Rae gave him when he had a different view. Will you mention this to them for me and ask them to drop me a line on it.

So, darling, here I am. You could imagine what a mess it is with all this going on (I had from 9–12:30 with M this evening) and to-morrow, and a document I am to do, how difficult it is to deal adequately with the new me that is solidly encased but exists. It is obvious that it will take a long period (weeks) with that as the main job. But meanwhile I go at it. I love you. Life without you now will be a horrible prospect. What would I do? And yet I flinch from your letter. What exactly causes this? I remember the night we saw Razor's Edge. You came in and sat in the living-room, and I knew you wanted me to come & talk to you & that I should. But I didn't. *What* is it? Sometimes I am tired. But then I just don't want to talk. And that is not often. But my response to your letter taught me something. I am defending myself—what? privacy? my concentration? But the letter would take only 15 minutes to read. I read the papers. Is it dread of emotional contact? As a little boy love-affairs were sternly forbidden—and I was always in love; I had to hide it. But that seems silly. It is a little early for me to begin figuring it out. I only recognised how wrong something or other is yesterday a.m. when the letter came. But now I know what, there remains to find out Why! Could you help me? I used to write & write to you about you. I have been sore too because I knew that about emotional things you were more gifted, and more resilient than I and I thought in fact I said you had much to teach me. I knew that. I was expecting it. But you seemed to demand that I take the initiative and then to get angry when I didn't. I said "After all, where is the equality in wh[ich] the responsibility for everything is thrust on me." I don't grumble any more. Not at all, not one little bit. But I still think that here you could be professor and I pupil and you take as much care and watch the pupil as carefully as I watch you and your writing and your development. I keep on thinking of "myself" as being encased in a wall—definitive armor. I have to break it in and peel it off and then find? I don't know. Maybe there is nothing there worthwhile. But I hope not, I don't think so, and in any case I want to see. We should get married. You know why I hesitate? Because I am terrified that after a little while you'll feel trapped again. That I don't make you happy, that I mean well but haven't got it in me. For my part I'd be the happiest man in the world to be Mr. Constance Webb to-morrow. Late now. I must go to bed. But I'll write again. I have my eye open for a present for you for my anniversary—April 14th. I'll buy it when I can. And our *real* anniversary May, we'll celebrate together with Turkey and *brandy*. Oh I forgot. To-day I was thinking of anniversaries and I thought of our Easter dinner. God! How good I felt. You looked wonderful. You were very sweet. But somehow I did not make the best of it for you. But we'll see. Till later.

N

L. Paine
629 Hudson St.
N.Y. N.Y.

Postmark April 23, 1947
Thursday

Dearest,

Your letters are met by a bold and stalwart warrior. Does he flinch? Not he! In fact he actually rejoices at the sight of them. Can you believe how perverse people can be? Anyway one thing only before I do my duty. I got up this a.m. suddenly frightened. I find that my reactions are delayed very often. But I was frightened for half an hour and off and on all day. Darling, get away from it, go to Freddie's, go to Frank's, go anywhere, but get away and send to tell me that you have. Otherwise I shall be without peace.

Otherwise I am well. I am tired in a way, but my stomach is wonderful. The stitches are taken out but it is swollen larger than ever. Ho! ho! ho! G says this will last two weeks or more. But I have had no pain. My hands are very tired. Writing is a pain. But I am well. I love you. I shall write to you later.

The trip here has been fabulous. 30 people came to Saturday night's meeting. Sunday p.m. there were almost as many. You heard how Helen A said she was with us, etc. You want to write to her—when I return I'll tell you more.

Well, Monday p.m. two people, Irving and wife from Minneapolis came for an interview. They had resigned from M'pls SWP because of "bureaucracy." They told a horrible story and it sounded pretty bad and true—name calling, brutality, personal ties to leadership demagogy, subservience, etc. I listened. They are people with money, devoted to the movement. They had gone to see Natalia [Trotsky].

I did not deny their stories. I did not minimise them. They were all wrought up and they were serious. I pictured to them instead [what] they had *not* done. They had not organised; had not clarified themselves; had not kept away from the monstrous behavior of Morrow,* etc.; and presented their grievances not in terms of bettering the party but of violations of their sense of justice, etc.

1) They should rejoin the SWP with a letter asserting their past services, their regrets at their resignation, their determination to serve.

2) They should fight like hell, but in a careful disciplined manner for their point of view.

3) These unity negotiations, etc., were merely preliminaries. They represented merely the preparation of the U.S. movement for a genuine struggle of all groups on how to build the party. They should get in and prepare for this.

They were, as Gogol told me afterward (he saw them) subdued for the afternoon. *I had told them exactly what Natalia had told them.* Only (and this must be kept *absolutely* quiet) she had said: In the course of the coming struggle there may well be another split—this time definitive. I was very pleased. This contact we shall hold. That night, Monday night, was the Negro meeting. Some 20-odd people came. Bessie and E were vastly pleased. The whole branch was turning out to hear the minority. Sat'y evening I pounded Hal. Sunday I pounded him harder. Now Monday, I ran him off his legs. I stood up to speak and spoke for 70 minutes at a great pace. I gave theory; the history of Negroes in the U.S.; developed the idea in half-a-dozen ways that the party by its action on the N'o question carved a way for itself to the leadership not of Negroes but of "the nation." It was not a "Negro" question at all. I ended with Negro work in the party as being a test of *all* work. I deliberately did what nobody expected—ignored the Majority and lifted the discussion to a plane none had conceived of.

The comrades and friends loved it. Hal? "I had *not* put forward the Minority position as such. He was glad to see it. The discussion should proceed along these unpolemical lines, etc." The upshot was a protest from the branch. He lost control of his stalwarts. One of them provoked me (undisciplined rank and filers are the worst torture—only less miserable than undisciplined leaders). So having been provoked I then opened fire against the Majority polemically. They were routed completely. Bart Abbott said that he was for the first time able to sit through a meeting without sleeping.

Mannie the Mexican was there with his wife. Bessie had worked heroically to get them. They were pleased. Anyway, Bart practically declared himself on our side; so did the Irvings. After the meeting we told the Irvings we wanted some money. They said they would see us to-day. Helen who is very poor, said she had a bed-spread

---

* Felix Morrow, who had remained a member of the SWP after the 1940 split, became increasingly critical of Cannon's leadership. He was expelled from the SWP in 1946, accused of holding secret meetings with Max Shachtman.

worth $100. She would try to sell it. The majority had crawled away. Bart and Helen and Jimmy, another longshoreman, went to Everett's house until 2:30 "talking as if they were J'ites already." The branch is in a mess. Nobody of our people had expected this. We had thought of a few, two or three coming to our discussions. We have Helen for certain and she is dead set on winning over Bart. He is committed on the R'n Q'n [Russian Question] but love can conquer all things. But joking apart, Helen is a formidable person aching to learn, to know, and act *for us*. They were due in Frisco on Friday. They are leaving earlier to be sure to have a discussion with me.

To-night is the unity meeting. I am writing from Everett's where I am spending the afternoon with himself and Washburn, M.Manon. Hal called me this a.m. "to make arrangements." He wanted to get the last word in at the meeting—I said I didn't mind. I proposed. I told him to be strictly political—I was not going to discuss anything else. He said O.K. So to-night there will be, we expect, another crowded house—this is a branch meeting—and this will end it. I am to meet a Negro SWPer to-morrow a.m. at 11 and catch the plane at 2.

I cannot write another line now. I love you.

            N

I didn't post after all. I am home from the meeting and 2 interviews after. I am pretty much exhausted. But we massacred them. On unity. We put forward political analysis and program. They shouted and screamed at the Cannonites and us. We said: Look at the two types of speeches, etc., etc. The Minneapolis people gave us $15.00. Helen did not sell the spread but will try. *Bart is definitely with us.*

So, darling, till to-morrow. Tom's present is wonderful. Mine is on the way. I hope you like it. I do. I also have got for you Pylon by Faulkner—1935.

           As ever
            N

L. Paine
629 Hudson St.
N.Y. N.Y.

                Postmark April 29, 1947
Darling,

I love you. I have an hour or two now and shall spend part of it in writing to you. Listen to about me. I am well—no stomach pains at all and fit—but dog tired. Friday night I had a meeting—after, we all went to Willie's—a hot discussion, 8 or 10 people. It lasted until 3. Then Bart and Helen who had come up a day earlier specially to meet me drove me to air-port. They left at 5:30. I got a plane to Denver at 7:30; slept on board for 4 hours; at Denver drove 30–40 miles to Boulder; shower; buffet dinner; meeting till 12. In bed at 12:30. Up at 4:45 to drive back to Denver. All the plane schedules changed. Got a special seat in a plane, one of the new ones, 300 miles an hour. Could not sleep at all; reached Chicago at about 2:15; dinner at about 5:30, talk talk talk; meeting at 7—lasted till after 12. Then came home with *S.W.P'er* and Dave (Zelnek); argument till 2 with SWP'er. Up at about 11—sleep at last; the Chicago people offered me a meeting of the club to-night; had to take it—people here begging to hear something. I had to start reorganising schedule. I have sent enough telegrams to make a bonfire these few days. But after reorganising schedule and putting a few things to rights here I am; have had one interview (our solitary supporter on R. Q.

[Russian Question] in branch; prospects he thinks are good) then firing away at SWP'er, a *splendid* guy but I.K.D.'er, Dave says we *must* win him; now I write you. Dave is waiting to talk to me about the R. Q. He has not *yet* decided. At 5 we prepare a special speech to suit the situation. At 6 dinner. At 7 go to meeting till midnight and then people. In between is keeping in touch and working out the coming campaign. The trouble is—my hands. I feel it there—writing is *hard*. But altogether am doing wonderful and I know that these last months with you have been the beginning of my salvation. I am standing the strain as I have not done for years. I have eaten hot dogs and drunk cokes. I have gone hours without eating—and I would like to see how anyone could have done differently on some of the flights I had to take, e.g., my plane to S.F. from Cleveland was late. They held the L.A. plane for us—we transferred in 2 minutes instead of the hour we hoped for and there was nothing to eat on the new plane but coffee. So that's me. The trip has been wonderful—flights intriguing and very successful. We have won far more contacts, etc., than I thought. I had not expected any. I hadn't come for that.

There are some things that I must take up.

First about you and me. You say that you are going to make an attack upon me and conquer the positions. Go ahead. I am willing to be conquered. It will not be so easy as you think—this old sinner is willing but tough. One thing, however, I know. I shall have no peace until you are at ease fundamentally. How it will be I don't know and to be frank I have been thinking of it only when I had time and not too much. It is there, the problem is recognised. I begin "by talking." I know I shall never "not talk" again. Maybe I shall in time talk "too much." I don't know. But *you* go ahead—*you* think and watch and tell me. I am thinking too but as I think I see that I have been disappointed in you—rightly or wrongly. I sensed my deficiencies and hoped that you would help, take the initiative, plan, scheme, and not leave it to me. We shall see.

Now about your "political activities." You wish to be *one* personality—you will find that very difficult. For weeks, if not months, I have watched with some misgivings your desire to be "active" in things. I said nothing, in my usual manner. Now I shall say something. The leaders of the faction are leaders because of years of study, devotion, and leadership in struggles. You cannot begin there; giving advice, entering into discussions of vital matters, instructing the youth, etc. Before you know where you are you will unloose such a crop of antagonisms of a personal and political nature as would take months to straighten out. When I bring back your letter you will see what is as clear as day to me already—the development of a grouping of Frank and Cecelia and perhaps Leon and Cuppy around you against or in passive opposition or reaction against Grace. Before you know where you are *it will find, for it will*, some shade of *difference*. Cecelia will, of course, desert you with the utmost speed as soon as it begins to assume the form of a clique. For these groupings, evanescent as they may appear, breed other groupings or talk, observations, counter-talks, counter-observations. I once saw in a meeting Grace force a point and get the votes of Ike, Harry, and Yonnie whom she brought in. All who had sense knew the falsity of the position she would soon find herself in. I didn't like Frank's remarks about Grace's 30 books at all. And you clarified Columbia for him when he was going to Staten and G and I pulled him back. He used to live at F'die & L's—day in day out. He then left them entirely and transferred to G who taught him most of what he knows in strict theory; now he is transferring his allegiance. He is a fine guy, I have always liked him a lot. But—*anything*; *anything* which will put you in a little clique that is even faintly anti-Grace would be wrong and unbelievably foolish for you.

Take another example. Grace is in charge of Phil's document. She is far and away the most capable person for it. Phil listens to you a great deal. That is O.K. But if you talk to him about this or that aspect of his stuff and then put him in a position where Grace is telling him one thing and you something else it would be very very wrong. Then add that to Frank and Cecelia and Leon on the one hand and that horrible Ike on the other and there is the making of a nice mess—and all quite unnecessary. Are people beginning to say "You ought to move." If so, I would be very sorry. Why do you think I let Ike get away with so much? Precisely because *at this time* above all I do not want any antagonisms.

Again. You attend faction meetings. I am glad, but the way it was done was wrong. A motion should have been made. Special circumstances. You act as my secretary, and are a channel of communication, etc., and therefore for these reasons you are allowed, without voice or vote except of course at open meetings. Why? Because to-morrow in P'a somebody will want to bring someone and the vote will be "No," and sure as day especially if the political issues are sharp, someone will say "In N.Y. J's wife was allowed." And it can become a source of scandal, and even antagonism inside the group. Yet if it is done in an orderly, dexterous manner, then one is ready. Yet I have said nothing to G. and R. I cannot be constantly preaching to them. It would create an irritation, unconscious even. But as soon as the opportunity presents itself I shall say something. You will hear. R and G. are very nice to you and let you in on everything. I welcome it. But you should lean backwards not to get entangled in any kind of conflict or opposition especially to G. who is the cornerstone of our organization. No great harm has been done. But these things flare up rapidly. I have been aware of it for some time in little things. One night when I broached the new turn, Rae was obviously upset. She began to talk. You wrote a note for me, which meant that you were in on it and on my side and giving me in all probability points and arguments against her. It is a little thing; but a lot of little things can pile up, until the sentiment will grow: She behaves as if she and Jimmy founded the faction. It can, you know.

Then there are ambitious people who want to be in and around the leadership. And will resent your being so close and throwing your weight around as if you were one already. You seem very much concerned about not being "Johnson's wife." Why? You could get *yourself* politically into an awful mess that way. For you would soon find if you were a member, sneers, etc., that you were always on my side, and then you would begin to feel the *necessity* of differentiating yourself on this or that point. I have seen it 99 times out of 100. I hope, darling, you are the hundredth.

Politics, rev'y politics, is a very serious business that takes years of hard work and conscious devotion of all efforts. I know a man who has been in for years—a journalist, high up in our organisation, does serious and *responsible* work, gives all he has. He can talk like a I. S. [International Socialist] resolution. But all of us, friends and enemies, know that he does not belong—that he is dilettante and does not understand really. He has never been through the mill. I asked G about him. His comment was superb "He does his work." I asked no more. We understood one another.

You want to be a politico? That's O.K. with me. Then I'll show you. It will take you five years. And the first thing you will have to do is to stop talking and begin listening, begin the exercise of a rigorous self-discipline, looking, watching, weighing—sitting in the last row for a long time and not coming up front even when you are invited. We'll talk about this and other things. But the moment *two* people come to you and tell you things about a leader of your group—that is a danger signal. Read Lord Raingo* again, I beg of you.

On the other hand, work. *Do* all you can. Choose low, nasty jobs—type and re-type; undertake the things wh[ich] demand sacrifice and renunciation of pleasures; those who watch and weigh and form opinions of people will note. I hope you have been to see Sarah and have written her a note or two or asked her if she wanted anything. And so on.

I have all these things in mind. I chose you for the Negro thing purposely. I have some other people I want you to correspond with. But I have chosen them carefully and the topics. I do not under any circumstances want any clashes. You have for the time being a modest function. You can do it best and build for the future if you rigidly keep out of everything which may begin something. A true maestro does not have to get out of things. He avoids getting into them.

I am working on the outline. I shall not write. I don't think it is good. It certainly is far below what I think is your best. But it is a beginning. I suggest that you keep the others out of it until I have spoken to you about it fully and completely. They do not understand what you are doing and on the whole it is much much better that way. I shall discuss everything with you but please get at it yourself. Don't wait for me. If when I come you have altered it top and bottom, O.K. with me.

About the case, sweets, I wish us luck.** Wouldn't that be *something*? Fingers crossed. But keep it quiet. I beg of you. And insist on secrecy from all including that gulf-stream Conrad.

The laundry: Come downstairs, go left; turn first left; then turn left at the first street; go down about 60 yards and it is on the opposite side. A little Jewish place, like something in Dickens. He never gives a ticket. Tell him the no. It *may* be the second street, not the first. Forgive me.

So my sugar, that's it for now. I think of you every second. You are my wife. Your letters mean much to me. Reversal eh? I am up to my eyes. And they give me a rest and promise long talks and clarification of all sorts of things.

One word about outline. Something *is* wrong. In your letters there are observations which are remarkable in their penetration and the possibilities they open up. But the outline somehow is stodgy and the great connecting links, the strong logical movement isn't there. We'll work it out.

N

L. Paine
629 Hudson St.
N.Y. N.Y.

---

* Arnold Bennett, 1926.
** Webb had brought a legal case against a club for injuries which prevented her from modelling.

WESTERN UNION
September 26, 1947

After a hard year I understand myself and so can understand you. You are wrong in thinking that I purposely put it aside for something else. A pattern which had moulded my whole life and not ineffectively fought against the new experiences I sought for personal reasons. My greatest discovery is that I need them in all aspects of my life. Both the violence of the last letters and the subsequent silence were the result of a primitive jealousy and the old reserve fighting a last battle for self-preservation. These things had never happened to me before. I tried to speak but couldn't. I could scarcely speak that morning at the Raskin's as I left and then outside to save my pride I swaggered in case you were looking. I called you one evening. Francesca said you were away for the weekend. I at once was jealous again and could not say anything. As soon as you left New York I understood. I called Palm Drive. I wrote to Bessie. I called her and asked her to contact you for me. I want you to know that the human being you sought and fought for exists. All that you wanted to hear I want to say. All that you wanted me to do I want to do. I shaped my life by yours for eight years and never failed you when things were bad. You remember those days when I helped you with Jack. Do the same for me now. I shall be in Los Angeles in two weeks. I shall not write to you the things I have to tell you I shall say in person. But I have a manuscript to send you which will say other things for me and I hope for you. Please wire me at Freddie's soon. I have missed you and have suffered just like any petty-bourgeois existentialist while I maintained a front outside. According to how you sign the wire I shall call and speak to you for a few minutes. Do not be afraid to be generous with me, Constance. I will not misunderstand it. I have never really loved you before until now. Any readiness you show I will take to mean that you are ready to do the things we planned, to fight hard, and never, never to settle for less. The information you ask for I shall send soon as I put my hand on it. But my lawyers say that if you take the step immediately you will hit my public life as hard a blow as I have hit my personal self. You now know everything. All other matters are progressing miraculously. Now that I see other things to do I can do them as well.

N

WESTERN UNION
October 6, 1947

I shall do what you wish tomorrow if you like. But how do you help the me you have created if you cannot restrain your antagonism. A month ago as you know I would have kept silent and maybe I will be able to do so in time but at present I must let you know I am fighting for something new and whatever decisions you make for yourself you must help me.

N

Terrified I was too old for you. You *cried* when we slept together.*
Relaxing with women never doing anything else
You came like a storm   You battered me   I was frightened
Too late?
How can it be
I have been searching
You " "
Now it is here
I have broken all ties
Immigration—*Social*
Every woman I've ...
Love *all day*

    Lights gone. Just enjoying your body. The intimate relationship, names for our private selves; when I love you *never*. . . . Kissing you there loving you there with my lips getting to know every inch of your body   Tenderness

Letters to wife
Never discussed what *we* liked
how we *liked* it
Our past sex lives
Never ...
(Share My Life)
I would like to go over my letters with you one by one
Sit Near to you   Meetings
     Chinese
     Freddie
Orchard St. was worse, narrowness and all callers
I have to clear that up
Days you were sweet
(I had wanted to write letters to my wife)
The person who gets you if it
  antagonism
  must come out
The change I had experienced
English gentlemen
James is against gentleness   superior person above *things*
So much love, so much happiness, so much attention

A selfish life   two *of us* alone   I need it
When you left ... Nothing mattered ... You loved me
I went away to Freddie. Allen was GPU agent of FBI. He was after me. When I went to Northport Eddie guarded me. They have murdered [?] and many of our young people

---

* Notes, according to Constance Webb, prepared by James for his meeting with her after she left him.

Never for one   how
Politics
You represented things in my life I thought the movement was depriving me of.
Orchard St.
Caucus: How *it happened*?
I couldn't work
you fought
When you left—what I wanted from you
If you have been looking for something all your life—suffered and fought
fought and have been   It is here now. You have only to stretch out your hand.

You have been thinking—you say well you have *tried*. 27. You are nervous of your youth fought for 10 years. Battered at me. Tremendo*us effo*rt. Seemed in *vain*—you are not . . .

The old me, the one who was destroyed at a stroke. . . . And the new one couldn't make it

The spell of the old was there   Caucus
The *Shock*   Talk to you
How it happened
Sexual Fear I had never had it
You are. . . .
Terrified I was too old for you
Financial worry
Your . . . director, if acting was your life
. . . and my
You hammered at me . . . I had lost my. . . . I couldn't *work*
If I had those days to live over now

The old me was destroyed and there were sometimes antagonisms passions hates
My sexual life went to *pieces*. . . . My political life was threatened
I couldn't work. It was all centered around you so the antagonisms . . .
But why you—whom I was in love with . . .
All I could do was to . . .
Antagonisms centered on you   Psycho analysis . . . When the suppressed things come up

Then *immediately we married* it started
    problem I was nobody I was nothing . . . that's what you did to me
You hit me with a . . . and savagery that bewildered me
I had no time to prepare. You hammered at me. You battered at me
Nobody
The old one was gone
1) Hurt you as a woman
2) *You think I fixed my work and then you*
3) *I have been rude, fierce*, doubted you
4) I have stood up talking to my caucus, have never done it before,
never lost my intellectual integrity, natural to me
    a) Caucus

Separation and Limbo (1947–8)

b) Cecelia (. . .)

I am talking to you for me . . . first time. By stages.

I wanted to to tell you, to talk to you for days and days and days   Sweet

Talked to others . . . I have become a talker

Don't tell him this   Don't tell him that . . . She will this and that

Most people's love letters cannot be read. Yours can be.

Raskins—know you

What I think of you. . . . Nobody loves you as I do, knows you as I do, nobody ever will . . . you know that

Raskins . . . I have to appeal to the girl *I know* . . . only I *know*

What a fool I have been

I am not going to reproach you with anything

If I thought I could find it I could go on. . . . In the last analysis only that will bring you back. But I can't find it

Orchard St.? *No.*

They . . . Vain selfish woman . . . dishonest, egocentric subjective, world revolves around you

For ten years you have suffered and sought

(You are thirty years beyond him)

If you hurt him if he cracks up for a bit. What does it matter? He will find someone. If you hurt *me*—weaken me, deprive me of strength, it matters. Where can I get anyone like you.

The attraction I have for people, etc., etc.—not for you. I seemed to sparkle for them.

No one will ever love you if I treble it—as I am trebly, I shall become . . .

We are made for each *other*. Never

want you to come out with me, one evening

let me write to you

If any love

Talk began about me then about you

Last thing

. . . If everything is dead, then

. . . But if it isn't if you

let me write to you

It seems easy way . . .

If he were a man just as he is working as a———would you marry him? or isn't he plus the life he offers

I wanted you to give me what the movement lacked. I tried to keep you from being a political drudge. Perhaps I used this. I don't know.

The crucial years they are   Now it is dead. It is we who made you. Those few who stand for something

They who have been holding you back . . . torturing you using your beauty and your charm, seeking to . . . from you. They use it as they use everything for their profit and their pleasure

I know how powerful I am. I know that once you feel secure you will sacrifice everything

No friends
I was badly beaten as a little boy. Father fierce Puritan.
Women I never trusted
Never wanted to be leader
worthwhile . . . wherever I went always a leader
Never spoken to anyone   I have changed
I will sign anything
The Immigration people are after me. The marriage will come up and I will say that my wife is challenging the marriage. They will say get out. I'll have to go. You are my chance.
Grace, etc., Gone. I declared war on all of them. I offer you . . .
300 dollars
200
House
Independent Life
We two
Kids
I may have to go   I want to know . . . If I That's what you want, I want

To put you to sit down and talk to you
You did it before—Jack and Stalinism
That world is dead. It is nothing. You cannot manage both. We have everything that matters.
Then you'll have some babies. You will have to accommodate yourself to him.
Strip him of all he buys for you—and then see
You cannot live a non-political life
Movement stopped
Nursing stopped
Modelling stopped
Acting stopped
Writing and ME stopped
Poetry
You will have an adjustment to make to the movement. I'll take you into caucus, my wife. I was scared of familiar, not right . . .
If you go I will never get over it. But you wouldn't either. It will remain. Why should we hurt each other so? You are just beginning.
All the hardness in your heart. I put it there. I have to take it out.
When I meet Connie.   American, etc.
Grace and I. We wanted you.
Cannon
Only shock. Jealousy—how it came out in those letters. Only shock.
Fighting for the preservation of the old life.
Norman. Fishler. Eddie. Jack a Stalinist. *Constance*. Married Training You made for me I for you

What Grace others. Go to N.Y. Write to Paula. Tell her that the shell is broken down and the man below has appeared. And ask her:

I wrote to you why? I could not speak.
In platform . . . private speech, private conversation, I am
Why? Nobody knows the power in me or if it will really give out. That depends on you. But if you don't I have plenty to go on with.
Some people saw through me. Paula did. Ask her. My publisher's wife: very acute but liked me all the same—after her husband I was her favorite man.
I couldn't speak.
The House. The morning after Philly. I'll fix things.
Talk to you. I am afraid of boring you, afraid of taking the conversation. I saw you with people to talk to them.
Failed.
You failed me.
I asked you for 2 months. I thought you had agreed. That was not honest. I knew.
Needle-pointed.
Fighting for preservation of old life. Only shock.

October 7, 1947

This is the man who loves you. I took up dialectic five years ago. I knew a lot of things before and I was able to master it. I know a lot of things about loving you. I am only just beginning to apply them. I can master that with the greatest rapidity—just give me a hand. I feel all sorts of new powers, *freedoms*, etc., surging in me. You released so many of my constrictions. What are you going to *do*? I am bursting all over with love for you. Who, who can give you anything like the love I have for you—any of those third-rate men? They haven't as much in all of them as I have in my finger. I'll make you feel like a queen of a tournament every hour of the day. We will *live*. This is our new world—where there is no distinction between political and personal any more. I would wash the dishes and sweep the floor so as to have you always with me, literally that. 50%. I *want* it that way. You make me twice as strong, my work will be easy, yours too—both of us sharing everything and making love every second of the day. Stop and think of my article. It is wonderful. I know it is. I did it in a few days—doing a thousand other things; I had a new energy, for things that had impeded me were broken down. Will you grow with me, or accommodate yourself to someone who lives on a different level. Darling, do not let past pain hold you back. Everything I have I'll put into loving you. And I have plenty. Come with me. In this ms. is a hint of me. But the real me is waiting for you. I know you will choose right. I owe you thousands of kisses. I want to pay the debt.

I think now neither of work, nor love, nor personal, nor public, nor any separation—only of you and me doing everything. I know now you are fully equal to anything that life will demand of us. I have confidence in you that I have in no one else. I know where you have come from to reach where you can begin. I know your power—who but I should. I felt it and broke down at last. I want now to be saying I love you every hour, to make up for the times I wanted to say it and didn't. I want to love you endlessly, never to let your lovely self be out of my sight for one minute more than I can help. Everything I think I can tell you—I know how good you are for me to talk to and whatever you say is precious for me. If we have worked hard and suffered, we have reached somewhere. My lovely, precious, Connie. The chains are broken. They only need to be shaken off. Already we have built a foundation that nothing can shake. Who comes into this is an intruder. When we look at each other think of the past that binds us. You love me, darling. Do not fight it. I want to proclaim to the whole world how I love you, and if we grasp the future, all the past pain will not only be bearable but will be remembered kindly because it helped us to find ourselves and each other. I read and reread your letters. One I shall frame and put on my desk. The others I shall bind. They are beautiful and were but the beginning. We shall write to each other again as I had always planned to do when we lived together. I couldn't, but I can now. How I shall write to you now!

One last word, darling, and I'll write it all here, for this is all of me. You might hesitate, thinking that I mean well but will slip into carelessness and leave the burdens to you. Remember 1944 to 1946. Was ever anyone, *anyone* so careful of you? Everything collapsed after because I collapsed. But the same care of you that I took then I will take again. It is the same me, only now strong and able to do things for you far far more than when you felt I did. I want to live as you want to live. Once I see it I can do it. And I see it now clearly. No one will take better care of you than I will. You are too lovely, too precious and too sweet for anything else. And I want to change, to use everything that I have in me and I know that it is only through the closest companionship and love with you that I can. Together, darling, a partnership, and I know that my partner is my most precious asset and I shall guard her from the things she fears as I shall guard my life; for her happiness and my life are the same. Let this brown-papered document be the beginning. In it, sweetheart, in mimeograph and in the writing in pencil is me—this day of October 7, 1947. As I am. This is me. Darling I am not so bad am I? I know my weaknesses and deficiencies but I know that I am a giant compared with the rest. I have said everything. You are the girl I know, you will let the love you bear me grow once more.

[unsigned]

October 10, 1947

Darling,

I am asking you to stay. Don't go back. Stay with me. Give up the job. You haven't to prove yourself that way. That is the right thing to do. I know it.

All through the eight years, I have doubted you. Why is not important any longer. I doubted you because I doubted myself, and all the time you were calling out to me to come to you and let us go together. You wrote to me in 1940 that you would like to come. You said you did not mean love. I accept that. But I did not wire you to come. I did not help you to come. That is clear enough. In 1944 and from then on I never asked you to come. Only at the last minute I did it and you responded immediately. Almost at once your love for me began to show itself—suppressed so far because I hadn't asked for it. Then when we knew we loved each other, it was you who with a confidence that stopped at nothing told me you wanted to come, and came. You talked about marriage. You talked about the baby. You talked about joining the party. You told me you would go to England with me. You fought me. Darling, you loved, you had courage, confidence, you went out. I did little. Now it is my turn. I love you, I am able to make demands on you because I have no doubts of you, or of myself to meet your love; all my hesitations are gone. Stay with me. And give up all your plans? Yes, all, give them up for me, for you, for us. For us. Yes, my dearest, dearest Constance, for us. Us. If you know what that word means for me now; it was never us before. I couldn't think it. I thought always of my decisions and if you would fit into them. That I could depend on you to work out a decision with me as to what *we* should do—I couldn't think that way. I distrusted you. You were petty-bourgeois, revolutionary it is true, but you—how could you understand what proletarian discipline meant; for me "obviously" you would not understand. There would be a clash. It would be asking too much of you. So that being so I had better be careful. If you made a move, then I could accept because if anything went wrong, the responsibility would have been yours. I was frightened at the responsibility of the marriage, until I was sure our sexual life was straightened out, until I was sure of your ability to live the hard life, until I was sure of every thing, all of which meant only until I was sure of myself.

I was afraid of letting you sit close to me in public. I was afraid it might not work out and then look at what would have been built up. I was afraid that people might know our sexual life was not good and that they would say I was too old for you and nod their heads and say "Yes. I thought so. That stupid James. Serves him right." Darling, they are all gone, gone with the wind and up in smoke. Gone. They can never come back.

Sweetheart, how I have wronged you and hurt myself. Your youth and beauty, your charm and style, darling I revel in them. You as you are, a work of art, to make me warm in my blood and delight in you aesthetically. Instead I fought you—fought your loveliness, all you had to give me as a woman. As if anything could be *wrong* in that. Now I have not only love and a burning glow inside of me for you but pride. My girl. I want to carry you around and let people see you and all the love and attention I shall lavish on you before everyone. They will be stunned into silence—if they want to criticize. But they will not want to. They will envy me my happiness. They will not think less of me. They will think more.

I did not get things for the house. I could have got them. I could have had the apartment decently furnished. I know that now. I could have got money for you to buy two nice dresses when your stock was running low. I see it all so clearly now. The antagonisms, hatreds, hostilities, fears that I had in me, all there for years, fought a last battle. They have been conquered, driven out. I know.

My friends spoiled me, and in return I developed a terrible need to justify it, to be the one who symbolised the sacrificial aspect of the movement. Many people are ready to sacrifice. I made a fetish of it at your expense. That Orchard St. menage, the 1306 barrack-room, what necessity was there to live like that? To submit you to it, right at the beginning, giving you nothing in return. You wanted to make contributions. I fought you. But as we drove on Wednesday and you talked so calmly and serenely (once you burnt with desire to write a pamphlet on the Negro question. I resented it. Thrust you aside. Instead of being happy and helping you) you sat driving and talking to me, so calm, so serene, so sure, and so splendid. All I could do was to thank my stars that you existed and I knew you; you said you could integrate me socially—I knew what you meant. You wanted people around—I have always wanted them too—the young ones in particular. They ought to be around. But the most important thing you said was that you and the others, Cuppy, Ceil, etc., could teach me how to apply the political line—but I wouldn't listen. Darling, I am going to listen. Something is terribly wrong with our movement and particularly in the

U.S. I have probed far, and we have something. But now to get it to people, that is a problem that is shaking the SWP After all their years of work they have little. There is the big question of the unions, but there is the question too of winning over individuals and integrating them—making them feel the party is theirs. We all have a lot to learn. You have plenty to learn too. But you can learn it. And I am beginning to feel all over that there is something which you and your particular friends can do, which some of us, more experienced and more developed ones can't. It is a tremendous problem but I notice that in Philadelphia (Nettie & Co.) and in Frisco Willie and Phil won people over. And Willie and Phil won workers. I am going to listen to you, darling, and we shall work it out. Bessie talks to me about it constantly. The people are around. They turn away from bourgeois society but they do not come. That bridge we must build—to help the objective movement. It will not be easy but you and Phil and Madeline, Yonny, Cecelia, Pete, Willie, have a role to play—I feel it strongly, first to learn, learn, learn, and then go out and bring them in and keep them. There is much in the Balance Sheet* that applies.

As you talked, however, something else emerged, your simple devotion, honesty, and elevated spirit. Darling, it burns now like an undying flame in my consciousness. These last few days, only since Sunday, have changed my attitude to you completely. But for that to happen, for me to see you as the rare and precious creature that you are I had to change. I have been wrong about you so often, always wrong, always falling short of you. My faith and confidence in you are not a roseate mirage of a man in love with a pretty girl. They come from experience—some of it hard and bitter. But I know you, now, darling, and my confidence is absolute.

So I want you to stay. I want you to meet me with the same confidence that of old you were ready to take every step.

You spoke of Lionel's belief that you would be back with me *in two years*. Two years, darling. Have we, you and I, struggled so hard, to wait now for two years? That is *wrong*. Two years suit his conceptions, not ours.

You want to do that work, to prove yourself, to get money to write. None of these is necessary. If you stay, within three weeks the introduction would be finished. If you work hard, within two weeks. And that will settle *everything*. It will put Dick in his place. I have the existentialist books. It will put them in their place. I trust your feeling about them absolutely. You will be revolutionary—this is not the time to delay; give them everything; and open fire on both Farrell and Howe.** It will hit the literary world and the rev'y movement like a bombshell and will make your reputation at one stroke. Sign it alone. We'll make it perfect. It will be *your* work. I'll see to that. Your ideas. I want *those*. Let us settle this once and for all. I'll teach you how to get the individual ideas down; and how to fuse them. It is time you did it, a complete concentrated piece of work. All the circumstances, Dick's work pirated, the impact the caucus has made everywhere, London and Paris, New York, all acts

---

* In 1947 James and his group published *The Balance Sheet*, a document justifying their split from the WP and tracing a history of American Trotskyism.

** In 1946 James T. Farrell and Irving Howe argued publicly over the interpretation of Lionel Trilling's "The Other Margaret," a story widely believed to have been prompted by Richard Wright's *Native Son*.

the stage for this right now. Malaquais and the rest, Sartre and all of them in Paris will get it hot and strong and in the vacuum that now exists in literature in the U.S., it will be like a rocket. It is your *duty*, Connie, *your duty* to stay here and put all you have into it. We shall do a publicity job on it, all languages into which Dick has been translated, which will startle these ineffective intellectuals. You have not one argument to oppose. There are things that I can see. What, when and how? The last year has proved that. This is one of them. Grab it with both hands.

Next, as soon as this is done, start with me on the book. The one will be splendid preparation for the other. I shall be on vacation for three months. Then I propose to tell JPC that I want to stay on here for three or four months more—working with the party. I shall fight if it is necessary every inch of the way. You say the word and I am here till Spring. By Spring, I am sure, long before, the book will be finished. And when you have it done, the world is then before you, before you and me, us.

I have $300, given to me for a purpose. I shall spend it if you say the word. I also expect to have $35.00 a week for the next few months. By the end of December I shall be on the SWP payroll again. There will not be luxury. There will be no grinding, shameful poverty. You have your mother. Ceil will be here. W and Phil and Marian in SF. These early weeks you can stay at home. Bessie will let us stay here, if we want, for a few weeks. We can get a place if we want one. You have your writing job. If Mr. K does not want it that way, let him go to hell. We, all of us, have struggled and suffered and helped each other and hurt each other to get someplace. Who is he to demand this and that and the other? I can see that this is a chance in a lifetime for us. I think of it this way. Gene and Francesca [Raskin], Ceil, Cuppy, Yonnie, Marian, Willie, Phil, Rae, your mother, yes, your mother too, all would say "That is the best thing for you and for him and for us, too." They would say that, wholeheartedly; it will not be a defeat for you darling. It will be a very great victory, and a victory for all of us. I love you, I want to love you. I want to take you in my arms and kiss you as I have never kissed you, to take pleasure and delight in you, and have communion with you as we have never had, as is impossible to people who have not gone through what we have gone through and who have not got to give what we have to give and can give only to each other. We could not give it to anyone else. How and when we shall work it out, we shall work out together. Together, without looking elsewhere when we speak, sure. Darling, there are I know other considerations. But weigh everything, put all we stand for on one side, as people, as revolutionaries, the work that is crying to be done and which only we can do, the people we have become, for during the drive darling, as your inner confidence was restored, you were a new person. Let others do some waiting, darling, it is time that they did. I need you. But I need you, not to lean on you, and drain you. I am finding my own way. But a man is to be judged, you remember, by what he needs in a woman. I need everything, and you have all that I need and more, far more, for you have not begun to expand as yet.

I feel already the stimulation to reach out and achieve, powers in me that you have awakened, to prepare and prepare and learn and build and pull people together for the time we are waiting for. I do not say that I cannot live without you, but now that I have allowed myself, have fought and am able to feel your loveliness and beauty and warmth, and have seen what a beautiful spirit you are, I know that without you the world for me would always be tinged with sadness, my life would always have an aching void. This tremendous period in which we live, the enormous demands on men, the tremendous potentialities created in us by the stage the world has reached, this makes us what we are. Men a generation ago, were and could be satisfied with less. It may seem that it was chance which brought us together. I don't think so. You in Fresno joined something. I thousands of miles away joined the same. I came, I saw, you conquered. And we have never been able to get away from each other. These last few days, God, dearest, what days they have been. We have helped to make each other what we are. We have reached maturity and understanding. All we have to do is to hold hands and exercise the courage and strength and experience that we now have. Darling, the love I have for you, the desire to enfold you with it constantly, is singing through me. I feel that if you only could sense it, you will cast all hesitation to the winds and come to me. I ask for a lot but it is because I have so much to give.

All my love, darling, for you, waking and sleeping, in joy or in sorrow, in public and in private life, never anything but loving you, holding you warm and safe in my heart.
Nello

October 11, 1947

I am in Gogol's office. I intended to stay at home and rest but he asked me to come down with him—he seems lonely and ready to be friendly. I wonder who are his *friends*. I am beginning to think that he is profoundly unhappy. I see how surrounded, I didn't want to use the word trapped, he is, emotionally.

Guess whom I just saw in the office. In 1940 when I stayed at your house, there lived in the next block or so a girl who had fine hands. She danced by herself rather well, too. But she was not goodlooking and she and her household were rather sloppy; wore glasses and her voice was low, with a certain precision of speech. She wore glasses and there was something peculiar in the way she looked at you—not very nice. I thought she was jealous of your youth and beauty. She was not in the party but close. However, she seems in now; she said she would see me to-night at the musicale. I said No. I shall go out or be down, upstairs, or something. But I wish to see no one. I just got her name. Anne Snipper. She is much much better dressed to-day than in 1940. She is not important. I saw her at your place and she remained in my mind. I want to tell you about me. I am not going to be tired any longer. No, Sirree. When the time comes for 20 hours a day I'll do it. Henceforth? Nothing doing. I'll have *time*. This hurry and strain. You said once that people should sit down and talk after the day's work—listen to some music, etc. I gave you some savage answer. Of course we do not live like bourgeois. But I propose to spend time on me and on us. Last year, this last one, I spent a deal of time, *doing nothing*, and fighting with myself. I could have spent it with you; book-buying, you remember? And I would so like you to go shopping with me. You went once in the Bronx and it was lovely.

Mice and bed-bugs. It was a scandal—a shame. Listen, sugar. If an apartment cost $60.00, we'll have it. I remember your asking me about Cuppy's place and my hesitating. Then you asked Tom to get a place and said $50.00 and asked me, looking at my face to see how I would take it. I don't want any wife of mine to ask me such questions in that way. It is *low*.

Bessie reminded me of one of Rae's famous jokes. The L. T. household in Coyoacan consisted of sometimes a dozen people. Serious financial crises would result in frantic discussions as to how to raise money and cut down expenses. Contribution of L. T. (organiser of the Red Army and originator of the plan for industrialization): Couldn't we use less ink?

I could do better than that.

Sugar, I am nervous. What is this hospital call and who in Frisco was calling, calling. Someone is *ill* and must see you. You have to go. This is me. I wonder what it is. Whatever happens, your place is *here* for the next three weeks at least. If someone is in hospital, then speak on the 'phone. Happiness is so near to me that I am full of alarms. Mice and bed-bugs. For Christ's sake. Sweetheart, in the backward W.I. my mother would have turned the house upside-down at the idea of bed-bugs. The place was always spotless. And bed-bugs, no love, and a jailer for a husband! I look at it and you and I wonder.

I just had hour with Jack Dale—as I saw him in 1940 he is to-day. He loves concrete dialectic, showing the d.l. at work in the life of the workers. Rather primitive stuff but useful, and does little harm if no good to speak of.

I want to share with you. On mornings, breakfast and making the bed—dinner, dishes; to talk, to work, to make demands. Darling, it is not only in books and in the future. It is here now. Somehow we were not satisfied with anything less. I can talk to you and accuse you of depreciating yourself in order to lessen your responsibility; but I can do this only because I now feel so confident about your organic integrity. I am sleepy.

But about you. You haven't begun yet. I *know* that. The tremendous crisis is due among other things to the need for doing something—your ideas have been stimulated, you have acquired knowledge, but you are now on the verge of a *leap*. You want to do so much that if you can't you'd rather die. All writers feel that at a certain stage. Maturity is near. Enough of talking; I want to do it. You think you want to justify yourself to your mother, etc. No. You want to do it for yourself, not to prove anything but fundamentally because the time has come. That is what is burning you up. And my vicious folly hit you hard. But you'll see the rush of ideas, the way your mind will jump, the building of the article—one complete whole. I'll tell you about others—Rae and Grace, and Bill. You know much less than they but you have learnt plenty in the past year and you are faster, more imagination, more *creative power* with a deeper logic than all of them except where Grace is concerned (logic). But you have not been trained in philosophy and you have the habit of the concrete. I am sitting pretty, to watch it during the next days, and then see you when it is finished. Want me to tell you something?

You lovely, tender-hearted darling? As soon as you felt it safe with me, *you*, you were ready to devastate Dick and put him in his place. You had it there all the time. You have no illusions about D really. Dick and J.T.F. and all of them, your judgment is sure and ruthless—*genuine Bolshevik*—much sharper, more severe than mine really. Don't you *know* that? Well, let it go. Hit hard. I'll keep the whole tidy and keep you from boners when you jump too far, and fill in the gaps in your knowledge, point new roads. You *always* understand immediately. Doing this sort of thing has been the greatest pleasure, or one of, in my life. But doing it with you, and watching your lovely face, and rich and voluptuous personality. This is to live. And all the time blows for our enemies and positive creative work for socialism. How is it possible to wish for more? We are lucky. It is ours. We fought for it, struggled, refused to settle for less. It is here.

I feel good, all set like match-day in my athletic days, or a convention in recent years, when I had everything well in hand; work, strenuous effort, difficulties, but the preparation and the training have been good and the aim will be achieved! Here's the best of luck to you, darling. Over the next weeks power will be exploding in you like a molecular chain reaction. This article will be famous, and it will be *good*. Gird yourself. Grace's, Willie's, mine on dialectic, and now yours. (Marian's? also). They are a series of explosions. (The woman question is next on the list by the way. See how it is stirring in the caucus, you can feel it.) But you are lucky in that the circumstances give you a dramatic setting. And yet it isn't luck. You talked and talked and talked to Dick and he finally gave it to you.

Well, miracle, I don't know what to do with this letter. I'll keep it till you call and then see if [I should] send it special.

Home after ride with Lou 10 p.m.

There have been happenings. Darling, you *have* to love me and keep on loving me and stick close, close to me.

I am now upstairs and there are a lot of people downstairs for the musicale. L and I have just returned. It is 10 o'clock. I have walked straight upstairs. You are here with me. I loved you very much this afternoon when you spoke to me on the 'phone.

Now all during the week B has been telling me about this musicale, some branch. I said *No*, I shall have nothing to do with it. I am going out. B said "The c'des will be glad to see you!" I said "*No*. I'll go to bed." She said "No, go upstairs and read." I said "No. They will come." She said: "A few c'des would like to say hello." (Here she comes again. No. It is Everett. This ends it. (hour later) Bessie has come up and we have quarrelled in front of Everett. I will not go down. She wants me to. I have refused. She is mad and I have told her off. She had gone down, come back for Everett and we didn't speak. We shall have it out finally. I'll leave here if necessary. When you hear the talk I had with L and link it up with this you will see something, sister, *something*. Bessie has a new black dress.

So this ends here. We must talk about this, for hours. You are in it with me, you know. And you have been holding out on me. But I have been on you too. So we are quits.

It is about two hours later. All have gone. I was lying on the couch upstairs covered with a blanket. Snipper, same girl, came up and talked a few minutes. But I wouldn't budge, so she left. Now I am downstairs, everybody is gone, and I am writing to you, most ostentatiously at the table in the dining room while Bessie cleans up. The atmosphere is freezing—I am contributing my share of the freezing. There were 60 people downstairs and I was to come down and relax with them! This was N.Y. all over again. You remember that meeting at which Rae made me speak? I was thinking of it. I saw Norman and Selma* that night outside on the roof. You came out. We talked a bit. It must have been horrible for you. Now I wanted you here to go on the roof and to talk to me. Tonight I wanted you all the time and I wanted you that night too, and only *a few people* would have said anything, 90% of the people there would have left us alone, and the *others* would have been stunned into silence. Times change but people change with them. If they can't, then they are lost. Imagine, my dear, 70

---

* Selma Weinstein became James's third wife in the 1950s.

people. I was to relax with them! How in the name of heaven was I to do that? 70 strange people. The request was not only unreasonable, it was subconsciously but very powerfully motivated. It was a protest against my preoccupation with you. I knew it as such and fought it as such. I think L knows it too. I am learning fast. I'll tell you, however, what I haven't learnt yet, when I see you. But things have happened, and they are not personal things at all. They are profoundly political—I know. But I have not worked them out completely as yet. I am still writing—B is in the living room smoking. L has gone in. *Your presence pervades the place???* Yes, you'll see. Darling, I have not been winning victories. I am sitting at your feet, but happy in this that like Portia, I am not bred so dull but I can learn. You are pushing deep into every fibre of my life. I write. B remains inside. The tension is enormous. A battle has been fought and a lot of people have been defeated. But they all don't know it yet. I have defeated people but defeats are no comfort to me. I have to win you, darling. Life without you is becoming impossible. We. To-night has been something. I write. B inside smoking. L is in bed. And she knows I am writing to you. *Everything, everything* to-day is the same thing—universality reigns. You are the centre of my life. I dreamt for years of someone like you, darling, glimpsed only part of you but enough to hold on for eight years. But now I see you I am that rarest of lovers, one who would not change a hair in his mistress's eyebrow.

Love
[unsigned]

P.S. B has gone in, without saying goodnight. I look out, the curtain is drawn, and he sits up in bed, reading. Darling, I cannot wait to tell you. He spoke to me tonight from out of his own frustrated life. He said "Life tends to drive you into a rut, into a depression, everyone. You can only meet it if you have someone knit to you in spirit, stimulating you to overcome..." I was dumbfounded.

He spoke of you. I told him what you were.

He said: "People like that are rare. You are lucky." "Yes," I said, "I know I am. But if I lose her."

"I think the situation is good for you," he said gravely. "I have been noting her magnetism, her spirit... you meet such people rarely.... I met one some years ago." He spoke a few words and then stopped. Look at what has happened! I let this household know that I am desperately in love with you, and want you above all things, and at once it opens up before me. But it must wait. One of the *less* astonishing things. He could have kept out of the war, but he went, he says, because of the relationship that had developed. He was hoping that a long absence would create a new situation. Darling, I can't get over that statement. And every second through this long evening I have wanted you near, wanted you near; knew that all this was happening through you—you were me and I was you. I *wanted* you so.

Bessie is back, reading your outline, 2 o'clock in the morning. She is reading it and reading it and reading it.... One conclusion I have *leapt* to. The revolutionary movement as such divides no couples. It exposes them, their own weaknesses of character, their inadequacies.... This is a *very* complicated business but we shall work it out. I am going to bed. I wish you were here for me to fold you to me. I feel so warm towards you, like a house all heated and fire glowing and you outside, in the cold, looking in but nervous that dangers lurk. Nothing lurks, darling. Come and search, in every nook and corner you will find cupboards, parcels, all done up in

various ways, but all of them when opened prove to contain nothing but love for you.
Sunday a.m.

Up early. Spun Judy and Eugene round holding them by the feet—how they don't get dizzy I don't know. Then breakfast—packed with drama—to this moment. I did my share—got over last night's difficulty. I'll tell you. But to go back.

First, I have worked out with finality the method of the way we shall work at the Outline. *Your* party. Wonderful it will be. And I was nervous about sex. If I had *talked* to you, worked *with you*, that is what you wanted, your nature craves it, a community, and then I would not have been afraid of you at all. By Monday one o'clock all will be well. In fact it is well already. Yes, already. I love you.

Now about last night. Where we shall get time to work (and *this* is going to be a dazzling piece of work—as soon as I tell you you will see—written from the *inside* out, *pure* dialectic, in itself, method and matter inseparable; *your* party, I attending to you, as a trainer his charge. You will have it all. And this being our challenge, it is to hit as hard at the intellectuals, Negroes and revolutionaries as we hit at the WP and SWP. But let me go on.)

Last night L said: "Since you came and this interest of yours in Constance began, B has changed. Her nervousness, tension and the way she shouts at the children and makes an issue of everything are worse than before. . . . You see you are a man who exercises a considerable fascination over women and along with politics and what you represent there is also mixed up sexual desires and jealousy of which the women themselves are not aware."

Sweetheart, I almost froze. He was as calm as ever. He said "That's why I asked you the other night." I couldn't say much. But what was there to say?

I have known now for three years that Rae is in love with me, and knows it; but does every mortal thing to hide it. I know one or two other people know too. And I think you know but were inhibited by my attitude. That's what I meant by holding out. . . . That whole business has to be probed. . . . B, he says, is jealous in a way of Rae. She is ambitious, he says. . . . But I think of something else. Rae could not bear to see me sitting or talking easily to anyone. She always found some urgent political issue that needed settling at once—that could not wait. Sometimes I had to be very firm.

There is also the question of the trip to Europe in 1945 and the question of "getting something out of it." I never told you, I never trusted you, I thought it might affect you, that through you I might be softened. It's over darling. We are each other's.

You know, the thing is this, simplified. If the decision is to be made: Should I go back to England or not (apart from the bourgeoisie persecuting me), the decision rests finally with the International. Then it rests with the SWP, then with the caucus, or now strictly speaking with the caucus members of the National C'tee of the SWP—we represent the caucus while it is disbanded. Finally with me. Now that is the hierarchy, the order of disciplinary power. In reality things work out quite differently. The I.E.C. [International Executive Committee] of set policy will not *insist* that the SWP send me somewhere *if* the SWP does not *want* to. The SWP normally would not *insist* on the caucus "sending" me away. The caucus would not force *me* against my wishes. We know that that sort of pressure does not work out. It is rarely exercised. If everybody is in favor of something, then we trust to time and good sense to make a comrade see that he should agree. (I am coming to us, darling.)

Now in a case like this if I start an agitation, *I* get the caucus to agree and bring pressure, I can get my way right up. If the I.E.C. starts pressure, or if the SWP does, I have great powers of resistance. In fact once the government leaves me alone, there is as good a case as any for my staying here. I have not worked at the problem at all. But where you and I come in is this. Any such decision depends to a large degree on me, on what I think. And I try always to act according to the interests of the movement. Always. But, not in any particular case, but in general I have had this attitude towards you. Will she understand? Is she devoted enough? Does she know what proletarian discipline is? Could she work it out with me and decide on the merits of the case and not from "flighty" personal prejudices? Darling, don't blame me too quickly. Think of this. Our finest people, Marx, Engels, L and T, had wives of the highest Bolshevik quality. But they said, let's go and the wives went. Somehow the action seemed, very often was dictated by political circumstances. But Rose Karsner, e.g., follows Cannon.* I have never felt that I wanted a wife who followed me around. I didn't want it. I am beginning to think I am a good person, I want so much from my woman. But the Bolshevik attitude is so difficult to learn, I distrusted you. These last days, however, I have jumped over all obstacles. In so far as I personally work out something, then take it to the caucus; then to the SWP, then listen to arguments, weigh and consider, agree, fight, procrastinate; in so far as they say something to me, I want you in. You have integrity and devotion, and simplicity. *We*. If you think I have been winning "victories" over you, you are wrong. The closed areas that I wanted opened are wide open. It was hard but I knew that I could not live that way any longer. I can talk to you. You have powerful contributions to make. These last few days have been like a rocket flight. I move so fast because of all our past. *We*. Partners. I feel doubled and trebled. Darling, it is hurting me horribly that I cannot hold you to me—just to feel for a minute that we are one. I know now what you wanted. I had to feel it before I could love you. And you see the terrible resistance I had to overcome.

[unsigned]

October 25, 1947

Well, precious, you must *not* be despondent. Sure you have been buffeted around, not for eighteen months but for eight years, and more. What you need now, and I too, is a vacation, a real one, *no work*, and we'll get it. Patience. And we'll sit around and take physical exercise and recover ourselves. You have undergone a great strain, violent and abrupt reversals of direction, that would shake up anybody—even the sexual experiences will have affected you. So, darling, don't decry yourself. Fight the feeling of needing reassurance (don't jump). Believe in yourself. I do. Why shouldn't *you* believe in yourself. The work is *not* good. Yes. *Not* good. So what! Tackle it again to-morrow. Have a little fun over the week-end reading, going into town, maybe a picnic on Sunday, perhaps a show, and then plug away on Monday again. Plug away. Keep plugging away. I believe in you absolutely. The thing will be

---

* Karsner was Cannon's wife.

Separation and Limbo (1947–8) 309

finished in three weeks, and if not in three weeks in four. So what! I am *not* going to impose my ideas on you. You dig something out of yourself. Sweat it out. I am in charge. Remember? I know what is required. This is your apprenticeship, your training period. Fight it. To-night you started to be ill-tempered (do *not* jump). You said "I don't want to sit around. I must read something," etc. You fought it off. Good. You *must* stop thinking about your weaknesses, your constant emotional upsets, your wasting of your time, the certainty that it will take months to finish the essay. You know what you are doing? You impugn *my* judgment at every step. *You are saying exactly what all our most hostile critics are saying.* She is no good, really. He is the one who is inflating her expectations. Well, precious, why should *you* do that to us? And you surely don't want me to baby you and pamper you. I shan't. I am absolutely certain and confident of myself and of you, and what I am doing. And you must pull yourself together out of a defeatist attitude. Any emotional break down, upset, sudden tears, doubts of our failure, as this morning I understand. They will come. You have cause to be doubtful, to fear the future. But with the work—*no. You inhibit yourself.* And if we are not careful, you will soon be forcing me into a position where I shall have to be coaxing you along inch by inch. I shall not do it. The work is *not* good. Tomorrow it may be bad; and all next week you may be struggling. But by Friday you will have something dug out of you. How do you think *good* work is done? No, no pampering from me here. You have to battle and learn strength, there is no other way. About ourselves, every time you falter I shall be there, helping you, trying to make you get over the doubts and fears. I understand completely this morning. I don't think you weak and silly. Christ, no. I think you are brave, and courageous and strong. There are other things we shall talk about, tough things, this question of Fil and Everett and his hostility to giving money, characteristic of workers as Bessie said, if he suspects that those he is giving it to are not as self-sacrificing as he is. I thought I noticed a reaction on your part. We'll talk about it in time, and our finances. One thing you can count on me—to talk *everything out*. I love you. You make me happy in a thousand ways I had not ever hoped to be. I respect your personality. In my own way, I respect Judy's and Eugene's. I offered you a partnership—because I believe that I can let myself go with you. I am ready to quarrel with you and disagree violently with you on any God damn question. I accept you inside of me as an equal. I am not afraid of you or anything connected with you. All that is over. You can do the work. The work will be done. Now stand up to it. If it is bad for two weeks I'll tell you so every day. I shall not fret over this. For it will mean that I shall begin having *serious* reservations with you. And that is over. I am learning fast, you see, and throwing down all the obstacles between us. Every time you feel emotionally upset, unhappy, doubtful, reacting to anything I have said, come and curl up in my arms and cry and tell me—come to me and tell me. I wouldn't think less of you, but more. Little by little, every day, we'll build up that confidence you need and that I helped so much to deprive you of. I didn't offer 50% of me to a baby or a weakling. No, sister, I offered it to you because I had confidence in you more than in anyone else. So that is why, on the work, forget that wretched letter. Bring it out, let us read it, talk about it and then burn it. To hell with it. I want you to tackle this work as you tackled the essay on the woman-hater. So sweets, pull yourself together, will you? I am not feeling so good. Do I care? Hell, no! I have the most wonderful girl in the world for my wife, and I know she is the most wonderful. But she needs to make an effort and pull herself out of something. Make it. I am seeing after everything. Strain and anxiety have caught up with me again. I feel it. I feel the pressure of work to be done. My hands are beginning to slip back. I shall have to fight to rebuild myself. I can see how tough it is going to be. But with you I can conquer all things. The old devil that was me is conquered. He is gone. I may sit quiet and preoccupied. But it isn't the old me. No, darling. The real me is coming out—and he is not so well, tired, needing a rest, with lots to do that he would rather not have to do now, but grateful for all the good fortune that has befallen him these two weeks and depending on you and confident of you. One last word. Don't be nervous about your rights. Give yourself to me completely. I'll meet you more than half-way. How far I am prepared to come to you will suprise you in time. I am not hesitating at any obstacle, though I may stop and think a bit, because of unfamiliarity. You'll see; *kisses, many of them, everywhere.*

[unsigned]

[August 1, 1948, enroute to Reno, Nevada]

Darling,

How are you and how is N?* I am improving. I hope you are good. You looked very sad at the very last moment. It stabbed me.

I went to bed at once—read Time—the story of the runners is very very interesting and explains a little about me. I slept from about 2:30–6:30. It was light—I got up—didn't know it was so early—but ate at 7. Dozed all morning and have just had lunch. Good enough—ham this a.m. and fish. But, oh, sweetie, it is a misfit compared to our breakfasts and dinners. I tell you, precious, I miss you at every turn. The people are interesting in a dull way and I am working out some ideas on my magnum opus, and some good ones too, but I wish it were different. The tum is good and ought to be, so much care is being taken. I am beginning to respond to the journey—just the journey—at the end of it begins something else. But henceforth all my long train journeys will be just 50%. I am not wanting to come back. I want *you* to be here. Then we would both perk up and do what we want to do and both miss the breakfasts and dinners, and make the best that we can of the substitutes. But we'll have it soon. We'll find a way or make it. Agreed? Agreed.

I remember the last time I traveled here—I was going to Detroit—and I wrote you from various spots. I don't write so much this time. But, sweetheart, you understand. The crises are so rapid. For years I had hoped to have *one* vacation—just one. But it was ruined, you remember. Then the case; the Negro Qu'n; the Convention. And everything underground, whispering. As soon as I leave N.Y. for a few hours I begin to see it in perspective. And you stick it, fighting to help me. Believe me I am very conscious of it, always. I know you are good and solid and faithful and true. I love you, more now than ever. And I now have a third addition—Nob. Already I think of us always as three. I am full of love for you, darling. Take care of yourself for the sake of the three of us. I am tired and tum is nervous. But I am on the road

---

* Throughout his Reno letters, James refers to N, Nob or Nobbie, the nickname he and Webb gave their son, C.L.R. James Jr.

up. And I hear by the grapevine that there *is* accommodation for people like me, where I am going—plenty of it. I haven't checked yet but I pass on the good news. I'll write again after I check up on things at Chicago.

                        Love,
                        N

New York Central System
En route

                        [August 2, 1948]
                        Sunday a.m.

Well, sugar. It was good to talk to you last night. You sounded a little tired. I hope everything is well with you and Nob. I wrote you by the way *before* Chicago; and once after that, on the train.

I had a good trip, was a bit "sick" at times, over-tired. But I read a little, talked to a few people, and learnt a lot about life, which I will tell you when I see you, except for one story which I shall tell later.

When I came to R [Reno], I consulted the Red Cap. He gave me an address at once. I went to eat first—not a bad lunch, giblets, rice, etc., 70 cents. Then I took a taxi—a white man and I asked him if *he* knew anywhere. He took me to a black parson's place. They are just completing the rooms—a kind of annex. $10.00 a week. The room is about 9 ft square and private. There is a bath and shower upstairs, but no hot water. There is hot water in the house though. I drove over to see the other place, it was a room in a house, I would have been a roomer, and there were a lot of women, probably curious, about the place. I preferred the other one, and took it. For the time being, the lady here tells me to buy my meals and she will cook them. That will stop soon, however, as she is going away. I hope the real mistress of the house will continue. If not I shall eat in restaurants. The Jim Crow here in restaurants is powerful. But there are 2 or 3 places set aside for Negroes—one joint, the Chinese restaurant, and a Negro place. However, one can eat.

After this I went to the Greyhound Station and "accosted" the Negro porter. He knew somewhere I could go if I wanted a room. Boy, the solidarity among Negroes is something. He asked if I was here for long. I said 6 weeks or so. He said Oh! Divorce. I said I wanted to see a Negro lawyer if there were any. He said there were none yet but one fellow was going to be soon, and I would find him at the Y.M.C.A. Off I went and sho' nuff at the Y.M.C.A. was a Negro, Mayfield, who takes his finals on Monday. I told him what I wanted. He recommended me to—a woman, a friend of his from law school in Oakland. He said she was a good lawyer and would not gouge my eyes out. I was a bit nervous. I asked him if her sex and my race would not prejudice matters. He said not at all. He called her and I am to see her on Monday at 3. I would prefer a man, but I may need a friend—and Mayfield is willing to be. I have to say if not to-day, perhaps to-morrow, certain things and I think here is a safe place. To-morrow I will see. So, sweetie, so far, so good. We'll hope for the best. But, for better or for worse, we go through. And honey, that was the packingest bag that was ever packed. If you had come out of it at the end I would not have been surprised.

                        Love,
                        N

C.L.R. James
c/o Mrs. Scott
539 Sierra
Reno, Nevada

Airmail Special Delivery
[August 2, 1948]

Well, honey, 11:30 or thereabouts. I had breakfast—and was reading the paper and listening to the radio—what a blessing it is. That and the clock. I am indebted to you every hour. It is tough here—lovely, lovely weather—hot but no humidity at all. But I feel exhausted somehow, I'll get over it I expect. I don't know if I'll complete this letter now. A sort of fatigue has me. I feel only to lie and read silly stuff—these silly papers—and the sillier radio. But about yesterday.

It began in the morning. The landlady introduced me to a young fellow 29, in dark glasses. Very good-looking, particularly a neat figure about 5 ft. 8. I was saying that I wanted to go to some seaside place or lake—if any. He then said he would take me, and when I asked frankly about cost, he said it would not cost me a penny. He asked if I minded whether he and his friends stopped for some highballs every now and then. I answered. He said I perhaps was religious. I said not very much. He told me afterwards that he did not want me to find myself in company whose procedures or conversation might embarrass me. He liked to get these things clear in advance. At about 10:30 he knocked at my door. We went out to a large car—Chev. '41 with a mulatto girl sitting in front—neat, short, and with a very large Negroid mouth. We went to pick up someone else, dark fellow who had a hangover, and who lived with two other Negro couples in a fairly nice house. One of the women had a brother, an orchestra leader who made records. But *the* thing about the house was a baby—a white baby, yellow-haired, blue-eyes, about a year old.

The parents had given him to this young woman to keep. *All* these Negroes loved him. They played with him and fondled him and just loved him. If he had been Nob he couldn't have been more secure. Paul, the mechanic in reply to a delicate enquiry from me, held forth while playing with the baby.

"Plenty of these whites do this. Many of the so-called white liberals grow up like this. After they grow up they can't forget where they come from and they don't go along with the rest of the whites. You see, he don't know anything about prejudice. If some of his own people came in here now, he wouldn't notice them. But when he grows up, you never know how they will turn out."

All the time playing most lovingly with the kid. Not one of them showed the slightest, the faintest hint of ill-feeling. I think they loved the kid more than usual because it was white and there could be warm feeling without prejudice. They overflowed. It was worth the whole day.

We set off.

The black fellow moaned for 20 minutes. He wanted a girl to go with him, but couldn't think up one who was available. I watched him. He said that there was no fun if he didn't have a girl to talk to.

We started to climb, 10,000 feet up, then 4000 feet down. A superb lake. All we did was to drive round it—about 80 miles. We stopped 3 or 4 times for whiskey and coke. They had brought half-a-bottle. The only lack of harmony was a period of jokes. I have to think this out but they made some extraordinarily stupid, dull, and vulgar jokes, and laughed uproariously. I distinguish between my prejudices and the jokes as jokes. None of our friends would have been other than very embarrassed. They felt *from the start* that I was not one to like these jokes. I said I was not good at that sort of thing and they told me another. Otherwise, they and I got on wonderfully. I made a few sprightly remarks as usual and they laughed uproariously and said that I was a "killer." They liked my jokes so that there was no distance between us.

The lake was lovely, the drive splendid. It should have been a perfect outing. Yet it wasn't. For there were no colored people in sight. We were excluded. All round were houses, people, cabins, cars, people bathing. But Negroes were out. The exclusion was always present. It did not ruin the day but it poisoned it. You and Dick between you have taught me much about the Negro question.

The girl worked behind the bar at the Dixie Club—a Negro club—a horrible joint. But she was a lady and very self-possessed, calm and sure of herself. She and Paul sat in front, saying pleasant things to one another. Paul is a peculiar man. He was making love to her all day. Jimmy, isn't she sweet? Honey talk to me, tell me something. Thelma, you liking this? Every minute. Very warm. But he was a tyrant. Darling, I want you to come in here with me. Come on, darling, I want you to come—you don't want breakfast? But I want some and I want you to have some with me. You must—talk to me, darling, tell me something, make me feel good. She was quiet but acquiescent. Swift was a notoriously savage man with his women, too, but was capable of great tenderness at times. A woman once told Thackeray that she would put up with all his savagery for the sake of his tenderness. Maybe that's why old-fashioned women loved to be beaten.

Half-way occurred something I am slowly learning to understand. Some man had gone to Thelma telling tales about Paul. Paul blew up—cursed the man, was angry with Thelma, spoke his mind about the guy. Melville behind stopped talking to listen, smiled and enjoyed it. Thelma pacified Paul, put her head on his shoulder. His anger was gone in a few minutes and all was as before. My past, my dear, has made all this very strange to me. But in the course of his grumbling Paul said some strange things.

"In this town, I can't find anything to do. As soon as I finish work I leave it and drive into the country—anywhere, I love it, and I want to get away. I feel I am going mad if I stay in it or go to the alley for all I can do there is to get drunk. Sometimes I don't even stop to eat. . . .

"Why should he *do* that? I don't trouble him. God! You cannot trust a friend. Live by yourself you are a recluse. Yet when you meet people you cannot trust them. They do things like this. You cannot have a friend. You cannot trust anyone. What is life without warm friendship?"

I was astonished, and watched him more closely. He asked me often if I was liking it. He apologised for any crudeness in their behavior—there was none. But they accepted me as a gentleman and an "intellectual"—tho' I said nothing, did nothing intellectual—discussed nothing. And yet they were very easy with me.

I sat alone while Paul drank at the bar. He insisted on waiting to take me home. On the way home and when we reached we talked.

He was from California. He had been a merchant seaman. His people were respectable and had some money. He married early but while he was away his wife wrecked the business and lived with another man. There was a divorce—that was why he had come to Reno. But having got his divorce he stayed. The rest had better be in his own words.

"When I came here for four weeks I was crazy almost. When I sat in the barber's chair for a minute I had to get up, I felt I was going mad. Then I decided to stay here. I am a machinist, I joined the union and worked. But here is no place. I drive out all the time. I love the country. All that matters here is money, and warm friendship. . . .

"And friendship is hard to get. Those two in the car to-day were not my friends really. He is not a friend and will never be anybody's friend. He is too clever. But he makes me laugh. And for that I will pay $10.00, $20.00, $50.00. I will pay for I want what he has. But he never holds up his end anytime. I don't mind. The girl, I know her only two weeks. To-day all day in the car she was trying to make me. Nobody can make me. I have been through too much, seen too much. Either you are in love, and then you don't have to make anybody, or you can be friends.

"I don't mind friendship with a woman. It can be the same as with a man. But it is hard. These girls, whether they like you or not, are always fishing for you to say things to them. Then when you say it, altho' it means nothing, they try to get you to make good on the promises. So soon you reach a spot where you either have to make love or go your way."

He then repeated the episode of the man who had slandered him.

"What can you do? There is no friendship. Sometimes you get bitter. When they behave like that you don't know who to trust. You meet a man, you want to be friends, but he can hurt you so you don't know what to do. So I go out and drive all round the country. Perhaps if we can know our destiny it would help. But I don't think so. When the evil that will happen to us is coming and we know it we might prefer to die. I do not expect as much good in the future as I have had evil in the past. But we have to struggle, that is every man's destiny, to go on and take it as it comes."

I have not done justice—he never hesitated for a word and he spoke beautifully. He has read but "Duel in the Sun," etc., are for him literature. It was quite a day, precious. He is an intensely human person, with nothing in his life to hold him. I said once "There should be some sort of revolution in this place." He replied quickly "Sure there should be." But I kept away from all politics because one thing leads to another.

I don't know the rights of the matter between him and the girl. But she wants him for she told me once when he went to get water for the trip.

"Jimmy, you think it's wise to fall in love?" I replied that *if* it was the right person it was fine. She said "I have fallen in love with Paul, and I wonder if I was wise. You think he is a good person to fall in love with?" I said I thought Paul was a fine guy, and time would tell.

Their easy relationship with one another, and with me, the sophistication, what Paul really thought and what he did all day, all this is very very different from the English workers I know. And Paul, I think, is a superior person. If he could exercise his savoir faire, his way of dealing with all sorts of people, and his terrible need for friendship in a movement of some kind he would accomplish great things for himself and his friends. It was wonderful to be with them just as ordinary people and not an object for politics. Paul has been in China, the Philippines, etc., over half the world. And he is a superb driver. Yet he is a plain, down-to-earth proletarian type—despite everything—one of the workers without a trace of intellectualism. He says he wants to arrange a party or picnic, something nice for me. I am a bit nervous. One of the necessities, it seems, is a girl. And I draw the line at being saddled with some dame brought for me, and whom I shall have to pay some attention to. I don't want but one dame, and she is far away. But these people somehow matter to me—I know because I have not forgotten them. They keep coming back to my mind. So sweetie, that's it. When I began I didn't think I could write a page. But I have made it. I love you. Tell me all about the Dick thing. Love for you and Nobbie.

N

C.L.J.
c/o Mrs. Scott
539 Sierra—Reno, Nevada

T'y

Dear Honey,

I have just received your letter with all the enclosures. Thank you. I hope you and N are O.K. I am better than yesterday, not so tired. Now for the news. I went to see the lawyer Charlotte Hunter yesterday at 3. She is in the thirties, active, friendly, knows all the Negroes in the place. I told her the elements of the story— mentioned that I was not a citizen. She said the divorce would be easy. She would write to J [Juanita James] at once. After my 6 weeks, we would give J notice again. In ten weeks it would be O.K. The law was that divorce could be granted if no cohabitation for 3 years. "Sixteen years!" she said, "No trouble." If J chose to cross-file, let her. After 6 weeks I could leave and come back to Reno. She gave me some other points about my stay here, leaving on Sat'y night and coming back Monday night, and not losing residence, etc. She also said that J might demand alimony, might ask for money from me so as to contest the case, etc. But all these were merely legal *possibilities*. We had no cause to worry about them. She had no reason to doubt that I would get the divorce.

Then came finances. She said she could not charge me as she did not know my financial status. She was very good and asked me finally if I could pay 300 all told. I said yes. Then she pressed me about writing J at once. I stalled. She seemed interested in me and asked about my financial status. The quicker she wrote to J, the easier it would be for me. (I should say that I began by asking her point-blank: would you as a white woman suffer from prejudice from the law. She said No, not at all. But if you feel doubtful, I can send you to a man. I decided to go on *discussing* and ask for time to decide.)

So, discussing finances, I told her I was a writer. She as I said seemed interested. Did I wish to work? I said I would be glad to. What? Did I want her to arrange a lecture for me? I said No, I preferred to be quiet. I said I would like to work outdoors on a ranch. She said she knew a rancher. She called him up at once, and said she could recommend me, I was well-educated, etc., etc. She gave me a boost. Sad results. He said he wanted to have nothing to do with well-educated people for that sort of work. He had tried it before and it had never worked out. She pressed him. He said if anything turned up at his place, he would see, and he would ask someone near. The ranch was 35 miles out, at Lake Pyramid, in the middle of the desert—warmish water, on an Indian reservation, isolated, guests, but otherwise uninhabited. Priceless for me.

Looking at everything I decided to go a little further. I told her the divorce would help me in my request for citizenship. What helped me was an incident which took place. The phone rang. She spoke, then put the receiver down and gestured. "The F.B.I.," she said. "They swarm all over the place and they are very efficient." I was startled. Reno is a little town, very few Negroes, and I stick out. She invited me to dinner at her house and then we would go at once to the man she had spoken to, the rancher. I said O.K. Then it was I told her some more.

Dinner was for 6, two other couples, friends of hers seeking divorces, her and me. After dinner we drove out. The place is marvellous. She wanted the man to see me, she said. We stayed there for a bit. The rancher introduced us to a Miss Howard who had the place next to his. She, her fiance, and a friend, wanted a man to take care of things. She spoke to me. I spoke my piece and she said she would think it over. I mentioned the *possibility* of my wife coming to help. We left and came home. She said she would see Miss Hunter to-day.

I saw H this a.m.; and (after long thinking) I told her that there was more to my case than met the eye—nothing dishonest but maybe she ought to know. After talking it over, she said she was not curious, as long as I was sure it would not affect the legal conduct of the case. I finally told her. I had written books the govt considered subversive. I was not a Communist nor a member of the C. P. The govt wanted to get me out on technical grounds. I wanted to clarify my marital status to force them to attack me politically. I was on bail. She said, "Keep quiet about it."

There were one or two things I didn't like. She had attended a Wallace* meeting and when Paul Robeson came thru', she entertained him. But she said in [the] course of casual conversation that she had never done anything subversive and probably wouldn't. . . . And she obviously is strong on the Negro question. Last night when the car stopped to drop me off she shouted to the red-cap "So and so, this is Mr. James. Take good care of him and help him." I listened to her carefully. She is in my view a liberal, sympathetic to the radicals and the Negroes. She said that she does not practice law; for her it is a form of service. The F.B.I. people had talked to her about her clients—immigration cases of Mexicans, etc. I was relieved. Furthermore Mayfield, the Negro, is not a Stalinist.

I feel fairly confident and this place is so small that I terribly wanted a lawyer who in case of any difficulty would be on my side so to speak. She seemed the type. However it isn't clinched yet.

Just an hour ago she called me to say that there seems some hitch on the job—and we will not know for certain for a few days—but if it comes through I alone will get board + $75.00; I and wife will get board + $100, to begin with. I hope it works out. We would be together, really hidden away; the money problem would be eased; and we'll have a chance to live quietly together. Otherwise, 10 weeks will be an awful long time to be away from you, sweetie. Now I am tired. I'll mail this. I love you.

N

R. J. c/o Scott
539 Sierra
Reno, Nevada

---

* Henry Wallace, who had been Vice President during the war, was influential in launching the Progressive Party, and became its Presidential candidate in 1948.

Tues'y [August 5, 1948]

Sugar, I love you. It is now 5:30. All day I have been lying in bed except going out for breakfast. The lady who cooked for me has left. I had a home lunch—salami and biscuits, etc. Now, no alarms. I have oranges, milk, cream, apple juice in an ice-box on this side of the place. I go out to eat. That's why I missed you last night. I went to the show—Duel in the Sun, a re-visit as I saw it months ago, in California. Still no good except for the astonishing way in which that Selznick has cliche after cliche, character, situation and spectacle, all trimmed down and served up. The only piece of real life in the thing was Walter Houston as a parson. The rest was all kitsch, I think the word is, but S is a maestro at it; and I noticed too that the actors, even the capable ones, play the parts as they are expected to play it by the audience. The whole thing is marvellously tailored, even to the bits of social significance. (I believe, however, that there was interwoven in this a very subtle piece of anti-racial prejudice.) The heroine is a half-Indian girl, of a whoring mother. Two sons of the senator one good, one bad fall in love with her. Even the bad one might have married her but that his father stopped it. But the good one is only prevented from marrying her because the bad one comes in between. Then the chief overseer, a *good* one, was about to marry her when the bad son shoots him. The mother of the boys loves her. Every good character loves her, and a bad character. She is the victim of race. But Selznick does not *preach* that and imperil his 4 million bucks. The production plays up the conflict between her good and evil instincts. But when you go home you *reflect* that she never had a break. But, sweetie, Walter Houston added something to our joint stock—a lecherous, lustful frontier parson—"genuine," his usual competence and imagination.

Sweetheart, why did I write the above? I didn't intend to. I have been so tired—but, I fear, a mental sickness. I could barely walk out this a.m. I read magazines, movie and True Romance, to go to bed. I found by the way that the stories in True Romance are much more significant than those in Collier's and the S.E. Post. Here it seems the proletariat scores heavily on the petty-bourgeoisie. People sleep before marriage, wives leave husbands, etc., live, come back; psychoanalysis is rampant; they are by no means literature but they are very very indicative. They are a curious grasping at the real problems, far, far removed from the slick S.E.P. stories.

I am tired, sort of psychologically sick. But I have managed to do a solid piece of reading of Guérin's Fr. Rev'n; I have made notes on L. T.'s thesis about plan. It will be a wreck when I am done; and I have thought about you and me. Plenty. In all spheres I am making progress. Ideas are beginning to flow—on all three. I am *doing nothing*—I am too weary. Things are just happening. And I know I shall in a day or two be well on my way. I had a bath, a cold one at 4; imagine; a shower. It freshened me up. I am going out to eat. I have to. But I said: I must write my wife I must communicate with her. All day I say. "But why can't I tell her she is lovely and terrific and I am proud of my beautiful wife? Why can't I" It isn't that I don't think so. I do. You are the most wonderful girl I know or have ever known. But somehow there is a barrier. I am going at it. Ideas are beginning to shoot up. But I love you. There is nobody else and I do not even imagine life without you. *We* go ahead, some way somehow, we'll come through, we, you, Nob and I.

N

318 *Separation and Limbo (1947–8)*

R. J. c/o Scott
539 Sierra
Reno, Nevada

Postmark August 9, 1948
Sunday Night

My dearest sweet,

I have just spoken to you and must now give you all the news. I love you and I want you to come. All these weeks—6 for the affair and then 30 days to give her time to file. It may even be longer. The climate is lovely, the lake is a few yards away, it is desert and hills—and a lake with the water not horribly cold but warm. Finances I'll go into in a moment. But it will mean much to us. The situation is. Miss Howard told the lawyer it's O.K. unless she called to say otherwise. I just spoke to Miss Hunter—she says she has heard nothing. I also asked her about you. She says it was understood that if the lease went thru'—that is the trouble—all will be well for you and me. I shall see her on Monday and settle it definitively and call or wire you. Now for finances. I am to get my keep for about 10 weeks . . . 450.00

We will live practically in isolation.

I would not spend a penny on the show even.

Two months and a half at 75 a month . . . *$187.50* . . . 637.50 . . . $637.50

Food is $5.00 a day and in that I include *everything*. You know how carefully I have to eat. Rent $10.00: That is $45, sweetie. If things go well, see what it means in cash. Now if you come, it means $100 for us both. Add 50 more in all and this may increase. Your food, etc., must be about $20.00 per week, $200. (You see, you can't spend money down there.) *That is nearly $900.* Will it work out? I only know that I am prepared to do my utmost. It is a sort of challenge. JPC at nearly 60 went to jail and came through. And if *you* come, then *I* cannot fail. The people may be impossible. But if they are not actually sub-human, we can make it. The chief danger is not my incompetence. The only serious problem I can foresee is that we make them uncomfortable by subtly letting them see that altho' we are servants we are superior to them. (Miss Howard, by the way, is a most notable frump.) But that, if we are on guard, we can handle. I have no pride of that kind—absolutely none. I have an aim. Everything will be subordinate to it. And you have worked around and know your way about. I suggest that when you come you arrive moderately attired. Miss H is a frump. She has a fiance and there is another man around. Dumb as I am, there are a lot of things I know that nobody else seems to know. She will be irritated if you come and overshadow her in her own house. Why the hell should she put up with it? You see the place is isolated and there will not be many people around. There are many people who should rise above it. My experience of life teaches me that as a rule people don't. And I have had to live watching these things. For the rest, when you come you will see. Sure it may fail. But that is a fine way to tackle something! It *may* fail. Ho! ho! Still, I go on Monday, have a look round and then I shall call you or wire you on Tuesday or Wednesday in the day.

Here are some ideas.

About rent, etc., all that is necessary is not to have to send the money from here. Also any money you have to draw, even later, should be drawn from N.Y. Tell Shorr of course.

Take your jewelery away from there. You *need* only working-clothes; bring anything else you want. I believe at the end of it you should go to California to see your mother. It is very near and you can do that on our way home.

Bring your type-writer. About the Dick thing, my advice to you, very considered, is to do nothing—just leave it. Put a dozen copies in your bag—that's all. Leave it—pay storage if necessary. Bring for me my personal copy of the Smaller Logic, the History of Philosophy by Hegel, and all the Sainte Beuves that have anything about Corneille, Racine, and Molière; also the Age of Corneille. Bring *one* of the books on Greece, preferably Rostovtzev, but if *you* prefer, the Cambridge Ancient History one. If you wish, bring also Poetique—I shall translate a lot for you. I have been reading a lot of things about Corneille, etc., and if we are lively, when you leave here you will have a grasp of Greek and French tragedy. After that you are on your own. Do *not* bring those tight overalls—they are too tight.

NOW. Go to Maurice as soon as you can and tell him *the facts*. I have only one message. My speech and the summary I hope are being organised. If they are ready let him give them to you for me to correct. If they are not, let him have them ready and as soon as I have a safe address I shall let him know.

time, jobs, you and me.

I haven't read your finance statement, of course. But as I see it, we shall gain a great deal of cash on the transaction. Your contribution alone is $200 in food, etc., + $50.00 extra wages: $250.00. To me it means safeguarding the job. And to spend this time together is worth plenty, plenty of money, darling. And do not, do *not start worrying about Nob*. You are always frightened about something. You and Nob will be taken care of. It's my stiff joints and aching back that I am going to be worried about—cleaning up that God-damned house and making beds. But $45.00 a week saved and $18.00 a week gained. For Christ's sake, ain't that something?

I am feeling good. Not tired any more. I can't work yet. Can only read; but have been reading hard. Fr Rev'n and Logic and Corneille, Racine, etc. And I have been thinking about you and me. Sweetie, I love you. I think of you all the time. Can't you see that? Don't you know it? Don't write until you hear from me. In fact as Shakespeare said—Do nothing till you hear from me. All my love, darling.

N

I was very pleased with what you wrote and said about Rae. I thought so a long time ago—but all that we'll talk about. I cannot understand it. I told her to say nothing about what she told the R's but she is all in prickles for months.

R. J.

c/o Scott, 539 Sierra, Reno, Nevada

Airmail Special Delivery
Postmark August 18, 1948
Monday Night

Sugar-pie: I have just spoken to you. And I want this letter to catch the mail in the a.m., if any. Mail does not go *every* day. Sweetie, I wouldn't trouble you about your hemorrhage—I can't spell the damn word. I hope you and Nob are O.K. I can't understand it. But you will let me know. I have written to you about what to bring. Here is some more. Clothes. Rain falls here once a year. Soon it will be cool on evenings. That is all. The book on Greece is Rostovtzev. History of the Ancient World. For the rest to hell with it. Bring your t-w, if you are sure you can get parties to lift it—if you have any doubt, don't. Don't mind if the books cost anything extra, bring them. About finances, bring all the money you can. We'll work it out.

You come. I asked if you could get work. Charlotte Hunter, the lawyer, said "Yes." If the work is too heavy, try some light work. If no light work, then no work. You must not stay up there away from me. We'll hold hands tight and come thru' somehow.

Now about me. I was waiting on Miss Howard. But I got tired of waiting. Money was slipping away fast. So I asked C. H. to ask Drackert if he would take me as a guest, so I would be on the spot. Miss H lives at Drackert's ranch and wanted to lease a house near. D finally said he would find something for me—so I came on Thursday night and am still here. Monday I was to begin with Miss H. *But she cannot get the house.* That is the latest. But D speaks as if he will leave me alone.

The ranch is a group of buildings on the shore of Lake Pyramid. P-d is some 12 x 6 miles, surrounded by low hills—the most wonderful spot you ever saw. But it belongs to an Indian tribe and is not commercialized or built up in any way. The ranch is the only spot in miles. It is 35 miles from Reno. You drive in in your own car or you take the ranch car when you can get it. It reaches Reno 3 or 4 times a week about 12 a.m. and leaves at about 4. There is 'phone communication, but no bus, no train, nothing. The ranch has everything—electric light, hot and cold water, a bar, etc. It serves about 30 people. Cabins vary from de luxe to simple ones. There are many people working here. I am gardener. I clean the yard—leaves and paper. I see after the water jets, for *irrigation* keeps the whole place alive. I mow the lawns and clean up the mess. I help put pormanteaux on the station wagon. I am handy man. I eat in the kitchen with the cook, the cowboy, two waitresses, the pantry-man and the house-maid. The food is good. I dry dishes twice a day.

I live in a cabin, but so far I have moved twice. That is the trouble. Drackert talks as if he is going to let me stay on. I want to—badly. The cowboy has a cot in the harness-room. I will stay there if necessary. Food is not the thing. I am useful—that is about all. But I may keep a guest away for the ranch is full these days. If the worst comes to the worst, I'll sleep in the stable. I am out in the sun and the dust for hours. I am very stiff sometimes—bending down constantly. *But it is good for me.* I read late at night but I sleep. And Drackert (about 50, an old rodeo man) is a gentleman and does not press me. When I am very tired, I go into my cabin and rest. The climate is wonderful. I get one day off a week—Wednesday. And I have to leave Reno at 5. We shall see very little of each other. But Charlotte H will help us out on a Sunday, I hope. *Maybe* you can get a job here, but the work of the waitresses is *hard*. But you come. (Bring half a pound of Hungarian and some bacc—if it doesn't smell.) You come honey. I want to see you. I love you. We'll fix up things. By the way, make a fuss about my speeches will you. I want them, to correct them. Take life *very* easy, honey. You are very precious to me. We'll make it somehow. Give the news to one or two and *demand absolute* silence. I'll write again every day. All my love and many kisses for you and N.

N

Honey-bunch. It is now a.m. and I have just had breakfast. I steal a few minutes before starting off to work. B'kfst is at 8. I don't overwork myself, but the sudden transition from sedentary habits *is* a jump. But between us, I am surprised at how well I am standing it. Seems all the old war-horse needs is some galloping and training and sun and bending down, particularly bending down. I wonder exactly how you got ill. I thought it would have been *months* before any such problem arose. Anyway—we'll go by the doctor. Does anybody, of your "attendants," know what is wrong and about Nob? You do what you want about that. I'll agree. I am looking forward to seeing the Dick thing. My sage experienced advice. Just leave things as they are. When you come I'll tell you how to handle it *exactly*. I love you, honey. I wish I could have you down here in the desert at last. But tho' it isn't quite as we pictured, it is still life moving. I don't quite, in fact I don't, see how we will be able to live together. But we'll be near, able to communicate every day and to see each other sometimes. And I'll know what is happening to you.

N

R. J.
Pyramid Ranch
c/o Mr. Drackert
Sutcliffe, Nevada

AIRMAIL SPECIAL
[1948, Reno]

Bring driver's license and social security card, if any; also marriage certificate, if findable.

Sugar, I have received only one letter—but this place is rather remote. I work hard, out in the sun, in the kitchen (the dish-washer left and I am helping out) and at the translation. But now every penny counts and I am satisfied with things. I hope I stay here for many weeks—there seems every sign of it. But one never knows. Bring all the cash we have.

Also typewriter, etc. *Lift nothing*, but bring them—it is warm in the day but chilly at nights and will grow colder.

What work you will get here I don't know. But we'll see. Charlotte H. was optimistic. Also I want you to type Guérin. I hope to make some good cash with this and quickly—besides *prospects* of doing the whole book. We have problems. We shall work them out. If we are lucky we shall rejoice. If we are not, we'll do the best with what chances we have. Nobbie will not suffer. Bring your Greek books and the Cambridge History of Ancient Times, the volume on Greece. When all is over here I wonder if you would care to go home by way of L.A. and S.F. You can see your mother and I would like this time to meet the party members—no more social business.

All the details I leave to you. Try and see Lyman and *Freddie before you leave. It is important*. So honey, take it easy. Do not expect to see me often. This is not going to be easy but it will be far better than your being so far away. And Reno is an easy-going place. If you get a job it will be near to where you live, you will have no steps after a long subway journey. Think of what you will need to wear for work. We have to see to it that we do not have to buy too many things now. Some things you can send by mail to be left till called for.

Does this letter seem serious? It is. But gloomy or doubtful? Not at all. We are acquiring new responsibilities and have to tighten up to meet them. Do not be afraid. I'll take care of you. I love you. But we'll have to be much more careful than in the past. Agreed? Agreed.

I am doing fine—I cannot complain and have much to be thankful for. *By the way, think over things.* Be prepared for the results of discrimination and our peculiar position. We want that decree—and we shall be on guard to do nothing to prejudice it. This is a very small place. I am sure we can manage it. It is only for a few weeks. But it helps when we know in advance and can adjust to it mentally. Charlotte Hewler, by the way, though a wonderful person, and a really wonderful person, is somewhat inexperienced in these matters. I came into Reno for my day off last W'y and lunched with her—in the Negro restaurant—a bit of a dump. She came willingly, but *she* wanted us to go to a big restaurant where she had influence, just to see if they would have the nerve, etc. Alas, I am a very modest, retiring person as you know, and cut a very humble figure persuading her not to. (Will that be forever my fate in life?) So that's it sweetie. I love you, more every day. I think you are wonderful, a wife to wear in my button-hole. If you want to please me, take care of yourself—arrive here safely—porters and taxis. There will be a place for you. Then settle down and take it easy. Don't worry. I shall try to arrange for us to meet briefly at least on Sunday. If not, then it will have to be Wednesday. There are all sorts of details—if you can stay somewhere where I can come to see you—what is your status when you come down here at Pyramid? You can think them out. They bristle with difficulties. But with a good and sharp lookout and a cheerful temper we'll make out until it is over. I shall be so glad to see you. I never looked forward to seeing you so much before.

N

I keep on remembering things. I need badly your little 25 cent Roget's Thesaurus.

I wash underwear, socks, and jeans. To-day I walked *miles*; up and down; and translated 6 pages, first draft. Isn't that something? It is now 11:15. I shall read the French to prepare for to-morrow and at 12 bed. Up at 8. I wish I could kiss you.

[1948]

Pyramid Lake Ranch,
Reno, Nevada.

Just for your note-book. The French Procession by Madame Mary Duclaux, Duffield and Co. A book to glance at; precious, rather, not our style at all, but she has read the stuff and thought long and lovingly over it.

Friday a.m. Sugar and I am waiting for some letters and to go for my day off—buy paper, press pants, put heel on shoes, notebooks, $3.00 in stamps, buy envelopes— the money goes and goes and goes. If I had not struck this haven, what a mess! Watch the pennies darling. We need them. I hope you and Nob are well. I am except my hands are rough and funny to hold.

Yesterday I had another talk with Budd. He is the cowboy, an Indian, dark, sharp-faced, from Montana. The Indians down here are short, thick, dumpy. Budd is nearer the type of fiction Indian. He is 37 or so, 5 ft 10; lean and hard. His girl, he says, is gone, Mary, and he misses her. The affair lasted only three or four weeks but Mary was a female who saw after her man. Budd says "It isn't good. I used to go till I dropped. But Mary made me take care of myself, clean shirt every day, wash up and clean up (himself he meant) all the time, brought me coffee, when I was sick, did everything, washed my clothes. When you [are] not accustomed to that and someone does it for you, it's bad, it spoils things, you get unsettled." I saw Mary myself taking care of Budd.

Budd wanted Mary to stay and Mary had promised. But she and the boss quarreled and Mary's passions conquered her passion. She refused to stay. She tried to persuade B to come to 'Frisco but B wouldn't. So the romance ended. That Mary! I believe she went because of bitterness—all her fine clothes and her consciousness of vitality; and excluded from the company of the guests. I asked Budd why she persecuted Viola so. Budd made a remarkable reply "I used to give her hell for doing it, but there is a streak of meanness in Mary's nature somewhere. Both of them had their "universal." If Mary had been allowed fraternisation she would have stayed. Budd on the other hand could get a fine job with a big saddlemaking firm in Frisco. His cowboy experience would be valuable, and he is a saddlemaker. But he cannot stand the city.

Now Joe, the Filippino cook, was sour for weeks. Budd, so friendly, helpful, and kind, if rather reserved, was sharp with Joe. I was scared of Joe—he disliked me, and I wanted no conflict between me and Drackert's cook, a valuable man. Though I was 100% right, Drackert needed his cook and did not need me. So I kept out of his way. But Joe was mean to everybody, and when I wanted ham instead of bacon, but didn't say so, Budd called for ham as if for himself and gave it to me.

Why was Joe so mean? Joe wanted to make Mary. His technique was simple. He had a quart of whiskey and continually offered her drinks in his cabin. Mary would not respond. So Joe, short, and very Filippinoish, was very dissatisfied and acted mean to everybody.

But others were not happy too. The help could not buy drinks at the bar or play pool or ping-pong—except Budd. Tho' Budd ate in the kitchen and fed the pigs and milked the cow, he rode and broke horses and took the guests out for riding. As he told me, his business was to fraternise with the guests, encourage them to ride "take care of them" he said, smiling. "But I didn't take care of *them*. I took care of Mary." Get it? So Mary had her revenge. On a dude ranch the cowboy is an aristocrat. The women here are not up to very much. But Mary had them defeated. *The day Mary left*, the *very day*, two of them offered to do Budd's laundry for him. He was taking it easy.

Next is the old cook I didn't know—a Chinaman who spent all his time making passes at Ramona. And then there is poor Viola the girl from Ioway, whom no one notices, and me. I am friendly, make some remarks at which they explode, but on the whole am reserved.

Finally there is Harry D himself, 50 odd, small, fit, still competes in rodeos, wrestling cows and riding bucking-horses, a good shot, busy with the ranch, but busy with the girls. There is always one around from Reno—Harry this and Harry that. And he takes them over to his private quarters at one end of the ranch; and the women who work here are mad. Ramona, Mary, yes, *Mary*, Viola, and Peggy, who is a big woman about 55 and takes care of the bar and is generally in charge when D is away in Reno. I hear little remarks that show how they resent these females who come around and monopolise D's attention, such as it is, for he does not spend too much time on them. Don't misunderstand me. Ramona and Mary, for example, had their own interests. But they would talk about "D's *extra* expenses" and "the way the place was managed" and "another one," etc., which showed that they felt it. Curious business. It was not their business whom D slept with. Peggy who lives here might feel it and as a sort of "partner" might legitimately resent these women. But the others—it seems curious to me, but then I am not a human being. I try to be reasonable and feel quite lost with the average citizen I see around me. Charlotte H told me that one night in the bar Harry D complimented her on her dress, and Peggy flashed at her before everybody "Did he buy it for you?" C. H. was a stranger here. C said she replied "If he were buying it for me, it wouldn't be cotton." But she told me she thought it strange. I too, I thought it very strange. But, as I say, I do not understand it.

So now I must go. I will read your letters (4) on the way up and if anything needs immediate handling I shall write and enclose it in this. I love you.

I have got your whole big bunch of letters, sweetie. I have read them. (I am now in Reno after 4 hours of running around.) All the time I was thinking of you, and how wonderful if you were here to run around with me. But I can't write. I am in CH's office. 1) We need the $300 by next Saturday. 2) Could you write to Bill and ask him to get my brother or one of them to get the exact dates of my marriage and cable it to you. Just the date. That is all the request. I would, in fact, write both: Eric's address is Eric James, Secretary T.A.F.A., Railway Dept. I would write in the letter just this: typed. Dear E. Could you find out at the Registrar's the exact date of my marriage and cable it to me. Just cable the date. Sign it N. Write Bill and ask the same request. I'll write to-night again.

Love,
N

Postmark August 21, 1948
Friday Night

Sweetie—how are you? Improving I hope. I am looking forward to hearing all the details. I am glad you are not alone. It is 10:45. I am in my cabin—tired as an old horse. All day I have been watering lawns, scraping up leaves, and helping in the kitchen. Started at 8, finished at 8:30, but I had long intervals of rest. During these I read voraciously—chiefly French literature. Also I think. Mr. Drackert said last night he would not send me away. So I am here for some weeks. The Howard deal is off—she cannot get the house. I worked this afternoon stripped to the waist. Mr. D said I looked so much better since I had come. I have not the slightest feeling of revulsion for the work I am doing—not the slightest. The climate and scenery are wonderful—six hours sleep is enough. No humidity—only the sun and the fresh air and the bright clear light—at nights it is cool and you sleep. My tummy gives me some pains but no more nor less than elsewhere. I eat, reasonably well—the food is good tho' not like ours. One finger is "wounded"—callouses all over and cracks—the effect of the rake, but otherwise these stiff bones of mine have responded astonishingly. I have not had any stiffness, though I bend down fifty times a day. Last night Charlotte Hunter and a friend came down to see me. Drackert invited them to stay over. We sat in his garden and played ping-pong. Otherwise I go to my cabin and read till one or two. It is hard to write. Sheer physical fatigue and the strain on my hands. But I have begun the translation.

Sugar I love you. I had intended all day to write you to tell you so. You said "I thought you had forgotten all about me." It is not a joke altogether. You have these fears. They are due to your past or your temperament. I think you are the most beautiful girl I know—no exaggeration. I believe you are the most wonderful wife. I like to see you, walking about the house. If I had a house and you weren't in it, I don't know what I would do. You are part of me. I am only sorry that I don't make you happier than I do. I make no plans in which you do not come in as naturally as if you were physically fastened to me. I haven't to remember you. You are just a part. So it is. So it will be. You have no rivals because you cannot have any. Your place in my life was created by you and me. From a solitary I have become part of a dual personality, you and me, and soon, in fact already we are three. The only serious problem in my life now is be sure that you are happy and remain so. I have no others. I have been reading Corneille, Racine, Molière and French literature from the beginning, its history, etc. I like it, it stimulates me and teaches me many things and brings back many happy days. But now I do it, thinking of you every hour, every minute. "This will be good for you. You must note this. I will tell you about this. When you read this I want to see how you will react." Every second. For you I read it again and satisfy my deep inner craving for literature. And I know you will do it wonderfully well. To this day I have never had the least doubt of that. Now I am really tired and must go to lie down. But I am not nervous. I am learning about agriculture, irrigation, and the early pioneers and the life of the West, and the people. It is an experience. When you come be prepared to live away from me. But we'll be near. Who will meet you? Charlotte Hunter *may be* able to. But call her. She expects you to come in and is very very kind. I will ask her to arrange for you to stay. You arrive whenever is convenient. Cash this cheque and bring the money. Also *if you can*, send me Saintsbury's History of Fr Lit by mail and if you can enclose Strachey's Hist of F Lit O.K. If you can't you can't. My love to Rae, John and the others. All my love for you and Nob.
                                    N

CH's no. is 24 227. Same number for home and for office. Her address at home is 239 Flint St., But of course I'll call you again.
R. J.
c/o Drackert
Pyramid Ranch
Sutcliffe, Nevada

                                          Postmark August 26, 1948

Sugar, it is 10:30, W'y, and I am breaking my schedule. Three pages remain, but there was a movie, Boyer and . . . (very stupid) and I saw it through. I can finish but I shall do so to-morrow.

To-day I did not go in. I shall have my day off on Friday. It was a day. Viola's day.

Viola is 46, from Ioway, divorced, middle-aged, plump, with a flat voice, and an incurable desire to talk but is so dull that nobody listens. She is the maid and from a.m. till p.m. goes from cabin to cabin, cleaning and making beds. She eats with the help in the kitchen. She helps in the doing of the dishes, but is somewhat erratic about it and in any case it is not her duty. Well to-day Ramona and Mary, two stalwart workers, left. The dish-washer had previously left. So that the place was in a minor crisis. I stayed and we got through the day. At five Viola returned and Drackert brought a new dish-washer (pearl-diver is the phrase). The cook was off to-day. Drackert cooked, we helped around, but Viola took over. She served at table, she made iced tea, she washed dishes, she put them away, she had to be called twice to eat, she left her food half-eaten, she spun around again, she was in 20 places at once, and only when everything was finished did she stop. Sweets, all of life is concentrated in this ranch at the back of beyond.

Viola is from Iowa—a country girl, brought up on a farm, with an agricultural mentality. Ramona and Mary were from California. Mary is about 28, here for a divorce. She is a waitress by profession; medium height, solidly built, a good face tho' drab in coloring. She worked like an engine, changed her clothes every day. She drives a car and when she puts her foot down does not take it off until she reaches where she is going. She eats enough for two. On her days off she went into Reno and got drunk—high as a kite. She appropriated Budd, the Indian cowboy, from all the hungry women swanking around. Once when there was no cook, she cooked for 30 people a day for a week and is as good a cook as the Filippino.

Ramona is 41, looks 30, except for gray in her hair; has a neat figure. She has a son 6 ft and a big daughter, but she too can work. And she and Mary as waitresses did a job, particularly when the dish-washer left (Kenny, another character).

Now Ramona was reserved but witty. Mary was aggressive. Mary was bitter because the guests "from the East" did not speak to her. Night after night, after work, they have nothing to do down here. Drackert also forbade fraternisation with the guests. Mary led Ramona in a constant complaint also that Drackert gave them too much work. She railed openly. She was in a state of constant or pregnant frustration and anger, and she took it out on Viola. Viola could not open her stupid mouth. Mary jumped on her and bawled her out. Nobody else did. Mary one day at dinner jumped up and held on to Ramona with both her arms to prevent R getting up and giving V some coffee. R was polite, reserved, helpful always. Mary's behavior was shocking and I in particular was revolted. But she was a gay, vigorous girl and she was nice to me. She and Ramona with their friendship, their clothes (particularly Mary) dominated the place and passed remarks about everybody including Drackert, the way he ran the place, the way he over-worked help, the guests, their inconsiderateness, the children whom Mary cursed day in and day out. Viola made her silly remarks, was jumped upon, was tolerated. Viola, the Ioway girl had an attitude of belonging to the place. She was deeply concerned at what would happen when all the people went away. Mary bawled her out fiercely for being concerned. Viola subsided.

But to-day M and R left: I did not know what fires burnt in Viola's dull bosom. They being gone, she was the only woman in the kitchen. Drackert depended on her. People called her. She was in the dining room among the guests. She was brilliant. She did the work of Mary and Ramona. And when it was all over she told the new dishwasher how to fix up everything and departed happy. God above us, I am continuously amazed at the volcano that is clamped down in every human being. That woman, properly handled, can do the work of both Mary and Ramona, who were remarkable workers. But she will not do it for money, nor could she be driven to it.

I, honey, am doing well. Don't worry if you are weak on the writing of letters. Just let it be. I am the last person in the world to check how many you write against mine. Let them be. I'll write to you. Next time I'll tell you about the romances here. The place is thick with them—no place more than in the kitchen. I, my precious, am out of it, tho' everyone seemed to think that Ramona and I would make a good match. I declined the gambit. No one but you.

I have just seen Viola. She is going to wait table all morning and make her beds. I know now, after seeing her, what the process was. Last night she was a star, she sparkled, she scintillated (while spinning on her very ample axis). To-day she is equally or nearly as busy, but she is calm, like one whose success is now assured. And now that I think of it, precious wifie, I'll be damned if half of V's concern for what would happen if the help all left was a vision of what would happen to her.

O.K. sweets. I love you.

[unsigned]

R. J.
c/o Drackert
Pyramid Lake
Sutcliffe, Nevada

Postmark August 27, 1948

Let me give you a fright I had. C. H. to-day told me Mr. D had said something to her about my staying on as guest at $40 per. I was, you can imagine, bowled over. I said I would speak to him. I just did so. He said that *she* had told him I had so much work (of my own) to get out that he had said "Then let him stop his work for me and stay on as a guest, etc." C. H. *talks*. Oh, sister, how she talks. But she is the extrovert to the nth. But I am safe; breathe freely.

Today C. H. carried on in a manner that shows how people can live in the world and know nothing about it. I meet her by appointment for lunch. Before I know where I am, she and I, and 4 other people lunch in the Negro Cafe—3 women, one of them the local candidate of the Progressive Party (she is no Stalinist). But Charlotte just goes along, multiplying contacts, discussions, and people, all along the street. I warned her last week and this week she admitted there had been talk. . . . It is extraordinary. They have no discipline at all. They are full of their "rights," "they would do it only to see," etc. Ten disciplined, alas, Stalinists, can run 10,000 of these people. And yet C is a fine person, honest, intelligent, frank, sympathetic, and will work her fingers to the bone for any cause or individual.

They spoke to the Negro owner of the Cafe—an officer in the last war—6 ft 6" a local Negro leader. He was, had been a CP'er in Chicago, and told the local white people so openly, and he told them too that there were about 10 Negro CP'ers in his local Negro organisation. He said that he was marked down as subversive in the army, but didn't know why. Anyway when on the coast he was in charge of two Japanese officers, prisoners. They went to a restaurant to eat and the Japanese officers were admitted but he was barred. So he threw a hand grenade in the place. That was subversive enough it seems to me.

Sweetie, I am so glad D isn't sending me away. I spent money like water to-day, stamps, paper, other stationery, pants press, shoes heeled, flask of whiskey (to entertain Budd and the rest), taxi to do all the messages, my own and what the others gave me. Laundry I am doing myself and I am waiting anxiously for my parcel of old clothes to save these I have. You see I am serious. And to think that I might have been thrown out. Phew. I *am* relieved.

On Saturday coming, sugar, I want to give Miss H $300 and on the Saturday after I will have been here 6 weeks and a large % of the job will have been done. She will begin to serve J the week before so that nothing will intervene in the decree being ready for me, as far as this side here is concerned. Let's just keep our fingers crossed. Little by little.

Your letters I shall read again and answer later. Meanwhile I'll go on with my folks here.

This morning Joe, the cook, was fired. He had been swearing he would *not* give breakfast after 10. The *boss* asked for it after 10 this a.m. Joe stuck to his guns and was fired on the spot. The after 10 business is a scandal, but Joe's principles were a bit excessive, I think. Anyway he had been grumbling for a long time.

Yesterday was the day. A new dish washer came—John, a Mexican, on 48 days leave *from the Navy*. Married, and has two kids in Oakland, but he wanted a holiday by himself and this is how he is taking it. A thick-set, noisy, active young man, has done a dozen jobs, accepts everything he sees and reads, ready to work, chattering away and making jokes. Then a middle-aged woman who is now cook, tho' she came as waitress yesterday. She is a talker; and Viola is once more busy with serving, but now has someone to talk to. Viola speaks like this: "In the Navy? I had a brother who had a friend in the Navy. This brother of mine married when he was 24. It was a girl he met in Sacramento. The two of them was . . ."

But the new cook tho' of a higher stage is of the same degree. She says: "Yes, I made chicken with wine-sauce at the Open House Ranch. It is a place larger than this, but they serve the food in open style—you come and get it. . . ."

They carry on like this to one another, and make jokes with John, who asks little from conversation except the sound of your voice and his fairly dividing the available time. The whole atmosphere of the kitchen is changed. *Budd can't take it.* He eats and goes out. I am tougher. I am accommodating myself to them. I sit and listen and talk about what they are talking about. I give it, very naturally, a little twist, that makes it more interesting to everybody, including themselves. I set them on the road of talking seriously about their own experiences of which they were just bobbling along. They see that I really want to know. I relate it to a very broad universal. They see themselves as having matter to contribute to something that is important. They talk up. Others talk up too. This morning we had half-an-hour on the organisation of service to feed 5,000 people, 30 people, 300 people; how it was organised, methods, etc. If I am alone with simple, uneducated people, I *never* fail, *never*; we *all* have a wonderful time—*they* have it. They talk more than they have talked before and to some purpose. I fit what they have to contribute into a framework—immediately, without thought, instinctively. I am not building them up. I *am* interested and they sense that, and talk. The only time, rarely, it goes wrong is when a sophisticate is there, who wants to talk about his subject or resents the fact that the talkers naturally talk to me. I am asking the questions, after all, and keeping it going. Like my speaking from the platform, this is a perfectly natural procedure with me. I do not think it out. I do the same with a bunch of highly sophisticated business-men, making them talk about their business, or musicians, making them talk about music. I have, my dear, made scientists talk to me about science, architects about architecture, gangsters about gangstering, and I have not the slightest doubt that if I met Gable, Tracy, e.g., Robinson and Humphrey B in a railway car, I could get them to talk for hours about acting. *They all have it in them.* The moment they see you really *want* to know they are attracted; as soon as they see that you have a comprehensive view of art and society and that their knowledge and experience are helping to deepen, broaden, clarify, or otherwise affect more things than they know, as soon as they see that their knowledge has significance far beyond what they dreamt, they *all* talk, *all*. I am *never* bored with people, and except they are self-centered, I never bore them. I am a little remote from all of them in the kitchen here, they sense or see for all I care that I am different—I am no American, I am reserved and formal, but I get on with all of them, all, and I am myself, not changed in the slightest degree. I remain myself. As I think it [this is] how I am going to be until my composition or the composition of people change. The Filippino was hostile, but I could have made him *talk*, not talk to him, about the Philippines, etc., *if* he would talk at all. O.K. sister, I hope by now the messages about the marriage date have gone off.

I just got up and went out. Sweetie, you should see. It is 10:05. Lights are on, doors open, and Viola and the new cook are discoursing in true social fashion. Glory be! Mary would retch with rage. And about what I was saying, [I] *never* impose my ideas or lecture the people I meet. In my own circle, among my friends I talk freely but with strangers or acquaintances I am careful. Now is that a correct portrait? I know that if I were among the guests, I would be exactly the same. Now you can imagine the analysis of the ego, and the instinct for domination, and the whole pile of crap that the average sharp-shooter can make of this. Let them. That is how I am. . . .

[unsigned]

R. J.
c/o Drackert
Pyramid Lake Ranch
Sutcliffe, Nevada

Postmark August 30, 1948

Only a thin letter, but lots of love, sweetie.

Dear Sweetie,

How are you and Nob? This is Monday a.m. I am ready for work. I did pages and pages of trans'l'n yesterday. To-day I shall write my notes on "House."

The kitchen is all changed. There is a woman cook 4 ft 11; about 55, fussy but friendly. The boy, Johnny is as lively as a kitten. He plagues her and she grumbles but loves it. Dot, the new maid, is an Irish girl of 22 or 23 who has lost her husband who left her with three kids. The kitchen is in a continuous racket. But I have noticed something:

Hazel the cook and Viola, who is still around a lot, are *loyal* to Mr. Drackert and the guests and the job. They work hard and wear themselves out for the job's sake and the boss's sake. It satisfies a social need for them. That is why that type can become fascist so easily. Joe, the previous cook, Mary and to some degree Ramona, were anti-job on principle. They were loyal to their rights. John the Navy . . . and

Dottie are in between. They are young, work hard, don't *know* much, and take their color from those around them. They could go either way and even Hazel and Viola, the feudalists can be torn away under a strong impulse. I can see all the signs.

These women here are a menagerie. God! How pathetic they are; Clare Luce's Women was sharp in its social satire and though Hollywoodish saw something clearly. You could say to a worker "Go see what the money your boss makes goes to keep up" and the future sociologist could get an insight into the lives of the rich. But the pathetic side, how empty and miserable they are, that she did not see, or if she saw could not combine with the savagery—she herself was too limited. But that is the chief thing that strikes me about them. I'll *tell* you about them sometime. But I am writing only about my co-workers as L. T. used to call them. O.K. sweetie. To-day "Horses" and I'll mail at once. It needs plenty done to it, I think. And take care of yourself. I love you and want you good and whole and active and healthy and lovely.

N

R. J. c/o Drackert
Pyramid Lake Ranch
Sutcliffe, Nevada

Curious thing. Since the new regime in the kitchen, the food in the kitchen, the organisation of *our* meals, the concern for us as help, has become hap-hazard. The employer has had nothing to do with it. He has not interfered. Twice already, there has not been enough meat for us remaining. No hardship. I had a huge turkey back-bone and the red beans were well cooked. But we eat how we can, etc. The Filippino had none of that in him. If meat ran short, and he took care as a rule that it didn't, he went into the ice-box, cut lamb-chops for each one of us and fried them at once. Nothing prevents this woman doing that. She is *personally* nice. When you come in she fusses round you and will do anything for you. But that strong sense of the help as a body with rights, none of them has. Budd by the way has walked off with the Irish girl who looks very well. Took her into the bar last night and sat drinking with her. How the other women must have fumed. The unorganised toilers are certainly defeating the petty-bourgeoisie in a very important local sphere.

Now here is something. I met a girl on the ranch here; watch it; thin, tall, bad complexion, Italian looking, by name Naomi, speaks French beautifully, also Italian, has visited France often; worked in international relief *and helped Jean not to come here*. Isn't the world small? I am sure she is no Stalinist but who she is I don't know. I saw her here but took no notice. Then on Friday on the way back from Reno, instead of my usual much-loved place in the back among the baggage, I found myself in the front next to her and Drackert. She was curious, in a friendly way. D who knows something about me was near. We talked. We know some people. Dwight McD, etc. She talked about Camus and Sartre. It was a mess. The rest of the waggon sitting behind with their ears cocked. That comes from letting people rob you of the back seat. O.K. Sweetie-pie. Give Nob a pat for me.

More news. The dinner in the kitchen to-night was a monstrosity—a catch as catch can. The food is still O.K. but no order. I shall observe these contrasting types closely.

[unsigned]

Postmark September 1, 1948

Sugar, just a note to tell you that I love you. Today, W'y, is day off for the help and a horrible jumble usually—I stay here and go on Friday so that somebody remains around. I wish I could see you for a little while but the grip of circumstances is strong. Anyway day by day, inch by inch they are slipping away; in a few days, we should have the decree, and then a great load will be lifted. *You* just take it easy. Take it easy. I don't want you to do any work now, sweetheart. Leave that to me. You type the stuff I send you; and see after yourself and N. Plenty of time to fix things. As long as you feel good, I am O.K. Much love and many, many kisses.

By the way I sent you the letters from R, etc. But, watch your step. Politicians are by nature unscrupulous. You see to it that you are not drawn into a sort of you and Rae admonishing G., or your opinions being quoted. You see there is always the tendency to draw someone in to strengthen the solidarity against someone else. And you can be useful to one "grouping" or another. I, my dear, am very very careful about these things. Many others are careless and are not. Particularly now you are really getting to know the people and establish good relations, just be on guard and do not let yourself be caught up in anything. Be quite rough if necessary. Say No. I am expressing no opinion. That is for you all to settle. This isn't "keeping you out," my dear. It is keeping you out of being "represented" to Gr as being "against" her. Not spitefully, not maliciously, not at all, but just the way politics go. The quieter you keep, the more you learn; then the more people tell you. Are you condemned to silence? No. The thing may come up and then *if you feel impelled to say something*, you say it to G., as you want to say it. Nobody will say "C said." This is the world we live in. I love you—many kisses, darling, many.

[unsigned]

R. J. c/o Drackert
Pyramid Lake Ranch
Sutcliffe, Nevada

Postmark September 3, 1948

Honeybunch. Thursday; to-morrow is my day off—a great event. I have this p.m., received the draft of my speech for correction—48 pages. At the same time I sweat at my translation. I read. And I go round and round six hours a day. My hands are better—healed, tho' they remain rough—who cares? Our cook is a fantastic creature. She does not feed us. Last night it was omelet and beets. Why? D tells her to cook so as not to have to throw away. D and his assistant, however, are very concerned about the staff's food. If they heard what she was doing they'd be mad as hell. But the real reason is that she is dying for praise and compliments—"the guests wanted seconds." That is her refrain and she embroiders on it. She manuevers and fishes and apologises so that someone might say "That was good." And I believe she is positively happy when she tells us "The meat is very little. The guests wanted seconds." The Filipino was twice as good a cook as she and nobody dreamt of asking for seconds. She maneuvers it. But don't misunderstand. There is plenty to eat. And if once a day the meat is shortish I don't feel it at all. I am merely comparing it with the old regime.

Now, sugar, I have been thinking about you. You write about our life together, that you want it above all things. So do I. It is our life. The food, the little pictures, the radio, the papers, the books, the music; it is wonderful. I have no hankering after anything else. It is a civilized life as I know it. I *want* to live that way. It is my *choice*. If you love it I feel happy and easy. But it isn't enough. Down here I am in the open, sun and the lake and physical exercise and dirt and sweat and fatigue. God! If you know what the afternoon shower is like. I haven't had that feeling for fifteen years. And we have not had it. We haven't been anywhere, walked on beaches, etc. I can. I am doing it here because I have to. But I get up in the a.m. and go round fixing my irrigation before eating—fitter than *after* breakfast at home. Somehow, sweetie, I have to live a more active life. I'll be better in myself and better for you. Don't mind about Nob. Nob is an interlude—very important but an interlude. I'll help you with Nob. We'll battle for that—going out, snow or sun, having three days or five days somewhere. I know how very different things would be for us if we could live together every now and then as I am living here.

That is one. The second is we haven't any friends except Bill. We don't drop in and gossip. I don't any more. I see R and G. and F & L, and we talk about something and I leave. We don't go anywhere on a Sat'y p.m. and eat and go out and maybe sleep over because it is too late and have breakfast. We have dinner and "discussions." True most of our conversation with friends is "discussions," but we miss it. Do you "bore" me? Never. I have never once felt the slightest fatigue in talking to you. But I think we need some friends. I have watched the division between us and my closest friends with resignation. Perhaps it is over now. I couldn't do anything about it. The responsibility is yours. Now don't jump. For instance, Freddie and L. Freddie, you say, does this and that and tells you this or that. She doesn't tell *me*. How could I interfere? But you, you handle her. You see, I know them, and they all are people who over the years I have learnt to like and to trust. They have their ways, but they are, the old brigade, R, G., L & F, solid people. Now I would, if I were you, put F in her place in the most uncompromising manner. Do not have the slightest fear of political complications. That is now over. You are established. They know that you are with me to stay. When I heard you say that you were going to settle the rumours about R, I was very very relieved. You go ahead. If any of them came to me with any tales or stories or intimacies about you, I would deal with it most promptly. When it was clear to me, what was to be done, I did it. Feel free to do what you want to do as far as they are concerned. You can discuss politics with them—only as I wrote in my last, avoid being drawn into sides, unless you want to go in. Your position is a hard one—everybody knows that—but if there is any place you have freedom, it is among us, our circle. This much I know, they are as good people as you will find anywhere.

Now about your friends. G and F, and now G [Gale Malaquais]. Why don't we see more of them? For the future. Jean [Malaquais] is a very trying person, his self-concentration is terrible. But we can manage it. Between us, G was flirtatious before even Jean began. But 1) I do not rush to such conclusions 2) I am scared of you on such subjects. But G and F, I am sorry we did not go on the boat. But I tell you one thing that you will find and you need not take it from me. Politics intervenes. That is why, to-day, your political associates are your best friends. The subject keeps cropping up. I usually keep silent. I know the dangers. And I know that they can't argue with me. Politics is my *business*. And it will mean a bad time for *them* if the subject intrudes or they intrude it. But it can be done. We must try.

These things all revolve around our central direction in life—work for the revolution. That is decisive, sweetie. You are my partner. You are ready to go through, to the end. I am learning to have confidence in you. Confidence grows with years and events. You cannot control it. It is an *instinctive* reaction; I love you, I think you are wonderful—I like to see you, you always seem beautiful to me, always. We talk, we go out, we look at pictures, we live the everyday life. I have an ultimate confidence in you. But the thing to have is confidence that I am able to take for granted that your reaction to any serious situation and mine will not clash and give a double problem, the problem itself and the problem of you and me in relation to the problem. This is not wrong or right. It is nothing so simple. If a crook and his Moll meet a child on a dark night and instinctively decide together to kidnap it, that's fine; or they instinctively feel that it isn't worth doing, that's fine; but if one feels to kidnap and is doubtful as to the other's reaction, then that's a hell of a mess for them. To take it farther, they can disagree, but have an instinctive confidence in each other. We don't make it so often. The trip here—who would make it; that horrible Convention; to mention only two. We have to overcome it somehow. But I want to—I don't weigh whether it's worthwhile as you seem to think. It never crosses my mind—well, we had better break it up. That never does. But little by little we bounce along, cannonading from side to side but holding on tight, and learning somehow. It is coming. As long as we hold on tight. And I am holding on. My reactions are simple where it comes to fundamental things. Note them. Proletarian revolution or ruin. I don't fool around with that. Jump high, jump low, I stay there. Nothing shakes me. Because after all these years, my whole experience, reading, thinking, amount to nothing else but a concretising, deepening, expansion of that simple truism. For you, it is the same. You are my wife—the wife I want. Without you, I don't know what. And everything that happens you come out closer to me, I am more certain than ever of the fundamental proposition I want you for my wife, my perpetual partner. Nothing has ever made me feel it less—always more. But I am not a shouting revolutionary, I just go ahead with my business; and I am not a shouting husband. We'll have our holiday when I return. Sure as day.

R showed you her letter to show you I had written to her. What the hell! You know, there are things that puzzle me. Why do you even notice them? Learn something about me. I am in my own way a psychologist—every man has to be. When A tells me something about B, do you know my invariable reaction? It is this. Why does A tell me this? I married you. I schemed and maneuvered and plotted 8 years. I could have married lots of other people. They were around. I didn't. You left. I came after you. I wrote R. I am going to write R plenty; long letters too. What the hell! You can say what you like but I know if R's name was Raymond and it was a man you wouldn't bother. I am not talking about this anecdote alone. I am in a real mess. They resent, of course they do, my marrying you, an outsider. But you are jealous of them. Don't try to bluff me. You want to argue. O.K. State your case. I'll argue. But you are nervous about them. I married you, of my own free will. I had a choice. I chose you. Not only I didn't choose some others. I never even squeezed their little finger. Never. So, my miracle, what's there to worry about. When you say you had a "wonderful" letter from me, I feel bad. Not too bad, but bad. I am nervous. It means that you are nervous, anxious, need reassurance, a "wonderful" letter proves something to you that you doubt. Don't doubt. Don't need assurance. Just be. Now that is what I think, good or bad. O.K.

N

Just had dinner. News: "Seconds" has been fired. She complained of the sailor whose animal spirits kept the kitchen in an uproar, so she said. She departs as she lived. The meat was tough to-night, leather. But she said to the kitchen, "They say they couldn't eat it but they asked for seconds." More news: D's wife has appeared. "She has come!" The news spread. "She is ill." Peggy, the assistant, took lunch into her over in D's quarters on a tray. I caught a glimpse of her this p.m.; young, as far as I could see, at a distance, a dramatic looking young woman. Later at the bar, at about 6:45, I saw a woman, in evening dress—and D in his cowboy outfit, and jeans. I am pretty sure it was she. The rumor is that the last time she came the result was the disruption of D for a week—the whole ranch felt it—the week after she left, to be precise. God! how they must hate her!

I met a man to-day whose father was chief engineer on board the Maraval, a boat that plied between U.S. and Trinidad. He knew the W-I well and we talked about the islands familiarly. Then there is the girl who got Jeannot over. How little it is after all. There was another couple here who lent me Partisan Review. They live in N.Y. No Stalinists so far. C. H. is no Stalinist. My dear, I watched that. She and the Wallace-ite argued bitterly before me. They always do. C distrusts politics. She is a "do-gooder."

I shall write again soon. I hope I interest you with my gossip. Imagine! I have never been in the kitchen nor in the pantry before, nor in the garden; working with them, from the inside. I have had intimate contacts with workers before, but they always knew who I was; these don't. I do not discuss politics. Furthermore the isolation of the ranch throws everybody on to everybody else. I am fascinated. The new cook is an oldish man, a hard-bitten American, and his Grant Woodish wife. I have to live with them. I hope they don't dislike me.

And by the way, my dear, the men in these parts, the farmers, the ones out in the open. I have seen some of the handsomest men I have seen in my life, face and figure. How well they look! I saw a cowboy to-day, about 35, about 6 ft exactly, so straight, so slim, his shoulders square, but almost as narrow as his hips, and his whole body as flat as a pancake, and his eyes blue; and they are slow, easy-going. I saw a man over fifty this a.m., a farmer, gassed in the last war, he farms and lives on his pension; 7 children; a farmer pretty dirty unkempt, but a beautiful figure, medium-sized, a tanned lined face, and a wonderful pair of blue eyes. He looked me in the eye, fair and square, and kept his eyes in mine, and I knew he didn't know I was a black man. People in France, strangers, look at you that way. Never in England and the U.S. It was a wonderful thing to see and to feel. This simple, honest Westerner. I shall never, never regret having come out here. I could have lived in Reno and been miserable—or at least just going to the show and scribbling in my room. We'll see it, sweetie, we'll see it. Remember what I wrote earlier. I love you sweetie. I have never thought that you "disappointed" me; why? We couldn't fit in easily, and many things are different. But I am different too—but that is not being disappointed in a person. No. I love you. I think you are as wonderful as I thought before we were married.

Red Skelton was on, and he was as funny as hell. And to-day, note the day, Thursday, I hear that the Council of Churches has decided against Communism and *against capitalism.* What then? Zero. But in the U.S. that is something. God help those who cannot see.

O.K., sweetie. Kisses innumerable. (And I am far from news, but I suspect that Zhdanov & Co. have been murdered.)*

N

Sweetie, forgive me. I wrote and put the sheets in my pocket to sort and add. Then I have been going round and round and now I have to rush. So sort them, please.

Yours as always,
N

R. J. c/o Drackert
Pyramid Lake Ranch
Sutcliff, Nevada

Postmark September 13, 1948

Sweetie,

As I hope to tell you on the 'phone before you get this, there has been a sharp change in our fortunes. My job is over. Really, D extended himself to make it so long. There are details or maybe they are not important. I have had no time to evaluate.

But I can stay on here as a paying guest—some $40 or $50.00 per week, all told. It is the chance of a life-time. Four or five weeks. I will have told you already, please send the $60.00 or rather make it $70, as I still have some more in the bank. Now I shall really finish off that translation and do all the other work I have to do. But the financial jam will be acute. You just don't bother your head about it. I shall arrange everything.

Now for some more *news*. The papers were sent off on Friday night to be served on J in the W.I. The first 6 weeks are up. The Govt can whisk me away, but my six weeks are made and I can always come back. Tho' there is little likelihood, as far as we can guess.

The charge, the question raised is: lack of cohabitation for 3 years. That is the law. Remote chance: She may demand that I pay her expenses here to contest the case. I don't expect too much from people in matters where their personal passions are concerned (my belief is in them always when they are taken out of themselves. They rarely fail me then.) As I say, I was always skeptical of anyone who *"knew"* what J would do. But I would be surprised if she went that far. *Secondly*: More remote. The Govt might hear of it in the W.I. or here. They could intervene as Govts always can directly or indirectly. But, frankly, I don't see it in this case, at this time. What I was scared of was their hauling me back to N.Y. and breaking up my 6 weeks. But that is now in the bag. I am beginning to feel a great deal more relieved. Cautious me.

You cheer up. Nob and you and me will have a big time when all this is over.

Between us I am glad. As I wrote to you, the work was too much for me. And when you see what I have been doing down here you will be astonished— writing work I mean. They will all be typed up and you will have all the copies in order. Meanwhile I send you one. Pass it on to R, as fast as you can will you?

---

* A. Zhdanov, a powerful and close collaborator of Stalin, who died under mysterious circumstances.

I shall now have ample time to *write*. I have one or two things to fix up first. I am still reading your two long letters. I shall arrange my ideas and my reply. I am trying to understand them or the mood or idea, or stage behind them. What is the word? Anyway I am managing; reading, comparing, working out. I shall answer everything answerable from here. So do send me the cash quickly. I have a confession. Don't tell *anyone*. You ought to know why by now. First they talk, they rush with the news. Secondly, enemies systematically use it against you; and even friends nourish their own egos with it. I gambled. Crime? Like hell. I lost. Crime? A hell of a crime. I hoped to make some money, not to buy drinks and give girls, etc., but to have a little more. My dear, I lost, but I am brave. I have forgiven myself.

I hope you are well. Give me the medical news in detail and often.

I am passing this on to R through you. Also I send the cheque. It did cost something to live down here. When I went to Reno, what with laundry, glasses fixed, clothes, shoes heeled, drinks I brought back, this that and the other, I spent a few dollars every week. Then there is a bar down here, etc. Now I shall spend some extra I expect. My stamp and paper bill is fantastic. I send you another cheque. Please cash and send for me. I'll write in detail to-morrow. I had to get this away. It was bothering me. I had planned to do it Sunday p.m., but I had to go off—came back late; and when he told me this a.m. about no more job, I just sat down and wrote this damn thing, finishing up the job in between. I was supposed to "think it over" to-day to tell him later. It is now nearly one but I am not sleepy. I love you, sweetie. I hope you are making out. Do tell me everything.

Love for you and N.
N

R. J. c/o Drackert, Pyramid Lake Ranch,
Sutcliffe, Nevada

Postmark September 20, 1948
Saturday

Speech. *NB*.

If the speech*es* are going to be printed . . . and perhaps, even if not, there are two things wh[ich] should come out.

I have seen the N'o question in many parts of the world: Change to I have a wide experience of the N'o qu'n.

And in the summary:

(When we were in the W. P. we taunted them) That ought to be out. To a sharp-eyed investigator, they could mean something.

Now just to show you that my letter of this morning was a letter which was *mild*, just read the enclosed.

C is to *work* for 3 months; *then* not to *work* to be my *secretary*. I would like to hear some comments from you on this. I really would. I wrote earlier to say: Leave C alone. But it seems I was too late.

I am pretty lonely to-night, my dear. I am thinking about writing you a long letter. I love you. Give Nob a little "feel" for me.

Love,
Nello

By the way, this same letter of R's contains 3 pages of analysis and some extracts on L. T. Anything more unlike G's stuff you never saw. It is close, tight, concrete, in order, pulled like a bow. You have to look twice and more often to see that very few, I doubt if *any* of L. T.'s followers from 1928, except those in Russia, could do anything like it. It is sweeping thru' decades, but never seems "*to make any jumps.*" It is wonderful stuff really. And she and G. It will be hard for them to respect and understand one another. J [John Dwyer] does not appreciate R at all. R is sometimes soft and silly, and subjective at times—there is a thwarted femininity there—but strictly politically she is tough as hell and she can work and think like a politico, *never* letting ideas run around as ideas. These two are going to find it hard to make it, with ease to themselves. The thing I have to do is to do what I can to adjust them, and the first thing is to make G respect R, in every way. Do you see one reason why I listen to our little character-analysts, and say nothing. I shall send you the letter soon. I did *not* write this for any "purpose." R's letter only brought home most sharply her strength and her weakness, and what I have been writing in the letters, trying to get G. to do, to stop throwing out ideas. It seems that Ike encourages her and tells her they are wonderful and she is wonderful and R isn't up to much, and probably that R is jealous. And that dumb G. probably believes it. During the last two weeks, in these notes, I have been putting before G another road—and in a *private* letter to her, I told her a few truths. Believe me, sweetie, I sent G abroad, I worked at R to go out. These are wonderful people. R's letter, I shall enclose it, send it back at once, is splendid. But historical circumstances have driven us into a little hole. Merely going here and there is not enough. They want scope, contact with the world, particularly workers, the movement, ideas tested in the actual struggle. Stalinism has us in that hole. It has killed a good many, just by this pressure. Squeezes them to pulp. That R could start afresh again 7 years ago and work as she has worked is as stern a test as is possible. When our little Filomena pops up and holds forth "I don't think R is much of a leader" I cannot *say* anything. What the hell can I say? I could say a lot of things about Filomena, who was born yesterday and knows nothing—yet is O.K. in her own way. If she had a *little* more experience, she wouldn't say that, not out of regard for R, but because she would know that such things reveal too much about F. I don't mean F is a criminal. Not at all. But I have enough to do to be bothered about everything. This business of watching them, and constantly adjusting. It is a hell of a business. And I keep it in the background as much as possible and as long as possible. I never obtrude it. They have their pride. (I just write, these are aspects, certain things which stand out at certain times.) I am tired. I'll write to-morrow. Take a picture, a new picture, not too big but not too small and send it, please. And tell Jean I would welcome a parcel of the Hegel Aesthetics. These free-wheeling gentlemen, *they* will not settle down and discipline themselves in a small narrow circle—it isn't easy or pleasant, you know—and fight for some ideas and hold some people together, and discipline yourself to a larger circle. No, *they* are their masters, free to abuse everybody. I listen and say nothing. I do my work, and with God be the rest. You are a great treasure to me, sweetie. And make that Jean sit up and get the books. Give my regards to him; Gale [Malaquais], Raskins and all. O.K. Sweets.
C. L. R. James
c/o Drackert
Pyramid Lake Ranch, Sutcliffe, Nevada

September 27 [1948]

And now, my miracle, a little examination of a great problem, tho' in itself it is no problem. I have seen you for a long time worrying about "a place for yourself," and your work, etc., and comparing yourself with R, and G., and wondering whether your literary work was worthwhile, your fits of typing and secretarialism, etc. Hints or rather clear indications have appeared in your recent letters.

I can't go into everything connected with this here. But I can go into some. One of your letters said how thrilled you were at the Greek plays, you began to see that there were possibilities for you, you wondered in the past if the study of literature was worthwhile when so much was going on. You always have been ready to compare literature with politics "in value." All this has been very painful to me. I had discussed it with you maybe not sufficiently. But I had told you my ideas. You had accepted them. I encouraged you to spend time, and money on books. I pointed out that G., Rae, Bill had all listened to me, Willie was listening. They were going places, after years of labour. I spent a lot of time on the thing myself. Put yourself in my place. Your queries meant (a) that I was faking and fooling you (b) or you were restless and dissatisfied and angling for me to reassure you and (c) or you were comparing yourself and your work with G and R; or a mixture of all three. And all the time you were saying "I am an unloved woman. Everything will be OK, but for that." Imagine me! A political task agreed upon, involving years of work and planning, rejection of this or that alternative course, and then this gigantic task made to rest on personal jealousy, personal considerations. Sweetie, I must write as I think, as I am, or I cannot write, I cannot speak. This was one aspect of a whole complex. Now I want to make some assertions here, positive statements—details we can talk about.

The literary career I have outlined for you is as serious a thing as the study of philosophy and the study of political economy. It is the job of a life-time. It will take years before you are fitted. Two years and two good years too, before you are equipped with a foundation. Five years before you are ready. (For one thing you have to *master* French. And that is no game.) It is a weapon in the class struggle, and given a mass party, a *powerful* weapon. In a preparatory stage as we are, it is a preparation as all we are doing is a preparation. I have looked for years for someone. In an irregular way I have never ceased to work at it. I tell you: devote yourself to it. You are my wife. I love you. Yet you doubt and challenge me on this, a profoundly serious matter. How do I feel? Or I am supposed to continually reassure you and reassure you whenever you feel like squealing.

Don't you read the New Masses or Old Masses or whatever it is. Didn't you see the Stalinists capture the field *in the U.S.* for ten years? Don't you see that L. T. himself, the second man in the U.S.S.R, had to leave the War Department work and write a book on this? Surely this field is big enough for you. And finally, to-day we above all preach universality. The struggle, we say, is total, embracing *everything*. We don't use these as phrases. We mean them. In this envelope is a letter to G. (in accompanying envelope rather. All my letters to you will be in ordinary envelopes henceforth). There you will see that philosophical method and dialectical logic are receiving my closest personal attention. If I were in charge of a party, I would publish such studies *for the general reader*. Lenin begged the academicians of 1921 to do the same. How is it possible to *underestimate* literature, literary criticism, the elaboration of a profoundly new method, and taking this to the masses, as one day, God willing, we shall take every God damn thing we are doing to the masses. Let them reject it. We will not assume that they will in advance.

This is a war, the literary field is a battlefield. Cecelia & Co. say that your work on D. W. [Richard Wright] can recruit. I am quite cold to it. If it recruits nobody, what? No, I don't look at it that way and that is the wrong spirit. Tho' they mean well. You are preparing yourself for something. Why? Because the something is valuable and because you have the capacity. Of that I have and have never had any doubt. I say as I said at the beginning. It is the will and the strength to grapple with the drudgery and shape the material. And that no one can know if you have unless you do it and until you do it. One more word on that and then I am done with it. R, G., to some extent, and B, all began with my ideas, lived on them, worked at them, listened, sat at my feet until they learnt, and then they flew. They had the will to stick it. *Nothing* turned them aside. That you must have.

Now, it isn't serious, it just isn't serious to say: Is my work as valuable as G's or R's? That means you don't respect it? Or you set out to type madly. "Now I am contributing." Fantastic. *FAN*-tastic. Peace or War, U.S. or Great Britain, one baby (good little Nob) or two; illness or health; poverty or balanced bills, that is your work. A crisis may cause all or any of us to throw all we have into some special job; everybody does that. G. & R are wonderful at it. So is Bill by the way. But the main objective always is the central task.

It must not be played with. If you wish to be a straight politico, then *drop this one*. Then you begin another set of reading, another set of thinking, buy other books, make other notes. . . . And literature becomes a mere avocation. You must join up as soon as I return—it was a *mistake* to go to the H. B. as you did—you do your chores, you live a regular party life, going to meetings, parties, etc. *And that is all.* (If you want to be 100% politico, OK. Training? General reading, etc.: 2 years. Fully equipped to do something: Five. Then you are a trained apprentice: nothing more.) Furthermore, and I mention this in passing. Your whole temperament unfits you for that business. You can learn, sure. But I don't think you really want to. I believe that your main motive would be a desire to feel that you are doing something, that you are not behind, that you have a place, that you will be with me, and G. & R, and not left out, etc., etc. That, sweetheart, is the lesser part of you. All of us have the two oppositions running through us. We can't drive them out, but we can know which is which.

You want your husband to be in love with you, admire you, respect you.

LE-gitimate. Absolutely *Le*-gitimate. I don't want a copy or the originals of G. and R. What I want is *you* doing *your* work, pushing aside narrow or small competition, learning something, learning, mastering it, filling a monstrous gap, and in time not only developing, elaborating something as new as what we are doing, *educating* everybody, but a terror to James T. F., Howe, Van Wyck Brooks, Albert Maltz, T. S. Eliot, Partisan Review, John Chamberlin, Orville Prescott (such tripe as Harvey Breit isn't worth a glance) and all others. When they see you coming they will run. And to cross the water and let Sartre and the rest of them have it. Do you think I propose to let William spend his days playing at being a workers' leader? Not if I can help it. He needed five years *discipline* and *experience*. You will have yours also, in a special way. We are having it, trouble enough. But respect your work. You are low down now in the scale. Young people always believe that the world is ending to-morrow. In a few years, whatever happens, in your particular field, you will be able to do what many others cannot do; go to the public. In fact you have begun. And the party will never stand in your way if you manage to get a bourgeois publication to take your work.

I said once: Ch'n should break out. That ass is so busy "splitting" or rather thinking about it, that he does not do it. We maneuvered R into a splendid controversy in the American Economic Review; G. has had a little show but not out. As you know we are hoping that W [William] will make it. Now you, I hope, will make this your *profession*. Then legitimately and without subterfuge or manuever, you can go out in the market-place, and do not only solid critical work but rough and tumble journalism, and any other writing that you please. So I have seen it always. And unless I feel that you see it that way, I shall not have any peace. It means sometimes sitting down and hearing others talk as if the world was theirs and theirs alone. Sweetie, *we all of us have been through that*, some alone, without anything except *the idea in their heads and hope in their hearts*. I know you can work patiently. But the comparisons with others must go. They poison me; and worse they wear you down. It is a demoralising business. And try as I can I cannot see it when you say: This is a great task, etc., etc., but you, Nello, spoil it. I stop for the time being. But I mean well. This is how I see it. When you say that, I haven't an argument, not one.

I sit quiet and can't begin. As a matter of fact, and you must take this seriously, I don't take it seriously. I say: well, let's wait and see. This *must* pass. And nothing I can say will help. For me to say "Darling, I love you," would seem to me like some mockery. As if I were telling a committee member "Please old chap, we like you. Don't leave the movement." I sometimes think I am a hard, bitter, cruel man who should not be married at all. But if I didn't take serious things seriously, I would be a different person, better or worse, but different. And it is hard to be different in fundamental things. I have to feel safe about certain things, and feel that they are right. My circle sometimes runs my patience to the last extremity, not for their personal characteristics—those I try to ignore. I am sure I have plenty. But it is when they do some of the things you have been hearing about, and you don't know half of them, that I get put out seriously, tho' I say nothing or little. But with you I want to feel absolutely at ease. And that for me means among other things that you are right with your work. I don't mean to be an ascetic or never to have little jealousies or despondencies, etc.—most people have them. But you seem at times to be ready to pose fundamental questions about it for insufficient reasons—and I react. I can't help it. But I believe you are serious. So this then must be a weapon in your struggle for my personal attention. I know that this is a serious matter for you. So where am I? And at bottom, in all the confusion I resent deeply that such matters should be weighed in the balance against our personal relations. If R ever said to me "I don't think I can go on—my personal life is so unhappy," I would try to persuade her otherwise, but I could never, never, feel the same about her. But you are my wife. I *have* to feel good about you. I feel ashamed to have to add: I do not doubt you. I never say: This is no good. I always say "Come what may, I shall see this through." I don't doubt you. But you do what are to me hurtful things. This just begins things, I know. Don't throw back things at me. These things are instinctive with me. I have lived by them. If they are inhuman or unreasonable then I have a long road to go; but I am ready to travel any road that I can see clearly.

Love and tickles to Nob. Kisses for you.

Nello

PUSSONAL
STRICKLY

Now, honey, don't you go straining yourself over all this stuff. Do Guérin and then take the rest in your stride.

Remember Nob is not to be made a B/K [Bolshevik] by force. *He* must decide. Also this letter to G., you enclose it in a little piece of Scotch tape. G is getting and is going to get some hard blows (fully deserved) but R is making some fine blunders in the course of her general strategy which is good. So I choose this *moment* to send G this stuff which I was going to do in any case. But I don't want to have to play those games with you. Then my whole life————. Christ.

Love, tickle for Nob.

[Letter to Lyman Paine]*

October 2, 1948

My dear Lyman,

Thanks for the money. I went into Reno and got it. The reasons for the crisis I wish to go into briefly.

I have to stay here at least five weeks longer than we planned and perhaps more. The final action can be begun only thirty days after notice of filing has been actually served on my ex-wife in the West Indies. Christ knows what tricks will be pulled out there. There may be days of delay. Living here is expensive. Even when all was found, my expenses as a "help," clothes, laundry, "conviviality," etc., mounted.

Then after I had carefully gained assurance that my job was safe, I lost it, and was allowed to stay on at $40.00 a week as guest. I stayed on for several reasons.

1) I was not sure where, or what, I could get as accommodation in Reno at all.

2) The meals were *regular in time* and not bad. If not exciting they were sound.

3) The chief reason however, is that even in the intervals of my gardening and cleaning, I found that for a variety of reasons I could work here as I have not worked for some dozen years. I don't know what the reasons all are, but the work has amazed me. I could do 10,000 words a day without stopping to put a comma, and then read all sorts of books, and start off again in the morning. It has not stopped. In fact I seem just to have begun. I could not risk going elsewhere and finding myself in some hole, having to go out for meals, without hot water, etc., as the first weeks.

I stayed but I stayed at a price. I have been as sick as a dog some days with my ulcer tearing the inside out of me. I became "a guest" but I have continued to eat in the kitchen. Spare me the labor of writing down the details, but I had to choose, and that was the better way. Unfortunately in addition to the strain, the kitchen fell into the hands of some barbarians and day after day I have gone in for my meals and had to clear a space out of pots, pans, potato-peelings, dirty dishes, etc., on the table of all work where we all eat. There were times when my stomach refused to take it. I

---

* A copy of this letter was sent to Constance Webb.

had a cup of soup and absolutely could not swallow—had to leave. The strain has been————. I hate even to write about it. But these are the fortunes of war.

It is a place of refuge. I am learning plenty and my work is unaffected. However *I* am affected. Whenever possible I rush into Reno, for this place is absolutely isolated, 35 miles from Reno. And I play the machine *and lose*. I am a gambler now. Then there are many opportunities here; there is riding, I can get taken in a car to places, I needed jeans, clothes, shoes, to buy many things but fifty dollars a week as living expenses and five and maybe more extra weeks, and extra expenses, legal, I mean (the lawyer is paid $250 already. I owe only $50, though there are other expenses waiting I am sure), all this makes a nice mess. To be quite frank, I could have bought many things with the money I played in the slot machine, but there you have the whole messy, sordid, Zola-esque details. These last few weeks are going to be grim. It is weeks since we sent the summons to the West Indies. There is no notice of service having been made as yet. But 1. The divorce is in sight and legal and solid, 2. The trip has given me a priceless insight into the West, and though I have missed so much, yet I have divined a great deal. 3. Work that would have taken six months in N.Y. has been done, and much more will be done, so that the tale of woe is silver-lined. Enough of that.

There is, however, another matter that I wish to bring to your careful attention. The matter has been preoccupying me for two years, and it is time that it was brought to an end.

I got a letter from Constance recently, last night in fact. In it she mentions 1) that Rae spoke to her about some lunch I had with you to talk about money matters 2) Rae mentioned it to her because Freddie had spoken to R about it "several times." 3) You had spoken to C herself about it, presuming that she "knew."

Closely connected with this is a scheme whereby F was to collect money for us for the baby and make all arrangements—not "factionally," only to expedite and help, etc. For this proposal R is responsible, and she in fact wrote to me about it when she learnt my first hostile reaction.

First of all, the question of money as such.

Money corrupts. Its ways of doing so are infinitely subtle. (His facility with finances *for the party* and friends was one of the sources of the destruction of Harry Allen.) Whoever has strenuous purposes or important associations should be extremely careful if there is any money about. That is a good general rule. In our case, however, the responsibilities are back-breaking. 1. It is a *political* responsibility of the first order. If it gets about at all that you have a little, just a little money, besides your regular income, or are expecting some, then God help us, God help us. It will form a part of the calculations of *all who are connected with us, or with whom we are connected*. It will be a source of intrigue, yes, intrigue and gossip, exaggeration, speculation and scandal. We will be harmed, no one else. We went through this in the W. P. In the SWP it could be incomparably *worse*. Then we have the responsibility to make some decisions about it. This involves, as I have told you, and as you have seen, the whole question of our political perspectives in the SWP At the Convention we came to a decision—into the SWP as deeply as we can and brush aside all other perspectives. But the final word in that matter does not rest with us. Circumstances bigger than we decide those things. It is a profoundly difficult problem. I am working at something. We shall discuss. But it is a political question

Separation and Limbo (1947–8) 343

with all sorts of moral implications; and involving the necessity of many safeguards whatever we do. It is not only what others may say two years from today; it is what all sorts of young people whom we are responsible for will say or may think, two years, five years, from today.

There is involved also the responsibilities of the tendency—at home, as a political group of people, its responsibility for individuals (e.g., the important question of Willie); and its responsibilities abroad. You have to know how what you do today will look three years from now.

Involved also is my personal situation. I have to find some means of livelihood. I have discussed that with you. I have to relate this to the SWP I *cannot* have any mystery about my income, and yet I am determined not to be a responsibility to the party and keep people like Hansen and all the field organisers out of a job. Abstract right has nothing to do with this, *absolutely nothing*. It would be a false position to be in, that would do infinitely more harm than good. At the same time I must not make the tendency feel responsible for me or that any "injustice" is being done to me. I came off the payroll as quickly as I could and during all the pre-convention period and before that, we lived on some money Constance had. I have to do some bourgeois work. Yet I must be free to do some party work and at the same time free to do the enormous work that devolves upon me. Three people *have* to do this work in the U.S. Cannon, Max, and myself. If the tendency were theoretically to gain a victory tomorrow, then I could take up a *department* and leave a lot of work of a general nature undone. But as long as the tendencies exist, someone has to keep incessantly coordinating everything in relation to our ideas—good or bad work it may be, but it is done as automatically as a man driving an automobile does things which the man sitting next to him does *not* do. If I were out of the way tomorrow, R would immediately and automatically begin. If half a dozen of us were wiped away, then soon enough the remaining senior would find himself doing it. Cannon leaves the international situation to the Europeans. I have to do *all*. I cannot let myself be overburdened with too much work of other kinds. I have superb assistance, but the ground I cover is twice what Cannon and Max even attempt. And their conditions of life are much easier than mine, in every way. Finally there is the Government. I have to be in a situation to make an open accounting to them; but this open accounting must be able to meet the scrutiny of the SWP This is a head-ache and a belly-ache, all in one, a burden beyond belief. I shall work it out. The only thing I ask for the time being is that it remain absolutely between us, every scrap of it. It adds too much to me when there is gossip and chatter of *any* kind. I have not consulted *Rae*. I don't want to. When you spoke to me you spoke to me confidentially. I took it as such. I spoke to you in the same way. You and *Freddie* are involved in one respect. But that is all. Nobody, absolutely nobody, has any right to be concerned with this, absolutely nobody. Whenever this sort of thing takes place, I feel it is a sort of political disgrace, and a terrible irritation. It is unbusinesslike, unprofessional, unpolitical.

Unfortunately, this is not all; and the whole thing is tangled up in my personal life, and my married life. I hope it is perfectly obvious now to everyone that I am in love with my wife, that it is neither infatuation nor episode, and that she is part of me and I of her. In our early months she was pestered by a continuous stream of information, gossip, advice, etc., about me, behind my back, what I thought, what I was doing, what I could do, what I could not do, my weaknesses, my strength, God knows what. And every bit of gossip was faithfully relayed to her—my past love affairs were not forgotten. We had our own troubles for which nobody was responsible but ourselves, but Constance is a very sensitive person, and to our own strictly personal problems, was added this constant interference, criticism, analysis, illumination of me, which made it doubly difficult for her to steer a road between me as a politician and as her husband. Much of it was stupidity, some of it well-meaning, and, I regret to say, a good bit of it was malicious. We struggled through this additional burden and in the whole mess, I nearly lost her. Now I am determined that nothing like this will happen again to complicate our personal relations. She has not complained to me—and for that matter if she had, that was O.K. with me. She merely wrote somewhat resignedly. But I do not want R or F or anybody else asking her questions about financial or any other arrangements which I am supposed to be making behind her back and about which it appears as if everybody knows and she does not know. We have had enough of all that, Lyman, more than enough. Further, I do not want any financial or any other arrangements to be made by Freddie or Rae, or any friends whatever, with her irrespective of me. I am opposed to the whole business because it builds up caucus solidarity, whatever may be in the heads of those who think it an innocent and friendly gesture. It strengthens some grave weaknesses I have seen among our people. Also it complicates for me the tangle I have outlined earlier. I have to know all that I am doing, getting, arranging, etc.

In addition, I must add, there is the implication that J cannot manage his finances. I have to spend some time on this. Politically, I have fought steadily against any attempt to limit or circumscribe the capacities of anyone. It is wrong. People can do anything within limits that they set their minds to and much more than they think. "That A can do this but is no good at that" is usually an analysis of the person who makes it, not of the person analysed. I have been shockingly careless in the past. The reason is simple. I have had too much work to do, and everybody automatically lets certain things slide. I let that side go its way, because I have no love for it. It was wrong. But that must stop now. My personal finances must become the attention of myself and my wife. Furthermore, Constance wants it that way. We have to work out these things and fix them the best way we can. I hope that both politically and personally this is clear, the reasons for it. Let me add also that I have been very angry at the way people speak of my habits, my preferences in personal associations, etc., to younger comrades, and loosely on the whole. All this is ammunition to enemies and disruption to our younger people.

We shall need help, but I am now responsible, directly. You and F have helped me in all sorts of ways in the past. I have made bills and you have paid them without even telling me. I have not said anything but I do not forget such things. But you see, I hope, that a new situation has arisen. Constance is pregnant and is far from well. The strain of the last two years has been almost unbearable. From now on, for a few months at least, insofar as the pressure, all pressure can be kept at bay, I propose to do so. Her personality has a right to be respected. We, she and I, do not see very much in that respect in regard to others. Rae and the others, I know, are burning with enthusiasm and affection, to help. That is wonderful and we expected it and are very happy about it. But if anyone wants to give some money, let him or her write out a cheque or get some cash and send it to me, or to both of us and say: this is for the baby or to help with expenses or something. The *official* handling of it I shall see after, taking all the circumstances into consideration, and they are many. I have mentioned only some.

Finally, Lyman, and I say this with much pain, as I think over the future in the light of the recent past, many or at least some aspects I think should be mentioned and should have been mentioned before. In the course of the past seven years I do not remember ever having consciously said anything which would harm relations between husband and wife; or cause doubt or unpleasantness between friends, or even acquaintances in our circle. I can remember innumerable occasions on which I have gone out of my way to do the opposite. Constance and I have not had the same extended to us. The thoughtlessness, the lack of control, and in some cases the venom with which our problems, weaknesses, and failings have been attacked and discussed are still an unpleasant memory. Older comrades have talked carelessly before younger ones, when at the very least they could have exercised restraint. Some of our personal experiences have been bitter enough. I think you should know a little of the strain under which we live. During the trip to California, part of which time we lived in a little room, there was the constant fear after the first few weeks, of the arrest; it means, my dear Lyman, that every knock on the door was a threat, every suspicious stranger a possible detective. Then came the arrest and the wearisome details of attorney, etc., day after day. We came back. One morning an F.B.I. man walked in, just walked in. After that, any morning an F.B.I. man can walk in. After that I was interrogated, and told to expect that a more official interrogation would take place within some weeks. The time is long overdue. In other words, at any time it can take place. The lawyer has warned me that my situation is as bad as it can be. The government, if it gets wind of this trip, can seek to stop it by yanking me back to jail. The serving of my ex-wife in Trinidad, through the American consul, *may* give them this information. Hanging over us is the threat of being yanked out in time. We still fear, and only when this marriage goes through we will be a little easier, that the government may raise complications about our marriage. In the best it means living here under constant uncertainty. For Constance it may mean being forced to fight to follow me, though the Reno divorce and Nobbie will help. It may mean going off to cold, hungry England, leaving everybody behind, and probable loss of citizenship for Constance. She has never wavered once, nor been anything else but brave and cheerful about the whole business. But we feel it, both of us, I can tell you. We feel it. The comrades stand by us faithfully and many with devotion. Of that there is no question. But we are entering a new stage. In all this mess of a life that we live, she now becomes the first object of my personal attention. And I want it as I have outlined it. Any kind of repetition of the past, with whatever good intentions, is out. And this Freddie to Rae to Constance to me; and the speed with which the "help" was organised, no. The dangers I know now.

I have written to you for two reasons. The first one is strictly political. I talked to you about it before I left. I may be sent off, maybe not, but no serious person takes chances on that. We, our tendency, live under great pressure. The pressure any small minority feels, worse still the pressure of a minority within a minority. The dangers for us in the SWP are *immense*, and all the more so because insidious. You see Novak told me after the Convention that he, i.e., they never expected the merger to work. I knew that and explained some of the reasons to you one day. Knowing them, and *knowing us*, I set myself to break a way for us. From the position I took in regard to the payroll, my votes and interventions at the club, on *all* topics; the whole Negro question, stage by stage, my personal relations, etc., ending with the Convention, when to speak, when not to speak, I cleared a road. They accept us now. The hard training and the documents of the interim period helped us; the comrades did *very* well. But that job was done *up above*, with the leadership, though the response of the membership at the Convention clinched it. But the plain fact of the matter is that, in the nature of things, *it is the task of the SWP to break us up, or dent us badly at any rate*. We have done all we could. That, by and large, is certain. And I do not accuse the SWP leaders of criminality. Simply one must operate on the basis that a majority automatically seeks to liquidate a minority, particularly a majority with the past experiences of the SWP Now, the task is to help the tendency in, as far in as it can go; absolutely in if possible; but the leadership, our leadership, must at the same time, maintain its own integrity, and maintain harmonious, progressive and yet nonconspiratorial relations within itself. Now our leading people have shown grave weaknesses, and not the least among them for me, is much that has taken place in connection with my marriage. In that respect you stand out. I cannot remember a single instance in which you behaved in any other way than a serious man would behave. We are petty-bourgeois, very much so, lacking the experience of not great, but large affairs; and some of our best people show it. Unless under the stimulus of political activity, and factional solidarity, they do not show the restraint and self-discipline that leaders have to show always, not 80% of the time, nor a high average, but *always*. We have developed a theory of astonishing range and vitality, due to our close consolidation, but this has taken its toll in other respects. There are certain things which I shall explain to you personally. But before I left, I told you, and am all the more certain of it since, that, whether I go or not, we need your sobriety and absence of violent personal prejudices. Rae is the unquestioned leader, not by seniority, but in experience and capacity. But she needs, all of them need, a stabilizing force, and a pole of observation, silence and personal authority. I don't know anyone so fitted for it as you. The prominent position occupied by two women, both married, and superior in political status to their husbands, offers possibilities of disorder, both internal and external. They all will be less intelligent than they ought to be, if they do not know that. I do not propose to go any further with this aspect of the matter now. But I leave the handling of this whole question to you, the questions that I have raised in this letter. Except for certain parts which are strictly between us, and nobody else, I do not care what use you make of it, whom you write to, whom you speak to, what you say; but at any rate you know how Constance and I feel about the past, what we think about the future, you will understand certain of my actions in the future and you can help us in many ways. When I return I shall have some conversations with you about these and kindred matters.

The second reason I write to you in particular, Lyman, is more personal, but as with me, the personal cannot be disentangled from the political. My wife is still somewhat of a stranger among us. Marrying me she married into a doubly difficult environment, the movement, my personal status here, and my race. We all, me included, are apt to forget that I am a Negro. Our child will be half-a-Negro. As long as I am around we can manage. But one must plan. Large insurances, etc., are for the time being beyond me. But that child will be a special responsibility. I am going to do my best to meet it.

But for me, the mother is more important than the child. Life, our life today, and our individual lives are full of turmoil and confusion. Comrades are comrades, some are very good; but many of these comrades are thoughtless and somewhat insensitive. I want to feel that in whatever circumstances she may find herself, with Nobbie, that Constance is able to come to you, and talk to you without doubt or hesitation; I feel that while others will be as generous as you are, they will not be as tolerant, as sympathetic, as ready to let people go their own way without necessarily thinking that that is the correct way. I want to feel at ease about a few elementary things. I want her to feel at ease also, as far as that is possible. And I do not want too much talk of any kind. I shall send this letter to Constance for her to read and then ask her to dispatch it to you. I shall be glad to hear from you.

Yours as always,

I wrote this letter on Friday. It is a difficult subject. I did not dispatch it at once. I left it and went over it on Saturday; much as has been said, yet much remains unsaid. I shall try to make it easier for you to understand the various points.

I have not gone "all psychological," but far from it. But I believe that I have kept silent about certain things too long, and that they have affected *me* personally. Also it is wrong for me to keep so many things to myself. Every single group and leadership suffers terrible blows whenever the accepted leader is removed, and this is part of the reason. Let me clear up a few things. The strain under which we have lived, Constance and I, has been too much. I am proposing now for her sake and mine that within the encircling pressures, and despite them, I shall make a certain normal life for ourselves, in every way, until Nob is born, weaned, and she is up and strong again, i.e., her usual self, this comes first with me. Constance has literary ambitions. I have encouraged them, confident of her ultimate success and the benefit to our movement. I have stood in the way of no one's attempt to do something—have stood out for ability of any kind to have the chance to express itself. I am going to foster hers. From our number 1306, an enormous amount of work and preparation for work in the future goes on. But it takes a heavy toll. Expenses mount. Personal expenses are hard to keep in check when every minute is spent with the thousand and one things that concern us both. I believe that we have spent a few hundred dollars in books recently, and the tale is not half over. She has to do the work. It will take years, she cannot go to university and lacks all training which must be made up for in the house here. The ordinary details of personal life suffer. This has to be changed. But we cannot change it by ourselves. There must be a better understanding all round. Constance is not an ordinary type. This constant struggle to adjust to me, a problem of great magnitude, if I may say so, and to everything else, is too much. I remember the tortures to which Grace was subjected, some of it through my own short-sightedness in regard to that miserable Allen. On the whole, the record has not been good. I know my share.

But there is something deeper going on here. During the days when I was working at the problem of the SWP and watching every step, knowing how much depended on the impression and the sense of confidence or non-confidence that all of them would be forming, during that time Rae behaved as if she was crazy. I had decided and told her that she was now on her own, and I would not try to exercise the firm restraint and control that I did at the W. P. You got only a hint of it at our meeting. There was a terrible, eating hostility against the SWP, which was at times uncontrollable. I'll give you the details. Some of the older comrades suffered from it (and you too did your share by the way). This at a time when so much depended upon the exactly opposite course. I said very little. I could not understand it. There was also a fierce hostility to Grace abroad. The pair of them blundered terribly while I was in California. And since I have been away Grace now, has gone crazy again, though in an opposite direction. There is the same lack of ability to watch a situation, detach your personal self from it, and do what is right, even if you personally are feeling wronged, and with considerable justification. Now today the situation between them is not good, due almost entirely to Grace's fault, but though Rae has made a splendid recovery, and *politically* develops every day—in many respects, in theory, *as related to political activity*, she is in class A, and lacks only the experience which our small movement cannot give her—she lacks that control of herself which a leader must have. She talks too much and too freely. And her task now demands the opposite. They will work together, because both are serious and trying, but I don't think it will ever be a completely harmonious combination and under political pressure it can explode. Furthermore, Rae has another grave weakness—a tendency to get our people together and hold them by close bonds. She never misses and automatically creates association, it is a touch of the old Abernism. Its positive side is one of her most remarkable characteristics, and has been a tower of strength to us, but at present it can do harm, to the others and to herself. Simple as it may seem I am very much concerned, for the strictest political reasons, that the tendency as a whole, lose any sort of feeling of responsibility for me. They have to learn to live alone, with their ideas, and a sense of personal responsibility and self-reliance. All this is very difficult.

Now as I look back at the last two years, the personal explosions that took place in regard to my marriage (There was one immortal formula that you and I will share. It was said that Constance had left the movement and gone and had a fine time as model and actress and had now come back and stolen the leader—stolen is a quote) and the violence of the reactions against the SWP leadership—in general—among some of the older comrades, I have come to see certain things and a pattern begins to form which embraces much of what is going on; though it is beginning to subside, there is no reason why it may not burst out again. There is a terrible discrepancy between the range, the boldness, the philosophical basis, the concreteness of our ideas, and the miserable little places we do hold, both as a group and individually. There is this constant underlying strain, exasperation, impotence and frustration. It is organic. The comrades by and large hold it in check, in fact looking back I see how much of our work and energy have been spent in holding down, inculcating discipline, subordination, restraint, opposition yet cooperation, etc. And periodically it explodes in bursts of anger and antagonism which sometimes takes absolutely unreasoning and crude personal forms. Sometimes it attacks an individual. I have seen some curious cases. Sometimes it takes a group of them together. But there must be one or two at least who will be aware and watch and analyse. Our people are serious people. And with serious people, serious things have serious causes. This is the road all of you have to live, Rae in particular. We have some weak spots. But someone must stand by, who is in a position and of a temperament to be detached, someone who can see, observe, maybe on rare occasions say a word here or two words there, and when necessary intervene to help Rae, and also to watch her, which is the same thing. I shall see to it that you are kept informed and take part in all our most intimate discussions. It will mean some effort. You will have to make it.

It is one of the most unwise things in political life to discuss the failings, so to speak, of your comrades. As a rule, little but harm comes of it, and harm which could have been avoided and is difficult to repair. I am making a change. But it is a very limited change, though it has great and important potentialities for us all. But it is limited in that I have told these things to you and to you alone. I would like to hear specifically from you on this point. I mean Freddie. Freddie has not the right to know my opinions of R and G. for example, to the extent that I have put them down here and hope to discuss with you further. Neither should she want to know. We have had enough of husband and wife among us, and it is time to put an end to it. You would be amazed at the distance that exists between JPC's secretariat and his *P.C.* He encourages no unnecessary talking—none; but he discusses with Moische and, I believe, Dobbs. It is absolutely certain that if you spread this any further, then even by implication it will begin to seep out and your possibilities of service will be seriously affected. Enough for the time being. The picture I hope begins to emerge.

With all the best,
J.

[C.L.R. James c/o Drackert
Pyramid Lake Ranch
Sutcliffe, Nevada]

Postmark October 11, 1948

Sweetie, I am very tired. Sunday night 12 p.m. I went into Reno on Friday; and from Friday night to now I have worked like a horse.

As I told you, I went gambling, hoping to make a lot of money. It is not so stupid as it sounds. But I made an awful fool of myself. After some heavy losses at the start, over and over again, three or four times running, I have won between $25 and $40.00 and if there had been a train I would have gone home. But there wasn't, there was nowhere I could go, and I just played and played and have lost every penny back. I did it on Friday again. You must wait until you hear all the details. So I work feverishly day and night to make up for the loss. It is not quite as simple as it sounds. I am going through something. You will now know, this and everything else.

I was glad to talk to you tonight. You sounded fine, happy and confident. I was not as bad as I sounded to you. I love you every day a little more; I think you are wonderful, in all sorts of ways. I have been very stupid about you, but I couldn't help it. The responsibility was always mine, but I think it is behind us now—its back is broken. Don't expect too much from me. I have been through plenty and it will take time to recover, but you will know everything, not only for your sake but for mine. I am satisfied with you. I wouldn't change a thing in you if I had the power to do so. Nothing. In many ways I think I have crossed a great milestone in my own life down here. I knew for years that something was wrong somewhere. The evil spirit, the demon, fought to hold me in the old groove. I know now exactly what the writers in Scripture wrote about, they and their demons. But I am sure now that that is over. But there are a lot of pieces to be picked up and patched together. I shall make it, I'll do the best I can. You loved me in a way that I used to wonder at. I couldn't understand it for I underestimated you. If you put half the tenacity into your work that you gave to me, you will be a wonderful writer. You are in fear of being patronised by me always. You need not be. I respect you, sister. I know you. Nobody else knows you as much as I do. And for me you are tops. Don't worry yourself about answering me about yourself and your working out of your problems. There is no dateline fixed.

I am going to talk to you. We'll see. I'll keep this open in case there is need to answer something quickly in the a.m. About my return, God knows. I *never* excite myself about these things because in case of disappointment I pay all the more. But I want badly to get out of here and start my new life with you. I'll have, maybe, some difficult moments and periods. The habits of a lifetime are not got rid of so easily, but I am master of the total situation. I am pretty sure of that, I am very sure. I am longing to see you. And don't be nervous about me, whether I am away from you or with you. Just be sure inside. That's all. You be sure.

N

Give Nob a little rub for me.
C.L.R. James [c/o Drackert]
Pyramid Lake Ranch
Sutcliffe, Nevada

Airmail Special Delivery
Postmark October 13, 1948,

Reno, Nevada

Monday *a.m.*

Dear Honey-bunch,

A whole mass of mail has come in, and the picture. You look wonderful, absolutely wonderful, my beautiful wife. I hope it isn't five weeks, sweetie pie. I am hoping that they will have served and are only late in sending to say. That happens. So I have your pictures spread out before me and little Richard's too and I am going to write you a long letter. I have sweated enough at that translation

Now, you take it easy, in every way, you do just as you please, just as you please, in regard to everything. Now and then I may say: do this immediately. That means do it before anything else, very rarely does it mean to hurry at once. Watch your eyes. If you *have* to wear glasses, then do so; but take it easy. I can only tell you a lot of things at this time if I know you are taking it easy and are not going to jump or worry. I see you say you are going to relax. Good. I am merely repeating it. Now I am going to take up everything I can. Some things I will just interject. Nothing is hostile. I'll just speak my mind. I have to begin, e.g., last night I was thinking. Do you know that knowing everything is going to be hard on your friendships? In spite of yourself you will have to have an "attitude" especially to the junior ones. I mentioned it before. I have been thinking of it. It will be hard on you. You will have to come closer to me. I am not afraid of you, or for you. They will in time begin to think you are a "wife." Ho! Ho! You will see how problems will arise, and the need for the poker-face. Funny, isn't it? But you will make it, I know you will. Then they'll get to understand you, and you will be able to help them—once you are sure of yourself.

About the Greek. Wonderful. I have been rejoicing at the way you have grabbed on to it; you see now, you can't make a step without them. And steady notes. We'll go to the library often, and have lunch and sit in the park. (I read the maternity book the same afternoon; fine; my conclusion? *Rest. Take it easy.*) Edith Hamilton, I don't know, but *if you like her*, that's good. Stick to Hegel tho'. I'll send some more translation later this week. Don't hurry or worry. If you want to stay there a year, stay there. Soon you will discover the books on the Greeks in the house.

You say that you don't say many things but you agree. I don't expect you to say too many things. I write and write. You read. You say enough and plenty. I am not ill—only low. My stomach is under control again. Love me but don't worry about me.

About R and G.. I am glad you told me what you did about R's attitude. You send and tell me what you see and think; and if you are uncertain then do as you wish but I would prefer to hear. I have to write to G.—I have been too silent in the past—and I am glad you wrote. I shall alter considerably the tone of my letter to G—in fact alter it completely—the tone. You see as long as I *know* that you are not concerned about them I welcome what you say. *And I am not worried about that any longer.* One day I'll tell you all about it. It is briefly this. I know them well enough—and their solid qualities, how irreplaceable they are. If I had to choose a political associate in the whole wide world, I would choose Rae. After her bad spell, she suddenly bursts out with a series of amazing theoretical work. And they are sound as people—very sound. So once I feel sure that you know this, feel it, we can talk. I am glad you pulled up R. G is in a mess. She'll be pulled out. I am going to write her a letter she'll remember. And you just watch and tell me—you are going to help me.

Now about you. The lesser self, sweetheart, is never demolished. It is always there. We have a name for it—petty-bourgeois. It is that lesser self that tears through all our people. They have it too. We all do. One thing I single out now. Nothing special is expected from you by me. You have to make no effort to justify my confidence in you. I *know* you were fighting to justify your new step. I saw it this way: that you stepped from one life into another and you saw the other as a place where you would *immediately* find a place and recognition and self-expression in the best sense of these words. You didn't, you couldn't, and it would have been ruinous for you in the end if you had. Unless you struggle, dig deep, project, discard, sweat, you have not become new. Don't I know? The other self was not a fraud. It isn't. I wrote to you about it last night. It is very real. That's what makes it so tough. However, you are on the way. Your work on R. W. is good work. It isn't *finished* work. But it is work dug out. G.'s evaluation of it should be precious to you. What I am concerned about now is that you take it easy and not tire yourself out with it.

Watch our friends and see how they explode. You need work, confidence, patience, and the courage to endure, and a close human relationship to enable you to meet the strains and the stresses. We'll get it, we are getting it. "I am worn out" you say. That we must avoid, darling. All this is very strenuous. Merely to read all these letters and keep track is exhausting. You just go ahead and let it take its course. You are not bound to explain at once. Only if you feel compelled to write it down, do it; but do it under no sense of obligation.

About Moishe! Good. One mistake. A *small* sum of money. Some money would have been enough. But that is one job done. About the pay-roll business, sweetie, I knew that. Think it over. You will see that I saved them from an embarrassing position. If I had pressed, *they had no alternative*. But it would have left a sore spot; and inasmuch as a) I cannot undertake full duties b) *I do not want to* (what an ass *I*

352 Separation and Limbo (1947–8)

would be), this thing would *constantly* be in the way and *come up*. Sweetie, it is impossible to get R to understand these things, impossible. And the reason, I see, is—hostility; anger at those who have the wrong position and are standing in the way. . . . I am glad *you* went and fixed it up. Little by little we'll fix up everything. To return to the topic. From any point of view, I on the payroll and the Detroit organiser not on it, on account of me, or as seemed probable once, Dobbs not on it. That is *wrong*. And only temper, frustration and hostility, not superficial, nothing *cheap*, can account for failure to see this. Then—it is easy to say—J has a weakness—he doesn't like these things. Sure I don't. But *if* there was a *gain*, a political *gain*, I'd make such a planned, organized stink as you never smelled. I feel at this moment very close and warm with you, sweetie. Never, *never*, in my life have I ever talked to anybody about everything. Never. And the last seven years I believe I have been the loneliest man in the world; our ideas and plans and perspectives are so big, our work, and our concrete sphere is so small. It is a terrible, a breaking strain upon the personality. We will share it.

The R's sweetie are Thomasites.* They will be perhaps good fellow-travellers. I would not embark on any campaign to destroy Norman Thomas with them. *They* must raise the questions and seriously. Carl Leo is a character. I believe you can at present get further with him. But I am cautious and skeptical. There is no reason why you should be. I only tell you what I think. I am not surprised about Jean and G either. But here arises a serious problem. I'll give you an example. I was skeptical about Ruth and Leah and the caucus. Rae said "*No*" and persisted and won them over. You are impatient and ready to pull some of your friends up if they are too slow, or you want to go ahead and see. You are absolutely right to do so. A great danger is that the older, more experienced, should check the younger, more adventurous. I stood aside and watched R—and genuinely wanted her to prove me wrong—and she did.

As for G wanting to go to P[ittsburg]. Jesus! Did you ever see such? You see behind it of course. The idea of being alone! Someone to talk to, the personal contact, the political contact, the reassurance, the salving of the frustration, and I do not mean personal, psychoanalytical tripe. In fact it is the reverse of that. Now you know more about me. I have had to hold them in check *for years*. And when you bounced around I was scared stiff. I could, I should have been easier on you, but I froze inside. G *knows* that this is wrong. But the internal strain becomes too much, and she makes this fantastic proposition. Yonnie [Feinberg] wants to contribute. He likes us, sure, but he feels left out, isolated. All this was behind my letter. And I know why I like William so much, in a personal way. W gets excited about *political* things. He says: This is needed at once, *at once*. I curb him. But he has a great detachment about many things, sensitive as he is. I am glad you checked her. But on the whole, sit back, watch, observe, and tell me. Don't get tangled up politically. Let it slide, watch and learn, and do your Greek. Lean backwards and let it be perfectly obvious that you are leaning backwards. Before ever you get into this, you have to establish a firm foundation of your own, your own *work*, your own *style*, your own outlook, not mine,

---

* Norman Thomas was the leader of the Socialist Party who ran for US President six times.

yours; and I want nothing to interfere with that. That is the only source of strength, and the overcoming of that demon. Make them come up to see you, and only when you want.

By the way, I wrote a long set of notes, Sep 15–20. I hope you have one—a special set is to be kept. Then R. F.'s book turns up.* The same thing I was striving at, there R. F. solves it for me; you will see it in a letter I wrote to R. You should read the notes and the letter together. Now lunch, and a letter to G. Thanks for doing all the business so promptly, sweetie. Your pictures are wonderful. You look terrific. You thought I don't admire you! Ho! But that demon, sweetie. If you know the dirty tricks he played on me. I think and have never thought otherwise, that you are woman No. 1; *nobody*, nobody else has even a look-in. I have thought so from the moment I saw you till to-day. My dearest Constance! Sugar, you must be very patient with me. You say you have to fight the demon. I have fought him. He fought me over you and my admiration of you. But you beat him. I love you and I *do* mean you. Ho! ho!

Just had some lunch and made some "hossies," paper hossies, for the kids. They have a field-day in my room, they are always in here, they come to me to button up their clothes, when they are hurt, to hear music, to go for walks, even to go to the ladies toilet in case of crisis; five of them, they run wild all over the place and do not trouble their parents—women who brought them here for the 6 weeks. But that is another story, and oh! sister, what a story!

By the way. You remember one day F'a came to you with some story about R and said, "I don't think she is much of a leader." From me: silence, absolute silence. Why? One reason is that I know R had been doing a lot of silly things and some terrible ones. But I have seen R, I know R, I appreciate R; she will have to do plenty to upset me. You remember L's [Lenin's] Testament. L. T. is not a Bolshevik; but make him the chief. You see L knew L. T., understood his value, but he knew his weaknesses. He could say the most awful things about him—and did—but as a colleague and say them and say "Make him chief." But the younger ones, and the more superficial ones cannot appreciate a leader. It takes years to do that and experience. They haven't got it. So the errors and mistakes and weaknesses loom large; and people use these to excuse their own weaknesses and backsliding. Erber** is another! God, how they come and go. And a bitter attack on a leader as leader is a bad sign—not a good sign I should say; you remember the Negro question at the Convention. I would not touch it with a 40-ft pole—all the grumbling. Why? Because they attacked "the party" as such. All this used to hurt me, for I have a sharp ear for criticism wh[ich] is meant to strike and criticism wh[ich] is meant to hurt or to bring people down. Between it all I used to be in a terrible mess; and could only sit still and take it. Particularly because no one has ever heard me or will ever hear me say "Cannon drinks to excess," nor do I like people who say it. Temperamentally I don't like it; and L. T. once told some of the friends that, even after Zinoviev had committed some of the most shameful crimes, he pulled up very sharply some young people in the Left Opposition who spoke disparagingly of him, although Z was a political enemy, ready to arrest L. T.

---

* Reference unknown to the editor.
** Ernest Erber, a prominent Trotskyist, who resigned suddenly from the WP in 1949.

That is how I am made up. It is strange—many British characteristics in me fit almost automatically into party responsibility, although I too was young and headstrong once. Further, the last years were tough. Very good people at any time could develop the most alarming symptoms. I tell you, between our entry into the SWP and the Convention, R was like a demented person. But she recovered. Naville once left the Fr[ench] Party and attacked it to the bourgeois press. The c'des hit the sky. L. T. said No. Naville is still a member, or at least one of the Fr Party. You must let me tell you about the Left Communists in 1918 one day. All this is very very hard to master *inside*. You need a very solid background and internal confidence in yourself. One day you said, "John on the P.C. I am surprised. I didn't think he was up to much." He is, as you say, not a Johnsonite; and in many respects he is very weak, but he has many remarkable qualities, political qualities, which are not often met with among us. A thousand things like that hurt me every day. The others do it and I am stoical. Much of the trouble between G. and R is the stupid way G refused to recognise R's ability. I never said a word to her. But I can't be stoical with you. But we'll dig it all out. I brought one Kierkegaard here with me; one of the sections in it has had a great influence on me.

About a trip for me back. G and I to raise the money. They are *crazy*, just crazy. I can't help wondering sometimes if *I* am the crazy one. Lovely for me to spend $350 to come back there for awhile and then be off again a few weeks later. Then G goes to P, R and J come in in December. On my way home, you go to P to meet me, we spend a week. *Isn't this a madhouse?* And after what happened between our entry and the Convention, I am very very concerned. I am writing a letter to G; you will see it and what she wrote to me. N.B. Get some of my type Scotch Tape and always close up the letters as if they came from me. And I am not doing you any favors. I want you to read them. I am opening up all round, you see; but it began with you. I look at your pictures again. I have showed them to 4 people already and I showed your other pictures to people too. Ho! ho! I laugh at the previous me.

This will stay until to-morrow. So long, sweetie. I kiss you many times, and Nob is practically born and waiting for me to see him as far as I am concerned. By the way; my phrase now; Dorothy Cheston Bennett, Arnold Bennett's mistress, wrote a book about her life with him. It is worth reading. Bear it in mind, and also that Greek book on politics and poetry. I am so glad you have caught hold of the Greek or rather it has caught hold of you. That is a big thing, sweetie, real big, don't worry to write me details, let them wait, tho' I want to hear what you have to say about the 35c book. Then one day we'll go to the Metropolitan and look at the casts of statues, the famous Greek ones. Then don't forget to bear in mind Spengler and his chapters on classical civilisation. Plenty of stuff and you have plenty of time. In all your reading and writing, notes, etc., observations, you show all the signs of a born writer, you never fail me. But you need internal calm. Don't be afraid for your work. Funny. You were eager to demonstrate. I was not. I was entirely *opposite*. I was eager to see you settle down to work and have the attitude—to hell with demonstrating anything. When you read the Greek this way, and books about it and get carried away by it, then I am "satisfied" and confident. When you are too eager to write and publish, even to do something to show *me*, I am unhappy. Let nothing shake you. War, revolution, you will do your share, but go out and work only if absolutely imperative to avoid starvation. Cultivate that calm, internal confidence and patience, and when in doubt, have confidence in me. I am glad you grabbed the Hamlet. Fine. And by the way, if anyone, *with money*, wants to give you a present, say the opera, Don Giovanni. In good time we have something rich there. Keep your eye open for a *cheap* Molière. If you see a copy of Man and Superman by G. B. Shaw, *grab it*. Any old *cheap* translations of Racine, Corneille, Seneca, grab them; *cheap* Goethe's Faust, grab it. And keep on looking for a Britannica; also a *cheap* Byron. Also, ask Simons to get you a copy of the Everyman's list, and a list, prospectus or whatnot of the Loeb Classical Library. Make *him* do the work. And when I come we'll have a party, after our own private party, you and me and Nob.

By the way, that Yonnie business and the letter to Freddie. I don't mind what Y and Pete and Filomena, and Cecelia, etc., do. Party members *always* gossip. Let them. Who worries about that will die young. What I object to is the responsible ones encouraging it, and giving rise to it. That gets me real mad. You see J.P.C.? Over and over again I see his P.C. as a whole is left out, knows nothing about what the Secretariat is thinking or working out. *Military*, J.P.C. says and he means it.

So, sugar, so long till later. And you worry about *nothing*.

N

P.S. Thanks for the enclosures. I read them all. Those women! The fighters. Think of the losses to society of all the marvellous people—that is the greatest loss.

That Jimmy Baldwin writes well. We must invite him to the party.

Honey, I got Bill's letter. It was terrible in parts. God! What misery we have to go through in this rotting society of ours. But there wasn't a note, not a line from you. I hope nothing is wrong. I love you. I send back one of Bill's letters for you to keep. About what happened there, about the information, let it stay there. I hope it didn't depress you. We will hear soon now. Courage, sweetie.

Well honey-bunch. Here is another job done. You see I am a new man I will no longer carry around all those burdens. G. has a hard struggle ahead of her. Good for her. Let her go through it. You give her the blue paper letter and this one, and seal it up nicely with my type of Scotch tape as if it came from me. And, honey, don't ever send me any enclosures without a word. I am *beginning* to feel so much freer.

Hi! I keep writin' and writin'—I lose track of the ms. I think I enclosed a long "notes" to R in a "personal" envelope. I intended to put it in this one. I love you. How is *Nob*?

Now I find R's letter after all. For Christ sake. I suffer.

C.L.R. James c/o Drackert
Pyramid Lake Ranch
Sutcliffe, Nevada

Postmark October 20, 1948

Sweetheart, I am back in Pyramid and want to write some more to you. Your last bunch of letters before this one startled me and made me spend a lot of time at night awake in bed wondering—is there something missing in me or what? No panic, none at all. Maybe it is something I shall come to. I was concerned also about the effect of what I had written. It was about the following.

Your letter showed how deeply you were affected by the extra five weeks and to-day's letter showed the same. Now I want to be back, I am anxious to begin afresh with you, I want to see you, I am sick of this place; but I began to think about ways and means of fixing up something. I said I would finish my dialectic thing, which expands beyond all previous planning, as has been the habit of years, I composed myself to it. I didn't work so well, and I have been sleeping badly. I spent two or three days in Reno; but I a) try to do something b) tell myself my usual "Anyway." This may be poison but I must say it. I say to myself. "I can take it. But God! What is happening to Constance." That is a simple sentence, my precious, but it means a lot to me. I have lived under the shadow of fear of just this "I can take it; what about you!" And somehow I feel that you resent the "I can take it." I feel that what you want is for me to say, to show that I am as miserable, as affected as you. To suggest that you are more affected is a reflection on you. I am taking it for granted that you are going to be more affected than I am. (Yet at the same time when something happens I feel that I am immediately supposed to comfort you. Like John Fredericks. Every time there is a crisis John fusses around, gives Rae hell, until some special meeting is arranged with him. He is patted and smoothed over and paid some attention and then everything settles down.)

This, by the way, is the exact opposite of the first feeling. But I get sometimes one, sometimes the other; and sometimes both. I cannot make rounded, organized, logical points. This is me. That is how I feel.

Now this last thing I say startled me. Why? When I heard I said "Oh! Jesus. This is going to hit Constance hard." Something like that. Then immediately I could visualize the challenge "Oh! it doesn't hit *you* hard! *You* don't care. It is only I who care enough to be hurt." The thing saddened me. I said to myself "Well, I presume one *has* to adjust." But my simple natural instincts, my character, my whole past life in the face of disappointment and crisis of every sort has always been "O.K. So it is. What shall we do next? That is so and either we can fix it, or try to fix it, or do something else—make the best of it somehow."

I thought this first. Then your letters came and when I saw the passionate grief and almost despair of your letters I again said: "Is something wrong with me?" I know that in politics, in business, in sports, and in ordinary life, I have generally been ready to say "Well, let's pick up the pieces and start again." Defeated? No. Only for the time being, temporary. That is how I have tried to live. I know it may not be as good as it sounds. It may be covering up the real wounds which fester below. All I know is this external fact. I have never played on a team, any team, yet where, whenever in a critical situation, my name came up, those in charge were not able to say "Jimmmy! He is O.K." Over and over again I have heard it, in games, in clubs, in parties "James is O.K. You can depend on him." "Don't worry about James. It's the others you have to worry about."

You have some idea of how I feel. Coupled with this is the deeply British instinct, hammered home in books, in education, in conduct and example: push *yourself* away. Get yourself and your problems out of the way. See what you can *contribute*, not what you *want*. Being intense[ly] serious and a *moral* person, I took these things seriously from childhood. You begin to see my problems? I think that perhaps I resented your need for some attention being paid to you and labelled you a "Mamma's Baby" like John F (who, by the way, as I know, has many sterling qualities, and I say this not to keep the balance, except that it is well to remember that a Mamma's Baby can be at the same time an extremely effective person). As I was saying: I resented, I think that you, as it seemed to me, were calling for my attention. But I am not *too dumb* darling. I know that the real deep and serious crisis between us, the clash between my old life and a new one, the period of transition, took all these things and transformed them into problems that held me by the throat.

Now why have I written to you about this? For this reason. I was in a mess when I read and re-read your letters. "Here," I said to myself "this is how Constance is. And me! I am busy with—dialectic! A whole big project. She is going to be shocked when she gets this—I am sitting down scribbling and working out theories, etc., while look at how she feels."

All the week-end, in between my work, this haunted me. I said to myself "What a shock to her! For Christ sake, am I inhuman or something?" But your letter comes this morning. It is not only that you say "Well, it can't be helped." But, you say "Where is the dialectic? I want to see it. Where is it?" Over and over again I have misjudged you. It is difficult, very difficult. But when I had been haunted by my sitting down and writing about dialectic and writing to you about it so enthusiastically; and then came your letter, sad, but eager about the dialectic. I knew something was wrong somewhere. I was not able to be myself; and I wasn't sure whether it was because the myself was a deficient character or whether he was O.K. (in this respect I mean) but had not adjusted to his environment. I wasn't too sure of the wisdom of writing to you about it. It could easily be mistaken for an attack on you. It isn't. I want to make no attacks on you, but I do things because of fears and doubts (or don't do them); doubts, inhibitions, the whole bag of complexes. It is because I fear you will do this or react this way; or I interpret something that way. Naturally that is not the *whole* story. I do not take these things as I should because I am what I am. These things, by another person, could be ignored, or turned aside or fought out, without casualties. But I have to begin with the fact as I see it, as I understand it in its first stage. If I am blocked there, then all I get is an abstraction: somewhere something is wrong. You see.

Honey, I sit and write. How I sit and write. Sometimes I say. This is an important principle, and should lead to concrete results. What results? *I don't know.* But I start tackling it there pen in hand, writing as I think. And without a break I work out something entirely new. Most times of course I know before I write, but I tackle it when I don't know. That's how I get on so fast. I know too that I am going to talk plainly to all who need it.

So I am hoping that I shall acquire the same ease of expression and reaction with you. You see I am confident with my work. I watch what seems a solid block of granite and I say: I am going to *dig* a pattern out of there; and I dig it out. Now that I am released I can talk to the others because whatever my short comings I know I am the chief. I was No. 1 on the list and over and over again I have made the correct decisions at the correct time.

But I am not, I have not been the same with you. Your fault? Ridiculous. You have done a lot of silly things and made a lot of mistakes. With an ordinary person you would have overcome them easily. But I am as I am, with a personality that has worked out a mode of existence for itself. You have had a tough time. I blame you for nothing. I thank you for everything. You have never failed me. I am building up a great confidence in you. It is perhaps the indispensable preliminary to building up confidence in myself.

One more point. I am not too much afraid of separation. Not really. They may put me in jail of course, they and their damned war, but that is a chance we all take. The separation of husband and wife and child, on immigration grounds, *that* I don't think likely. In a few weeks that I hope will be impossible, as far as anything is impossible. I am not trying to console you. I am hoping that one day I'll be able to talk to you very freely about crises, external crises and personal crises. Some of this is due to my fear of your reactions, but some of this is due to my own inability to come out with things. Some I *know* you will not complain [about], but I haven't the strength to make the effort. The calls on my strength are many. I am not being sorry for myself, but I doubt if among us anyone has the problems that I have. So sometimes I let one or two things go, till later. I get a little rest that way.

I'll write you again to-morrow, about things in general, things you wrote about. I put $10.00 in the envelope just for you. You must not skimp. To-morrow I shall enclose another cheque. So sweetie, make what you can of this. I know you'll read it with sympathy. And I don't mean that your ways of reacting must be changed. Absolutely not. Absolutely not. You live your own life. But I am not sure of mine. You need not hurry to write back about this. No. (And when I came in and saw you and Ceil gossiping in a corner I was not put out.) I let people go their own way. I am not quick to take offense. Not in general. If you and Ceil are happy talking you can go on for the whole night. That is one of my weaknesses. I have so many things that concern me that I am quick enough to look, say "anyway" and get on with something else. Perhaps it is a form of escapism. At least I don't take opium or sit and weep about my misery. But I know the things about Ceil that got me angry and wary. Sometimes I would talk to her about this or that, and whenever I saw you next, she had told you everything. *That* amazed me. But you and she talking in a corner—absolutely not. You could tell me to sit in the next room, you all want to talk—I'd go, and as far as I know, I doubt if I would be angry.

Sugar-pie. The picture, *not* in the bathing-suit, the other one—the whole movement about the waist-line—absolutely wonderful. The breasts are very big—as if Nob is up there, but be like that after Nob, and whenever I am preoccupied just point to it. I am learning not to hide what I feel even from myself. So now back to dialectic.

About Grace, one word. I am sure you can handle the situation. Do as you think fit. I know you'll be kind to her. I tell you one thing, however, that will help. Ask her to go out with you. You say nothing or little or whatever you wish about her talks with you. You seem to be doing pretty well. But by just regularly seeking her out for a little amusement together, altho' you *say* nothing perhaps about her special troubles, she will feel the sympathy. Grace is a remarkable person. But she is lonely and torn and now has to face herself. If you show her that you genuinely appreciate her you will see some very rare qualities. Her generosity, you know. It is genuine. Her power of work. But she is also a genuine *intellectual*—a rare type, with a passion for theory and intellectual effort for their own sake. You can help a remarkable person, and she can help you too.

All my love, sweetie, and tickle Nob for me.
N

The Philosophy of History we have at home.
C.L.R. James c/o Drackert
Pyramid Lake Ranch, Sutcliffe, Nevada

Postmark October 21, 1948
Monday

My dearest precious,

I am writing and writing and writing, and thinking and thinking and thinking. I went for a ride to-day. I needed it. But the work comes pouring out. I cannot stop it. Many days I rise at 9. Am back from breakfast at 10. Work till 1; come back at 2; I sleep sometimes from 3–5; work till 7; come back at 8:15 and work till 3, sometimes 4. Continuously. If I do not sleep in the afternoon I work till about 2. I sit at the table and do not move for hours on end. The people here look on me as some freak, the natives and the visitors. The ride to-day was a sort of intervention—"You cannot sit in there like that all day." It is 20 years since I have worked like this. I feel no mental or manual fatigue—absolutely none. It is not my bachelorhood. I was a bachelor for many many years. I have in between mastered at last the Hegelian logic. I know what I am doing in it. I stopped the translation when I received your telegram, turned over the pad to a new page and began a work on dialectic. I have written 15,000 words of it.

And all the time, consciously, sometimes subconsciously, I am thinking of you. Page after page on the dialectic, I am saying how you will be amazed and pleased; and I am hoping you will be able to use it for yourself. I think about us. I take a little walk around the place sometimes. Or I stop writing, or I lie in bed after turning off the light, or in bed on mornings. I am working on two planes—it and us. Some of it I write to you, some to Lyman in that letter. Plenty of it went into that letter. But I feel it all one place—when I go to Reno and play the machine. I seem to have no control. But I am getting that in hand at last.

There are things I do not write. I haven't the strength yet. It will be some time. But I feel very strong on the whole. David used to play for Saul to appease the demon. But nobody could help me. Only your determination and all that you showed me of yourself drove me to keep on at it. I had something to fight for. When I come, by degrees, we'll purge the carcass. And then we'll see what's there. One reason I am working this way is because when I return I don't want to be bothered with work of *this* kind. I am clearing the decks.

I am happy for you and the Greek. That is what I was looking for, what I planned for you to do; to read and read and read, to ignore everything else that you could ignore, to pursue it from book to book, stirred and uplifted. Every writer, thinker, artist must go through that. You build power and the knowledge. I wanted you to have it. You will have it. Two years. I have the whole "course" planned. If you choose to stay two years at Greek, stay there. Then you will have in time an actual study to do. Maybe you will feel it is something on the Greek you want to say. I have one or two others in mind. To hell with publication and "a place for yourself." I am confident of your future. Bourgeois society and its organised crimes can break our course. Nothing else can.

Let me write as I please. I relax with you. I just write about this, that, the other.

My attorney cabled this morning, or rather spoke to the consulate. They said they would serve her on Monday. We are now waiting. She says they were merely careless or stupid. I *suspect* collusion to delay. But I'll make her call again at the slightest delay. Meanwhile you wrote to my father; but if by this time you have not heard write to Bill and ask him to get J's private address and cable it to you, just in case. The

Consulate said it would serve to the office address and we don't want to start a new complication. If my father went he could give them the private address. But we'll call them and there will be no three weeks delay of sending letters to us thru' Washington saying they didn't know. It is hard, darling, but we will stick it. And if there is any further delay and uncertainty, then I shall move all forces I can for us to meet in California somewhere. That is the best I can see, and I know that you will make it. But once I come, it will be quite a while before I go again. We learn through experience, we achieve through suffering. We are tied tight now; our life has been and is such that we'll not go through anything like this again.

Rae comes into my mind. Yes, that sister frightens you, and you have cause. *I* know. That is what I was opposing these last days. She acts too quickly and she talks too quickly. Her qualities in those fields are remarkable—*but*, not for a leader; a leader, a *proletarian* leader has to stop and think and watch and consider. R acts and speaks too much on impulse, and this is communicated to the people around who all start doing the same. We'll get round to it, she and I. Her *crimes* in that field . . . and I mean crimes, have been too many. As long as I was around in charge and keeping an eye I didn't mind many things. And I dislike lecturing people about their personal practices. Furthermore, they knew I was there watching. All this has to change. They must begin to bear responsibility for themselves. You understand now why I so sharply put a stop to any organisation of anything for N. The room in Pittsburgh can be all the colors of the rainbow. R will keep herself quiet and *reserved*, and not be constantly starting this, proposing that, throwing off an idea here, starting off somebody there, etc., etc. At the Convention talks I was going to let her hear a few plain words in the presence of J. Z. But *she* reported her blunders, and I let it pass, tho' I was not too satisfied. I have started with G. And while I watch them I have to watch *myself*. Sugar-pie, you are already a pillar of strength for me. I'll talk to you, and not be worried that you will misunderstand or misuse (for yourself) what I tell you. People say "I will not be taken for granted." There is something to that. But I know that I could not be intimate with anyone whom I did not take for granted. I have heard nothing from Lyman. It is horrible that he does not want to take responsibility; or he does not want to take it alone. F [Freddy Paine] may have got hold of the letter and is fighting her case with him. I have made it quite clear to him and I shall stick to it. If I am to discuss and integrate him into a responsible position, he must assure me that F will not be included. I started to break up this husband and wife business and I shall break it up. It is not serious politics. And Lyman will be in a position where what I tell him remains where it is until he decides to speak about it. But I will not have F knowing everything, *my* most personal estimates of character, etc., and giving hints and gossiping, etc. There may be some trouble there—I don't know. But if there is, I took it into consideration when I wrote, and am quite prepared for it. You just show *no sign of anything*. Honey, about Academy.* That letter went astray. The mail here is taken in M'y, W'ys, and Fr'ys. But sometimes, in between, a trustworthy visitor, or someone who is going in, is given letters. *For our type of*

---

* Academy was the term used by James and Webb to refer to the pamphlet they were planning to publish on Richard Wright. Alongside Webb's essay, they intended to include the sections of *Black Boy* omitted by the publishers from the 1945 book.

letters, this is very irregular, and henceforth I shall trust only the M. W. and F. when Drackert himself takes them in. Briefly, what I said at length was this.

1) Do not circulate among the party members now; and R, and whoever has any must be strictly warned. I would not give *one* to my dearest friend, not now. Why? You should circulate *first* to Dick, and *hear from him* (about that more in a minute). *Then* to friends, writers, newspapers, etc. Let it be known outside and stamped as a *literary* venture on your part. Let *all* party members hear of it this way. Then let *them* ask. Then you let them have some (of course they were going to get it). But they, and the party authorities must feel that this had nothing to do with them at all. I would be rigid in this matter. And those who have already must not even leave them lying about. What would be a terrible blunder would be for the Johnsonites, or some Johnsonites, everywhere to have them at a certain time. I say it with bitterness: they cannot be trusted. And if even they could be, *in this case*, they must take their turn. *The public first, away from the party*, and then the party hearing of it from the public.

2) Dick. My view is: take no chances. Before you send to the press, etc., send half-a-dozen copies to Dick. Write to him and tell him you want to hear from him. Tell him that you have given out copies to friends like Malaquais, Guérin, Bernie Wolfe, James Farrell, Himes, *Ellison, and a few private friends, but you have sent to no newspapers*. Send to these people *at once*, so that Dick will know that a number of people, important people, have read the thing. That pins him down. He cannot retreat. Then wait until you hear from him. If he is friendly, then you send to some carefully chosen literary journals, etc. You do not want to irritate the publishers by sending to the Times, etc., which will only start enquiries. That we will go into.

Suppose Dick raises a stink. Then you go right ahead to private people, keeping out of the press. When you said to him "I have sent to X, Y, Z, and a few private friends," you are well covered. He makes a stink? You just keep on sending to your "few private friends." Also send him a separate parcel with copies for Camus, Sartre, and Simone de Beauvoir, *with their names written in*, coming from you, and letters, *brief*, saying you hope to hear from them. Put that responsibility on Dick.

Meanwhile watch carefully every one you send out. We have to make back *every penny*, every *penny*. *All* must give something, except me, your mother, and one or two others. *All*. But this is to be carefully done and in no hurry. I have an idea you should open a separate account somewhere for this, and put all that money there, for books, files, etc.

Then bear in mind the libraries. You can send at once to the Bibliotheque Nationale, Paris, France; the British Museum Library, London; the Bodleian, Oxford, England. Ask them to acknowledge. Let the American libraries wait until you hear from Dick. Send a copy to Harry and Mrs Spencer,* inscribed, and along with it inscribed copies of Black Boy and Native Son. Look up some old copies of Partisan Review and see who wrote on Existentialism. Send one to him, or them, with a brief note saying: not for review, but you think it may interest him. Send one to Sinclair Lewis, with a reference in a brief note to Kingsblood Royal. Send one to

---

* Harry and Elizabeth Spencer owned a tea shop in Nelson, the Lancashire town where James lived during his first year in England in 1932. The Spencers supported James's research into the 1791 San Domingo revolution and *The Black Jacobins* is dedicated to them.

Cox. Ask his publisher for his address. Send one to Reddick and ask him for Ira Reid's address. Tell him: your husband, C.L.R. J. told you he would be interested. Send one to Sterling North—he is professor of English Literature at Howard U'y. Tell him C.L.R. said, etc. I am not sure of the name. I have it: Sterling Brown. Say that it isn't for review. Also if you find in Life, Good Housekeeping, etc., people who wrote on Existentialism, send to them with a *brief* note. N.B. *Meyer Shapiro*. He is Professor of Art at Columbia University. Mention me, say I told you. Horace Cayton c/o Pittsburgh Courier. Mention me. Tell him not for review. There are many others we will work out. Of every 10, you will get a reply from 1. Don't let that worry you. Some will read, they will talk, they will put it aside, they will lend. To-morrow, next year, you write something else, or Dick writes something. You are remembered, the thing is taken up. A little ball starts rolling. Send to the girl who is having the baby. Send to one person at Conover's and *one* in the model agency you worked for. Take your time. Get your envelopes to suit, your mass of stamps and systematically send them out, a few every day, keeping tab. But get Himes, Bernie Wolfe, etc., *all* the friends of Dick quickly, or rather *first*. You have it? You see what a useful husband I am!

Now about money. What have you got? I ask you to buy this and do that. Tell me, please, how much money you have! You say you grabbed up Hamlet. OK! But can you buy books for H.S., etc.? I am terribly glad $250 and $100 were paid into the account. I send you a cheque for $20.00 to have around. About the doctor. $300 would be a mistake, my dear. We have all sorts of expenses between now and February, not to mention now and November. Still it would be nice to give some money—one visits with more assurance. I propose I write a cheque for $100 and give you to give it to him with a letter. Tell me, if that's OK with you. *Perhaps* better would be to wait till I come, we go in to see him, and I give him a cheque then. But we must pay him by installments. $300 is too big a lump out of our slender resources. (So darling, that is it.) 1:30—I have been writing to you since eleven. The pace slowed down a bit. I am worried about your ulcer. What about concentrating on it a bit! Willing it away. Take a week off from people, diet your diet rigidly, and put it in its place. All my love darling, you and Nob, or two. We'll give them all the names in the book if need be. I love you, honey.

N

Tape up G.'s as usual.* I hope you grasp it. If you don't now, you will soon.
C.L.R. James c/o Drackert
Pyramid Lake Ranch, Sutcliffe, Nevada

[October 1948]

Sweetheart,
Service was made yesterday, or rather Monday. Count from then for 30 days. But I am taking no chances. I am on the alert. Be calm, precious.

I brought this mail in myself. I cannot risk it any more. The large parcel contains of Part I of my dialectic study. I wrote it and had to rewrite it almost entirely.

---

* In his letters to Webb, James also enclosed unsealed letters which she read before forwarding them to his political associates.

Darling, I want you to know. Not a line in it was written without your being present in my mind. I wrote out all the quotes so that you could read it. Those that I left out will keep. It is a *very bold* attempt. I would like if you and G. made a date, with Ike, if you like, and read it together; tho' you can read it when you like, how you like. Tell G, no hurry about typing.

Also honey, set the bookshops agoing for any copies of Johnson and Struther's Translation of *The Science of Logic*. If you get the volumes separate buy them. It would be wonderful for you to give Rae a present of them. If you get *two* sets at a reasonable price, buy them. As for you and dialectic, rest assured, you will master it and use it. I am *impatient* for comments; from you and from G. *Impatient*. (Also in one of the translation bunches of papers I wrote a long note, paper stuck to paper, which should be handed to G.) I shall finish Part Second of Part I, I have to rewrite that too; and then into Part II. I am excited about the thing and I want to know how you all think about it.

All my love,
N

Strange how we commented about the ulcer. I got salami, ate it all off and couldn't eat my dinner.

November 8, 1948

Honey, I must answer your dialectic questions at once. I presume you know the questions. I want you to see something.

1) Norman Thomas and Co. do *not* reach the truth about Trotskyism, *nor* about bourgeois society. They reach the truth about *nothing*. The real creative Reason for the bourgeoisie is—Hitler. He destroyed the old categories, consciously, brutally, ruthlessly. But the only *need* categories open to him were—barbarism. And this proves that bourgeois society has no Creative Reason that is really reasonable. Thomas attacks Trotskyism and attacks Hitlerism. He understands neither, so his attacks, *his negative* has no real *positive* in it. It is only a show.

2) Mind *is* the highest level of truth. Stalin is in the same position as Hitler. His Creative Reason is—barbarism. But the question you ask, whether he is not able to see more than L. T. is sound and I answered it a few days ago in the later stages of the document.

Every time a new set of categories come, in *capitalist* society, a new group of people find them satisfactory, and wish to preserve them. They deprive them of revolutionary dialectical content merely because they wish to preserve them. But up to a point they do see things better than those who try to preserve the categories with no objective basis. These latter live *entirely* in abstractions. The first have a concrete basis and this gives them the advantage. Neither, however, sees real truth. *If* Stalinism could see the real power of the masses it would not be Stalinism, it would become revolutionary.

3) In *every* age, incapacity to see the Universal concretely, *must* lead to Individualism. In the declining Middle Ages the neurotic went into the monastery. God was his analyst. This is so *in every age*. Trotsky's weakness, his individualism, was not so much in My Life, which he wrote for cash, but in the way he made his individual struggle with Stalinism, the basis of the whole F. In'l [Fourth International]. That

was his basic error. It is *reflected* in *My Life*. All intellectuals, in *every* age, behave like that.

4) You are anxious about the backwardness of the American proletariat. You will see soon that I treat this in the second part of the Notion in general. There is a law of Historical Compensation, so I call it. Politically backward France produced the French Revolution. Politically backward Germany produced the Classical philosophy (Kant—Hegel) and Marxism. Politically backward Russia produced the great Russian writers and Bolshevism. Politically backward U.S. will produce an incomparable *new* literature and a *new* proletarian formation. As I see it, the *Other* of the age finds its greatest freedom and power where the resistance is weak or backward, i.e., the new form for 1948, will break out more easily where the resistance, i.e., the already established is weak. Get it? Honey, you just ask me the questions. I am glad to answer. And as for mastering the logic,

DON'T WORRY
DON'T WORRY

You will. You are one of those I have in mind as I write it, in *some* respects, more than all the others. In other respects I wrote it primarily for Rae and her study of American economy, which is going to hit hard—a very big thing for us, very big. In fact I want to hear more from you (for many reasons) and G (who is censor) than anyone else. We shall have sessions on it. You'll get it, *all of it*.

O.K. honey

N

And don't you be bullied into that typing.

C.L.R. James c/o Drackert
Pyramid Lake Ranch
Sutcliffe, Nevada

Postmark November 3, 1948
Thursday

I shall mail this by someone else.

Sweetheart, I was angry yesterday with you. As I thought over things and the old bitterness, pain, came back I was angry. I wanted to say: you hurt me; you were unreasonable; you did a lot of things to me.

I wanted to but I couldn't. And then I was angry with myself. For I kept them in. And I remember a picture with Ingrid B and Gregory P in which it was made clear that G. P. would be angry with the woman who was forcing him to dig down into the buried past; but that was the only way. And I knew that even as I shouted the things at you, they would disappear. That I shouted them at you, i.e., told you in anger, would not mean that in essence I believed them. But that way they were buried and that way perhaps it is easier for some to come out. But then there is the prospect of your anger and not a release for me but a quarrel. I know now why people go to psychiatrists (which does not in the least lessen my desire to stick a long pin into the whole tribe).

I came home, with a bottle of brandy. (I am not succumbing to drink.) I had 2 or 3 shots before dinner. It was Hennessey and in the cold I drank them off and had a good dinner. Then it hit me. I tried to read but was all sleepy. I dozed off for an hour or so; awoke, still sleepy or rather sleepish. I listened to Mr. District Attorney who sounded just like Dewey in this last campaign. My books were on the bed, and suddenly I began to make notes on Trotskyism for the last part of the dialectic. Honey bunch, they came out "incredible." I struck a vein. Dialectic. Opposites. Then I read a key passage in the Logic. I read others. I had the last part *tight*, rolled up, sealed, and pocketed. I nearly sent you a night-letter, as I nearly called you late election night, you were so close to me, as you have been all through this dialectic thing.

Then I read your sex letter again. I am going to take my time to answer; once you know that everything is OK, I think that's all right. There are problems in it, but I understand it, I think. Don't sweat, sweetie. Write some more if you want to. I understand it, in general. It is myself I do not understand. But about the girl in Life? I imagined her coming up to see me, and my going down to see her, love-making like mad, calling on the 'phone; but as I think of it, it was that God-damn demon again. She lived in her house and I in mine. She came and went. I came and went. You see how clever he is. It was the old life.

So I read it and felt very warm to you. If you were here I would have made love to you. Then to sleep. I had a curious dream.

I was working out problems of my life in a marvellous dialectical manner. Problem after problem came, *the method* was applied, the problem solved.

Then I was on a train, which had stopped. F and L were on the train. Suddenly a big branch of a tree bent over and smashed our carriage, and somehow the carriage still whole in outline was lifted up to an embankment.

Now the significance of that is this. In 1915 I was in a train-wreck. 14 people killed and 44 wounded. I was 14. When it happened I was miraculously unhurt—miraculously is the word. Some of my school-friends were killed. I got up and went looking for my friends. There was a scare that the boiler of one of the engines would burst and people ran. I didn't run. I found the boy I was looking for, made him comfortable and stayed with him until the ambulance came for him. Then I walked away to the road and went to my god-mother's who lived about a mile or so away. I was never frightened at any time. If to do what I think is the thing that ought to be done is neurotic fakery with me, then it goes very deep. If most people would have run away from the boiler I might have run. But as long as some stayed doing the work I was going to stay.

I was not frightened; but last night the carriage which cracked up from the tree, even in the dream, was the image of the broken carriage out of which I crawled that night, nearly 35 years ago. I have never dreamt of it since, as far as I know. But there it was. I wonder if there was some release.

What makes me think so is the last part of the dream. There was a school. The principal was away and Lyman was acting principal. I was teacher (or school boy) or something around. Then I walked down the steps and one day there was a detective waiting for me (Don't get startled; the dream is good.) He arrested me, and two others, examined me—for being an alien who had overstayed his time, and with much detailed examination, etc., they took me off to prison. The arrest was a surprise but the threat had been hanging over me a long time.

I was quite cheerful all through and very cheerful this a.m. about it. These fears I had in the old days, constantly; I thought the arrest in Cfa would have fixed them, but we have had no peace really. But somehow I feel too that that is now in the open—gone. That is how I feel to-day at any rate. I think it will continue.

Don't worry about the typing. Take your time. Pass this round for me. a), and perhaps b) too.

a) Something has happened in the country. What it is I don't know exactly, tho' I can guess. The reason is that the pollsters were wrong. That is no light matter. The Literary Digest was right for years until the country changed. Gallup and Co. examined, codified, etc., but the social categories and their representatives have shifted. The shift is *enormous*. If Wallace and Thurmond had not been there, Dewey would have been beaten shockingly, almost as surprisingly as Landon was beaten in '36. I believe that if I were investigating I would investigate the petty-bourgeoisie, not labor *particularly*. This is why. In 1931 in Britain the L [Labour] P'ty lost nearly all its seats. From some 135 or something it went to 31. But the labor vote stood steady—6 million. The workers did not budge. Pleased or angry, it votes *against* the Tories. It is clear that the American p't [proletariat] has reached that stage.

It is the petty-bourgeoisie which has changed. It is not frightened by blarney about Communists. It does not care about the projected repeal of Taft-Hartley. It does not care a damn. I would investigate along the following lines:

1) On the Negro issue the D'ctic [Democratic] Convention came alive again.

2) The petty-bourgeoisie could get nothing from Dewey on prices, housing, or anything.

As soon as it saw that labor was going down the line with the President on these things, it turned swiftly and went with him and labor. The poll-takers are uppish but not stupid. If some fundamental change had not taken place they would have been more or less accurate as usual.

b) The Truman campaign impressed me, and since the victory, more so. It has a great lesson for us, socialists, though for me less than for most of the others. The power that is in men, each individual man, however poor a thing he may seem to be. This Harry T. is a poor creature in many ways. He does not understand foreign policy; he doesn't know what a police state is. He blunders on serious issues, he cannot write anything, he can't read properly. But he has a profession, it is politics, to go to the people and slug it out. Prendergast machine or no, he must go to the people, find some issues, make his black, white, and his opponents white black. There you must win—after that back to Washington where the intrigue and the graft and the lobbying begin, and the speechmaking. There Truman is a big zero.

He finds himself Vice President, a compromise, which means that in serious politics he is a colourless person. As politico and administrator he is a mess. Comes election time and everybody, EVERYBODY, except his own immediate entourage says that he is going and that he ought to go. He is *obviously* unfitted for the post.

But just here the little man finds himself. This is *his* milieu. It is an *election*, and he knows about elections. The local sheriff, the local dog-catcher, does not give up without a fight; and the little haberdasher has the biggest job of all—he loves being President. He will *fight*. Boys, writing the speeches, make it hot and strong. We'll fight. The demoralisation in the D'c Party was enormous. They couldn't get money at one time to pay for broadcasts. Nobody helped Truman. Many of the cabinet members shrugged their shoulders and looked for a new job. For a long time the labor leaders wouldn't go near him. Many an administrative politico would have wilted, been unable to galvanize his people into an effort. It is clear that little Harry wouldn't. You see he *had* the job, and a new porch beside. He went at it. He has the trained politician's knack of talking to the people, making them feel he was one of them. Behind the incompetent, blundering rendition of the speeches on the radio, as I listened to them I could feel a vibration. In the pictures too, in the press and on the screen, little Harry was throwing all he had into it, to keep the big job history had shoved into his pocket. I think it would be a great mistake to underestimate the role he played. He had a line, and he went to the people. Fundamental forces, even, need something through which they can express themselves. He did it almost alone. Good old Harry. He will now proceed to bungle up his politics more than ever, and the mess he is going to get into over prices, the Taft-Hartley bill, etc., will be something to see. I doubt if he had the faintest expectation or any desire for the landslide in the Senate and the House of Representatives. Personally I don't think Harry has saved the D'c Party. I am of the opinion that in the course of the next four years, he will repeat the last two on a rich and multitudinous scale. He is going to make bitter and final enemies of workers, Negroes, house-wives and farmers.

But that should not blind us to the fact that little Harry Haberdasher has carved himself a place in history. As far as I know it is the most surprising election in the history of the country. All came to bury Harry and now have to praise him. I have seen it many times in my life, and most often on the field of sport. All men have the spark in them somewhere, and few things amaze me so much as the casual way many people have of dismissing A, B, or C. "He's no good." Usually I say to myself "*You* are no good." If Harry Haberdasher could rise to *his* measure so well, we need not doubt that the most insignificant of our people will rise to *their* occasion, if and when they see it, and their leaders believe in *them* and in the occasion. Sometime or other I shall put my hand on an essay by Georges Sorel on Corneille Desmoulins, with some vicious quotations from Renan. They have a marvellous time at Corneille's expense, and they really make Corneille look a fool. But Corneille had something in him that they didn't understand. And as Hegel in a very fine passage in the smaller (p. . .) says: The *real* (Corneille) is the one who did the big things. That is the *Essence* of the man the rest is Appearance. I nearly quoted it but refrained. I didn't want to make people uncomfortable. As I say: I think we can learn something important ourselves from the Show (capital S) put up by Harry Haberdasher. Show it is in the true Hegelian sense, for it is only a show. The classes as I say have moved. Of that I am certain and I hope the c'des will examine carefully; but neither John L. Lewis, nor Murray, nor Reuther, nor Eleanor Roosevelt, nor anybody *did* anything for it. Harry Haberdasher put on the show and it was spectacular. Which will not prevent it like all genuine Shows being from Nothing, through Nothing, to Nothing again.

OK, sweetie, I love you. Tickle Nob for me.

N

C.L.R. James c/o Drackert
Pyramid Lake Ranch, Sutcliffe, Nevada

[Reno, Nevada, 1948]

First Letter

Honey, my attorney spoke to J. J says No. She wants 900 dollars, and my attorney tho' saying I haven't the money, left her with the belief that we were trying to get the money. But we learnt the main thing: she gave no impression whatever of wishing or planning to contest the case.

So make some enquiries as to where we can most easily be married. I do not wish to be bothered with New York and its Wasserman laws.* Perhaps it will not be wise to go back to Fort Worth or wherever was that miserable place. But just enquire. I'll come back by 'plane, and we can see if we can go straight from the plane and get that fixed. Just take it easy, darling, and ask. We have time (unfortunately) but once this is done, then it is going to be tough to part us. And even if—the worst—the authorities say they want to see me, I can now leave and come back. So be of good faith, my co-warrior. A port is in sight. I am seeing it.

Tell old Schorr exactly how matters stand so he'll be prepared, if need be, for anything that *may* turn up in the next weeks. But, soon, sweetheart, soon, you will always have someone to lean on whenever you go up those steps.

Now let me put everything in order. First a cheque for rent. (I am writing to him about Cyril L.R. and C.L.R. James, to-day, but meanwhile I'll continue C.L.R.) Two cheques—one for rent and one for the doctor. I take it, sweetie, that you are paying in the $100 as you said. Now let me write to the bank. Bank written to. Now, my precious, a few words; everything *in order*. Orderly.

1. I love you.

2. Thanks for your note about the dialectic. It *pleases* me mightily. You see: I want to write and send, and write and write without being concerned about a) Constance is mad that she is not writing something; that she seems to be only an appendage 2) She is going to say: Why! I am suffering here and he sits down, living his old life, writing away, happy, feeding his ego.

Be prepared over the next few weeks for these *explosions* of sentiments. I am not saying: You did this. You did that. You are guilty, your fault. I am saying: this is how I felt, this is how I feel. As they come to me, if I am in the mood, they'll be dragged up to the surface. I take no responsibility. I don't know the procedure. But I suppose after a period of this, one loses the fears and can sit back and live. Or, if not, what? I don't know. But this way we shall try. And above all don't argue with me to prove you were right or I misjudged you. You put me on the defensive, *I* start to argue, and I say nothing more. Yet I want you to say something—and yet I don't want you to be writing reams and reams—too tiring. You do what you want—that is best. If you write me insincerely that is to say, working out ways and means to put me at my ease, I'll be very unhappy. And by the way: One time you were very hard at work "trying to make me feel good." Useless. USELESS.

You know when I have felt best, some of the times at any rate.

1) One night, very early, you stopped writing and went inside and painted a plate—just painted a plate.

2) When you get a book about Negroes and you say "Oh boy! I am going to settle down to this," all excited. Or when you are gobbling up that Greek? I love you most then and I feel very happy. Then I ask you about the dialectic, and you write and say it's fine. I am satisfied. I trust your judgment. But never you try, waste your energy,

---

* Public health regulations requiring anyone wishing to be married to undergo a test.

and lower your self-respect by looking to help my ego. I am very very suspicious on that side, and *except deep down inside*, inclined to scepticism and under-statement where I am concerned. When I see you relaxed and happy and busy about something, without thought of you or me, except to report the good news, I am just glowing inside, and I remember it for months. Problem? Is that because *that* is my personal ideal? And if so? TO HELL WITH IT. That is how it is. The more you go your own way, *joyfully*, the happier I am.

3) Order. (You can imagine the mess I was in, the disorder, papers, etc., which demanded "order." But order it is and will be.)

After I wrote to you about dialectic and expression of sorrow, etc., I was unhappy. It was, I thought, a messy business. But there has been so much fear and misunderstanding that I said: Out with it, try *this* this time. Do you know next morning I was up at 8 and lay in bed till nine? Thinking of you and how tough you had it, recognising your tendency to have outbursts, but seeing the long, miserable months, years you have had. And I felt very different from the night before, I really understood it and wanted to be near to you to help you out of it; and will remember that in future.

4) Order. I have no sympathy whatever for anybody who gets into any trouble in Detroit. If the SWP is pissed-off, that is their misfortune: I mean about the no of J'ites in Detroit. But anyone with a little, a little restraint, a little capacity to think, would see that precisely because of the numbers of J'ites, who could upset the balance of the branch, then, because of that, the J'ites had to take *special pains* to let the leaders see that this lack of balance need not trouble them. But these young people are young—let us put it at that. They should watch how they vote, *follow* the leadership. *If* they did that, they would see that the SWP would appreciate it. But their God-damned egos puff them out and everything becomes a question of principle in which they must state or indicate their point of view.

Irving had a similar situation in Philly, worse: he could have had a majority. Irving did not play with it. He saw to it that they did not use the majority. You can do that without caucusing. And to keep things in order, he collaborated with the SWP organiser and dispatched some six of our people over the country. He told us *after* he had done it. I was *very much impressed*. He said: Integration and integration it was. I don't want any majority in any branch of the SWP I don't want any minority large enough to be able to influence affairs. I have written and talked enough. But I say this with absolute confidence: If the SWP is pissed off because there are so many J in Detroit, it is *entirely* the fault of the Johnsonites, entirely. For it means that either positively or negatively they show that they are an alien element. I don't care all that they *say*. I made the people in N.Y. feel that tho' I was the chief of the political opposition I was *not* an alien element. I went out of my way to do so. I sat up nights and sweated and restrained myself. Those egomaniacs in Detroit do not impress me very much. That *is* Bolshevism by the way—precisely that. Bolshevism says: We are now agreed that we must subordinate ourselves to the SWP Long discussion. Agreed? Agreed? Agreed. Then no excuse, no injustice, no crimes, no sufferings, must excuse you. You have an ultimate purpose. You take a decision. Pay attention to it. If the people persecute you so much that you cannot make it, then something new is needed. You say: this policy of ours is a failure. It cannot *work*; a new policy is needed. But all that Cuppy business with the Negroes and the scandal in the branch, that, sweetheart was petty-bourgeois nonsense and child's play. *If* the SWP did not know how to treat Negroes—*if* the branch was suffering—*if* your personal feelings were outraged—*if, if, if*, yet the Detroit branch is a powerful branch, with trained leaders. Let them be responsible. Their work in Detroit is of tremendous importance. They do their best. If they are bungling up the Negro question—as it might have seemed—a new minority cannot correct them. You pull yourself *away* from entanglement. The branch loses 2, 3, 4 Negroes. The leadership sees this. It will raise the question. It is not *blind*. It is not a minority's business to champion anything or anybody. I was disgusted I can tell you. And if the SWP is pissed-off about something then a serious Bolshevik says: My policy is that the SWP should *not* be pissed-off about us. If they are, why? This must be checked. In the *last* analysis, the responsibility is with the Majority, because they have power, and power is responsibility. But you can always tell how people are reacting and I do not like *anything*, not one single thing I have heard from Detroit. Bolshevism is a line and a line which never complains about what the other is doing to prevent the line being carried out.

Order (Turn up the pages and put in the number for me. I have forgotten.) About the dialectic, I am sending some more, as I say, with some odds and ends I have here, Willie's letter and so forth; also I *may* include a letter for G.; also I *may* finish one for R. As for Lyman and F, let that wait. Only if you get a *good*, *clear*, chance say for me "J-y and I agreed that he would handle *all* financial matters." And R's treatment of G; ah! sweetheart, I shall drop you a line on personality and leadership one day soon. Subjectivity, lack of control of yourself, impatience, I'll tell you what these mean politically in leaders. Let it wait for next time.

Sugar-pie, some more order. Here I start off again.

First: seal up G's letter tight; and R's letter also. Pause. To write R's letter. R's letter now written.

Honey-pie. Enjoy your Aristophanes. You have the political book on him well noted, I expect. Good times ahead. Now to two things, to begin with.

Lyman's talk with you. 1) Did you go to R with financial troubles? *No*. Did I ask him *not* to come to you? Yes. Two to three weeks, he has not written to me. Freddie has most probably wormed something out of him. But I shall be blackmailed no longer. I want when Lyman writes to be able to say that you wrote me about this, the conversation. I'll remind him once more of what I asked him. The letter will not be long. It will be short. *If* Freddie interferes, then I know precisely what I shall not say, but write. If there is a racket to come, I shall have the whole thing well documented. You just do everything I ask you and keep a straight face. If the price of financial assistance is a constant meddling, joint planning, discussion, in and out and to and fro, then I do not want it, and shall say so without mincing matters. I am in no hurry to say so, I shall say it at the last possible minute, I shall do all I can not to have to say so, but if we are headed for that then we are. I made up my mind as to that before I wrote the letter. When you start something you must know where you are going.

Which brings me to the second part. My main personal problem, strange tho' it may seem is Rae, *not* Grace. I am afraid that G in a crisis can lose her head, discover that she is in serious disagreement, and then backed by *Ike*, unloose forces she had no intention of doing. She will be beaten in the end, but she *may be* lost and much mischief may be done. Because if every few months you do something, one day you will do something that is SOMETHING.

Without Ike G can manage. She *means* no harm I am sure. But with Ike telling her she's wonderful, unable to tell her plainly that she is an infant to R in politics *and* in strict political theory (which does *not* consist of brilliant *ideas*), and fancying himself as an organiser, there is a danger. We are not in the W. P. any longer. I could control it. But R cannot control herself and therefore cannot control anybody.

Look at how I am handling Grace—my last letter was hard. It was an indictment. But I told G, she could see that I was full of concern for her. I keep up our logical studies, etc., I want her to correct herself, but I do not want to have any wounds, I do not want to crush her spirit. It is because I think all the time of our little organisation.

But R is brutal. Imagine not talking to *G*, and shaming G. in front of *you*. You know what it meant: "*Politically* I am obliged to talk with you, but *now* I am talking to my friends." I have been watching this and similar things in other fields and I do not like it. Why? Why does a genuine leader *never* do these things? Because his first thought, his *universal*, is always the organisation, and everyone is part of it and any impatience or anger *always* has that censor which says "No, think again. This may affect. . . ." Now pitiable as Shachtman is, he has it. Cannon has it. R is devoted *to* the organisation, sacrifices anything *for* it, does all sorts of splendid work, but precisely the *one* thing that is required, she has not learnt. She always and always must say what is bothering her. At our collaboration talks Irving had to pull her up sharply for her loose tongue, just at the same God-damn meeting that I was building her up.

Now for me that is a very serious thing. R has shot off her mouth *in the P.C.*, attacking Cannon who was not even there. And I know that all this takes place because her subjective responses are not governed, dominated by something larger. If I were Rae's enemy, I would always have around her in politics or discussions someone whom she hated. I would rub her raw. (She is on a level with Grace, she dislikes Grace, but she is in competition with Grace.) I have said nothing for over a year. Now this is where my two chief theoretical collaborators are. I turn to Lyman. He does not answer for weeks. So the temptation is great to go on *by myself*, but I am not going to. It's started and I am going on with it stage by stage until we come out a little bruised but on a higher level. Kisses, sugar. I can take it easy with you. I should have known . . .

N

Sweetie, this is still Wednesday. I dispatched to you this afternoon in *one* big envelope—the end of Part I of my dialectic; *two* checks, both made out to Constance Webb James; and a whole lot of stuff. It was not registered. Over eight ounces is 10 cents an ounce by the zone. I just ignored the whole business. It is a brown envelope all taped up with the stamps plastered all over the front. It was addressed to you and had my address behind—a brown envelope, so if it does not turn up by Friday morning

MAKE A ROW and ASK THEM ABOUT THE OTHER ONE

And always give me a little memo like this of any important letter.

I am somewhat tired. I have been beating at the Doctrine of Being, there is my peculiar self—between wind and water. All I can think of is just writing down a lot of things. About money, about you and the party and me, you and clothes, our monthly expenses, everything boiling in my head. What a mess! I wish I could take a brush and scrub it out, scrub it out, but I can't. I have to dig it out. And the demon. Jesus! He says "You are writing because you can't talk." But I ain't budging. I shall write *to-day* otherwise I shall be putting it off for *to-morrow*. But it is shaking me. I don't know what. Will there be an end to it or have I now embarked upon a self-questioning that will be endless, you and I always nursing each other? No. I don't think so. We'll *find* some spot. What is good is that I am working. I read a page of the Logic—and oh, sister, some of it is tough—and I translate it like French—French is *much* easier. I write. I develop things. So I say: get with it. Nothing is *wrong* with you. You work O.K. And you are closer to your wife than ever before. What a mess I am in, however, I'll *tell* you sometime. I couldn't write it. And that sex. God! To be free and normal and not have the feeling of you wanting. You do wonderfully. Honey, I am worried about you being in a turmoil, papers, letters, typing, *a strain*. Take it easy. If you forget a letter, to mail it, let it stay till the next day. When you are tired rest. And *hide behind your pregnancy*. People will wear you out. Say you are tired and you don't want to go out. I have found people ready to do everything for me, wear themselves out to the bone, everything except leave me alone. Do you know one of my secret admirations is for Greta Garbo? Her time and energy are her own. And Hegel has a habit of writing "Such and such is the case. Those who think otherwise can be ignored" and going on without another word. A politician cannot do that. But how enviable are people who can. You be firm.

When I finish this dialectic, I shall be happy. *If it comes out as I aim it to do*, then a great job will have been done, a big big step. And for you too. You must master it, master it in its political form. And then you can transfer it to literature. Some news. Irving Howe wrote an article on Edmund Wilson in the Nation. I shall send it to you. I could have taught that boy something—seriousness, method, dig down deep, wrestle with ideas, help the proletariat, help himself. I always used to tell him, years ago: "You, I am sorry for. You are being ruined." I used to tell him so openly, in debate. For I had my eye on him many years ago. He is a *literary* person, by nature. And yet I wonder. Jimmy Baldwin, the outcast little Negro switch and Bohemian *writes*—he is as different from Howe as genuine orange-juice is from the stuff in cans. What I wonder is: Is a man fixed? Is Howe as he is because he just is that? I can't believe it. I believe that the proletarian revolution, the creative proletariat, will transform men. All of us have two men inside of us. And with the proper environment, the proper friends, few though we are, Howe could have been more than he is. And yet, he *could* have come. Others came. But he is *your* special baby. Watch him. Read his work (or put it away to read). He will teach you a lot—negatively tho' far more than positively. You see, ultimately, I see you, after having gone through a training, chiefly European, and writing your own stuff, whatever that may turn out to be, after all that, coming back home, and opening out on the great American classics, Whitman, Melville, Hawthorne, Poe, Mark Twain. They are there waiting, as the Negro question was waiting. American culture, the specifically American, will have to wait for the proletariat. When you read a history of French literature, 700 years of it—an unbroken stream, or the Greek, or the English, a complete whole, you see that America has not found expression. Gifted men, men of genius, yes. They always come. But the milieu was hard, they could not find themselves. Only a dialectical method can unravel this past. Take your time, Greek drama, French drama, Elizabethan drama, the Romantic Movement, the Moderns; develop *an aesthetic* of your own, and then carry the war into the enemy's ranks. Internal confidence, patience, and the courage to endure; to be happy not only when the ultimate goal is achieved, but to enjoy the road there. Honey, you are the wife I wanted. My restrained, cramped, narrow self could see in you at first glance the vitality and passionate nature that I needed. *I knew*. Whatever is in front, the worst is behind.

I am just writing you. When I began I didn't know what I was going to write, I just had some time and wanted to write to you. Sometimes my judgments of people will read harshly. I judged Grace rigorously. I have been silent for so many years. But I *am* never harsh with them, or cruel or spiteful. And I only want to see them realise the best in themselves. But they can be *very* trying. Somehow I feel that if Grace could get herself *right* she will be wonderful. She can keep still, hold her tongue, watch and say nothing. She does not shout out whatever comes into her head. If she finds herself, that will be *somebody*. But Rae is getting *worse*. Sweetie, when I tell you the story of Rae, you will be *shocked*. And I am disturbed and ashamed at the state Grace is in—abject, praising Rae extravagantly, etc. It is a rush of feeling, but it is perilously near to a loss of human dignity, and worse still, a loss of judgment. And that Rae, who is the leader and therefore *responsible*, should be so insensitive to all this is not good. She behaves as if she had a troublesome rival and has *defeated* her. Rae is about 38. She is not a kid.

Did you get a letter telling you about my playing the machine? If you did, why have you said nothing? Is it too much for you?

You must remember me to Paul and Sylvia, Gene and Francesca, and the cleaner and his wife. The next thing is the marriage. Oh boy, what a day! We shall not waste an hour.

You look out for these turbulent, explosive bursts of letter-writing from me over the next few weeks. Then you can take them up when I come. I'll go over them, you ask me anything you wish. I want you to ask me, clear up all that old mess, thirty years and perhaps more. But God! How tired I am in some parts of me. One day in Los Angeles we went to see that lawyer, Lawrence Miller. And I

(Harry Spencer
Wyndclyffe
Halifax Road
Nelson, Lancashire
Tell him within four weeks
I shall be able to write)

said "My wife something" and you spoke up your piece. And after, you said "You gave me a little chance to say something." Honey, I was in the mud. I said "Jesus, look at what my wife is reduced to." That I felt. And the night we quarrelled and I said "I'll leave now" and you said "O.K. I accept. I am sorry. I'll do the best I can." Again, I hit low. I couldn't say anything. I didn't know what to say. But I knew that it was terrible; that your spirit should be beaten down. And sometimes when we quarrelled and I remained glum, and you would make the effort and say something and take the blame so to speak. Those were my worst moments. I should have said something. I felt them. They must never happen again.

I am writing by association. My pen wanders. But I think of you all the time, all the time. I wonder when I return, how it will be. The demon is waiting for me, I know the old habits, sitting down and reading and all the time so nervous about you, so nervous, nervous fifteen hours out of eighteen. I *know*, I shall have to break resolutely out of it. I am preparing. As long as I am nervous something is wrong. I think often of my return, and how it is going to be. You should know the long, long solitary hours I have spent, reading—reading—reading, thinking, writing. Since I was about four years old. It is the ingrained pattern of a life-time. You must talk to me. Take the letters, let us go over them. There are other ways too. It is a battle. I have to get out of it. For our sake, for your sake, and for my own; or I shall sit there, apparently doing my business, but strained and tense and frightened inside. And my sex life too. I feel that it will get itself right, the more we break down, or rather clear away, all the barriers, the restraints, the nervousness, the doubts and fears. We'll do a thorough job, a thorough job, not as in a confessional box, but making me stop thinking everything inside. Clemenceau, the old cynic, once said of Lloyd George "Ah! Si je pouvais pisser comme il parle!" = "Ah, if I could only pee as he talks." I have been writing so easily and reading so easily I say "Jesus. If I could only express myself to you as easily, as naturally." It is something to strive for. You are O.K. You have angers and passions and disappointments; and a certain harshness of outlook that exists on this side of the barricades which you must get accustomed to. But nothing serious, nothing that is not too hard. But I am different. Years and years, and the British bourgeois training ingrained. I remember some poems by D. H. Lawrence in Poesies. One of them said "See that British bourgeois, washed and clean and strong. But put him in a situation where a little human understanding and feeling are required. He is a good for nothing." I know what he is talking about. I am not indulging in an orgy of confessionalism and self-abnegation. Not at all. That, as you very rightly said about G., solves nothing. It just makes you feel good and sometimes leaves you worse than before. As I go over these things it is with a view to get myself prepared to break these old patterns once and for all, once and for all. Here comes our man—good-bye, darling.

N

C.L.R. James
c/o Drackert
Pyramid Lake Ranch
Sutcliffe, Nevada

Postmark November 8, 1948
Sunday Night

Sweetie, I love you. Everything is normal. I spent the weekend in Sacramento. Drackert took a party there to see a football match. I arranged to meet William and we had a very profitable day and a half. We discussed a) dialectic b) his Abolition Study c) SWP. Everything was exciting and pleasant. This is my second football match. I have thought a great deal about it and the differences between it and soccer, also baseball and cricket. Both pairs are expressions of national character. More of that another time.

Honey, I am pretty OK. I love you. I saw all the women at the football match. How I wished you were there—to have you near me, to love you, and to show you off. I used to be so stupid. About dialectic. If you understand the abstract you *cannot* fail to master it. Don't mind the terms or the names. Just read it and tell me it's wonderful. By now you have read the concluding part of Essence. It is massive. The first part was merely hors d'oeuvre. I am still waiting for The Notion section I sent for G.'s OK. I have the last part written in sections, a draft. I'll finish it this week, maybe Saturday. I have to work like hell all week. I have no urge to go to Reno anymore. Jesus, honey, that was a nightmare. The letters are coming and there is nothing I can do now. You got the cheques? I suppose so.

I wrote you a note about your questions. Don't worry about dialectic, sweetie you will have it. Don't type the thing. You take it easy, and don't go out too much and get tired. I am glad your friend's baby has arrived safely. Give her my regards.

I love you, honey, and I am getting myself in some sort of order. Don't bother about those women. Forget them, honey. Ignore them. I never loved any of them. I love only you. This letter will be short. I am tired.

William admired your R. W. very very much.

So, sweetie! You have a smaller Logic, haven't you? That is why I leave out some of the quotes. The pages I forgot to write in, in the letter, are p. 255–256. That is the code I live by. I have read that passage often.

Here is R's letter. I knew that not only she but all of us, including you and me, needed that dialectic thing. I am so glad when I send it off and calculate whether you have got it yet, and count the days until a letter from you is due. There is nothing, *nothing* you will not thoroughly understand.

So, honey, so long. I enclose $5.00 to buy anything you want or do what you want. I leave the marriage things to you. Soon I'll tell you the exact day of my arrival. And then, honey, we will be very happy.

Look at this peculiar tangent R has about G. and dialectic. G does not know her own powers in philosophy—this will help her to realise it. We shall have some sessions and G will go through the thing. You will hear some things. And if of any section she says: no good, then I am in trouble. Anyway I shall manage these relations. All my love, honey. And we shall *both* feel Nob kicking. When he grows up we shall tell him about it.

[unsigned]

C.L.R. James
c/o Drackert
Pyramid Lake Ranch
Sutcliffe, Nevada

Postmark November 9, 1948
Tuesday

Honey, I see a chance of getting a letter off, an inoffensive one, i.e., not too private. I therefore scribble this to tell you that I love you. I dreamt of you last night, vague and shadowy but calm and peaceful—almost I saw you coming into my little cabin at one stage. It has been cold down here at times. When I go out to the foot-ball match, D lends me a coat.

Whom do I go out with? Nobody. Sad but true, for all I care. The guests, or some of them go. We have seats that D has reserved. They are—guests, and I am a kind of nondescript. The formalities are observed, but even in walking from the carpark to the seats for the game, our isolation from each other stands out. I am not hostile, but I am not over-friendly. As soon as we reach Reno from Pyramid I go my way, library, Negro restaurant, drugstore to play the machine. I drop in sometimes to my attorney's office. I have not been to her house for months. I am not boasting about it but I simply live my own life. I talk to the servants, the help a bit. There are women around but I don't see them—a pleasant word or two. Barbara, about 3, is my genuine friend and now and then asks me if she still is my cutiepie.

I am deep in the last part of my thesis. And when I say deep, I mean deep, morning, noon, and night, I think of it and can only *not* think of it, by reading something else very stimulating. Last night I read a detective story which I am sending to you to-morrow. I read it last night from cover to cover. I laughed and laughed. The book was so British. I did not laugh at it but with it. I had been reading Cain's Serenade, Double Indemnity, etc. The two books, or authors, rather, were vastly different. But he is a very poor creature who could not read both.

I got your letter about the races, honey. I am glad you had a good time and *did not go home that night*. I always see you and the steps.

I also read Cass Timberlane. It is *not* an absurd book in general. It is an absurd book for the author of Babbitt to write.* Of itself I found it not interesting but instructive. The quarrels between husband and wife, and many of the things the wife said and did I saw with interest and they made me stop and think.

So, honey, that's all for this little billet. Somehow I don't feel like writing explanatory letters these days, so I just don't. A lot of barriers are broken down. Let it stay awhile. I do not want to have any of this dialectic on my hands when I return. I am feeling much better inside.

I dropped two lines to Lyman, saying I would be glad to hear from him. He wants to wait and talk it over, *not* make the effort to say something on his own. He may do that if he wishes, but he will do it without any assistance from me.

I have written a letter to R—but I shall keep it and mail it myself to-morrow.

That is all, sweetie, I love you and every little note from you, even on half a sheet of paper, means plenty to me. Tickle Nob for me—Nob the kicker.

N

C.L.R. James c/o Drackert
Pyramid Lake Ranch
Sutcliffe, Nevada

[Reno, Nevada, 1948]

Honey, all things being in order I shall leave here Thursday or Friday. I shall probably get the Wasserman through. But you wait: when I know for certain I'll wire you. Now you know all about the marriage arrangements. Just plan them. I am responsible to nobody but myself and you and when I go out it will be to see after finances—on a large scale. I don't want any delay on that. For the rest plan as soon as you wish, early if you wish, for a few days at Bear Mountain, but be sure to get it clear that I am a Negro. I think, however, that is O.K. there. But do not risk it. I'll have the money.

---

* Sinclair Lewis.

Here is this letter from H. V. *You* see if we shall have time to talk to her. I would like to, and I am sure you would like it—this was my first good look at a lot of American people and it was something, I assure you. Also Helen has genuine gifts. And she is a lonely soul just about to make a leap. Bud too is a man. Something began and I'd like to finish it. Will you call her or write her or arrange something. I can't from here. I love you, honey, and will do the best I can for everything.

[unsigned]

C.L.R. James c/o Drackert
Pyramid Lake Ranch
Sutcliffe, Nevada

Abbreviations

Personal Names:

(Brother) Bernardo	Bernard Adams
Bessie, B	Bessie Gogol
Bill	Eric Williams
C.H.	Charlotte Hunter
Ceil	Cecelia Daitch
Conrad	Conrad Lynn
D.	Harry Drackert
Dick	Richard Wright
Dr. F.	Dr. Harry Fishler
Dwight MacD	Dwight MacDonald
Eddie, Eddy, Edward	Edward Keller
E.W.	Ethel Waters
E., E.W.	Everett Washburn
F., Freddie, Freddy	Freddie Paine
F'a, Fil, Filomena	Philomena Daddario
Gale	Gale Malaquais
G and F	Eugene and Francesca Raskin
Grace, G.	Grace Lee
G's	Gogols
Harry C	Harry Conover
I, Ike	Ike Blackman
Jack, J	Jack Gilford
Jean	Jean Malaquais
Jimmy, J.	C.L.R. James
John	John Dwyer
Johnny Z, JZ	Johnny Zupan
JPC	James P. Cannon
J.R. Johnson	C.L.R. James

JTF	James T. Farrell
J.	Juanita James
Judie, Judy	Judy Gogol
L.	Lenin
L.D.	Lev Davidovich Bronstein (Trotsky)
L., Louis	Louis Gogol
L.T.	Leon Trotsky
L, Lyman	Lyman Paine
Madeline	Madeline Patterson
Manon	Manon Washburn
Max	Max Shachtman
Mrs. G.	Bessie Gogol
Monica	Constance Webb
Marty, M.	Martin Glaberman
N, Nello	C.L.R. James
Nettie	Nettie Kravitz
N, Nob, Nobbie	C.L.R. James Jnr.
Norman	Norman Henderson
Old Man	Leon Trotsky
Paul R.	Paul Robeson
(Sister) Paula	Paula de Aragon
Phil	Philomena Daddario
Phil	Phil Romano
R.W.	Richard Wright
Rae, R.	Raya Dunayevskaya
R's	Eugene and Francesca Raskin
Sol	Sol Babitz
S-ky	Stanislavsky
Sylvia	Sylvia Nesson
T.	Trotsky
W, Willie, William	William Gorman

Other:

AWP	American Workers' Party
Appeal	Socialist Appeal
BJ, Bl.Ja	The Black Jacobins
c'des	comrades
c'tee	committee
CIO	Congress of Industrial Organizations
CP	Communist Party
(Ency.) Brit.	Encyclopedia Britannica
Fr. Rev'n	French Revolution
J'ites	Johnson Forest Tendency
N, N'o	Negro
NI	New International
PC	Pittsburgh Courier

PC	Political Committee
RQ, R'n Q'n	Russian Question
SA	Socialist Appeal
SEP, SE Post	Saturday Evening Post
SWP	Socialist Workers' Party
WI	West Indies
WP	Workers' Party
WPA	Workers' Party of America

Glossary

In compiling these notes I have been greatly assisted by the work of Alan Wald, *The New York Intellectuals* (Chapel Hill 1987); Paul Buhle, *The Artist As Revolutionary* (London and New York: Verso, 1988) and *Marxism in the USA* (London: Verso, 1987); Scott McLemee and Paul Le Blanc, eds, *C.L.R. James and Revolutionary Marxism: Selected Writings of C.L.R. James 1939-1949* (New Jersey: Humanities Press, 1994); and Kent Worcester, *C.L.R. James: A Political Biography* (Albany: SUNY Press, 1995). The reader may also find these sources valuable in supplying a fuller discussion of the political and intellectual climate, and more detailed biographical accounts of leading figures, for the period which frames James's Webb letters. Other important sources include: *The C.L.R. James Reader; American Civilization; C.L.R. James: His Intellectual Legacies*, Selwyn Cudjoe and William Cain eds. (Amherst: Univ. of Massachusetts Press, 1995); *Rethinking C.L.R. James*, Grant Farred, ed. (Oxford, UK and Cambridge, Mass.: Blackwell Publishers, 1995).

de ARAGON, Paula — friend of Constance Webb.
ABERN, Martin — leading member, with James Cannon and Max Shachtman, of the American SWP; but in 1939 he joined the opposition to Cannon's position on the Russian Question.
ADAMS, Bernard — husband of Raya Dunayevskaya.
ALLEN, James S. — one of the Communist Party's leading intellectuals and historians, author of *Reconstruction — The Battle for Democracy* (1937).
APTHEKER, Herbert — a leading figure in black history who was closely associated with the Communist Party. Under the pseudonym J. Meyer, James later wrote a critical review of Aptheker's work "Herbert Aptheker's Distortions," *Fourth International*, December 1949.
BALDWIN, James — African-American novelist and critic, author of such classic works as *Go Tell It on the Mountain* (1953), *Giovanni's Room* (1956) and *Nobody Knows My Name* (1961), briefly flirted with Trotskyism during the early 1940s; but his connection with James is said to have stemmed from his job as a waiter

at the Greenwich Village restaurant which James frequented. Moreover Baldwin's growing reputation as a young writer brought him into the literary circles of Philip Rahv *(Partisan Review)* and Dwight MacDonald *(Politics)* with which James was familiar.

BEARD, Charles — a prominent liberal historian whose collaboration with Mary Beard produced the widely-read two volume work *The Rise of American Civilization* (1927).

BENET, S.V. — American poet and fiction writer, whose work expressed themes from American history and politics. This extract is taken from his poem, *Litany for Dictatorships* (1935).

BLACKMAN, Ike — close associate of Grace Lee and part of James's political circle.

BROWDER, Earl — leader of the American Communist Party.

BURNHAM, James — taught philosophy at New York University and moved into revolutionary politics during the 1930s. He became an important figure in the organization of the American Workers' Party, and later in the Trotskyist Socialist Workers' Party. Burnham joined Max Shachtman in opposing James Cannon's position on the Soviet Union; and although he left the SWP to join the Workers' Party after the split over the Russian Question, his new political allegiance was shortlived. He resigned from the WP in 1940 and a year later published a hugely successful book, *The Managerial Revolution*. Burnham rapidly repudiated his revolutionary past, moving to the kind of right-wing position he himself had identified in a 1939 pamphlet "Intellectuals in Retreat," co-authored with Shachtman.

CANNON, James — one of the figures most identified with Trotskyism in the United States. He was distinguished more by his organizational skills than by his political originality; but for two decades his strengths were complemented by those of his close colleague, Max Shachtman. Cannon lost many political associates following the split in the Socialist Workers Party over the Russian question; but, under his leadership, the SWP continued to be a significant force in the Trotskyist movement. Unlike many others, Cannon remained committed to and active in socialist politics to the end of his life.

CARLO — a cartoonist for the Trotskyist press.

CONOVER, Harry — head of Conover model agency in New York and for whom Constance Webb worked (sometimes spelt by James as Connover).

CURTISS, Charles — member of the Trotskyist movement and participant in James's discussions with Trotsky in 1939.

DADDARIO, Philomena — member of James's political circle.

DAITCH, Cecelia — member of James's political circle.

DRACKERT, Harry — Nevada ranch-owner who provided James with accommodation while he sought a divorce from Juanita James in 1948.

DRAKE, St. Clair — leading black sociologist who, with Horace Cayton, co-authored *Black Metropolis* (1945).

DUNAYEVSKAYA, Raya — James's collaborator in the Johnson-Forest Tendency. Dunayevskaya (nom de guerre — Freddie Forest), a Russian emigre, began her lifelong engagement with revolutionary politics during the 1920s. She worked as secretary and translator to the exiled Leon Trotsky before joining forces with C.L.R. James and later Grace Lee to carve out an independent

revolutionary Marxist position. In 1955 Dunayevskaya broke with James and established her own political organization and newspaper, *News and Letters*.
DWYER, John — close associate of Raya Dunayevskaya.
ELLISON, Ralph — novelist and author of the classic *Invisible Man* (1952).
FARRELL, James T. — literary critic and novelist (most well known for his harshly realist *Studs Lonigan* trilogy, 1935) was a member of the Communist Party during the early 1930s. He subsequently moved to an anti-Stalinist position; and although he never formally joined the Trotskyist movement, he wrote extensively for its different publications. From the later 1940s, however, Farrell increasingly drifted away from the radical political engagement of his youth.
FISHLER, Harry — a doctor on the fringe of James's circle.
GARVEY, Amy — wife of Marcus Garvey and active with James in the London-based International African Service Bureau.
GILFORD, Jack — Hollywood actor, and one-time companion of Constance Webb.
GLABERMAN, Martin — member of James's political circle during the 1940s; later he became a leading figure in the political groups which succeeded the Johnson Forest Tendency. Glaberman remained loyal to James throughout the fissures of the 1950s and 1960s, becoming one of the leading disseminators of James's work.
GODFREY, Peter — director of the 1936 production of James's play, *Toussaint L'Ouverture* at the Westminster Theatre, London.
GOGOL, Bessie and Louis — James met the Gogols in Los Angeles during his first American speaking tour. They became friends, and James often stayed at their house on his visits to the west coast. Bessie Gogol was the sister of Raya Dunayevskaya; her husband, a physician, became professionally involved in James's medical problems, particularly concerning his ulcer.
GOGOL, Judy — daughter of Bessie and Louis Gogol.
GORMAN, William — member of the Johnson Forest Tendency whom James regarded as a personal protege.
GUÉRIN, Daniel — historian and prominent figure in the French Trotskyist movement. During his stay in Nevada, James began an English translation of Guérin's *History of the French Revolution*.
HENDERSON, Norman — Constance Webb's first husband. Their marriage broke up in 1940.
HIMES, Chester — author of novels ranging from Harlem detective stories to works of social criticism. He began to write while serving a prison term in the early 1940s; and in 1953 he emigrated to Europe where he lived until his death in 1984.
HOWE, Irving — literary critic and essayist, became active in socialist politics while a student in New York during the 1920s. He joined Shachtman's Workers' Party and became one of its leading writers. In 1946-47 Howe fiercely attacked James for his maneuvers within the WP and SWP; but by the late 1940s Howe himself was at odds with the WP leadership.
HUNTER, Charlotte — James's attorney for the months he spent living in Reno, Nevada during 1948. James sought her help in securing a divorce from his first wife Juanita.
JAMES, Eric — brother of C.L.R. James.

JAMES, Juanita — first wife of C.L.R. James. Married in Trinidad during the 1920s.
KELLER, Edward — Constance Webb's second husband.
KRAVITZ, Nettie — member of James's political circle.
LEE, Grace — a Chinese-American who trained in philosophy at Bryn Mawr. Her political activity began in Max Shachtman's Workers' Party; and through it she became acquainted with James's work. During the 1940s Lee was, with Raya Dunayevskaya, a leading figure in the Johnson Forest Tendency. She remained with James following Dunayevskaya's split in 1955; but a decade later, with her husband James Boggs, Lee too broke away from what remained of James's group.
McCARTHY, Desmond — English writer and critic; literary editor of the *New Statesman*.
MACDONALD, Dwight — a Yale graduate, was drawn to the Communist Party during the early 1930s; but following the political persecutions in the Soviet Union he moved to an anti-Stalinist position. MacDonald served on the editorial board of the Partisan Review, a literary journal which by the late 1930s had a developed Trotskyist orientation. In 1939 he joined the Socialist Workers' Party; but, after the split in the Trotskyist movement over the Russian Question, he allied himself with Shachtman and James in the newly formed Workers' Party. In 1941, after disagreements with the WP leadership, including James, he resigned from the party. MacDonald later he founded his own journal *Politics* (1944–9); but he began to move away from radical issues and in 1951 became a writer for the *New Yorker*.
MALAQUAIS, Jean — writer and translator.
MORROW, Felix — a philosophy student and journalist, he became a member of the Communist Party in 1931. He wrote for the Daily Worker and the New Masses; but increasingly he developed Trotskyist sympathies. In 1934 he joined a small group of Trotskyists in the Communist League of America. Later Morrow followed James Cannon and Max Shachtman into the Socialist Workers' Party, remaining a member until 1946.
NAVILLE, Pierre — leading figure in the French Trotskyist movement.
PAINE, Freddy and Lyman — close associates of James and his political group during the 1940s. James spent much time at their summer house in Northport, Long Island. For many years the Paines provided James with financial support; but in the 1960s they broke away, joining Grace Lee and James Boggs in a new political organization.
PARRINGTON, Vernon — prominent American literary critic.
PATTERSON, Madeline — friend of Constance Webb during the period she worked as a model in New York.
RASKIN, Eugene and Francesca — literary critics, and friends of James and Webb.
RIVERA, Diego — the Mexican painter and muralist, who was influenced by the revolutionary developments in Russia, and became committed to radical artistic practice. During the 1930s Rivera painted murals in a number of major American cities (Detroit, New York and San Francisco). Later he was instrumental in Trotsky being granted refuge by the Mexican government. In 1939 Trotsky and his wife, Natalia, moved into the household in Coyoacan which Rivera shared with his companion, Frida Kahlo; but, in the following year, personal and political disagreements led to a break between Trotsky and Rivera.

ROBESON, Paul — leading black American singer, actor and public figure whose stand on questions of race and politics became the focus of much controversy. Robeson played the title role in James's 1936 London production of *Toussaint L'Ouverture*; but his association with the Communist Party led to a breach with James.

RUKEYSER, Muriel — American poet and fiction writer. Her work was distinguished by its social commitment; and she herself was known for political activism, most notably in the protest which followed the 1931 Scottsboro rape trial in Alabama.

SCHUYLER, George — editor of the *Pittsburgh Courier*.

SHACHTMAN, Max — a charismatic figure of the Trotskyist movement. He began his political career in the Communist Party; but, following his expulsion, he joined James Cannon in the Trotskyist Communist League of America and later in the Socialist Workers' Party. For almost two decades he collaborated closely with Cannon. In 1940 their disagreement over the defence of the Soviet Union led to Shachtman's break with the SWP. He became the leader of a rival Trotskyist group, the Workers' Party, remaining a dominant figure in radical politics until the late 1950s when he began, like many others, to endorse right wing positions.

SOUVARINE, Boris. Towards the end of his stay in Britain, James undertook a translation from French of Boris Souvarine's monumental biography, *Stalin*. It was published on the eve of the Hitler-Stalin pact. Souvarine, Russian born, but a resident of Paris for many years, had been a leading member of the Communist International in the early 1920s. Following his expulsion from the French Communist Party, he moved closer to the exiled Trotsky; and in his study of Stalin, Souvarine benefited from Trotsky's first hand knowledge of developments in the Soviet Union.

STANISLAVSKY, Konstantin — Russian born theatre director, actor and co-founder of the Moscow Arts Theatre. In 1923 he moved to the United States where he lived and worked until his death in 1938. Stanislavsky was a highly influential teacher and writer who developed a distinctive approach to dramatic interpretation, emphasizing the necessity for an actor to internalize a role, to identify completely with a character and eliminate all artifice from acting style.

THOMAS, Norman — leader of the American Socialist Party from 1926–1955. On six occasions he stood as a presidential candidate.

TROTSKY, Leon — Russian revolutionary leader who participated in the first uprising of 1905; subsequently lived in exile in Europe and America before returning to Russia in 1917. With Lenin, Trotsky was one of the most important figures of the revolutionary period which saw the foundation of the new workers' state. After Lenin's death in 1924 and Stalin's assumption of power, Trotsky was increasingly marginalized within Soviet politics. He was forced into exile in 1929, living first of all in Norway and later establishing headquarters in Mexico. He was murdered by Ramon Mercader in August 1940.

VAN VECHTEN, Carl — American novelist and critic. Author of the classic *Nigger Heaven* (1926).

WASHBURN, Everett and Manon — members of the Californian political circle associated with James and participants in discussions over the Johnson Forest's allegiance to the SWP and WP.

WEINSTEIN, Norman and Selma — members of James's political group. Selma Weinstein later became James's third wife.

WILLIAMS, Eric — a Trinidadian like James who studied for a D.Phil at Oxford University during the 1930s. His research into the economies of the slave trade developed a number of themes which James himself first raised in *The Black Jacobins*. James had taught Williams as a boy at Queen's Royal College, and continued to consider himself Williams' teacher and mentor throughout the 1930s and 1940s. In 1939 Williams followed James to America, taking up a teaching post at Howard University; and in 1944 *Capitalism and Slavery* was published. Later, following Williams's rise to power as the first Prime Minister of Trinidad and Tobago, James was forced to break his longstanding relationship with him.

WOLFE, Bernie — novelist and critic, was active in Trotskyist politics during the 1930s. In 1946 he published *Really The Blues*, a biography of a Jewish jazz musician; and he became involved in Wright's attempt to establish the black literary journal, *American Pages*.

WOODSON, Carter G. — founder of *The Journal of Negro History* and author of important works in black history, including *The Mind of the Negro As Reflected in Letters Written During the Crisis 1800–1860*, 1926.

WRIGHT, Ellen — wife of Richard Wright

WRIGHT, Richard — African-American writer born in Mississippi in 1908. He moved to Chicago in 1934 and began to publish novels which explored the black experience in segregated American society. A set of four novellas, *Uncle Tom's Children* (1938) was followed in 1940 by his most widely known work, *Native Son*. Wright had been a member of the Communist Party for a decade; but when James met him in New York in the early 1940s, he was on the verge of breaking his political allegiance. At this time Wright was preparing his autobiography, later published as *Black Boy* (1945).

ZUPAN, Johnny — a member of James's political group.

Index of Names

Abern, M., 9, 58, 61, 348
Adams, B., 175
Aeschylus, 14, 221
Allen, H., 342, 347
Allen, J., 53, 59
Aptheker, H., 53, 59
Aquinas, St. T., 191
de Aragon, P., 116, 219, 243, 297-298
Aristotle, 221, 223
Arthur, J., 74
Auden, W.H., 25, 136-138, 155, 160-161, 164, 176, 249
Babitz, S., 38, 48, 63
Bacall, L., 216
Bach, J.S., 145, 238
Baldwin, J., 355, 372
Barrymore, J., 89
Beethoven, L.V., 25-26, 42, 65, 74, 78, 89, 91, 112, 115, 128, 133, 135, 139, 145, 216
Bell, C., 210
Bennett, A., 4, 218, 292, 354
Bennett, D.C., 354
Bierce, A., 42
Birchman, 61
Bogart, H., 13, 22
du Boissière, R., 5
Boyer, C., 22, 73, 325
Breit, H., 340
Brooks, V.W., 339

Brown, J., 83-84, 97
Buhle, P., 33-34
Burnham, J., 53, 58, 64-65, 69
Byron, L., 159, 355
Cannon, J.P., 8-9, 12, 58, 64, 279-280, 284, 288-289, 297, 302, 308, 318, 343, 349, 353, 355, 371
Carlo, 46, 51, 87-88, 92, 94
Castro, F., 15
Cayton, H., 184, 362
Césaire, A., 7
Chamberlin, J., 339
Chekhov, A., 28, 203-206
Chopin, F., 139, 197, 247
Churchill, W., 147, 219, 248
Cipriani, A., 5, 33
Coleridge, S., 25, 165
Conover, H., 131, 153, 362
Constantine, L., 6
Corneille, P., 319, 325, 355, 367
Cornell, 37
Cromwell, O., 14
Curtiss, C., 8, 34, 58
Curtiss, L., 40
Daddario, P., 34, 283, 301-302, 309, 337, 353, 355
Daitch, C., 34, 272, 290-291, 295, 300-302, 339, 355, 358
Dali, S., 193
Davenport, 185

Index of Names

Davis, B., 13, 22, 73, 178
Descartes, R., 223
Desdemona, 24, 82-83, 90-91, 124
Dewey, T., 175, 365-366
Dickens, C., 292
Dietrich, M., 73, 140, 268
Dobbs, 349, 352
Dobson, 221
Dostoevsky, F., 14
Douglass, F., 83, 96-97
Drackert, H., 31-32, 259, 281, 320-321, 323-327, 329-331, 335-336, 338, 349-350, 355, 359, 361-362, 364, 367, 374-377
Drake, St. C., 13, 184, 189
Dryden, J., 221, 238-239
Du Bois, W.E.B., 7
Dunayevskaya, R., 10, 17, 28, 32, 152, 163, 188-189, 230, 280-282, 291, 331-333, 336-344, 349, 351-355, 360-361, 370-371, 375-376
Dürer, A., 187
Dwyer, 285, 325
Eden, A., 212
Eliot, T.S., 110, 138, 145, 164, 221, 237, 339
Ellison, R., 12, 184, 361
Engels, F., 9, 80, 106, 137, 161, 187, 194, 230, 308
Erasmus, D., 161, 192
Erber, E., 58, 353
Ernst, M., 193
Farrell, J.T., 13, 208, 226, 228, 231-232, 237, 301, 304, 339, 361
Feuerbach, L., 160, 176
Fishler, H., 49, 52, 286, 297
Fitelsen, 233
Forest, F. (Raya Dunayevskaya), 10-12, 17, 19, 27-28, 30, 32, 34, 280
Frederick the Great, 222
Fredericks, 356
Freud, S., 80, 271
Gabin, J., 73
Gable, C., 46, 268, 329
Garbo, G., 22, 73, 372
Garrison, W.L., 83-84, 96-98
Garvey, A., 190

Garvey, M., 225-226
Gautier, T., 42
George, L., 374
Gide, A. 196
Gielgud, J., 90
Gilford, J., 23, 28, 149, 151, 156, 160, 184-186, 197, 200-201, 203, 208-209, 214-215, 217-218, 226, 228-230, 232, 235, 246, 248, 252-256, 266, 293, 297
Glaberman, M., 34, 272, 279-281, 286
Glover, M., 4
Godfrey, P., 33, 108
Goethe, J.W. von, 133, 161, 355
Gogol, B., 99, 101, 110, 204, 229, 259, 283, 286, 288, 293, 301-303, 305-306, 309
Gomes, A., 5
Gorman, W., 28, 34, 151, 217, 229, 249, 283, 286, 289, 301-302, 305, 338, 340, 343, 352, 370, 374
Gould, 58
Grimshaw, A., 1, 33-34
Guérin, D., 32, 317, 321, 341, 361
Hagen, U., 24, 90-91
Harris, W., 15, 35
Hart, K., 34, 366-367
Hayworth, R., 13
Hegel, G.W.F., 2, 9, 11, 22, 24, 26, 32, 34, 70, 73, 79-80, 91, 95, 103, 113, 123, 133, 140-141, 155, 160, 166, 176, 192, 195, 206, 211, 221, 223, 235, 238-239, 255, 281-282, 319, 337, 351, 359, 364, 367, 372
Heine, H., 215
Hemingway, E., 165, 193, 196
Henderson, N., 37, 39, 50, 201, 208, 217, 246, 248, 257, 297
Henderson, W., 37
Himes, C., 361-362
Hopkins, H., 180, 213
Houston, W., 276, 317
Howe, I., 46, 55, 69, 79, 81, 99, 154, 158, 177, 202, 204, 210, 242, 244, 263, 301, 303, 311, 316, 339, 342, 351, 372
Hume, D., 176
Hunter, C., 315-316, 318, 320-322, 324-325, 327, 334
Ike (Saul Blackman), 29, 227, 290-291,

337, 363, 371
James, C.L.R., 1-35, 40, 51, 59-60, 71, 97-98, 122, 142, 184, 244, 246, 279, 293-294, 300-301, 305, 311, 316, 338, 349-350, 355-356, 359-362, 364, 367-368, 371, 374-377
James, C.L.R. Jnr (Nobbie), 12, 17, 310-312, 315, 318-322, 325, 329-330, 332, 335, 337, 339, 341, 345, 347, 350, 354-355, 358, 362, 367, 375-376
James, Eric, 324
James, Juanita, 12, 315
Jimmy (C.L.R. James), 21, 200, 202, 239, 280, 291, 313-314
Johnson, J.R. (C.L.R. James), 10-12, 17, 19, 27-28, 30, 32, 34, 179, 188, 280, 291, 354, 361, 363, 369
Jones, J., 237
Joyce, J., 145
Judy (Gogol), 99, 101, 285, 306, 309
Kant, I., 160, 176, 192, 223-224, 364
Keats, W.B., 25, 122, 140, 159, 165, 242, 281
Keller, E., 63, 69, 170, 185, 208, 217-218, 246, 248, 252, 294, 297
Kierkegaard, S., 354
Koestler, A., 155
Konokov, 60
Kravitz, N., 29, 34, 227-228, 241, 255, 301
Lamming, G., 15
Lang, C., 34, 158
Langtry, L., 117
Laski, H., 122-123, 142, 145
Lawrence, D.H., 110, 117, 166, 169, 209, 257
Lee, G., 10-12, 17, 28-29, 117, 138, 163, 188-189, 196, 217, 223, 227, 230, 238-239, 244, 268-269, 279-280, 282-283, 285-286, 290-291, 297, 304-305, 331, 332, 337-341, 347-349, 351, 353-355, 358, 360, 362-363, 370-371, 373-375
Lenin, V.I., 9, 11, 14, 18, 34, 57, 112, 128, 140-141, 146-148, 195, 243, 339, 353
Leo, C., 352
Lewis, J.L., 155, 160, 176, 362, 367, 376
Louis, J., 117

L'Ouverture, Toussaint, 7, 15, 23, 33, 88
Luce, H., 330
Luther, M., 91, 161, 188, 192
Lynn, C., 267, 292
MacDonald, D., 62, 226, 330
Machiavelli, N., 188
Malaquais, G., 332, 337
Malaquais, J., 301, 332, 337, 352, 361
Malraux, A., 155
Maltz, 339
Marx, K., 6-11, 17, 34, 38, 51-53, 57, 61-62, 64, 70, 72, 78, 80, 102, 123, 138, 140-142, 147-148, 152, 155, 160-161, 176, 181, 186, 190, 192, 195, 203, 211, 230, 232-233, 236, 245, 308, 364
Mayakovsky, V., 159
Melville, H., 14, 31, 35, 166-167, 313, 372
Mendes, A., 5
Miller, L., 373
Milton, J., 14, 161
Molière, 79, 319, 325, 355
Monica (Constance Webb), 131, 133, 136, 138-139, 141-142, 152, 154, 157, 163, 174-175, 177-179, 186, 200, 202, 209-210, 214, 222, 229, 268
More, Sir T., 161, 192, 260
Morrow, F., 61, 288
Mozart, W.A., 25, 145, 216, 238
Mussolini, B., 6-7, 193, 212
Myrdal, G., 190, 210
Nello (C.L.R. James), 4, 21, 38, 43, 52, 54, 60, 62, 65, 71, 84, 89, 94, 99, 101, 109-110, 122, 129, 131, 138, 140, 142, 144, 157, 164, 167, 187, 195, 199, 207, 213, 223, 232, 241, 249, 251, 255, 303, 337, 340-341
Nettie (Kravitz), 29, 34, 227-228, 241, 255, 301
Nesson, S., 286
Nkrumah, F., 14, 34
O'Brien, E.W., 5
O'Neill, E., 193-194, 199
Padmore, G., 7-8, 14
Paine, F., 10, 115, 142, 144, 175, 219, 222, 226, 228, 233, 247, 263, 267-268,

283-287, 292-294, 321, 332, 342-343, 349, 355, 360, 370
Paine, L., 32-33, 66, 143-144, 175, 210, 226, 266, 289, 321, 341, 344-346, 359-360, 365, 370-371, 376
Parrington, V., 221
Patterson, M., 222, 239, 245, 253, 301
Petrarch, 192
Phillips, W., 83, 96-99
Picasso, P., 40, 177
Poe, E.A., 42, 120, 126, 132-133, 138, 156, 161, 221, 265, 274, 297, 319, 372, 374
Pope, A., 25, 155, 164-165, 238
Prescott, O., 339
Primus, 155
Proust, M., 221, 237
Pushkin, A., 42
Rachmaninov, S., 238
Racine, J., 319, 325, 355
Rae (Raya Dunayevskaya), 29, 110, 152, 163, 167, 175, 187-188, 217, 223, 226-227, 237, 282, 285-286, 291, 302-305, 307, 319, 325, 331, 338, 342-346, 348-349, 351-352, 356, 360, 363-364, 371, 373
Raleigh, W., 161
Raskin, 293, 296, 302, 337
Reich, W., 250, 253, 259-260
Rivera, D., 38
Robeson, P., 7, 24, 28, 78, 88, 90, 96, 108, 123, 178, 249, 316
Robinson, E.G., 13, 77, 179, 329
Rodin, A., 268
Romano, P., 280, 283, 291
Roosevelt, E., 86
Roosevelt, F.D., 108, 143, 147-148, 175-176, 212, 367
Rousseau, J.-J., 14
Rukeyser, M., 125, 136-137, 213, 222
Sartre, J.-P., 301, 330, 340, 361
Schuyler, G., 37, 53
Schwarz, 237
Scott, H., 223
Selznick, D., 317
Serge, V., 214
Shachtman, M., 9, 39, 58-59, 63-65, 280, 288, 343, 371
Shakespeare, W., 4, 14, 24-26, 35, 70, 76, 78, 82, 89-91, 123-124, 133-135, 155, 161, 164-165, 168, 172, 196, 238, 319
Shaw, G.B., 111, 114, 149, 355
Shelley, P.B., 25, 122, 128, 133, 144, 146, 159, 163-166, 169, 221, 241-242, 281
Sheridan, A., 276
Smith, A., 223
Sobers, G., 15
Sophocles, 268
Sorel, G., 367
Spencer, H., 361, 373
Spender, S., 25, 118, 126, 160, 176, 249
Stalin, J., 8-10, 12, 21, 24-25, 32, 51, 55-59, 115, 122, 124, 142, 147-148, 156, 158, 161, 168, 177, 191, 196, 214, 229-231, 237, 248-249, 276, 297, 316, 327, 330, 334-335, 337-338, 363-364
Stanislavsky, K., 80-81, 177, 211-212, 216
Stanley, 61
Stone, Ria (Grace Lee), 10
Stravinsky, I., 197, 238
Swift, J., 313
Tchaikovsky, P.,197
Tennyson, A., 238
Thackeray, W.M., 4-5, 313
Thomas, N., 190, 196, 352, 363
Thompson, D., 221, 248
Tibbett, L., 41
Tierney, G., 223
de Tocqueville, A., 13
Tolstoy, L., 50, 155, 196, 205
Trotsky, L., 1, 6, 8-9, 11-12, 19-22, 26, 30, 34, 38-39, 49, 51, 53, 57-58, 64, 66, 85, 112, 115, 117, 136, 161-162, 174, 190-191, 212, 223, 226, 230, 243, 248, 271, 284, 288, 301, 303, 317, 330, 337-338, 353-354, 363-365
Truman, H., 366-367
Tubman, H., 23, 82-84, 96, 115
Turgenev, I., 205
Turner, L., 13, 33, 73
Turner, W.J., 160
Twain, M., 196, 372
Van Gogh, V., 281

Van Vechten, 13, 104, 107
da Vinci, L., 131, 187
Voltaire, 222
Wallace, H., 158, 175, 316, 334, 366
Washburn, E., 284, 289, 305, 309
Waters, E., 92, 96, 99, 107-108
Webb, Constance, 1-4, 8, 10-13, 15, 17-34, 37-39, 42, 46-47, 49-55, 57, 59-67, 69-72, 74-77, 79-82, 85-86, 89, 91-95, 99-101, 103, 105-106, 110, 113, 120, 128, 131-132, 136, 139, 141, 149, 152, 154, 157-158, 160, 181, 195, 197, 199-200, 203, 208-209, 214, 218, 220, 223, 232, 235, 239-240, 242, 244, 248, 253, 257-260, 266-269, 282, 287, 292-293, 297-299, 301, 307, 310, 341-348, 353, 356 357, 360, 362, 368, 371
Weinstein, S., 34, 305
Wellesley, D., 160
Whitman, W., 25, 164-167, 372
Wilcox, E.W., 221
Wilkie, W., 157, 175
Williams, E., 5, 14-15, 28, 50, 63, 88, 124, 163, 186, 203, 209, 217, 220-221, 226, 232, 235, 243-244, 249, 272-273, 283, 304, 324, 332, 338-339, 355, 360
Wolfe, B., 226, 361-362
Woodson, 59
Woolf, L., 33
Woolf, V., 150, 227
Wordsworth, W., 25, 165, 221, 238-239, 242, 259
Worrell, F., 15
Wright, R., 12, 27, 29, 124, 148, 155, 160, 162, 184, 189-190, 194, 196, 208-209, 214, 221-222, 226, 228, 231, 236-237, 239, 245-246, 248, 251-252, 256, 282, 301, 304-305, 313, 315, 319, 321, 339, 351, 360-362, 375
Wright, E., 222, 246
Yeats, W.B., 144, 176
Zupan, J., 360